OECD Reviews of Regulatory Ref

GW00494212

Regulatory Reform
in Ireland

OECD

ORGANISATION FOR ECONOMIC CO-OPERATION AND DEVELOPMENT

ORGANISATION FOR ECONOMIC CO-OPERATION AND DEVELOPMENT

Pursuant to Article 1 of the Convention signed in Paris on 14th December 1960, and which came into force on 30th September 1961, the Organisation for Economic Co-operation and Development (OECD) shall promote policies designed:

- to achieve the highest sustainable economic growth and employment and a rising standard of living in Member countries, while maintaining financial stability, and thus to contribute to the development of the world economy;

- to contribute to sound economic expansion in Member as well as non-member countries in the process of economic development; and

- to contribute to the expansion of world trade on a multilateral, non-discriminatory basis in accordance with international obligations.

The original Member countries of the OECD are Austria, Belgium, Canada, Denmark, France, Germany, Greece, Iceland, Ireland, Italy, Luxembourg, the Netherlands, Norway, Portugal, Spain, Sweden, Switzerland, Turkey, the United Kingdom and the United States. The following countries became Members subsequently through accession at the dates indicated hereafter: Japan (28th April 1964), Finland (28th January 1969), Australia (7th June 1971), New Zealand (29th May 1973), Mexico (18th May 1994), the Czech Republic (21st December 1995), Hungary (7th May 1996), Poland (22nd November 1996), Korea (12th December 1996) and the Slovak Republic (14th December 2000). The Commission of the European Communities takes part in the work of the OECD (Article 13 of the OECD Convention).

Publié en français sous le titre:
LA RÉFORME DE LA RÉGLEMENTATION EN IRLANDE

FOREWORD

The OECD Review of Regulatory Reform in Ireland is one of a series of country reports carried out under the OECD's Regulatory Reform Programme, launched in 1998 in response to a mandate by OECD Ministers.

The Regulatory Reform Programme is aimed at helping governments improve regulatory quality – that is, reforming regulations which raise unnecessary obstacles to competition, innovation and growth, while ensuring that regulations efficiently serve important social objectives.

The Programme is part of a broader effort at the OECD to support sustained economic development, job creation and good governance. It fits with other initiatives such as our annual country economic surveys; the Jobs Strategy; the OECD Principles of Corporate Governance; and the fight against corruption, hard-core cartels and harmful tax competition.

Drawing on the analysis and recommendations of good regulatory practices contained in the 1997 OECD *Report to Ministers on Regulatory Reform*, the Regulatory Reform Programme is a multi-disciplinary process of in-depth country reviews, based on self-assessment and on peer evaluation by several OECD committees.

The country Reviews are not comprehensive, but, rather, targeted at key reform areas. Each Review has the same structure, including three thematic chapters on the quality of regulatory institutions and government processes; competition policy and enforcement; and the enhancement of market openness through regulatory reform. Each Review also contains chapters on sectors such as electricity and tele-communications, and an assessment of the macroeconomic context for reform in the country under review.

The country Reviews benefited from a process of extensive consultations with a wide range of government officials (including elected officials) from the country reviewed, business and trade union representatives, consumer groups, and academic experts from many backgrounds.

These Reviews demonstrate clearly that in many areas, a well-structured and implemented programme of regulatory reform has brought lower prices and more choice for consumers, helped stimulate innovation, investment, and new industries, and thereby aided in boosting economic growth and overall job creation. Comprehensive regulatory reforms have produced results more quickly than piece-meal approaches; and such reforms over the longer-term helped countries to adjust more quickly and easily to changing circumstances and external shocks. At the same time, a balanced reform programme must take into account important social concerns. Adjustment costs in some sectors have been painful, although experience shows that these costs can be reduced if reform is accompanied by supportive policies, including active labour market policies, to cushion adjustment.

While reducing and reforming regulations is a key element of a broad programme of regulatory reform, country experience also shows that in a more competitive and efficient market, new regulations and institutions are sometimes necessary to assure that private anticompetitive behaviour does not delay or block the benefits of reform and that health, environmental and consumer protection is assured. In countries pursuing reform, which is often difficult and opposed by vested interests, sustained and consistent political leadership is an essential element of successful reform efforts, and transparent and informed public dialogue on the benefits and costs of reform is necessary for building and maintaining broad public support for reform.

The policy options presented in the Reviews may pose challenges for each country concerned, but they do not ignore wide differences between national cultures, legal and institutional traditions and economic circumstances. The in-depth nature of the Reviews and the efforts made to consult with a wide range of stakeholders reflect the emphasis placed by the OECD on ensuring that the policy options presented are relevant and attainable within the specific context and policy priorities of each country reviewed.

The OECD Reviews of Regulatory Reform are published on the responsibility of the Secretary-General of the OECD, but their policy options and accompanying analysis reflect input and commentary provided during peer review by all 30 OECD Member countries and the European Commission and during consultations with other interested parties.

The Secretariat would like to express its gratitude for the support of the Government of Ireland, for the OECD Regulatory Reform Programme and its consistent co-operation during the review process. It also would like to thank the many OECD committee and country delegates, representatives from the OECD's Trade Union Advisory Committee (TUAC) and Business and Industry Advisory Committee (BIAC), and other experts whose comments and suggestions were essential to this report.

ACKNOWLEDGEMENTS

This series of Reviews of Regulatory Reform in OECD countries was completed under the responsibility of Deputy Secretary-General **Sally Shelton-Colby**. The Review of Ireland reflects contributions from many sources, including the Government of Ireland. Major contributions were also made by the Committees of the OECD, representatives of Member governments, and members of the Business and Industry Advisory Committee (BIAC) and the Trade Union Advisory Committee (TUAC), as well as other groups. This report was peer reviewed on 23 March 2001 in the OECD's Ad Hoc Multidisciplinary Group on Regulatory Reform.

In the OECD Secretariat, the following people contributed substantially to the review of Ireland: the former **Head of Programme on Regulatory Reform and lead drafter**: Scott H. Jacobs; **Document preparation**: Jennifer Stein; **Economics Department**: Chapter 1 was principally prepared by a consultant, John Fitzgerald, and, in the OECD Secretariat, Rick Imai and Grant Kirkpatrick, and benefited from work by Giuseppe Nicoletti on regulatory indicators; **Public Management Service**: Cesar Córdova-Novion, benefiting from work by Edward Donelan, Office of the Attorney General, Dublin, Ireland, on secondment to the OECD; **Trade Directorate**: Denis Audet, Didier Campion, Anthony Kleitz; **Directorate for Financial, Fiscal and Enterprise Affairs**: Patricia Heriard-Dubreuil, Bernard J. Phillips, Sally Van Siclen, Michael Wise; **Directorate for Science, Technology, and Industry**: Takashi Yamada, Dimitri Ypsilanti; **General Secretariat**: Steve Cutts. The Head of the Programme on Regulatory Reform is Rolf Alter.

TABLE OF CONTENTS

List of Boxes

List of Tables

List of Figures

Part II

Part I

OECD REVIEW
OF REGULATORY REFORM
IN IRELAND

EXECUTIVE SUMMARY

Regulatory reform in Ireland gathered speed over the 1990s and is moving ahead on a broad front. From one perspective, Ireland's regulatory reforms are the familiar story of an OECD country moving away from statist policies focussed on producer supports toward market-oriented policies focused on consumer welfare and dynamic economic growth. But the Irish story is in some ways different, because regulatory reform is occurring in the context of fast growth, and its dynamics are unusual. Ireland experienced remarkable economic performance in the last decade, with average annual growth of 8.3% in 1997-1999. This stellar growth performance reflected an array of policy commitments and reforms. For example, large and sustained foreign investment, lured by increased market openness spiced with generous incentives, transformed Ireland's production capacity and broadened its trading interests beyond the EU market. Growth boomed, unemployment fell, and the government's chronic budget deficits turned into surpluses.

Regulatory reform is helping Ireland to manage the consequences of fast growth, and to build new capacities to sustain growth into the future. For example, regulatory reform is seen as a way to open up important infrastructure and policy bottlenecks to further growth and to attain efficiency improvements that can help manage inflationary pressures. The main bottlenecks where regulatory reform is useful are in physical infrastructure, labour supply, and inefficient administration of business policies. The Irish government is also using reform to establish a more competitive and flexible economy that can innovate, adapt and prosper even as the sources of its current prosperity change. The challenge is to move from growth based on using more resources (mostly more labour) to growth based on using resources better, that is, on productivity improvements. This shift in sources of growth requires a more nimble and dynamic economy rooted in a modern regulatory environment that is consistent with market forces, rewards productivity and innovation, and responds to consumer needs and changing market opportunities, domestic and international. The current Irish regulatory environment is making progress, but does not yet meet that need. Large-scale change to domestic competition is still necessary.

Chapter 1. The macroeconomic context for regulatory reform. Ireland's economic traditions lie in protection and domestic monopolies in which agriculture was the dominant sector. With membership in the European Union in 1973, the policy bias toward producer interests began to be balanced by consumer interests and competition. The Irish model became increasingly embattled in the 1980s with financial difficulties and recession which induced privatisation, reduction of state aids, and some deregulation. The turning point came in the 1990s, with a remarkable economic resurgence. The resurgence was due mostly to fundamentals such as free investment and trade, infrastructure and human capital investment, combined with a rising labour supply, and agreements among the social partners for pay moderation, combined with relatively flexible labour markets. EU integration, European liberalising and market openness reforms, and now the EMU play a vital role in Irish economic performance. By the end of 1997, Ireland was one of the less regulated OECD countries in terms of barriers to entry and entrepreneurship, market openness, and labour markets, though policy biases of producer over consumer interests, and of control over competition, still linger in some areas.

Assessing the impacts of recent regulatory reforms in Ireland is not easy, but a few reforms seem already to contribute to the country's economic success. Reform in telecommunications came late compared to other OECD countries, but has proceeded quickly and is now reducing prices. Transport costs are important for Irish competitiveness, and much progress has been made in road freight, airlines, and airports, though little progress has been made in improving the competitiveness of Irish ports. Reform of bus transport has had some success, in contrast with taxis, where restrictive regulations have until now imposed a high cost on consumers. Reform of the energy sector has been slower, though potential benefits are large.

The reform agenda is still long. Bottlenecks in physical infrastructure such as housing, transport, and environmental services are fueling inflation and constraining future growth. Labour shortages, too, are emerging and are likely to worsen as the supply drops. Capacities in the public sector are not sufficient to deliver the volume of decisions and services needed to address the infrastructure deficit. Weak competition in key sectors is another risk to future performance. Completion of the privatisation agenda, within appropriate regulatory frameworks, is a high priority. Irish local government services supply many essential public services, but tend to be inefficient and fragmented, hence market-oriented reforms in delivery of public services can result in targeted services and substantial cost savings. Cost savings in public services result from efficiency gains through better management, increased job flexibility and economies of scale and scope, not from social dumping or reductions in quality. Lifting of quantitative restrictions on entry into taxi and pub sectors can produce significant one-off reductions in price levels.

Chapter 2. Government capacity to assure high quality regulation. Pragmatism and steady progress have characterised Irish reforms to the public sector. The Strategic Management Initiative in particular is fostering a new culture in government regulatory practices. Yet reform of Ireland's regulatory governance lag behind dynamic market and social changes, and hence could be a bottleneck to sustained growth. Irish regulatory reform policy is broad and includes most of the OECD's recommended regulatory quality tools, such as regulatory review, but implementation is still weak. Significant improvements have been made to consultation and transparency, and further action can pre-empt the risk of capture by insider groups. By contrast, RIA has not yet been implemented effectively, and economic assessment of proposed rules is missing. Alternatives to regulations, such as economic instruments, have replaced few traditional "command and control" approaches. Implementation and enforcement of the Reducing Red Tape policy may need to be stronger to make a real impact on administrative burdens. The Irish government has launched a constructive debate on the design and governance of the new independent regulators, and modernisation of other state institutions merits further attention, as does regulatory quality at the local government level.

Chapter 3. The role of competition policy in regulatory reform. Competition policy has been a key weakness that undermined Ireland's move to sustainable market-based growth. Through the 1990s, competition policy had a difficult time taking root in the domestic economy. Today, competition principles are integrated to some extent into the general regulatory reform programme but market reforms of utilities and infrastructure services still do not consistently apply competition principles. Anti-competitive licensing schemes survive, but some prominent ones, in taxis and pubs, were recently relaxed. The Competition Authority has a continuing role in curbing abuses in traditional utility and infrastructure industries. Ireland's basic tool kit in its competition law is comparable to those of other OECD countries, and is increasingly focussed on horizontal cartels. The possibility of contradiction and confusion in merger reviews has made that process clearly unsatisfactory, and moves to reform are welcome. There are no explicit exemptions from the Competition Act, but many other laws and programmes restrict entry to protect incumbent firms. Enforcement capacities are still being tested, and private litigation has sometimes been the only recourse. The Authority is perhaps too reliant on the ministry for its resources, and staffing will require continuing attention in Ireland's tight labour market. The Authority has tried to move into an advocacy role, but making advocacy effective will require more resources and clearer independence.

Chapter 4. Enhancing market openness through regulatory reform. Ireland has gained substantial benefits by pursuing trade liberalisation, welcoming foreign-owned firms and integrating in the world economy. Irish growth was fueled by openness in Irish labour markets, which allowed substantial immigration of valuable labour. Today, Ireland relies more on trade than almost any other OECD country. Ireland has also been successful in attracting foreign investment, though its investment incentives have prompted some complaints. Nevertheless, global and regional economic markets will pose many surprises ahead, and further reform to Ireland's domestic regulatory framework can help it better prepare for shocks. Ireland has integrated many of the OECD's efficient regulation principles into its domestic regulations. Transparency in market rules has improved, but is still vulnerable to insider interests, increasing uncertainty for foreign actors. By contrast, elaboration of technical regulations and standards under EU and WTO procedures is sufficiently transparent, and Ireland has an excellent record in the use of internationally harmonised measures and open government procurement. Continued attention is warranted to ensuring respect to market openness principles by local governments.

Chapter 5. Regulatory Reform in electricity, gas, pharmacies, and legal services. Reform of the Irish electricity and gas sectors has begun, but is far from finished. The Irish energy sectors are dominated by two state-owned firms. Restructuring to induce competition in generation is a high priority, in parallel with restructuring to separate networks from potentially competitive activities. The natural direction is development of an all-island energy market, of which co-ordinated regulatory reform is one part. The independent regulator for electricity, and the planned extension of its authority to gas, will speed competition and investment, as will adopting regulatory instruments to promote commercial incentives for efficiency. Liberalisation of all consumers should proceed as planned and acceleration might be considered. Likewise, regulatory reform in important professional services would boost efficiency and quality, though reforms have already gone a long way to helping consumers choose from more competitive legal services. Further reforms should remove remaining impediments to healthy competition. Pharmacies are highly regulated in Ireland to ensure safety and availability of services to rural areas, but more sensible regulation could bring down prices without endangering safety or accessibility. The restriction on economic freedom of pharmacists educated in other EU countries should be eliminated, as should restrictions on the location and number of pharmacies.

Chapter 6. Regulatory reform in the telecommunications industry. Ireland gave up its derogation and liberalised telecommunications earlier than planned, a wise move that has placed its communications market on par with many OECD countries. Liberalisation has rapidly increased investment in new technologies and services, while consumers are beginning to see concrete results in terms of prices and quality. A long-term strength is that the Irish regulatory regime is designed to evolve as conditions change and this flexibility is particularly useful since important regulatory issues must be tackled to complete the regulatory environment for competition. To further open the market, it is timely to move to a class licensing system, replacing the existing individual licensing system. Ireland should continue its efforts to reduce interconnection prices to meet best practices, while delays in obtaining capacity from the incumbent should be reduced. Price rebalancing has been slow, and should be completed rapidly. Local loop unbundling has been an issue for the regulator for some time, but lack of supportive legislation has resulted in a missed opportunity to take the lead. Competition in the cellular market has been delayed partly due to weak enforcement powers of the independent regulator. Legislation relating to rights of way for telecommunication operators over public highways should be adopted as soon as possible. A universal service costing methodology should be implemented and, if necessary a universal service fund set up.

Chapter 7. Conclusions and policy options for regulatory reform. The coming cycle in Irish economic development justifies a more coherent and determined approach to regulatory reform than seen to date. Ireland's future strengths lie in continued attention to domestic competitiveness through regulatory efficiency and flexibility, good governance, and competition policy. Success will require Ireland to benchmark itself to a higher standard than its neighbours, that is, to be a leader in regulatory reform. To speed up results, a broad and co-ordinated approach across product, labour, and financial markets is needed, with governance reforms. Major steps recommended in this report include:

– *Remove licensing constraints on free entry, particularly those with quantitative limits.* The challenge is to identify and eliminate regulatory programmes and licensing schemes that have the effect of preventing entry and permitting non-competitive behaviour.

– *Eliminate special-interest rules that inhibit efficient competition, such as the Groceries Order.* The potentially anti-competitive effects of the Groceries Order are well recognised.

– *Strengthen implementation of the regulatory reform policy by creating stronger disciplines and performance assessment of regulatory quality within the departments and agencies, and by enforcing the disciplines through a high level committee.* Current mechanisms to implement the regulatory reform policy are too weak to change long-established habits and culture, to protect the regulatory system from pressures from special interests, to offset perverse incentives within the ministries and agencies, and to co-ordinate the difficult agenda of regulatory reform.

– *Strengthen the accountability of sectoral regulators by building capacities for appropriate overview by Parliamentary committees, and clarify the roles of sectoral regulators and the Competition Authority to ensure a uniform competition policy in the regulated sectors.* Market-oriented institutions have developed along with liberalisation of several sectors. However, the powers, nature, and accountability mechanisms of sectoral regulators are challenging the general public governance and institutional balance. Ireland was one of the first countries to start addressing the complex issues of accountability raised by this situation, and this progress should be maintained.

– *Strengthen disciplines on regulatory quality in the departments by i) reinforcing the central review unit; ii) refining tools for regulatory impact analysis, iii) adopting an explicit benefit-cost principle, iv) increasing the assessment of alternatives to regulation, v) integrating these tools into public consultation processes and vi) training public servants in how to use them.* The Regulatory Quality Checklist that accompanies memoranda for a proposed law is a crucial step forward. However, important weaknesses and gaps exist in the Irish process for regulatory quality controls.

– *Increase transparency by standardising public consultation and more use of the Internet.* Consideration should be given to establishing a "notice and comment" mandatory requirement for all regulatory proposals, and to establishing minimum criteria and disciplines for the public consultation required by the Reduce Red Tape action plan.

– *Enhance the current programme of restating and consolidating existing laws and regulations with a target review programme based on pro-competition and regulatory high-quality criteria.* The 1995 OECD regulatory quality checklist could be used to verify the continued necessity and appropriateness of the existing stock of regulations.

– *Expand competition in the provision of public services at local authority levels. An effective means would be competitive tendering of public services, within the framework of quality standards and monitoring.* The large role of Irish local governments in providing public services has a significant impact on the economy because the level of efficiency in public services helps determine overall price levels. Improving the quality and cost of services will require more contracting out and more intense competition.

– *Strengthen the application of competition policy economy-wide through a series of reforms.* Vigorous enforcement of competition policy in the self-regulated professions is a priority, and advocacy by the competition authority throughout the public administration would strengthen attention to market principles. The merger process should be streamlined and responsibility for competition policy reviews for all mergers clearly assigned to the Authority. A leniency programme should be implemented to help attack cartels. Judicial expertise needs attention. The Authority should be more independent on budget and staffing.

– *Encourage better regulatory practices at regional and local levels of government.* Safeguarding the gains made at the national level through regulatory reform will require intensive efforts to promote regulatory quality at sub-national levels.

– *Continue to encourage the use of international standards in national standardisation activities and to promote international harmonisation in European and international fora.* Strong commitment to an efficient and reliable standardisation system not only enhances market opportunities for Irish firms but also contributes to world-wide consolidation of efficient and transparent markets for industry and consumers.

– *Continue to work to develop regional and island-wide regulatory solutions where those improve efficiency.* Optimal regulatory frameworks for Ireland might in some cases extend beyond Irish borders into Northern Ireland and Britain.

– In the pharmacy sector, eliminate the restriction on economic freedom of pharmacists educated in other EU countries, and location restrictions on pharmacies.

– In legal services, move the control of education and entry of legal professionals from the self-governing bodies, but maintain close ties as regards quality of entrants and content of education and training, and maintain the freedom of solicitors to advertise their fees and areas of specialisation.

– Complete the process of introducing competition, and the application of general competition policy, in traditional monopoly sectors, including electricity. A series of steps would boost market performance in the energy sector. While retaining regulatory responsibility for electricity tariffs, specific license conditions and transmission access, the Commission for Electricity Regulation should also take responsibility for regulating transmission access for gas. Enforcement of the competition law in these sectors should remain with the Competition Authority. Tariff structures should be modified to improve efficiency in the energy sector by making regulated tariffs cost-reflective. Barriers to entry for gas importers and sellers should be reduced by ownership separation of transmission from potentially competitive activities. Efficiency should be increased by eliminating the subsidies for peat.

– In the telecommunications sector, take a number of steps to complete the regulatory framework. These include streamlining the licensing regime using general authorisations, rather than individual licensing, establishing concrete procedures with standard time frame for handling consumer complaints, accelerating the introduction of appropriate rights of way legislation to facilitate the construction of new networks on public highways, eliminating the "in platform exclusivity" granted to cable operators after the five-year period has expired in April 2004, using an agreed method to determine the costs of providing universal service, and developing explicit and concrete provisions governing forbearance and withdrawal from sector specific regulation.

Chapter 1

REGULATORY REFORM IN IRELAND

INTRODUCTION

The Irish story is in some ways unique, because regulatory reform is occurring in the context of fast growth, and its dynamics are unusual.

Regulatory reform in Ireland gathered speed over the 1990s and is currently moving ahead on a broad front. From one perspective, Ireland's regulatory reforms are the familiar story of an OECD country moving away from statist policies focussed on producer supports toward market-oriented policies focused on consumer welfare and dynamic economic growth. But the Irish story is in some ways quite different, because regulatory reform is occurring in the context of fast growth, and its dynamics are unusual.

Ireland experienced remarkable economic performance in the last decade, with average annual growth of 8.3% in 1997-1999. This stellar growth performance reflected an array of policy commitments and reforms[1]. Contributing factors included a favourable tax regime for corporations; social consensus; and Ireland's commitments in the ongoing EU integration, notably the European single market programme and the Economic and Monetary Union. Massive investments were made to improve the education level of the baby boom generation that entered the labour market in the 1990s, while skilled emigrants returned. Large and sustained foreign investment, lured by increased market openness spiced with generous incentives, transformed Ireland's production capacity and broadened its trading interests beyond the EU market. As a result, growth boomed, unemployment fell, and the government's chronic budget deficits turned into surpluses.

Regulatory reform is helping Ireland to manage the consequences of fast growth, and to build new capacities to sustain growth into the future.

Regulatory reform is helping Ireland manage the negative consequences of exuberant economic performance...

In the Irish context, regulatory reform is not seen as a way to reduce high levels of unemployment or boost slow growth, which are the main drivers in many other OECD countries. Rather, regulatory reform is seen as a way to open up important infrastructure and policy bottlenecks to further growth and to attain efficiency improvements that can help manage inflationary pressures. That is, regulatory reform is helping the government manage the negative consequences of years of exuberant economic performance and establish new ways to sustain high future growth. The main bottlenecks where regulatory reform is being useful are in physical infrastructure, labour supply, and inefficient administration of business policies.

15

...and to establish a more competitive and flexible economy that can innovate, adapt and prosper.

Irish regulatory reform is not only a defensive strategy. It is also positive, because the Irish government is using reform as a means of establishing a more competitive and flexible economy that can innovate, adapt and prosper as the sources of its current prosperity change. Essentially, the challenge is to move from growth based on using more resources (mostly more labour) to growth based on using resources better, that is, on productivity improvements. This shift in sources of growth requires a more nimble and dynamic economy rooted in a modern regulatory environment that is consistent with market forces, rewards productivity and innovation, and responds to consumer needs and changing market opportunities, domestic and international. The current Irish regulatory environment is making progress, but does not yet meet that need.

Ireland has today a golden opportunity to catch up by pushing forward with the deepest structural reforms possible.

Success seems well within reach, though, if social consensus and political will for reform can be sustained. Ireland has today a golden opportunity to catch up with OECD leaders by proceeding with the deepest structural reforms possible to sustain growth and soften the downturns ahead. This is because, relative to OECD countries where regulatory reform is occurring in a low-growth climate, regulatory reform can go faster and deeper in Ireland with minimal transition costs. The experiences of some other OECD countries who missed the upward economic cycle, only to face structural reforms when the political and social costs of change are the greatest, are cautionary.

The reform agenda in Ireland is more complex than traditional deregulation, because it involves large-scale change to domestic competition.

In addressing these concerns, the Irish agenda is tackling both over-regulation and under-regulation.

In addressing these concerns, the Irish agenda is tackling both over-regulation and under-regulation. The nature of the regulatory challenges facing Ireland are not largely the traditional regulatory inefficiencies associated with state ownership, legal monopolies, and explicit barriers to entry, although there are important areas for reform here. The major priorities in Ireland today are the more difficult issues of re-regulation, quality regulatory administration, complex and onerous licensing regimes, and, in general, establishment of a robust domestic environment for competition.

Regulatory reform has not been easy to initiate or sustain in Ireland. Until late in the 20th century, the economy was based on low-wage agriculture and basic manufacturing, and exported large amounts of labour to other countries in the form of emigration. Price controls remained a common policy tool until the early 1980s and the central role of competition policy in a modern economy was not fully recognised in public policy until the 1990s. Indeed, as Chapter 3 points out, competition law is not fully implemented even today. Irish regulatory reforms did not become broad until the 1990s, often under the spur of European Union reforms, and even then reform was reluctant and often slow. Most reforms are just now beginning to yield benefits, and producer groups are still strongly vested in protecting their sectors from entry.

Today, regulatory reform seems firmly on track to build the rules and institutions for a modern, competitive economy.

For these reasons, reform has been a halting and sometimes inconsistent process. Today, however, regulatory reform seems firmly on track, as part of the largest domestic reform programme since Irish independence early in the 20th century, to build the rules and institutions for a modern, competitive economy.

Box 1.1. What is regulation and regulatory reform?

There is no generally accepted definition of regulation applicable to the very different regulatory systems in OECD countries. In the OECD work, regulation refers to the diverse set of instruments by which governments set requirements on enterprises and citizens. Regulations include laws, formal and informal orders and subordinate rules issued by all levels of government, and rules issued by non-governmental or self-regulatory bodies to whom governments have delegated regulatory powers. Regulations fall into three categories:

– *Economic regulations* intervene directly in market decisions such as pricing, competition, market entry, or exit. Reform aims to increase economic efficiency by reducing barriers to competition and innovation, often through deregulation and use of efficiency-promoting regulation, and by improving regulatory frameworks for market functioning and prudential oversight.

– *Social regulations* protect public interests such as health, safety, the environment, and social cohesion. The economic effects of social regulations may be secondary concerns or even unexpected, but can be substantial. Reform aims to verify that regulation is needed, and to design regulatory and other instruments, such as market incentives and goal-based approaches, that are more flexible, simpler, and more effective at lower cost.

– *Administrative regulations* are paperwork and administrative formalities – so-called "red tape" – through which governments collect information and intervene in individual economic decisions. They can have substantial impacts on private sector performance. Reform aims at eliminating those no longer needed, streamlining and simplifying those that are needed, and improving the transparency of application.

Regulatory reform is used in the OECD work to refer to changes that improve regulatory quality, that is, enhance the performance, cost-effectiveness, or legal quality of regulations and related government formalities. Reform can mean revision of a single regulation, the scrapping and rebuilding of an entire regulatory regime and its institutions, or improvement of processes for making regulations and managing reform. Deregulation is a subset of regulatory reform and refers to complete or partial elimination of regulation in a sector to improve economic performance.

Source: OECD (1997), OECD *Report on Regulatory Reform*, Paris.

THE MACROECONOMIC CONTEXT FOR SECTORAL REGULATORY REFORM

The Irish economy, after many decades of underdevelopment, enjoyed a major turnaround in the 1990s.

The Irish economy, after many decades of relative underdevelopment in the OECD, enjoyed a major turnaround in the 1990s. A sustained rise in output, remarkable growth in employment and the resulting convergence in living standards to the EU average all happened rapidly. Unemployment, which had been chronically high for a long time, fell dramatically, putting Ireland at the lower end of the EU spectrum of jobless rates. Irish regulatory reform was not a significant contributor to this turnaround, but the regional integration of Ireland into Europe through EU membership and particularly the European single market programme, which was essentially a regulatory reform programme, were major factors in the revival of the Irish economy.

By 2000, signs of overheating were apparent throughout the economy.

By 2000, signs of overheating, which had been present in the housing market for two years, were apparent throughout the economy. The rise in consumer price inflation in 2000 was preceded by a rise in the GDP deflator. It is now accompanied by rapid acceleration in the rate of wage inflation. In this context, regulatory reform is seen today as a non-inflationary way to sustain growth and raise real income by strengthening efficiency, market performance and competitiveness, and by removing specific bottlenecks to growth.

Ireland's economic traditions were protection and domestic monopolies…

Ireland's protectionist self-sufficiency economic strategy was maintained until the 1950s…

While the rest of Western Europe began a process of trade liberalisation and integration in the immediate post-war years, Ireland maintained a protectionist self-sufficiency strategy. Tariffs on imports were maintained at very high levels until the end of the 1950s and quota restrictions were an important part of the protective milieu in which Irish business operated.

…which meant that manufacturing developed under cover of a very high protective barrier against external competition.

In manufacturing, much of the sector had developed since the late 1920s under the cover of a very high protective barrier against external competition. With a small domestic market, the granting of protection could ensure a domestic monopoly for production. In addition, the right to import goods that were restricted by quotas was valuable, conferring a local monopoly on the recipient. Thus the regime of high protective tariffs fostered a milieu where monopolies were not unusual and where the rights of consumers were always subservient to the rights of producers. The exclusive right to import the many products not produced in Ireland was frequently a more profitable pursuit than engaging in manufacturing.

…in which agriculture was the dominant sector…

Agriculture was by far the most important sector and much of its output was exported.

Agriculture was by far the most important sector and much of its output was exported. However, the external climate for food exports was unfavourable in the post-war years, with much of the European market protected against competition. Only the UK market was open to Irish agricultural produce and maintaining and improving this access was a key driver of external economic policy. Domestic economic policy centred on the importance of maintaining export earnings of agricultural producers[2]. Here too the rights of consumers came low on policy-makers' list of national priorities.

The importance for economic policy of maximising the price received by agricultural producers was explicitly recognised at the time of the decision to join the EU in 1972[3]. In the debate on membership, it was made clear that this would entail big price rises for consumers. The Government white paper, *The Accession of Ireland to the European Communities*, estimated that the changeover to the EU system of agricultural price support would add around 5 percentage points to consumer prices over five years. However, the expected gains to farmers outweighed the loss to consumers by such a large margin that the change in regime was accepted by the electorate with a large majority.

...and state ownership became increasingly prevalent.

From the 1930s on, a series of state-owned companies was engaged in commercial activities.

As shown in Table 1.1, from the 1930s on a series of state-owned companies was engaged in commercial activities that were not being undertaken by the private sector or which were felt to be outside the expertise of existing firms. State-owned banking firms catering to sectoral needs, a state-owned shipping company and a state-owned airline, state-owned electricity and peat producing utilities, a state-owned insurance company, a state-owned distillery,[4] and a state-owned food processing company were all started between 1930 and 1950.

Table 1.1.   The rise and fall of state-owned enterprises in Ireland

Establishment of state companies	Privatisation/restructuring of state companies
1927 – ESB (Electricity), Aer Rianta (airports), ACC (bank)	1984 – Irish Shipping (In receivership)
1933 – ICC (bank), Greencore (food processing)	1991 – Irish Life, Greencore
1936 – Aer Lingus (airline)	1996 – Irish Steel
1939 – Irish Life (Assurance)	1999 – Telecom Éireann (Telephones)
1944 – CIE (Public Transport)	2000 – ACC, ICC, TSB (bank), Aer Lingus to be privatised as market circumstances permit
1947 – Irish Steel (Steel)	
1961 – NET (Fertiliser)	
1975 – Bord Gáis (Gas)	

With membership in the European Union, the policy bias toward producer interests began to be balanced by consumer interests and competition.

EU membership in 1973, by freeing trade, was a significant step toward market competition.

EU membership in 1973 represented a significant step in redressing the balance in favour of consumer rights and competition. In freeing all trade in goods it ended any remaining monopoly power for domestic industrial firms, greatly enhancing competition. The result was a dramatic increase in the share of imports in personal consumption[5]. It also brought the growing corpus of EU legislation favouring competition and consumer rights.

But the market philosophy was not embraced whole-heartedly. In the 1970s, instead of proceeding with comprehensive legislation on competition, reliance was placed on such mechanisms as the *National Prices Commission* to monitor, and occasionally to try to control prices. An attempt to control the price of oil in the late 1970s proved unfortunate, resulting in supply shortages (at the regulated price), as oil companies diverted product to more profitable markets elsewhere.

The Irish model became increasingly embattled in the 1980s with financial difficulties and recession…

The 1980s were a difficult time for the Irish economy, as government spending was out of control.

The 1980s were a difficult time for the Irish economy. Following an unwise fiscal expansion in the late 1970s, Ireland began the 1980s with a very high level of public debt, a record level of government borrowing and an unsustainable balance of payments deficit. The slow response of policy makers aggravated these problems until fiscal policy was finally tightened dramatically in 1983, with this stance broadly continuing over the rest of the decade as successive governments sought to bring the financial crisis under control.[6]

The 1983 budget was probably the most deflationary of the last 30 years, with major increases in tax rates and big cuts in public capital expenditure. Over the period 1982-86 the cumulative impact of fiscal tightening amounted to around 5% of GDP. Output stagnated, employment declined, and despite sizeable outward migration and low labour force participation, the unemployment rate reached 17%, the second highest in the OECD. Even so, the earlier fiscal retrenchment still left the public finances in serious condition. The general government deficit was nearly 11% of GDP and gross debt approached 120% of GDP. Further consolidation from 1987, focusing this time on major cuts in current expenditure rather than tax increases and cuts in capital spending, dramatically reduced the deficit to below 2% of GDP by the end of the 1980s.

The worsening government financial situation coincided with domestic recession and removal of the last protections for Irish manufacturers.

Fiscal correction in the 1980s was only one factor contributing to an unfavourable environment for the Irish economy. By the beginning of the 1980s the worsening government financial situation coincided with domestic recession and the removal of the last vestiges of protection for Irish manufacturing industry.[7] The combined effects of a deterioration in competitiveness in the 1970s and the delayed impact of EU entry on the exposed tradable sector would, in any event, have posed problems. When added to the recession in Europe in the early 1980s and the effects on a very indebted economy of a rapid rise in world real interest rates, this proved a poisonous cocktail.

…which induced privatisation, reduction of state aids, and even some deregulation.

As protection declined, many domestic firms closed…

The result of the crisis was the closure of many domestic firms operating in more traditional sectors of manufacturing. In the 1970s the state had taken action through state aids to help some of these firms continue trading, but it could no longer afford such a policy in the 1980s. The state agency charged with rescuing domestic manufacturing firms, *Fóir Teoranta*, was closed in 1982. An even more striking sign of the changing environment was the decision to allow the state owned shipping company to go bankrupt in 1984. This sent a signal to other state owned commercial companies that they had to learn to survive with a hard budget constraint in a competitive environment, and it also ensured that the financial sector would help maintain financial discipline in such firms.

The changing environment of the 1980s saw the abolition of the *National Prices Commission*, as increasing competition from abroad took over much of its role. The completion of the internal EU market was widely welcomed as potentially enhancing domestic competitive pressures.

...but not until the 1990s was there a significant retreat in state involvement in the commercial sector.

Late in the 1980s the state began the process of divesting or closing a range of state owned commercial firms (Table 1.1), but only in the 1990s has there been a significant retreat in state involvement in the commercial sector. The main state-owned food-processing company was privatised in 1991 and in 1999, the remaining government stake in *Eircom* was floated. Even today, while the government has declared its intention of selling the state-owned banks and airline, technical problems have delayed actual implementation of this policy. Of the three state-owned banks (ICC, ACC and TSB), the ICC was sold in February 2001, and sale of TSB is expected to be concluded by late April 2001. The government has authorised an initial public offering of shares in the state-owned airline (*Aer Lingus*). The timing of the IPO will be influenced by market conditions and enactment of relevant legislation.

The turning point came in the 1990s.

Since 1994, real GNP has grown at an average rate of just under 8% a year...

Following the recession, widespread in much of Western Europe in the early 1990s, the Irish economy began its recovery relatively early in 1994. This followed a series of social partnership agreements initiated in 1987. Since 1994, real GNP has grown at an average rate of just under 8% a year.[8] Employment growth over the seven years to 2000 averaged around 4.7% a year, well ahead of any other EU country. Even with significant immigration of skilled labour in recent years, the unemployment rate, which peaked at 15.7% in 1993, had fallen to 3.9% by the winter of 2000.

...and by 2001 was running into capacity constraints.

Rapid growth in the economy appears to be continuing into 2001, but there are signs that it is running into capacity constraints. The rate of inflation, which remained low throughout the period of rapid growth up to 1999,[9] averaged 5.6% in 2000. House prices, which rose dramatically over the period of economic recovery, are still rising rapidly at an annual rate of around 15%. The rate of unemployment is now very low and still falling, and increasing signs of tightness have emerged in the labour market. Not least, there is rapid acceleration in the rate of wage inflation with average earnings estimated to rise by 8% in 2000.

Following large deficits in the 1980s, the balance of payments first moved into surplus in 1991. It continued in the black throughout the 1990s, reflecting strong improvement in public finances and significant private sector savings. Latest estimates for 2000 suggest that the balance of payments showed a small deficit.

The rapid growth in the economy in recent years has boosted tax revenue at a time when falling unemployment and other demographic changes reduced pressures on public expenditure. Declining debt and interest rates contributed to the budget turnaround. The General Government Surplus in 2000 was 4.6% of GDP.

21

The public sector first moved into surplus in 1997, and the continuing rapid economic growth steadily increased the surpluses. The debt to GDP ratio was 39% of GDP by the end of 2000.

The remarkable economic resurgence of Ireland was due mostly to the fundamentals...

In examining the sources of growth, it is clear that Ireland is experiencing belatedly the fruits of free trade and investment in human capital that the rest of Europe enjoyed in the 1960s and the 1970s.

The sustained rapid growth in the economy in the 1990s has raised questions as to where the growth came from. To some extent, it reflects the past failures of the economy. With better policies and better luck, Ireland might have converged toward the EU average standard of living much earlier. The failure to adopt free trade and to participate in the European integration process in the immediate post-war years was a serious setback. The state failed to invest in education in the 1950s and 1960s, at a time when neighbouring countries in Europe had embraced the need to invest in human capital. In a sense, Ireland is experiencing belatedly the fruits of free trade and investment in human capital, fruits that the rest of Europe enjoyed in the 1960s and the 1970s.

The factors underlying long-term success can be divided into those affecting the supply of labour and other factors.[10] Important measures, aimed at increasing the productive potential of the economy, have been implemented over the years.

...such as free investment and trade, which became more significant as the European market developed...

Promoting foreign direct investment to modernise the economy had considerable success.

The policy of promoting foreign direct investment to modernise the economy has had considerable success. Foreign investment was also supported by a positive Irish reputation for policy stability and a welcoming environment for foreign businesses (Chapter 4).

The first tentative movement towards an opening up of the economy to the outside world was the introduction in the late 1950s of an exemption from corporation tax for profits from exporting. This policy was aimed at attracting foreign direct investment. Successive Irish governments have developed and pursued this policy of promoting foreign direct investment. The primary instruments deployed to attract investment have been a consistently low rate of corporation tax for the last 40 years, the simplification of administrative procedures to facilitate such investment, and, more recently, the rapid rise in the supply of skilled labour.[11] All governments for the last 40 years have pursued the policy of attracting FDI with vigour, and considerable success. In particular, in the 1990s there has been a big inflow of foreign firms in high technology sectors, such as pharmaceuticals and information technology.

The importance attached to this policy, and its acceptance as central to government supply-side economic policies, has been reflected in a widespread welcome for such firms. There has been little or no pressure on governments to alter the policy, and incoming firms have felt certain that the environment for their business will not change once investment has been committed.[12] The public has come to accept the importance of free trade, and access to the EU market in particular, as central to the Irish success story.

...infrastructure investment...

A wide range of measures to improve physical infrastructure was pursued...

In addition, most recently in the 1990s, a wide range of detailed measures to improve the physical infrastructure of the economy have been pursued within the context of successive National Development Plans. While not an exciting topic for political debate, nonetheless investment in areas such as sewerage and water supply are going to play a vital role in expanding the productive potential of the economy in the coming years.

...investments in human capital, combined with a rising labour supply...

...with major investments in human capital.

As discussed, Ireland was a late but enthusiastic convert to the importance of investing in human capital. Investment in education, rising female participation, the lagged effects of a high birth rate up to 1980, and, in the 1990s, significant net immigration of skilled labour, has meant that labour supply has risen, and is rising rapidly. This rapid growth in labour supply makes Ireland different from its EU partners. In the 1990s, the labour force in Ireland increased by an average of 2.7% a year, expanding the capacity output of the economy.

The increase in educational participation contributed up to 1% a year to the growth rate of output.

While belated, the conversion after 1970[13] of policy makers to the belief that human capital is important to economic growth has been important. It is estimated that the rapid increase in educational participation contributed up to 1% a year to the growth rate of output in recent years by raising the productivity of labour.[14] The increase in educational participation continued in the 1990s. In 1988, 17% of the population aged 25 to 29 had third level education (both university and non-university). By 1999 this had doubled to nearly 34%.[15] The proportion of the population aged 20 in 1996 who were benefiting from third level education was 47%.[16] This indicates that the impact on productivity of rising human capital will continue to be important for much of the current decade as those currently in the education system replace older retiring workers.

Female labour force participation was low in Ireland in 1980. However, cultural change and rising educational attainment[17] have created a major change over the last 20 years. The increase in participation has been most rapid in recent years, but for older women the rate in Ireland is still well below the EU average (see Figure 1.1).

The birth rate in Ireland was high until 1980 but cultural changes and the developing demographic structure saw a very rapid fall over that decade (Figure 1.2). The high birth rate in the 1970s led to rapid increase in young entrants to the labour force in the 1990s. Over the next few years, the lagged effects of the 1980s slow-down will begin to impact on the growth in labour supply and, hence, on the economy's potential growth rate.

Figure 1.1. **Female labour force participation**

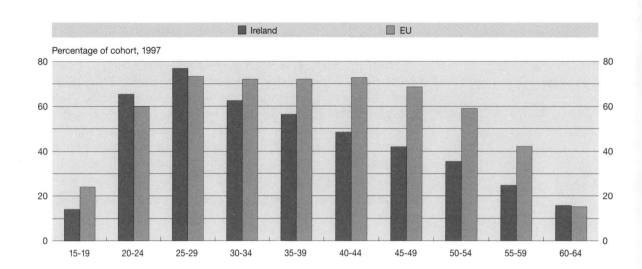

Immigration played an important role in expanding the productive capacity of the economy.

Finally, net immigration, especially of skilled people, has played an important role in expanding the productive capacity of the economy. The majority of those coming to Ireland, whether returning emigrants or immigrants, have a high level of education.[18] In addition, for returning emigrants the skills and expertise they acquired abroad enhance their earning power, reflecting their higher productivity.[19] This has further expanded labour supply, keeping wage inflation for skilled workers down, and improving the competitiveness of the economy.

...agreements among the social partners for pay moderation...

A "partnership agreement" with the social partners involved a trade-off of tax cuts in return for pay moderation.

As part of a strategy for economic recovery in the late 1980s the government in 1987 entered into a "partnership agreement" with the social partners – the trade unions and the employers. This agreement involved a trade off of tax cuts in return for pay moderation and a reduction in public service employment (see Box 1.2). Successive governments have continued this partnership approach to policy making until the present day, though in recent years the trade off has consisted of increases in public services as well as tax cuts in return for pay moderation. The tax cuts, which were an integral part of the agreements, meant that the budgets for 1997 to 1999 were more expansive than would otherwise have been the case (i.e. the baseline budget) and the same is certainly true in 2000.[20]

...combined with relatively flexible labour markets.

Importantly, the Irish labour market is relatively unregulated by EU standards.

The labour market is relatively unregulated by EU standards.[21] While standard EU employment protection legislation has been implemented, purely domestic regulations are relatively limited. A minimum wage was introduced from April of 2000. While it was anticipated that this would adversely affect employment, the rapid rise in wage rates for the unskilled over the last two years has minimised potential damage from this policy. In Ireland, the elasticity of supply of skilled labour through immigration is very high by EU standards. As discussed above, immigration of skilled labour has been important in allowing the economy to expand rapidly and in enhancing the flexibility of the economy.

Figure 1.2. **Birth rate**

Per thousand population

Source: CSO Vital Statistics

Box 1.2. Social partnership in Ireland

As successive governments in the 1980s sought to tackle the crisis facing the Irish economy due to burgeoning public debt, it became apparent to the social partners (government, employers, trade unions, and farming organisations) that fighting over shares of a declining income was fruitless. A report by the *National Economic and Social Council* set the scene for a more constructive approach to policy formation, including wage formation. As a result, in the Programme for National Recovery (PNR) agreed between the social partners in 1987, a three-year strategy for tackling the government's financial crisis was mapped out.

The PNR included detailed targets on controlling public expenditure and stabilising the debt/GNP ratio. It was agreed that, in return for significant pay moderation, there would be a reversal of the policy of increasing taxation. This agreement to trade off tax cuts against pay moderation has become a hallmark of all subsequent agreements. The agreement also provided a framework in which the government cut employment in the public sector over a two-year period by 7%. Thanks to the agreement this cut was achieved without significant industrial unrest.

Social partnership in Ireland (*Cont.*)

Since 1987 there have been a series of similar agreements between the government and the social partners culminating in the *Programme for Prosperity and Fairness* agreed early in 2000. The content of these agreements has been similar, including an explicit trade-off of wage moderation for tax cuts. However, over time, they have become much more detailed agreements on the development of a wide range of state services, including social welfare transfers. In addition, policies on privatisation have been developed in close consultation with trade unions and effected, in some cases, through "strategic alliances" where their support is linked to immediate benefits, often in the form of direct participation in the privatised company.

The extension in scope of policy areas covered by the agreements has been partly driven by the inclusion in recent negotiations of a fourth "partner" – the community and voluntary sector. This sector broadly represents, the unemployed, and other groups not represented by employers and trade unions. Their inclusion was intended to ensure a balance of representation in the "partnership process". Consumers, as such, are not represented in the process, reflecting the limited role of consumer groups and lobbies in the economy as a whole.

The econometric evidence suggests a movement towards more moderate growth in wage settlements early in the first half of the 1980s – before the partnership agreements began.[23] This undermines the frequently made assertion that the partnership process is responsible for moderating wages. It may be the case that for a year or two wage settlements were achieved below levels that would otherwise have occurred as a result of market forces. However, over the period since 1987 the cumulative rise in wage rates was largely determined by market forces, with periods of below-trend growth compensated by periods of "catch up".

There are other benefits of the agreements. Even if market forces might have delivered a similar path for pay rates in the private sector, the partnership agreements ensured that the appropriate rate was reached without major industrial disputes. This was in marked contrast with the earlier period from 1970 to the mid-1980s and it encompassed the period of major reduction in public expenditure. The partnership agreement, together with the support of the major opposition parties, gave the incoming government in 1987 the capacity to undertake the radical reduction in expenditure that it planned. In addition, over the 1990s, the agreement has involved a multi-annual planning process for taxes and government expenditure. This has helped improve the coherence of public policy formation.

Against these benefits, concerns have been raised that the commitments entered into by the social partners infringe on the role of the Parliament. In particular, the extension of the agreements to a wide range of other areas, apart from pay rates, raises questions of democratic accountability. However, in practice the agreements on these other measures have either covered non-contentious developments in public services or else have been sufficiently flexible to allow continuing freedom of action to the government and the Parliament. As a result, incoming governments have not had major problems implementing agreements reached by their predecessors.

The tightening of the labour market, as reflected in the reduction in unemployment to 4% or less of the labour force, has been putting the current agreement under serious pressure. With inflation in Ireland rising from a low level at the end of 1999 (the agreement was signed in early 2000) to be the highest in the Euro area in mid-2000, pressure for higher pay increases in the private and the public sectors mounted. The income-related elements of the PPF were adjusted in December 2000, with additional wage increases in April 2001 and measures to enhance stability in industrial relations.

ECONOMIC IMPACTS OF SECTORAL REGULATORY REFORM[24]

Regulatory reform in Ireland began later than in many OECD members, beginning in the 1980s and slowly spreading through the economy in the 1990s.

As noted, regulatory reform in Ireland began later than in many of its EU neighbours, beginning in the 1980s and slowly spreading through the economy in the 1990s (Table 1.2). The initial impetus for state withdrawal from the economy in the 1980s derived from the serious financial crisis facing the economy rather than from a strategy for structural adjustment. The need to reduce unlimited support for failing state-owned commercial enterprises was driven by the inability of the state to continue funding such losses. In addition, in the 1980s the state was not able to continue supporting ailing private sector firms in the way it had done in the 1970s. Membership in the European Union, particularly the competitive and liberalising forces of the single market programme, further supported the development of a more market-oriented policy framework.

Introduction of competition into the airline market in the 1980s achieved a dramatic effect by reducing prices and increasing output (Box 1.3). The demonstration effect of this success story made a big public impact. However, in spite of the large benefits to the public, progress in introducing competition elsewhere was slow. Road haulage was deregulated at the end of the 1980s, but telecommunications was not until 1998. The energy sector awaits effective liberalisation, and some other sectors where efficiency gains are clearly possible, such as pub licenses, have not yet been tackled.

By the end of 1997, Ireland was one of the less regulated OECD countries in terms of barriers to entry and entrepreneurship, market openness, and labour markets.

By end 1997, Ireland's light-handed regulation, its flexible labour markets, and its market openness had placed it among the less regulated countries in the OECD...

International comparative indicators, shown in Figure 1.3, indicate that, by the end of 1997, Ireland was among the less regulated countries in the OECD. The synthetic indicators in Table 1.3, which combine measures of different kinds of regulation across the economy, indicate that on a series of dimensions Ireland had a light-handed regulatory environment. These indicators confirm the main points of this review: the remaining regulatory problems in Ireland are primarily those associated with an inefficient state sector, weak competition policy, and unfinished pro-market regulatory regimes, rather than the traditional agenda of state ownership, legal monopolies, and explicit barriers to entry.

The underlying policy biases of producer over consumer interests, and of control over competition, still linger in some areas.

...though Irish economic policy remains more favourable to producer interests than to consumers.

Despite the reforms of the past decade, Irish economic policy remains more favourable to producer interests than to consumers, evidence of an underlying social caution about change, as well as the power of vested producer interests. The important social partnership process (Box 1.2) involves government, trade unions, employers, farmers and the community and voluntary sector. Consumers are not considered as an independent social partner. While their interests may often be represented by differing coalitions of the other participants, their interest in enhanced competition is not formally recognised.

With rising inflation in 2000, there have been renewed calls for regulation of prices, especially pub prices, rather than enhancing competition as a way to reduce price levels. Price controls have found greater political favour than the more effective move to abolish restrictions on entry to the market. The high value of the right to operate a pub (price of the license) indicates the serious upward pressure on prices that arises from restricted entry.

27

Creation of the Competitiveness Council, and the work of Forfas, have been useful in raising awareness of the broader benefits and costs of market reforms.

Competitiveness became a higher priority in the later 1990s.

The establishment of the National Competitiveness Council in 1997 was an interesting innovation. It includes individuals from the business community, some trade union officials and some civil servants, and its remit is to examine the competitiveness of the economy and how it can be improved. While similar in representation to the bodies established under the partnership process, its focus on improving competitiveness has provided a useful counterbalance to other lobby groups, as it focuses on reducing input costs to business. In successive reports it has promoted increased competition in energy, telecommunications, transport and many other areas of the Irish economy. In particular, it has highlighted areas where costs for Irish business (and generally also for private consumers) are out of line with those in competitor countries. Its annual reports bring together a wide range of useful measures of competitiveness, helping focus attention on the areas most in need of reform.

Table 1.2.   Sectoral regulatory reforms in Ireland

Sector	Status of reforms
Telecommunications	June 1997, Telecommunications regulator established. Full liberalisation. 1 December 1998. Remaining Government stake (51%) in largest service provider, Eircom, sold June 1999.
Electricity	July 1999, Electricity Regulation Act established independent regulator. From February 2000, competition is permitted for 30% of market. Full liberalisation by 2005. Further legislation to complete implementation of the EU directive was brought into force in December 2000. Largest incumbent remains state-owned, vertically-integrated, and dominant.
Gas	Third party access for large industrial consumers since 1995. Network code of operations and pricing regime in place. Review of tariff methodology nearing completion. Electricity regulator to be given responsibility also for gas.
Airports	Legislation establishing an independent regulator was passed by the Parliament in February 2001.
Public Transport	Proposals for new institutional and regulatory framework published August 2000.
Taxis	A High Court decision in October 2000 led to the introduction of a new regulatory regime on 21 November 2000 which liberalised entry to the sector. The new regulations were the subject of High Court judicial review proceedings and a judgement is awaited. Taxi licences continue to be issued under the new regulations until the Court decides otherwise.
Pubs	Some changes in licensing regulations in 2000 with the creation of a nation-wide licensing area. With assess further reform, the Commission on Liquor Licensing was established in November 2000.
Distribution	Ban on below cost selling still in force.
Financial Sector	A new structure for financial services regulation was announced by the overnment on 20 February 2001.
Competition Authority	Established 1991. From 1996 it has investigative powers and can bring civil and criminal court actions.

Forfas, the policy advisory board of the Department of Enterprise, Trade and Employment for enterprise, trade, science, technology and innovation, has been a key analyst and promoter of reforms. Forfas serves as the secretariat of the National Competitiveness Council.

Assessing the impacts of recent regulatory reforms in Ireland is not easy, but reforms seem already to contribute to the country's economic success.

Regulatory reform seems to have played a significant but not central role in Ireland's success to date.

There has been very little economic assessment, either *ex ante* or *ex post*, of the impact of regulatory reform in Ireland over the last twenty years. This reflects the relatively low priority given to this aspect of supply side policy by successive governments. Generally, the arguments in favour of reform have been couched in theoretical terms, or using evidence on experience in other economies, rather than through systematic studies of the circumstances in Ireland. Most commentaries suggest that regulatory reform has played a significant part in Ireland's recent success but the major driving forces lie elsewhere.[25] Evidence is available on the effects of some of the many regulatory changes that have occurred, but even these partial studies are limited in scope. Table 1.3 summarises the limited evidence available.

Table 1.3. Economic effects of sectoral regulatory reform

Sector	Status	Expected impact
Public procurement liberalisation	Implemented 1992	GDP +2%
Single market "supply effects"	Implemented 1992	GDP + 0.6%
Ports	Increased competition beginning in 1990s	
Airline Deregulation	Beginning in 1986	1998, passenger numbers in Dublin-London route are up 410% from 1985
Taxis	Entry was liberalised in November 2000 following a High Court decision, which could be reversed by further adjudication	Cost, higher price level for consumers of at least 0.1% of private consumption
Pubs	Still regulated	Cost, higher price level for consumers of at least 0.3% of private consumption
Telecommunications	Liberalisation completed in December 1998	Telecommunications costs had fallen 16% by autumn 1999

EU integration, European liberalising and market openness reforms, and now the EMU are playing a vital role in Irish economic performance.

The opening of the Irish economy played a vital role in the rapid rise in living standards.

The opening-up of the Irish economy as part of European integration has played a vital role in the rapid rise in living standards. In addition, it has been an important factor in introducing competitive forces into what would otherwise be a small national market.

Fears were expressed in the EU that the completion of the single market in 1992 would be bad for peripheral locations, but

In public procurement, Ireland had little to lose and much to gain from European reform.

The EMU has increased competitive forces in Ireland.

this was not expected to be the case *ex ante* for Ireland. In a report published in 1992,[26] using the approach underlying the Cecchini report and a specially developed macro-economic model of the Irish economy, the potential impact of the single market on Ireland was examined. In particular, the reform of public procurement practices within the EU and the increased competition and productivity effects (supply effects) of completion of the market were expected to confer significant benefits on Ireland.

In public procurement, the small size of the Irish public sector market meant that a "buy Irish policy" was not possible, as well as being inefficient. Thus Ireland had little to lose and much to gain from regulatory reform in this area. It was anticipated that as a result of the single market programme there would be increased production of telecommunications equipment and health care products in Ireland for sale into the public sector markets of the EU.

Following the Cecchini report, the supply effects were composed of a competition effect and a productivity effect. The competition effect was expected to result from the abolition of customs barriers, allowing freer movement of goods, and facilitating parallel importing. The expected GDP gains took account of some losses in sectors that were expected to suffer from the abolition of borders, *e.g.* import agents and the wholesale sector.

It was estimated that the "supply effects" of the single market would increase the volume of GDP once-off by around 2%. In the case of public procurement the positive effect was expected to be around 0.6%. The total effects of the completion of the internal market, including all other effects, were expected to amount to around 4.5% of GDP, achievable over a number of years.

The "supply effects" were also estimated to result in a once-off reduction in the price level in Ireland of around 2.3%. In total, the single market reforms were expected to reduce the price level by around 6% over a number of years.

Parallel importing was expected to increase competitive disciplines on the retail sector in what is by EU standards quite a small retail market. A substantial share of the retail sector in Ireland is owned by UK companies. As a result, quite a high proportion of the goods sold in shops are sourced through the United Kingdom. This has meant that Irish consumer prices have tended to follow those in the United Kingdom, with an adjustment for the exchange rate. Generally, changes in the UK price were passed through rapidly into Irish prices, with delays of between one and two years in carrying through what were perceived as "permanent" changes in the exchange rate.[27] However, there is evidence that, with the advent of the Euro, the pricing behaviour of UK firms selling into the Irish market changed, with a growing share of product being priced in Euros.[28] This is reflected in the unexpectedly low inflation rate in 1998, after sterling strengthened, with UK firms (manufacturers and retailers) holding their prices in Euros on the Irish market for fear that their Irish competitors would shift sourcing of products to suppliers in the Euro zone. Experience to date in Ireland would suggest that EMU has increased competitive forces in Ireland.

Transport costs are important for Irish competitiveness...

An efficient transport system is particularly important for Ireland...

Because of Ireland's peripheral location as an island within the EU there has long been concern that high transport costs were having a negative impact on the competitiveness of the economy. While firms in France or Germany have only to pay for a limited road journey to get their products to the major EU markets, Irish firms have to pay for at least one ferry or air journey. In addition, the cost of access transport is felt particularly keenly by the tourism sector, and concern about this aspect of transport costs was reflected in the first *National Development Plan*[29] covering the years 1989-1993.

A study published in 1992 indicated that the share of manufacturing industry costs accounted for by the transport sector was slightly higher than in the UK. However, it also showed that Irish industry had specialised into sectors with high value-added to weight ratios, reflecting the competitive penalty they suffered from their location in the periphery of the EU.[30] This highlighted the importance to Ireland of having an efficient transport system.

...however, little progress has been made in improving the competitiveness of Irish ports...

...which illustrates the importance of more progress on reform of ports.

To counter this cost disadvantage it was initially envisaged that the state would provide direct aid for access transport (*National Development Plan*, 1989-1993). However, reports by the independent external evaluator of the EU funded Operational Programme for Peripherality recommended against such investment, which was also opposed by the European Commission. Instead it was suggested that priority in developing the port system be given to introducing competition.

Because of greater efficiency in ports in Northern Ireland, by the early 1990s much of Ireland's freight exports went through them. Over the course of 1990s, there were significant developments in introducing competition into the supply of port services, bringing about a noticeable improvement in service. However, even in 1997, the proportion of freight units using the Northern Ireland ports was still surprisingly large at 47% of the total.[31]

...in contrast to road freight...

Trucking, by contrast, is fully liberalised.

By 1980 the scarcity value of a road freight license was £12 000 (or just under 40 000 Euros at 1999 prices). Legislation was not passed until 1986 to deregulate the sector, legislation that was phased in over two years. The effect of the regulation had been to force many firms to extend their activities into own account haulage. However, after deregulation there was a major increase in the share of the market accounted for by the hired haulage sector.[32] The EU single market reforms resulted in the sector being fully opened to competition from abroad.

...airlines...

The most notable success in deregulation, and one of the earliest to change, was the deregulation of the air transport sector (see

Box 1.3). This occurred in 1986 and it has resulted in a dramatic fall in fares on the busier routes and a huge volume response in traffic. As outlined in Box 1.2, the tourism industry is very price sensitive, and its success in the 1990s owes much to the reduction in the cost of access transport arising from deregulation.

…and airports.

Airlines provided an early example of the consumer benefits of market reforms.

The Department of Public Enterprise recently established a new airports regulatory body called the Commission for Aviation Regulation. The role of this regulator will be to set a price cap for airport charges. The regulator will also have responsibility for other tasks such as implementing EU regulations on slots.

Reform of bus transport has had some success…

Informal bus deregulation for inter-city services has had some success.

An informal bus deregulation for inter-city services has had some success. On routes that are contested fares are notably lower. Before deregulation in the 1970s, there were indications that the system was inefficient. Barrett, 1982,[33] estimated that savings of 40 to 50% would result from deregulation. With the introduction of some *de facto* deregulation since the late 1980s, the state owned inter-city bus company has faced continuing pressures to improve efficiency and reduce fares.

In August 2000, the Department of Public Enterprise published proposals for a new institutional and regulatory framework for the public transport system. This document proposed the establishment of a separate regulatory authority to ensure an integrated public transport system of high quality. In particular for urban buses, it suggests a franchise type model to introduce competition into the process of supplying bus services. This document forms the basis for a consultative process that is still under way.

…in contrast with taxis, where restrictive regulations have until now imposed a high cost on consumers.

New regulations, introduced in November 2000 following a court decision, have removed quantitative restrictions on taxi licences and liberalised entry to the market.

Under the regulatory regime in place before 21 November 2000, individual licensing authorities could restrict the number of licenses for taxis and wheelchair-accessible taxis granted in their taximeter areas. In Dublin the cost of a licence traded in the open market prior to 2000 was close to 101 000 Euros (a pre-2000 market figure in the region of £80 000 has been mentioned, or around 101 579 Euros). In response to an October 2000 High Court judgement, new regulations made on 21 November 2000 revise the basis for taxi licensing. They do not place or authorise any restriction on the numbers of new taxi licences granted by local licensing authorities, and revoke all earlier restrictions of this kind. National licence fees were introduced. The fee for an ordinary taxi licence is 6 300 Euros, and a fee for a wheelchair-accessible taxi licence is 125 Euros. High Court judicial review proceedings were initiated in relation to the new regulations and the case was heard in December 2000 and January 2001. The High Court has allowed taxi licenses to be issued under the new regulatory regime until it decides on the case.

Box 1.3.   Reforming the Irish aviation market

The most notable success in the area of deregulation has been the air transport market. The revolution which occurred in the mid-1980s happened more by accident than by design. As documented by Barrett,[1] in 1984 a Bill was introduced into the Dáil (Lower House of Parliament) to control the discounting of air fares. However, a popular revolt among members of the Dáil (TDs) ensued and, while the Bill was still progressing through parliament, the government announced their intention of deregulating air transport.

Competition effectively began in 1986 under the new regime. The result was new entry into the market resulting in an immediate dramatic fall in air fares on the Dublin-London route. Barrett estimates that in 1995 the real fare on the Dublin-London route was around 25% of the 1985 fare. Barrett notes that this contrasts with estimates of a 15% overall reduction in fares due to deregulation in the United States.

Already in 1987 passenger numbers on the Dublin-London route were up 65% on the regulated world of 1985 and the rapid growth has continued through the 1990s.

Barrett, 1999[2] remarks that the success of the major new entrant to the market *Ryanair* "has been based on expanding the market rather than diverting a static market". With the benefit of hindsight it would appear that the state-owned incumbent (*Aer Lingus*), prior to deregulation, was not maximising profits through a fundamental misunderstanding of the shape of the demand curve which it faced for its product.

The experience on the Dublin-London market was replicated on other routes once new entrants started competition on the relevant route. The volume of traffic on the Dublin to Glasgow route more than trebled in the five years after competition began in 1994 (Barrett[3]). Competition on other routes from Dublin to the North of England also saw a remarkable increase in the volume of traffic. While the relevant period examined here saw recovery in both the UK and the Irish economies from recession in the early 1990s, a recovery that would in any event have increased the volume of traffic, deregulation clearly still had a major impact.

No assessment has yet been made of the wider economic impact of deregulation in this one sector of the economy. However, tourism is notoriously sensitive to price competitiveness. The current version of the HERMES model[4] of the Irish economy indicates that this is certainly true in the case of Ireland. It suggests a long run own price elasticity of –3.4, *i.e.* a 1% fall in the cost of the tourism product increases the volume of expenditure by 3.4%.

As an island, Ireland's tourism industry is extremely sensitive to the cost of air transport. The dramatic reduction in the cost of this form of transport consequent on deregulation has clearly made a major contribution to the exceptional growth in tourism numbers in recent years. According to Barrett (1999), "Irish tourism grew faster than any other country in the OECD in the decade after deregulation". In 1998 there were 18.5 million passenger journeys into and out of Irish airports compared to 8.3 million in 1988. Of these, 74% were by air compared to 66% a decade ago.

Barrett, 1999 concludes from this experience of deregulation in the airline market that potential market entry was not enough to affect price. Even after the experience with competition on the Dublin-London route in the late 1980s, it was only after new entry on other routes to UK regional airports in the early 1990s that fares there also fell.

This experience of deregulation in Ireland was not part of an overall strategy of introducing competition. The timing of the change was almost accidental. However, it provided a clear demonstration of the potential benefits of competition to all consumers in Ireland, having a significant effect on public opinion.

1. Barrett, S. (1997), "The Implications of the Ireland-UK Airline Deregulation for an EU Internal Market", *Journal of Air Transport Management*, Vol. 3, No. 2, pp. 67-73.
2. S. Barrett (1999), pp. 21-30.
3. S. Barrett (2000a), pp. 13-27.
4. Bradley, J., J. Fitz Gerald, D. Hurley, L. O'Sullivan and A. Storey (1993).

Due to the previous restrictive regulatory regime, the number of licenses in Dublin has not risen in line with the growth of activity and wealth in the city and, as a result, there are frequently shortages of supply, with substantial queues. This imposes a substantial loss of welfare on those seeking taxis. It also has knock-on effect on business activity.

Reform in telecommunications came late compared to other OECD countries, but has already produced lower prices.

In telecommunications, the state owned monopoly producer lost its monopoly status gradually over the period 1992-1998 and was privatised partially in 1996 and fully in 1999. The sector has been subjected to regulation by an independent regulatory authority and the rapid rate of technical change and advent of new entrants has produced a substantial reduction in costs for consumers (see Chapter 6). While Ireland negotiated a two year derogation from the EU directive to fully liberalise the telecommunications market from January 1998, the government actually implemented full liberalisation of the sector in December 1998. In June 1999 the government sold its remaining shareholding in the ex-monopoly telecommunications company, now called *Eircom*. The Office of the Director of Telecommunications Regulation was established in 1997, prior to full liberalisation and privatisation, to oversee the sector.

As a result of the entry of new firms into the sector, and the possibility of further new entrants, the cost of telecommunications has fallen significantly.

As a result of the entry of new firms into the sector, and the possibility of further new entrants, the cost of telecommunications has fallen significantly. The cost of telecommunications, measured in the appropriate CSO price index, had by Autumn 1999 fallen 16% in nominal terms on November 1996. Since that date further significant falls have taken place.

The speed of deployment of a third mobile phone license was delayed by court action. This delay slowed the introduction of competition from the new entrant, and was much against the public interest. The result has been higher tariffs for consumers.

Reform of the energy sector has been slower, though potential benefits are large.

Progress on reform of energy utilities has been slow.

As discussed in Chapter 5, progress on reform of the monopoly producer of electricity has been slow. However, the opening in February 2000 of 30% of the market to competition and the commitment to move to full market opening by early 2005, should see new entrants in the next few years. The need for change in the energy sector, to introduce a more competitive environment, has been widely recognised since the early 1990s. However, change in the sector was accorded a lower priority than for other sectors, such as telecommunications and transport, where the potential gains from deregulation were perceived to be larger. The fact that electricity prices were not out of line with those in many other EU countries limited the pressures for change. In addition, the potential cost of mistakes was perceived to be high.[34]

*Electricity liberalisation
could have a significant positive
effect on GNP, by increasing
the competitiveness of the economy.*

A study suggested that in the long run electricity liberalisation could have a significant positive effect on GNP, through increasing the overall competitiveness of the economy, while probably leaving overall employment unchanged.[35] The jobs lost through restructuring in the energy sector would be compensated for by new jobs created elsewhere as a result of the expansion in output.

The Electricity Regulation Act, which partially implements the EU directive on liberalisation, came into effect in July 1999. It set up an independent regulator who oversaw the introduction of competition into 30% of the market from February 2000, which will rise to 40% in 2002, moving to full market liberalisation in February 2005. Further legislative measures brought into effect in December 2000 implemented the rest of the directive, including establishment of an independent transmission system operator.

Box 1.4.   Promoting reform: the Irish Company Law Review Groups

Ireland's reliance on high level advisory groups in key reform areas has helped advance regulatory reform. Some of the most influential have been the Competition and Mergers Review Group, which examined competition policy and enforcement processes (see Chapter 3), and a series of Company Law Review Groups.

The first Company Law Review Group, established in 1994, was asked to examine seven aspects of Irish company law. The Group represented interests such as the accounting professions, the Law Society and Bar Council, the Irish Association of Investment Managers, the Irish Bankers Federation, the Irish Stock Exchange, the business community and the trade unions. Also represented were two government departments, the Revenue Commissioners and the Minister for Finance. The creation of a forum representing all interests in company law was a departure from the usual means of reforming legislation.

The final report, published in December 1994, made broad recommendations on the reform and simplification of company law, including contentious issues such as disclosure of directors' remuneration, disqualification and restriction of rogue directors, and creditor protection. Implementation of many of their recommendations was, however, delayed until the publication of the 1999 Companies (Amendment) (No. 2) Act.

Another Review Group was established in 1998 to recommend reforms in company law compliance and enforcement, and reported in November 1998. Following from a parliamentary inquiry into the non-payment of Deposit Interest Retention Tax, a Review Group on Auditing was established to examine the regulation of and rules governing auditors and accountants, and reported in July 2000. The recommendations of both these groups are being implemented. Yet another Company Law Review Group was set up in 2000 to review aspects of company law not covered by the original Group. This Group has been set up on an ongoing basis to review company law and support *"the enactment every two years of a Company Law Review Bill which will update, streamline and otherwise bring the Companies Code in Ireland into line with international best practice on corporate governance, having regard to the principles of compliance and simplification."*

Inefficient pub regulations substantially increase the costs of drinks for consumers.

Pubs have been a continuing problem, with poor regulation contributing to high prices...

A widely discussed problem in Ireland is the regulation of pubs. To open a new pub, a license has to be acquired from an existing pub owner. Around 10 400 pubs are authorised in Ireland. The current value of a pub license is at least 140 000 Euros. The capitalised value of pub licenses in Ireland is around 1 500 million Euros or between 1.5 and 1.75% of GDP. At current interest rates the cost of remunerating this capital amounts to around 0.3% of the value of personal consumption. At a very minimum this is the potential gain from deregulation, a one-off fall in the consumption deflator of 0.3%.[36]

The cost to society of regulation of this form is substantially higher. The restriction on entry into the market greatly reduces the potential for competition. With new entry difficult, it makes it easier for local cartels to operate and the substantial capital needed for entrants to finance the purchase of a license also provides an unnecessary barrier to entry.

...and regulatory inefficiencies such as a shifting of investment to cafés and restaurants.

The effect of the licensing regime has also been to force a change in the traditional character of pubs in Ireland. Because a single license is required for each pub, irrespective of surface area, the high cost of the license has resulted in a shift to larger pubs. In particular, in growing urban areas, the result has been the growth of "industrial" pubs with huge surface area. The restriction is also contributing to the rapid growth in restaurants and cafés, which are an imperfect substitute for pubs. The changes in the licensing system introduced in 2000 should permit greater mobility of licences from over-provided, mainly rural, areas to locations with a demonstrable need for such licences. This should result in more licensed premises in areas of greatest need, and reduce market distortions.

ANTICIPATED EFFECTS
OF FURTHER REGULATORY REFORM

Significant progress was made on regulatory reform over the last decade, but Ireland faces a large and unfinished reform agenda. Further progress will be required over the coming decade if the potential growth rate of the economy is to be realised, and if the rise in living standards is to be shared fully by consumers.

Further regulatory reform founded on market principles can help create new foundations for long-term growth in Ireland. Large potential gains are possible in many sectors.

Regulatory reform founded on market principles can help create new foundations for long-term growth in Ireland. Future growth will require improving the efficiency with which the economy uses inputs, organises production, innovates new technology and generates new products and profit opportunities. Experience in other OECD countries shows that regulatory reform can generate rapid increases in productivity and efficiency. If Ireland's experiences are similar to those seen elsewhere, large potential productivity gains are possible in many sectors, including electricity, telecommunications, transport, and distribution. Synergistic effects are important, both between sectors and between reforms in individual product markets and labour, land and capital markets, suggesting that broad-based regulatory reform will amplify the gains in individual sectors.

Declining prices will mean greater consumer income and demand, helping sustain growth in the long run.

Regulatory reform will generate large gains for consumers and exporters as price levels drop substantially and the variety and quality of services improves. Declining prices, in turn, mean greater consumer income and demand. These demand effects, complementing the supply side effects of regulatory reform, can be multiplied by further reducing prices through rapid implementation of reforms, helping to sustain growth in the longer run.

In the current high-growth economy, the transitional costs of job losses due to reform will be minimal, while more jobs will be created throughout the economy.

From the viewpoint of transitional costs for employees, the changed circumstances of the Irish economy make it an appropriate time to actively pursue regulatory reform.

The changed circumstances of the Irish economy make it an appropriate time to actively pursue regulatory reform. Whereas in the past the temporary job losses that might occur in the face of restructuring could have added to unemployment, this is not the case today. The economy is now highly constrained in the labour market. This means that anyone losing a job will immediately find productive employment elsewhere in the economy. In the case of regulatory reform, the change should, if anything, enhance output and productivity in the relevant sector. At the same time, the labour resources released as part of the reform will expand productive capacity elsewhere in the economy, allowing more rapid growth in GDP. This reflects the fact that employing people in unproductive activities or in an inefficient way is particularly wasteful in an economy where there is full employment.

This change in circumstances was reflected in a study, published in 1998,[37] which examined criteria to be used in making decisions on industrial policy. It argued that, whereas in the past the creation of new jobs in an economy with high unemployment conferred benefits on society over and above the increase in output, this is no longer the case. Since publication, Ireland has moved to a situation of full employment, further strengthening this conclusion.

Bottlenecks in physical infrastructure such as housing, transport, and environmental services are fueling inflation and constraining future growth.

Rapid convergence to EU average living standards could be brought to a premature halt by bottlenecks in the economy.

There is a danger that rapid convergence to EU average living standards could be brought to a premature halt by bottlenecks in the economy. There are three main areas where bottlenecks are already apparent: physical infrastructure, labour supply, and problems in the structure of administration and regulation.

One of the most obvious areas where the economy is running into physical constraints is in housing.

One of the most obvious areas where the economy is running into physical constraints is in housing. Demand for housing increased substantially due to many factors and, despite the fact that completions of dwellings are at an all time high, house prices are up more than 100% since 1996. Though data for 2000 show a moderation in the rate of increase, continuing high demand is likely to put persistent pressure on the housing market. The price increases are driven partly by the fact that Ireland has had, and continues to have, more adults per dwelling than is the case for most other EU countries, with the exception of Spain. Combined with a disproportionate share of the population in its late teens or 20s, this requires a major increase in the number of dwellings. The rapid increase in real incomes for this group is also encouraging a rise in the proportion of a cohort that is a head of an independent household. The number of dwellings built in Ireland in 1998/99 was around an eighth of that in Germany in 1994, in spite of their very different populations. This reflects the extent to which the government and the building sector have responded to demand, but rapidly rising prices, especially for skilled labour, suggest that any further increase in output will prove difficult if no measures are taken to increase the capacity of the sector. In line with the response of the building sector to the increase in demand for houses, the planning authorities have also improved their productivity to cope with the greatly increased demand.

Problems in the housing market are indicative of a wider shortage of physical infrastructure. A report commissioned as an input into the current *National Development Plan*[38] identified shortages of infrastructure in environmental services, public transport and roads as serious underlying constraints on expanding housing output. In addition, it indicated that sclerosis in the physical planning system was seriously delaying progress in implementing plans for major infrastructural investment and in producing more dwellings.

There is a need for a rapid increase in public physical infrastructure.

The report on *National Investment Priorities 2000 to 2006* found a need for a rapid increase in public physical infrastructure, broadly defined, to accommodate the growth that has already taken place, and which is in prospect. While many of the recommendations for infrastructure investment are being implemented, or are likely to be implemented in line with the National Plan, there remain concerns about the ability of the planning system and the civil engineering industry to deliver. A report by the CSF Evaluation Unit for the EU Commission, *Ex Ante Evaluation of the National Development Plan, 2000-2006*, expressed concerns about the ability to deliver on plans, not because of inadequate funding, but because of supply constraints in the building industry. These constraints are reflected in the inflationary pressures particularly affecting that sector.

Labour shortages, too, are emerging and are likely to worsen as the supply drops.

Labour shortages, too, will slow future growth.

The second area where bottlenecks are clearly emerging is labour supply. The labour force has risen rapidly in the last decade, but the rate of growth seems likely to slow in the immediate future. Growing problems in the availability of childcare[39] are affecting the supply of female labour. While participation rates for younger women are above the EU average,[40] there remains some room for catching up among older women.

In the late 1990s returning emigrants and growing immigration of skilled labour were important factors in expanding the productive capacity of the economy. However, the cost of accommodation and the growing congestion in urban areas is slowing this inflow.

While the unemployment rate has fallen dramatically in recent years, there remain a significant number of individuals who are marginally attached to the labour force and whose lack of appropriate human capital discourages their long-term employment prospects.

Capacities in the public sector are not sufficient to deliver the volume of decisions and services needed to address the infrastructure deficit.

Sclerosis in physical planning is delaying important public infrastructure projects.

A major obstacle to redressing the infrastructure deficit is sclerosis in the system of physical planning. This is especially important for major public infrastructure projects, such as roads and urban public transport. The combination of many layers in the planning approval process with subsequent recourse to the courts means that, for many major infrastructure projects, it may take many years from inception to commencement of construction. The costs of such delays imposed on the country are growing steadily.

Decisions on major infrastructure projects are now made by an independent planning appeals board, and a new planning law enacted in 2000 aims to further streamline the planning control and infrastructure consent systems. It may also help control lengthy appeals. But there are grounds to believe that long delays will continue. In particular, shortage of appropriate staff to implement improved procedures could be a major bottleneck. Even after the appeals process within the planning system is exhausted, there remains the possibility of even more lengthy appeals through the court system. In the past, this obstacle resulted in lengthy postponement in some important infrastructure projects.

Weak competition in key sectors is another risk to future performance.

Ireland's history of a weak "competition culture" still leads to a lack of competition in key sectors of the economy...

In a competitive world, a lack of competition in key sectors of the economy raises serious concerns. To some extent, this is the product of a weak "competition culture" in the past. In spite of recent successful reforms several areas, including stronger laws in the 1990s about competition, further change has been slow to come about, partly because of well-organised and powerful lobby groups.

...which pushes up costs for businesses.

Continued restraints on competition can have a negative effect on national competitiveness, by pushing up the costs and wage levels of businesses. For example, the slow rate of change in the energy sector, and restrictive licensing laws in the case of pubs, pharmacies, and the taxi market created an environment lacking in competition. Over the medium term, measures need to be taken to deregulate certain key areas in the economy to allow real competition to develop. Successful liberalisation in both the

39

telecommunications and aviation sectors has shown the gains that can be had from liberalisation. As a result of allowing competition in these areas, considerable restructuring and change took place as incumbents sought to improve efficiency and as new entrants sought to get a foothold in markets. Ultimately such competition has resulted in more choice, improved services, and lower prices for consumers. Recent changes in the regulation of taxis and pubs may produce similarly beneficial changes in those sectors.

Completion of the privatisation agenda, within appropriate regulatory frameworks, is a high priority.

Privatisation should be completed.

In the 1980s, progress on privatisation arose from a desire to realise the value of assets held by the state at a time when public finances were severely stressed. However, more recently, the focus has shifted to the issue of how services can be provided more efficiently. It is this latter issue which assumes the greatest economic importance[41] today, since experience shows that the private sector generally produces goods and services more efficiently in a competitive market. Given the potential for efficiency gains, it was appropriate for the state to privatise Greencore (a food processing company) and Irish Life (Assurance Company), and most recently *Telecom Eireann (Eircom)*. Similarly the state should probably privatise its remaining assets in the banking sector.

In the case of monopolies, privatisation of a dominant integrated firm is unlikely to prove the best route. While external regulation can help to modify the damaging effects of a monopoly, regulation is often ineffective, leaving considerable power in the hands of the monopolist. The best way of dealing with this situation is to restructure the dominant firm so that market competition can emerge for competitive activities. In the case of "natural monopoly" a second best solution is to force the monopoly to limit its role to managing the business and to buy inputs through a competitive tendering process. This approach is being pursued in the United Kingdom by the regulator of the water industry. In the Irish case, B*ord Gáis Eireann* (the gas utility) and B*ord na Móna* (the peat production utility) have also pursued this strategy, gradually restricting their business to the core management of their activities, and buying in services, such as pipe-laying and maintenance. This makes the accounts of the firms much more transparent, greatly facilitating the task of the regulator.

Stronger competition policy is key to success after liberalisation.

In the aftermath of privatisation and liberalisation, strengthening competition policy is key to ensuring that consumers benefit, as recommended in Chapter 3.

Irish local government services supply many essential public services, but tend to be inefficient and fragmented.

Reform of local government services should be a priority.

There has been little reform of local government services. This sector is both a producer and a supplier of public services in Ireland. Many areas such as maintenance of social housing, road maintenance, engineering and architectural design of public infrastructure, waste disposal and water supply, which in other countries are produced by the private sector, are produced in Ireland by a fragmented local government sector. The operation of the community employment programme is a particular example.

In many other EU countries, economies of scale have seen the growth of significant utilities, whether in public or private ownership, charged with providing essential sanitary services. In Ireland, each small local government unit is responsible for both the production and supply of sanitary services to local communities. In many cases in rural areas such services are provided on a limited basis by local co-operatives. The fragmentation of the industry has meant that it has never reaped the scale economies that have been exploited elsewhere.

As well as the small scale of the utilities in the sanitary services sector, the production, as well as supply, of a range of public services by the local government sector is not efficient. The absence of competition, for example in housing maintenance services provided by local governments, reduces quality and raises costs. As a result, there is wide scope for efficiency gains in this area.

Market-oriented reforms in delivery of public services can result in targeted services and substantial cost savings.

Outsourcing in OECD countries has usually been successful in lowering costs.

Outsourcing, when and where introduced in OECD countries, has usually been successful in lowering costs though consumers have not seen lower prices as gains have usually been absorbed by municipal budgets (either reducing pressures for tax increases or increasing service quantity or quality). In urban transport in Denmark, for example, the costs of operating the Copenhagen bus system dropped by 24% since public tenders were introduced in 1990.[42] Transition expenses involved in the tendering process, including compensation costs involved in laying off workers, where this has occurred, have usually been a fraction of annual savings.[43] In Sweden, outsourcing of elderly care in the early 1990s resulted in prices falling by one third. In most countries, the documented cost savings from contracting out are typically quite large, at around 20% (see Table 1.4).

There is some debate whether levels or quality of service were always maintained while these savings were achieved, but what does seem clear is that effectively implemented contracting out can improve productivity. Experience also suggests that the requirement to market-test can act as the catalyst to other reforms which improve the productivity of ongoing in-house production by about the same order of magnitude (OECD, 1998).

Cost savings in public services result from efficiency gains through better management, increased job flexibility and economies of scale and scope, not from social dumping or reductions in quality.

Concerns about service quality must be addressed in the framework for outsourcing.

Use of outsourcing has been hampered by concerns that it results in job loss, lower wages, social dumping, and downgrading of skill levels, hurting workers and lowering service quality. Past

41

experiences in some countries seemed to support these important concerns. In Denmark, observations of declines in quality derive from cases where municipalities outsourced services and simultaneously cut service quality to increase cost savings.

A growing body of evidence, however, shows that these concerns can be met through appropriate design of outsourcing. Outsourcing has not usually led to lower quality and can increase service quality. In the United Kingdom, the Labour Government has made clear that "retaining work in-house without subjecting it to real competitive pressure can rarely be justified,"[44] and its Best Value programme combines cost and efficiency targets with quality targets.

The evidence shows that outsourcing has not usually led to lower quality.

Outsourcing has allowed local governments to more explicitly choose the quality of service they wish to provide for a given level of spending, thereby increasing transparency and government accountability. Thanks to the tendering process, the market has generated quality standards for results. Private contractors, working with interested local governments, have developed technical performance standards for a variety of operational services. Some countries have seen the development of specialised consulting firms that work with local authorities to specify quality standards in their tenders. To out source effectively, local governments needed to become more proficient in tendering and contract specification, management, and oversight to be sufficiently confident about using outsourcing. As both market actors and local governments gain expertise in working within this system, the results in terms of service quality depend on choices made by the local authority.

Table 1.4. Cost savings in the wake of contracting-out in selected countries

	Estimated savings (per cent)	Source
United States	20	OECD (1991), "The United States Experience with Contracting Out under Circular A-76", by L.S. Dudley, *Public Management Occasional Papers* No. 2.
	20-50	OECD (1993), *Economic Outlook* 54.
	22	Stiglitz (1991).
United Kingdom	20	*Market Testing Bulletin: Special Report*, 9th January 1995, Cabinet Office.
	6.25	OECD (1993), *Economic Outlook* No. 54.
	21	Office of Public Service (1995) "Government Opportunities Publication".
Australia	20	M. Lambert, "Contracting Out Initiatives and Opportunities in New South Wales", *Making the Australian Public Sector Count in the 1990s*, IIR Conference, February 1995.
	15	OECD (1993), *Economic Outlook* 54.
	*	Industry Commission (1996) *Competition Tendering and Contracting by Public Sector Agencies*.
Sweden	9-15	OECD (1992), OECD *Economic Surveys* 1991/1992, *Sweden*.
	9-25	OECD (1993), *Economic Outlook* No. 54.
Iceland	20-25	National Authorities.
Denmark	5-30, average of 14.5	*Erfaringer med udbud og udlicitering*. Finansministeriet, August 1995. PLS Consult (1997), published by the Danish Ministry of Interior.

* Potential overall addition to GDP of 0.3 to 1.7%

Lifting of quantitative restrictions on entry into service sectors such as the pub sector could produce significant one-off reductions in price levels.

Removing restrictions on entry in service sectors will reduce price pressures.

The damage done to the interests of consumers by the restriction of entry into these businesses is significant. In mid-2000 there was again some recourse to the use of price regulation. However, such measures will fail in inducing the entry, efficient and innovation needed to bring down prices. The appropriate way forward is to remove restrictions on entry. In the current inflationary climate, such an implementation of competition could produce a significant once-off reduction in the price level, contributing to the broader needs of fiscal policy.

Further liberalisation of the retailing sector might be possible following a recent review of planning regulations.

The retail sector is generally competitive, but its heavy dependence on UK retailers, combined with restrictions on entry because of planning regulations, may prevent new entry by retailers in the Euro area. If such retailers were to enter the market, sourcing products from suppliers within the Euro area, this could immediately increase competition. However, possible gains from new entry have to be weighed against the need to plan for an orderly spatial development of urban areas. As part of the process of drawing up new planning guidelines, and to address concerns about the effect of planning restrictions on retail competition, a study was commissioned by the government to examine the likely impact of the proposed guidelines on competition in the Irish retail sector, on the supply of products to consumers at lower prices, on consumer choice, and on the supplier base. Results of the study were considered in finalising the Retail Planning Guidelines issued in January 2001.

There is need for further action in transport sectors.

Competitive pressures in most transport sectors should be boosted.

Progress in deregulating air transport was early and impressive, but there is need for further action to increase competitive pressures in other transport sectors. The ongoing debate on the appropriate method of providing public transport services is important. Once this debate is concluded, reforms should be implemented rapidly. Experience with the sector is that change has been very slow to materialise. While the road haulage sector has been deregulated, the report by the Department of Public Enterprise published in 1999[45] on the sector concentrated on the interests of the road haulage sector itself and not on the interests of consumers and the wider economy.

Figure 1.3. **Comparative indicators of product market regulation in OECD countries, end-1997
Overall regulatory approaches[1]**

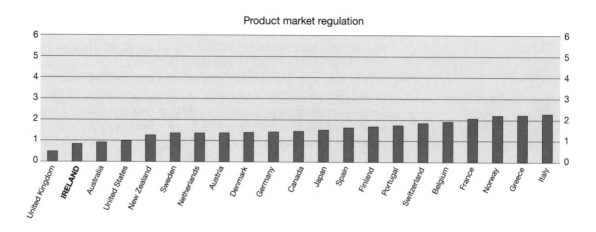

Product market regulation

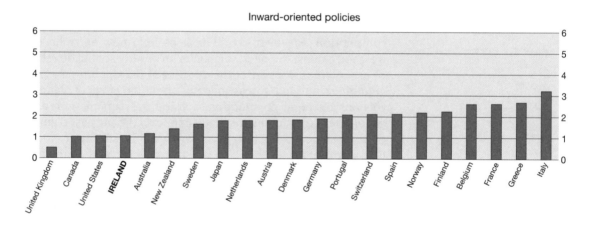

Inward-oriented policies

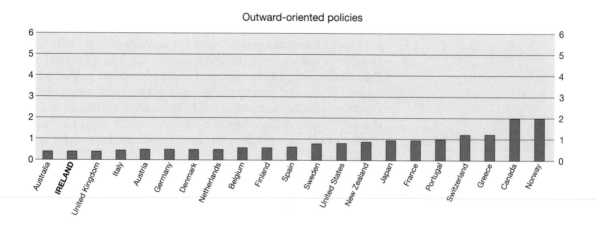

Outward-oriented policies

1. The scale of indicators is 0-6 from least to most restrictive.
Source: OECD.

Figure 1.3.   **Comparative indicators of product market regulation in OECD countries, end-1997** *(cont.)*
Inward-oriented regulations[1]

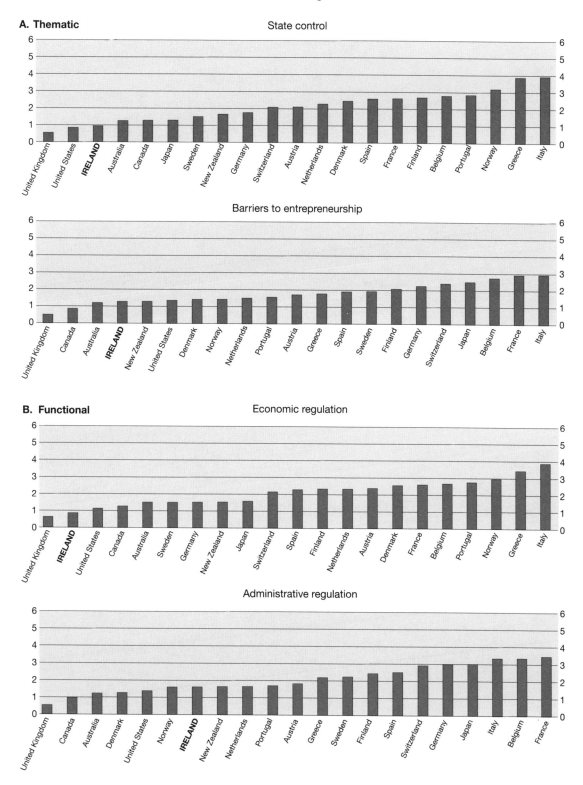

A. Thematic

State control

Barriers to entrepreneurship

B. Functional

Economic regulation

Administrative regulation

1.   The scale of indicators is 0-6 from least to most restrictive.
Source: OECD.

45

Chapter 2

GOVERNMENT CAPACITY TO ASSURE HIGH QUALITY REGULATION

The awakening of the "Celtic Tiger" was supported by a public administration that has taken steps to adapt policies to the changing market environment. In addition to the policies of privatisation and liberalisation described in Chapter 1, significant improvements were made to the Irish public service and the national regulatory environment (Box 2.1).

Pragmatism and steady progress have characterised Irish reforms to the public sector.

In a step-by-step transformation, the roles of the state, markets and society have steadily shifted toward consumer interests and market competition.

The Irish approach to modernisation of the public sector during the past decade was based on pragmatic steps. Successive Irish governments based their efforts on building consensus through processes of national partnership. Hence, the Irish reform style is closer to the experience of the Netherlands and Denmark than to countries that have taken a "Big Bang" approach. In this step-by-step transformation, the roles of the state, markets and society have steadily, if slowly, shifted toward consumer interests and market competition.

Accountability and transparency have been enhanced, through traditional participatory and consensus-building mechanisms characterised by the social partnership approach, and through new mechanisms such as enforcement and compliance with the *Freedom of Information Act*. The Strategic Management Initiative is fostering a new culture in government regulatory practices. New market-oriented institutions have been set up or strengthened, such as sectoral regulators and the competition authority.

Yet reform of Ireland's regulatory governance lag behind dynamic market and social changes, and hence could be a bottleneck to sustained growth.

Yet decades of statist policies and attitudes have left their mark...

The fundamental shift to new styles of governance has not been completed, due to the difficulty of reversing many decades of statist policies and attitudes. Over most of the life of the Irish state, government policies were aimed at redistribution, protection of producers, and managing slow growth and high unemployment. The market-led growth of the past decade evolved so rapidly that it has strained the capacities of government institutions to perform urgent new tasks:

47

repair market failures, support dynamic competition, protect consumer interests, and target social welfare at new needs. Skills gaps and institutional and cultural rigidities persist in the public administration that could create bottlenecks to future growth.

Box 2.1. Managing regulatory quality in Ireland

Ensuring regulatory transparency:

– Since the advent of the Public Service Management Act 1997 and the Freedom of Information Act 1997, the flow of information between departments and the public has been considerably enhanced. In the past few years, prior consultation at an early stage in the development of regulations has become more common in many departments. However, most consultation and transparency practices is still at the discretion of ministries.

– Since 1999, a Regulatory Quality Checklist requires that proponent departments outline the extent to which interested parties have been consulted.

– Notice of new legislation (primary and secondary) is given in the *Iris Oifigiuil* (Official Journal). In many cases, notice is also published in national newspapers circulating throughout the country. There are bound volumes of the Acts for each year. Current plans include making statute book available on the Web and preparing updated CD-ROMs. In 2000 the government presented a Statute Law (Restatement) Bill to enable it to produce administrative consolidations of laws.

Promoting regulatory reform and quality within the administration and the Parliament:

– The Strategic Management Initiative (SMI) has promoted quality across all government activities, including the preparation of laws and regulations. In particular, each department needs to undertake on a regular basis a systematic review of all its operations and ask whether each policy was necessary or whether it could best be achieved by alternative means. This process has resulted in some regulatory reforms.

– The government adopted in July 1999 the Reducing Red Tape policy which requires that each department and office assess all new laws and regulations based on a "Quality Regulation Checklist" and assigns responsibility for implementing the programme at a senior management level. It called for the listing of relevant legislation (primary and secondary) to identify the scope for consolidation, revision or repeal.

– A Statute Law Revision Unit was established in the Office of the Attorney General in 1999 to improve the quality of existing legislation in term of public accessibility. The Unit also drafts consolidation bills and supervises the preparation of indexes.

Assessing regulatory impacts:

– As part of the Checklist, since 1999 departments need to indicate if the proposed law and regulations has impacts on competition, market entry and administrative burdens, as well as the distribution impacts they may have on SMEs.

Toward accountable and results-oriented regulation:

– Judicial review in Ireland has been more vigorous than in other countries, and thus forms part of the central regulatory management armoury.[1]

– SMI requires that each department and office prepare a Strategy Statement at least every three years. In 1997, the Implementation Group of Secretaries was given responsibility for implementing and monitoring SMI and reporting progress across departments to the *Parliament*.

---

1. In the last 30 years, an increased willingness of the courts to strike down legislation as being unconstitutional has increased awareness by public servants of the need to draft legislation that is constitutionally robust.

...and new challenges to public sector quality such as skills shortages are arising.

In short, governance in Ireland still faces important challenges in adapting its practices, culture, and relations to a high-growth and pro-market environment in which consumer interests are dominant. For example, one challenge facing the Irish government is a shortage of skills and personnel resulting from rapid economic growth. The number of applicants for entry-level positions in the civil service is declining as more opportunities open up in the private sector. Key institutions are experiencing difficulties in recruiting and retaining staff. Labour shortages are compounded by skills mismatches. At local and national levels, shortages have hit the staffing of the planning authorities and the appeals board.

A second challenge is that interventionist practices that reduce market efficiency linger in the Irish public sector. There is still suspicion of market mechanisms and a cautious attitude toward market-based approaches. The "command and control" reflex, looking first to a regulatory solution rather than to other types of policy instruments (or no intervention), is still present among parliamentarians and regulators. Competition principles are not widely used in public debates and policy statements. Producer interests tend to take precedence over consumer interests (see Chapters 1 and 3). In this respect, the public statement by the minister responsible for sectoral regulation that, as a general principle, competition rules should apply throughout the public enterprise sectors, is a useful guide for the government. Regulatory bodies need to be vigilant to avoid capture by producer interests who, in the aftermath of more intensive competition policy enforcement, will intensify their efforts to use regulatory regimes for private advantage.

Irish regulatory reform policy is broad and includes most of the OECD's recommended regulatory quality tools...

Reforms underway since 1994 establish a broad programme of action to reform the regulatory system.

The 1997 OECD *Report on Regulatory Reform* recommends that countries "adopt at the political level broad programmes of regulatory reform that establish clear objectives and frameworks for implementation." A public sector reform programme called the Strategic Management Initiative (SMI) has, since 1994, been the vehicle to promote quality across the government, including regulatory reforms (Box 2.2). In addition, the government adopted in July 1999 a report, *Reducing Red Tape – An Action Programme of Regulatory Reform in Ireland*.

The *Reducing Red Tape* policy and its programme of action are comprehensive and in line with regulatory quality standards in place across the OECD area. It sets out the policy of deepening public consultation with a department's "customers and other interested parties" through existing mechanisms and establishment of new user groups. It requires that each department and office assess all new laws and regulations based on a "Quality Regulation Checklist" and assigns responsibility for implementing the programme at a senior management level. It called for the listing of relevant legislation (primary and secondary) to identify the scope for consolidation, revision or repeal.

The breadth of the programme is slowly expanding, following a decentralised approach in which the ministries have the main role.

The programme is slowly materialising, following the SMI's decentralised approach. The Assistant Secretary General of the Department of the Prime Minister in charge of SMI is responsible for co-ordinating policy on regulatory reform. Senior officials are responsible within each department. In Summer 2000, two officials were appointed in the Department of the Prime Minister as the first staff of the new central resource unit to co-ordinate the regulatory reform agenda. An *Ad Hoc* high level group of senior officials has begun to examine implementation of recommendations on administrative simplification accepted by the government.

...such as regulatory review...

Reviews of the large stock of existing laws and regulations are proceeding, and could pick up speed.

In parallel with the regulatory quality policy, the government has made progress in reviewing existing laws and regulations. A Statute Law Revision Unit was established in the Office of the Attorney General in February 1999 to draft statute law reform and consolidation bills and undertake related work, including supervising the preparation of indexes to the statutes and statutory instruments. Approval will be sought for the introduction of changes in the procedures of Parliament so that revision bills may be enacted on a fast track procedure.

A recent initiative, the *Statute Law (Restatement) Bill*, currently being discussed in Parliament, will strengthen the review policy. It proposes that the Attorney General prepare and make available (in hard copy and electronic form) Acts that restate the statute law in any given area in a more intelligible form without any change being made to that law except in its presentation. To speed the process, instead of proceeding through the Parliament, it is proposed that restatements be certified by the Attorney General. This policy will also be of particular benefit where a series of Acts has been consolidated and the consolidation has been superseded by an amending Act. Parliament has yet to develop a specific role in relation to this novel procedure.

...but implementation is still weak...

Implementation of regulatory reform, however, is weakened by lack of clear priorities and incentives strong enough to transform deep-seated regulatory traditions and practices.

However, implementation is weak. Regulatory reform is only one of many SMI projects, with unclear priorities. Reliance on the SMI approach, based on self-assessment and peer pressure, may provide too few incentives (positive and negative) to effectively transform deep-seated regulatory traditions and practices. Establishment of a small unit in the Department of the Prime Minister to drive the agenda and monitor progress is good practice. However, the smallness of the unit raises questions about political commitment and effectiveness. The Unit is not a true watchdog over regulatory quality because it does not have capacities nor a mandate to assess the quality of answers to the Checklist.

Moreover, no explicit links seem to exist between the implementation of the regulatory reform policy and related policies such as structural adjustment policies, competition policy or trade openness.

...and there is an important gap in regulatory quality principles.

Secondly, the OECD has recommended as an essential principle that regulations should "produce benefits that justify costs" and "consider the distribution of effects across society." This principle is referred to in various countries as the "proportionality" principle or, in a more rigorous and quantitative form, as the benefit-cost test. Such a test is the preferred method for considering regulatory impacts because it aims to produce public policy that meets the criterion of being "socially optimal" (*i.e.*, maximising welfare).[46] This key principle is insufficiently developed in the policy of the government of Ireland and in the Checklist.

Box 2.2.   The Strategic Management Initiative: changing the civil service culture in Ireland

The main vehicle for modernising the public service was the launching in 1994 of the *Strategic Management Initiative* (SMI). This is regarded as the first successful reform of the Irish public service since the foundation of the independent state.

The SMI contains initiatives aimed at improving customer service and delivery of policies, including simplification of administrative procedures and regulatory reform, and aimed at internal improvements of the administration, such as devolving authority and accountability.

The programme is based on a "bottom-up" approach, where "shared ownership" by public administrators is favoured over a "top down" approach. The government implements SMI through self-assessment, that is, a requirement that each department and office identify its strengths and weaknesses and put into place a process of strategic management. Strategy Statements are prepared each three years, or after the election of a new government. Departmental strategies are consistent with the current policies of the government, and international and EU obligations. Departments are requested to implement sectoral programmes that follow the core initiatives.

To oversee the SMI, the government appointed nine top-level civil servants to serve on a steering group, supported by specialised working groups of senior officials and experts from public and private sectors. This group has now evolved to become an Implementation Group of Secretaries General comprising the Heads of all Government Departments and Offices. Their mandate is to manage the overall implementation and further development of the SMI. Two small executive units support the programme. In 1999, a Change Management Fund of IR£ 5 million per annum was established to support departments and offices (up to 50% of the project costs) to implement the programme.

From some perspectives, the SMI has been successful, though no comprehensive, external evaluation has yet been undertaken. The SMI helped to reverse low morale in the public service, resulting from the perception that public management was centred on the goal of cutting the number of public servants. A recent evaluation of the departments' strategic statements showed progress, finding significant improvements in strategic capacities, a reduction of "aspirational expressions", better focus on customers and a significant effort on performance measurement. The study, however, stressed that there was room for improvement. The SMI has also helped change the culture of public service and its public dealings. Concrete improvements are felt by citizens dealing with the Department of Social Community and Family Affairs and Revenue Commissioners, and transparency and accountability have improved. Some departments have undertaken strategic examination of particular policies in light of external changes, such as policy papers on critical aspects of accountability, transparency and ethics (such as the *Freedom of Information Act*). SMI has also helped to improve the degree of formality in administrative procedures across the government.

The Strategic Management Initiative: changing the civil service culture in Ireland(*cont.*)

Critics have pointed out, however, that the SMI has been slow to show concrete results and that outcomes only became tangible in 1999, five years after its launch. Lack of uniform compliance by departments and offices has raised questions about the drawbacks of a "bottom up" approach based on self-assessment and peer pressure to achieve objectives rather than on incentives and a standardised approach. The lack of precise indicators and targets and of an explicit auditing mechanism by an independent overview body have hampered the development of objective measures of performance. The ability of central oversight to challenge progress is unproven. The effectiveness of the new collaboration mechanisms to deal with cross-cutting issues, such as children policy, asylum seekers and regional development, is still to show results. Anticipation of needs and adaptation to change, monitoring and evaluation of policy and effective reward for performance are yet to be engrained in the operation of services. Equally, application of the SMI has had little impact on local government capacities as yet.

Significant improvements have been made to consultation and transparency, but further action can pre-empt the risk of capture by insider groups.

Consultation with affected parties has long traditions in Ireland, and its practice is improving.

The Irish public service attaches great importance to public consultation. Consensus building, anchored in extensive dialogue with the social partners is considered a central element of the economic and social successes of the country. Since the advent of the *Public Service Management Act* 1997 and the *Freedom of Information Act* 1997, the flow of information between departments and the public has been considerably enhanced. In the past few years, prior consultation at an early stage in the development of regulations has become more common in many departments.

Recent measures, such as the enactment of the *Freedom of Information Act*, a new *Electoral Act* and codes of conduct, and the role of the Ombudsman have further improved transparency and accountability. These tools would be strengthened by further reducing the influence of informal mechanisms and processes that provide opportunities for interests to monopolise information, and thus favour "insiders", and by strengthening government-wide "watchdog" functions such as competition advocacy by the competition authority (Chapter 3).

Yet rent-seeking attitudes increase the risk of capture and insider-outsider problems...

Improving transparency continues to be a challenge in Ireland because policy-making still confronts rent-seeking attitudes, typically in the form of close relationships between elected representatives and particular producer interests which usually act against market principles. This environment reduces market confidence and increases the risk of investment, which might be costly for Ireland as competitiveness becomes more intense.

...which are heightened by inconsistency in consultation processes.

The risk of capture is exacerbated by the fact that there is little consistency in consultation processes; and consultation tends to be *ad hoc* and informal. There are no formal written procedures to prescribe as a matter of course who should be consulted, and in practice it is often producer groups. Important interests, notably consumer groups, report that they have not been able to participate and defend their interests. Consultation processes on zoning or reforming local public transportation have raised criticism that the policies can be unduly influenced by influential groups. Hence, consultation may be vulnerable to "insiders" or powerful interest groups, relative to smaller or new actors such as consumers or market entrants.

Clear guidelines and training, establishing "notice and comments" requirements and improvement in the quality of the documents subject to consultation may be required.

Clear guidelines and training, establishing "notice and comments" requirements and general improvement in the quality of the documents subject to consultation may be required, without unduly formalising the processes. On the other hand, too much of the wrong kind of consultation can be equally damaging. As the Netherlands discovered in the 1990s, too many advisory bodies focusing on details reduce accountability, the quality of public consultation and slow government responsiveness to a changing environment. The establishment in Ireland of more than 90 groups under the last Social Partnership Agreement raises these kinds of concerns.

Existing institutions and procedures for consensus building may not be adequate to deal with a rapidly-changing society. Some interests such as unions and "big business" representatives may play too large a role.[47] Changing priorities and strategies involve re-assessing whose interests are affected. A new pro-competition stance should require a re-balancing of powers between the views of producers and those of consumers – an interest group which does not participate in the Partnership process.

RIA has not been implemented effectively, and economic assessment of proposed rules is missing.

The use of RIA is in its infancy in Ireland.

The 1995 *Recommendation of the Council of the* OECD *on Improving the Quality of Government Regulation* emphasised the role of regulatory impact analysis (RIA) in systematically ensuring that the most efficient and effective policy options were chosen, and most OECD countries use RIA. The use of RIA is in its infancy in Ireland. The government adopted RIA only in July 1999, later than most OECD countries, and it is not yet consistently implemented. Hence, regulatory quality disciplines in Ireland are still primarily aimed at legal quality rather than regulatory efficiency and performance.

A standardised Quality Regulation Checklist includes various tests on the quality of the future regulation...

In November 1999, the *Cabinet Handbook*, which guides departments on the administrative procedures to follow when making laws, was amended. According to the *Cabinet Handbook*, when presenting a Memorandum for the government all departments and offices must "indicate clearly, as appropriate, the impact of the proposal" based on a standardised Quality Regulation Checklist which includes various tests on the quality of the future regulation, such as its efficiency and need. Such tests include impacts on 1) relations, co-operation or common action between North and South of Ireland, and between Ireland and Britain; 2) employment; 3) women, 4) persons in poverty or risk of falling into poverty, 5) industry costs and cost to small business; 6) rural communities and 7) costs to the Budget and

...and could easily be the basis for the development of more rigorous regulatory impact assessment.

staffing implications (in consultation with the Department of Finance).[48]

Among other aspects, the Checklist establishes a clear test concerning the impact of legislation on market entry, restriction on competition and increase in administrative burdens, which gives it a market-oriented and pro-competition stance. It could easily be the basis for the development of more rigorous regulatory impact assessment, but additional steps are needed. For example, secondary regulations seem to be exempted. The Irish RIA does not include specific methodologies or even guidance. Analysis and quality control should be more developed, particularly for economic impacts, with a broader scope, appropriate skills, and adequate incentives for different stakeholders. The Checklist asks if affected parties have been consulted, but should also ask how the ministry responded. The extensive list of impacts to be considered should be shortened to establish clear priorities with respect to benefits and costs, in line with adoption of the benefit-cost principle. It is currently so long, imprecise, and difficult to assess that it has little analytical credibility, and the criteria for regulatory efficiency are not clear.

Alternatives to regulations, such as economic instruments, have replaced few traditional "command and control" approaches.

Ireland has been slow to use policy instruments that work more efficiently and effectively than traditional regulatory controls.

Much reform of the regulatory process in other OECD countries is based on the use of wider range of policy instruments that work more efficiently and effectively than traditional regulatory controls. Ireland has been slow in promoting the use of policy instruments that have been proved to work more efficiently. In general, regulators still tend to rely on "command and control" mechanisms. This may reflect the conservatism of the Irish administration, and in some sectors, a rigid regulatory approach taken by European regulation. Progress nevertheless is seen in some areas, such as voluntary codes of conduct organised by industry groups, and this trend will be accelerated if the Regulatory Quality Checklist embedded in new regulatory policy is adequately implemented and enforced.

Implementation and enforcement of the Reducing Red Tape policy may need to be stronger to make a real impact on administrative burdens.

Some results have been accomplished in tackling administrative burdens through the Reducing Red Tape programme...

A focus of current Irish policy is control of administrative burdens. The recent programme, *Reducing Red Tape*, is an important addition to an array of initiatives and policies, stretching back more than a decade. Some evidence exists of significant results: business licences and permits have been reduced and improved in some areas. Efforts by the Revenue Commission have streamlined and simplified the information requirements provided by firms. Registration of companies has been simplified, permitting the registration of a company in one week. Ireland has been praised for implementing a sophisticated and efficient environmental licensing system covering air, water, noise and waste/soil.[49] The setting up of a one-stop-shop by the Industrial Development Authority and simplified administrative procedures to help foreign investors have been recognised as useful in attracting foreign investment.

...but substantial improvement is still needed in the use of licenses and co-ordination across levels of government.

Nonetheless, such initiatives tend to be piecemeal and lack a systematic approach. Anti-competitive licensing schemes still govern activities such as utilities, public transport, banking, lotteries, places of public amusement, professions, and are frequent policy tools in areas such as environment and health. The extent and number of licenses and permits are not known with certainty. A particular concern is the lack of consistency across the central administrations and local governments when establishing formalities, and the lack of co-ordination of information required by departments and agencies.[50] These inefficiencies have disproportionately higher impact on SMEs.[51]

The Irish government has launched a constructive debate on the design and governance of the new independent regulators.

Ireland is building a series of market-based institutions to separate ownership, policy development and day-to-day regulatory overview in key economic sectors.

As have most OECD countries, Ireland is building market-based institutions to separate ownership, policy development and day-to-day regulatory overview in key economic sectors. In 1997, regulatory functions for telecommunications were transferred to the Director of Telecommunications Regulation. Two years later, the Commission for Electricity Regulation was established and the Government now plans to enlarge its remit to include regulation of the gas sector. In February 2001, legislation was enacted to establish a regulatory body to deal, among other things, with airport charges; a regulator-designate had been appointed in late 1999 in anticipation of the legislation. In September 2000, regulation of postal services was assigned to the telecommunications regulator. Regulatory arrangements for surface transport are still under consideration.[52] In February 2001, the government announced the establishment of a new sectoral regulator for financial services: the Irish Financial Services Regulatory Authority (IFSRA). The new authority will have its own board and an independent chair, who will report to the Minister for Finance and to the Prime Minister.[53]

Good design means that their functional independence is working properly.

These regulatory authorities operate within policies laid down by the minister responsible for policy in the sector. Practice in Ireland indicates that with respect to functional independence, the design is mostly working properly. For instance, in terms of financial independence, the independent regulators are funded by the industry on the basis of fees for licences and levies. This has allowed the regulators to have adequate staff, premises, equipment, services and other resources necessary for their operation. Oddly, the independence of sectoral regulators in utilities in the public sector contrasts with the position of the Competition Authority (see Chapter 3). A problem is that some of the energy regulator's powers are granted by statutory instrument rather than law, and hence could be removed by a single minister. Independence will be more credible when these provisions are incorporated into statute.

The regulatory framework is being modified to improve accountability to the parliament...

Important accountability issues have received attention, and the regulatory framework has undergone development. The 1997 legislation establishing the independent telecommunications regulator made no provision for accountability to Parliament, apart from the production of an annual report and accounts. However, the 1999 legislation for the electricity regulator requires the Commission for Electricity Regulation to account to parliamentary committees for its performance. Although there is no statutory obligation, the Director of Telecommunications Regulation has appeared before parliamentary committees on several occasions. Proposed legislation for regulation of the communications sector will include a statutory obligation in this regard. It is important that the accountability requirements are balanced with the necessary operational independence of the regulators. Also, Parliament's committees may not have the capacities to materially respond to such a responsibility, due to lack of financial and human resources.

...and further discussion is underway about the transparency, fairness, efficiency and effectiveness of decision-making by the regulators, their relationship with stakeholders and their enforcement powers.

In March 2000, the discussion was expanded with publication by the Minister for Public Enterprise of a policy paper on *Governance and Accountability in the Regulatory Process.* The document develops the regulatory framework to resolve perceptions about "democratic deficit" which could have had an impact on the credibility and legitimacy of the new regulatory institutions.[54] The document discusses the transparency, fairness, efficiency and effectiveness of decision-making by the regulators, their relationships with stakeholders and their enforcement powers. The document proposes:

– Introduction of legislation to clarify the right to judicial review of the decisions of regulatory bodies, and propose that, unless otherwise decided by the courts, the decision of a regulator should stand while under review.

– Updating relevant legislation on fines and penalties so that punitive measures reflect the nature and consequences of a breach of regulatory rules.

– Adoption of a model of regulatory commissions comprising three persons, as in the case of the Commission for Electricity Regulation.

– Strengthening of consultation mechanisms between the Competition Authority and sectoral regulators.

– Setting of public service/social requirements should remain a function of the minister, but regulators and interested parties should be invited to make suggestions to the minister.

The report recommends periodic reviews, a good practice to maintain flexibility in domestic regulatory regimes.

Given the changing nature of technologies and evolution in markets, the policy requires that a review should take place on a regular and systematic basis, possibly every three to four years, though aspects of telecommunications may require more frequent review. An important concern that the report tends to make worse affects the core objectives for regulators. The report justifies regulatory intervention as a way to "to facilitate market entry, ensure fair market conditions and customer protection and ensure that all users have access to a basic level of services at reasonable prices. In this way, economic regulation can comprehend social and regional objectives". These objectives are commendable, but the report does not consider their potential contradictions and does not set priorities or mechanisms to help the regulator resolve discrepancies. Hence, the performance criteria for the regulator are not clear.

Some issues are still to be settled. In 1996, the government announced its intention to establish a multi-sector regulator for the energy and communications sectors.[55] Since then, a shortage of appropriate expertise has appeared, yet the political position has shifted away from the multi-sector regulator approach to setting up independent regulators for each regulated sector. This is a less than optimal use of scarce human resources and poses risks of duplication between bodies. Proliferation of sectoral regulators may also increase institutional rigidity and fragmentation, and augment the risk of capture by powerful interests.[56]

Governance and Accountability in the Regulatory Process concluded that, for the present, regulation at the sectoral level was probably the most appropriate for the utilities in Ireland, given that it would allow for an approach focused on the particular circumstances of the various markets while comprehending the competition/complementarity between industries operating (or potentially operating) in the same market. However, *Governance and Accountability* noted that, as markets develop the justification for detailed sectoral regulatory intervention might diminish over time and the question of a supra-sectoral regulatory authority could be re-examined, at a future date.[57]

Modernisation of other state institutions merits further attention.

The judiciary, Parliament, even the regions require faster institutional adaptation.

The judiciary, the new market-based institutions, including the competition authority, the Parliament and its committees, even the new regional powers need institutional adaptation in terms of their efficiency, accountability and overall co-ordination.

Judicial review has helped in some respects to improve the quality of regulation, but must also confront new challenges to adapt to the new Irish context. Through judicial reviews and appeals, judges increasingly make key regulatory decisions. This has raised concern about judicial trespass into the field of the legislature.[58] Not dissimilar to debates in other countries, this complex issue requires continuing attention to the selection, appointment and training of judges. Further, application to a court of competent jurisdiction is regarded by businesses as slow, complex and expensive. Ireland has been slow to develop private arbitration and other alternative dispute resolution mechanisms (see Chapter 5). A recent reform, the *Courts Service Act, 1998*, may improve the administration of justice by emphasising user quality and investment in information technologies.

Compared to the pace of change in the executive branch, the Parliament has been slow to assume its new accountability responsibilities.

Compared to the pace of change in the executive branch, the Parliament has been slow to assume its new regulatory accountability responsibilities. Parliamentary committees exercise extensive powers and prerogatives to oversee regulators. However, adequate resources have not accompanied these new competencies. The lack of resources and research capacities means that members of the Parliament are dependent for information on the government and interest groups. Changing institutions, the transfer of competencies to European levels, new domestic consultation processes and the setting up of independent regulators further complicate Parliamentary overview, and contribute to a loss of influence by the Parliament over national regulatory policy.

Regulatory quality at the local government level merits more attention.

Local governments enjoy a range of new responsibilities, some of them regulatory…

Ireland is one of the most centralised countries in Europe, as its 114 local authorities have a more limited range of powers than their counterparts in other EU countries.[59] As described in Chapter 1,

---

Box 2.3. Regional regulatory frameworks and Northern Ireland

Optimal regulatory frameworks for Ireland might in some cases extend beyond Irish borders into Northern Ireland. This may be the case, for example, with network industries such as telecommunications, transport, energy, and water, and with policies such as environmental quality and SME development. In energy, since 1993, gas is increasingly imported through a gas interconnector from Scotland, but gas demand is soon expected to exceed the interconnector capacity. The Irish electricity transmission system is linked to the Northern Ireland system but net imports accounted for less than 2% of total electricity supply in 2000. Except for Northern Ireland, there are currently no possibilities for interconnecting the Irish electricity grid on a commercial basis due to the geographical location of the island. Hence, further developing the interconnection with Northern Ireland offers possibilities for realising added efficiency gains in electricity generation, transportation and distribution on the island. The authorities in the Republic and Northern Ireland are aware of the potential offered by an all island energy market and the two administrations have jointly commissioned consultants to examine the operation of the markets in each jurisdiction with a view to creating an all-island energy market in a European context. This report is expected by mid 2001.

Progress in underway in establishing the political capacities for island-wide regulatory co-ordination. While institutional relations and co-ordination between the Irish and Northern Irish authorities were rare, the Good Friday Agreement of 1998 changed this situation. Since the Agreement, the discharge of a range of public functions is undertaken in close co-operation with the devolved government in Northern Ireland, while certain functions are now carried out on an all-island or cross-border basis. These co-operation arrangements are set out in and governed by the *British-Irish Agreement Act, 1999*.

A North/South Ministerial Council (NSMC) has been established to bring Ministers, north and south, together to develop consultation, co-operation and action within the island, including through implementation on an all-island and cross-border basis. The Ministerial Council has a range of modes of operation, including exchanging information and consulting, reaching agreement on adoption of common policies, and taking decisions by agreement on policies and actions at an all island and cross-border level to be implemented either (a) separately in each jurisdiction, North and South or (b) by implementation bodies operating on a cross-border or all-island level. Six such bodies have been established, many with regulatory relevance, with defined executive functions in the areas of Inland Waterways throughout the island, Food Safety Promotion throughout the island, Special EU Programmes, Language (Irish and Ulster Scots), Trade and Business Development and Lough Foyle and Carlingford Lough (inland fisheries and aquaculture in these river basins). Six areas have been identified for co-operation in the first mode described above: Agriculture, Education, Transport, Environment, Tourism and Health.

In line with the Good Friday Agreement, a British-Irish Council (BIC) has also been established, comprising representatives of the British and Irish Governments, of the devolved governments in Northern Ireland, Scotland and Wales, together with representatives of the Isle of Man and the Channel Islands Priorities identified for co-operation under the BIC include the fight against drugs, social inclusion, transport links and the knowledge economy.

---

local governments provide many public services, and have some authority in building construction and traffic management. New responsibilities have been added to local governments, in areas such as environment, planning, urban renewal, housing and general development, while others have been reduced, such as health functions that were moved to regional health boards and primary environmental protection transferred to a specialised agency.[60] Local governments have a limited role in the fields of education, health, public transport (except taxis). Their involvement in social programmes is growing. In terms of regulatory powers, local authorities' competencies concentrate on licensing and permitting (*e.g.* land use) and control of nuisance and litter.

...yet there are few explicit quality principles for local regulatory decisions.

Few explicit quality principles to be observed when preparing new local rules existed until recently. The *Local Government Bill* being discussed in Parliament will make further changes to ensure transparency and wider consultation on local decisions, for example by ensuring that almost all meetings of the local elected members be in public. In 2000, the Planning code was overhauled to improve transparency and accountability of local authorities in respect of decisions concerning the preparation of the draft development plan. These reforms may help local governments modernise management, streamline administrative procedures and reduce duplication.[61]

Two particular concerns arise. Inefficient spatial and housing planning is becoming an important obstacle to growth, impeding greater employment mobility and emigration and exacerbating inflation and transport problems. The problem is rooted in the many layers in the planning approval process, with recourse to courts.[62] Second, as noted in Chapter I, many local governments are simultaneously producer, supplier and regulator, a confusion that impedes the delivery of high quality public services. The sheer number of local governments has fragmented industries so they are incapable of reaping scale economies in maintenance of social housing, road repair, engineering and architectural design, disposal and water supply.

Chapter 3

THE ROLE OF COMPETITION POLICY
IN REGULATORY REFORM

Competition policy is central to regulatory reform.

Competition policy is central to regulatory reform, because, as regulatory reform stimulates structural change, vigorous enforcement of competition policy is needed to prevent private market abuses from reversing the benefits of reform. Competition principles and analysis provide a benchmark for assessing the quality of economic and social regulations, as well as motivate the application of the laws that protect competition.

Competition policy continues to be a key weakness that is undermining Ireland's move to sustainable market-based growth.

Ireland has moved to implement best practices in competition policy and enforcement, but its efforts have suffered from missed opportunities and uncertain commitment. Ireland's present prosperity offers an opportunity to strengthen its commitment to effective competition policy.

Small business traditions supported control, not competition.

From a history and tradition of protecting small producers and fair competition, Ireland has tried for the past decade to establish a competition policy founded on promoting efficiency and consumer welfare. This new approach should be congenial to reform, as economic policy has abandoned autarky and embraced the goal of a market-led and open economy. But the process of developing this new approach and creating the institutions to apply it has encountered difficulties, while lingering tradition of concern about supposedly unfair competition impedes reform in some non-traded sectors. Despite Ireland's leap into the international economy over the last 20 years, the tradition of protecting small enterprises against competition remains strong.

Through the 1990s, competition policy had a difficult time taking root in the domestic economy. Policy and institutions continue to evolve.

The "prohibition" approach was adopted in 1991 At first, enforcement was too weak...

In 1991, a new Competition Act prohibited restrictive agreements and abuses of dominance, and the old Fair Trade Commission was succeeded by a new Competition Authority ("Authority"). But the means provided for enforcing these new prohibitions were ineffective. The Minister for Industry and Commerce could file suit in court, but never did. Private parties could sue for damages or injunctions, but few succeeded. The independent Authority had only an advisory role in enforcing the prohibitions or controlling mergers. The weakness of the initial enforcement system suggests that, despite the change in the statute, the commitment to stronger competition policy was ambivalent.

... but now sanctions are tougher and enforcement is independent.

Concern about the lack of public competition law enforcement led to calls for further reform in the mid-1990s. One obvious step was to give the independent Authority the power to seek court orders to stop prohibited conduct. The Competition (Amendment) Act of 1996 also made all violations of the law potentially criminal offences and set fines and even imprisonment as available sanctions. Ireland thus provides in principle for some of the toughest sanctions in OECD countries for similar violations.

More institutional reforms are proposed.

At the same time, the Minister appointed an advisory panel, the Competition and Mergers Review Group ("CMRG"), to examine competition policy and enforcement processes. The CMRG issued its final report in early 2000, making 40 detailed recommendations about applying competition law and about the relationship between competition policy and other regulatory institutions and policies. Its recommendations often parallel the actions recommended by the OECD in this report.

Competition principles are integrated to some extent into the general regulatory reform programme...

The government's reform programme makes competition a top goal.

In the government's general regulatory reform programme, competition policy is a main substantive theme. As Chapter 2 notes, the Strategic Management Initiative's "quality regulation checklist" asks whether each regulatory proposal "will affect market entry, result in any restrictions on competition or increase the administrative burden." The 1996 Report of the SMI's Working Group on Regulatory Reform calls for "removing entry restrictions" in existing regulations, because "better quality regulation must address issues such as licences and permits". In general, the Working Group Report found that reform should "aim at the targeted dismantling of burdens to market entry and exit, price controls and other restrictions on competition."

...but market reforms of utilities and infrastructure services still do not consistently apply competition principles, and anti-competitive licensing schemes survive.

Structural reform plans depend on competition, but also pursue potentially inconsistent goals.

Plans to restructure utilities and infrastructure services aim at relying more on competition. The Department of Public Enterprise (DPE) has developed proposals to manage the relationship between regulation and competition policy. The DPE proposals recognise that the general competition law will apply in the sectors it regulates. DPE stresses the use of economic regulation during the transition to liberalised markets to accomplish some goals that are typically the function of competition policy, while also emphasising other goals and concepts, such as fairness and social and regional objectives, that can be inconsistent with competition policy based on consumer welfare or that are better addressed directly by other means.

Control, not competition,
is still invoked for
difficult problems.

Ireland's best-known competition policy problems result from anti-competitive licensing schemes, even though the SMI Working Group said such regulations should be eliminated. In mid-2000, as the economy's continued strength produced very high inflation indicators, the government's response to demands for action included imposing temporary price control prices for drinks at pubs, and relaxing, but not eliminating, the anti-competitive licensing controls against new entry. The Minister acknowledged, however, that the sustainable solution to reducing pub prices lay in greater competition. Ministers reportedly met with industry groups to emphasise the need for "social responsibility" in setting prices. Such official admonition risks encouraging potentially vulnerable industries to agree on target prices – that is, to flout the most basic principle of modern competition policy.

Ireland's basic tool kit in its competition law is comparable to those of other OECD countries...

Ireland's basic substantive law about restrictive agreements and abuse of dominance, which was explicitly crafted by analogy to EU law (Competition Act 1991), is comparable to standard practice in OECD countries. The methods for dealing with mergers, though, should be streamlined. And reliance on court proceedings and criminal sanctions, necessary for imposing fines under Ireland's constitution, introduces some technical hurdles and uncertainties.

...and is increasingly focussed on horizontal cartels.

Enforcement attention has concentrated on horizontal cartels. The Authority has announced that it will seek criminal penalties, rather than just civil relief, when it finds such conduct. However, proving secret agreements usually requires first-hand admissions, particularly when the criminal law's high standard must be met. The Authority lacks the authority to implement a leniency programme to encourage parties to make these disclosures. That will require the assent of the Director of Public Prosecutions (DPP), who recently indicated that he would support it.

Self-regulation is not allowed
to restrain competition.

Self-regulation by professional and trade associations has often been found to restrain competition in many countries. In Ireland, several associations have notified their agreements and sought licences permitting them to continue. Early decisions rejected association rules that restricted fees or advertising and found that restraints on premises and limits on training opportunities were unacceptable barriers to entry.

There are no explicit exemptions from the Competition Act, but many other laws and programmes restrict entry to protect incumbent firms.

State owned firms may be subject
to suit under the competition law.

State-owned firms are subject to the competition law, and some of them have been sued for abuse of dominance. State monopolies may operate under laws that authorise non-competitive practices or conditions, though. Non-competitive practices and conditions that have been authorised in Ireland have occurred in several sectors, including gas and water service, forestry, airport management, and road and rail passenger transport, as well as the telecoms, electric power, broadcasting, and postal sectors, where reform programmes are making the transition to competitive markets.

Local authorities may prevent competition.

Enforcement of the Competition Act cannot redress the anti-competitive effects of actions by local authorities. Such actions are typically undertaken through advisory boards that include local officials and other appointees. Areas where problems have appeared include land use, health care, and licensing. Anti-competitive effects of decisions by these bodies may not be subject to challenge as violations of the competition law. To correct these problems requires advocacy and legislation.

No de minimis principle shelters small businesses.

Ireland's competition policy makes no special provision for small business, and the Authority has advocated repealing one vestige of small-business protection, the Groceries Order. The Authority's first decision denied that the law should not be concerned about the conduct of smaller firms. On the contrary, in a small country with a dispersed population, consumers may be more vulnerable to anti-competitive behaviour by small firms such as local retailers, professionals, and service providers.[63] Nonetheless, some observers continue to advocate adopting a *de minimis* rule, perhaps to make Ireland's rules consistent with the EU's in this respect. But it would be difficult to devise safe-harbour tests that would not shield some notorious competition problems from effective enforcement.

…but enforcement capacities are still being tested.

Requirements of criminal law complicate enforcement.

The Authority must resort to the courts to obtain enforceable orders and sanctions, even in non-criminal matters. Resort to courts and criminal sanctions introduces complexities and difficulties. The scope of application of criminal sanctions remains to be determined authoritatively. A particular concern could be that government efforts to control inflation by persuasion might insulate price fixing agreements from liability, if the parties to the agreement contend that the intended effect of their conduct was to respond to the Ministers' wishes in the public interest. There will be continuing uncertainty about the standards to be applied, at least until the courts have more experience and have issued more decisions. An opportunity was missed in 1996 to assign jurisdiction for Competition Act prosecutions to the central criminal court, where the president of the Court could assign an expert judge.

Criminal penalties have been applied only recently.

The Authority itself can bring summary actions in the lower, District court, seeking penalties up to a fine of IR£ 1 500 or six months imprisonment. Summary procedures must be brought quickly, though, and thus they may not be appropriate for complex cases, which will take more time for investigation and trial. The Authority did not obtain a conviction in a summary prosecution until late 2000. For more serious cases, the Authority may refer its investigative results to the DPP, who may seek an indictment and much higher penalties, fines of IR£ 3 million or 10% of turnover, whichever is greater, and imprisonment up to 2 years. Criminal liability may attach both to individuals and to firms. As of early 2001, no indictments had been authorised yet. In general, courts have rarely imposed high penalties in white collar crime cases.

Private litigation has sometimes been the only recourse.

Private lawsuits could be important.

Private enforcement has been unusually significant in Ireland. For the first 5 years after the Competition Act was passed, private actions were the only form of enforcement. The 1996 Amendment Act created a wider personal liability for directors, shadow directors, managers and other officers of the defendants. Private plaintiffs can now sue those individuals, as well as their firms.

But private suits have encountered difficulty.

High costs and legal uncertainty have discouraged some potential plaintiffs. Courts have struggled with the complex economic issues, and the experience has led members of the bar to believe that competition cases are difficult to win. But the private right of action may still have tactical value, in putting additional pressure on adversaries and in gathering evidence. Although plaintiffs have rarely won outright-the courts often find there is dominance, but not abuse-the decisions have established some sound and useful precedents about the application of the Competition Act.

The Competition Authority has a continuing role in curbing abuses in traditional utility and infrastructure industries.

Some applications to network monopoly have been controversial...

Since 1996, there have been many occasions to challenge the abuse of dominance by traditional network and infrastructure monopolies, in telecoms, electric power, gas, and air transport. Notably, the Authority claimed, in an April 1999 lawsuit, that Telecom Eireann's refusal to grant unbundled access to the local loop constituted an abuse of a dominant position.

...but restructuring tools have not been used.

Special provisions of the competition law could be used to restructure dominant firms and infrastructure monopolies, through processes that depend on political decisions rather than law enforcement. But the power has not been used. Ireland's utility monopolies, which are under the jurisdiction of a different minister, are being restructured by sector-specific legislative programmes, and the CMRG has recommended that this unused power be deleted from the competition law. But if that is done, there may be no other means of achieving structural changes to correct and remedy violations. The powers of Irish courts to impose a structural remedy to control or undo a position of dominance are not yet clear.

The possibility of contradiction and confusion in merger reviews makes the process clearly unsatisfactory.

Separate laws control mergers.

The process of applying competition policy to mergers is clearly unsatisfactory. Large mergers must be approved pursuant to the Mergers and Take-Overs (Control) Acts. The Department of Enterprise, Trade and Employment (DETE), not the Authority, administers the Mergers Acts, and decisions to authorise or prohibit mergers are made by the Minister. The Mergers Acts' substantive standard includes a competition policy test and a general criterion, whether the transaction would be likely to operate against the "common good", which makes the range of policy concerns that the Minister might consider virtually limitless.

The Authority also claims Competition Act powers.

The Authority has contended that all agreements, even those governed by the Mergers Acts, may be restrictive agreements that the Competition Act would prohibit unless the parties notify the Authority and receive a licence. Based on this claim of jurisdiction, the Authority has propounded a general merger analysis and enforcement policy via a category certificate and licence. The overlapping notification systems expose parties to uncertainty and risk. The risk may be considered low, as few firms bother to make notifications to the Authority.

The potentially conflicting processes should be streamlined.

The review process should be more transparent and the role of the independent body should be strengthened. The CMRG recommends shifting roles, so that the Authority would receive all merger notifications and would be responsible for competition policy analysis in every case. A standard two-phase competition policy review would involve a quick examination to identify possible competition issues, and a more thorough investigation for the small proportion of filings that present them. The Minister would retain full power to permit, or prohibit, a merger on the basis of other permitted policy criteria, but the Minister could not over-rule the Authority's conclusions and decision on the grounds of competition policy. This process would bring Ireland more into line with practice in many other OECD countries that have merger review provisions in their competition statutes. The government has decided that a new Competition Act will take merger control out of the political arena and, except in the case of media mergers, give it entirely to the Competition Authority.

Box 3.1.   The groceries order: time for reform

In one sector, grocery retailing, special rules based on principles of unfair competition, in place since 1956, have led to anti-competitive conditions and calls for reform. One rule is similar to a prohibition of below-cost sales, but because it is based on invoice price, its actual effect is an anti-competitive form of resale price maintenance.

Some of the Order's other provisions may also be inconsistent with general competition policy principles. Its rule[1] against refusal to supply ignores costs, justifications, the parties' market positions, or the actual effect on the customer or on competition. On the other hand, provisions to equalise bargaining strength might be useful in some market settings, although they may not be flexible enough to take account of innovative marketing strategies and relationships.

The CMRG recommended repealing the Order; however, the government has determined to retain it. To support the consumer-welfare goals of competition policy, rules about marketing practices and discrimination should be sensitive to actual effects in particular circumstances. Thus, a rule against discrimination should permit consideration of differences in costs, available alternatives, and competitive responses and effects, rather than punish every price difference as an offence.

1.   Art. 13(1)(a).

The Authority is perhaps too reliant on the ministry for its resources...

The Authority's independence is limited.

The Authority is independent in decision-making, but in other respects it is strongly dependent on DETE, to which it is attached for administration, personnel, and budget. Experience in other OECD countries shows that competition policy bodies which depend on ministry decisions for budget and personnel may be exposed to indirect ministerial control over their priorities, while agencies with hiring authority and separate budget authorisation from parliament or other sources of funds may have more effective decision-making independence.

...and critical understaffing has appeared, which will require continuing attention in Ireland's tight labour market.

The Authority has suffered a crisis in personnel.

Uncertainty about personnel has hindered the Authority's work. The Authority had difficulties through 1998 and 1999, and by mid-2000 it was critically understaffed. The principal reasons for the problems appear to be the expiration of limited-term personnel contracts, which had discouraged retention of professional staff, and increased demand for people with these skills at the new sectoral regulators and private sector firms involved with regulation, as well as disruptions that accompanied the resignation and replacement of the chair in early 2000. Appointments restored the Authority to its full 5 member complement in the third quarter of 2000, and by the end of the year nearly all authorised professional positions were filled.

The Authority has tried to move into an advocacy role, but making advocacy effective will require more resources and clearer independence.

Independent advocacy power has been limited.

The Authority has had the power to study and report on practices and methods of competition since 1991; since 1996, it has been able to do so on its own initiative. But the law does not clearly provide for Authority comments on particular policy proposals. Nonetheless, DETE has tried to provide some means for the Authority's views to be considered in policy development. The CMRG recommended that the Authority should have statutory powers to issue opinions on regulations and existing and proposed legislation and to advise public bodies. The new competition act now being drafted should consider this recommendation.

Responsibility for competition policy impacts is diffused.

Pro-competitive reform has been a theme at DETE, which is responsible for policy issues related to the competition law (Ireland, 2000). In intra-government deliberations, DETE can call attention to the impact of regulation on competition. But other demands can affect DETE's competition policy priorities. DETE is also responsible for consumer protection policy and enforcement, which can include controlling prices under the Prices Act. The competition policy office in DETE has been undertaking, as of mid-2000, a review of existing legislation and regulatory programmes to identify state-promoted legal and other restrictions on competition in all areas of the economy. In some sectors, the issues are already well recognised.

67

Box 3.2. Independent regulators and competition policy

Sectoral reforms moving from monopoly toward competition have highlighted the relationships between general competition policy and special sectoral regulators. Independent regulators for telecoms, electric power, and aviation already exist. Responsibility for postal services has been assigned to the telecoms regulator (soon to become the Commission for Communications Regulation), and for gas, to the electric power regulator (to become the Commission for Energy Regulation). Regulatory arrangements for surface transport are under consideration, while in February 2001 the government announced the establishment of a new sectoral regulator, the Irish Financial Services Regulatory Authority.

The Authority's relationships with these sectoral regulators are still developing. Efficient sharing of responsibilities is hampered by constraints on sharing information and the lack of clear means for one agency to defer to another about a particular complaint. Potentially overlapping actions by the Authority and the telecoms regulator, ODTR, highlighted the co-ordination problem. In 1999, the Authority initiated proceedings against the incumbent wireline provider, contending that its refusal to unbundle local loop services was an abuse of dominance in violation of the Competition Act. At about the same time, ODTR initiated a process of public consultation to consider whether, and on what terms, the incumbent should be required to unbundle these services by regulation. Legislative measures to facilitate further co-operation between the Authority and sectoral regulators is under development by DPE and DETE.

As these sectoral regulators have begun to proliferate, Ireland has engaged in a debate about the implications of institutional independence and the relationship with competition policy.[1] The Minister for Public Enterprise called for comment in September 1999 on regulatory governance and accountability. Her proposals appeared in March 2000. DPE's proposals include means for promoting accountability to the public, such as formal decision procedures, consultation requirements, comment opportunities, publication of comments and decisions, and protection of confidentiality. Regulators would be accountable to the Minister through regular strategy statements and work programmes. And the parliament could request regulators to account to parliamentary committees at least annually. This review would deal with implementation of plans and overall performance, but not, in theory, with individual decisions.

DPE recognises that regulators' tasks now call for interventions to facilitate entry and ensure fair market conditions and consumer protections. DPE notes that sectoral regulators have powers over licensing conditions that necessarily involve them in competition issues. This suggests the potential use of those powers to enforce compliance with competition rules, if the enforcement methods of competition law are considered too time-consuming and legalistic. DPE acknowledges that sector-specific rules should not, in principle, conflict with generally applicable competition rules, but rather than try to resolve remaining tensions between them, the proposals take advantage of the contemporaneous appearance of the CMRG report to call for more consultations between the ministries and for continued consultations between sectoral regulators and the Authority.

The CMRG makes detailed recommendations for managing the relationship between sectoral regulation and general competition policy. To emphasise the generality of competition policy, the Competition Act should continue to apply to regulated sectors, without any substantive exclusion or exemption. A single public body, the Authority, should enforce it. To avoid putting firms in impossible positions where regulatory decisions overlap competition issues, conduct undertaken pursuant to a regulator's decision or approval should not be subject to the most serious sanctions, of criminal liability or damages, though it might still be enjoined as a violation of the law. These recommendations have the net effect of giving competition policy a general priority while leaving to the courts the task of working out the balance between competition policy and regulatory decisions in particular cases. CMRG recommendations would also encourage co-ordination among enforcers, to prevent serious conflicts from developing. A new competition act currently being drafted should take account of the CMRG recommendation in this area.

---

1. The more general problem, of establishing the right balance among independent decision-making and political accountability, is taken up in Chapter 2.

Analysis and advocacy are languishing because of resource constraints.

Authority comments have aided the process of reforming traditional utility sectors, notably electric power and natural gas. Previous industry studies such as the Authority's 1998 papers about competition problems in the taxicab and retail drinks industries were influential factors in public debate. But the Authority's policy work is being pushed aside because of resource constraints. A general study of surface passenger transport issues, begun in 1999, has been deferred because of lack of resources. Re-establishing this function is a high priority.

Chapter 4

ENHANCING MARKET OPENNESS THROUGH REGULATORY REFORM

Market openness further increases the benefits of regulatory reform for consumers and national economic performance. Reducing regulatory barriers to trade and investment enables countries in a global economy to benefit more fully from comparative advantage and innovation. With the progressive dismantling of traditional barriers to trade, "behind the border" measures are more relevant to market access, and national regulations are exposed to unprecedented international scrutiny by trade and investment partners. Regulatory quality is no longer (if ever it was) a purely "domestic" affair.

Ireland has gained substantial benefits by pursuing trade liberalisation, welcoming foreign-owned firms and integrating in the world economy.

Ireland's growth performance in the 1990s reflects Ireland's commitment to integration in the European Union and global markets.

Ireland's stellar growth performance in the 1990s reflects an array of policy reforms, but in particular Ireland's commitment to integration in the European Union, through the single market programme and EMU. Foreign investors, partly lured by generous incentives, have recognised the attractiveness of Ireland and made significant investment in skilled-labour-intensive and export-oriented sectors that have transformed Irish production capacity and broadened Ireland's trading interest beyond the EU market. Despite the scope and depth of EU integration, Ireland increasingly trades with non-EU states, taking advantage of competitive input sourcing on a world basis and further re-enforcing the competitiveness of Irish production capacity.

Today, Ireland relies more on trade than almost any other OECD country.

Trade is increasingly important to the Irish economy.

Trade is increasingly important to the Irish economy. Total merchandise trade amounted to 125.1% of GDP in 1999, up from 102.4% in 1993 (Table 4.1). This ratio is about twice as high as for other OECD countries with small populations – New Zealand (44.1%), Norway (54.8%), Portugal (58.2%), Finland (60.2%) and Sweden (65.2%). This high ratio reflects the strong and growing integration of Ireland within the world economy.

Despite the scope and depth of EU integration, the EU's share of Ireland's imports and exports dropped between 1988 and 1998, with a corresponding increase in exports to the United States and larger imports from Singapore and the rest of the world. The Irish trade pattern suggests that the Irish integration process within the EU has not been detrimental to non-EU trading partners. It also highlights that Ireland has gained commensurate benefits in pursuing integration within the world economy.

Table 4.1. Merchandise trade in Ireland

Trade (% of GDP)	1993	1995	1999
Exports	58.5%	67.2%	75.4%
Imports	43.9%	49.8%	49.7%
Export + Imports	102.4%	117.0%	125.1%

Source: Ireland's Central Statistics Office.

Ireland has also been successful in attracting foreign investment, though its investment incentives have prompted some complaints.

Foreign-owned firms were responsible for two-thirds of manufacturing employment and more than three-quarters of Irish imports and exports in 1996.

Foreign-owned firms have profoundly modified the structure of the Irish economy. They were responsible for two-thirds of the manufacturing employment and more than three-quarters of its imports and exports in 1996. Ireland, together with Hungary, has the highest shares of both production and trade accounted for by foreign affiliated firms among all OECD countries. Prior to 1995, FDI originating from the United States accounted for about half of total FDI and this share exceeded three-quarters in 1995-1998 (Table 4.2). Reflecting the relative attractiveness of Ireland among OECD countries, Ireland's share of total OECD inward FDI increased by a factor of six during 1988-1998. The presence of foreign affiliates brought tangible linkages and spin-offs to the Irish economy, in terms of improved human skills in high value-added activities, improved access to the world marketing networks of these firms and diversified export destinations.

Ireland was late in enhancing its attractiveness as a host country for foreign direct investment (Box 4.1), but mainly since the 1960s programmes were set up to encourage FDI. More recently, several factors have been instrumental in Ireland's success in attracting greenfield investments in skilled-labour-intensive and export-oriented sectors such as information and communications technologies, financial services, healthcare and pharmaceuticals. Among the explanatory factors are access to the EU-wide market, the availability of high skilled labour at a reasonable cost, a preferential tax system, an industrial agglomeration in electronics and pharmaceuticals, and linguistic affinity with US investors. To maintain its attractiveness, the National Development Plan was published in 1999 and aims to raise the quality of Ireland's physical, educational and social infrastructure to continental European standards.

Irish programmes to attract foreign investment have caused some controversy.

Irish programmes to attract foreign investment have caused some controversy. EU members have complained about the competition-distorting impact of the Irish preferential tax system. In July 1998, an agreement was reached between the European Commission and Ireland that removed the discriminatory provisions and addressed concerns about the state aid aspects of the Irish corporation tax regime.

Table 4.2.   Foreign Direct Investment, Inflows

FDI	1988	1990	1995	1996	1997	1998
Direct Investment (Million Irish Pounds)	169	125	235	360	383	415
Origins (% of total)						
Europe	41%	36%	12%	13%	13%	21%
USA	51%	52%	78%	83%	84%	78%
Others	6%	12%	10%	3%	1%	1%
Ireland/Total OECD	0.07%	0.14%	0.27%	0.78%	0.58%	0.48%

Source: OECD, International Direct Investment Statistics Yearbook, 1999.

Irish growth was fueled by openness in Irish labour markets which allowed substantial immigration of valuable labour.

Employment creation was supported by a net migration inflow.

As described in Chapter 1, Ireland maintained between 1994 and 1999 an average annual rate of employment creation of 5.1%, outstripping the OECD average of 1.16%, and bringing its unemployment rate to 3.7% in October 2000 – down from 15.7% in 1993. This employment creation was supported by a net migration inflow. To ease labour shortages, firms are recruiting on a world-wide basis, using EU labour mobility and a new work visa that was established to make it easier for people originating from outside the European Economic Area to take jobs in Ireland.

Continued focus on encouraging labour immigration is necessary for sustaining future economic prosperity.

As labour shortages are spreading through the economy, wage and residential cost pressures are creeping up and are gradually eroding some of the perceived Irish comparative advantages. The consumer price index reached 6.2% in the year to July 2000, outstripping the EU average of 2.2%. Continuous focus on encouraging labour immigration to Ireland is necessary for sustaining its future economic prosperity.

In the context of the EU-wide Schedule of commitments under the WTO General Agreement on Trade in Services (GATS), Ireland maintains few additional limitations concerning certain professional services, mainly relating to commercial presence. For example, market access is limited to partnerships for auditing services. For medical, dental and veterinary services market access is limited to partnerships or natural persons. Regarding cross-border supply, real estate services are unbound. For financial services, the right of establishment in Ireland does not cover the creation of represen-tative offices for insurance companies. These limitations should be reconsidered in the context of the ongoing multilateral trade in services negotiations in the WTO.

Box 4.1. The surprising opening of the Irish economy

The openness of the Irish economy is astonishing, given the ideologically contrary policies in place for many years after independence. As Chapter 1 notes, while the rest of Western Europe began a process of trade liberalisation and integration in the immediate post-war years, Ireland maintained a protectionist eco-nomic strategy aimed at self-sufficiency. Tariffs on imports were maintained at very high levels until the end of the 1950s and quota restrictions established a protective fence around Irish businesses.

Ireland acceded to the European Economic Communities (EEC) in 1973, ten years after its initial application to join was withdrawn when the simultaneous application by the United Kingdom was rejected. The setback and the search for alternative trade arrangements led to a series of unilateral across-the-board tariff cuts in 1963 and 1964 and the Anglo-Irish Free Trade Agreement in December 1965, which provided for a gradual phase out of reciprocal tariff protection over a ten-year period. Closer economic integration with its main trading partners, through market openness, was considered a necessary policy to improve its economic prosperity and to curb a long-term trend of emigration – in the 1950s, around 1.5% of the popula-tion in net terms was departing every year.[1]

With its EU membership, Ireland has foregone the right to follow an independent trade policy but in return it has gained improved market access to other EU member markets and a voice in the process of elaborating the EU's common external trade policy. Accession meant that it had to assume all prevailing EU rights and obligations, the *Acquis communautaire*, some of it immediately upon accession and the rest over a transitional period. These reforms rapidly brought positive results with higher economic growth and lower unemployment.

As EU countries deepened integration, Ireland was required to provide free movement for goods, serv-ices, capital and people – the four freedoms – to other EU countries. The single market program acted as a strong policy anchor and was instrumental in the Irish success in attracting foreign investment in projects designed to serve the EU-wide market and beyond. The single market directives put downward pressure on costs and prices and encouraged rationalisation in several sectors. Ireland may have grown at about one percentage point faster per year than it would otherwise have done.[2]

Since 1989, Ireland's transition to an open and liberal economy benefited considerably from EU structural and cohesion funds aimed at reducing economic and social disparities among EU members. Annual transfers to Ireland from Community Structural Funds was estimated at 2.8% of GDP between 1989 and 1993. The level declined afterwards, but amounted to 2.25% in 1997 and 1998 (Barry et al., 1997). More than half of the transfers was allocated to human resource development and physical infrastructure projects, which enhanced productive potential without adding budget pressures. Although Ireland's success has brought its per capita GDP above the EU average, its eligibility under the EU Community Support Framework will continue for the period 2000-2006, but on a different basis than previously, with eligibility criteria now varying depending on the regional location of projects.

---

1. The cumulative total of net emigration from Ireland in the 110 years up to 1991 was 2.8 million persons. OECD (1999a), p. 36.
2. Barry, Frank, et al. (1997).

Nevertheless, global and regional economic markets will pose many surprises ahead. Further reform to Ireland's regulatory framework can help it better prepare for shocks.

As Ireland's international cost competitiveness disappears, the quality of its domestic regulatory regime will be increasingly important.

Ireland's recent economic expansion has overshadowed the need to put in place a more rules-based regulatory regime that fosters economic efficiency, minimises obstacles to growth and promotes sound competitive conditions. Yet these reforms are perhaps more urgent today than ten years ago. As Ireland's cost competitiveness comes under pressure in the wake of rising labour costs and infrastructure bottlenecks, the quality of its domestic regulatory regime will be increasingly important to traders and investors. Inefficiencies, uncertainties, rigidities, and unnecessary business costs will become more influential in determining overall competitiveness.

Regulatory reform is an investment in the shock absorption capacities and sustained competitiveness of the Irish economy.

Even more important is economic flexibility. Ireland, as a small open economy, is more vulnerable to external shocks than are larger economies. Ireland will be able to deal more effectively with eventual external shocks and a less favourable global economic environ-

---

Box 4.2. The OECD efficient regulation principles for market openness

To ensure that regulations do not unnecessarily reduce market openness, "efficient regulation" principles should be built into domestic regulatory processes for social and economic regulations, and for administrative practices. These principles, described in T*he* OECD *Report on Regulatory Reform* and developed in the OECD Trade Committee, have been identified by trade policy makers as key to market-oriented, trade and investment-friendly regulation. They reflect basic principles underpinning the multilateral trading system. This review does not judge the extent to which Ireland has complied with international commitments, but assesses whether and how domestic regulations and procedures give effect to these principles.

- *Transparency and openness of decision-making.* Foreign firms, individuals, and investors seeking access to a market must have adequate information on new or revised regulations so they can base decisions on accurate assessments of potential costs, risks, and market opportunities.

- *Non-discrimination.* Non-discrimination means equality of competitive opportunities between like products and services irrespective of country of origin.

- *Avoidance of unnecessary trade restrictiveness.* Governments should use regulations that are not more trade restrictive than necessary to fulfil legitimate objectives. For example, performance-based rather than design standards should be used as the basis of technical regulation, and taxes or tradable permits should be used in lieu of regulations, where appropriate.

- *Use of internationally harmonised measures.* Compliance with different standards and regulations for like products can burden firms engaged in international trade with significant costs. When appropriate and feasible, internationally harmonised measures should be used as the basis of domestic regulations.

- *Recognition of equivalence of other countries' regulatory measures.* When internationally harmonised measures are not possible, necessary or desirable, the negative trade effects of cross-country disparities in regulation and duplicative conformity assessment systems can be reduced by recognising the equivalence of trading partners' regulatory measures or the results of conformity assessment performed in other countries.

- *Application of competition principles.* Market access can be reduced by regulatory action condoning anti-competitive conduct or by failure to correct anticompetitive private actions. Competition institutions should enable domestic and foreign firms affected by anti-competitive practices to present their positions.

ment by strengthening domestic market forces through more market-oriented regulatory regimes. In this sense, regulatory reform is a vital investment in the shock absorption capacities and sustained competitiveness of the Irish economy.

Ireland has integrated many of the OECD's efficient regulation principles into its domestic regulations.

Most of the OECD's six efficient regulation principles for market openness are integrated into domestic regulation.

Not all of the six efficient regulation principles examined in this review are expressly codified in Irish administrative and regulatory oversight procedures to the same degree. However, evidence suggests that the important principles of non-discrimination, use of international standards and recognition of equivalence are given ample expression in practice.

Transparency in market rules has improved, but is still vulnerable to insider interests, increasing uncertainty for foreign actors.

As discussed in Chapter 2, the Strategic Management Initiatives and the ensuing action plan for regulatory reform are broadly in line with regulatory standards in place across the OECD area. The policy fosters transparency and accountability by stressing the need for consultation and rules-based procedures.

Market openness for both domestic and foreign actors would be enhanced by a more formalised public consultation process.

However, market openness for both domestic and foreign actors would be enhanced by a more formalised public consultation process. Public consultation on regulatory matters remains too discretionary in terms of its duration and timing, and the selection of interested parties. There are no common criteria for evaluating the quality of either the consultation or the decisions taken by the regulators on how to consult. Although there are no specific requirements to ensure that the views of foreign parties are sought and taken into consideration during the regulatory process, the government increasingly uses the Internet for consultation, thereby reaching out to a larger audience.

In Ireland, as a small economy, the informality in relations between the market and the state was traditionally perceived as a flexible means for facilitating consensus, all the more acceptable given the producer bias in policy. Easy accessibility to government information, senior decision-makers and Irish ministers contributed to this informality, characteristics that are less likely to occur in large economies. Although informality underpins flexibility and quick responsiveness, it is often mirrored by procedures lacking in transparency with inevitable risks of regulatory capture and larger transactions costs for outsiders.

By contrast, elaboration of technical regulations and standards under EU and WTO procedures is sufficiently transparent...

Transparency in technical regulations and standards has been strengthened by regional and international discipline mechanisms.

In contrast to domestic consultation procedures, transparency in technical regulations and standards has been strengthened by regional and international discipline mechanisms. Divergent national product regulations can be major obstacles to access to domestic markets, and information is essential to firms to reduce uncertainties over applicable requirements and facilitate understanding of market conditions.

As part of its notification obligations to the European Commission and the WTO, Ireland provides information to its trading partners on the making of national technical regulations and standards, and gives them opportunity to comment. The National Standards Authority of Ireland (NSAI) elaborates Irish standards with the open participation of all interested parties, without any discrimination. The elaboration process of Irish standards and EU standards are subject to a series of check and balance features that minimise the emergence of obstacles to the free movement of goods within the EU.

…and Ireland has an excellent record in the use of internationally harmonised measures…

The harmonisation of technical regulations and standards with the EU is almost total.

As an EU state, Ireland takes part in the EU harmonisation process. Reflecting EU harmonisation, Irish indigenous standards account for less than 3% of total standards enforced. Of about 9 600 standards, there are 286 indigenous standards, concentrated in the construction and food sectors. Adoption of an indigenous standard is rare (less than four times a year on average). The decline in the production of specific regulations is reflected in the number of draft technical regulations notified to the European Commission. Since January 1993, Ireland notified 23 technical regulations, compared to a total of 4 653 for all EU members. With only three technical regulations notified by Ireland in 1999, the harmonisation of technical regulations and standards with the EU is almost total.

…as it does in open government procurement.

Irish public authorities have diligently implemented relevant EU directives for public procurement.

The Irish legal framework on government procurement transposes the guiding principles provided by the EU Government Procurement Framework. They provide for transparency, non-discrimination and equal treatment, which enhance competitive conditions and are mutually beneficial for concerned parties. Irish public authorities have diligently implemented the relevant EU directives, as illustrated by the near absence of infringement procedures launched by the European Commission against Ireland for incorrect application. A voluntary chapter of best practices on debriefing of suppliers, approved in 1999 by the Forum on Public Procurement in Ireland,[64] provides for common access to information and a common debriefing policy while ensuring respect for confidential information made available to contracting entities by suppliers.

Continued attention is warranted to ensuring respect to market openness principles by local governments.

Respect for the efficient regulation principles by local and regional administrations is essential.

Assessing the application of the efficient regulation principles by local and regional bodies is not in the scope of this review. The central government should, however, continue to promote the awareness and to encourage respect of the efficient regulation principles by local and regional communities.

A focus in the new regulatory impact assessments on competition and market entry will help keep Irish markets open against pressure from domestic producers.

Chapter 2 describes new procedures for regulatory impact analysis being put into place within the Irish public administration. The RIA discipline is important, because it can help resist the influence of producer and other inside groups who seek regulatory protection from competition, including foreign competition. The Irish RIA procedures are in many respects compatible with OECD best practices, but in other respects they seem to be too discretionary and qualitative to provide consistent and transparent information to decision-makers.

The RIA defence against new barriers to market openness is unlikely to function well in its current state.

In principle, the RIA requires an assessment of the market entry and competition impacts of proposed regulations. This is good practice, as such competition criteria could be given wide interpretation by considering the least-trade restrictiveness aspects of regulations. These criteria should encourage regulators to select regulatory instruments that minimise negative impact on

---

Box 4.3.   Ireland in the new economy: its booming market in telecommunications equipment

Ireland's ability to prosper in the new global economy, and its dependence on remaining flexible enough to adapt to new market opportunities, is illustrated by its cross-border trade in telecommunications equipment. Exports of communications-related equipment from Ireland tripled in value between 1996 and 1999 and Ireland maintains a sizeable trade surplus in this sector. Imports doubled during the same period and were instrumental for the vitality and competitiveness of the Irish communications sector.

Irish trade in communications equipment

Communications equipment (in US$)	HS Numbers	Imports		Exports	
		1996	1999	1996	1999
Telephone equipment					
Telephone sets	85.17.11+19	20 463 637	55 008 473	48 850 781	63 114 933
Switching equipment	85.17.30	9 516 903	16 629 804	39 534 762	24 480 889
Other equipment	85.17.80+90	207 821 369	640 164 664	331 468 463	1 782 124 439
Radio, Telephony, Broadcasting					
Tramsmission apparatus	85.25.10.+20	53 373 908	89 801 761	184 038 357	135 194 321
Receivers (radio/tel/broad)	85.27	56 936 948	32 529 664	117 660 998	26 545 242
Television receivers	85.28	66 173 586	67 528 444	5 127 439	77 905 934
Other equipment	85.29	141 291 121	84 538 773	30 461 966	120 124 633
Total		555 577 472	986 201 583	757 142 766	2 229 490 391

Source: OECD, Foreign Trade Statistics, Harmonised System of Classification.

competitive conditions. But, as Chapter 2 notes, the methods are not yet spelled out as to how such impacts will be assessed. In practice, recent regulatory decisions regarding the licensing of pubs suggest that the competition criterion has not been interpreted as requiring the minimising of barriers to entry. Hence, the RIA defence against new barriers to market openness is unlikely to function well in its current state.

Irish customs procedures have worked well in handling the huge increases in volume.

Customs declarations can be cleared within a few seconds, instead of six to eight hours per transaction before 1991.

Irish Customs authorities oversee 41 customs entry ports distributed through the Irish territory. A paperless system of electronic exchange was fully operational in May 1996.[65] The use of the EU Single Administrative Document (SAD) as a declaration form and electronic exchanges has drastically reduced the time required for goods to clear customs. Declarations can be cleared within a few seconds, instead of six to eight hours per transaction before 1991.

The use rate of electronic declaration forms in Ireland grew from 81% to 92% of total import declarations between May 1996 and the end 2000, and from 23% to 80% of total export declarations during the same period. Efficient customs procedures are necessary for Ireland given the important role played by imports and exports in its overall economy. The volume of total customs declarations more than doubled between 1993 and 1999, reflecting the booming Irish economy.

A weak area for market openness is competition policy. It should be strengthened to protect market openness in liberalising sectors.

The benefits of market access may be reduced by regulatory action condoning anti-competitive conduct or by failure to correct anti-competitive private actions that have the same effect. Ireland needs to remain vigilant in applying competition policy to newly deregulated sectors and privatised enterprises to ensure that access and entry are not impeded.

Dominant firms in telecom and energy can have an unfair advantage against their foreign rivals.

Efforts now underway in Ireland to reduce the role of government in economic activities by exposing sheltered sectors to competition forces are described in Chapters 1 and 3. As is true in most countries in similar phases of reform, incumbent and former state-owned enterprises still hold dominant positions in the telecommunications and energy sectors. Without careful competition oversight that is co-ordinated with trading partners, this may afford an unfair advantage in foreign markets where such firms compete against their foreign rivals.

An area of particular interest for foreign firms wishing to expand activities in Ireland relates to the Irish merger law. Due to overlapping notification requirements for merger agreements under the Mergers and Take-Overs Act and the Competition Act, parties are exposed to undue legal uncertainty and risk (see Chapter 3).

Chapter 5

REGULATORY REFORM IN ELECTRICITY, GAS, PHARMACIES, AND LEGAL SERVICES

Sectoral reforms in Ireland have been an important part of the move toward market-based growth but progress has varied among sectors. A range of key regulatory and competition issues remain in many sectors.

Reform of the Irish electricity and gas sectors has begun, but is far from finished.

Ireland is closer to the start than the finish in establishing an energy sector where private investment, innovation and lower prices are driven by competition.

Ireland has begun major reform of its gas and electricity sectors. Much has been accomplished, but delays and partial reforms have been frequent. Hence, Ireland is still closer to the starting blocks than the finishing line in establishing an energy sector where private investment, innovation and lower prices are driven by competition. In the interim, the regulatory uncertainty is an obstacle to private investment in the gas sectors.

The future agenda is a broad one. No single reform will enable the Irish electricity and gas sectors to become competitive. The economy, and its demand for energy, is relatively small on a global scale and the location is not conducive to imported competition. However, by combining structural change in generation and enhanced transmission to allow access by generation in Northern Ireland, in combination with the institutional and regulatory changes, the Irish electricity market can become competitive.

The Irish energy sectors are dominated by two state-owned firms.

One big firm dominates all activities in each of the electricity and gas sectors.

The Electricity Supply Board (ESB) and Bord Gáis Éireann (Irish Gas Board) dominate all activities in their sectors. ESB consumes about half of all gas consumed in Ireland. Both ESB and Bord Gáis are fully state-owned and vertically integrated. Electricity and gas demand are growing rapidly, reflecting GDP growth. The shift toward gas in electricity generation means that incremental electricity generation requires incremental natural gas supply. By 2010, or earlier, 70% of electricity is likely to be generated by gas and in 2000 shortages of gas were projected for winter 2002.

Ensuring efficiency and investment in these dynamic sectors can result in large cost differences and improve security and regional development.

Prices of electricity for both industrial and domestic customers are low by European standards, and about median among International Energy Agency members. Hence, reform of the energy sector might seem unimportant to Irish competitiveness. However, ensuring efficiency and investment in these dynamic sectors can result in large cost differences and improve security and regional development. For example, in spite of earlier warnings, a law that addressed the allocation of gas capacity was passed only after supply shortage concerns had become imminent. This delay benefited the incumbent because competition objectives were subordinated to short-term issues of supply security.

Restructuring to induce competition in generation is a high priority...

Decisive structural change is an integral part of reform.

Decisive structural change, including the diminution of ESB's dominant position in generation, is an integral part of a reform package. Whether that diminution takes the form of a capacity cap or divestiture is a decision that needs to rest on the experience of market entry, competition from Northern Ireland generation, and assessments of market prices and performance. It may be advisable to create separate, competing generation companies, or it may be sufficient to develop an all-island market and promote competitive entry into electricity generation. In gas, structural change means a similar separation of transmission from supply, or alternatively to retain vertical integration while selling rights to transmission capacity, thereby introducing competition in transmission.

The small scale of the Republic of Ireland's electricity system has raised the question of whether a competitive generation market is feasible. Existing plants are large relative to the size of demand, so ESB's plants could, at most, be split among two or three independent companies. Facilitating competition from generation in Northern Ireland, such as through transmission infrastructure investments and compatible regulatory regimes, would introduce two sizeable independent competitors to the Republican market.

Box 5.1. **Why restructuring matters: experience in other OECD countries**

Both the United Kingdom and Spain had electricity sectors with structures more conducive to competition than Ireland will have under present proposals, and in both countries there was evidence that market prices were well above competitive prices. The United Kingdom had three and Spain had two large electricity generators. In the United Kingdom, for some time the main generators were not vertically integrated, but in Spain they were integrated into distribution-supply, and partly owned the transmission grid.

Experience in the United Kingdom, Spain and New Zealand indicates that further increasing the number of independent generating companies would induce yet lower prices and higher productivity. Such an increase in numbers of competitors could be effected by having distinct owners of distinct generator sets within a given plant, for example. Similarly, experience in New Zealand showed that imposing a capacity cap and relying on new entrants to provide competition did not develop effective competition.

In Ireland, contracts for "virtual independent power producers" have been auctioned. These are financial instruments; neither ownership nor operational control of any generation assets will change hands. The idea is that owners of these VIPP contracts will compete in the supply market to re-sell electricity to liberalised consumers. VIPPs cannot be relied upon to provide competition to ESB, though, particularly when ESB has itself has bought some.

...in parallel with restructuring to separate networks from potentially competitive activities.

Access to electricity and gas transmission networks should be non-discriminatory, at prices that induce efficient use, and subject to independent regulation...

Access to electricity and gas transmission networks needs to be non-discriminatory, at prices that induce efficient use, and subject to independent regulation, as is already the case for electricity. This will not be easy as long as both ESB and Bord Gáis continue to be vertically integrated into both competitive activities (generation for ESB and supply) and monopolistic activities (transmission and distribution). This integration gives them incentives to exercise their market power by discriminating against non-integrated rivals. Three possible concerns are discriminatory maintenance of transmission, insufficient investment in transmission, and misattribution of costs to the regulated activity.

To counteract the potential for these abuses, access to the electricity grid is regulated, by the Commission for Electricity Regulation (CER) for electricity and through government directives for gas. To ease regulatory oversight, the integrated electricity firms are to keep separate accounts for their generation, transmission, distribution and supply activities. Also, Eirgrid rather than ESB is responsible for operation of the transmission grid.

...but this will not easy under accounting separation.

However, accounting separation has proved, in other countries, to be the least effective way to reduce discrimination against competitors. This form of separation can reduce the ability to discriminate, provided appropriate regulation is in place and the regulator is vigilant, but divestiture, that is, separation of ownership of generation from transmission, is the only form of separation that eliminates incentives to discriminate. If discriminatory access is detected, that should be further evidence of the need to separate potentially competitive activities from the networks.

Some warning signs have already emerged. Congestion of the Irish transmission network means that there are only a few points where a new generating plant could be physically connected. For example, it is estimated that only two generating plants can be added in the Dublin area under current arrangements without further reinforcements. Thus, the granting by ESB of a grid connection to its joint venture with Statoil before other potential entrants could enter a grid connection agreement has been seen by potential competitors as having serious repercussions on the future development of competition in the Irish electricity market. The arrangements for grid connections are being examined by CER, however, in a process involving public consultation.

83

Development of an all-island electricity market is necessary.

The natural direction is development of an all-island energy market, of which co-ordinated regulatory reform is one part.

Development of an all-island electricity market is necessary to develop competition in generation for consumers in the Republic, as well as in Northern Ireland. In 1999, economists at the ESRI said that an all-island market "could give rise to substantial savings in the very long run for consumers in both jurisdictions."[66]

Indeed, an all-island electricity market is already developing. Before it can proceed, the transmission grid needs substantial reinforcement. Besides enhancing competition, this will also increase security of supply and fuel diversification and reduce the need for, and cost of, operational reserve of generation. Continuing the co-ordination between the regulators on the island will also aid the increases in efficiency from cross-border trade and investment.

Strengthening the independent regulator for electricity will speed competition and investment...

Independent regulation provides a safeguard to competition.

Another integral part of an effective reform package is putting in place appropriate regulatory institutions, in particular an independent regulator. Independent regulation provides a safeguard to competition especially in sectors where there is an essential facility to which all firms need access. Independent, well-resourced and well-respected regulatory institutions attract investment since investors can feel they will be treated fairly and consistently.

In Ireland, three institutions – the Department of Public Enterprise, the Commission for Electricity Regulation (An *Coimisiún um Rialáil Leictreachais* or CER), and the Competition Authority – are involved in regulating the sectors. The Minister for Public Enterprise is the primary regulator of gas. For electricity, the CER regulates entry into generation, transmission, and trading. CER has been granted power, by the Minister, to regulate final tariffs to captive consumers and the agreement between Eirgrid and ESB. CER is expected to begin, in 2001, to regulate final electricity tariffs for captive consumers. The CER has structural independence, is independent in the performance of its functions and has financial independence since it may impose a levy on electricity undertakings. However, some of its key regulatory powers are granted – and thus withdrawable – by the Minister. Legislation is expected in 2001 to transfer these powers to the CER. The CER is accountable to both the Minister and a Joint Committee of the Parliament. To the extent that the market is integrated across national borders, such institutions are needed in each jurisdiction, and increasing co-ordination will be needed between these institutions.

...as will adopting regulatory instruments to promote commercial incentives for efficiency.

The regulation of ESB is less formal and complete than that in many other OECD countries.

The regulation of ESB is less formal and complete than that in many other OECD countries though, as noted, this may be remedied by new legislation in 2001. ESB must "break-even."[67] Within that framework condition, the regulation of ESB's tariffs is changing in 2001. Under the earlier system, ESB may apply to the Minister for Public Enterprise for increases in the tariffs charged customers, and the Minister may grant or deny the application. However, in December 2000 CER was granted, by the Minister, the power to set and change tariffs, in addition to its regulatory powers under the primary legislation as regards transmission access and generation licensing. Changes in regulation mean proceeding with the transformation of the entities into limited liability companies, imposing on their boards commercial objectives and incentives, and introducing economic regulation that provides incentives for efficiency and competition, such as a price cap regime.

The performance of Eirgrid and the Energy Procurer will be difficult to improve.

It will be difficult to provide Eirgrid, the transmission system operator (TSO) with incentives for efficiency. Since Eirgrid should seek innovative ways to reduce system cost, command and control regulation is unsuitable. Further, it will be difficult for Eirgrid to ensure that ESB Transmission is fulfilling its maintenance and development tasks in a non-discriminatory way.

Entities such as a Public Electricity Supply Business are difficult to regulate. While it would seem "fair" to pass onto consumers the costs of the energy procured for them, this would mean the Public Electricity Supply Business would not have incentives to bargain for better prices or to seek alternative lower cost suppliers. From February 2005, the Public Electricity Supplier will have an economic purchase obligation, *i.e.* it will not be supplied in the first instance by ESB generation.

Liberalisation of all consumers should proceed as planned and further acceleration might be considered.

Ireland should consider speeding up liberalisation in consumer choice.

The liberalisation of large consumers is an important first step, but was unaccountably delayed. The Minister announced in June 1995 that, from 1 January 1998, very large electricity users could buy from generators other than ESB, yet the change in the law to allow this took effect only in February 2000. The government has announced that electricity users totalling 40% of demand will be free to choose supplier in 2002, and 100% by 2005. This degree of consumer liberalisation meets or exceeds that specified in the directives agreed by EU members, though the EU electricity directive allowed Ireland an additional year to implement the first phase of liberalisation. Given the powerful forces for efficiency and quality engendered by consumer choice, Ireland should consider speeding up liberalisation in this area.

Regulatory reform in important professional services would boost efficiency and quality.

A significant part of the Irish economy depends upon, or consists of, professional services.

A significant part of the Irish economy depends upon, or consists of, professional services. As the economy has boomed, demand for these services has experienced a corresponding expansion. More

85

providers are needed to meet this increased demand, and supply has come from several sources: expanding places for professional education at Irish universities and other programmes, Irish citizens going abroad for professional education, return of Irish expatriate professionals, and immigration of foreign professionals. Previous studies have called for reforms in Ireland's professions (see background report in this volume). The main problems – unnecessarily restrictive conditions for entry and rules about advertising and location, and implicit collective fee-setting – are common to many professions.

The market for solicitors' services raises more regulatory concerns than does the market for barristers' services.

The legal profession in Ireland is divided into solicitors and barristers. Solicitors, who deal directly with clients, provide legal advice, prepare paperwork for legal proceedings, retain barristers, manage legal cases, and advocate in the District Court. They engage in other work not directly related to court, such as property conveyancing, testacy, and commercial contract work. Barristers provide legal advice and advocate in court as well as in tribunals.

Box 5.2. Alternative fuels in Ireland: clean green and polluting peat

Renewable energy generation. Ireland has set an ambitious target for increasing the amount of electricity generated by renewable sources of energy. In its Green Paper on Sustainable Energy, this target was increased by 500MW (about one-eighth of total installed generation in Ireland). Ireland has relied on auctions to build generation using specified technologies. It is expected that these projects and the 2005 target will deliver a total capacity in excess of 600MWe in 2005, the vast majority of which (over 80%) will be wind powered (ESB, 1998). Since February 2000, this mechanism has been augmented by allowing any electricity supplier supplying from renewable energy sources (green electricity) to supply any final consumer. The ERA, 1999 requires the CER to have regard to the need, "to promote the use of renewable, sustainable or alternative forms of energy." CER recently amended the trading regulation to allow green operators to mix with non-green sources, thus facilitating their activities. However, the expansion of wind powered generation is hampered by the lack of verified published data on site-specific and overall grid capacity acceptance limits from wind powered sources. Until resolved, this will hinder growth in the liberalised green market.

Peat, the traditional fuel in Ireland, is supplied by Bord na Móna, a State-sponsored body, to ESB under long term agreement.[1] The International Energy Agency estimates that, in 1999, the cost of generating electricity from peat was 50% higher than doing so from alternative fuel (coal). The IEA notes, however, that the producer subsidy for peat was far lower than the producer subsidy equivalent for coal in, say, Germany or Spain (IEA, 1999). Peat emits more CO_2 per unit electricity generated, 1 467g/kWh as compared with 851g/kWh for coal or 492g/kWh for gas. However, since the exploitation of peat for electricity generation takes place in an area of higher than average unemployment, it was originally considered to form part of the social safety net. Current plans call for the six old peat-fuelled plants to be replaced by two new peat plants, bringing the total to three. The Minister for Public Enterprise may direct the CER to impose on ESB the requirement, as a public service obligation, that up to 15% peat, as a primary fuel source, is used in the fuel mix of electricity generation in any year (ERA, Sect. 39). This requirement is intended to ensure that Ireland is reasonably self-sufficient in electricity generation. Gas from the Irish seabed and from other European Union Members also ensures this self-sufficiency.

1. To compare size of operation, the turnover of Bord na Móna in the year ended March 1999 was IR£153m, of which some was not from the energy market, whereas the turnover of Bord Gais in 1998 was IR£313m. [http://www.bge.ie/htm/faces/fac_fs6c.htm on 12 June 2000].

Since the market for legal services is subdivided, market failures and the rationale for regulation differ.

Since the market for legal services is subdivided, market failures and the rationale for regulation differ, too. Clients hire legal professionals, making choices among solicitors but, with few exceptions, not among barristers. Solicitors choose among barristers, except when experienced clients make that choice. Hence, from an economic perspective, for inexperienced clients, solicitors compete for clients, and barristers compete for solicitors.

In the market for barristers' professional services, the clients or solicitors tend to be well informed. The quality of a barrister's advocacy is relatively apparent to solicitors. The market for solicitors' professional services is different. The difference is largely that solicitors' clients are relatively uninformed. While clients have begun to "comparison shop" for relatively straightforward tasks, such as conveyancing, this is impractical where the legal task is non-standardised. Further, at present there is excess demand for solicitors' training. These characteristics mean that the market for solicitors' services raises more concerns than does the market for barristers' services.

Reforms have already gone a long way to helping consumers choose from more competitive legal services. Further reforms should remove remaining impediments to healthy competition.

Ireland has already implemented substantial reform in the legal professions...

Ireland has already implemented substantial reform in the legal professions. Advertising by solicitors is already liberalised, and recommending scale fees has been suppressed by the Competition Authority for a decade. Further, the self-governing body of solicitors has already taken steps to increase the capacity of its law school. Still, there are unnecessary restrictions. For example, the self-governing bodies of solicitors and barristers, respectively, control entry into their respective professions. Ireland restricts the form of business in which solicitors and barristers may practice. Solicitors may practice only in partnerships (with other solicitors) while barristers operate as independent entities.

...however, further reform could have positive effects.

However, further reform can have positive effects. The priorities are to remove remaining impediments to competition among solicitors, or indeed between solicitors and barristers, and provide incentives for solicitors to ensure that even inexperienced clients receive barristers' services at competitive fees.

– Opening up the service of conveyancing to, for example, banks and financial institutions, would provide additional options to consumers.

– Continued freedom of advertising for solicitors – recently being questioned – will encourage consumers to shop around for cost-efficient legal services, which in turn encourages competition among solicitors. Advertising by solicitors and newspaper articles overcome a market failure by providing information about the cost and benefits of professional services, thus expanding services and access to justice to under-served populations. If the underlying issue of concern to those who would restrict advertising is that too many tort suits damage Irish competitiveness, a more direct tort reform would result in a more efficient justice system.

87

– Making solicitors responsible for paying barristers their fees would increase solicitors' incentives to ensure cost-effective barristers services. Enabling clients to instruct barristers directly would increase efficiency.

– Allowing solicitors and barristers to practice in other business forms could increase efficiency, and other common law systems give legal professional greater scope in this dimension than does Ireland's.

– Any publication of, *e.g.*, a survey of costs, that could help to form solicitors' or barristers' expectations about a standard price should be suppressed.

– The control of education and entry of legal professionals should be moved from the self-governing bodies, but close ties as regards quality of entrants and content of education should be maintained.

Pharmacies are highly regulated in Ireland to ensure safety and availability of services to rural areas, but more sensible regulation could bring down prices without endangering safety or accessibility.

Reform of economic regulations for pharmacies could bring about lower prices and more efficient provision.

The pharmacy sector has a vital role in promoting the health of Irish citizens. Pharmacies are highly regulated in Ireland, as in many countries. However, the evidence suggests that reform of some of the economic regulations could bring about lower prices and more efficient provision. The retail margin on medicines in Ireland is higher than in any other EU country (Bacon, pp. 10-11). Community pharmacists can receive salaries high enough to impair the supply of pharmacists to hospital pharmacies and industry (Forum). Pharmacies are changing hands at high prices. Competition is limited by preventing new pharmacies from locating near existing pharmacies. Reducing barriers to competition among pharmacists is expected to increase competition, which in turn would induce pharmacists to identify more efficient ways of performing their professional tasks and thus reduce the cost to consumers.

One reason given for current restrictions is that they will ensure that each pharmacy has sufficient scale to make the investments to strengthen its delivery of more sophisticated health care services such as patient advice and counselling. Another reason given is to improve the delivery of health care services in rural areas. Thus, it is fair to compare the actual effects of the restrictions with these objectives, and to ask whether a different approach might be less costly to the Irish.

The restriction on economic freedom of pharmacists educated in other EU countries should be eliminated...

A substantial flow of pharmacists from the UK to Ireland, and the provision of pharmacist education in the UK to Irish students, is made possible by EU directives. These directives say that persons holding a comparable certification from a Member state may practice pharmacy in other Member states, subject to some restrictions. In Ireland, the main constraint, in practice, has been that such a person cannot, throughout his/her career, ever manage or supervise a pharmacy that has been in existence for less than three years. This constraint was put into place to ensure that lifting the entry restraints on EU-trained pharmacists would not result in unrestricted opening of new pharmacies in Ireland, openings that were restricted in many other EU members. Ireland's current rules on "contractor pharmacies" perform essentially the same function.

The Irish restriction on pharmacists educated in other EU countries does not promote health care delivery.

The Irish restriction on pharmacists educated in other EU countries does not promote health care delivery. It simply restricts entry, and thus has anti-competitive effect. In particular, it restricts entry of new pharmacies – those that would have opened if foreign-trained pharmacists were unrestricted – and employment possibilities for a subset of pharmacists.

…as should restrictions on the location and number of pharmacies.

Before 1996, Ireland did not restrict entry of pharmacies. This resulted in Ireland having one of the highest ratios of pharmacies to population in Europe. Today, however, limits on the location of pharmacies effectively limit the number of pharmacies. Pharmacies that wish to be contractors under the state health plan must comply with the location restrictions. The reasons are put forward by the Department of Health for location restrictions are (1) to bring Ireland into line with other EEA countries where such controls exist in form or another; (2) to improve standards in pharmacies; and (3) to promote patient access to pharmacy services in areas currently without such services.

The logic for restricting the location and number of pharmacies is flawed.

The logic for restricting the location and number of pharmacies is flawed. Incumbents in other sectors in other economies make similar arguments, that if they are protected from competition then they will perform a variety of good works. In fact, competition – keeping up with the competitors – is what induces quality-improving investments.

Where there is a genuine public service obligation, such as loss-making provision of a service to rural areas, the solution is not creation of a protected monopoly to cross-subsidise the unprofitable activity. Rather, the solution is to split the task into two parts, of providing the service and of paying for the part that must be subsidised. The provider is chosen by auction for minimum subsidy, where the auction terms specify the services to be provided. The funds are provided either by the state budget, or by a small fee like a tax on some set of persons. If there are rural areas that would not have a pharmacy under such conditions, but that need one according to public policy criteria, those may have to be subsidised directly. For example, the United Kingdom subsidises some pharmacies to be open on Sundays and bank holidays.

Chapter 6

REGULATORY REFORM IN
THE TELECOMMUNICATIONS INDUSTRY

The telecommunications industry is extraordinarily dynamic. Rapid evolution of technologies has shaken up industries and regulatory regimes long based on older technologies and market theories. Twenty-four OECD countries have unrestricted market access to all forms of telecommunications, including voice telephony, infrastructure investment and investment by foreign enterprises, compared to only a handful a few years ago. The industry's boundaries are blurring and merging with other industries such as broadcasting and information services.

Regulatory regimes must simultaneously promote competition and protect other social interests in dynamic markets.

Strong competition policies and efficiency-promoting regulatory regimes are crucial to the future development of the industry.

Strong competition policies and efficiency-promoting regulatory regimes that work well in dynamic and global markets are crucial to the performance and future development of the industry. The central regulatory task is to enable the development of competition in local markets, while protecting other public interests such as reliability, universal service and consumer interests. Entry must be actively promoted in markets where formerly regulated monopolists remain dominant, and consideration must be given to convergence of separate regulatory frameworks applicable to telecommunications and broadcasting infrastructures and services.

Ireland gave up its derogation and liberalised telecommunications earlier than planned, a wise move that has placed its communications market on par with many OECD countries.

Recent acceleration in liberalisation brought the Irish regulatory framework to par with many other OECD countries, and in some areas ahead of countries that had opened their markets earlier to competition.

Market access in the telecommunications sector of Ireland is relatively liberalised and its regulatory framework has moved steadily to implement best practice regulation. Originally, on the basis of a European Commission derogation, Ireland had committed to open its market to full competition on 1 January 2000. A turning point was Ireland's decision in May 1998 to end the derogation on 1 December 1998, shortening the remaining period for completing full liberalisation from nineteen to six months. This acceleration in liberalisation brought the Irish regulatory framework to par with many other OECD countries, and in some areas ahead of countries that had opened their markets earlier to competition.

91

The market has responded well. Over forty operators now compete in the Irish market, and the new entrants' share in the fixed line market has expanded to more than 17% (measured by revenue). Due to development of solid competition for international calls, the regulator removed these services from price cap regulations. Introduction of Wireless Local Loop services and telephony over cable TV networks has already begun to develop in the local call market. Competition in the mobile market is weak, but a third market entrant entering at the end of February 2001 will improve this situation and several airtime resellers are beginning to place competitive pressure on prices.

Irish authorities hope to reach the top decile of OECD countries in performance in the sector, to become a communications hub linking Europe and North America, and to develop electronic commerce. Further reforms will help Ireland attain these ambitious goals.

Liberalisation has rapidly increased investment in new technologies and services...

Since liberalisation, the Irish telecommunication market has shown dynamic growth in terms of new market entry, investment and development of services.

Since liberalisation of the Irish telecommunication market in late 1998, the market has shown dynamic growth in terms of new market entry, investment and development of services. Revenues in the telecommunication service sector increased by almost 60% from 1995 to 1999, and its share in GDP increased. Ireland rapidly digitalised its network since the 1980s, stimulating the emergence of new technologies, in particular ISDN. By end-1999, Ireland had 596 000 CATV subscribers, a 38% increase since 1997. The CATV penetration rate as measured by the proportion of households with access to cable was 49%. Cellular mobile penetration increased from 14.4 per 100 inhabitants in 1997 (OECD average was 15.6) to 42.7 by 1999 (OECD average was 32.4), and by mid-2000 to 49.7.

The licensing of wireless local loop services will also ensure the more rapid development of competition in the local market. The independent regulator of telecommunications, the Office of the Director of Telecommunications Regulation (ODTR), has issued wireless local loop (WLL) licences for broadband services to four entities, two of which also have been granted WLL licences in narrow band, earlier than many other OECD countries.

...while consumers are beginning to see concrete results in terms of prices and quality.

In liberalised areas, Irish consumers and users have already seen some price decreases, and a wider range of services...

Although full liberalisation has been in place for only 24 months some benefits have accrued to Irish consumers and users. These have been mainly from price decreases, and an expansion in the range of services. Ireland had relatively high international collection charges, which were above the OECD average in the past, but continuous reductions since 1994 (mainly through indirect competition *e.g.* call-back services) improved Ireland's position significantly. The OECD basket of international telephone charges as of August 2000 shows that Ireland's international charges are less than half of the OECD average both for business and residential calls in USD/PPP (Table 6.1).

...though, where markets are still weak, Irish performance lags other OECD countries.

Where markets have not been strong, Irish performance lags other OECD countries. Delay in the third mobile licence becoming operational reduced the impact of price competition in that market, and as a result Ireland is the ninth most expensive OECD country (in PPP), above the OECD average (Figure 6.1). The lack of vigorous mobile competition in the Irish mobile market, which had a monopoly until 1997 and a duopoly since then, is the main reason for the lack of price competition. The costs of services in the business basket are also high (the ninth highest), above the OECD average for the same reason.

Table 6.1.   OECD basket of international telephone charges, August 2000

	Business Excluding tax		Residential Including tax	
	USD	USD PPP	USD	USD PPP
Australia	0.80	1.03	1.12	1.44
Austria	0.80	0.87	1.21	1.32
Belgium	1.17	1.34	1.56	1.79
Canada	0.21	0.26	0.74	0.92
Czech Republic	1.18	3.11	1.26	3.31
Denmark	0.50	0.44	0.81	0.71
Finland	0.77	0.74	1.08	1.04
France	0.60	0.65	0.75	0.81
Germany	0.79	0.86	1.16	1.26
Greece	0.89	1.26	1.35	1.90
Hungary	1.11	2.77	1.77	4.43
Iceland	0.79	0.63	1.25	1.00
Ireland	0.55	**0.65**	0.76	**0.89**
Italy	0.93	1.18	1.35	1.71
Japan	2.90	1.78	3.25	1.99
Korea	2.38	3.83	2.77	4.46
Luxembourg	0.52	0.58	0.66	0.74
Mexico	3.25	4.51	3.94	5.47
Netherlands	0.33	0.38	0.48	0.55
New Zealand	0.77	1.09	1.06	1.50
Norway	0.46	0.40	0.71	0.62
Poland	1.49	2.87	2.35	4.51
Portugal	0.97	1.49	1.38	2.12
Spain	1.09	1.49	1.52	2.08
Sweden	0.39	0.35	0.61	0.56
Switzerland	0.30	0.25	0.37	0.31
Turkey	1.67	3.10	2.07	3.84
United Kingdom	0.87	0.80	0.94	0.87
United States	0.55	0.55	0.87	0.87
OECD average	1.00	**1.35**	1.35	**1.38**

Source: OECD and Teligen.

A long-term strength is that the Irish regulatory regime is designed to evolve as conditions change...

The regulator's practice of conducting and publishing a quarterly review of the Irish telecommunications market will boost flexibility...

While sector-specific regulations are necessary to steer and facilitate the transition of the market from monopoly to full competition, it is necessary to consider when it is appropriate to streamline regulations and to withdraw sector-specific regulations as the market becomes competitive. The ODTR's practice of conducting and publishing a quarterly review of the Irish telecommunications market is commendable from this perspective. The review should focus on the impact of market changes on users and the benefits that they are deriving from competition. Another strong point is that the government and the regulator have effectively used public consultation process both in the development of legislation and in regulation.

...and this flexibility is particularly useful since important regulatory issues must be tackled to complete the regulatory environment for competition.

...and this will help Ireland more quickly resolve lingering weaknesses in both regulations and institutions.

The reform agenda is not yet finished. Rapid transition to create a competitive environment has inevitably left issues unresolved. The Department of Public Enterprise and the regulator, ODTR, have recognised weaknesses in both regulations and institutions, and have proposed corrective action by preparing legislation to make major changes in institutional and regulatory frameworks. This

Figure 6.1. **OECD Basket of consumer mobile telephone charges, November 2000**
(in US$/PPP)

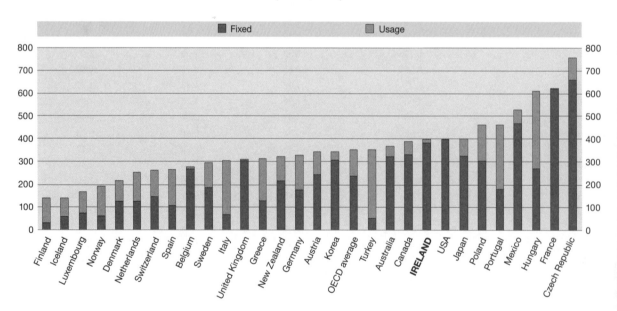

Note: The basket includes 50 minutes per month and includes international calls. VAT is included.
Source: OECD and Teligen.

important legislation was in early 2001 not yet adopted. New entrants' market share in fixed line services should increase further as the impact of the development of a new interconnection regime, based on a long run average incremental costs (LRAIC) methodology, and the introduction of carrier pre-selection, and geographic number portability take effect.

To further open the market, it is timely to move to a class licensing system, replacing the existing individual licensing system.

The Irish licensing regime is open, but unnecessarily onerous, complex and costly.

The Irish licensing regime is open, but unnecessarily onerous, complex and costly. To further reduce barriers to market entry and attract more investment by improving transparency, simplicity, and efficiency of regulation, Ireland should change its individual licensing regime toward a system of general authorisation. A good practice in this regard is found in Denmark. In Denmark, all telecommunications operators, except for those providing public mobile communications, can enter the market freely without the need even to register with the regulatory authority as long as they satisfy the general conditions.

In this dynamic sector, it is also necessary to ensure that licenses do not freeze competition. Current terms of cable licences issued in 1999 grant cable operators five years of exclusivity (a monopoly in each operating area), out of fifteen years duration of licence, to provide programming services. This policy of limited monopoly was employed so that the CATV infrastructure in Ireland, particularly for digital services, could develop quickly and licensees could invest actively in building infrastructure requiring enormous capital investment. That aim has been partly achieved. The penetration rate of cable infrastructure is now relatively high. In the next phase of reform, upgrading cable to provide broadband access and telephony would more likely occur in a competitive market. It is necessary to ensure that this exclusive period will end as planned.

An interconnection framework reflecting best practices should be adopted, while delays in obtaining capacity from the incumbent should be reduced.

Ireland is one of the first OECD countries to implement LRAIC accounting methods for interconnection, but could further reduce local and single tandem prices and encourage more competition in the local loop...

New entrants still rely on Eircom's networks to provide services to end-users. Such dependence will continue for some time, especially for the local network. The method used to determine interconnect charges offered by Eircom has been based on historical costs, which has produced relatively good results. A general consensus has emerged, however, on the theoretical superiority in dynamic markets of the LRAIC accounting methodology as closely approximating costs of the most efficient operators and as bringing the rates to the level of a fully competitive market. Ireland has become one of the few OECD countries to implement the LRAIC methodology, and indeed, Ireland's interconnection rates are currently below EU benchmarks and among the lowest in the EU. With this method, Ireland could further reduce local and single tandem prices to meet best practice.

...and sterner steps are needed to improve availability of leased lines.

Another important requirement in market access and interconnection is the availability of leased lines. Eircom had reached an agreement with new entrants on detailed delivery deadlines and other terms and conditions, with the penalties to be paid by Eircom to operators if it failed to meet the targets. However, many new entrants have complained of delays.[68] The ODTR proposed to increase the level of fines as an incentive for the incumbent to meet its commitments, but these fines were delayed as a result of a court appeal by Eircom. At the same time, the ODTR has launched a review to find solutions to improve the provision of leased circuits and the performance of Eircom.

Price rebalancing has been slow, and should be completed rapidly.

The regulator should ensure that subscriber line charges become cost-oriented as soon as possible...

Price rebalancing should be completed as rapidly as possible to attain cost-orientation and eliminate any cross-subsidies. This will also facilitate the implementation of local loop unbundling. The incumbent's line rental charges have been subject to only minor changes over seven years, although significant changes have taken place in local call charges. It is important for the ODTR to ensure that subscriber line charges are cost-oriented as soon as possible. It would be preferable that this takes place before full local loop unbundling is introduced, but this is unlikely to occur given the low increase allowed by the current price cap.

...through stronger market competition, if possible.

There appears to be a consensus among OECD countries that the most effective way to achieve cost-based prices is through effective competition and not through price regulation. However, in tariff re-balancing of residential and local services, the regulator has to handle the sensitive issue of how quickly to manage the transition since price changes can have social costs even while they produce overall social benefits. Constant review of market competition and price developments is important.

Local loop unbundling has been an issue for the regulator for some time, but lack of supportive legislation has resulted in a missed opportunity to take the lead.

Ireland tackled unbundling earlier than many other OECD countries.

The regulator began to tackle the issue of unbundling earlier than many other OECD countries, and announced that it planned to develop a framework for full local loop unbundling by April 2001. Developments in the EU and the decision to implement full local loop unbundling will be important in upgrading the network to provide broadband access and help fulfil Ireland's policy goal to develop a knowledge based economy and become a European hub for electronic commerce. It is unfortunate that these wider economic goals were not supplemented earlier by specific legislation to allow important developments such as full LLU (Local Loop Unbundling) to be implemented, thus giving Ireland a head start. A decision on pricing of unbundled local loops also needs to be made rapidly and in this context price rebalancing will be important.

Competition in the cellular market has been delayed...

The costs of uneven market opening in slowing growth and benefits to users are most apparent in the cellular mobile sector.

The costs of uneven market opening in slowing growth and benefits to users are most apparent in the cellular mobile sector, still suffering from insufficient competition. A third licence is only now becoming operational because of litigation lasting well over a year. This has had a negative impact on price performance and mobile penetration rates. Entry of the third operator is expected shortly, but the ODTR needs to maintain this market under review to ensure that a competitive market for mobile services develops. This will be assisted by the announced intention to offer four licences for the UMTS services.

...partly due to the weak enforcement power...

In some respects, Irish regulatory institutions are solid. There is general consensus that ODTR has acted fairly and independently of politics and of industry. Unlike ministries in many other OECD countries the Department did not attempt to retain regulatory power over the sector. ODTR has emphasised market evaluation as a basis for making timely and appropriate regulatory decisions.

The regulator has not been rated highly in terms of its ability to follow-up on decisions, monitor compliance and enforce decisions.

Yet ODTR has not been rated highly in terms of its ability to follow-up on decisions, monitor compliance and enforce decisions. One reason for this has been the lack of staff and the need for the regulator to concentrate on rapidly developing the regulatory framework, following the decision in 1998 to fully liberalise the market 13 months before the end of the derogation period. A second, more fundamental reason, has been a lack of sufficient enforcement powers.

The ODTR needs to be strengthened to make and enforce binding decisions. The Irish regulatory landscape has been characterised by lengthy court cases that slowed liberalisation, because, before March 2000, appeals against decisions of ODTR on licensing and interconnection resulted in suspension of the decision until the outcome of the appeal. The challenge to ODTR's decision to award the third cellular mobile licence, which ended when the Supreme Court upheld the decision of the ODTR in May 2000, delayed the introduction of the third mobile licence by eighteen months. Since March 2000, however, following amendments to regulations on interconnection and licensing, an appealed decision can be implemented unless the court expressly decides to suspend it.

Proposed provisions of the Communications Regulations bill will further reduce resort to the courts by restricting judicial review of ODTR's decisions to its compliance with legal procedures rather than the merits of the decision, by placing a time limit on applying for reviews, and by ensuring that judicial review takes into account "the interests of the public in the efficient regulation of the market".

...and inadequate resources of the ODTR.

Recruitment of staff has been a major issue for the regulator.

Effective regulation is not possible without adequate human resources. Recruitment of staff has been a major issue for the ODTR and there has always been a shortage of personnel relative to the required amount, quality, and speed of work. ODTR needs to continue its focus on completing its staffing needs. Lack of staffing is partially responsible for the fact that the ODTR has not been sufficiently pro-active in certain areas, *e.g.* in consumer protection and enforcement of the decisions.

Improvements in institutional relations with the Competition Authority are also necessary. The draft legal proposals currently

---

Box 6.1. Improving the effectiveness and accountability of an independent telecom regulator

Accountability of the new independent regulators has received much attention in Ireland. The Department of Public Enterprise noted a need to overcome a perceived "democratic deficit"[1] that could have an impact on the credibility and legitimacy of the new regulatory institutions. The 1996 Act establishing the ODTR did not have a provision regarding accountability to the Parliament other than production of an annual report and accounts, but later legislation did address this for other sectoral regulators, such as in electricity. In March 2000, the Department published "Governance and Accountability in the Regulatory Process: Policy Proposals"[2] to address the governance and accountability aspects of the regulatory framework across all sectors within its remit.

In telecommunications, the Department published in September 2000 a consultation paper for a new communications act.[3] It proposed to:

– Replace the current single regulator structure of the ODTR with a three-person Commission and bring postal regulation within the ambit of the regulator.[4]

– Explicitly require the "Commission" to report to a relevant parliamentary committee on a regular basis in relation to its plans and overall performance, as is provided for the Commission for Electricity Regulation.[5]

The proposals are based on the argument that a commission can be more effective than a single regulator, and indeed it may be. There is no evidence from other OECD countries, however, to indicate that a "commission" structure for a telecommunication regulatory body is more or less effective than a single-person regulator. This will depend on how a Commission is structured and frequency of meetings. Criticism that a single person regulator can result in "undue personalisation" may not be of concern if good accountability procedures are put in place. Effective regulation may sometimes require that the regulator has an authoritative public profile.

The proposals improve accountability of regulation by more clearly defining the objectives of regulation, the powers of the regulatory body, and its answerability. By requiring the regulatory body to provide a general review of its performance to a committee of parliament, the proposed act increases transparency and accountability, and enhances the independence of the regulatory body. However, the draft act states that it should have "regard to any recommendation of such Committee [of parliament] relevant to its functions".[6] In this context it is also important to note that the Minister is responsible for overall policy in the communications sector. This new clause can cause difficulties for the Commission since it is subject to policy directions from the Minister and these policy directions may differ from "recommendations" of a Committee of parliament, and the two together from the statutory policy mandates to promote competition.

---

1. See, Department of Public Enterprise (1998), "Statement of Strategy", April, at the Section "Accountability of regulatory system" available at www.irlgov.ie/tec/publications/dpe13.htm.
2. Available at www.irlgov.ie/tec/publications/regulatory.htm.
3. This document is available on the website of the Department of Public Enterprise at www.irlgov.ie/tec/communications/commconsultation.pdf. The discussion and analysis in the "Governance and Accountability" document is of a cross-sectoral, generic nature, but implementation of the policy proposals is being done by means of sector-specific measures.
4. The Department of Public Enterprise, *op. cit.* note 36 at Item 3(a)(b). Postal regulation has already been transferred to the ODTR under a statutory instrument of 27 September 2000.
5. *Ibid.* at Item 4(h).
6. *Ibid.* at Head 25.

underway explicitly recognise the need to ensure that ODTR and the Competition Authority work together through deferring, consulting, and trading confidential information.

Legislation relating to rights of way for telecommunication operators over public highways should be adopted as soon as possible.

New entrants face major difficulties in meeting demands by local and municipal authorities on their requests for rights of way over public highways.

New entrants face major difficulties in meeting demands by local and municipal authorities on their requests for rights of way over public highways. Some municipalities have requested that extra ducts be provided and made available to other new entrants. Obtaining rights of way to public highways requires, for local roads, permission from local road authorities (over thirty of them in Ireland) or the National Roads Authority for national roads. In 1999, the Minister for Public Enterprise prepared a bill to reform the system for telecommunications network operators to access public and private land. This bill would have provided a benchmark for many countries with open telecommunication markets, since rights of way have become a key stumbling block in the development of competitive networks. In light of public concerns about access by telecom operators to private land, the bill was withdrawn in December 2000.

A universal service costing methodology should be implemented and, if necessary a universal service fund set up...

Funding for provision of universal services should be carefully designed to avoid distortions.

Eircom is obliged by the ODTR, under law, to provide certain universal services. Irish services are comparable to those of many OECD countries, including access to the fixed public telephone network and services, directory services, and public pay telephones. The universal service obligation (USO) operator may receive funding for the net cost of meeting the USO. Eircom can be reimbursed by either of two mechanisms: establishing a fund to which all operators contribute and from which the USO operator is reimbursed, or adding a supplementary charge to interconnection fees.

Experience from other countries has shown that the first option tends to be preferable since it avoids distortion in interconnection, tends to be more transparent and allows designation of another operator, instead of the incumbent, to provide universal service in specific areas. Accounting separation should be ensured to prevent the possibility of cross-subsidisation with other competitive services offered by the USO operator. The second option, if implemented, should clearly separate interconnection payments from any access deficit charges. This option could create structural inflexibility in prices and in the way interconnection is charged.

...and the market would function more effectively if ODTR focussed more on consumer issues.

Some aspects of consumer protection have been neglected.

Consumer interests are best enhanced through effective competition, which will deliver lower prices, improved choice and better quality. However, there is a continuing role for the government

99

to ensure that consumer interests are protected. The government and the ODTR have worked to ensure that consumers benefit from increased competition, but some aspects of consumer protection have been left behind.

Consumer groups have argued that complaints regarding tele-communications services have not been handled in a satisfactory manner. Consumer complaints, such as on billing, are dealt with in the first instance by the same telecommunications operators who are the object of the complaint. Consumers unsatisfied with the operator's handling have requested the intervention of the Office of the Director of Consumer Affairs (ODCA), an independent statutory body responsible for a wide range of consumer protection laws. However, most complaints on telecommunications fall outside of the remit of the ODCA. The ODTR, who has regulatory responsibilities in complaints on telecommunications, handles complaints, and in many cases has referred problems back to the operators for investigation before ascertaining what action if any can be taken.

A more direct focus on consumer interests would boost the benefits of markets. In particular, an effective framework is needed to handle consumer complaints and resolve disputes, while bench-marks for quality of service and the publication of relative quality of service indicators can also facilitate consumer choice. The ODTR and the Department of Public Enterprise have been working to establish a formal mechanism to handle consumer complaints. An industry wide code would also help ensure consistency in the market. An ODTR programme called "Measuring Licensed Operator Performance", which will require operators to publish reports on the complaints received, and data on the time taken for resolution, the number of cases resolved satisfactorily and the number not resolved, will improve market transparency.

Chapter 7

CONCLUSIONS AND POLICY OPTIONS FOR REGULATORY REFORM

Although it was slow in coming, the Irish performance of the 1990s is evidence that, sooner or later, sensible structural reforms will pay off. Ireland's tranquil, agricultural economy of post-war years has mostly disappeared, and a modern, vibrant, open market has taken its place. A rising social consensus backs the further structural reforms that are necessary to maintain growth, and the visibly positive results of liberalising trade, inviting foreign investment, and strengthening competition should build even broader support. The result is that regulatory reform in Ireland is no longer the reform that dare not speak its name, but instead is increasingly central to policy prescriptions and public expectations.

A flexible and dynamic domestic economy, backed up by high quality regulatory and competition regimes, will help sustain growth...

The remaining challenges of reform are not entirely unpleasant to face, since they are partly results of rapidly rising prosperity that has changed the basis of the Irish economy. A "virtuous circle" has emerged, as increases in take-home pay and improved cost competitiveness led to substantial job creation and a turnaround in public finances. These trends freed up resources for spending on health, education and social welfare that will support continued growth. An essential ingredient to maintain the virtuous circle is a flexible and dynamic domestic economy, backed up by high quality regulatory and competition regimes.

The coming cycle in Irish economic development justifies a more coherent and determined approach to regulatory reform than seen to date.

...and Ireland will increase the cost and length of future downswings if it does not over haul its regulatory regimes.

The converse is also true. The cost and length of future downswings will increase if Ireland does not overhaul its regulatory regimes during this window of opportunity. Economic prosperity has reduced the visible costs of weaknesses in Irish regulatory approaches, but these costs are now emerging. Capacity constraints and the emergence of "bottlenecks" in many sectors are undermining the sustainability of the economic expansion and the competitiveness of domestic industry, and are exposing the weak points of the Irish economic strategy. Ireland, being a small open economy, is more vulnerable to external shocks than larger economies. Ireland will deal more effectively with eventual external shocks and a less favourable global economic environment if it improves its regulatory approaches. The coming cycle in Irish economic development justifies a more coherent and determined approach to regulatory reform than seen to date.

Ireland's future strengths lie in continued attention to domestic competitiveness through regulatory efficiency and flexibility…

Ireland will maximise the return of its market openness approach by pursuing efficient regulation.

Ireland and others in the Euro area no longer have the option of devaluating domestic currencies to improve the international competitiveness of their domestic firms. However, Ireland remains particularly vulnerable to large fluctuations in the external value of the Euro since its largest trading partners are not Euro members. The United Kingdom and the United States together account for more than a third of total exports and almost half of total imports. In this context, the importance of establishing a sound regulatory framework that minimises domestic obstacles to growth and maximises competitive conditions is more crucial than ever. Ireland will maximise the return of its market openness approach by pursuing efficient regulation.

…good governance…

Ireland's governance institutions are coming into line with market and social changes.

Ireland has long had a robust rule of law that is attractive for foreign players. Ireland's governance institutions are coming into line with market and social changes. Like many OECD countries, Ireland faces important challenges in adjusting its governance arrangements to the new realities of globalisation, demands of civil society, and new technologies.

…and competition policy.

The importance of competition policy in market reform is recognised and supported at the highest levels in Ireland. Competition law and institutions are mostly based on international good practices. Competition policy is a principal criterion of regulatory quality in the SMI reform programme of the Prime Minister's office. The Ministers with the largest stake, at DETE and DPE, support the competition policy principles of reform.

Strengths in competition laws and institutions have been compromised by a lack of resources, unclear independence, and inconsistent leadership.

But these strengths of laws and institutions have been compromised by a lack of resources, unclear independence, and inconsistent leadership. The Authority's history of resource problems suggest that the relationship between the Authority and the department that controls its budget and shares many of its powers needs improvement, though the apparent resolution of the 1999-2000 staffing crisis is a promising sign. Still, competition policy institutions have been employed only sporadically in the process of reforming economic regulations. For mergers, the decision process has appeared to permit politicisation and risks some uncertainty. Some provision for public interest judgements may well be appropriate, but the process should be more transparent, and the trade-offs should be recognised more forthrightly. The plan to give nearly all merger control responsibility to the Authority is another promising step.

Ireland can now see some concrete benefits of regulatory reform, as well as the costs of not reforming.

Already, in Ireland, implementation of reforms generates concrete benefits...

Experience in OECD countries indicates that structural reforms can remove institutional biases that, by inhibiting competition and misallocating resources, result in higher prices and low levels of efficiency. Reforms can lower costs, encourage greater efficiency and stimulate business dynamism and entrepreneurial activity. The benefits of sectoral reform are amplified when competition is vigorous in upstream and downstream sectors, in service as well as manufacturing sectors. Already, in Ireland, implementation of reforms in different sectors is beginning to generate benefits in some areas:

...by boosting consumer demand and welfare through lower prices, better service quality, and greater choice... ·

– *Boosting consumer demand and welfare through lower prices, better service quality, and a greater variety of goods and services.* Lower prices come partly from productivity increases. The annual benefits from reform in airlines and telecoms have been estimated to be IR£ 1 billion. Productivity in the telecommunications sector rose by almost 50% from 1995 to 1999, measured by operating revenue per employee. Opening up the airline market to competition reduced fares and expanded service. Eliminating the constraints on entry in pubs and taxis could produce a one-time saving of 0.4% of total personal expenditure. The opposite is also true, where reform has not occurred. Prices for package retail sale of beer, where competition is strong, have declined, while prices in pubs, where regulation reduces competition, have increased, so that the indexes of the prices in the competitive package sector and the non-competitive pub sector have diverged by as much as 25%, for a product on which Ireland spends 5% of its GDP.

...reducing the domestic cost structure of exporting sectors to improve their competitiveness...

– *Reducing the domestic cost structure of exporting sectors to improve their competitiveness* in regional and global markets, while reducing the risk of trade tensions due to possible regulatory barriers. Continuing focus in Ireland on market openness through import competition will contribute to reduce inflationary pressures in wages and costs of building materials and of services, and hence maintain competitiveness. Import competition can play a crucial role in government procurement by facilitating the completion of projects on time and keeping downward cost pressure on goods and services purchased. Facilitating labour mobility within the EU and from abroad through the recognition of professional qualifications will be instrumental in improving the availability of required skills and for easing inflationary pressures, particularly in services-related sectors where demand is expected to remain strong in the foreseeable future.

– *Improving the flexibility of the supply-side of the economy* by stimulating investment, by increasing the efficiency of the allocation of capital, and by lowering barriers to the creation of new firms, products and services. This is particularly impor-

...increasing the potential employment by creating new job opportunities...

...maintaining and increasing high levels of regulatory protections for citizens and the environment.

tant in Ireland as it loses its low-wage advantage, in light of its exchange rate vulnerability.

– *Helping to increase employment by creating new job opportunities.* The economy-wide employment effects of regulatory reform are expected to be positive as competitiveness and innovation improve. Employment increased in airlines as demand rose. In the Irish telecommunications sector, employment dropped from 1995 to 1998, and then after liberalisation began to rise. In 1999, employment was higher than in 1995.

– *Maintaining and increasing high levels of regulatory protections* in areas such as health and safety, the environment, and consumer interests by introducing more flexible and efficient regulatory and non-regulatory instruments, such as market approaches.

To speed up results, a broad and co-ordinated approach across product, labour, and financial markets is needed, with governance reforms.

It will be necessary to maintain a broad approach to reform that includes initiatives in labour, financial and product markets, and, crucially, the quality of market governance. The OECD recommends a comprehensive approach to reform because synergistic effects increase and speed up benefits, thereby easing the transition pains of adjustment. Liberalisation of product markets has its greatest effect, for example, when the labour market is more flexible.

The unfinished reform agenda is lengthy.

Concerns remain about the potential abuse of dominant position in the telecommunications and energy sectors.

Considerable efforts have been made to reduce the role of government in economic activities in exposing previously sheltered firms to competition forces. Yet Ireland faces the same difficulties plaguing other OECD countries in introducing competition into network sectors that were formerly monopolies. Two independent regulators have been established, for the telecommunications and the electricity sectors respectively. Although the Irish government is committed to liberalising these two sectors, two large players hold dominant positions in the telecommunications sector and state-owned enterprises still dominate the energy sector. Concerns remain about the potential abuse of their dominant position in these sectors.

Policy must move away from emphasis on protection of incumbents against innovation and competition.

Policy must move away from emphasis on protection of incumbents against innovation and competition. The strength of this tendency to protect incumbents was illustrated by the persistence of barriers to new entry in pubs and taxi services (though recent actions, sometimes spurred by court orders, are finally leading to changes in these regulatory regime), continued support for anti-competitive regulations like the Groceries Order, and the appearance of new constraints on competition in pharmacies and retail trade. The Prices Acts and Groceries Order, in fact, survived the three major legislative reforms, in 1987, 1991, and again in 1996, showing that where interest are strong, opportunities for reform have been repeatedly missed.

Consumer voices are still weak in the policy process.

Consumer interests are not well represented in policy debate and deliberation in Ireland, which remain dominated by producer interests.

Consumer interests are not well represented in policy debate and deliberation in Ireland, which remain dominated by producer interests. Consultation with consumer groups tends to come late, asking for pro forma comment on a finished product rather than help in creating it. No consumer group is among the nearly 40 bodies identified as participants in the negotiation of the social partners' "Programme for Prosperity and Fairness." The "social partnership" process has expanded beyond the traditional economic interests, but it still does not incorporate the most inclusive interest, with the most to gain from pro-competitive reform, namely the consuming public at large.

Changes to the institutions and culture of the public sector are still lagging policy reforms.

Governance changes have lagged behind economic changes, and could pose a bottleneck sustained growth...

Governance changes have also been significant, but have lagged behind economic changes, and could pose a bottleneck to sustained growth. Ireland will need continued regulatory reform to improve the market environment and resolve emerging challenges such as skills and housing shortages.

...though, within a few years, the Irish regulatory environment and framework have been significantly improved.

Improvements have been gradual and incremental, and in some case piecemeal, but recently the rate of changes in the modernisation of the public sector accelerated. Within a matter of a few years, the Irish regulatory environment and framework have been significantly improved. Within the broad framework of public service reforms and market developments, new regulatory regimes have evolved. New market-oriented institutions have been set up or strengthened, such as the sectoral regulators and the competition authority. Accountability and transparency have been enhanced through new mechanisms such as enforcement and compliance with the Freedom of Information Act. The Irish judicial review process has helped to identify poor-quality laws and regulations.[69]

However, Ireland lags behind many OECD countries in terms of its capacities to ensure high quality regulation. Economic assessment of proposed legislation is missing. Alternative means of regulation, such as economic instruments, have replaced very few traditional "command and control" approaches. Implementation mechanisms and enforcement powers of the Reducing Red Tape policy may need to be enhanced if anti-competitive styles of regulations in non-traded sectors and interventionist tendencies are to be reversed. A particular challenge concerns the search for a new balance between public consultation, flexibility and rapidity in rulemaking.

Reform of the state must include the judiciary, the new market-based institutions, the Parliament and its committees, even the new regional powers.

Reform of the state is a broader task than modernisation of the public administration. The judiciary, the new market-based institutions, including the competition authority, the Parliament and its committees, even the new regional powers still need institutional adaptations in term of their efficiency, accountability and overall co-ordination.

POLICY OPTIONS FOR REGULATORY REFORM

This section identifies actions that, based on international consensus on good regulatory practices and on concrete experiences in OECD countries, are likely to be beneficial to improving regulation in Ireland. The summary recommendations presented here are discussed in more detail in the background reports to Chapters 2-6, published in this volume. They are based on the recommendations and policy framework in the OECD Report on Regulatory Reform.

Remove licensing constraints on free entry, particularly those with quantitative limits

Licensing restraints should be removed...

The SMI Working Group set this goal several years ago. The challenge is to identify and eliminate regulatory programmes and licensing schemes that have the effect of preventing entry and permitting non-competitive behaviour. A 1994 report by the Minister for Enterprise and Employment claimed progress concerning lawyers, opticians, electric power, telecoms, oil, gas, air and bus transport, broadcasting, taxi and hackney licensing, ports, and casual trade licences. Seven years later, constraints on competition persist in nearly all of these sectors.

Eliminate special-interest rules that inhibit efficient competition, such as the Groceries Order

...and the Groceries Order eliminated.

The potentially anti-competitive effects of the Groceries Order are well recognised. The CMRG's proposal, to eliminate rules aimed at sales supposedly below cost but retain some rules against anti-competitive discrimination and assertion of buyer power, seems sensible.

Strengthen implementation of the regulatory reform policy by creating stronger disciplines and performance assessment of regulatory quality within the departments and agencies, and by enforcing the disciplines through a high level committee

To boost implementation of regulatory quality disciplines...

Reducing Red Tape originated in the SMI as one of the elements to modernise the Irish public administration. The enforcement and compliance approaches of *Reducing Red Tape* are based on self-assessment and peer pressure. Contrary to the implementation approach used for other flagship policies, such as the *Freedom of Information Act*, the modernisation of the regulatory management system has lacked resources, training and resolve, and has yielded few concrete benefits for citizens and business. Accountability mechanisms of the new policy are based on vague internal procedures, supervised by an over-busy co-ordinating group. Such mechanisms are too weak and remote to change long-established habits and culture, to protect the regulatory system from influence and pressures from powerful special interests, to offset perverse incentives within the ministries and agencies, and to co-ordinate the difficult agenda of regulatory reform.

...a high-level regulatory committee might be created at the cabinet level...

An option that might be considered, for example, is creation of a high-level regulatory committee for these tasks with adequate powers to influence decisions at the cabinet level. Its role could be to advocate and promote implementation of the regulatory reform policy, to initiate key regulatory reform decisions, and to co-ordinate regulatory reform across government.[70] Participants on the committee could include the Department of the Prime Minister and the Ministry of Finance, and the Office of the Attorney General, and the Competition Authority. Regulatory departments and offices and sectoral regulators should be invited on an *ad hoc* basis. The committee may be supplemented by an advisory body where social partners (including consumer groups) and key institutions, like Forfas, could discuss regulatory affairs. The committee's work could be co-ordinated with other horizontal policies, such as SMI or budgeting. It could also prepare an annual report to the Parliament. This political body could be modelled on the Netherlands' Ministerial Committee in charge of the influential MDW ("Functioning of Markets, Deregulation and Legislative Quality") programme.[71]

...and performance standards should be set.

In parallel with a strong central promoter, Ireland could raise accountability for results within the departments and agencies through measurable and public performance standards for regulatory reform. One possible model to be explored is the U.S. *Government Performance and Results Act* of 1993, which established a government-wide system, including for regulators, to set goals for programme performance, measurement, and publication of results.[72]

Strengthen the accountability of sectoral regulators by building capacities for appropriate overview by Parliamentary committees, and clarify the roles of sectoral regulators and the Competition Authority to ensure a uniform competition policy in the regulated sectors.

Creation of independent regulators should be accompanied by a strategy to improve their accountability to the Parliament and ensure co-ordination with the Competition Authority.

Market-oriented bodies and institutions have developed along with liberalisation, privatisation and regulatory reform. However, the powers, nature, and accountability mechanisms of the sectoral regulators are challenging the general public governance and institutional balance. In some respects, these bodies have become a "fourth branch of the State" beside the Executive, Legislative and Judiciary.[73] Ireland was one of the first countries to start addressing the complex issues of accountability raised by this situation. Early in 2000, the Minister for Public Enterprise published a policy proposal on *Governance and Accountability in the Regulatory Process* which among other things, strongly advocated a more important role for Parliament in overseeing them. However, the Parliament and its committees lack capacities to do so. In light of this and past reports,[74] Ireland should consider a strategy to improve Parliamentary accountability procedures, including appropriate resources. Attention should be paid to managing information to permit the committees to focus on strategic policy decisions. A step in that direction could be the development of an impact assessment of policy decisions along the lines of a RIA.

With respect to co-ordination between the competition authority and the sectoral regulators, many of the CMRG recommendations should be followed, to provide for a structured process of co-ordination and a legal basis for the agencies to defer to each other without risk and without diluting or compromising the application of competition policy. The Authority and sectoral regulators should advise each other about matters that may come under the others' jurisdiction, and consult when they find they are both pursuing the same matter.[75] To do this meaningfully, they must have the right to exchange information with each other. Having someone from the Authority sit on appeals panels for sectoral regulator decisions can help integrate policy perspectives.

Strengthen disciplines on regulatory quality in the departments by i) reinforcing the central review unit; ii) refining tools for regulatory impact analysis, iii) adopting an explicit benefit-cost principle, iv) increasing the assessment of alternatives to regulation, v) integrating these tools into public consultation processes and vi) training public servants in how to use them.

The Regulatory Quality Checklist is a crucial step forward, but weaknesses and gaps should be corrected in putting it into practice.

The Regulatory Quality Checklist that accompanies memoranda for a proposed law is a crucial step forward. However, important weaknesses and gaps exist in the Irish process. Particularly important is the need, on one hand, to clearly differentiate between the mandatory Checklist and the "proofing" of impacts as, *inter alia*, employment, women, persons in poverty, and on the other hand, the need to consolidate in an extended RIA some key assessment, such as the impacts on industry and small business costs. The laundry list of economic and social impacts to be explored is too long and vague to provide a consistent framework for analysis, and will undermine the value of the programme. As the central principle for the RIA, a benefit-cost test should be adopted. It should be implemented by a step by step strategy to gradually improve the quantification of regulatory impacts for the most important regulations, while making qualitative assessments more consistent and reliable. These tools also need to be incorporated into day to day administrative practices. Based on OECD best practices, five key steps would improve effectiveness.

– Ireland should consider reinforcing the Central Unit in the Department of the Prime Minister, or otherwise strengthening independent quality control mechanisms on ministerial regulatory decisions.

– Development of effective ways to apply the *Reducing Red Tape* programme to subordinate regulations is necessary.

– Methodological rigour in the answers to the Checklist can be increased by providing training, written guidance, and minimum analytical standards, including for the benefit-cost tests, to departments and agencies.

– RIA should be expanded to incorporate detailed consideration of alternatives to be analysed and compared with the regulatory proposal. Because Ireland has been slow in incorporating regulatory and non-regulatory alternatives that can increase policy effectiveness at lower cost, regulators must be motivated through results-oriented management. This requires strong encouragement from the centre of government, supported by training, guidelines and expert assistance where necessary. Where rigid laws and legal culture inhibit use of more effective alternatives, broader legal reforms to allow more innovation and experimentation may be necessary.

– The effectiveness of the Irish regulatory management system would be enhanced by integration of RIA with public consultation processes. Such integration should, however, be carefully designed so that additional delays to the policy process are not introduced.

Increase transparency by standardising public consultation and more use of the Internet.

– *Standardise administrative procedures, including those concerning public consultation and rulemaking.*

Transparency is good, but could be better...

The small size of Ireland, the political culture of openness, the social partnership process, the number of elected representatives relative to the size of the population, and the *Freedom of Information Act* contribute to a climate of openness that facilitates consultation. However, as relationships evolve, new participants, including non-nationals, are affected by Irish regulatory affairs. Likewise, lack of minimum rules may complicate public consultation and regulatory procedures reducing effectiveness, speed and timeliness of regulatory responses. The recognition of such new circumstances is reflected in the increasing formalisation of basic administration duties (*e.g. the Cabinet Handbook, the Public Service Management Act*).

...by, for example, establishing a "notice and comment" requirement for all regulatory proposals.

Consideration should be given to establishing a "notice and comment" mandatory requirement for all regulatory proposals (perhaps managed by the RIA central unit mentioned previously). As a complementary measure, Ireland may wish to establish the minimum criteria and disciplines for the public consultation required by the *Reduce Red Tape* action plan. Furthermore, these efforts may be integrated into an encompassing initiative to prepare an Administrative Procedure Act. This would consolidate the recent effort to publish the basic rule making procedures in the *Cabinet Handbook*, and on the other hand would provide in a single text clear rights to citizens and businesses to know and challenge the rules to be followed when making regulations (RIA, consultation, publication, etc.) and when adjudicating regulatory matters (make a decision on a formality).

– *Make the QRC widely available to consulted parties, possibly through the Internet.*

A revamped QRC would provide a more coherent regulatory tool to assist regulators in the exercise of the regulatory choices. Current deficiencies in enforcement of the QRC are undermining its effectiveness as a useful regulatory tool.

Enhance the current programme of restating and consolidating existing laws and regulations with a target review programme based on pro-competition and regulatory high-quality criteria.

The 1995 OECD regulatory quality checklist could be used to verify the continued necessity and appropriateness of the existing stock of regulations.

The enactment *Statute Law (Restatement) Bill* and its full application is an important step to enhance the Irish regulatory framework. Adding specific regulatory quality criteria to the review process would enhance this mechanism. For such reviews, the 1995 OECD regulatory quality checklist could be used as a reference to verify the continued necessity and appropriateness of the existing stock of regulations. To support the review, the Parliament or government could directly or via an independent commission review the main areas of legislation and produce a rolling programme of reform spanning various years. As a prerequisite for such an endeavour, the government should provide enough human and technical resources to the unit in charge of the review. Such a unit could be merged with the enhanced RIA unit previously mentioned. The review process undertaken in Australia as part of its National Competition Policy is illustrative. Under that policy, all legislation was reviewed and anti-competitive restrictions were required to be removed unless it could be demonstrated that those restrictions were in the public interest and that there was no other way to achieve public policy objectives.[76]

Expand competition in the provision of public services at the municipal levels. An effective means would be competitive tendering of public services, within the framework of quality standards and monitoring.

Outsourcing by local governments can improve consumer choice and service quality, and allocates resources where they are most needed.

The large role of Irish local governments in providing public services has a significant impact on the economy because the level of efficiency in public services helps determine overall price levels. Improving the quality and cost of services will require more contracting out and more intense competition. Available evidence suggests that in most cases outsourcing improves consumer choice and service quality, allocates resources where they are most needed, with little if any negative impact on wages or employment. Where it has been applied, outsourcing in many OECD countries has generated substantial cost savings and increases in efficiency through improved management and economies of scale and scope.

Such initiatives are not without their problems as regards the regulatory framework to ensure quality of service, rights of access and cost control. The public service may require additional training and preparation, as in many countries, in administering contracts for those services where a significant degree of discretion is inevitable in providing the service. A more formal and specific statement of objectives and targets for such programmes is desirable, but experience in writing and monitoring such contracts is limited.

Strengthen the application of competition policy economy-wide through a series of reforms.

Vigorous enforcement of competition policy in the self-regulated professions is a priority...

– *Apply competition policy against non-transparent, anti-competitive self-regulation of professions and services.* These problems have already been the subject of enforcement action. Vigorous enforcement may be necessary, but the risk of backlash must also be managed. That is, the professions may seek legislative protection against further enforcement. To resist that plea, the Authority should be able to demonstrate how its action have yielded concrete consumer benefits.

...and advocacy by the competition authority throughout the public administration would strengthen attention to market principles.

– Improve advocacy powers, with clearer authorisation for more independent, wide-ranging analysis, clearer responsibilities on other agencies to consult with the Authority, and more resources to do the job. The statute should be amended, if needed to authorise more clearly a broad-ranging analysis and advocacy role for the Authority. Already, a new competition act is in preparation, which will statutorily support an advocacy role for the Authority. The Authority should act on its own right, and it should participate at the outset, rather than at the end of the process. The CMRG recommendation presents a useful model for advocacy powers. Ministers sponsoring legislation should be free to request the Authority's views directly, without going through DETE, about a proposal's implications for competition. Ministers should explain their views about the proposals' likely impacts and the reasons why restraints on competition could be justified in the public interest, and they should state whether they have consulted the Authority. The Authority's opinion would become public when the bill is published. Similarly, Ministers should be free to consult the Authority about the effects of proposed regulations, and the Authority's views about them would be made public along with the regulations. Providing for more systematic competition analysis of regulations and decisions below the level of legislation could be particularly important. Input from the Authority should be routine before departments adopt rules that limit entry and competition. More broadly, the CMRG calls for empowering the Authority to publish general discussion papers, to participate in the development of national policies that may affect competition, to co-operate with sectoral regulators, and to appear before parliamentary committees on issues that may affect competition.

– Clarify and make operational the criteria about competitive effects in the SMI checklist and standards. The competition policy criteria in the SMI checklist may be too general to guide non-experts. Either through additional guidance or training, they could be made more practical and specific. For example, they might operationalise the Working Group's recommendation to eliminate constraints that act like quotas limiting entry.

The merger process should be streamlined and responsibility for competition policy reviews for all mergers clearly assigned to the Authority...

– Make merger processes consistent, and eliminate the risks of overlap, uncertainty, and conflict. Maintaining two notification systems risks contradictory orders from two regulators. The process should be streamlined and responsibility for competition policy reviews for all mergers clearly assigned to the Authority. Application of other public interest factors would then be up to the Minister. This change might require transferring some of the personnel at the Department, who now do

111

the initial merger screenings, to the Authority, anticipating that they would continue performing that function there. In November 2000, the government indicated it planned to change the review process so that the Authority would have sole decision-making responsibility, except for mergers involving the media.

...and cartels broken up through a leniency programme.

– *Authorise a "whistleblower" or leniency programme.* Effective pursuit of the Authority's top priority will be aided greatly by an offer of leniency to cartel members to give evidence against their co-conspirators. Implementing this would require close co-ordination between the Authority and the DPP, which would ultimately make any leniency determinations. Here, Ireland may wish to study the Canadian programme. Generally applicable criminal procedures might support such a program. If not, special legislation or an authoritative policy statement would be needed.

Judicial expertise needs attention.

– *Consider ways to develop judicial expertise in competition matters.* Competition law may still be novel for many Irish judges. The CMRG has recommended that competition cases be assigned to judges on the basis of their expertise in competition matters, both in the High Court and in Circuit Courts. This may accomplish the same thing as establishing a specialised competition court, but without the need for structural changes in the judicial system. Rather, it could presumably be accomplished by court rule, adopted by the judges themselves.

The Authority should be more independent on budget and staffing.

– *Make the Authority more independent with respect to budget and staffing decisions.* Advocacy and especially a formal review role could only work if there is a statutory basis for Authority independence, as well as independence from indirect control throug the government budget. The Authority should have the same hiring flexibility that is enjoyed by the regulatory bodies under DPE. Permitting the Authority to exceed civil service salary caps could improve its retention experience. After the crisis of 1999 and early 2000, DETE has taken steps to bring the Authority and its staff up to authorised levels. At a minimum, that process should be completed. Additional investigative staff from the gardaí will aid the enforcement program. And additional economic resources will enable the Authority to revive its analysis and advocacy functions.

Encourage better regulatory practices at regional and local levels of government.

– *Co-ordinate regulatory reform initiatives with the regions and municipalities, and assist them to develop management capacities for quality regulation.*

Safeguarding the gains made at the national level through regulatory reform will require intensive efforts to promote regulatory quality at regional and local levels.

Managing regulations at different levels creates potential concerns for the future coherence and efficiency of the national regulatory system. Safeguarding the gains made at the national level through regulatory reform will require intensive efforts to promote regulatory quality at sub-national levels. In Ireland, the SMI has not improved local government capacities very much. New responsibilities have been added to local governments, in areas such as environment, planning, urban renewal, housing and general development. Adoption by regions and municipalities of programmes of reform based on consistent principles should form the basis for more formal co-operation measures. Other strategies to help regions and local government launch regulatory reform programmes include: establish and enforce good regulation tools, such as RIA and "notice and comments" procedures and benchmarking exercises.

– *Heighten awareness of and encourage respect for the efficient regulation principles by the county councils, regional bodies and large cities in their regulatory activities affecting international trade and investment. Through the co-operation institutions between the central government and sub-central bodies, the central government should promote the awareness and encourage respect of efficient regulation principles.*

Continue to encourage the use of international standards in national standardisation activities and to promote international harmonisation in European and international fora.

A strong commitment to an efficient and reliable standardisation system not only enhances market opportunities for Irish firms but also contributes to the world-wide consolidation of efficient and transparent markets for industry and consumers.

Continue to work to develop regional and island-wide regulatory solutions where those improve efficiency.

Optimal regulatory frameworks for Ireland might in some cases extend beyond Irish borders into Northern Ireland and Britain.

Optimal regulatory frameworks for Ireland might in some cases extend beyond Irish borders into Northern Ireland and Britain. This may be the case, for example, with network industries such as telecommunications, transport, energy, and water, and with policies such as environmental quality and SME development. For example, further developing the electricity interconnection with Northern Ireland offers possibilities for realising added efficiency gains in electricity generation, transportation and distribution on the island. Progress is underway in establishing the political capacities for island-wide regulatory co-ordination, and to the extent that these are successful they could have big payoffs for the Irish.

In the pharmacy sector...

Reform in the pharmacy sector...

– *Eliminate the restriction on economic freedom of pharmacists educated in other EU countries.*

– *Eliminate the location restrictions on pharmacies. Assess the exit and entry in the sector, and provide transparent subsidies to pharmacies that are desirable on the basis of public policy objectives, but are not forthcoming under free entry.*

113

In the area of legal services...

...and in legal services would help consumers.

– *Move the control of education and entry of legal professionals from the self-governing bodies, but maintain close ties as regards quality of entrants and content of education and training.* Entry and education are in the hands of the professions' self-governing body. While their stated purpose is to guarantee a minimal quality of professional knowledge and skills, the logical connection between the input, education, and output, quality enhancement, is tenuous. The contrast with the absence of mandatory continuing legal education is marked.[77] There is also a difference in the interests of the professional bodies and the public, where the latter would prefer a wider choice of professionals at lower cost.

– *Maintain the freedom of solicitors to advertise their fees and areas of specialisation.* Advertising by solicitors encourages consumers to shop around for cost-efficient legal services, which in turn encourages competition among solicitors.

Complete the process of introducing competition, and the application of general competition policy, in traditional monopoly sectors, including electricity and telecommunications. Increase competition in the market for electricity by:

A series of steps would boost market performance in he energy sector.

– *Prohibiting, in the short and medium term, further additions to ESB's generating plant.* In the longer term, if effective competition develops, then remove this limit on ESB so that all generators can compete across the entire market.

– *Requiring divestiture of some generation plant by ESB.* If market prices to liberalised customers are above competitive levels after the generation fuelled by the existing gas capacity comes on line, and if the amount of entry then expected and import capacity are together insufficient for effective competition, require further divestiture.

– *Ensuring by establishment of appropriate access tariffs and terms, that conditions of access to the transmission and distribution grid, including for example ancillary services, are cost-reflective and non-discriminatory.*

– *Requiring divestiture of transmission from generation if transmission constraints are not relieved or if there is discrimination in access.*

– *Proceeding with plans to increase the capacity of transmission of electricity between the Republic and Northern Ireland.*

– *Ensuring that any long-term contracts do not block further liberalisation of consumers.*

– *Liberalising choice for all electricity and gas consumers by 2005, or sooner if there is evidence of liberalised customers being subsidised by captive customers.*

Ensure well-resourced and independent regulation of the electricity and gas sectors by:

– *For gas, shifting regulatory responsibility for transmission access to the Commission for Electricity Regulation.*

– Retaining enforcement of the competition law in the sectors, however, with the Competition Authority.

Modify the tariff structure to improve efficiency in the sector by:

– Making regulated tariffs cost-reflective. Consider eliminating the requirement that tariffs be geographically uniform in light of the non-uniformity of cost of supply.

Reduce barriers to entry for gas importers and sellers

– The corporate separation of transmission should be a first step toward ownership separation of transmission from the potentially competitive activities.

Increase efficiency of regional employment support by:

– Putting into place more efficient support for employment and eliminate the subsidies to peat.

In the telecommunications sector, take a number of steps to complete the regulatory framework.

– Streamline the licensing regime using general authorisations, rather than individual licensing.

The telecommunications sector would also benefit from a more efficient and market-oriented regulatory framework.

Ireland needs to shift further towards a framework for market entry based on general authorisation rather than individual licensing. This will help to further reduce barriers to entry and to free scarce human resources in the ODTR. The requirement for a high-level business plan with the financial sources and projections, as well as for adequacy of managerial and technical resources, in obtaining a General Licence is questionable.

– The ODTR should establish concrete procedures with standard time frame for handling consumer complaints.

The procedure should be speedy, simple, and inexpensive for ordinary consumers. It should also ensure that telecommunications operators implement and make public an appropriate code of practice for consumer. Operators should be required to provide a published report on their handling of the complaints. The Department of Public Enterprise and the ODTR have been aware of the problem in dealing with consumer complaints and this issue has been covered in the draft legislation. The ODTR should develop concrete procedures to deal with consumer interests. The telecommunications industry, in particular, should be required to develop adequate and simple procedures to resolve disputes and respond to complaints.

– Accelerate the introduction of appropriate rights of way legislation to facilitate the construction of new networks on public highways.

The Irish government proposed benchmark legislation in 1999 to reform the system for telecommunications network operators to access public and private land. The Telecommunications

(Infrastructure) Bill provided that the network operators could apply for and possibly compulsorily acquire rights of way over private land in the event that negotiations with landowners were unsuccessful. It also addressed the issue of the use of public roads for infrastructure, and provided a legislative basis for sharing of ducts. The Bill proposed to set up a Telecommunications Infrastructure Board, a quasi-judicial body with the power to facilitate access to private land. Now that the Infrastructure Bill is withdrawn because of the issues over compulsory access to private land, and the provisions relating to access to public highways and sharing of infrastructure are to be included in the new Communications (Regulation) Bill, the government needs to take appropriate action to ensure its enactment.

- *The "in platform exclusivity" granted to cable operators should not be continued after the five-year period has expired in April 2004. The industry should be informed of such a decision at an early stage.*

Intended as a means to provided an incentive to develop digital networks, the "in platform exclusivity" period also serves to limit competition. As a tool to stimulate investment, the strength of the policy lies in the time limitation imposed. Clarifying that the exclusive privilege will not be extended is more likely to provide CATV operators with incentives to upgrade their networks for broadband access and telephony.

- *The costs of providing universal service should be determined on an agreed methodology. If net costs are found and deemed as an unfair burden on the incumbent then a universal service fund should be created through contributions of market participants.*

Appropriate policies to rebalancing prices should be given the first priority in the context of universal service. A methodology agreed to by the industry should be used to determine the cost of providing universal service. If the ODTR determines that the costs of universal service are high, taking into account any benefits that may accrue to the incumbent from providing universal service, then a funding system should be implemented to allow for appropriate compensation. If this is required, it is more appropriate to set up a universal service fund to which market players contribute than to use access deficit charges, which would also be in line with the European Commission's proposals in the draft new Directive on Universal Service.

- *Explicit and concrete provisions governing forbearance and withdrawal from sector specific regulation should be developed. From this perspective, the ODTR's practice of reviewing the telecommunications market should be strengthened and enhanced as a measure to enable the ODTR to evaluate the state of competition in the market to determine when and how sectoral regulations can be withdrawn leaving incumbent power to be disciplined by the market and the general competition law.*

Even though there may be scope for the introduction of further regulations in the market, the requirement to streamline regulations and forbear from regulation, when and where appropriate, remains an important task for the ODTR as does the need for continuous consultation with the Competition Authority. The market reviews of the ODTR are an important initial step in this process. These should be strengthened and the ODTR should be required to undertake regular reviews of regulation to ascertain where streamlining can take place.

MANAGING REGULATORY REFORM

Success will require Ireland to benchmark itself to a higher standard than its neighbours, to be a leader in regulatory reform.

The moment is right to take action with long-term benefits, for prosperity and full employment will cushion short-term adjustment shocks.[78] The next policy steps to be taken need to focus on issues of sustainability and the development of a robust regulatory policy. Success permits Ireland to be more assertive and forthcoming. But success will require it to think differently; not just differently from what it did before, but differently from its closest "peers". Ireland should benchmark itself to a higher standard than its neighbours.

These efforts will require a new political commitment. Although its contribution has been essential, regulatory reform is not a political "hot topic", and some reforms lack the external imperative that is often needed to overcome internal resistance. Hence, the government will need to employ all its persuasive and communication skills necessary to pursue the regulatory reform agenda.

NOTES

1. OECD (1999*a*). See also Fitz Gerald. J. (1999*a*); L*es études du* CERI, No. 56, November.

2. Much of the agricultural produce was exported unprocessed or with very limited processing.

3. The referendum deciding on membership took place in 1972 with accession occurring from the beginning of 1973.

4. To produce alcohol for industrial purposes from potatoes.

5. Using the CSO Input-Output Tables for Ireland, it can be seen that the direct and indirect import content of consumption rose from 29.5% in 1969 to 34.5% in 1975.

6. I. Kearney, D. McCoy, D. Duffy, M. McMahon, and D. Smyth (2000) and P. Honohan (1999).

7. Ireland had received a derogation allowing it to continue protection of the motor vehicle assembly industry till the beginning of the 1980s.

8. GNP is a better measure of rising living standards in Ireland as it excludes profit repatriations by foreign multinationals, which are very large in Ireland. The average growth rate for GDP for the six years 1994-99 was 8.7% whereas for GNP it was 7.8%.

9. Over the six years ending in 1999 it averaged 2% a year.

10. J. Bradley, J. Fitz Gerald, P. Honohan and I. Kearney (1997); OECD (1999*a*).

11. The rate of corporation tax on profits from exporting was zero until 1980. Thereafter, in line with EU requirements on eliminating discriminatory tax regimes, a common 10% rate has been charged on all profits from manufacturing activity. The commitment is now to unify tax rates for all business at 12 1/2%. The Industrial Development Authority has provided a "one stop shop" for potential investors successfully smoothing the path through the domestic bureaucracy for incoming firms.

12. Ruane, F. and H. Görg (1997).

13. Free second level education was only introduced in 1967.

14. Durkan, J. D. Fitzgerald and C. Harmon (1999).

15. CSO Labour Force Survey micro data.

16. D. Duffy, J. Fitz Gerald, I. Kearney, and D. Smyth (1999).

17. Generally women in Ireland have a higher level of educational attainment than men, D. Duffy, J. Fitz Gerald, I. Kearney, and D. Smyth (1999).

18. Barrett, A. and F. Trace (1998).

19. Barrett, A. and O'Connell, P. (2000).

20. I. Kearney, D. McCoy, D. Duffy, M. McMahon, and D. Smyth (2000). The OECD's calculations give a somewhat different picture, however, underlining the caution to be placed on these estimates.

21. For a detailed discussion of the regulation of the labour market see Sexton, J.J., and P. O'Connell (1997).

22. National Economic and Social Council (1986).

23. FitzGerald, J. (1999*b*).

24. This section covers reforms of economic regulations only.

25. OECD (1999*a*); Barry, F. (ed.) (1999).

26. Bradley, J., J. Fitz Gerald and I. Kearney (eds.) (1992).

27. FitzGerald, J. and F. Shortall (1998).

28. McArdle, P. (2000).

29. This plan was the document on which the provision of EU structural funds to Ireland was based.

30. Durkan J., and A. Reynolds-Feighan (1992).

31. T. Ferris (2000*a*).

32. S. Barrett (2000*b*).

33. Barrett, S., *Transport Policy in Ireland*, The Irish Management Institute, Dublin.

34. See M. McGurnaghan (1995).

35. J. Fitz Gerald and J. Johnston (1995).

36. See the footnote on taxi licenses for further details on how this is derived. This is very much a lower bound of the cost of licensing. The restriction on entry will allow owners of licenses to extract a rent over and above the cost of remunerating the capital tied up in the license.

37. P. Honohan (1998).

38. J. Fitz Gerald, I. Kearney, E. Morgenroth and D. Smyth (1999).

39. These problems have been aggravated because of the introduction of strict regulatory procedures for businesses offering child-care facilities at a time when the market for such services was already very tight.

40. Partly because the average age of women who have children is high by EU standards.

41. National Economic and Social Council (1999).

42. See OECD (1999*a*), p. 78. The Survey states that: "Costs are 55 and 30% below those of two other metropolitan areas (Århus and Odense) using in-house production."

43. *Ibid.* Costs appear to be around ¼ – ½ of the annual savings, though there are clearly economies of scales. In a few cases no costs were involved, while in a very few cases costs equalled or exceeded initial annual savings.

44. UK Department of the Environment, Transport, and the Regions (1998), para. 7.28.

45. Department of Public Enterprise (1999).

46. OECD (1997), p. 221

47. Irish Small and Medium-sized Enterprises – ISME, (2000), *Sustaining FDI let Economic Development. An ISME Response.* Document presented to the OECD delegation, June.

48. Department of the Prime Minister (2000), *Cabinet Handbook*, Rule 3.1j.

49. OECD (2000).

50. High Level Group on Administrative Simplification. *Report of the Meeting held 8 February, 2000, Answers to a Small Business Federation Recommendation.* A particular complain raised by SMEs is that departments and agencies tend to duplicate information requirement despite the Central Statistical Office (CSO) powers to be previously consulted (states in Section 31 of Statistical Act, 1993).

51. ISME – The Enterprise Association (2000), *op. cit.*

52. For Postal services see www.irlgov.ie/tec/communications/commconsultation.pdf; for transport proposals, see www.irlgov.ie/tec/transport/2117 DPE.pdf.

53. For more details see http://www.irlgov.ie/finance/News/sra/srap1.htm.

54. For a fuller discussion of "democratic deficit" in the regulatory process, see Ferris, Tom (2000*b*).

55. Parliamentary Debates, Dáil Éireann, Vol. 466, cols. 2244-6, 13 June 1996.

56. Jacobs, Scott H. (2000), "Regulatory Governance: Improving the Institutional Basis for Sectoral Regulation", OECD, Paris. The paper can be found at http://www.oecd.org/subject/regreform/Products/Sectoral_regulation.pdf.

57. *Governance and Accountability*, Chapter 3, pp. 9 and 10.

58. Morgan, D.G. (1999), pp. 8 and 12.

59. Local authorities are categorised in five legal classes 29 County councils, 5 county borough corporations (cities), 5 borough corporations, 49 urban districts, 26 town commissioners.

60. Council of Europe (1998); OECD (2000).

61. Until now, semi-autonomous and local agencies have rarely been merged or eliminated.

62. Examples of co-ordination difficulties go from the propensity of local authorities to create industrial and commercial zones instead of housing zones (for tax reasons) to the difficulties in securing permission to lay telecom cables or plan the Eastern Bypass highway around Dublin. Criticism of the lack of strategic spatial planning is being addressed through placing regional planning guidelines on a statutory footing under the 2000 Planning Act and through the preparation of a National Spatial Strategy by the Department of the Environment and Local Government. This Strategy is due to be published at the end of 2001.

63. Competition Authority Decision No.1, Notification No. CA/8/91, Nallen/O'Toole (1992). The statement was dictum in the particular decision, which approved a non-competition agreement that accompanied the sale of a small repair shop.

64. See the Forum on Public Procurement's website http://www.fpp.ie.

65. The computerised system is based on the United Nations Electronic Data Interchange Protocol and harmonised data-set (UN/EDIFACT) and it enables users to submit their import and/or export declarations to Customs authorities and to receive customs permissions through electronic exchange.

66. ESRI (1999), p. 252.

67. Section 21(2) of the Electricity (Supply) Act 1927 requires ESB to fix charges for the sale of electricity and for goods and services rendered by it so that the revenues derived in any year from such sales and services will be sufficient and only sufficient to pay all salaries, working expenses, and other outgoings properly chargeable to income in that year and such sums as the Board may think proper to set aside in that year for reserve fund, extensions, renewals, depreciation, loans and other like purposes (ESB, 2000*b*).

68. The ODTR states that in September 2000, delivery of circuits was 20% less than in August 2000, and 25% less than the target for September set by Eircom under its transformation programme. See ODTR 00/78, Consultation Paper on Service Levels Provided to Other Licensed Operators by Licensees with Significant Market Power.

69. For instance, the High Court decision in October 2000, which repealed quantitative limits on taxi licenses.

70. This body could build on the Council of Regulation and Competition proposed by Forfas

71. See OECD (1999*b*).

72. See US Government, General Accounting Office (1997).

73. Some of the questions raised may also be applicable to the accountability of other "recent" institution such as an independent central bank, competition authority, ombudsman office or electoral institutions.

74. For instance, the 1997 report of the Comptroller and Auditor General, the 1995 Delivering Better Government Report.

75. Making the agencies meet together quarterly to make sure they really do this seems like an oddly precise requirement, but its inclusion in the CMRG recommendation recognises, unfortunately, the history of suspicious relations among these agencies.

76. For further information see, Hilmer, F, Raynor, M., and Taperell, G. (1993), The Independent Committee of Inquiry, *National Competition Policy*, AGPS, Canberra, Australia.

    Or http://www.ncc.gov.au/nationalcompet/Legislation%20Review/Legislation%20Review.htm.

77. "21 Years On: The Changing Face Of CLE" by Sarah O'Reilly in the Law Society Gazette December 1999 on http://www.lawsociety.ie/GazDec1999.htm on 9 June 2000. "The future development of CLE is currently under review by a Law Society task force. The law societies of England & Wales and Scotland have in recent years introduced mandatory CLE. While the suggestion of mandatory CLE in Ireland has previously been discounted, there are some signs of change of attitude among the profession."

78. From Fingleton (2000). Although producer interests trump consumer interests, there are signs that this is changing. The positive experience in deregulating areas like telecommunications and air travel makes clear the enormous benefits from reform, and also removes fears concerning the dire scenarios predicted by the vested interests in such markets. As such, this early success builds momentum or constituencies for further change and makes it easier to argue for more extensive reform. In the first half of 2000, the Government finally started to tackle the problem in the Dublin taxi market, and has announced plans to introduce competition in the bus market in Dublin. A major review of competition law has recommended sweeping changes that would also benefit consumers, several of which were mentioned above and includes the abolition of the Groceries Order. On the other hand, greater competition increases the incentive for vested interests to seek protection by special regulation. As a result, we can expect exciting debates that raise complex economic, legal and political issues to continue in this area.

BIBLIOGRAPHY

Barrett, A. and F. Trace (1998), "Who is Coming Back? The Educational Profile of Returning Migrants in the 1990s", *Irish Banking Review*, Summer.

Barrett, A. and O'Connell, P. (2000), "Is There a Wage Premium for Returning Irish Migrants?", The Economic and Social Research Institute, Working Paper No. 125, Dublin.

Barrett, S. (1997), "The Implications of the Ireland-UK Airline Deregulation for an EU Internal Market", *Journal of Air Transport Management*, Vol. 3, No. 2.

Barrett S. (1999), "Peripheral Market Entry, Product Differentiation, Supplier Rents and Sustainability in the Deregulated European Aviation Market – A Case Study", *Journal of Air Transport Management*, Vol. 5, No. 1.

Barrett S. (2000a), "Airport Competition in the Deregulated European Aviation Market", *Journal of Air Transport Management*, Vol. 6 No. 1,

Barrett S. (2000b), "Regulation and Deregulation", in J. Mangan and K. Hannigan (eds), *Logistics and Transport in a Fast Growing Economy*, The Irish Management Institute, Dublin.

Barry, Frank, *et al.* (1997), *Single Market Review: Aggregate and Regional Impact – the cases of Greece, Spain, Ireland and Portugal*, Kogan Page, London.

Barry, Frank. (ed.) (1999), *Understanding Ireland's Economic Growth*, Macmillan Press Ltd.

Bradley, J., J. FitzGerald, P. Honohan and I. Kearney (1997), "Interpreting the Recent Irish Growth Experience", in D. Duffy, J. Fitz Gerald, I. Kearney, and F. Shortall (eds.), *Medium-Term Review: 1997-2003*, The Economic and Social Research Institute, Dublin.

Bradley, J., J. FitzGerald, D. Hurley, L. O'Sullivan and A. Storey (1993), "HERMES: A Macrosectoral Model for the Irish Economy", in Commission of the European Communities ed., HERMES: *Harmonised Econometric Research for Modelling Economic Systems*, North Holland.

Bradley, J., J. FitzGerald and I. Kearney (eds.) (1992), *The Role of the Structural Funds: Analysis of Consequences for Ireland in the Context of 1992*, Policy Research Series, Paper No. 13, The Economic and Social Research Institute, Dublin.

Council of Europe (1998), *Report on Structure and Operation of Local and Regional Democracy in Ireland*, Strasbourg.

Department of Public Enterprise (1999), A *Strategy for the Successful Development of the Irish Road Haulage Industry*, The Stationery Office, Dublin.

Duffy, D., J. FitzGerald, I. Kearney, and D. Smyth (1999), *Medium-Term Review 1999-2005*, The Economic and Social Research Institute, Dublin.

Durkan J., and A. Reynolds-Feighan (1992), "Irish Manufacturers' Transport Costs", in Bradley, J., J. Fitz Gerald and I. Kearney (eds.) (1992), *The Role of the Structural Funds: Analysis of Consequences for Ireland in the Context of 1992*, Policy Research Series, Paper No. 13, The Economic and Social Research Institute, Dublin.

Durkan, J., D. FitzGerald and C. Harmon (1999), "Education and Growth in the Irish Economy", in F. Barry (ed.), *Understanding Ireland's Economic Growth*, Macmillan Press Ltd.

Ferris Tom (2000a), "The Role of Government", in J. Mangan and K. Hannigan (eds.), *Logistics and Transport in a Fast Growing Economy*, The Irish Management Institute, Dublin.

Ferris, Tom (2000b), "Regulation of Public Utilities in Ireland", *Irish Banking Review*, Spring.

FitzGerald. J. (1999a), *The Irish Economic Boom*.

FitzGerald, J. (1999b), "Wage Formation in the Irish Labour Market", in F. Barry ed., *Understanding Ireland's Economic Growth*, Macmillan Press Ltd.

FitzGerald, J., I. Kearney, E. Morgenroth and D. Smyth (1999), *National Investment Priorities for the Period 2000-2006*, The Economic and Social Research Institute, Policy Research Series No. 33, Dublin.

FitzGerald, J. and F. Shortall (1998), "Pricing to Market, Exchange Rate Changes and the Transmission of Inflation", *The Economic and Social Review*, Vol. 29, No. 4.

Fitz Gerald J. and J. Johnston (1995), "Restructuring Irish Energy Utilities", in J. Fitz Gerald and J. Johnston (eds.), *Energy Utilities and Competitiveness*, The Economic and Social Research Institute, Policy Research Series No. 24, Dublin.

Forfás (2000), "Enterprise 2010: A New Strategy for the promotion of Irish Enterprise in the 21st Century", Dublin.

Hilmer, F, Raynor, M., and Taperell, G. (1993), "The Independent Committee of Inquiry", *National Competition Policy*, AGPS, Canberra, Australia.

Honohan P. (1998), *Key Issues of Cost-Benefit Methodology for Irish Industrial Policy*, The Economic and Social Research Institute, General Research Series No. 172, Dublin.

Honohan P. (1999), "Fiscal Adjustment and Disinflation in Ireland", in F. Barry (ed.), *Understanding Ireland's Economic Growth*, Macmillan Press Ltd.

Jacobs, Scott H. (2000), "Regulatory Governance: Improving the Institutional Basis for Sectoral Regulation", OECD, Paris.

Kearney, I., D. McCoy, D. Duffy, M. McMahon, and D. Smyth (2000), "Assessing the Stance of Fiscal Policy", in A. Barrett (ed.), *Budget Perspectives*, The Economic and Social Research Institute, Dublin

McArdle, P. (2000), "Living With the Euro: A preliminary View", *Irish Banking Review*, Spring.

M. McGurnaghan (1995), "Electricity Privatisation: The Northern Ireland Experience", in J. Fitz Gerald and J. Johnston (eds.), *Energy Utilities and Competitiveness*, The Economic and Social Research Institute, Policy Research Series No. 24, Dublin.

National Competitiveness Council (2000), "Statement on Regulatory Reform", Forfás, Dublin.

National Competitiveness Council (1998,1999, 2000), "Annual Competitiveness Report", Forfas, Dublin.

National Competitiveness Council (1998, 2000), "The Competitiveness Challenge", Forfás, Dublin.

National Economic and Social Council (1986), *A Strategy for Development 1986-1990*, The Stationery Office, Dublin.

National Economic and Social Council (1999), *Opportunities, Challenges and Capacities for Choice*, Report No. 105, The Stationery Office, Dublin.

OECD (1997), *Regulatory Impact Analysis: Best Practices in OECD Countries*, Paris,

OECD (1999a), *Economic Surveys: Ireland*, Paris.

OECD (1999b), "Background Report on Government Capacities to Produce High Quality Regulations" in OECD *Reviews on Regulatory Reform: Regulatory Reform in the Netherlands*, Paris.

OECD (2000), *Environmental Performance Review of Ireland*, Paris.

ODTR (2000), "Measuring Licensed Operator Performance: Report on Consultation", Document No. ODTR 00/04, 27 January.

Ruane, F. and H. Görg (1997), "The Impact of Foreign Direct Investment on Sectoral Adjustment in the Irish Economy", *National Institute Economic Review*, No. 160, April.

Sexton, J.J. and P. O'Connell (1997), *Labour Market Studies: Ireland European Commission*, DG V, Brussels.

US Government, General Accounting Office (1997), "Managing for Results: Regulatory Agencies Identified Significant Barriers to Focusing on Results", Washington, D.C.

Part II

BACKGROUND REPORTS

BACKGROUND REPORT ON GOVERNMENT CAPACITY TO ASSURE HIGH QUALITY REGULATION*

---

* This report was principally prepared by **Cesar Córdova-Novion**, Principal Administrator for Regulatory Management and Reform, with the participation of **Edward Donelan**, Consultant, and **Scott H. Jacobs**, then-Head of Programme on Regulatory Reform, in the Public Management Service. It has benefited from extensive comments provided by colleagues throughout the OECD Secretariat, by the Government of Ireland, by Member countries as part of the peer review process, and by the Trade Union Advisory Committee and the Business Industry Advisory Committee. This report was peer reviewed in December 2000 in the OECD's Working Party on Regulatory Management and Reform of the Public Management Committee.

TABLE OF CONTENTS

List of Boxes

Executive Summary

Background Report on Government Capacity to Assure High Quality Regulation

Can the national administration ensure that social and economic regulations are based on core principles of good regulation? Regulatory reform requires clear policies and the administrative machinery to carry them out, backed up by concrete political support. Good regulatory practices must be built into the administration itself if the public sector is to use regulation to carry out public policies efficiently and effectively. Such practices include administrative capacities to judge when and how to regulate in a highly complex world, transparency, flexibility, policy co-ordination, understanding of markets, and responsiveness to changing conditions.

Closely connected to the outstanding economic performance and transformation of the economic, social and cultural environment of the country in the last fifteen years, is the significant improvement of the Irish regulatory environment and framework. Accountability and transparency have been strongly enhanced, not only through traditional participatory and consensus-building mechanisms characterised by the social partnership approach, but also through new mechanisms such as enforcement and compliance with the *Freedom of Information Act*. The remarkable Strategic Management Initiative is fostering a new culture in government practices, including rule making. New market-oriented institutions have been set up or strengthened, such as the sectoral regulators and the competition authority.

But the Irish regulatory system continues to have some weaknesses. Ireland lags behind many OECD countries in terms of its capacities to ensure high quality regulation. Economic assessment of proposed legislation is missing. Alternatives to regulations, such as economic instruments, have replaced few traditional "command and control" approaches. Critically, implementation mechanisms and enforcement powers of the 1999 *Reducing Red Tape policy* may need to be enhanced if anti-competitive styles of regulations in non-traded sectors and interventionist tendencies are to be reversed. Like other small and participative countries, Ireland should acknowledge that globalisation and openness require a certain degree of formalism in the national regulatory management system to support market confidence and avoid undue preferences for insiders or "big players". A particular challenge concerns the search for a new balance between public consultation, flexibility and rapidity in rulemaking. The modernisation of other state institutions needs further attention. The Judiciary, the new market-based institutions, including the competition authority, the Parliament and its committees, even the new regional powers still need institutional adaptation in terms of their efficiency, accountability and overall co-ordination. Lastly, the Irish policy-making culture continues to be highly risk adverse, with a tendency to follow rather than lead.

While initiatives are underway across a wide range of areas, attention to implementation, evaluation, and refinement is essential to ensure that potential benefits are realised. Moreover, important gaps remain unaddressed. Policy options that should be considered by the Irish government are the following:

– *Strengthen implementation of the regulatory reform policy by creating stronger disciplines and performance assessment of regulatory quality within the departments and agencies, and by enforcing the disciplines through a high level committee*

The modernisation of the regulatory management system has lacked resources, training and resolve. Accountability mechanisms of the new policy have been based on vague internal procedures and have been too weak and remote to change long-established habits and culture, to protect the regulatory system from influence and pressures from powerful special interests, to offset perverse incentives within the ministries and agencies, and to co-ordinate the difficult agenda of regulatory reform. Measurable and public performance standards for regulatory reform should create feedbacks and incentives to transform culture and practice across the government. A high-level regulatory committee should be created for these tasks with adequate powers to influence decisions at the cabinet level.

– *Strengthen the accountability of sectoral regulators by building capacities for overview by the Parliamentary committees, and clarify the respective roles of sectoral regulators and the Competition Authority to ensure a co-ordinated, uniform competition policy approach in the regulated sectors.*

Executive Summary (*cont.*)

While Ireland has been one of the first countries to start to tackle the complex issues raised by the impact of sectoral regulators in terms of governance and accountability in the regulatory process, the government should strengthen effective review capacities of the Parliament and its committees to complete the new framework. As the new system stabilises, a second issue concerns the process of co-ordination and the need for a legal basis for the sectoral regulators and the Competition Authority to defer to each other without risk and without compromising the application of competition and high quality regulation policies.

– *Strengthen disciplines for regulatory quality in the departments and offices by reinforcing the central review unit and refining and integrating tools for regulatory impact analysis, increasing the use of alternatives to regulation, integrating these tools into public consultation processes and training public servants in how to use them.*

Use of regulatory impact assessment in Ireland is at an early stage and, unsurprisingly, requires strengthening if the potential benefits of this policy tool in improving regulatory quality are to be achieved. As a key step, the Central Unit in the Department of the Prime Minister should be reinforced with enough resources and analytical expertise to provide an independent opinion on regulatory matters. RIA should also be improved in four dimensions. First, a single assessment, based on a universal benefit-cost principle, should be adopted, merging the various existing assessments currently required. Second, application of the full RIA discipline should be extended to lower level rules as well as primary legislation. Third, the expanded RIA should incorporate detailed consideration for alternatives to be analysed and compared with the regulatory proposal. Fourth, the transition cost of implementing RIA would be reduced, and its quality increased, if it were routinely integrated with public consultation processes.

– *Increase transparency by formalising administrative procedures, including those concerning public consultation and rule making.*

As relationships evolve and new participants, including non-nationals, become affected by Irish regulatory affairs, minimum rules will improve public consultation and regulatory procedures enhancing effectiveness, speed and timeliness of regulatory responses. As a precautionary step, consideration should be given to establish as a safeguard a "notice and comment" mandatory requirement for all regulatory proposals (perhaps managed by the RIA central unit mentioned previously). As a complementary measure, Ireland may wish to establish the minimum criteria and disciplines for the public consultation required by the *Reduce Red Tape* action plan. Furthermore, these efforts may be integrated into an encompassing initiative to prepare an Administrative Procedure Act, which establishes in particular the rights of citizens and businesses to know and challenge the rules to be followed when making regulations (RIA, consultation, publication, etc.) and when adjudicating regulatory matters (make a decision on a formality).

– *Enhance the current programme of restating of existing laws and regulations with a target review programme based on pro-competition and regulatory high-quality criteria.*

Adding specific regulatory quality criteria, based on the 1995 OECD regulatory quality checklist, to the review programme of existing laws and regulations would enhance its impact. To support the review, the Parliament or government could directly or via an independent commission review the main areas of legislation and produce a rolling programme of reform spanning various years. As a prerequisite for such an endeavour, the government should provide enough human and technical resources to the unit in charge of the review. Such a unit could be merged with the enhanced RIA unit previously mentioned.

1. REGULATORY REFORM IN A NATIONAL CONTEXT

1.1. The administrative and legal environment in Ireland

Good public governance in Ireland faces important challenges in adapting its practices, culture, and relations to a high-growth and pro-market environment in which consumer interests are dominant. Over most of the life of the Irish state, government policies have been aimed at redistribution, protection of producers, and managing slow growth and high unemployment. Important reforms, such as abandoning protectionist policies, have been made. Undoubtedly the public sector and its institutions have changed in the past decade and half. However, further reform are still needed to sustain and consolidate the market-led growth of the past decade, which has evolved so rapidly that it has strained the capacities and flexibility of existing government institutions to repair market failures, protect consumers, and target social welfare policies at new needs. That is, reform of Ireland's governance structure is lagging behind dynamic market and social changes, and hence could be a bottleneck to sustained growth.

This challenge is not an unpleasant challenge to face, since it is a result of rapidly rising prosperity. Ireland experienced remarkable economic performance in the last decade, with an average annual growth of 8.5% in 1997-1999. A "virtuous circle" has emerged, as increases in take-home pay and improved cost competitiveness led to substantial job creation and a turnaround in public finances. These trends freed up resources for spending on health, education and social welfare that will support continued growth.[1] Irish performance is even more striking when set in a European context of slow growth (see Chapter 1).

Several factors contributed to this success: a successful policy on inward investment and increased openness of the economy; a favourable tax regime for corporations; massive investment on education and human capital; favourable demographic factors; the return of skilled emigrants; significant social consensus; and Ireland's robust rule of law.[2] The fact that Ireland is an English-speaking country might have made it more attractive for foreign firms as an entry point into Europe. Accession in 1973 to the EU and the consistent adoption of pro-EU policies proved helpful to the creation of a favourable climate for growth and development. In addition to the significant boost provided by the EU Structural and Cohesion Funds,[3] a substantial number of policies were brought up to European standards, including, health and safety at work, environment and consumer policies in keeping with the rest of the members states of the EU. Membership also transformed the regulatory environment and framework as, for example, some product markets and network industries were subjected to Single Market disciplines.

In addition to these factors, which some other countries have shared, the awakening of the "Celtic Tiger" has been supported by a public administration that has taken steps to adapt policies to the changing market environment. Following radical decisions in the late 50s and 60s to abandon inward and protectionist policies that had been in place since independence and intensified in the 30's, successive governments have transformed Ireland into one of the OECD's most open economies.[4] Accompanying decisions, such as investing in education and basing industrial policy on attractive tax rates, have borne impressive fruit after a few decades. Capacity to learn from mistakes and use crises to overcome barriers also played parts.[5]

The Irish approach to modernisation of the public sector during the past decade was based on pragmatic steps. Some other countries, such as the UK and New Zealand, pursued a rather contentious, ideological, and legalistic approach to reform (which may have been necessary in their particular circumstances), but successive Irish governments based their efforts on building consensus through processes of national partnership. A process begun in 1987 has developed through a succession of complex national concordats on pay into a permanent conference on wider economic and social policies (see Box 7 in Section 3.1 below). In this respect, the Irish reform style is closer to the experience of the Netherlands and Denmark. The development of policies in Ireland is characterised by prudence, pragmatism, and an incremental approach to change rather than the adoption of "big projects".

In this step-by-step transformation, the roles of the State, markets and society have shifted. State-market intervention in Ireland, formerly characterised by direct involvement in the economy through

133

ownership of public monopolies and direct intervention, has changed to acceptance of free market forces and the development of pro-competitive policy regimes that support market forces notably in aviation, electricity and telecommunication. Driven largely by the European single market programme, the last decade has seen restructuring, privatising and deregulating, and construction of new market institutions such as independent regulators. Today, governments on all sides of the political spectrum acknowledge the benefits of competitive and open markets.

Yet skills gaps and institutional and cultural rigidities persist in the public administration that could create bottlenecks to future growth. An emerging challenge facing the Irish government is a shortage of skills and personnel resulting from rapid economic growth. The number of applicants for entry-level positions in the civil service is declining as more opportunities open up in the private sector. Some key institutions are experiencing difficulties in recruiting and retaining staff.[7] The labour shortages are compounded by skills mismatches. At local level and national level shortages have hit the staffing of the planning authorities and the planning appeals boards. The labour shortages are compounded by skills mismatches. Although this is changing, the traditional Irish civil servant is more a generalist who lacks specific training in economic and analytical expertise needed in key regulatory positions.

Second, interventionist practices that reduce market efficiency linger in the Irish public sector, and this habit of market intervention presents a challenge for further reforms.[7] Although these habits are changing, there is still suspicion of market mechanisms and a cautious attitude toward market-based approaches, perhaps reflecting the view of the general electorate. Many Irish still believe that government can and should solve all problems. For example, although the recent voluminous Social Partnership pact, the *Programme for Prosperity and Fairness*, makes general reference to implement the

---

Box 1.   Good practices for improving the capacities of national administrations
to assure high quality regulation

The OECD Report on Regulatory Reform, which was welcomed by ministers in May 1997, includes a co-ordinated set of strategies for improving regulatory quality, many of which were based on the 1995 Recommendation of the OECD Council on Improving the Quality of Government Regulation. These form the basis of the analysis undertaken in this report, and are reproduced below.

A.   BUILDING A REGULATORY MANAGEMENT SYSTEM

1. Adopt regulatory reform policy at the highest political levels.

2. Establish explicit standards for regulatory quality and principles of regulatory decision-making.

3. Build regulatory management capacities.

B.   IMPROVING THE QUALITY OF NEW REGULATIONS

1. Assess regulatory impacts.

2. Consult systematically with affected interests.

3. Use alternatives to regulation.

4. Improve regulatory co-ordination.

C.   UPGRADING THE QUALITY OF EXISTING REGULATIONS

(In addition to the strategies listed above)

1. Review and update existing regulations.

2. Reduce red tape and government formalities.

regulatory reform agenda and fostering competition policy, little specific mentions are made to fostering market functioning, consumer choice, and price mechanisms as solutions to bottlenecks and shortages, instead focussing on state actions and market interventions. Indeed, though this policy document focuses on the need to increase competitiveness of Irish enterprises, the role of competition as a central means to achieve this goal is nearly absent. Competition principles are not widely used in public debates and policy statements. Producer interests tend to take precedence over consumer interests in many policies (see Chapter 1 and background report to Chapter 3), and governance institutions are still vulnerable to "capture" by producer interests who, in the aftermath of more intensive competition policy enforcement, will intensify their efforts to use regulatory regimes for private advantage. The "command and control" reflex, looking first to a regulatory solution rather than other types of policy instruments (or no intervention), is still present among parliamentarians and rule-makers. For instance, licences and price controls are still common reactions when problems arise, accompanied by strong resistance to elimination of protectionist and corporatist regulations.[8]

Policy-making in Ireland still confronts rent-seeking attitudes, typically in the form of strong and close relationships between elected representatives and particular groups of interests. Functioning as a broker at the local level, and directly connected to the electoral constituency, the Irish politician becomes a specialist on governmental information and contacts, to, for example, help citizens obtain a house or a scholarship,[9] or to resist changes that would reduce regulatory rents. This type of lobbying, often assimilated to brokerage', or even "Clientelism" was shown recently to be a powerful ingredient in the opposition to reforms to the agriculture policy, the introduction of some "polluter pays" instruments, and the liberalisation of taxis and public houses. Land-use planning by local governments, in particular in Dublin, seems to have been particularly vulnerable.[10] Recent measures, such as the enactment of the *Freedom of Information Act*, a new *Electoral Act* and codes of conduct, the incisive role of the Ombudsman and of an aggressive media, have raised awareness and brought a climate of change. These important transparency and accountability steps would be strengthened by further reducing the influence of informal mechanisms and processes that provide opportunities for interests to monopolise information, and thus favour "insiders", and by strengthening government-wide "watchdog" functions such as competition advocacy by the competition authority (3).

Box 2.   The legal and regulatory framework in Ireland

Ireland is a common law country with a written Constitution. While much of Irish public law is similar to that of other common law jurisdictions the existence of a written Constitution and judicial review of legislation has meant that the Irish legal system has developed its own distinctive characteristics.[1]

There are essentially two classes of legislation: primary legislation consisting of acts enacted by the Parliament (*Oireachtas*), and secondary legislation (regulations, rules, orders and "bye-laws" made by ministers and other bodies under a power conferred by an Act.[2] Ireland enacts between 50 – 60 Acts and some 500 – 600 regulations in any one year.[3]

In addition, departments and offices produce a significant number of administrative circulars (such as schemes, standards, licenses and formalities) which although not recognised by the courts as binding law, for many practical reasons impose similar administrative burdens.

---

1. Hogan, Gerard (1994), in Chapter 2.
2. In addition to the Acts of the Houses of the *Oireachtas* (Parliament), Ireland's statute book is composed of Acts of the Parliament of *Saorstat Eireann*, Acts of the Parliament of the United Kingdom of Great Britain and Ireland passed in the period 1801 to 1937, Acts of the Parliament of Great Britain passed in the period 1707 to 1800, Acts of the Parliament of England passed in the period 1226 to 1707, Acts passed by any Parliament sitting in Ireland before the Union with Great Britain in 1801.
3. See the volumes of the Statutes and Statutory instruments published since 1990. It is significant to note also that some orders may be kept on the Statute Book even if its primary act has been repealed (*e.g.*, Groceries Order).

A third challenge for progress on regulatory reform is upgrading the effectiveness of what is now a regulatory management system aimed at legal quality rather than regulatory efficiency and perform-ance. Where there are controls, they tend to be based on tradition or informal practices rather than on written standards and consistent rules. Considerable discretion is left to ministers when making new rules. There are almost no written standards and rules for quality regulation, apart from the legal requi-rement that regulations be authorised by a parent statute. Challenges to regulations must be done by judicial review, a costly and time consuming process[11]. Judicial review cannot be regarded as an effec-tive quality control mechanism in view of the 500 to 600 regulations made each year. An additional pro-blem is that there is no body independent from the regulating ministries (see Section 2.1) to oversee the preparation of secondary regulations. As a result, there is a natural tendency for the regulatory fra-mework to fragment and inflate. For example, the legal and regulatory system for the communications sector is spread among many individual pieces of secondary legislation. Irish regulation is vulnerable to the vicious cycle seen also in the United States: more regulations attempt to remedy more problems, and when performance falls short, even more regulations are triggered.

The larger picture is one of adjustment of governance institutions in line with market and social changes. Like many OECD countries, Ireland faces important challenges in adjusting its governance arrangements to the new realities of globalisation, demands of civil society, and new technologies. In particular, the effectiveness of existing institutions is tied to the relationships between the three exe-cutive, legislative, and judiciary branches of the state ("horizontal coherence") and the relationships between central and local levels of government ("vertical coherence").[12]

Compared to the pace of change in the executive branch, the Parliament has been slow to assume its new accountability responsibilities. Since 1997 a reform strengthened Parliamentary committees fair-ly extensive powers and prerogatives to oversee bodies under the aegis of government departments.[13] However, adequate resources have not accompanied these new competencies to provide effective over-seeing mechanisms.[14] Members of Parliament receive a flood of official reports, but the sheer number of these reports and the lack of staff to help assess them reduce accountability and parliamentary capaci-ty to focus on important issues.[15] The lack of resources and research capacities means that members of the Parliament are dependent for information on the government and interest groups. The more power-ful of the latter are well served by independent, expert advice and research support and may exercise undue influence through these information resources. Localism and the "brokerage' system referred to above in Irish parliamentary culture tends to further hinder the Parliament from concentrating on "big picture" issues. Changing institutions, the transferral of competencies to European levels, new domestic consultation processes and the setting up of independent regulators further complicate Parliamentary overview, and contribute to a loss of effective influence by the Parliament over national policy.

The judiciary must also confront new challenges to adapt to the new Irish context. Through judicial reviews or court appeals, judges increasingly make key regulatory decisions. This has raised concern about judicial trespass into the field of the legislature[16]. Not dissimilar to debates in other countries, this complex issue has raised questions about the accountability of judges, and their selection, appointment and training.

Questions remain open on the need to improve vertical coherence. Ireland has been confronted by the difficult choices in balancing a demand for devolution (advocated by EU regional policy), and on the other hand, the dangers of fragmentation and diseconomies in a small country of 3.7 million inhabitants (of which 1 million live in Dublin).[17]

1.2. Recent regulatory reform initiatives to improve public administration capacities

A recently approved regulatory reform programme *Reducing Red Tape* is an important addition to an array of initiatives and policies, stretching back more than a decade, that are intended to increase, efficiency, transparency and accountability of the Irish public administration. The main vehicle for these improvements was the launching in 1994 of the Strategic Management Initiative (SMI). Its main objectives were:

reforming [the] institutions at national and local level to provide services, accountability, transparency and freedom of information. In so doing [the government is] committed to extending the opportunities for democratic participation by citizens in all aspects of life.[18]

SMI is the third attempt to reform the Irish administration. Earlier attempts to reform the public service were of value in diagnosing the problems of the public service and raising awareness about new management approaches and tools.[19] The first attempt to reform the public service followed the publication of the *Report of the Public Services Organisation Review Group* 1966-1969, (commonly referred to as the Devlin Report). The *Devlin Report* presented a series of recommendations to permit the administration to cope with new demands generated by the creation of a European welfare state providing more services to a wider array of citizens. It concentrated on key functional elements, the most important of which was a separation of policy making from implementation and service delivery functions. For several reasons, notably, a lack of involvement from the administration and partisanship in the political spheres, the reform initiative failed. Its legacy was a series of piecemeal results.

In 1985, the government launched a second reform programme through publication of a White Paper: *Serving the Country Better*. That reform aimed to introduce new public management concepts and policy tools. It advocated greater decentralisation, improved budgetary management and greater mobility across departments of top level administrators. While the programme permitted the introduction of some important changes, by the time of the economic crisis of 1987, the political level and highest level of administration had withdrawn their support, and basic structural changes were not implemented.

Though the successive reforms built robust foundations for change and a wealth of experience, the continuing need for deeper and wider reform of the public sector led in 1994 to the SMI. Today, the SMI is regarded as the first successful reform of the Irish Public Service since the foundation of the independent state. One of the reasons for the success of the SMI is that it has had strong support, not only from senior civil servants, but also from three successive governments.[20] Another reason is that many of its central policies were underpinned by legislation in the *Public Service Management Act, 1997, the Freedom of Information Act, 1997 and the Committee of the Houses of the Oireachtas [Parliament] (Compellability, Privileges and Immunities of Witness) Act, 1997*. In many ways, the laws provided formal structure and content to informal and heterogeneous procedures and practices.

The SMI has been converted into a series of policy documents and guidelines that build on the principles laid down at the outset.[21] Currently, eight initiatives form the core of SMI. Four are aimed at improving customer service and delivery of policies:

– Quality services for customers.

– Simplification of administrative procedures and regulatory reform.

– Open and transparent service delivery.

– Effective management of cross-cutting issues.

Four initiatives are aimed at internal improvements of the administration:

– Devolving authority and accountability;

– New approaches to human resource management;

– More effective financial management, and

– Improved use of information technology to meet business and organisational needs.

The programme is based mainly on a 'bottom-up' approach, where 'shared ownership' by public administrators is favoured over an exclusively "top down" approach, and where goals and priorities are to be achieved with the help of positive and negative feedback. This participative approach intends to focus on behaviours and empowerment of the civil servants. Basically, the government implements SMI through self-assessment, that is, a requirement that each department and office identify in an iterative way, its own strengths and weaknesses and put into place a process of strategic management. This process is ongoing. In particular the preparation of Strategy Statements is undertaken every three years, or after the election of a new government, through the preparation of a statement of strategy by each department and office and by the setting out of a business plan by which the strategy will be delivered. Individual departments' strategies are consistent with the current policies of the government of the day and international and EU obligations. Departments are also requested to implement sectoral programmes that follow the eight core initiatives noted above.

To oversee the SMI process the government appointed nine top-level civil servants from different departments to serve on the steering group known as the Co-ordinating Group of Secretaries. This group is itself supported by specialised working groups of senior officials and experts, from both the public and private sectors, focusing on particular actions or issues. A specific working group focuses on legal reforms, where the Attorney General Office has been working since the beginning. In 1997, a new group, the Implementation Group of Secretaries was given responsibility for implementing and monitoring SMI and reporting progress across departments to the Congress. Two small executive units support the programme: a unit in the Department of the Prime Minister's Office has responsibility for central co-ordination of the programme, and another within the Department of Finance provides financial support to the programme. In each department and office, a specific implementation group has been created. In 1999, a Change Management Fund of IR£ 5 million per annum was established to support departments and offices (up to 50% of the project costs) in their efforts to implement the programmes.

Assessment. From some perspectives, the SMI seems to have been a successful programme but no external and comprehensive evaluation has yet been undertaken to evaluate it.[22] The SMI helped to reverse low morale in the public service resulting from the perception that public management policies were centred on the overall goal of continuously cutting the number of public servants. A recent evaluation of the departments' strategic statements prepared during the first (1995-1996) and second (1998-1999) iteration of the SMI showed progress. Focusing in three key elements, the evaluation found significant and clear improvements in strategic capacities, a reduction of "aspirational expressions", better focus on customers and a significant effort to set up a performance measurements framework in most departments and offices. The study, however, stressed that there was room for improvement, in particular many departments have failed to link their analysis to internal change and restructuring.[23] Another clear impact of the SMI has been changes in the culture of public service and in the manner by which it deals with the public. Concrete improvements are felt by citizens dealing with the Department of Social Community and Family Affairs and the Revenue Commissioners, and transparency and accountability have improved. A new culture is patent in the fact that some departments have undertaken strategic examination of particular policies in the light of developments within the relevant environment; examples of this include the policy papers on critical aspects of accountability (of sectoral regulators, see Section 3.4)[24] and transparency and ethics (see the design and implementation of the *Freedom of Information Act*). SMI has also helped to improve the degree of formality in administrative procedures across the government.[25]

Critics have pointed out, however, that the SMI has been slow to show concrete results and that outcomes only became tangible in 1999, five years after its launch. Lack of uniform compliance by departments and offices has raised questions about the drawbacks of a 'bottom up' approach based on self-assessment and peer pressure to achieve its objectives rather than on incentives and a standardised approach. The lack of precise indicators and targets and the lack of an explicit auditing mechanism by an independent overview body have hampered the development of objective measures of performance in the programme. The ability and will of the Implementation Group of Secretaries, whose members are judge and part of the programme, to challenge, check and stir advancements of the programme across the whole government are as yet unproven. The effectiveness of the new collaboration mechanisms to deal with cross-cutting issues, such as children policy, asylum seekers and regional development are still to show results. Anticipation of needs and adaptation to change, monitoring and evaluation of policy and effective reward for performance are yet to be engrained in the operation of services.[26] Equally, the SMI has not yet proven its impact on the improvement of local government capacities (see Section 2.3). While the "bottom up" approach to reform has benefits, it could be supplemented by other more direct and speedier approaches to change based on clearer disciplines, rights and obligations.

E-*government*. As with most OECD countries, Ireland has invested in new information and communication technologies to improve transparency and delivery of government services. An infrastructure exists which interconnects all agencies in central government. It is intended to replace this infrastruc-

---

Box 3. Chronology of regulatory reforms and important laws in Ireland

1924: *Ministers and Secretaries Act* creates the Civil service and basic accountability mechanisms.

1969: Publication of *Report of Public Services Organisation Review Group* (Devlin).

1980: *Ombudsman Act.* The Ombudsman's remit was extended in 1985 to Local Authorities, Health Boards, Telecom Eireann and An Post.

1984: Government White Paper *Serving the Country Better.*

1986: New Judicial Review Procedures introduced.

1991: *Competition Act.* The Act establishes a competition authority. The Act was later amended and strengthened in 1996 by the introduction of criminal offences and penalties (see background report to Chapter 3).

1993: *Comptroller and Auditor General's Act.*

1994: Strategic Management Initiative Launched.

1995 *Ethics in Public Service Act*: new enforcement accountability mechanisms. Also provides for a register of interests and other procedures against corrupt practices.

1996: Publication of the Report *Delivering Better Government.*

1996: *Telecommunication (Miscellaneous Provisions) Act.* The Act makes provision for the establishment of the Office of the Director of Telecommunications Regulation, (an independent regulator); transfers functions and pricing authority from the minister to the Director; provides for the imposition of a levy on providers of telecommunications services to finance the regulator.

1997: *Freedom of Information Act.* The Act enables members of the public to obtain access, to the greatest extent possible consistent with the public interest and the right to privacy, to information in the possession of public bodies; to have personal information relating to them in the possession of public bodies corrected; to have the right of access to records held by public bodies; to be entitled to an independent review of decisions of public bodies. The Act also establishes an the office of information commissioner.

1997: *Public Service Management Act.* The Act provides for a new management structure to enhance the management, effectiveness and transparency of operations of departments of state and certain other offices of the public service. It also increases the accountability of civil servants while preserving the discretion of the government in relation to their responsibility to Parliament.

1997: *Committees of the Houses of the Oireachtas (Compellability, Privileges and Immunities of Witness Act.)* The Act together with the Public Service Management Act provides the framework for accountability of civil servants to committees of the Parliament.

1999: *Electricity Regulation Act.* The Act establishes the Commission for Electricity Regulation (independent regulator), transfers certain regulatory functions from the Minister to the Commission, and provides for the imposition of an industry levy to finance the regulator.

1999: Reducing Red Tape – An Action Programme for Regulatory Reform in Ireland.

2000: Publication of *Governance and Accountability in the Regulatory Process: Policy Proposals.*

---

ture in 2001 with a countrywide virtual private network, which will cover all of the government sector. This network will be used to support the delivery of E-government, and for the Intranet and Extranet needs of government.

Deregulation, privatisation and liberalisation. Derived in large measure from EU directives, Ireland has exceeded EU directives in aspects of its privatisation and market liberalisation programme. Aviation and telecommunications have been fully liberalised. Markets for gas, electricity and postal services are in the process of liberalisation and proposed arrangements for public transport have been issued for public consultation. However, the Irish economy is still characterised by state monopolies in some sectors, where Ireland has been slower than other OECD countries to sell. The Irish government still retains monopoly control of Irish Rail and bus companies serving Dublin and the provinces. The state also owns a commercial bank and controls big utilities including electricity, gas, water and peat. Based on a practical, non-ideological and case by case approach, policies on privatisation have been developed in close consultation with trade unions and effected, in some cases, through "strategic alliances" where their support is linked to immediate benefits, often in the form of direct participation in the privatised company. In terms of competition law and policies, Ireland has been slowly converging to EU standards, though implementation has not been sufficiently integrated into the general policy framework for regulation (see background report to Chapter 3).

2. DRIVERS OF REGULATORY REFORM: NATIONAL POLICIES AND INSTITUTIONS

2.1. Regulatory reform policies and core principles

The 1997 OECD *Report on Regulatory Reform* recommends that countries "adopt at the political level broad programmes of regulatory reform that establish clear objectives and frameworks for implementation."[27] The 1995 OECD *Council Recommendation on Improving the Quality of Government Regulation* contains a set of best practice principles against which reform policies can be measured.[28] The recent policy on *Reducing Red Tape: An Action Programme of Regulatory Reform in Ireland* adopted by the government in July 1999 is based on these principles.[29] The following sections consider whether the goals and strategies set out in this programme meet Ireland's regulatory needs and priorities, and whether the mechanisms proposed are likely to allow them to be put into practice.

The current policy has its root in previous initiatives and programmes, in addition to the long established quality standards that laws and regulations have a legal basis and are clear, consistent, comprehensible and accessible to all users. A strong judicial review mechanism has also promoted reforms and quality regulation (see Box 4). In terms of explicit policies, substantive reforms can be traced to the 1980s, when attempts to reduce the burden of regulations were launched through the work of *ad hoc* groups such as the Industrial Costs Monitoring Group in the Department of Industry and Commerce, and the Task Force Report on Small Business and Services, set by the Department of Enterprise, Trade and Employment. More recently, the SMI has been a vehicle to promote quality across all government activities, including laws and regulations. For this task, each department was asked to undertake on a regular basis a systematic review of all its operations and ask whether each policy was necessary or whether it could best be achieved by alternative means. This process has resulted in many regulatory reforms.

Regulatory reform became an explicit policy objective in the mid-1990s. In May 1996, the Government published a policy document on public service modernisation (*Delivering Better Government*) which devoted a specific section to regulatory reform and set out a programme of action for administrative simplification. The policy outlined four principles of reform:

- To improve the quality, rather than reduce the quantity, of regulations;

- To eliminate unnecessary and/or inefficient regulations (including legislation);

- To simplify necessary regulation and related procedures as much as possible, and

– To lower the cost of regulatory compliance, and to make regulations more accessible.

The policy was not implemented at the time. However, a Regulatory Reform Working Group was set up to propose a detailed programme of action. Three years later, based on the recommendations of the Working Group, the government adopted in July 1999 the report, *Reducing Red Tape – An Action Programme of Regulatory Reform in Ireland*.[30] The social partners in the recent partnership programmes – *Partnership 2000 and the Programme for Prosperity and Fairness* – later endorsed the policy, as well as this OECD review of regulatory practices in Ireland.[31]

The heart of *Reducing Red Tape* is to establish a programme of action to reform the regulatory management system. The programme institutionalises new regulatory procedures and requires a series of actions. It sets out the policy of deepening public consultation with a department's "customers and other interested parties" through existing mechanisms or the establishment of new user groups. It requires that each department and office assess all new laws and regulations based on a "Quality Regulation Checklist" (see Section 3.3) and assigns responsibility for implementing the programme at a senior management level. It called for the listing "by Autumn 1999" of relevant legislation (both primary and secondary) to identify the scope for consolidation, revision /or repeal. Lastly, it recommended the establishment of a small Central Regulatory Reform Resource Unit in the Department of the Prime Minister to drive the agenda and monitor progress, and an *ad hoc* High Level Group to monitor, to the extent possible, implementation of the remaining recommendations of the Small Business Forum.

The programme is slowly materialising, following the SMI's decentralised approach and based on "bottom up" implementation mechanisms. In November 1999, the *Cabinet Handbook*, which guides departments on the principal administrative procedures to follow when making laws, was amended.[32]

Box 4. Judicial Review in Ireland

Judicial review in Ireland has been more vigorous than in other countries, and has been a deterrent against "bad quality" laws and regulations, and thus form part of the central regulatory management armoury. Similar to the practice in other countries such as the United States, a judge may declare legislation to be unconstitutional,[1] and the High and Supreme Courts ensure that government and Parliament, in the enactment of primary legislation, respect principles of natural and constitutional justice. These principles include principles of proportionality, the right to be heard, and the right to have decisions taken without bias. The courts also ensure that secondary legislation and other acts of public bodies are consistent or go beyond the authorising primary legislation. In this regard, the courts will be concerned with how, for example, a decision was taken by a regulator, rather than with the merits of the decision itself.

Courts review the constitutionality of legislation through two methods: the first is set out in Article 26 of the Constitution which provides that the President may, after consultation with the Council of State, refer any bill to the Supreme Court for a decision on the question as to whether any such bill or any provision of the bill is repugnant to the Constitution or any provision of it. The second method is set out in Article 34.3.2 of the Constitution which enables the High or Supreme Court on appeal to question the validity of any law having regard to the provisions of the Constitution.

First, judicial review can be costly and time consuming. In addition, a single judge sitting in a particular court handling certain types of cases can become a *de facto* regulator with little accountability constraints. Judges performing this task may lack technical expertise or experience in solving such problems. In addition, since review by the courts increases uncertainties and delay in regulatory policies, it may undermine the responsiveness and transparency of the regulatory system. The costs in terms of money, time and risk may deter small regulatory cases of concern to individuals or less well off groups in society.

---

1. Moran, David (1999), p. 8.

In addition to other proofing and impacts assessment (such as on women, poverty or rural communities), departments and offices must verify, prior to presentation to government, that their proposed legislation meets the Checklist criteria (see Section 3.3). The Checklist should be completed together with the other six impact assessments.[33] This self-assessment must then be reported in the Memorandum for the Government, which Ministers present for Cabinet approval. The Assistant Secretary General of the Department of the Prime Minister in charge of SMI was made responsible for the implementation of a policy on regulatory reform. Senior Officials of equal rank are responsible for this area within each department. They are responsible for implementation of the regulatory reform programme in their respective Departments and report through the Department of the Prime Minister to the Implementation Group, which in turn has responsibility to report to the Government on overall progress. In the Summer 2000, two officials were appointed in the Department of the Prime Minister as the first staff of the new central resource unit to co-ordinate the regulatory reform agenda. Their remit includes developing a work programme for the unit and identifying human resource requirements which are to be provided initially through consultancies, secondments and contracts funded by the change management fund. They both also have other duties to perform. The Ad Hoc High Level Group of senior officials set up to examine the remaining recommendations of the Small Business and Services Forum has begun to examine the implementation of the recommendations on administrative simplification accepted by the government.

In conjunction with the new regulatory quality policy the government has made progress in reviewing existing laws and regulations.[34] A Statute Law Revision Unit was established in the Office of the Attorney General in February 1999. The Unit will have five full time and one part time officials when it is fully functioning. The objective of the Unit is to draft statute law reform and consolidation bills and undertake related work, including supervising the preparation of indexes to the statutes and statutory instruments (See Section 4). The Unit has worked closely with the Department of the Prime Minister to ensure that each department and office has reviewed its legislative stock and identified laws in need of consolidation, revision or repeal. The Unit has also obtained government approval for publishing administrative consolidations of Acts. Approval will be sought for the introduction of changes in the procedures of Parliament so that revision bills may be enacted on a fast track procedure.

The content of the *Reducing Red Tape* policy and its programme of action are comprehensive and are in line with regulatory quality standards in place across the OECD area. They adequately cover the preparation of new regulations and the revision of existing regulations. The policy also fosters transparency and accountability by stressing the need for consultation and reforming the rule-making process. The Checklist articulates a clear test concerning the impact of legislation on market entry, restriction on competition and increase in administrative burdens. In that sense, the policy has a market-oriented and pro-competition stance. It could easily be basis for the development of regulatory impact assessment.

However, the implementation strategy and institutional drivers for reform are weak. From the perspective of the departments of state and of the ministers concerned, regulatory reform is one of many SMI projects, with unclear priorities. But reliance on the SMI approach, based on self-assessment and peer pressure, may provide too few incentives (positive and negative) to effectively transform regulatory traditions and practices. From the perspective of the departments of state and of the ministers concerned, regulatory reform is one of many SMI projects, with unclear priorities. The distinction between the Checklist and the ever extending list of issues to be assessed or proofed is not clear. And this might be an important reason to explain why during the first year of operation the Checklist has often been ignored or been perceived as a formality in the internal red tape of governmental procedures rather than a genuine regulatory decision making tool.

The establishment of a small Central Regulatory Reform Resource Unit at the Department of the Prime Minister to drive the agenda of regulatory reform and monitor progress represents best practice in this field. However, the small size of the Unit raises questions about the political commitment to the process and about its effectiveness. The Unit does not have a statutory mandate to assess the quality of the answers to the Checklist nor a statutory duty to report on the outcome of its work. In fact, the

Unit would appear to have less powers than those recommended by the 1996 Working Group. The Working Group recommended that the central resource unit would produce an annual report and provide an independent assessment of new proposals, in particular of compliance costs. It remains to be seen whether or not the central resource unit will be in a position to deliver these responses in its current configuration. Moreover, the delay in the articulation of the policy and programme, the small size of the Central Regulatory Reform Resource Unit, and a perceived lack of support in terms of staffing the Unit may reduce its credibility during the crucial transition phase of establishing a regulatory management system.[35]

Furthermore, while many OECD recommendations have been adopted, others have not. Some important gaps may be identified. In practice, this means that departments preparing secondary regulations will not provide written answers to the Checklist Although the Reducing Red Tape explicitly indicates that the Checklist applies to the preparation of new laws and subordinate regulations, its enforcement mechanism is the Memorandum for Government, and the Memorandum needs to be completed only for the preparation of laws and exceptionally for secondary regulations. This contradiction implies that departments preparing subordinate regulations have not a clear obligation to use the Checklist. Secondly, the OECD has recommended as an essential principle that regulations should "produce benefits that justify costs" and "consider the distribution of effects across society." This principle is referred to in various countries as the "proportionality" principle or, in a more rigorous and quantitative form, as the benefit-cost test. Such a test is the preferred method for considering regulatory impacts because it aims to produce public policy that meets the criterion of being "socially optimal" (i.e., maximising welfare).[36] This key principle is insufficiently developed in the policy of the government of Ireland and in the Checklist. Third, sufficient consideration does not seem to be given to the determination of the distributive effects of proposed regulations across society. Moreover, no explicit links seem to exist between the implementation of the policy and related policies such as structural adjustment policies, competition policy or trade openness (though the second test in the Checklist refers to market entry and restrictions on competition.) Finally, there are no standards and parameters for the operation of the Unit. No training has been provided in the specialist work of regulatory reform, in particular training on public consultation and RIA (for a further discussion of the Checklist see Section 3.3).

Modernising regulatory bodies and regulatory institutions. In parallel to the policies focussed on improving existing and new regulations, the Department of Public Enterprise recently developed a set of policy proposals to improve the performance, transparency and accountability of the recently created sectoral regulators (see Section 3.4).

Competition advocacy. Competition advocacy by the Authority, which in many countries has been a primary driver for reforms of regulation, has been meagre in Ireland, principally due to resources constraints, although this issue has been the subject of a recent examination and additional staff are in the process of being recruited (see background report to Chapter 3).

2.2. Mechanisms to promote regulatory reform within the public administration

Mechanisms for managing and tracking reform inside the administration are needed to keep reform on schedule and to avoid a recurrence of over-regulation. It is often difficult for ministries to reform themselves, given countervailing pressures, and maintaining consistency and systematic approaches across the entire administration is necessary if reform is to be broad-based. This requires the allocation of specific responsibilities and powers to agencies at the centre of government.

Ireland has a strong decentralised rulemaking process, where the proponent Ministry assumes most of the regulatory decisions before the Cabinet approves a bill (see Box 5 on the Irish rulemaking process). Procedures tend to be quite permissive and be seen as guides rather than rules to be complied with. At the centre the *Department of the Prime Minister* co-ordinates the discussion through the management of the fundamental regulatory documents: the Memorandum for the Government. The Cabinet Secretariat discharges the role of co-ordinating co-operation between departments and acts

Box 5. The regulatory decision making process in Ireland

The Irish regulatory reform management process is shared between the Department of the Prime Minister (*Taoiseach* in Irish) and each department promoting regulations in consultation with the Attorney General Office. There are essentially three stages in respect of the making of new primary legislation. The first stage is a decision in principle to proceed with the development of a new law. After approval of the policy, the next step is to draft legislation on the basis of an approved general scheme. The third is the approval of text and publication. At each stage, the Memorandum for the Government (the document that forms the basis for the discussion and decisions) is circulated for comments to all concerned departments and the Office of the Attorney General. In the case of primary legislation, the decision to draft and publish legislation rests with Government. The Government acts on the basis of a proposal put forward by a Minister and based on a document known as a Memorandum for Government. The Memorandum is prepared following an iterative process in which the officials concerned identify the problem to be solved, research and consider policy options and hold consultations inside and outside the administration to be sure that the proposal for Government is soundly based.

Under the government procedure rules, set out in the *Cabinet Handbook*, all departments are consulted sufficiently in advance... to allow proper consultation and consideration (para. 1.3) at each stage of the legislative drafting process.[1] Public consultation is often done in parallel to the interministerial discussions.[2]

After government approval of the draft heads, the department concerned sends a complete file to the Office of the Government Parliamentary Counsel (OGPC), part of the Office of the Attorney General. OGPC is responsible for the drafting of all government bills. The main element of the file is the draft heads of bill accompanied by explanatory memoranda. In the formal drafting process by the OGPC, there is a continuous dialogue with the policy division of the department to ensure that the final legal text reflects the intention of the proposed legislation. The evolution of a draft from idea to law is very much an iterative process. Essentially, the drafter analyses legislative proposals from the point of view of constitutionality and effectiveness. He or she then prepares a series of drafts in consultation with officials in the department or office promoting the legislation and lawyers from the advisory side of the Office of the Attorney General.

After the text is ready, the proponent department draws up the final Memorandum setting out the proposal for legislation and the background with a clear statement of the problem to be solved and appends the draft Bill. Since November 1999, the Memorandum must also state whether or not the department has completed the Regulatory Quality Checklist, which appears as Appendix VI of to the *Cabinet Handbook*. Lastly the draft Bill and Memorandum and appendices are presented and approved at Cabinet level.

The preparation of secondary regulation (regulations, orders, rules and "bye-laws") follows the same principles laid down in the *Cabinet Handbook*. The process is one of custom and follows no set rules, though. A Minister has full responsibility to prepare secondary regulation according to the parent Act. A majority of departments tend to involve the OPCG. For limited purposes, specified by the legislation, a limited number of bodies, such as the Law Society and the sectoral regulators, may also prepare and issue regulations. When published they are usually laid before the Parliament which in many cases has 21 days to invalidate them.

After approval by the Cabinet, a bill is submitted to each House of the Parliament (in Irish, *Oireachtas*) for a five-stage process that leads to its eventual enactment. Notice of making of regulations is published in the *Iris Oifigiúil* (Official Journal) and in many cases notice is also published in national newspapers circulating throughout the country.

---

1. Collective authority responsibilities, set up in the Constitution, Article 28.4.2 requires that Ministers should inform their colleagues in Government of proposals, they, or Ministers of State at their Departments intend to announce and if necessary, seek their agreement (Cabinet Handbook, para. 1.1)

2. Two further important sources for law are Green and White Papers. Green or White Papers set out Government plans in advance and permit a high level of public consultation to take place before the enactment of legislation. Green Papers were invented by the Labour Government in England in 1967. They essentially set out the Government proposals without committing themselves. White Papers tend to be definite statements of Government policy. These documents were used with great effect for the formulation of recent education policy and the Education Act, 1998, was developed following a process that includes both Green and White Papers.

as mediator in the case of disputes. As noted, a small *Central Regulatory Reform Resource Unit* implements and oversees regulatory reform policy.

A second important participant in the legislative drafting process is the *Office of the Attorney General*. The Office provides an independent legal review of legislative proposals, both primary (bills) and secondary regulations.[37] Its main objective is to ensure that constitutional principles and relevant international obligations are respected (*e.g.* fair procedures, proportionality and equality of treatment of citizens). It also verifies the legal quality of legislation. A special unit, called the *Office of Parliamentary Counsel to the Government* at the Attorney General Office drafts all Bills (proposed primary legislation) initiated by government and most secondary legislation.[38]

The *Department of Finance* also provides advice to Government on all proposals submitted by other Department regarding primary legislation. It verifies in particular, the "Explanatory and Financial Memoranda" that accompany the bills on presentation to the Parliament prepared by sponsoring Departments.[39] However, the Department does not examine subordinated regulations that do not to have to be co-signed by the Minister of Finance. There are no published guidelines as to the criteria used in these reviews but they seem to be confined to minimising expenditure.

A few other bodies have participated as advocates for reform. The *Government Legislation Committee* (a committee composed of the Government Chief Whip, the Attorney General, the Office of the Government Parliamentary Counsel and the programme managers of each political party in Government) meets weekly to monitor the implementation of the government's published legislation programme. The committee also manages the flow of legislation into the Parliament. It has, however, no role in reviewing the quality of the bills. A well respected Ombudsman, who also is the Commissioner of the *Freedom of Information Act*, and the Comptroller and Audit General play a valuable surveillance role in strengthening accountability of the administration.

Forfas, as the policy advisory board of the Department of Enterprise, Trade and Employment for enterprise, trade, science, technology and innovation, has been a key promoter of reforms.[40] In particular, *Forfas* serves as the secretariat of the influential *National Competitiveness Council* established in 1997 whose members include both employers and trade union representatives. Senior government officials attend as observers. The Council's focus on improving competitiveness has provided a useful counterbalance to other lobby groups, as it focuses on reducing input costs to business. In successive reports it has promoted increased competition in energy, telecommunications, transport and many other areas of the Irish economy. In particular, it has highlighted areas where costs for Irish business (and generally also for private consumers) are out of line with those in other competitor countries. Its annual reports bring together a wide range of useful measures of competitiveness, helping focus attention on the areas most in need of reform. Equally, the Institute of Public Administration (IPA) has contributed to the debate on the modernisation of the public administration and the dissemination of new public management techniques including regulatory management tools.[40]

2.3. Co-ordination between levels of government

Ireland is considered as one of the most centralised countries in Europe. There are 114 elected local authorities, which have a more limited range of powers than their counterparts in other EU countries.[428] The present-day system of local government differs little structurally from the one established by the *Local Government (Ireland) Act, 1898 by the Westminster Parliament*. Under the general supervision of the Department of the Environment and Local Government, local governments mainly provide public services, such as social housing, water, waste removal and treatment, roads, fire services and recreational facilities for local communities. In recent years, a certain amount of discretion has been decentralised in the areas of personnel, building construction, and traffic management. At the same time, new responsibilities have been added to local governments, in areas such as environment, planning, urban renewal, housing and general development, while others have been reduced, such as health functions that were moved to regional health boards and primary environmental protection transferred to a specialised agency.[43] Local governments have limited powers in the fields of education, health, and public transport (except taxis). Their involvement in social programmes is growing. In terms of regulatory powers, local authorities' competencies concentrate on licensing and permitting (e.g. land use) and control of nuisance and litter. Few explicit quality principles to be observed when preparing new local rules existed until recently.

A significant number of semi-autonomous single purpose public regional bodies operate in the health, tourism promotion and fisheries areas in addition to the local authorities.[44] While these bodies operate separately from local government, elected members are represented on the boards of some of these bodies. In addition, more than 100 other local development bodies operate at local level supported by EU programmes and are concerned with rural development, micro enterprise and community development/social exclusion.

In the last decade, a series of functional, rather than structural, reforms have been launched. In particular, the government has made important efforts to improve the managerial capacities of local governments' administration and co-ordination between local governments and between local governments and local development bodies. Based on the SMI, the programme 1996 *Better Local Government* created strategic policy committees for all counties.[45] In 2000, county/city development boards were set up to improve co-ordination between local government, local development and state agencies and reduce policy and service delivery fragmentation at the local level. In 2000, the Planning Act was overhauled to improve transparency and accountability of local authority in respect of decisions concerning the preparation of the draft development plan. For example, the Act ensures pre-draft discussions with relevant interest groups and requires all submissions on the draft plan to be in writing. The *Local Government Bill*, 2000 will also make further changes in respect of local authority procedures to ensure wide consultation on local decisions, for example through the Strategic Policy Committees, and transparency in the system, for example by ensuring that almost all meetings of the local elected members must be in public.

Since the early 90s, the government has also been building second-tier bodies to improve co-ordination and maximise the effectiveness of EU funds at the regional level (as well as to ensure their reinstatement). In 1991, the country was divided into eight regional authorities and in 1998, the country was further divided into two regions. Two new regional assemblies were created for the latter. Although the newest structure was designed to avoid conflicts and overlaps with existing regional authorities, a certain amount of scepticism greeted the new bodies as they were considered additional talking shops.[46]

The new arrangements may help local governments modernise management capacities, streamline administrative procedures and reduce duplication from the proliferation of semi-autonomous and local agencies (some of them funded by EU) and local governments with partial objectives.[47] Two particular concerns have been detected. Inefficient spatial and housing planning is becoming an important obstacle to growth, impeding greater employment mobility and emigration as well as exacerbating inflation and transport problems. The problem is rooted on the many layers in the planning approval process with subsequent recourse to courts.[48] Secondly, the fact that many local governments are producer, supplier and regulator impede the delivery of high quality public services. The sheer number of local governments has created fragmented industries incapable of reaping scale economies, for instance in the maintenance of social housing, road repair, engineering and architectural design, or disposal and water supply.

Ireland joined the European Union in 1973 as part of the first enlargement of the Union. The effects of its membership have been huge and essentially beneficial. The economic and political opening and subsequent growth and diversification of trade and investment have been a powerful driver of Ireland's economic success (see background report to Chapter 4). However, EU membership has added an additional layer of government and policymaking.

The obligations of each EU Member State are to ensure that national law guarantees that directives have been given full effect. A key element has thus been the development of the machinery needed implement the *acquis communautaire* (see Box 6). This process necessitates the drafting of measures in precise and clear language.[49] The choice of form and methods is left to Member States to decide. In Ireland, this has meant implementation by using one of two choices: primary legislation or secondary regulation.[50] The bulk of Directives have been implemented by means of regulations made under the *European Communities Act*, 1972. This route has not been without controversy.[51] Some directives have been implemented by primary legislation. The choice of primary or secondary legislation is usually determined by reference to whether the policy proposals are entirely within or go beyond the terms of the directive. The tendency is to copy out directives into Irish law, that is, to replicate as far as possible the wording of the directive in Irish legislation. This contrasts with the approach in other Member States, notably the United Kingdom, where the directives are rewritten to fit in more closely with English law.

In addition to transposing the body of EU legislation into their own national law, countries must ensure that it is properly implemented and enforced. The record of Ireland in transposing directives has been fair. By November 1999, Ireland needed to transpose 4.4%. In terms of the Single Market Scoreboard table, it occupied the 11th position, with delays in particular in the Transport and Veterinary sectors. Where there is action by the Commission for failure to implement directives the reason is often due to lack of staff resources to work on implementation projects rather than any ideological objections.

The Department of Foreign Affairs in conjunction with other relevant Departments has responsibility for monitoring the development of EU policy across the government and ensuring that there is sufficient coherence in Ireland's stance in Brussels. In addition, the Department of the Prime Minister through the Cabinet Committee on European Affairs provides overall direction to Government policy. Day to day co-ordination is done through working groups of senior officials. As other Member States have experience on this matter, public consultation on draft directives and EU regulation is mostly left at the discretion of concerned departments. Important interests, such as business associations tend to intervene directly in Brussels through specialised lobbies.

Relationship with Northern Ireland. Institutional relations and co-ordination between the national government and regional governments were rare. The Good Friday Agreement of 1998 changed this situation. Since the Agreement, the discharge of a range of public functions is undertaken in close co-operation with the devolved government in Northern Ireland, while certain functions are now carried out on an all-island or cross-border basis. These co-operation arrangements are set out in and governed by the *British-Irish Agreement Act*, 1999.

A North/South Ministerial Council (NSMC) has been established bringing Ministers, North and South, together to develop consultation, co-operation and action within the island of Ireland-including through implementation on an all-island and cross-border basis. The Council meets in different ways:

Box 6.   The European *acquis communautaire*

The *Acquis communautaire* comprises the entire body of legislation of the European Communities that has accumulated, and been revised, over the last 40 years. It includes:

The founding Treaty of Rome as revised by the Maastricht and Amsterdam Treaties.

The Regulations and Directives passed by the Council of Ministers, most of which concern the single market.

The judgements of the European Court of Justice.

The Acquis has expanded considerably in recent years, and now includes the Common Foreign and Security Policy (CFSP) and justice and home affairs (JHA), as well as the objectives and realisation of political, economic and monetary union.

147

- In plenary or summit format twice a year, with both sides represented by the Heads of Government;

- In specific sectoral format – so far eleven[52] – with each side represented by the appropriate Ministers; these meetings take place quarterly; and

- In an institutional format to consider institutional or cross-sectoral matters (including in relation to the EU) and to resolve disagreement. This format, in which Ireland is to be represented by the Minister for Foreign Affairs, has yet to meet.

All Council decisions are by agreement between the two sides. The Ministerial Council has a range of modes of operation, from exchange of information and consultation, through using best endeavours to reach agreement on the adoption of common policies, to taking decisions by agreement on policies and actions at an all island and cross-border level to be implemented either (a) separately in each jurisdiction, North and South or (b) by implementation bodies operating on a cross-border or all-island level. Six such bodies have been established with defined executive functions in the areas of Inland Waterways throughout the island, Food Safety Promotion throughout the island, Special EU Programmes, Language (Irish and Ulster Scots), Trade and Business Development and Lough Foyle and Carlingford Lough (inland fisheries and aquaculture in these river basins). Six areas have been identified for co-operation in the first mode described above: Agriculture, Education, Transport, Environment, Tourism and Health.

In line with the Good Friday Agreement, a British-Irish Council (BIC) has also been established, comprising representatives of the British and Irish Governments, of the devolved governments in Northern Ireland, Scotland and Wales, together with representatives of the Isle of Man and the Channel Islands. The BIC is also to meet in different formats, mirroring the situation with the NSMC. The BIC will exchange information, consult and use best endeavours to reach agreement on co-operation on matters of mutual interest. It is open to the BIC to agree common policies or common actions. Individual members may opt not to participate in such common policies and common actions. There are no implementation bodies with executive functions reporting to the BIC. A number of priority subjects have been identified for co-operation under the BIC -the fight against drugs, social inclusion, transport links and the knowledge economy.

3. ADMINISTRATIVE CAPACITIES FOR MAKING NEW REGULATION OF HIGH QUALITY

3.1. Administrative transparency and predictability

Transparency of the regulatory system is essential to establishing a stable and accessible regulatory environment that promotes competition, trade, and investment, and helps ensure against undue influence by special interests. Transparency also reinforces legitimacy and fairness of regulatory processes. Transparency is not easy to implement in practice. It involves a wide range of practices, including standardised processes for making and changing regulations; consultation with interested parties; plain language in drafting; publication, codification, and other ways of making rules easy to find and understand; controls on administrative discretion; and implementation and appeals processes that are predictable and consistent.

Openness and consultation are integral elements of public life and government procedures in Ireland. The *Freedom of Information Act, 1997*, has expanded these values. Transparency is further reinforced by the fact that the Irish administration is small and interrelated. However, there is little consistency in the consultative processes; and because consultation tends to be *ad hoc* and informal, it might be vulnerable to "insiders" or powerful interest groups, relative to smaller or new actors such as consumer groups.

Transparency of rule-making procedures. Ireland does not have a law setting out procedures for the legislative drafting process. However, since 1998 |the Department of the Prime Minister has been publishing and up-dating a *Cabinet Handbook* that details the required procedures to present proposals for legislation for approval by the government. Previously the rules, or rather guidelines, were set out in confidential internal circulars. The Handbook also sets out the requirements to be followed when Ministerial or Departmental Orders (*i.e.* regulations, rules, schemes and by-laws) need to be submitted to the government.

Transparency as dialogue with affected groups: use of public consultation. The Irish public service attaches great importance to public consultation. Consensus building, anchored in extensive dialogue with the social partners is considered a central element of the economic and social successes of the country (see Box 7). Since the advent of the *Public Service Management Act* 1997 and the *Freedom of Information Act* 1997, the flow of information between departments and the public has been considerably enhanced. In the past few years, the practice of prior consultation at an early stage in the development of regulations has become for many departments a well-anchored custom.

In terms of formal requirements for the government to produce Bills and subordinate regulations, the *Cabinet Handbook* provides that proponent departments may consult with outside persons/bodies "if necessary", although they should refrain from disclosing the actual legal text prior to approval by the Cabinet and presentation to the Parliament in the case of bills.[53] Furthermore, the 1999 *Reducing Red Tape* policy, incorporated in the *Cabinet Handbook*, requires as an element of the Quality Regulation Checklist that departments "outline the extent to which interested groups or representative bodies have been consulted".62 In practice, the consultation process is *ad hoc* and unsystematic. Consultation procedures vary in accordance with the circumstances. There are no formal written procedures to prescribe as a matter of course who should be consulted before the making of legislation. Departments regard it to be part of their responsibility to identify key players in the areas for which they have responsibility and to keep in touch with them and their concerns. In some cases, the public is consulted widely and views are sought by means of advertisements in the national newspapers. In other cases where the proposals are industry or sector specific, the proposals are discussed with known industry or sector representatives. The process of consultation might involve the publication of a Green Paper, setting out the options for regulation and inviting formal submissions from the general public. This would be followed by a White Paper setting out the government's policy intentions. Some policy changes are preceded by discussion documents, and when published these documents would set out with some particularity the nature of the issues considered and how problems were solved.[54]

Departments also rely on an array of advisory and liaison bodies. For instance, the Revenue Commissioners have a standing committee (called the Tax Administration Liaison Committee) comprising members of the accounting and legal profession which consider issues relating to tax regulation and administration. Most of the times, these bodies have been set up within the Social Partnership system to introduce checks and balances into decision-making, to increase the legitimacy of legislation, to identify and discuss policies, and to improve the level of voluntary compliance, including a smooth and rapid implementation of new legislation, once agreed. The official aim for the consultation is also to ensure that affected parties are well-informed of new regulation in advance and are able to minimise adjustment costs through forward planning.

Occasionally, after the Cabinet has approved the text, draft legislation is published in advance of its initiation in Parliament, with a general invitation to comment. The objective of this is to nurture national debate in Parliament. This has happened for example with consolidated tax legislation and with some significant changes to VAT legislation.

Assessment of public consultation. The nearly universal support for the social partner mechanism signals a general satisfaction with existing consultation and participation practices.

Although the processes are transparent, the efficiency and expediency of the consultation process could be enhanced by improved information and though the creation of safeguard mechanisms to

---

avoid potential abuse. It can then be counter-argued that in a small open economy, with a strong media and a strong tradition of local politicians' accessibility, formalised procedures would be costly and counter-productive. But important interests, notably consumer groups, report that they have not been able to participate and defend their interests.[55] Equally, consultation processes on zoning or reforming local public transportation have raised criticism that the consultation system can be unduly influenced by influential groups. In this sense, clear guidelines and training, establishing "notice and comments" requirements prior to acceptance at the Cabinet and general improvement in the quality of the documents subject to consultation may be required, without unnecessarily formalising the processes.

Rethinking the institutional setting might also be desirable to sustain public support on reforms and adapt Irish institutions to new circumstances. As the Netherlands discovered in the early 90s, too many advisory bodies focusing on details do not increase the quality of the public consultation and slow down government responsiveness to a changing environment. The existence of more than 90 different groups established under the last Social Partnership Agreement, for instance, makes it difficult for a newcomer to the process to understand where the decisions will be made, before considering the substance of the decision.

Lastly, existing institutions and procedures for consensus building, either formalised or *ad hoc*, may not be adequate to deal with a rapidly changing society. Some interlocutors such as the unions or "big business" representatives may play too large a role.[56] Changing priorities and strategies involve asses-

---

Box 7.   Social Partnership in Ireland

Since 1987, the Social Partnership process in Ireland has been the catalyst for stable change in both economic and social spheres. The first social partnership, the *Programme for National Recovery* (PNR) was prompted by a number of crises – principally a fiscal crisis in which the debt/GNP ratio was around 125%. In return for moderate wage growth, competitiveness was restored and some control over public finance achieved. The view was taken that the trade unions would gain in the long term from these corrections and, additionally, the government accepted that the value of social welfare payments would be maintained and that the income tax regime would be reformed to the benefit of trade union members.

Four other social partnership agreements followed. An important aspect of social partnership in Ireland has been the consciousness that the process must have an inherent dynamic to respond the changing needs and new challenges. For example, under the second programme (1990-1993), the *Programme for Economic and Social Progress* (PESP). Partnership companies were established, on a pilot basis, in 12 disadvantaged areas in order to achieve a more co-ordinated approach to social inclusion. Under *Partnership 2000*, community and voluntary interests were included for the first time in the negotiations and social inclusion issues were given much greater emphasis than before. Under the most recent Agreement *Programme for Prosperity and Fairness*, a change of format was introduced, in addition to an extended participation from the unions, farmers and the community and voluntary sector.[1] Each section begins with a small number of overall objectives followed by a number of specific actions working towards these objectives. This was to take account of criticisms that earlier agreements focussed too much on detail and not enough on the bigger picture.

---

1. The parties to the negotiations for the *Programme for Prosperity and Fairness* included:

    Trade Union Pillar: Irish Congress of Trade Unions (ICTU)

    Employer and Business Pillar: Irish Business and Employers Confederation (IBEC); Construction Industry Federation (CIF) ;Small Firms Association (SFA); Irish Exporters Association (IEA); Irish Tourist Industry Confederation (ITIC); Chamber of Commerce of Ireland (CCI)

    Farming Organisation Pillar: Irish Farmers Association (IFA); Irish Creamery Milk Suppliers Association (ICMSA); Irish Co-operative Organisation Society Ltd. (ICOS); Macra na Feirme

    Community and Voluntary Pillar: Irish National Organisation of the Unemployed (INOU); Congress Centres for the Unemployed; The Community Platform; Conference of Religious of Ireland (CORI); National Women's Council of Ireland (NWCI); National Youth Council of Ireland (NYCI); Society of Saint Vincent de Paul; Protestant Aid.

sing the representativeness of traditional participants. For instance, a new pro-competition stance should require a re-balancing of powers between the views of producers and those of consumers – an interest group which do not participate to the Partnership process. Economic and social developments also mean that new interest groups can become increasingly vocal, and require further transparency and accountability safeguards. Interest groups, sometimes supported internationally or in the case of local issues nationally, may exert a significant influence and control over the policy-making and the law-making processes.[57] Here again precautionary steps, as full disclosure of interests, can be the best way to maintain a healthy consultation process.

Transparency in implementation of regulation: Communication. Transparency and regulatory compliance require that the government and Parliament effectively communicate the existence and content of laws and regulations to the public, and that enforcement policies are clear and equitable. As part of its modernisation programme, Ireland has been deepening and improving the accessibility of the regulatory framework, reversing a situation in which access to the law was a preserve of specialists. As is the case in most jurisdictions, notice of new legislation (primary and secondary) is given in the Iris *Oifigiuil* (Official Journal). In many cases, notice is also published in national newspapers circulating throughout the country. There are bound volumes of the Acts for each year. These are published chronologically, not according to subject, which makes it hard to identify precise obligations. *Statutory Instruments* are bound separately. Currently, the Office of the Attorney General, the Parliament, the Department of Finance and the Government Publications Office are formulating a policy to ensure that appropriate indexes (including Chronological Tables to the Statutes)[58] be made available in hard copy and electronically on a regular and updated basis. Making available the statute book on the Web and preparing updated CD-ROMs of all statute law for sale will accompany this programme. To complement such initiatives the government presented a *Statute Law (Restatement)* Bill in June 2000 to enable the Attorney General Office to produce administrative consolidations of laws (see Section 4).

While there is no central database for circulars, licences, permits and other administrative procedures, individual Customer Service Action Plans (CSAPs) published every two years by each department and office describe the services, including the required formalities, and set out standards of service delivery to which they are committed over the period of the Plan.

Irish departments have been keen to organise public information campaigns about new legislation that affects the public widely. For instance, when major new legislation or policies are introduced information seminars are held nation-wide. This was the case when the policy document *Social Housing – The Way Ahead* was published in 1995. Similarly, when the 1998 Traveller *Accommodation* Act was enacted the responsible department held a series of nation-wide seminars with local authorities to explain the impact of the legislation. Information leaflets in plain language are updated and published on a regular basis to take account of changes to the terms and conditions of the various schemes. The Department of the Environment and Local Government has also been publishing explanatory guides to its regulations. There are a series of 11 leaflets on the planning system which are available free of charge. One of them in the series is "A Guide to the Building Regulations". Technical Guidance Documents covering all parts of the building code and explaining how compliance with the buildings regulations can be achieved have been issued in 1997 by the department, following a two year review process, which included public consultation.

Use of Plain language. As a matter of policy, the *Cabinet Handbook* encourages regulators to avoid jargon and technical language when possible.[59] Recently the Law Reform Commission published a Consultation Paper on the subject of Statutory Drafting and Interpretation.[60] Although the Commission did not find major faults in the process of drafting legislation that would give rise to interpretation difficulties, it recommended the adoption of standard drafting practices, which would ensure consistency in the statute book and better understanding of the legal texts. The Paper also recommended that as far as possible all legislation be drafted in clear language. The Office of the Attorney General broadly welcomed the Paper and started work on a style guide for the drafting of legislation and the use of plain language to be published in the Autumn 2000.

Compliance, application and enforcement of regulations. The adoption and communication of a law or regulation is only part of the regulatory framework. The framework can achieve its intended objective only if each law is adequately implemented, applied, enforced and complied with. A mechanism to redress regulatory abuse must also be in place, not only as a fair and democratic safeguard of a rule-based society, but as a feedback mechanism to improve regulations. Ireland in all these issues shows results, commitment and intention for further progress.

A fundamental feature of regulatory justice is the existence of clear, fair and efficient administrative procedures. A clear trend among OECD countries towards the establishment and achievement of these goals has been the development or updating of administrative procedure acts. Ireland does not have such an instrument, though. Its administrative "law" is still scattered widely across diverse legislative acts and rulings of courts. Enforcement and dealing with complaints practices vary significantly across departments and offices, and there are no over-arching generic procedures for ensuring fairness or transparency of the administrative process. For instance, in the case of enforcing labour law, a variety of approaches have been adopted in individual labour law over the years reflecting both differences in the laws to be enforced and the development of the institutional framework over time. Earlier legislation relied for enforcement on criminal sanctions with power given to the Minister to appoint inspectors to investigate complaints and initiate prosecutions. A more proactive approach was taken in the administration of the enforcement regime in employment covered by newer acts. In addition, most employment legislation of the modern era relies for enforcement primarily on civil remedies by means of special procedures created to provide speedy and inexpensive redress.

Since the late-1970s, Irish administrative law has become more coherent.[61] In the past five years, further progresses have been achieved through the enactment of new acts, such as the *Freedom of Information Act, 1997*. The possibility to enshrine in a single Act basic administrative justice principles and administrative procedures, as is the case in many other common law jurisdictions, may improve consistency, coherence and transparency in the interpretation and application of the rules.[62] An initiative of this kind could also be an opportunity to review, codify and reduce, if needed, any excessive discretionary powers delegated to regulators or local governments in preparing or designing regulations.[63]

A second essential element in the effectiveness of the legal and regulatory framework is the existence of a timely and effective appeal system. The method for challenging administrative decisions is an application to a court of competent jurisdiction. This process is undoubtedly transparent and fair but is regarded by businesspersons as slow, complex and expensive. In addition, remedies are often unclear and rarely justify the costs of legal proceedings. Ireland has also been slow to develop private arbitration or other alternative dispute resolution mechanisms (see background report to Chapter 5).

A recent reform, the *Courts Service Act, 1998*, may bring improvements to the administration of justice.[64] The Act provides for the establishment of an independent agency named the *Courts Service* that will have management and financial autonomy for the day-to-day operation of the Courts. Of particular importance, the agency will invest almost £12 million in information technology systems. In its three year Strategic Plan, the Courts Service is planning a review of Court Rules to ensure that persons seeking a legal remedy are provided with an efficient and user-friendly court service with minimum delay. The Plan sets also the strategies which must be undertaken to fulfil the mandate, the outputs to be achieved, with corresponding key performance indicators, on different services provided by the courts.

Regulatory compliance and enforcement. Assessments of compliance are seldom part of the rulemaking process. Compliance nevertheless is perhaps one of the most important performance indicators of a good quality regulation.[65] Ireland, as most OECD countries, has rarely systematically studied or evaluated the issue. Even if recent evidence shows increasing efficiency in enforcing regulations, strong informal relationships and persistence of effective lobbies at local level, may indicate the need for further efforts on this issue.

Some interesting initiatives to improve compliance may be identified in current practices. Following increasing evidence of corporate misconduct, the government accepted the thrust of most of the recommendations presented by the Working Group on Company Law Compliance and Enforcement.[66] One of the Group's principal recommendations is the establishment of a new statutory office to be known as the Office of the Director of Corporate Enforcement. The Office will have specific powers and responsibilities for the investigation of instances of suspected reckless or fraudulent trading and of suspected offences under the Companies Acts (false accounting, offences relating to insolvency, etc.). In relation to tax evasion, and based on the findings of the Comptroller and Auditor General 1997 annual report, the government has also recently given the Revenue Commissioners more powers to combat tax evasion, including the power to examine bank accounts without court approval and to pursue tax evaders. Related to other policy areas, an interesting pilot scheme launched in 1999 enables businesses to comply with a voluntary code of conduct for workplace safety to qualify for preferential insurance rates.[67]

3.2. Choice of policy instruments: regulation and alternatives

Much reform of the regulatory process in other OECD countries is based on the use of wider range of policy instruments that work more efficiently and effectively than traditional regulatory controls. The range of policy tools and their use is expanding as experimentation occurs, learning is diffused, and understanding of the markets increases. At the same time, rule-makers and regulators often face risks in using relatively untried tools, bureaucracies are highly conservative, and there are typically strong disincentives for public servants to be innovative. Reform authorities must take a clear leading and supportive role, if alternatives to traditional regulations are to make serious headway into the policy system. Ireland in this respect has been slow in promoting the use of policy instruments that have been proved to work more efficiently. In general, regulators still tend to relay on "command and control" mechanisms. This may reflect the conservatism of the Irish administration. Progress nevertheless is seen in some areas, and this trend may be accelerated if the Regulatory Quality Checklist embedded in new regulatory policy is adequately implemented and enforced.

Some progress in using alternatives to regulations can be found in particular areas. The most used instruments seem to be the voluntary codes of conduct organised by industry groups. Voluntary codes for instance have been used for instance to implement the guidelines contemplated by the *Broadcasting Act of* 1990, or for the pensions guidelines issued under the *Pensions Act,* of 1990, and of artists' tax exemption guidelines issued under the *Finance Act,* 1994. Voluntary codes have also been issued under the *Safety Health and Welfare at Work Act,* 1989. However, the use of voluntary codes have been criticised as having the character of legislation without any of the safeguards of legislation,[68] and have raised questions about potential collusive effects and corporatist attitudes

Ireland has also promoted self-regulation schemes, for example in the field of advertising. A complaint may be made to the Advertising Standards Authority about an advertisement. This self-regulatory body, may hear the complaint and if it considers that its Code of Conduct has been breached it may issue a ruling calling on the advertiser to withdraw the advertisement. In the majority of cases the offending advertisement is withdrawn. On the other hand, Irish regulatory authorities seldom use economic instruments. A recent report by the OECD states that "Ireland has made only limited use of economic instruments in environmental management so far. While some funding is provided for incentive payments and remuneration of environmental services, particularly in the context of agricultural policy, charges are of marginal importance. To some extent, present practice recent decisions are inconsistent with the intention to make polluters pay and to confront consumers of scarce resources with their actual costs".[69] Recent episodes in establishing user charges on domestic waste in Dublin show how powerful vocal local opposition may hinder important regulatory innovations.

Ireland has also delegated regulatory powers to non-governmental bodies or other self-regulatory bodies, where powers are usually to be exercised within a broad policy framework laid down in a the parent act. For example, some of the enforcement provisions of the tax collection system are delegated to a network of Revenue sheriffs and external solicitors. The Law Society has also been empowered as a self-regulatory body to overview and to regulate solicitors. Joint Labour Committees (JLCs) can as well be considered as non-governmental bodies with limited regulatory capacities in the area of industrial relations and statutory minimum and conditions of employment for the workers involved. The supervision of company auditors has also been delegated by law to a number of recognised accountancy bodies that monitor, investigate and (where appropriate) discipline its members practising as auditors. The supervision by recognised accountancy bodies of their auditing members has recently formed part of a detailed review. The Report of the Review Group on Auditing (July 2000) has suggested that the monitoring arrangements in place up to recently have not been effective in deterring a number of significant instances of corporate malpractice over a prolonged period. The Group has recommended that an independent and more rigorous system of regulation and accountability should be established and maintained in the public interest, in order to ensure that the structures, procedures and professional standards in the recognised accountancy bodies are operating to high standards.[70]

3.3. Understanding regulatory effects: the use of Regulatory Impact Analysis (RIA)

The 1995 *Recommendation of the Council of the* OECD *on Improving the Quality of Government Regulation* emphasised the role of RIA in systematically ensuring that the most efficient and effective policy options were chosen. The 1997 OECD *Report on Regulatory Reform* recommended that governments "integrate regulatory impact analysis into the development, review, and reform of regulations." A list of RIA best practices is discussed in detail in *Regulatory Impact Analysis: Best Practices in* OECD *Countries*.[71]

The use of RIA is currently in its infancy in Ireland. The government adopted RIA only in July 1999, which was later than most OECD countries. The process of approving this policy was in itself slow. The policy was established three years after being proposed by the Working Group on Regulatory Reform. The implementation of the programme of action has also been laborious, as many months were requi-

---

Box 8.   Quality Regulation Checklist in Annex VI of the Cabinet Handbook

1.   Is the proposed legislation and/or regulation absolutely necessary *i.e.* is the problem correctly defined and can the objective be achieved by other means (*i.e.* improved information, voluntary schemes, codes of practice, self regulation, procedural instructions)?

2.   Will the legislation affect market entry, result in any restrictions on competition or increase the administrative burden?

3.   Is the legislation compatible with developments in the Information Society, particularly as regards electronic Government and electronic commerce?

4.   Outline the consideration which has been given to exemptions or simplified procedures for particular economic or social sectors which may be disproportionately burdened by the proposal, including the small business sector.

5.   Outline the consideration which has been given to application of the following principles:

–   Sunsetting *i.e.* establishing a date by which the measure will expire unless renewed

–   Review date *i.e.* a predetermined date on which the efficacy and impact of the proposed new measure will be reviewed.

–   The "Replacement" principle *i.e.* where the body of regulations/legislation in a particular area will not be added to without a corresponding reduction through repeal of an existing measure

6.   Outline the extent to which interested or affected parties have been consulted, including interest groups or representative bodies where such exist. A summary of the views of such parties should be provided.

red before the *Cabinet Handbook* stipulated the completion of the Quality Regulation Checklist and the Central Regulatory Resource Unit was assigned its first administrator. This contrasts with the elaborate procedures for financial and budgetary control mechanisms, which include accountability assessments applied by the Ministry of Finance and external overview by the Comptroller and Auditor General and the Parliament.[72]

According to the *Cabinet Handbook*, when presenting a Memorandum for the Government all departments and offices must "indicate clearly, as appropriate, the impact of the proposal" based on a standard Quality Regulation Checklist (see Box 8). They must also self-assess, through a "proofing" if during the preparation of the proposal consideration was given to for 1) relations, co-operation or common action between North and South of Ireland, and between Ireland and Britain; 2) employment; 3) women, 4) persons in poverty or risk of falling into poverty, 5) industry costs and cost to small business; 6) rural communities and 7) costs to the Budget and staffing implications (in consultation with the Department of Finance).[73] This section will concentrate mainly on the Quality Regulation Checklist rather than on the other impact issues. Moreover, as the information available about the actual implementation of the Checklist in Ireland shows that for the moment most of the departments have considered that their legal proposals passed the tests and that the Department of the Prime Minister accepted their assurance, it will focus on the formal instruments described in the *Reducing Red Tape* programme against OECD best practice recommendation rather than its practice.

Assessment

Maximise political commitment to RIA. Use of RIA to support reform should be endorsed at the highest levels of government. The Irish system obtains an average mark on this criterion. On the one hand, the Memorandum for the Government, which implements the Checklist, is presented and discussed at Cabinet level and thus must endorsed by ministers. However, the *Cabinet Handbook* gives discretion to the proponent ministers whether or not to include the Checklist ("as appropriate"). More problematic, most of the secondary regulations (*i.e.* Orders) are not reviewed by the Cabinet and thus will be automatically exempted from the Checklist altogether.

Allocate responsibilities for RIA programme elements carefully. To ensure "ownership" by regulators, while at the same time establishing quality control and consistency, responsibilities for RIA should be shared between regulators and a central quality control unit. Here too, the Irish system receives a mixed result. On the positive side, the programme is embedded in the SMI approach, where a key component is to produce an endogenous cultural change from regulators, strengthening accountability and transparency. The policy also provides for the establishment of a small central unit in the Department of the Prime Minister to drive and monitor progress. Although the central unit (currently two persons) could have access to the Memoranda for Government by being located in the Department of the Prime Minister, it is not clear that it has the capacities to review and assess hundreds of Checklists a year covering a variety of issues and areas, some of which are very technical (*e.g.* new regulation on food safety). Furthermore, due to its hierarchical ranking and the high level of autonomy of each ministry, the unit or even the Department of the Prime Minister may find it difficult and politically expensive to challenge ministers' answers to the Checklist. Experience of other countries like the Netherlands and Denmark show that the "check and balance" function that a RIA should play can be substantially enhanced when institutional "heaviness" and/or a tacit and strong alliance between powerful institutions (traditionally the Department of Finance) raises the cost for proponent departments of confronting the overseeing unit.

Train the regulators. Regulators must have the skills to do high quality economic assessments, including an understanding of the role of impact assessment in assuring regulatory quality, and an understanding of methodological requirements and data collection strategies. Currently no formal training programmes or guidelines are in place in Ireland to help implement the Checklist. Given the fact that impact assessment is at an early stage, training should be a high priority, both to develop specific skills and to contribute to longer term cultural changes among regulators. Training and guidance

155

are also essential to ensure methodological consistency between assessments. The Dutch experience of having a specific help desk at the disposal of regulators might also be applicable to Irish circumstances.

Use a consistent but flexible analytical method. Irish requirements do not include specific methodological standards or guidance to help proponent departments answer the Checklist's items 2 and 4 concerning impacts on market entry and administrative burdens, as the distribution impacts on SMEs. This area should be a high priority one, as economic valuation has been detected as being a weak point of the Irish administration. Fostering analytical methods for completing the Checklist could also be seen as an important step to comply with Section 4(1)g of the *Public Service Management Act*, 1997 which specifies that all ministries need to "examine and develop the means to improve service delivery at the lowest costs".

At any rate, the absence of a requirement to use quantitative methodologies means that consistency in assessments cannot be assured. Attention to developing detailed methodological requirements for impact assessments, and supporting them with relevant training, guidance and expert assistance, is key if impact assessment is to achieve its potential in improving the quality of Irish regulation. As a clear goal of the policy, the RIA system should aim in the longer-term to establish benefit-cost analysis as the primary method for assessing regulations. This could benefit from the growing experience on evaluation techniques concerning many EU programmes, where Brussels requires a cost/benefit analysis.

Develop and implement data collection strategies. As RIA seems in the Checklist to have been confined to qualitative analysis, data collection strategies have not been developed. Since data issues are among the most consistently problematic aspects in conducting quantitative RIA, the development of strategies and guidance for departments and offices is essential if a successful programme of quantitative RIA is to be developed. However, the programme of action anticipates the establishment of "user groups", whose role is not defined. According to the 1996 Working Group's recommendations accompanying the policy, their main function should be to provide advice on "the quality and quantity of regulation".[74] In that sense, it would be advisable if such user groups could be assimilated to the existing Danish Business Test Panels, where a cross-section of businesses is asked directly about expected administrative burdens of proposed legislation.[75]

Target RIA efforts. RIA resources should be targeted to those regulations where impacts are most significant, and where the prospects are best for altering outcomes. In all cases, the amount of time and effort spent on regulatory analysis should be commensurate with the improvement in the regulation that the analysis is expected to provide.[76] In reality, the Irish RIA is almost totally focussed on primary legislation, as the *Cabinet Handbook* does not required the preparation of a Memorandum for the Government (and thus a Checklist) for most secondary regulations. While in theory subordinate regulations cannot go beyond their parent Act, in practice many requirements set in secondary legislation have major impacts. A major improvement will thus be to broaden the scope of RIA to all type of instruments, but in parallel to design a targeting system to focus only on those with potentially high impact. For instance, the Korean RIA defines as "significant" regulations those that have an annual impact exceeding 10 billion won (US$ 0.9 million), an impact on more than 1 million people (approximate 2% of the Korean population), a clear restriction on market competition, or a clear departure from international standards. In general terms, the assessment is made by the proponent department, which needs to justify its request for an exemption from the requirement of cost-benefit analysis, but the central unit, through a "is consent" rule, can contest the self-estimate and require a complete RIA.

Integrate RIA with the policy making process, beginning as early as possible. Integrating RIA with the policy-making process is meant to ensure that the disciplines of weighing costs and benefits, identifying and considering alternatives and choosing policy in accordance with its ability to meet objectives are a routine part of policy development. In some countries where RIA has not been integrated into policy-making, impact assessment has become merely an *ex post* justification of decisions or meaningless internal paperwork. Integration is a long-term process, which often implies significant cultural changes within regulatory ministries. Here again Ireland gets a mixed mark given that the Checklist must accompany the Memorandum for the Government before the Office of the Attorney General drafts the legal text. But the difference between complying with the Checklist and the various assessments or proofs that departments need to report in the Memorandum, such as employment, impact on women, affect on persons in poverty, industry costs and cost to small businesses are unclear. Too many goals and assessments create confusion and overlap. In addition, the tests are so imprecise and difficult to assess that it has little analytical credibility, and the criteria for regulatory efficiency are not clear. If the Checklist is intended to be a true RIA, steps should be taken to either consolidate some of the impacts currently "proofed" or clearly differentiate the type of compliance required for the Checklist and for the other general considerations. For instance, the justification of the foreseen impacts on "industry costs and the cost to small business" or the impact on "employment" could be easily integrated into the Checklist.

Involve the public extensively. Public involvement in RIA has several significant benefits. The public, and especially those affected by regulations, can provide the valuable data necessary to complete RIA. Consultation can also provide important checks on the feasibility of proposals, on the range of alternatives considered, and on the degree of acceptance of the proposed regulation by affected parties. The Programme of Action emphasises in three out its seven main actions the need for consulting with "customers". However, the *Cabinet Handbook* does not impose a requirement to hold consultations with third parties in respect of the Checklist. The *Freedom of Information Act* states that Memoranda for the Government may be withheld from access for five years.[77] Ireland should consider making it a statutory requirement to publish RIAs at the earliest possible stage. For this, a first step could be to dissociate the Checklist from the Memorandum which is kept confidential for the sake of the Cabinet effectiveness and cohesion. The publication of the Checklist could also be a powerful way for Ireland to formalise public consultation and at the same time improve rapidly the quality of RIAs – and foster accountability across regulators. Indeed, a "name and shame" mechanism is often the strongest incentive and/or sanction for public servants.

In conclusion, Ireland has not yet incorporated into its policy making process a well-functioning RIA process, but a start has been made. The checklist constitutes an important step in this process Nevertheless, the checklist and the institutions for implementing it have significant weaknesses. Additional steps are needed to make the analysis more rigorous, with a broader scope, developing appropriate methods and adequate incentives for different stakeholders. Critics have claimed that Irish adoption of RIA was only to "keep pace with developments" in other countries, without being convinced that a RIA is a crucial element for efficient, transparent and accountable regulatory decisions. Development of RIA in the coming months may prove them wrong.

3.4. Institutional design

As have most OECD countries, Ireland is building market-based institutions to separate ownership, policy development and day-to-day regulatory overview in key economic sectors. This is in line with EU requirements.[78]

In June 1997, regulatory functions for telecommunications were transferred to the Director of Telecommunications Regulation (DTR). Two years later, the Commission for Electricity Regulation (CER) was formally established. Legislation for the setting up of an airports regulatory body was enacted in February 2001; a regulator-designate was appointed in late 1999 in anticipation of the legislation. In September 2000, the regulation of postal services was assigned to the telecommunications regulator. Regulatory arrangements for gas and for surface transport are under consideration at present.[79] In February 2001, the government announced the establishment of a new sectoral regulator for financial services: the Irish Financial Services Regulatory Authority (IFSRA). The new authority will have its own board and an independent chair, who will report to the Minister for Finance and to the Prime Minister.[80]

These regulatory authorities operate within the policy parameters of the regulatory framework laid down by the minister responsible for policy in the sector. Part of the minister's policy role is to undertake an ongoing evaluation of the appropriate extent and range of utilities regulation, having regard to developments within the sectors and within the economic environment generally. As the Department of Public Enterprise's Strategy Statement (1998) states, the regulatory objective is "to provide for an effective regulatory framework for each sector in such a way as to strike a balance between independence and accountability".

Although recent, the practice in Ireland indicates that with respect to independence, the design is working properly. For instance, in terms of financial independence, the independent regulators are funded by the industry on the basis of fees for licences and levies. This has allowed the regulators to have adequate staff, premises, equipment, services and other resources necessary for their operation.

Oddly, the independence of sectoral regulators in utilities in the public sector contrasts with the position of the Competition Authority. Although the Authority is independent in decision-making, in other respects it is strongly dependent on the Department of Enterprise, Trade and Employment, to which it is attached for administration, personnel, and budget.[81] This has important consequences on the institutional architecture (*e.g.* salary levels at the Authority are lower than in the sectoral regulators, and thus create recruitment difficulties and reduce credibility.) The relationship between the Competition Authorities and the sectoral regulators was unclear in the early days of independent sectoral regulation. However, in the context of development of the regulatory framework, the issue of the management of overlapping jurisdiction is now being addressed. Some proposals in this regard were made both by the Minister for Public Enterprise in her *Governance and Accountability* document of March 2000 and by the Competition and Mergers Review Group in its Report of May 2000. The various regulatory agencies are already engaged in administrative arrangements to deal with such matters, and some legislative measures are also proposed by the Minister for Public Enterprise and the Minister for Enterprise, Trade and Employment. (see background report to Chapter 3).

Important issues concerning **accountability** have received attention in recent times, and the regulatory framework has undergone some development in this regard. For example, the 1996 legislation establishing the independent telecommunications regulator made no provision in relation to accountability to Parliament. However, the 1999 legislation for the electricity regulator demonstrates how this lacunae in the regulatory framework, once discovered, was filled. That legislation makes specific provision requiring the Commission for Electricity Regulation to account to parliamentary committees for the performance of its functions. Although there is no statutory obligation, the Director of Telecommunications Regulation has, in fact, appeared before parliamentary committees on several occasions. Forthcoming legislation for regulation of the communications sector will include provision for a statutory obligation in this regard.[82]

As other countries have found, replacing direct political accountability based on ministerial responsibility with managerial/technical accountability between regulators and ministries as well as parliament can create new potential problems. There is both the risk that such parliamentary overview will either be too loose, allowing the regulator too much or inappropriate discretion, forcing the regulator into specific market decisions not linked to the regulatory mission. It is important that the accountability requirements are balanced with the necessary operational independence of the regulators.[83] The fact that independent sector-specific regulation in relation to certain public utilities is a new advent in Ireland – the first such sectoral regulator was only established in 1997 – means that it is yet too early to assess the effectiveness of parliamentary overview.

In March 2000, the discussion was expanded with the publication by the Minister for Public Enterprise of a policy paper entitled *Governance and Accountability in the Regulatory Process: Policy Proposals*. This paper sets out the Minister's policy proposals on the governance and accountability aspects of the regulatory framework for the sectors within her portfolio. The policy proposals drew on the views expressed in the submissions received in response to the Minister's call in September 1999 for public comments on these arrangements; they were also informed by the experience gained to-date in the independent regulation of the utilities in Ireland, and by international experience. The proposals are reflected in the various legislative documents that the Minister has been bringing forward recently for the regulation of the individual sectors.

In general terms, the *Governance and Accountability* document develops the regulatory framework so as to resolve perceptions about "democratic deficit" which could have had an impact on the credibility and legitimacy of the new regulatory institutions.[84] Some of the issues analysed by the document concern the "top-level" structure and composition of regulatory authorities, the relative merits of regulatory boards over a single regulator, the methods of selection, appointment and removal or regulators, and the relationship between appointment and independence and accountability. The document also discusses the transparency, fairness, efficiency and effectiveness of decision-making mechanisms of regulators, and the relationship with important stakeholders and the question of enforcement powers. In conclusion, the document proposes:

- The introduction of legislation to clarify the right to judicial review of the decisions of regulatory bodies, and proposes that, unless otherwise decided by the Courts, the decision of a regulator should stand while under review.[85]

- The updating of the relevant legislation in the area of fines and penalties in order that punitive measures reflect both the nature and the consequences of a breach of the regulatory rules.

- The adoption of a model of regulatory commissions comprising three persons, as in the case of the Commission for Electricity Regulation.

- The strengthening of consultation mechanisms between the Competition Authority and the sectoral regulators.[86]

- That the setting of public service/social requirements remain a function of the Minister (subject to public notification, in the interests of openness and transparency), but that, in addition, regulators and other interested parties be invited to make suggestions to the Minister in relation to such comments.

The discussion and analysis in the Governance and Accountability Report is of a cross-sectoral, generic nature, but it is proposed that the implementation of the policy proposals be done by means of sector-specific measures in each of the various sectors to which the document relates. This will allow the exact manner of the implementation to vary from sector to sector, in order to take account of each sector's individual circumstances.[87] In areas for which legislative arrangements are already in place (*e.g.* telecommunications, electricity) the existing legislation is being reviewed so that future legislation can include provisions which bring it into line with the policy set out in the Governance and Accountability document. In the areas for which legislation post-dates the publication of Governance and Accountability (*e.g.* aviation), such legislative measures are being drawn up in accordance with the principles set out in that policy document. Moreover, given the changing nature of technologies and evolution in markets, the policy requires that a review should take place on a regular and systematic basis, possibly every three to four years, though some aspects of telecommunications may require more frequent review.

The Governance and Accountability Report can be considered one of the more interesting exercises about these issues undertaken in OECD countries. Still, it leaves important questions unclear. First of all, a central proposal concerns the clarification about the accountability role played by Parliament. But Parliament's committees do not have yet the capacities to materially respond to such a responsibility, in part due to lack of financial and human resources. A second concern relates to the quality of the regulations produced by the regulators. Although not systematic, the Office of the Government Parliamentary Counsel and the newly established Central Regulatory Reform Unit provide a quality check on proposals concerning secondary regulations prepared by all departments (see Section 2.2). With independent regulatory authorities having the power to make regulations in specified areas, central *ex ante* overview on the quality and impact regulations could be eroded.

159|

A third important concern that is unresolved (and perhaps accentuated) by the Governance and Accountability Report refers to the core objectives for such bodies. The report justifies regulatory intervention "to facilitate market entry, ensure fair market conditions and customer protection and ensure that all users have access to a basic level of services at reasonable prices. In this way, economic regulation can comprehend social and regional objectives" (p.6). Although these objectives are commendable, the Report does not consider their potential contradictory effects and does not set priorities or mechanisms to help regulators resolve discrepancies when they implement strategies to attain each one of these goals.

Lastly, some issues that go beyond accountability issues and refer to effectiveness of the regulators are still to be settled. In 1996, the government announced its intention to establish a multi-sector regulator for the energy and communications sectors.[88] The thinking behind this was that for a small country connected to a larger EU regulatory framework, synergies between the different fields of expertise could be found to maximise the output of the scarce number of expert regulators. Since then, a shortage of appropriate expertise has appeared, yet the current political position has shifted away from the multi-sector regulator approach to setting up independent regulators for each of the regulated sectors. In addition to a less than optimal use of scarce human resources and possibilities of duplication between bodies, the proliferation of sectoral regulators may increase institutional rigidity and fragmentation, and augment the risk of capture by powerful interests.

Governance and Accountability in the Regulatory Process concluded that, for the present, regulation at the sectoral level was probably the most appropriate for the utilities in Ireland, given that it would allow for an approach focused on the particular circumstances of the various markets while comprehending the competition/complementarity between industries operating (or potentially operating) in the same market. However, *Governance and Accountability* noted that, as markets develop the justification for detailed sectoral regulatory intervention might diminish over time and the question of a supra-sectoral regulatory authority could be re-examined, at a future date.[89]

4. DYNAMIC CHANGE: KEEPING REGULATIONS UP-TO-DATE

The OECD *Report on Regulatory Reform* recommends that governments "review regulations systematically to ensure that they continue to meet their intended objectives efficiently and effectively". Ireland until recently did not have a systematic policy to review its existing laws and regulations. Review and reform of its stock of regulations and administrative formalities were done by each department and office, and consisted mainly of harmonising with EU directives and conforming to the SMI programme.

But until the last two years Ireland did not have a comprehensive and explicit policy to deal with the stock of laws and regulations. Following the recommendations of the Report of the Review Group on the Law Offices of the State, a small unit was established in 1999 at the Office of the Attorney General. Based on that policy, in July 1999, the *Reducing Red Tape* Programme of Action required "that each department/office... list, by autumn 1999, the relevant legislation (both primary and secondary) and identify the scope which exists for its consolidation, revision and/or repeal". For example, the Department of Enterprise, Trade and Employment set up in 1999 a Company Law Review and Consolidation working group with the double objective of modernising the statutes, procedures and supervision of companies and also consolidating all rules and regulations into a basic company law. As a first step, departments and offices have been required by the Department of the Prime Minister and the Statute Law Revision Unit to list by the spring of 2000 relevant legislation identifying the scope for consolidation, revision or repeal. The second stage, to be completed in the autumn of 2000, will consist in prioritising consolidation work. The initiative however, remains limited to clarity and transparency of the legal system. The review strategy did not encompass principles of good regulation (*i.e.* proportionality, impact assessment, choice of policy instruments), nor it is linked to broader structural review programmes based on the implementation of competition principles.

Ireland has also relied on high level advisory groups in key reform areas has helped advance regulatory reform. Some of the most influential have been the *Competition and Mergers Review Group*, which examined competition policy and enforcement processes (see background report to Chapter 3), and a series of *Company Law Review Groups*. The First of the Company Law Review Group was established in 1994 to examine seven aspects of Irish company law. The Group represented interests such as the accounting professions, the Law Society and Bar Council, the Irish Association of Investment Managers, the Irish Bankers Federation, the Irish Stock Exchange, the business community and the trade unions. Also represented were two government departments, the Revenue Commissioners and the Minister for Finance. The creation of a forum representing all interests in company law was a departure from the usual means of reforming legislation. Another Review Group was established in 1998 to recommend reforms in company law compliance and enforcement, and reported in November 1998. Following from a parliamentary inquiry into the non-payment of Deposit Interest Retention Tax, a Review Group on Auditing was established to examine the regulation of and rules governing auditors and accountants, and reported in July 2000. The recommendations of both these groups are being implemented. Yet another Company Law Review Group was set up in 2000 to review aspects of company law not covered by the original Group. Interestingly, the Group has been set up on an ongoing basis to review company law and support "the enactment every two years of a Company Law Review Bill which will update, streamline and otherwise bring the Companies Code in Ireland into line with international best practice on corporate governance, having regard to the principles of compliance and simplification."

A recent initiative, the *Statute Law (Restatement) Bill*, currently being discussed in Parliament, will strengthen the review policy. It proposes that the Attorney General prepare and make available (in hard copy and electronic form) Acts that restate the statute law in any given area in a more intelligible form without any change being made to that law except in its presentation. To speed the process, instead of proceeding through the Parliament, it is proposed that restatements be certified by the Attorney General.[90] This policy will also be of particular benefit where a series of Acts has been consolidated and the consolidation has been superseded by an amending Act. Parliament has yet to develop a specific role in relation to this novel procedure.

Sunsetting and automatic reviewing mechanisms. The new Regulatory Reform programme requires through the Regulatory Quality Checklist that rule-makers verify if new laws and regulation can incorporate automatic review mechanisms, such as sunsetting, a precise review date or mandatory substitution (adding a rule only when a corresponding reduction or repeal accompany it). Until now, application criteria or guidance has not supported these mechanisms.

Systematic use of sunsetting and mandatory periodic reviews places Ireland among a very small group of OECD Member countries. Information on the effectiveness and efficiency of sunsetting, and on the challenges of managing it in practice is quite limited. Sunsetting laws and regulations may create unforeseen problems and wrong incentives, especially if too brief a period is established. Indeed a badly designed sunsetting mechanism may lower compliance and predictability of the regulatory framework. However, a recent OECD/PUMA study reviewed the use of sunsetting in several Australian States and concluded that its use has removed much redundant regulation from the statute books and played a significant role in encouraging the updating and rewriting of much that has remained. The report noted, though, that a review cycle of five years might be too short, leading to a waste of review resources and reducing the predictability of the legal system.[91] Ireland may refer to this experience when establishing the criteria and guidelines to implement the new requirement.

As noted above, at the sectoral level, the Minister for Public Enterprise proposed in the Governance and Accountability Report a periodic formal evaluation of regulatory developments, including an assessment of the continued justification for intervention in the context of the achievement of national economic, social and regional objectives.

Reducing administrative burdens. An important focus of the current Irish policy is the control of administrative burdens. As such, it incorporates past thrust and initiatives, such as the mid-1990s recommendations of the Task Force on Small Business and Services. Some evidence exists of significant results:

business licences and permits have been reduced and gradually improved in some areas. For instance, the recent efforts by the Revenue Commissioners have significantly streamlined and simplified the information requirements provided by firms. The registration of companies has also been simplified, permitting the registration of a company in one week.[92] Ireland has also been praised by the implementation of a sophisticated and efficient environmental licensing system requiring integrated permits for medium to large industries covering air, water, noise and waste/soil.[93] The setting up of a one-stop-shop by the Industrial Development Authority and simplified administrative procedures to help foreign investors have also been recognised as a significant factor in attracting foreign investment.

Nonetheless, initiatives in Ireland in this field tend to be piecemeal and lack an overall and systematic approach. Anti-competitive and entry-controlling licensing schemes still govern activities such as utilities, public transport, banking, lotteries, places of public amusement, professions, housing, and policy areas such as environment and health. The extent and number of licences and permits is not known with certainty. Although the Ad Hoc High Level Group on Administrative Simplification to be set up under the agaeis of the *Reducing Red Tape* Policy should address the issue, a particular concern is still the lack of consistency across the administrations when establishing formalities and the duplication and lack of co-ordination of information required by departments and agencies.[94] One reason for this relates to the large discretion that departments, agencies, sectoral regulators, and local governments have in the design of their formalities without any central overview. This has disproportionately higher impact on SMEs.[95]

5. CONCLUSIONS AND RECOMMENDATIONS FOR ACTION

5.1. General assessment of current strengths and weaknesses

Ireland has transformed its economy in the last 15 years. From a low-skilled and low-wage population with high levels of emigration, and a protected and highly regulated economy, Ireland today is enjoying market-driven prosperity and low unemployment. Governance changes have also been significant, but have lagged behind economic changes, and could pose a bottleneck to sustained high levels of growth. Good economic performance explains part of the transformation of the economic, social and cultural environment. But external and perhaps one-off factors were also at play. In sustaining its development, Ireland will need continued regulatory reform to improve the market environment and resolve emerging success-related challenges such as skills and housing shortages.

The Irish regulatory environment and framework has been significantly improved. Major legal reforms have produced fundamental changes in important sectors such as financial services, telecommunications, electricity, transport, and in the roles of local governments. Within the broad framework of public service reforms and market developments, new regulatory regimes have evolved. New market-oriented institutions have been set up or strengthened, such as the sectoral regulators and the competition authority.

Accountability and transparency have been strongly enhanced, not only through traditional participatory and consensus-building mechanisms characterised by the social partnership approach, but also through new mechanisms such as enforcement and compliance with the *Freedom of Information* Act. Improvements have been gradual and incremental, and in some case piecemeal, but recently the rate of changes in the modernisation of the public sector has accelerated. The high-level support by the administration and by successive governments of the remarkable SMI is fostering a new culture in government culture, including rule making. The Irish judicial review process is in many ways exemplary, and has helped to identify poor laws and regulations.[96]

This progress in government capacities has been accomplished without an external crisis, but instead through pressures from the European Union and an internal, non-partisan initiative sustained through several governments. Ireland provides a lesson in the strategies of regulatory reform. Prolonged, consistent policies that are broadly supportive across policy areas can create a stable microeconomic environment that enables new institutions to produce positive outcomes. For instance, the sustained policies to foster market openness and attract FDI, as well as EU integration, have trickled down to most policy areas.

However, new challenges in the short and medium term need to be addressed. In the next few years, a range of success-related difficulties, such as shortages and bottlenecks, in a context of fiscal constraints and anti-inflation controls, may require that Ireland regulate "better and smarter" than in the past or than its trading partners. Rapid growth may be masking significant regulatory weaknesses. In a high-growth environment, discerning regulatory failures and acting against high regulatory costs are more difficult. A cyclical down-turn may reveal costly burdens due to low quality and rigidity of laws and regulations. As durable anti-market regulatory regimes in pubs, taxis or land zoning show, interventionist policies and influence by interest groups are still powerful.

Second, Ireland lags behind many OECD countries in terms of its capacities to ensure high quality regulation. Economic assessment of proposed legislation is missing. Alternatives to regulations, such as economic instruments, have replaced few traditional "command and control" approaches. Critically, implementation mechanisms and enforcement powers of the *Reducing Red Tape* policy may need to be enhanced if anti-competitive styles of regulations in non-traded sectors and interventionist tendencies are to be reversed. In particular, self-assessment and peer review seem to be too weak to create incentives for newer and more effective regulatory approaches. Like other small and participative countries, Ireland should acknowledge that globalisation and openness require a certain degree of formalism in the national regulatory management system to support market confidence and avoid undue preferences for insiders or "big players". A particular challenge concerns the search for a new balance between public consultation, flexibility and rapidity in rulemaking.

Third, Ireland's reforms have mainly concentrated on the modernisation of the public administration. These developments have gone further than those concerning other governance actors. While progresses are visible, the Judiciary, the new market-based institutions, including the competition authority, the Parliament and its committees, even the new regional powers still need institutional adaptations in term of their efficiency, accountability and overall co-ordination.

Lastly, the Irish policy-making culture continues to be highly risk adverse, with a tendency to follow rather than lead. The adoption of a formal regulatory reform policy only in 1999, years after most OECD countries, is striking evidence. In global environments, small countries will need to increasingly exploit their nimbleness in adapting to changing markets and technologies. Ireland should seek ways to become an innovator in the next generation of governance reforms.

5.2. Policy options for consideration

The policy options below suggest concrete actions that should be considered to address the challenges identified above. The strategies recommended are in accord with basic good practices in other countries. Some of the recommendations can be carried out quickly, while others would take some years to complete.

- *Strengthen implementation of the regulatory reform policy by creating stronger disciplines and performance assessment of regulatory quality within the departments and agencies, and by enforcing the disciplines through a high level committee.*

Reducing Red Tape originated in the SMI as one of the elements to modernise the Irish public administration. The new policy and action plan inherited the management and implementation mechanisms as well as the accountability structure of SMI. In particular, the enforcement and compliance approaches of *Reducing Red Tape* are based on self-assessment and peer pressure. Contrary to the implementation approach used for other flagship policies, such as the *Freedom of Information Act*, the modernisation of the regulatory management system has lacked resources, training and resolve, and has yielded few concrete benefits for citizens and business. Accountability mechanisms of the new policy have been based on vague internal procedures, supervised by an over busy SMI Co-ordinating Group of Secretaries. Such mechanisms are too weak and remote to change long-established habits and culture, to protect the regulatory system from influence and pressures from powerful special interests, to offset perverse incentives within the ministries and agencies, and to co-ordinate the difficult agenda of regulatory reform.

A high-level regulatory committee should be created for these tasks with adequate powers to influence decisions at the cabinet level. Its role should be to advocate and promote implementation of the regulatory reform policy, to initiate key regulatory reform decisions, and to co-ordinate regulatory reform across government.[97] Participants on the committee could include the Department of the Prime Minister and the Ministry of Finance, and the General Attorney Office, and the Competition Authority. Regulatory departments and offices and sectoral regulators should be invited on an *ad hoc* basis. The committee may be supplemented by an advisory body where social partners (including consumer groups) and key institutions, like *Forfas*, could discuss regulatory affairs. The committee's work should be co-ordinated with other horizontal policies, such as SMI or budgeting. It should also prepare an annual report to the Parliament. This political body could be modelled on the Netherlands' Ministerial Committee in charge of the influential MDW (Functioning of Markets, Deregulation and Legislative Quality) programme.[98]

In parallel with a strong central promoter, Ireland could raise accountability for results within the departments and agencies through measurable and public performance standards for regulatory reform. Indeed, control mechanisms are not balanced by effective incentives for the departments to change themselves, particularly given contrary pressures from their constituencies and the political level. At present, the objectives of the regulatory reform programme are formulated at a high level of generality, and transparent measures of performance for each department have not been adopted. That is, objectives are strategic rather than results-oriented. Hence, accountability for results is over-centralised, whereas the skills and resources for reform are decentralised. The fact that incentives for the departments to produce good regulation are still not very strong may be one explanation why the regulatory habits of the administration have not changed very much. One possible model to be explored is the U.S. *Government Performance and Results Act* of 1993, which established a government-wide system, including for regulators, to set goals for programme performance, measurement, and publication of results.[99]

- *Strengthen the accountability of sectoral regulators by building capacities for appropriate overview by the Parliamentary committees, and clarify the respective roles of sectoral regulators and the Competition Authority to ensure a co-ordinated, uniform competition policy approach in the regulated sectors.*

Market-oriented bodies and institutions have developed along with liberalisation, privatisation and regulatory reform. However, the powers, nature, and accountability mechanisms of the sectoral regulators are challenging the general public governance and institutional balance. In some respects, these bodies have become a "fourth branch of the State" beside the Executive, Legislative and Judiciary.[100] Ireland has been one of the first countries to start addressing the complex issues of accountability raised by this situation. In March 2000, the Minister of Public Enterprises published policy proposals on *Governance and Accountability in the Regulatory Process* which among other things, advocated a clearer role for Parliament in overseeing sectoral regulators. However, the Parliament and its committees lack capacities to do so. In light of this and past reports,[101] Ireland should consider a strategy to improve Parliament accountability procedures, including appropriate resources. Attention should be paid to managing the information to permit the committees to focus on strategic policy decisions. A step in that direction could be the development of a succinct impact assessment of policy decisions along the line of a RIA.

As background report to Chapter 3 argues, many of the Competition and Mergers Review Group recommendations should be followed, to provide for a structured process of co-ordination and a legal basis for the sectoral regulators and the Competition Authority to defer to each other without risk and without diluting or compromising the application of competition policy. The Authority and sectoral regulators should advise each other about matters that may come under the others' jurisdiction, and consult when they find they are both pursuing the same matter. To do this meaningfully, they must have the right to exchange information with each other.[102] Having someone from the Authority sit on appeal panels for sectoral regulator decision is an excellent idea for integrating policy perspectives.

- *Strengthen disciplines on regulatory quality in the departments and offices by reinforcing the central review unit and refining and integrating tools for regulatory impact analysis, based on a benefit-cost principle, increasing the use of alternatives to regulation, integrating these tools into public consultation processes and training public servants in how to use them.*

The Regulatory Quality Checklist that accompanies memoranda for a proposed law is a crucial step forward in the modernisation of the Irish regulatory management system. However, important weaknesses and gaps exist in the Irish process. Particularly important is the need, on one hand, to clearly differentiate between the mandatory Checklist and the "proofing" of impacts as, *inter alia*, employment, women, persons in poverty, and on the other hand, the need to consolidate in an extended RIA some key assessment, such as the impacts on industry and small business costs. As the central principle, a universal benefit-cost test should be adopted, with step by step strategies to gradually improve the quantification of regulatory impacts for the most important regulations, while making qualitative assessments more consistent and reliable. Moreover, these tools should not only be well-designed but well-used, that is, incorporated into day to day administrative practices. Based on OECD best practices, five key steps are needed to improve effectiveness. As a first, step, Ireland should reinforce the Central Unit in the Department of the Prime Minister. Concrete steps could be to provide it with (i) statutory authority to make recommendations on the quality of checklist responses to the high-level regulatory committee as recommended, (ii) adequate capacities to collect information and co-ordinate the reform programme throughout the public administration, and (iii) enough resources and analytical expertise to provide an independent opinion on regulatory matters.

A second challenge is the development of effective ways to apply the *Reducing Red Tape* programme to subordinate regulations. Parliamentary and judicial review are the only quality check on this kind of regulation (not including the non-mandatory legal review undertaken by the Attorney General Office). However, these mechanisms are in many ways either theoretical, too rigid or politically, too late in the process, or too expensive to assure that lower level rules comply with criteria of high quality. Hence, an important improvement would be to apply and enforce the *Reducing Red Tape* disciplines on subordinate regulations (*i.e.* the preparation and external review of the checklist, mandatory public consultation, centralised publication, etc.). A delicate but vital element to be considered concerns the need to develop a mechanism that should permit third-party review of the quality of sectoral regulators' rules without impinging on the independence of these bodies. A first step could be to require them to implement a "notice and comment" procedure for an expanded RIA for their draft regulations.

Third, increase methodological rigour in the answers to the Checklist by providing training, written guidance, and minimum analytical standards, including for the benefit-cost tests, to departments and agencies. The practical and conceptual difficulties of a formal benefit-cost analysis suggest that a step-by-step approach is needed in Ireland, in which the RIA programme is gradually improved, integrating both qualitative and quantitative elements of the analysis, so that over time it better supports application of the benefit-cost principle.

Fourth, expand RIA to incorporate detailed consideration for alternatives to be analysed and compared with the regulatory proposal. Because Ireland has been slow in incorporating regulatory and non-regulatory alternatives that can increase policy effectiveness at lower cost, regulators must be motivated through results-oriented management. This requires strong encouragement from the centre of government, supported by training, guidelines and expert assistance where necessary. Where rigid laws and legal culture inhibit use of more effective alternatives, broader legal reforms to allow more innovation and experimentation may be necessary.

Fifth, the effectiveness of the Irish regulatory management system would be enhanced by integration of RIA with public consultation processes. Publication of RIA through a procedure that required regulators to respond to comments from affected parties would enable consultation to function more effectively as a means of cost-effective information gathering, and thereby improve the information needed for good RIA. Public exposure of RIAs would also be a mighty incentive for departments to raise rapidly the quality of their answers to the checklist. Access to RIA would also improve the quality of consultation by permitting the public to react to more concrete information. Such integration should, however, be carefully designed so that additional delays to the policy process are not introduced.

- *Increase transparency by formalising administrative procedures, including those concerning public consultation and rule making.*

It is accepted that the small size of the country, the political culture of openness, the number of elected representatives relative to the size of the population and the *Freedom of Information Act* contribute to a climate of openness that facilitates an effective consultation process. However, as relationships evolve, new participants, including non-nationals, become affected by Irish regulatory affairs. Likewise, lack of minimum rules may complicate public consultation and regulatory procedures reducing effectiveness, speed and timeliness of regulatory responses. The recognition of such new circumstances is reflected in the increasing formalisation of basic administration duties (*e.g.*, the *Cabinet Handbook*, the *Public Service Management Act*). However, accessibility may still needed. As a precautionary step, consideration should be given to establish as a safeguard a "notice and comment" mandatory requirement for all regulatory proposals (perhaps managed by the RIA central unit mentioned previously). As a complementary measure, Ireland may wish to establish the minimum criteria and disciplines for the public consultation required by the *Reduce Red Tape* action plan. Furthermore, these efforts may be integrated into an encompassing initiative to prepare an Administrative Procedure Act. This would consolidate the recent effort to publish the basic rule making procedures in the *Cabinet Handbook*, and on the other hand would provide in a single text clear rights to citizens and businesses to know and challenge the rules to be followed when making regulations (RIA, consultation, publication, etc.) and when adjudicating regulatory matters (make a decision on a formality).

- *Enhance the current programme of restating of existing laws and regulations with a target review programme based on pro-competition and regulatory high-quality criteria.*

The enactment *Statute Law (Restatement) Bill* and its full application is an important step to enhance the Irish regulatory framework. Adding specific regulatory quality criteria to the review process would enhance this mechanism. For such reviews, the 1995 OECD regulatory quality checklist could be used as a reference to verify the continued necessity and appropriateness of the existing stock of regulations. To support the review, the Parliament or government could directly or via an independent commission review the main areas of legislation and produce a rolling programme of reform spanning various years. As a prerequisite for such an endeavour, the government should provide enough human and technical resources to the unit in charge of the review. Such a unit could be merged with the enhanced RIA unit previously mentioned. The review process undertaken in Australia as part of its National Competition Policy is illustrative. Under that policy, all legislation was reviewed and anti-competitive restrictions were required to be removed unless it could be demonstrated that those restrictions were in the public interest and that there was no other way to achieve public policy objectives.[103]

5.3. Managing regulatory reform

The next policy steps to be taken need to focus on issues of sustainability and the development of a robust regulatory policy. An important driver for an effort to modernise regulatory management is that Ireland recognises that not only regulatory capacities in other countries have been changing faster, but that the recent economic success permits a more innovative approach to regulatory affairs. Ireland is falling behind in the "race" for "regulatory quality". Success permits it to be more assertive and forthcoming. But success will require it to think differently; not just differently from what it did before, but differently from its closest "peers". Ireland should benchmark itself to a higher standard than its neighbours should.

These efforts will require a new political commitment. Although its contribution has been essential, regulatory reform is not a political "hot topic", and some reforms lack the external imperative that is often needed to overcome internal resistance. Hence, the government will need all the convincing and communication skills necessary to push beyond a sceptical administration and public.

NOTES

1. Total employment has risen from just one million in 1988 to 1 737 900 in 1999, and unemployment has dropped from 15% in 1994 to 4.1% in 2000. Debt/GDP ratio had been reduced from 120% in the mid-1980s to about 39% in 2000. The Irish living standards are converging with the EU average, with GNP per capita at 97% in 1999 compared with less than 70% in 1987. In terms of GDP per head (PPP basis), Ireland ranked 8th in 1999, above Netherlands, Germany or Sweden. OECD, 2000 and Irish Government.

2. OECD (1999*a*). See also Fitz Gerald. J. (1999), Les Études du CERI, No. 56, November.

3. During the 90s, EU yearly transfers represented more than 4% of GDP.

4. The first decades of independence from UK saw the erection of very high tariff barriers against the outside world. Fitz Gerald, J (1999), pp. 6 and 24.

5. The macro-economic stability of the 90s was a result of the painful adjustments of the 80s to solve the late 70s "dash for growth" policy, that involved a huge fiscal injection which turned out to be unsustainable and almost wrecked the economy Fitz Gerald, J. (1999), p. 14.

6. For example, although this is being addressed, the Competition Authority had until recently difficulties recruiting high level professionals.

7. Interventionism can be traced to Article 45 of the Constitution which stipulates that "the State shall favour and, where necessary supplement private initiative in industry and commerce" and "the State shall endeavour to secure that private enterprise shall be so conducted as to ensure reasonable efficiency in the production and distribution of goods and as to protect the public against unjust exploitation" Millar, Michelle, Onik Karapchian and Tony Verheijen (1998), p. 283.

8. Such as in the case of the recent implementing price control in pubs to fight inflation or the permanence of the old Groceries Order which prevents full competition in the retailing market, see background report to Chapter 3.

9. The "brokerage" system is not only related to the electoral system based on proportional representation in multi-seat constituencies but to the political environment where ideology plays a minor part compared to direct contact and knowledge of the constituency's needs. Collins, Neil and Patrick Butler (1999), p. 41. O'Halpin, E and E. Connolly (1999), p. 135.

10. Laffan, Brigid (1999), p. 94; and Collins, Neil (1999), p. 73. About the taxi and pub market see Chapter 1 and Chapter 3 of the review.

11. See Kelly, M. (1999), p. 69 on this point.

12. An additional issue concerns the inter-temporal coherence of dealing with policies with impact on different generations.

13. Powers to compel appearance by public servants at Parliamentarian committees predated 1997 in particular in relations to reviews of public accounts.

14. The reform permitted Parliament's committees to require senior public servants to appear to give evidence to them Committees of the Houses of the *Oireachtas* (Compellability, Privileges and Immunities of Witnesses) Act of 1997.

15. O'Halpin, E and E. Connolly (1999), p. 133. N. Collins, for instance has underlined the "declining parliamentary supervision", Collins, Neil (1999), p. 78.

16. Morgan, D.G, (1999), p. 8 and 12.

17. A case clearly shown by the Department of Education in its findings of the high costs of creating decentralised local boards.

18. Government of Ireland (1996), p. 6.

19. Millar, Michelle Onik Karapchian and Tony Verheijen (1998), pp.285-291 and Kelly, M. (1999), pp. 82-85

20. An important contribution to the development of SMI was a joint thesis produced by a group of senior civil servants who were undertaking a special Masters programme in Strategic Management in the Public Sector from 1992 -1994 in Trinity College Dublin with the support of the Civil Service Training Centre in the Department of Finance. Based on the courses and work visit to New Zealand and Australia, the "Masters Group" submitted a joint thesis stressing the need to develop strategic capacities for policy development in the public service. The thesis, published in 1995 an academic journal, contained the basis of what became the policy document Delivering Better Government. (Kelly, M. 1999, p. 86.)

21. For instance, Delivering Better Government – Strategic Management Initiative (1996); Better Local Government – A Programme for Change (1996), Reducing Ted Tape – An Action Programme for Regulatory Reform (1999), etc.

22. The Department of the Prime Minister issued at the end of 2000 a Request for Tenders for a major external assessment of SMI.

23. For instance, see Keogan Justin and David McKevitt (1999), pp. 3-25.

24. Department of Public Enterprise (2000).

25. Kelly, M. (1999), p. 90.

26. Based on a NESC Strategy Report reported in Boyle, R. et al. (1999), "Review of Developments in the Public Sector in 1999", Administration 48(4), p.10.

27. OECD (1997a), p. 37.

28. OECD (1995).

29. Reducing Red Tape: An Action Programme of Regulatory Reform in Ireland, Government Publications, Dublin, July 1999.

30. The report of the Working Party was published together with the policy document Reducing Red Tape.

31. Government Publications, Dublin, July 1999.

32. http://www.irlgov.ie/taoiseach/publication/cabinethandbook/contents.htm

33. All Memorandum for the Government must indicate clearly, as appropriate, the impact of the proposal for:

   (i) Relations, co-operation or common action, North/South in Ireland, or East/West, as between Ireland and Britain

   (ii) Employment.

   (iii) Women.

   (iv) Persons in poverty or at risk of falling into poverty, in the case of significant policy proposals.

   (v) Industry costs (except in the case of measures relating to the Budget) and the cost to small business.

   (vi) Exchequer costs and staffing implications, and

   (vii) Quality regulation by reference to the notes in Appendix VI The Quality Regulation Checklist.

   Department of the Taoiseach, 2000, Cabinet Handbook, paragraph 3.1.

34. The policy was first launched based on the recommendations of the Report of the Review Group on the Law Offices of the State.

35. The attitude towards the programme of the Department of Finance seems to have been mixed. According to interviews, funds and resources to support the development of the Central Unit and the Statute Law Revision Unit have been reluctantly allocated and there are substantial delays in the recruitment and putting in place of trained personnel. Interviews during the OECD Mission to Ireland, June 2000.

36. OECD (1997b), p. 221.

37. The mandate derives from the constitutional role of the Attorney General as legal adviser to the Government. There is therefore an implicit obligation that laws that are drafted are legally sound and consistent with the constitution. This seems so inherent to the system that it is not written down. See Donelan. E. (1992), p. 1.

38. Up to September 2000 this was called the Office of the Parliamentary Draftsman.

39. Department of the Prime Minister, *Cabinet Handbook*, Rule 4.5.

40. See Statement on Regulatory Reform, July 2000 http://www.forfas.ie

41. Boyle, R. (1998).

42. Local authorities are categorised in five legal classes 29 County councils, 5 county borough corporations (cities), 5 borough corporations, 49 urban districts, 26 town commissioners.

43. Council of Europe (1998) and OECD (2000a).

44. A quasi-autonomous non-governmental organisation or non-departmental public body has been defined as a body which has a role in the processes of national government, but is not a governmental department or part of one, and which accordingly operates to a greater or lesser extent at arm's length for the Ministers' Cabinet Office, Officer of Public Service, 1997.

45. By 1999, the Chambers of Commerce of Ireland (CCI) published a CCI *Local Government Policy. From Local Administration to Real Local Government* where they indicated that the "... local government must be strengthened... and [make] it more accountable to the community it serves and offer value for money in the services it provides." The 3rd recommendation (out of 12) was "The principles of the SMI should be applied to local government – guaranteeing customer focus, accountability and the search for efficiency".

46. Boyle, R. *et al.* (1998), p. 10-11. Knox, Colin, Richard Haslam (1999), p. 30.

47. Until now, local agencies and bodies have rarely been merged of eliminated.

48. Examples of co-ordination difficulties go from the propensity of local authorities to create industrial and commercial zones instead of housing zones (for tax reasons) to the difficulties in securing permission to lay telecom cables or plan the Eastern By Pass highway around Dublin.

49. See case 29/84 (Commission -v- Germany) and see case 365/93

50. Initially, it was believed that directives could be given effect to by administrative circulars as well as by primary and secondary legislation and some Directives were implemented by means of administrative circulars. However, the Court of Justice has rejected this policy as an appropriate means of implementation CF Case 116/86 Commission -v- Italy [1988] ECR 1223, Case 236/85 Commission -v- Netherlands [1987] ECR 4637 Case 381/92 Commission -v- Ireland [1994] ECR 1-215

51. Some doubt was cast as to the validity of the European Communities Act by the challenge to regulations made under the European Communities Act in the case of Meagher -v- the Minister for Agriculture and Food. [1994] ILRMI. In that case, the applicant challenged the validity of two statutory instruments made by the Minister pursuant to section 3(2) of the European Communities Act 1972. That section provides that: "Regulations under this section may contain such incidental, supplementary and consequential provisions as appear to the Minister making the regulations to be necessary for the purposes of the regulations (including repealing, amending or applying, with or without modification, other law, exclusive of this Act)." The two statutory instruments in question had purported to amend section 10 (4) of the Petty Sessions (Ireland) Act, 1851. The High Court held that the regulations were ultra vires the European Communities Act on the basis that they purported to amend the primary legislation by means of secondary legislation. This decision was reversed in the Supreme Court.

52. Agriculture, Education, Transport, Environment, Tourism, Health/Food Safety, Inland Waterways, Language (Irish and Ulster Scots), Special EU Programmes, Trade and Business Development, Lough Foyle and Carlingford Loughs (aquaculture and fisheries).

53. Department of the Prime Minister, *Cabinet Handbook*, Rule 4.8.

54. For example, the Ombudsman's Act, 1980, implemented the recommendations of the Report All-Party Informal Committee on Administrative Justice 1977. The Safety, Health and Welfare at Work Act, 1987, followed the recommendation of the Barrington report into that area.

55. Consumer groups reported frustration that Ministers have refused to meet with them about particular concerns such as on pharmacy licenses and other health care regulations (see Chapter 3).

56. Irish Small and Medium-sized Enterprises – ISME, (2000). Document presented to the OECD delegation, June.

57. Overt exercise of sectoral influence concentrated in few powerful interest groups, including the Catholic Church, trade unions, farmers and domestic industry and professional interests have been replaced by "a myriad of organi-

169|

sation, groups and movements demanding a say in public policy at local, national and European level". O'Halpin, E. and E. Connolly (1999), p. 126.

58. These are publications that enable users of statutes and statutory instruments identify whether a particular law has been amended, repealed or otherwise affected since publication.

59. Department of the Prime Minister, *Cabinet Handbook*, Rule 6 and Appendix II.

60. The Law Reform Commission (1999), *Statutory Drafting and Interpretation – Plain Language and the Law*. Consultation Paper

61. Before that time, Irish administrative law was described as "a collection of shreds and patches, with no coherent statement of principle or in-build dynamism", Hogan, G. (1995).

62. Recent proposals for an Irish Administrative Procedure Act can be found on the policy document, A *Government Renewal* (section 71) or the Law Reform Commission, 1999, *Statutory Drafting and Interpretation – Plain Language and the Law*, Consultation Paper, p. 122.

63. In part because redress for a single case of excessive discretion of administrative sometimes is too costly and unpredictable through courts, in general Irish citizens acting in their own interest do not seek redress in the courts for mal-administration (Verheijen and Millar (1998),*op. cit.* p. 113). However, in 1993, a case was won against an environmental regulation more restrictive than the framing EU directive. More recently, the Ombudsman reported about a secondary regulation going beyond the primary law in a case of Pension and Welfare. Ombudsman (1997).

64. There have been some substantive proposals to solve the problem. For instance, the Devlin Report of 1969 recommended a systematic scheme for reviews and appeals for the decision of public authorities under a "Commissioner for Administrative Justice" acting like an Ombudsman (Verheijen and Millar (1998), *op. cit.* p. 113).

65. See OECD (2000*b*).

66. The working party was established in 1998.

67. The initiative has been backed by the unions, (Congress), the business association (IBEC), the Department of Enterprises, Trade and Employment, the Health and Safety Authority and the Irish Insurance Federation.

68. Administrative Law in Ireland, Hogan and Morgan Dublin, 1988.

69. OECD (2000*a*).

70. Chapter 6 of *The Report of the Review Group on Auditing*.

71. OECD (1997*a*), Paris.

72. Verheijen and Millar (1998), *op. cit.* p. 107.

73. Department of the Prime Minister, 2000, *Cabinet Handbook*, Rule 3.1j.

74. See point 4.1 of the recommendations of the Working Party report in *Reducing Red Tape*, 1999.

75. OECD (2000*c*).

76. Morrall, John and Ivy Broder (1997), p. 245.

77. Section 19 of the *Freedom of Information Act* and Department of the Prime Minister (2000), *Cabinet Handbook*, Rule 1.7

78. For instance in the case of telecommunications, independence of the regulator from the shareholder is an EU requirement set out in Directive 90/388/EEC and subsequently amplified by the Court of Justice and the Licensing Directive 97/13/EC.

79. The functions of the telecommunications, electricity and aviation regulators are set out respectively in the *Telecommunications (Miscellaneous Provisions) Act*, 1996 the *Electricity Regulation Act*, 1999 and the Aviation Regulation Act 2001. The assignment of postal functions was effected by the European Communities (Postal Services) Regulations 2000. The outline legislative proposals to amend current arrangements in the communications sector are available at www.irlgov.ie/tec/communications/commconsultation.pdf. The proposals in relation to the regulation of surface transport are at www.irlgov.ie/tec/transport/2117 DPE.pdf.

80. For more details see http://www.irlgov.ie/finance/News/sra/srap1.htm.

81. A similar situation pertains to the Office of the Director of Consumer Affairs.

82. The proposals for the new legislation, as issued for public consultation, are available on the website of the Department of Public Enterprise at http://www.irlgov.ie/tec/communications/commconsultation.pdf.

83. For discussion of governance and accountability see Tuohy, Brendan (2000).

84. For a fuller discussion of "democratic deficit" in the regulatory process, see Ferris, Tom (2000).

85. At present, decisions of both the Director of Telecommunications Regulation and the Commission for Electricity Regulation are subject to judicial review, but only in the latter case is there express statutory provision in this regard.

86. A point further discussed in the May 2000 Report of the Competition and Mergers Review Group requested by the Minister for Enterprise, Trade and Employment.

87. In this regard, the implementation mechanism could be viewed as akin to that for EU Directives, where the policy direction and end result is decided at a central level, but the means of reaching that result are left to the discretion of the Member States in light of their individual circumstances.

88. Parliamentary Debates, Dail Eireann, Vol. 466, cols 2244-9, 13 June 1996.

89. *Governance and Accountability*, Chapter 3, pp. 9 and 10.

90. By virtue of a change to the law proposed by this Bill the text of a restatement will be prima facie evidence of the relevant law and as such will be capable of being presented in court. This expedited approach would allow Acts to be restated at regular intervals.

91. OECD (1999*b*). See especially pp. 38-40.

92. Government of Ireland, communication to the OECD, May 2000.

93. OECD (2000*b*).

94. See High Level Group on Administrative Simplification. Report of the Meeting held 8 February, 2000, *Answers to a Small Business Federation Recommendation*. A particular complain raised by SMEs is that departments and agencies tend to duplicate information requirement despite the Central Statistical Office (CSO) powers to be previously consulted (states in section 31 of Statistical Act, 1993).

95. ISME -The Enterprise Association (2000), *op. cit.*

96. For instance, the High Court decision in October 2000, which repealed quantitative limits on taxi licenses.

97. This body could build on the Council of Regulation and Competition proposed by *Forfas*

98. See OECD (1999*c*).

99. See US Government, General Accounting Office (1997).

100. Some of the questions raised may also be applicable to the accountability of other "recent" institution such as an independent central bank, competition authority, ombudsman office or electoral institutions.

101. For instance, the 1997 report of the Comptroller and Auditor General, the 1995 Delivering Better Government Report.

102. Making the agencies meet together quarterly to make sure they really do this seems like an oddly precise requirement, but its inclusion in the CMRG recommendation recognises, unfortunately, the history of suspicious relations among these agencies.

103. For further information see, Hilmer, F, Raynor, M., and Taperell, G. (1993), The Independent Committee of Inquiry, *National Competition Policy*, AGPS, Canberra, Australia. Or http://www.ncc.gov.au/nationalcompet/Legislation%20Review/Legislation%20Review.htm.

BIBLIOGRAPHY

Boyle, R. *et al.* (1999),
   "Review of Developments in the Public Sector in 1999", Administration 48(4).

Collins, Neil (1999),
   "Corruption in Ireland: a Review of Recent Cases" in Collins, Neil ed.

Collins, Neil and Patrick Butler (1999),
   "Public Services in Ireland: Social Marketing Management" in Collins, Neil ed.

Council of Europe (1998),
   Report on *Structure and Operation of Local and Regional Democracy in Ireland*, Strasbourg.

Department of Public Enterprise (2000),
   Governance and Accountability in the Regulatory Process: Policy Proposals, March.

Donelan, Edward (1992),
   "The Role of the Parliamentary Draftsman in the Preparation of Legislation in Ireland", *Dublin University Law Journal*.

Donelan, Edward (1992),
   "The Role of the Parliamentary Draftsman in the Implementation of European Union Directives" in *Ireland: Statute Law Review*, Volume 18.

Ferris, Tom (2000),
   "Regulation of Public Utilities", *Irish Banking Review*, Winter.

Fitz Gerald. J. (1999),
   The Irish Economic Boom.

Government of Ireland (1996),
   Delivering Better Government. The Strategic Management Initiative, Second Report to Government of the Co-ordinating Group of Secretaries, May.

Hogan, Gerard (1994),
   "An introduction to Irish Public Law", in European *Public Law*.

Irish Small and Medium-sized Enterprises – ISME, (2000),
   Sustaining FDI let Economic Development. An ISME Response, June.

Keogan Justin and David McKevitt (1999),
   "Another Set of Strategy Statements: What is the Evidence on Implementation?" in *Administration* 47(1).

Knox, Colin and Richard Haslam (1999),
   "Local and Regional Reforms" in Collins, Neil ed.

Laffan, Brigid (1999),
   "The European Union and Ireland", in Collins, Neil ed.

Millar, Michelle, Onik Karapchian and Tony Verheijen (1998), in Tony Verheijen and David Coombes (eds),
   Innovations in Public Management. Perspective from East and West Europe, Edward Elgar, Cheltenham, UK and Northampton, MA, USA.

Morrall, John and Ivy Broder (1997),
   "Collecting and Using Data for Regulatory Decision-making" in OECD (1997b), *Regulatory Impact Analysis: Best Practices in OECD Countries*, Paris,

Moran, David (1999),
"The future of the Irish Constitution" in Collins, Neil, *Political Issues in Ireland Today*, Manchester University Press, Manchester and New York.

OECD (2000*a*),
Environmental Performance Review of Ireland, Paris.

OECD (2000*b*),
Reducing the Risk of Policy Failure: Challenges for Regulatory Compliance, Paris.

OECD (2000*c*),
"Background Report on Government Capacity to Assure High Quality Regulation" in OECD *Reviews of Regulatory Reform, Regulatory Reform in Denmark*, Paris.

OECD (1999*a*),
Economic Surveys: Ireland, Paris.

OECD (1999*b*),
Report by the Public Management Service of the OECD on *Regulatory Impact Assessment in New South Wales*, Published by the Regulation Review Committee, Parliament of New South Wales, Report No. 18/51, January 1999.

OECD (1999*c*),
"Background Report on Government Capacities to Produce High Quality Regulations" in OECD *Reviews on Regulatory Reform: Regulatory Reform in the Netherlands*, Paris.

OECD (1997*a*),
The OECD *Report on Regulatory Reform: Synthesis*, Paris.

OECD (1997*b*),
Regulatory Impact Analysis: Best Practices in OECD Countries, Paris.

OECD (1995), *Recommendation of the Council of the OECD on Improving the Quality of Government Regulation*, OCDE/GD(95)95, Paris.

O'Halpin, E. and E. Connolly (1999),
"Parliaments and Pressure Groups: The Irish Experience of Change", in *Parliaments and Pressure Groups in Western Europe*, Ed. Nolton P., London.

Ombudsman (1997),
Report on the Non-Payment of Arrears of Social Welfare Contributory Pension, March.

Tuohy, Brendan (2000),
"Evolving towards and Excellence Regulatory Framework through Review, Reassessment and Reform", paper delivered to the Conference on "Managing for Performance for Excellence", University College Cork, September.

US Government, General Accounting Office (1997),
"Managing for Results: Regulatory Agencies Identified Significant Barriers to Focusing on Results", Washington, D.C.

173

BACKGROUND REPORT ON THE ROLE OF COMPETITION POLICY IN REGULATORY REFORM*

* This report was principally prepared by **Michael Wise** in the Directorate for Financial and Fiscal Affairs of the OECD. It has benefited from extensive comments provided by colleagues throughout the OECD Secretariat, by the Government of Ireland, and by Member countries as part of the peer review process. This report was peer reviewed in October 2000 in the OECD's Competition Law and Policy Committee.

TABLE OF CONTENTS

List of Boxes

List of Tables

Executive Summary

Background Report on the Role of Competition Policy in Regulatory Reform

Competition policy is central to regulatory reform. Its principles and analysis provide a benchmark for assessing the quality of economic and social regulations. It motivates the application of laws that protect competition, which must be applied vigorously as regulatory reform stimulates structural change so that private market abuses do not reverse the benefits of reform. A complement to enforcement is advocacy, the promotion of competitive, market principles in policy and regulatory processes.

Effective competition policy is important to stimulating innovation and production while keeping price increases in check. It can thus help eliminate some of the bottlenecks to achieving growth without inflation, which include weak price competition and insufficient entry and innovation. Ireland has moved in the direction of implementing best practices in competition policy and enforcement, but its efforts have suffered from missed opportunities and uncertain commitments. Ireland's present prosperity offers an opportunity to strengthen its commitment to effective competition policy.

Ireland's conception of competition policy is still evolving. Some aspects of Ireland's competition policy support pro-competitive reform. These include the principles announced in the Prime Minister's regulatory reform programme, the government's plans for restructuring infrastructure industries, and the enforcement priorities of the Competition Authority (the "Authority"), which emphasise the goal of consumer welfare. These programmes and policies, which are based on promoting free competition, entry, and efficiency, represent a new departure in the last decade. They have accompanied, and in some respects responded to, reform initiatives from the EU. For most of the 20th century, Ireland's history and its economic and political culture fostered a different conception of competition policy, one which emphasised fairness and the protection of incumbent interests, particularly small businesses, more than efficiency and consumer interests. Producer interests have dominated policy debate, while consumer interests have been neglected. Tensions between the older and newer conceptions explain the difficulties Ireland is facing now in applying its competition policy to problems in domestic, non-traded sectors.

Ireland's national institutions have most of the tools needed to promote competition policy effectively. The substance of the competition laws, which follows the EU-based model, is fully adequate. But important gaps remain. The Authority has dealt with the flood of applications, mainly about vertical restraints, that followed adoption of the competition law in 1991. Since it obtained the power to initiate enforcement action in 1996, the Authority has made horizontal cartels its top priority. But in part because the Authority depends upon the Department of Trade, Enterprise and Employment ("DETE") for appointments, budget, and staff, it has suffered from personnel problems that have hampered its efforts. DETE, not the Authority, has decision power concerning the competitive impact of mergers. Whether sanctions to ensure compliance are adequate depends entirely on the courts. Treating competition law violations as crimes shows that they are taken seriously – and is the only way to apply pecuniary sanctions in Ireland – but it complicates enforcement processes.

Competition policy is not yet sufficiently integrated into the general policy framework for regulation. The overall reform programme calls for evaluating regulatory proposals based on their competitive effects, but it is not yet clear how this criterion will be applied in practice. Many entities play some role. DETE oversees competition policy issues, but another body, the Department of Public Enterprise ("DPE"), is responsible for reform in major infrastructure sectors. The Authority itself has only limited advocacy powers and insufficient resources to perform that role effectively. Despite the fragmentation of responsibility, reforms in many government programmes and policies to encourage more competition have shown positive results, particularly in traded sectors. But as attention turns now to the more difficult problems of domestically-imposed constraints and non-traded sectors, the independent Authority plays an *ad hoc* role in policy deliberations.

Regulations have produced long-standing and well-known competition problems, notably in Dublin's pub and taxi sectors. To counter inflation, though, the government has relied more on controlling pub prices

Executive Summary (*cont.*)

than on promoting competition. Recent reforms move toward greater reliance on competition in the long run, by permitting more flexibility in pub licensing – but retaining numerical limits – and opening up the taxi market to free entry – prompting strong protests by the current license holders. The durability of these restraints demonstrates the continued political influence of the older tradition, of protecting incumbent interests and small business. It is thus all the more important that competition policy decision-making be clearly and effectively independent.

Box 1. Competition policy's roles in regulatory reform

In addition to the threshold, general issue, which is whether regulatory policy is consistent with the conception and purpose of competition policy, there are four particular ways in which competition policy and regulatory problems interact:

- Regulation can **contradict** competition policy. Regulations may have encouraged, or even required, conduct or conditions that would otherwise be in violation of the competition law. For example, regulations may have permitted price co-ordination, prevented advertising or other avenues of competition, or required territorial market division. Other examples include laws banning sales below costs, which purport to promote competition but are often interpreted in anti-competitive ways, and the very broad category of regulations that restrict competition more than is necessary to achieve the regulatory goals. When such regulations are changed or removed, firms affected must change their habits and expectations.

- Regulation can **replace** competition policy. Especially where monopoly has appeared inevitable, regulation may try to control market power directly, by setting prices and controlling entry and access. Changes in technology and other institutions may lead to reconsideration of the basic premise in support of regulation, that competition policy and institutions would be inadequate to the task of preventing monopoly and the exercise of market power.

- Regulation can **reproduce** competition policy. Regulators may have tried to prevent co-ordination or abuse in an industry, just as competition policy does. For example, regulations may set standards of fair competition or tendering rules to ensure competitive bidding. Different regulators may apply different standards, though, and changes in regulatory institutions may reveal that seemingly duplicate policies may have led to different outcomes.

- Regulation can **use** competition policy methods. Instruments to achieve regulatory objectives can be designed to take advantage of market incentives and competitive dynamics. Co-ordination may be necessary, to ensure that these instruments work as intended in the context of competition law requirements.

1. COMPETITION POLICY FOUNDATIONS

From a history and tradition of protecting small producers and fair competition, Ireland has been trying for the past decade to establish a competition policy founded on promoting efficiency and consumer welfare. This new approach should be congenial to reform, as economic policy has abandoned autarky and embraced the goal of a market-led and open economy. But the process of developing this policy approach and creating the institutions to apply it has encountered difficulties, while the lingering tradition of concern about supposedly unfair competition impedes reform in some non-traded sectors.

1.1. Context and history

Ireland's traditional economic policy approach did not emphasise market competition. The Irish Republic tried to be economically self-sufficient for most of the 20th century, following a model of state-directed centralisation. The state was involved directly as an investor or operator in some major industries. In others, such as the cement industry, it granted monopoly privileges to private operators. Enterprises in agriculture and commerce were typically small-scale, and the small business culture supported political demands for protecting and preserving it. Despite Ireland's leap into the international economy over the last 20 years, the tradition of protecting small enterprises against competition remains strong.

The traditional approach to market regulation in Ireland tended to rely on control rather than competition. The Prices Acts, which date from 1958, provide for fixing prices by ministerial order. Price orders were in effect through the 1970s and into the 1980s. Most of the structure of price orders was dismantled in the 1990s, but the government still occasionally tries to control prices directly, and not just in infrastructure utility sectors.

Ireland's first competition act, the Restrictive Practices Act of 1953 law, protected fair trade. This statute supplemented the common law's principles governing business behaviour. It was designed to control abuses, not to prohibit particular types of conduct. The statute was applied through orders prescribing fair practices for an industry and through decisions about applications for exemption. These actions were taken by a Minister based on recommendations from the Restrictive Practices Commission (Ireland, 2000). The three Commissioners were not full-time appointees until the 1970s, when the body was renamed as the Fair Trade Commission, and they had no professional staff support.

As Ireland's economic policy direction shifted in the late 1980s, a different competition culture began to appear. One stimulus for change has been the EU directives calling for liberalisation in industries that were traditionally cartels and state-run monopolies. Changes in policy direction in Ireland coincided with similar changes elsewhere, as many EU and OECD Member countries moved toward more market-based regulatory systems. Support for change in Ireland has been reinforced by Irish emigrants returning home, bringing with them their experiences of market-oriented alternatives to Ireland's traditional approach. Other events, such as the success of airline liberalisation in expanding service and reducing fares, tended to build support for the direction of change among decision-makers as well as the general public.

There had already been calls for reform of competition policy in the 1970s. The Fair Trade Commission issued a report in 1989 recommending fundamental changes. In 1991, the old Restrictive Practices Act was replaced by a new Competition Act,[1] which prohibited restrictive agreements and abuses of dominance, and the Fair Trade Commission was succeeded by a new Competition Authority ("Authority"). All of the "restrictive practices" orders were eliminated, except the one covering the grocery industry.

But the means provided for enforcing these new prohibitions were ineffective. The Minister for Industry and Commerce could file suit in court seeking an order to stop prohibited behaviour; during the 5 years that the Minister had the sole authority to take enforcement action, it took none. Private parties harmed by prohibited conduct could sue for damages or injunctions; several parties filed suits, at considerable cost but with limited success. Meanwhile, the independent Authority had only an advisory role. The Authority could license agreements, but there were no consequences if parties did not notify the Authority of their agreement. The Authority could not investigate a cartel unless the agreement was submitted for approval. The Authority could not deal with abuse of dominance or mergers unless the Minister requested advice. Under the merger laws, the Minister issued orders and the Director of Consumer Affairs, not the Authority, enforced them. These first years without enforcement provided a transition period during which businesses could become accustomed to the new policy regime. But the weakness of the initial enforcement system suggests that, despite the change in the statute, the commitment to stronger competition policy was ambivalent.

Concern about the lack of public competition law enforcement led to calls for further reform in the mid-1990s. One obvious step was to give the independent Authority the same power the Minister had, that is, to seek court orders to stop prohibited conduct. Debate about reform featured increasingly vigorous claims about the need for stronger enforcement. As a result, and somewhat unexpectedly, the Competition (Amendment) Act of 1996 not only provided for independent enforcement power and a Director of Competition Enforcement, but it also made all violations of the law potentially criminal offences and set fines and even imprisonment as available sanctions. Ireland thus provides in principle for some of the toughest sanctions in OECD countries for similar violations.

At the same time that enforcement powers were dramatically expanded, and before there was any experience applying them, the Minister appointed an outside advisory panel, the Competition and Mergers Review Group ("CMRG"), to examine competition policy and enforcement processes. The CMRG's broad assignment included the merger laws, the effectiveness of the competition laws, "cultural matters" related to the application of the Competition Act (particularly its provisions for exemption from the prohibition against restrictive agreements), and appropriate means of implementing the law (Ireland, 2000). The timing of the CMRG's creation suggests that the Minister thought it prudent to maintain continuous monitoring of the enforcement process, both to gain support for assigning enforcement to an independent body as well as to work through some of the implications of making competition violations criminal offences. The CMRG issued its final report in early 2000, making 40 detailed recommendations about applying competition law and about the relationship between competition policy and other regulatory institutions and policies.

1.2. Policy goals

Official statements about the goals of competition policy permit many interpretations. Ireland's constitution contains "Directive Principles of Social Policy", which are intended to guide legislation, but not to control it.[2] These constitutional directives call for the state to favour private initiative and ensure "reasonable" efficiency in production, but "where necessary" the state is also to "supplement" private enterprise. The state is to protect the public against "unjust exploitation", and to aim toward distribution of ownership and control to serve "the common good". Moreover, and "especially," policy must not permit free competition to result in concentration of ownership or control of "essential commodities in a few individuals to the common detriment." Taken together, the constitutional aspirations appear to authorise a competition policy of controlling monopoly and abuse, more than a policy of supporting free competition and efficiency. The statement of purpose in the Competition Act too is general and perhaps indecisive, echoing the constitution in saying that restrictive agreements and abuse of dominance are prohibited "in the interests of the common good" (Competition Act). The use of the term "common good" might be taken to imply that protecting public interests should take precedence over protecting private interests.

To guide its application of competition policy, the Authority has adopted a Mission Statement that implies a preference for consumer interests. The Mission Statement describes enforcement as "contributing to an improvement in economic welfare," and the Authority treats consumer welfare and economic efficiency as its main priorities (Ireland, 2000). In this context, the emphasis is usually on allocative efficiency, except that dynamic efficiency could be more important for subjects such as intellectual property licensing.

1.3. Competition policy in reform

In promoting an approach based on efficiency and consumer welfare, Ireland's competition policy institutions are trying to take the lead in changing the traditional solicitude for the interests of producers and the protection of incumbents. But this new direction has been feasible only "because the welfare of exporters is often coincident with that of domestic consumers and because of Ireland's EU membership" (Fingleton, 1997, p. 112). Producer interests that benefit from the fair-competition tradition have resisted change. As a result, features of regulatory programmes that protect incumbents have often survived the government's reform efforts.

In the government's general regulatory reform programme, competition policy is a main substantive theme. The Strategic Management Initiative ("SMI") is devoted mostly to process, rather than the substance of regulations. But in the SMI's "quality regulation checklist", which departments must complete for each proposed new law or subordinate regulation, the second criterion is whether the proposal "will affect market entry, result in any restrictions on competition or increase the administrative burden" (Ireland, 2000). (The first criterion is whether the regulation is absolutely necessary.) The 1996 Report of the SMI's Working Group on Regulatory Reform is more pointed. It calls for "removing entry restrictions" in existing regulations, because "better quality regulation must address issues such as licences and permits". In general, the Working Group Report found that reform should "aim at the targeted dismantling of burdens to market entry and exit, price controls and other restrictions on competition."

Plans to restructure utilities and infrastructure services would rely more on competition. The Department of Public Enterprise ("DPE"), which has principal responsibility for the regulatory framework over many of these sectors, has developed proposals to manage the relationship between regulation and competition policy. These proposals may lead to legislation to deal with potential overlaps between the Authority's responsibilities to ensure compliance with the rules of competition and the sectoral regulators' responsibilities to ensure that competitive markets exist (Ireland, 2000); in September 2000, DPE issued Outline Legislative Proposals for the Regulation of the Telecommunications Sector which include provisions about co-operation. The DPE proposals recognise that the general competition law will apply in these sectors. DPE's statement of objectives emphasises the use of regulation during the transition to liberalised markets to accomplish goals, such as ensuring free market entry, that are typically the function of competition policy. In addition, though, it also emphasises such goals for economic regulation as "fair market conditions", a notion whose application can be inconsistent with competition policy based on consumer welfare, as well as public service requirements. And it contends that "economic regulation can comprehend social and regional objectives" (Ireland, 2000*b*, p. 6), a position that seems contradicted by experiences in other OECD countries. Rather, economic regulation proves to be best suited for problems of market power and asymmetric information, while social and regional policy goals are addressed more effectively and efficiently by other means (OECD, 1997).

The Department of Enterprise, Trade and Employment ("DETE") is responsible for policy issues related to the competition law (Ireland, 2000). Pro-competitive reform has been a theme at DETE, following the leadership of its Minister (who is also the Deputy Prime Minister).[3] In intra-government deliberations, DETE can call attention to the impact of regulation on competition. But other demands can affect DETE's competition policy priorities. DETE is also responsible for consumer protection policy and enforcement, which includes the occasional application of the Prices Act. And the consumer protection office in DETE is responsible for applying one of the remaining potentially anti-competitive aspects of the pre-1991 competition policy approach, the Groceries Order.

The well-intentioned goals of reform do not always determine policy choices, though. Some of Ireland's principal competition policy problems result from the anti-competitive entry-controlling licensing schemes that the SMI Working Group said should be eliminated. But in mid-2000, as the economy's continued strength produced very high inflation indicators (3 times the EU average), the government's response to demands for action included imposing temporary price control prices for drinks at pubs, rather than eliminating the anti-competitive licensing controls against new entry. The Minister acknowledged, however, that the sustainable solution to reducing pub prices lay in greater competition. Ministers reportedly met with industry groups to emphasise the need for "social responsibility" in setting prices.[4] The groups involved – in construction, homebuilding, auctions, motor vehicle sales, medical and legal professions, brokerage, and banking – comprise a roster of sectors where it would not be surprising, based on experiences in other countries, to find explicit or implicit price co-ordination, entry control, or market division. Such official admonition to be "responsible" risks encouraging potentially vulnerable industries to agree on target prices – that is, to flout the most basic principle of modern competition policy.

2. SUBSTANTIVE ISSUES: CONTENT OF THE COMPETITION LAW

Ireland's basic substantive law about restrictive agreements and abuse of dominance, which was explicitly crafted by analogy to EU law (Competition Act 1991, long title), is comparable to standard practice in other OECD countries. The methods for dealing with mergers, though, should be streamlined. And reliance on court proceedings and criminal sanctions, necessary for imposing fines under Ireland's constitution, introduces some technical hurdles and uncertainties.

Box 2. The competition policy toolkit

General competition laws usually address the problems of monopoly power in three formal settings: relationships and agreements among otherwise independent firms, actions by a single firm, and structural combinations of independent firms. The first category, **agreements**, is often subdivided for analytic purposes into two groups: "horizontal" agreements among firms that do the same things, and "vertical" agreements among firms at different stages of production or distribution. The second category is termed "**monopolisation**" in some laws, and "**abuse of dominant position**" in others; the legal systems that use different labels have developed somewhat different approaches to the problem of single-firm economic power. The third category, often called "**mergers**" or "**concentrations**," usually includes other kinds of structural combination, such as share or asset acquisitions, joint ventures, cross-shareholdings and interlocking directorates.

Agreements may permit the group of firms acting together to achieve some of the attributes of monopoly, of raising prices, limiting output, and preventing entry or innovation. The most troublesome **horizontal** agreements are those that prevent rivalry about the fundamental dynamics of market competition, price and output. Most contemporary competition laws treat naked agreements to fix prices, limit output, rig bids, or divide markets very harshly. To enforce such agreements, competitors may also agree on tactics to prevent new competition or to discipline firms that do not go along; thus, the laws also try to prevent and punish boycotts. Horizontal co-operation on other issues, such as product standards, research, and quality, may also affect competition, but whether the effect is positive or negative can depend on market conditions. Thus, most laws deal with these other kinds of agreement by assessing a larger range of possible benefits and harms, or by trying to design more detailed rules to identify and exempt beneficial conduct.

Vertical agreements try to control aspects of distribution. The reasons for concern are the same – that the agreements might lead to increased prices, lower quantity (or poorer quality), or prevention of entry and innovation. Because the competitive effects of vertical agreements can be more complex than those of horizontal agreements, the legal treatment of different kinds of vertical agreements varies even more than for horizontal agreements. One basic type of agreement is resale price maintenance: vertical agreements can control minimum, or maximum, prices. In some settings, the result can be to curb market abuses by distributors. In others, though, it can be to duplicate or enforce a horizontal cartel. Agreements granting exclusive dealing rights or territories can encourage greater effort to sell the supplier's product, or they can protect

The competition policy toolkit (*cont.*)

distributors from competition or prevent entry by other suppliers. Depending on the circumstances, agreements about product combinations, such as requiring distributors to carry full lines or tying different products together, can either facilitate or discourage introduction of new products. Franchising often involves a complex of vertical agreements with potential competitive significance: a franchise agreement may contain provisions about competition within geographic territories, about exclusive dealing for supplies, and about rights to intellectual property such as trademarks.

Abuse of dominance or **monopolisation** are categories that are concerned principally with the conduct and circumstances of individual firms. A true monopoly, which faces no competition or threat of competition, will charge higher prices and produce less or lower quality output; it may also be less likely to introduce more efficient methods or innovative products. Laws against monopolisation are typically aimed at exclusionary tactics by which firms might try to obtain or protect monopoly positions. Laws against abuse of dominance address the same issues, and may also try to address the actual exercise of market power. For example under some abuse of dominance systems, charging unreasonably high prices can be a violation of the law.

Merger control tries to prevent the creation, through acquisitions or other structural combinations, of undertakings that will have the incentive and ability to exercise market power. In some cases, the test of legality is derived from the laws about dominance or restraints; in others, there is a separate test phrased in terms of likely effect on competition generally. The analytic process applied typically calls for characterising the products that compete, the firms that might offer competition, and the relative shares and strategic importance of those firms with respect to the product markets. An important factor is the likelihood of new entry and the existence of effective barriers to new entry. Most systems apply some form of market share test, either to guide further investigation or as a presumption about legality. Mergers in unusually concentrated markets, or that create firms with unusually high market shares, are thought more likely to affect competition. And most systems specify procedures for pre-notification to enforcement authorities in advance of larger, more important transactions, and special processes for expedited investigation, so problems can be identified and resolved before the restructuring is actually undertaken.

2.1. Horizontal agreements

Agreements that restrict competition are prohibited (Sec. 4). The statute does not distinguish between horizontal and vertical agreements, but enforcement attention has concentrated on horizontal cartels. Anti-competitive agreements are legally void and unenforceable. Since the 1996 statute strengthened enforcement powers, they may also be treated as crimes. (Ireland's constitution does not generally permit administrative or civil "fines"; instead, financial or other penalties against improper conduct may only be imposed by a court, after conviction of a crime). The maximum possible penalty is a fine of IR£ 3 million or 10% of turnover (whichever is greater), and imprisonment up to 2 years.

Stern treatment of horizontal restraints is consistent with efficiency-based policy. Agreements to fix prices, limit output, or divide markets virtually always harm consumer welfare. Therefore, the Authority has announced that it will seek criminal penalties, rather than just civil relief, when it finds such conduct. The Authority believes that, by contrast, the effects of other kinds of agreements among competitors may not be presumed with as much confidence, so in those cases civil remedies such as a court injunction to stop the forbidden conduct could be more appropriate. There is thus enough flexibility for enforcers and decision-makers to punish anti-competitive collusion but permit pro-competitive co-operation.

On finding that an agreement's benefits outweigh its harm to competition, the Authority may grant a licence authorising it (Sec. 4.2). If examination shows that the agreement would not violate the Act at all, the Authority can issue a certificate to that effect (Sec. 4.4). A licence or certificate may apply to a defined category of agreements, so an agreement that meets the category's terms need not be notified

(Sec. 4.3(b)). (Thus "category" licences or certificates correspond to what are called "block exemptions" elsewhere). Few horizontal agreements are notified now, because firms are unlikely to have any honest doubts now about whether agreements to control price or output are prohibited. But some other kinds of plans for horizontal co-operation have been licensed. A performing rights society set common prices and demanded exclusive representation, but collected royalties more efficiently; because this arrangement was, on balance, pro-competitive, it received a 15 year licence (OECD CLP, 2000). Agreements among banks about clearing arrangements were considered facially anti-competitive, but they were licensed because they did not prevent entry and they had significant efficiency benefits (Fingleton, 1997).

Horizontal cartels became the Authority's top priority when it gained independent enforcement authority. Since 1998, price-fixing proceedings have been initiated against five trade associations, one professional association, and more than thirty separate undertakings. In three cases, the parties have consented to corrections. Since mid-1999, the Authority has forwarded three recommendations for indictments to the Director of Public Prosecutions ("DPP") (Ireland, 2000). Among the industries and sectors in which horizontal agreements have been subject to investigation and enforcement action are:

– Petroleum products: In response to dozens of complaints since 1997 about motor fuel prices, on-site investigations of distributors and a trade association have led to summary prosecution against one distributor, while other investigations continue, as do investigations about home heating oil.

– Dairies: Cases begun in 1998 are pending. Meanwhile, a threat of boycott by the Irish Farmer's Association, aimed at a German retail chain's low milk prices, was averted by the Authority's investigation and related publicity. Another chain then started offering the same low retail prices.

– Airlines: Travel agents tried to boycott Ryanair, because it cut their commissions. The national trade association was originally involved in the 1997 action, but it promised to stop and to instruct its members to stop. Some of the association's members did not follow that instruction, and the Authority brought another enforcement action against them, which was settled through assurances of future compliance (OECD CLP, 1999).

– Wholesale beer and soft drink distribution: The Authority recommended prosecution following investigation. It appears that the investigation may have been triggered by newspaper reports of a claim by a disgruntled former employee, that he was punished for refusing to participate in meeting of an alleged cartel.

– Pubs: The Authority instituted civil proceedings in 1998 against the Licensed Vintners Association and Vintners Federation of Ireland and their members (the first association covers the pubs in Dublin, and the other covers those in the rest of the country).

Self-regulation by professional and trade associations has often been found to restrain competition in many countries. In Ireland, several associations have notified their agreements and sought licences permitting them to continue.[5] These have included associations in optometry, accounting, medicine, engineering,[6] law, and journalism. Early decisions rejected association rules that restricted fees or advertising[7] and found that restraints on premises and limits on training opportunities were unacceptable barriers to entry.[8] Enforcement actions illustrate the extent of the problems. The association of veterinary surgeons promoted "recommended" minimum fees. It advised its members that they could charge more, but not less, than those recommended levels, exhorted members to co-operate with their neighbours about fees, and offered to help them do so (OECD CLP, 1999). The Authority's civil suit was settled by the association's promise that it would comply with the law in the future. Another action targeted the association of truckers, which agreed on rates for serving the Dublin port and announced that its members would boycott anyone who paid less. The boycott escalated into a blockade, which ended only after the Authority applied to the court for an injunction. This case too was eventually resolved by the parties' admission that their conduct was a concerted practice in violation of the law and their promise, to the court, to cease from future violation – and to pay the Authority's costs.

Collusive tendering was an early enforcement target. In late 1997, the Authority sent guidelines about detecting collusive tendering to 200 public sector agencies and made a presentation about procurement collusion to local government officials. Complaints that followed disclosed that the Construction Industry Federation encouraged co-ordination by publicising its members' bidding intentions. Following a protest from the Authority's Director of Enforcement, the Federation promised to stop this practice (OECD CLP, 1998).

Box 3. The EU competition law toolkit

The law of Ireland follows closely the basic elements of competition law that have developed under the Treaty of Rome (now the Treaty of Amsterdam):

- **Agreements**: Article 81 (formerly Article 85) prohibits agreements that have the effect or intent of preventing, restricting, or distorting competition. The term "agreement" is understood broadly, so that the prohibition extends to concerted actions and other arrangements that fall short of formal contracts enforceable at civil law. Some prohibited agreements are identified explicitly: direct or indirect fixing of prices or trading conditions, limitation or control of production, markets, investment, or technical development; sharing of markets or suppliers, discrimination that places trading parties at a competitive disadvantage, and tying or imposing non-germane conditions under contracts. And decisions have further clarified the scope of Article 81's coverage. Joint purchasing has been permitted (in some market conditions) because of resulting efficiencies, but joint selling usually has been forbidden because it amounts to a cartel. All forms of agreements to divide markets and control prices, including profit pooling and mark-up agreements and private "fair trade practice" rules, are rejected. Exchange of price information is permitted only after time has passed, and only if the exchange does not permit identification of particular enterprises. Exclusionary devices like aggregate rebate cartels are disallowed, even if they make some allowance for dealings with third parties.

- **Exemptions**: An agreement that would otherwise be prohibited may nonetheless be permitted, if it improves production or distribution or promotes technical or economic progress and allows consumers a fair share of the benefit, imposes only such restrictions as are indispensable to attaining the beneficial objectives, and does not permit the elimination of competition for a substantial part of the products in question. Exemptions may be granted in response to particular case-by-case applications. In addition, there are generally applicable "block" exemptions, which specify conditions or criteria for permitted agreements, including clauses that either may or may not appear in agreements (the "white lists" and "black lists"). Any agreement that meets those conditions is exempt, without need for particular application. Some of the most important exemptions apply to types of vertical relationships, including exclusive distribution, exclusive purchasing, and franchising.

- **Abuse of dominance:** Article 82 (formerly Article 86) prohibits the abuse of a dominant position, and lists some acts that would be considered abuse of dominance: imposing unfair purchase or selling prices or trading conditions (either directly or indirectly), limiting production, markets, or technological development in ways that harm consumers, discrimination that places trading parties at a competitive disadvantage, and imposing non-germane contract conditions. In the presence of dominance, many types of conduct that disadvantage other parties in the market might be considered abuse. Dominance is often presumed at market shares over 50%, and may be found at lower levels depending on other factors. The prohibition can extend to abuse by several firms acting together, even if no single firm had such a high market share itself.

- **Reforms in administration:** Recent and proposed reforms of EU competition policy reduce the scope of the prohibition against vertical agreements and would eliminate the process of applying for exemptions for particular agreements. Instead, exemption criteria would apply directly in decisions applying the law, and these decisions would increasingly become the responsibility of national competition authorities.

Using criminal law processes and penalties against horizontal agreements leads to difficulties and complications. But there is no other way to achieve deterrence through effective sanctions under Ireland's constitution, so the problems will have to be faced and solved. It is too soon to suggest particular changes, before Ireland's courts have had an adequate opportunity to devise solutions in particular cases. One source of potential difficulty relates to knowledge and intent, which are characteristic requirements of criminal laws. The Authority's enforcement policy presumes that cartels harm competition, but nonetheless the law permits parties to defend on the grounds that they did not know (or could not reasonably have known) that the effect of their conduct would be to prevent or distort competition (Competition (Amendment) Act, Sec. 2(2)(c)(i)).[9] It remains to be seen what kinds of defensive claims Irish courts will accept in this context. A particular concern could be that government efforts to control inflation by persuasion might insulate price fixing agreements from liability, if the parties to the agreement contend that the intended effect of their conduct was to respond to the Ministers' wishes in the public interest. Here, too, it remains to be seen whether Irish courts would accept this argument. There will be continuing uncertainty about the standards to be applied, at least until the courts have more experience and have issued more decisions.

Proving secret agreements usually requires first-hand admissions, particularly when the criminal law's high standard must be met. The Authority lacks the authority to implement a leniency programme to encourage parties to make these disclosures. Discussions are underway about how to accomplish this within Ireland's institutions, and the Authority hosted a public conference on the subject in November 2000.[10] In serious cases, decisions to grant leniency would be up to the DPP, not the Authority. The DPP normally has discretion to authorise leniency in particular cases, based on such considerations as the value of the evidence that the recipient can provide about other violations. The DPP has supported the concept of a formal, publicised programme that offered leniency under general terms. Such a program would need to be supported by an official policy statement, if not legislation.

2.2. Vertical agreements

In principle, restraints on competition imposed between firms in a vertical supplier-customer elationship are also prohibited. In practice, the absolute prohibition applies only to resale price maintenance, territorial protections, and non-compete clauses. Although the statute sets the same kinds of sanctions, including criminal punishments, for vertical restraints as for horizontal ones, as a matter of enforcement policy the Authority would seek only civil remedies, that is, injunctions, for most kinds of anti-competitive vertical agreements.

The efficiency-based policy approach motivates application of the rules about vertical restraints (Competition Authority, 1998d). Recognising that most agreements along the distribution chain are likely to be efficient, a general Category Certificate-Licence[11] permits a wide range of vertical restraints. Its short list of forbidden subjects includes resale price maintenance, absolute territorial protections, and non-compete commitments that extend beyond the contract term. (Franchise agreements may contain a one-year post-term non-compete clause, to protect the franchisor's goodwill). For other kinds of practices, if both undertakings have a market share below 20% then the category certificate applies and the practice is deemed not to be prohibited. If their shares are higher, the agreement is deemed to violate Section 4(1), but if the market share of neither party exceeds 40% then the category licence applies and the agreement is permitted. At low market shares, most vertical agreements are unlikely to foreclose market access or have other anti-competitive effects. Benefits of reduced costs and increased incentives are likely to outweigh any impairment of competition even if market shares are somewhat higher. Non-price restraints that are characteristic of exclusive and selective distribution and franchising can benefit consumers by improving efficiency and increasing choice. Thus, a licence might be granted in a particular case even if the firms' market shares exceed 40% (Ireland, 2000).

The Authority has consistently prohibited vertical agreements that impose resale price maintenance, regardless of market share. Even agreements limiting maximum resale prices have been rejected, despite the claim that they keep consumer prices down, because they limit the downstream sellers' competitive strategies (Fingleton, 1997). A supplier may recommend a resale price, but the recommendation may be no more than that; the supplier must advise the reseller that he may set a different price, must not indicate the margin resulting from using it, may not require the reseller to display it, and may not do anything to make the reseller charge it. Other policy concerns rarely can outweigh competition issues. The Authority rejected the Net Book Agreement, which was then in force among UK publishers, because vertical price fixing was likely to contribute to horizontal co-ordination.[12] The proffered justifications, such as the purported need to cross-subsidise unsuccessful titles and smaller booksellers, failed because cross-subsidisation distorts relative prices and the law was not intended to protect particular competitors.

Most of the 1 400 notifications to the Authority since 1991 concerned vertical agreements, and most of those were submitted in the early years, to meet the 1-year deadline for notifying agreements that were already in existence when the law became effective. Now that these matters have nearly all been decided and the Authority has issued authoritative guidance about the issues, the number of notifications and cases about vertical issues is declining. But the first successful criminal prosecution under the Competition Act, a summary proceeding in October 2000 resulting in a fine of IR£ 1 000, was against resale price maintenance.

2.3. Abuse of dominance

The basic prohibition against abuse of dominance parallels the EU prohibition (Sec. 5).[13] Until the 1996 revisions, this prohibition was enforced principally by private lawsuits for injunctions or damages. The Authority could only deal with issues of dominance when requested by the Minister in a particular case; moreover, that request was to be founded on the Minister's prior determination that there was an abuse to be investigated (Sec. 14). Since 1996, the Authority can go to court for injunctive relief on its own initiative.[14]

Efforts to apply the law consistently with a policy of emphasising consumer welfare and efficiency have sometimes encountered difficulty. Many complaints about abuse of dominance seek actions that could be inconsistent with the Authority's policy of emphasising efficiency rather than protection of competitors. About 15% of complaints are from small businesses about refusals to supply, under conditions that are unlikely to be violations of the law. The Authority has tried to make clear that one firm's refusal to supply another would not violate the law unless the firm has a dominant position or is a party to a boycott, and it has helped to resolve some of these disputes informally.

On the only occasion when the Minister used the statutory power to seek the Authority's views about an abuse of dominance, competition policy analysis ended up being subordinated to other interests. The Minister asked first for a general study of competition in the newspaper market in late 1994, and then, shortly afterwards, for an interim report on cross-border competition with UK firms and on a newspaper acquisition in Ireland. The Authority responded in March 1995 with the conclusion that the low pricing of UK newspapers in Ireland did not constitute anti-competitive predation, but that the acquisition by the Irish firm was an abuse of dominance in the Irish market. Although the Minister stated that he accepted the Authority's findings, he did not implement them and did not ask the Authority to complete its investigation. (At that time, the Authority did not yet have enforcement authority). Instead, the Minister appointed a new ad hoc commission on the newspaper industry, to report on "the competitiveness of the industry in Ireland which faces growing challenge from imports", among other topics. The newspaper commission's report disagreed with the Authority's analysis of the relevant markets, found that UK newspapers were being sold "below cost" and recommended legislation to control prices, and absolved the acquiring firm in Ireland from the Authority's finding of abuse of dominance (Fingleton, 1997). It also recommended applying special substantive criteria to media sector transactions, to consider ownership and viewpoint diversity.[15]

Since 1996, there have been many occasions to apply the prohibition to claims about abuse by traditional network and infrastructure monopolies.

189

– Telecommunications (*Telecom Eireann*): The Authority claimed, in an April 1999 lawsuit, that Telecom Eireann's refusal to grant unbundled access to the local loop constituted an abuse of a dominant position (Ireland, 2000). This suit, brought following a complaint, was intended in part to bridge an apparent jurisdictional lacuna in the telecoms rules. An EU draft regulation would bring this issue under sectoral rules, rather than the competition law.

– Electricity (*Electricity Supply Board*): In the period before access would be opened according to the terms of the EU Electricity Directive, ESB proposed a pricing scheme for its larger customers, which would have given ESB the right to match any lower price offer from another supplier and to lock in customers for 6 months even if ESB did not match the lower price. This arrangement could have blocked competitive entry. Opposition from DPE and the Authority's threat of enforcement action led to ESB removing the price-matching right and reducing the notice period to 3 months (Ireland, 2000).

– Gas (*Bord Gais Eireann*): In 1997, the Authority communicated its concerns about a power plant proposal that could have involved price discrimination among firms that competed at the downstream stage, and that favoured the incumbent supplier's own operations and those of firms in which it had an interest.

– Airlines (*Aer Lingus*): An investigation of the response to Cityjet's competing service between Dublin and London City airports was pending as of mid-2000.

Special provisions of the competition law could be used to restructure dominant firms and infrastructure monopolies, through processes that depend on political decisions rather than law enforcement. After the Authority has completed an investigation at the request of the Minister, the Minister may, "if the interests of the common good so warrant," prohibit the continuance of the dominant position, place conditions on its continuance, or "require adjustment" by sale of assets or otherwise (Sec. 14(3).[16] The Minister may consult first with other Ministers, and each house of parliament must confirm the action. The power has not been used to undo a position of dominance. Ireland's utility monopolies, which are under the jurisdiction of a different Minister, are being restructured by sector-specific legislative programmes, and the CMRG has recommended that this unused power be deleted from the competition law. But if that is done, there may be no other means of achieving structural changes to correct and remedy violations. The powers of Irish courts to impose a structural remedy to control or undo a position of dominance are not yet clear. Providing some means in the law could be a useful basis for finding solutions in particular cases, even if the power is rarely, or never, formally invoked.

2.4. Mergers

Large mergers must be approved pursuant to the Mergers and Take-Overs (Control) Acts, 1978 to 1996 ("Mergers Acts"). DETE, not the Authority, administers the Mergers Acts, and decisions to authorise or prohibit mergers are made by the Minister. The Mergers Acts' substantive standard includes a competition policy test, whether the transaction would be likely to prevent or restrict competition or restrain trade in any goods or services. (This test evidently does not depend upon finding that the merged firms would enjoy a dominant position). There is also a general criterion, whether the transaction would be likely to operate against the "common good", which makes the range of policy concerns that the Minister might consider virtually limitless.

Smaller mergers, falling below the Mergers Acts' thresholds, can be reviewed as agreements under the Competition Act.[17] In addition, the Authority has contended that all merger agreements, even those for transactions large enough to be governed by the Mergers Acts, may be restrictive agreements that the Competition Act would prohibit unless the parties notify the Authority and receive a licence. Based on this claim of jurisdiction, the Authority has propounded a general merger analysis and enforcement policy. Most merger agreements have no anti-competitive effects, so notification, review, and issuance of a licence could impose unnecessary delays and burdens. Thus, the Authority's Category Certificate for Agreements Involving a Merger or Sale of Business sets out a general framework for merger policy mostly by defining the kinds of agreements about the sale of a business that need not be notified individually (OECD CLP, 1998).

The main source of substantive guidance about merger policy is the category certificate. DETE has not issued guidelines or other explanations of its decisions under the Mergers Acts; instead, DETE evidently starts with the analysis set out in the category certificate. There is no prescribed methodology for defining product or geographic markets; treatment of potential imports as a separate factor implies a presumption that geographic markets are presumed to be national (or smaller). A three-part "safe harbour" test is based on HHI[18]: the law will not be concerned about a transaction leading to a post-merger HHI below 1000, or an increase in HHI of less than 50 regardless of the level, or a post-merger HHI between 1000 and 1800 resulting from an increase of less than 100.[19] An alternative criterion, based on plain market share, is post-merger four-firm concentration below 40%. Because of concern about dominance, no horizontal merger involving a firm with a pre-merger share over 35% qualifies for safe-harbour treatment. In general, though, if there are no entry barriers, then the level of concentration is not relevant.

Transactions covered by the Mergers Acts must be notified in advance to DETE.[20] The Mergers Acts apply if two (or more) firms involved each have assets over IR£ 10 million or annual turnover over IR£ 20 million.[21] Intra-group restructuring and transactions in receivership or liquidation are exempt. DETE may request that the parties submit additional information. The Minister may refer the transaction to the Authority. The referral must be made within 30 days after the notification is completed, and the Authority must have 30 days to investigate and issue its report. The transaction may not be closed unless the Minister approves it; however, the parties may proceed if the Minister has not acted within 3 months (Ireland 2000). This deadline begins to run when the parties have submitted a complete notification (or a complete response to the request for further information). Non-compliance can lead to fines ranging from IR£ 1 000 (or IR£ 100 per day of continued violation), up to IR£ 200 000 (IR£ 20 000) for violations serious enough to call for indictment. By contrast, the Authority's process under the Competition Act would also involve notification to request a licence. There is no deadline for the Authority to act on such a notification. The sanction for failing to notify the Authority would be the risk of substantive consequences under the Competition Act for an unlicensed agreement that does not qualify for the category certificate.

The Minister has wide discretion to apply the criterion of the "common good". The Merger Acts' list of subjects to consider includes the transaction's effects on continuity of supply or service, employment, regional development, rationalisation and efficiency, research and development, increased production, access to markets, shareholders and partners, employees, and consumers. Constraints on the Minister's discretion are procedural and indirect. Before issuing an order prohibiting a transaction or subjecting it to conditions, the Minister must consider the Authority's report. Thus, to take any action other than approval requires referring the matter to the Authority, and its report may address all of these statutory factors, not just competition policy. The Minister need not follow that advice or recommendation; however, the report must be made public, and disagreement could be embarrassing. In addition, either house of parliament may pass a resolution with the effect of annulling the Minister's prohibition or conditions. By managing the process, DETE can control the balancing of policies. The process is illustrated by the application of the "common good" criterion in connection with a combination of milk producers. DETE did not refer the transaction to the Authority for review, because the Minister had decided that the firms should be permitted to combine in order to make the Irish industry more competitive in a European market. Because there was no referral and no Authority report, there was no public airing of views about the potential impact on competition within Ireland.

Mergers in industries subject to sectoral regulation are also covered by the Mergers Acts, rather than special sectoral legislation. The Minister consults with other ministries, departments, or regulators who might be concerned. A recent major merger review (and the only merger issue referred to the Authority in the reporting year 1999) demonstrates the synergy with regulation. In late 1999, the Authority reviewed two mergers, at the same time, involving television distribution systems. The Authority noted that regulatory constraints prevented different MMDS and cable firms from offering consumers substitutable products. Even though the transactions reduced the number of different providers in Ireland to 2, the Authority determined that there was no effect on current competition. But the effects in related markets for telecommunications were potentially positive. A principal reason that the Authority recommended approval of both mergers was that each opened the possibility of introducing new telecoms technologies more quickly and over a wider geographic area (OECD CLP, 2000).

The basic substantive merger law and the guidelines for applying it are adequate, from the perspective of competition policy. Ireland's standard is slightly different from the EU merger regulation, and the CMRG recommended that Ireland adopt the European rule to make them formally consistent. The principal practical difference is that Ireland's standard could reject a merger on competition policy grounds even if it did not involve a dominant position. To reach the same result under European law requires invoking doctrines about "collective" dominance. Ireland's rule is thus more general. But if consistency is thought to be very important, adopting the European rule would probably not lead to substantially different decisions.

By contrast, the process of applying competition policy to mergers is clearly unsatisfactory. The overlapping notification systems expose parties to uncertainty and risk. The risk may be considered low, as few firms bother to make notifications to the Authority. But the system should be simplified, if only to eliminate the possibility that DETE and the Authority could issue contradictory orders about the same transaction. The CMRG has recommended that a single notification process apply to all mergers over a defined threshold, and that mergers no longer be treated as potentially restrictive "agreements" under the Competition Act. Mergers that fell below notification thresholds might still be subject to the Competition Act, but only if they involved an abuse of dominance.

The review process should be more transparent. Now, the Minister need not disclose the details of notified mergers, explain the reasons for not referring a transaction to the Authority, nor explain the reasons for approving a merger that has been notified. A low rate of referral would not, by itself, indicate a lax approach to anti-competitive mergers. But in the absence of explanation, failure to refer transactions that appear facially anti-competitive would tend to support that conclusion. To make competition policy more effective, the role of the independent body in this process should be strengthened. The CMRG recommends shifting roles, so that the Authority would receive all merger notifications and would be responsible for competition policy analysis in every case. A standard two-phase competition policy review would involve a quick examination to identify possible competition issues, and a more thorough investigation for the small proportion of filings that present them. The Minister would retain full power to permit, or prohibit, a merger on the basis of other permitted policy criteria, but the Minister could not over-rule the Authority's conclusions and decision on the grounds of competition policy. This process would bring Ireland more into line with practice in many other OECD countries that have merger review provisions in their competition statutes. The result may be to leave the Minister with the less attractive role of defending what may appear to be special interests. But the result would also be stronger support for competition policy exercised in the interest of consumers.

2.5. Unfair competition

Because Ireland is a common law country, some of the basic legal principles governing unfair competition are covered by tort doctrines of misrepresentation and deceit (Ireland, 2000). Some issues involving trademark may be covered by the Trade Marks Acts. In general, the competition law is not applied to most traditional types of unfair competition – false advertising, deception, unfair practices, trademark abuse and passing off, sales below cost, and abuse of economic dependence.

In one sector, grocery retailing, special rules based on principles of unfair competition have led to anti-competitive conditions and calls for reform. The grocery sector has been the subject of a series of Restrictive Practices Orders since 1956. As innovative market practices appeared in the sector, new orders were issued to regulate them, in 1958, 1973, 1981 and 1987. One rule under the current, 1987 Order is similar to a prohibition of below-cost sales, but that is not its actual effect. The reference "floor" is based on the invoice price, and it does not adequately take account of other factors that determine the true net price, such as off-invoice adjustments, allowances, discounts, or rebates. The effect of the rule requiring prices at or above invoice level, while permitting allowances and other measures so that actual intermediate sales are at non-invoice prices, is that distributors or manufacturers can control both downstream margins and final consumer prices. Suppliers might use these powers to reward customers who comply with preferred marketing strategies while preventing retailers from competing by lowering consumer prices. That is, the effect is an anti-competitive form of resale price maintenance.

Some of the Order's other provisions may also be inconsistent with general competition policy principles. Its rule[22] against refusal to supply apparently makes that a *per se* offence, regardless of costs, justifications, the parties' market positions, or the actual effect on the customer or on competition. On the other hand, provisions to equalise bargaining strength might be useful in some market settings, although they may not be flexible enough to take account of innovative marketing strategies and relationships. The Order tries to curb the practice of "hello" money, that is, paying, or demanding, inducements to retailers to stock the goods of suppliers. It prohibits discriminating among retailers in terms and conditions of supply or threatening or coercing retailers by withholding supplies, and to police that prohibition it requires suppliers to maintain published terms and conditions of supply and to maintain a register of supplementary terms. Suppliers may not give retailers any benefit for advertising the suppliers' goods. And retailers must pay suppliers on time.

The Groceries Order is a holdover from the era before Ireland had a comprehensive Competition Act. Enforcement responsibility is still assigned to the Director of Consumer Affairs. The original intention was that all the Restrictive Practices Orders would be revoked in 1991, as the Competition Act would become the means for dealing with anti-competitive practices in all areas of the economy. But this one alone survived, probably due to the influence of the wholesale sector, which was concerned about increased competition from firms that bypass wholesalers and source centrally. The chair of the Authority has been critical of the Groceries Order for distorting the groceries market and for promoting policy goals that are inconsistent with competition:

> [T]he Groceries Order ... exists to prevent multiple supermarkets from undercutting smaller shops and driving them out of business. While this may seem reasonable, it has been argued that it restricts competition in the sector for two reasons. First, off-invoice discounts can be used by upstream distributors to set minimum resale prices downstream. Second, it prevents retailers from pricing their goods optimally in what is a multi-product market, whereas loss-leading on certain products may in fact be more competitive. The main motivation for the Groceries Order is an idea of fairness, but this ultimately protects small shops from competition, which may not be desirable in the long run. Moreover, it increases the incentive for other groups to lobby for such protection based on fairness (Fingleton, 2000).

The legal status of the Groceries Order is peculiar. The law under which it was issued has been repealed. The Order cannot be amended by the same processes that were used to establish it; instead, change would require repealing the Order[23] and then replacing it with something else. The CMRG recommended repealing the Order without replacing it with any new rule against "below cost sales". A minority of the CMRG dissented from that recommendation. The CMRG does not object to new rules requiring retailers to honour suppliers' credit terms and banning discrimination and "hello" money. To support the consumer-welfare goals of competition policy, rules about marketing practices and discrimination should be sensitive to actual effects in particular circumstances. Thus, a rule against discrimination should permit consideration of differences in costs, available alternatives, and competitive responses and effects, rather than punish every price difference as an offence.

2.6. Consumer protection

There is some potential for co-ordinating competition and consumer policies. The same Division of DETE is responsible for competition policy and consumer protection policy (Ireland, 2000). The Director of Consumer Affairs is responsible for enforcing the laws about false and misleading advertising, unfair contract terms, consumer credit, food labelling, and product safety. Although the Authority and the Director of Consumer Affairs are attached to the same Department, and the two often contact each other informally, there is no formal process for co-operation between them.

At one time, the Office of Consumer Affairs and Fair Trade combined both functions. Now that competition enforcement has been shifted elsewhere since 1991, the "fair trade" tradition survives in the Groceries Order, enforced by the Director of Consumer Affairs. In addition to enforcing laws about consumer contracts and information, her office polices rules about price posting and accuracy, which can improve consumer information and improve market functioning (but which can also help a cartel control defection), as well as the Groceries Order and orders under the Prices Act.

Consumer protection organisations outside the government have not been included in policy consultations, and their efforts to present concerns directly have sometimes been unsuccessful. Labour groups believe that they have been the *de facto* representative of consumer interests in that setting. (Yet consumer groups tend to support the Groceries Order, despite its likely effect of dampening price competition, out of a belief that it prevents market domination by large firms). A more significant Irish consumer movement, supporting pro-competitive reform, may develop as increasing affluence is leading to greater consumer awareness, beginning with demands to recognise consumers' rights in commercial transactions.

3. INSTITUTIONAL ISSUES: ENFORCEMENT STRUCTURES AND PRACTICES

Benefits from reforming economic regulation can be lost if competition law and policy are not applied vigorously to prevent abuses in restructuring and developing markets. After devoting much of its attention for several years to vertical issues and notifications, since 1996 the Authority has made an enforcement campaign against price fixing cartels its top priority. The strength of enforcement depends crucially on courts and other institutions, which are being tested now for the first time.

3.1. Competition policy institutions

The Authority is the public body with principal responsibility for applying and enforcing competition law and policy. It has 5 permanent members, the maximum authorised number (the minimum is 3). They serve terms of up to 5 years, which may be renewed. The Minister recruits and appoints the members. The chair's authority is limited to calling meetings and presiding. This may represent a weakness, as the Authority has sometimes found itself attending to managerial details as a body. The CMRG has proposed that the chair assume responsibility for managing the Authority's operation. One of the Authority's permanent members may be designated by the Minister as the Director of Competition Enforcement. The Director is responsible for conducting investigations into violations and advising the Authority about enforcement proceedings. The chair is now also serving as the Director of Competition Enforcement.[24]

Although the Authority in its present form was created by the 1991 Competition Act, it is the lineal successor of the Fair Trade Commission and, before that, the Restrictive Practices Commission, dating from 1953. All of these commissions appear to have had only limited participation in the policy process. Those commissions served advisory roles and lacked staff support, and their members did not serve full-time until the 1970s. At first, the Authority followed that pattern too, serving first in an essentially advisory role and lacking staff support. The Authority's chairs have all come from academia. Filling positions promptly has sometimes been a problem. Even as the Authority was getting authority to act independently, the Authority was unable to make any decisions because it could not muster a quorum – of 3 members – in the second half of 1996 (OECD CLP, 1997).

The Authority is independent in decision-making, but in other respects it is strongly dependent on DETE, to which it is attached for administration, personnel, and budget. Experience in other OECD countries shows that competition policy bodies which depend on ministry decisions for budget and personnel may be exposed to indirect ministerial control over their priorities, while agencies with hiring authority and separate budget authorisation from parliament or other sources of funds may have more effective decision-making independence. In principle, the Authority is not subject to DETE direction in its law enforcement actions. But as long as the Authority operates under DETE's budget, for which the Minister is accountable to parliament, the Authority will not be fully independent of DETE's control. That control is manifested in decisions about membership, staff personnel, and budget. Compensation and employment terms of members and staff are determined by DETE in consultation with the Department of Finance. The members' conditions of service, including their pay, and the length of their terms of service depend on individual contracts negotiated with the Minister (Competition Act, Schedule, Sec.1). The Minister has the power to appoint "temporary members" to step in when a permanent member is unable to discharge his duties. The Minister may remove a member when that appears "necessary in the interests of the effective and economical performance of the functions of the Authority". If the Minister removes a member, a statement of the reasons for the action must be submitted to parliament (Competition Act, Schedule, Sec. 4(1)). Of course, if a Member chooses to resign, no such statement is needed.

Competition policies are formulated in DETE, which is also responsible for monitoring the impact of other laws and regulations on competition. The Authority has no statutory responsibility here. It has had the power to study and report on practices and methods of competition since 1991; since 1996, it has been able to do so on its own initiative. But the law does not clearly provide for Authority comments on particular policy proposals. Nonetheless, DETE has tried to provide some means for the Authority's views to be considered in policy development. Under the "Financial Autonomy Agreement" between DETE and the Authority, DETE has undertaken to "seek the views of the Authority on the competition implications of new legislation, whether originating within the Department or elsewhere, with a view to improving its capacity for policy formulation." (Ireland, 2000). Other departments do not formally consult the Authority, although there are indirect channels of communication, through DETE.

3.2. Competition law enforcement

In applying competition policy, the Authority plays different roles in different kinds of cases. The Authority is the deliberative decision-maker for applications for licences or exemptions. It acts as a policy analyst and advisor concerning the merger matters that are decided by the Minister. And it acts in a more executive capacity, as investigator, plaintiff, or prosecutor. when orders must be sought from a court. The Director of Competition Enforcement may investigate matters in response to a complaint or on his own initiative. The Authority's general enforcement guidelines and a note about procedures in cartel investigations detail its approach to investigations. Hearings in the courts follow Ireland's generally applicable judicial procedures.

The Authority can require production of information, books, documents and other records, and it can summon witnesses and examine them under oath (Competition Act, Schedule, Sec. 7). After obtaining a warrant from a District Court Judge, it can enter and inspect premises without notice (the so-called "dawn raid" power), require production of books and documents, and provide other information which the inspecting office may reasonably require in that process (Competition Act, Sec. 21). These powers appear broad, but assembling evidence for prosecutions requires particular sensitivity to the special requirements of the criminal law and process, including its high standards of proof. For this purpose, the plan to hire several *gardaí*[25] to assist the Authority's staff and membership, most of whom have backgrounds in economics rather than litigation, should help.[26]

The Authority tries to review complaints quickly and to contact complainants within a month if it necessary to get more information. Complainants are notified when the Authority decides to close a matter, either because the complaint does not state a claim under the Competition Act or because further investigation has found insufficient evidence to make a case. Some concerns have been expressed about delays in high-profile cases, but these complaints may result from misunderstanding about the difficulty of successful criminal prosecutions, when something that may seem obvious to the

195

man in the street must be proved beyond a reasonable doubt in the face of a vigorous defence. Both the Authority and the DPP are still engaged in a learning process.[27]

The Authority must resort to the courts to obtain enforceable orders and sanctions. The Authority (or DETE) can bring cases in the Irish High Court seeking injunctions or orders declaring the defendant's conduct to be illegal. The burden of proof is the normal civil standard, of balance of probabilities. Civil cases may be settled before judgement, through an admission of wrongdoing and undertaking not to repeat it.

Box 4.   The "Elective Hearing" proposal

The CMRG proposed a complex new procedure for hearing and deciding complaints, creating a quasi-adjudicative "elective hearing" before the Authority for what would otherwise be criminal cases (CMRG, 2000, Chaptrer 4).

The proposal

For violations that would otherwise be subject to criminal proceedings, potential defendants would have the option to request a hearing first before a panel of the Authority. At the end, the Authority could set a (recommended) fine, but not a term of imprisonment or any civil remedy, such as an injunction. If the party did not pay it, the Authority's recourse would be to proceed with the prosecution in court. If the party paid the "fine" (or if the elective hearing concluded there was no violation), it would gain immunity from actual criminal prosecution, although the Authority or a private party might still seek civil sanctions, and the Authority could use the evidence and findings of the elective hearing in such a civil proceeding. The CMRG recommended that decisions reached in the elective hearing be kept confidential, at least until the final determination of actual criminal proceedings. And the CMRG suggested that DETE might appoint temporary members to assist in this process, such as experienced lawyers who could deal with admissibility of evidence and similar procedural issues in this "quasi-trial."

Motivation and intention

The proposal is intended to provide some kind of expert adjudication of competition cases, consistent with the constitution's requirement that only courts can issue mandatory orders and fines. It also anticipates that changes in EU enforcement policies will increase the workload of national authorities, and that national competition agencies will have to be constituted as adjudicative bodies. It reinforces the CMRG's proposal to separate the enforcement function from the adjudication function. In addition, some observers believe that expanding the Authority's "adjudicative" function is a response to concerns that the Authority pays too little attention to small business complaints about unfair competition and refusals to supply.

Evaluation

The CMRG proposal would give the Authority a function that looks like what an independent, collegial, adjudicative body would typically do. Because the notification-licensing function is becoming less important, and it may disappear if the EU white paper is adopted and Ireland follows that lead, virtually all important decisions would otherwise move to the courts. But the "elective hearing" does not solve any clearly identified present problem. It appears to be motivated by a desire to reduce the resort to actual criminal proceedings and fines. It is hard to understand why a defendant that "lost" this decision would pay the fine or change its behaviour. There might be some risk that a court would impose a higher fine than the Authority had sought, and might even impose prison sentences as well. But until there is more experience with actual sentences in competition trials, the extent of that risk is entirely a matter for speculation. The provision for temporary Authority members risks the appearance that decision-makers will be appointed based on expectations about their decisions.

Imaginative effort has been side-tracked on a hypothetical problem. Ireland's laws have been on the books for a decade, and enforcement and sanctions were strengthened nearly 5 years ago. Only now are courts actually facing the need to make decision in enforcement actions. It would be better to try to make the present system work. The government has evidently decided not to proceed with this proposal at this time.

Violations may also be subject to criminal penalties. The Authority itself can bring summary actions in the lower, District court, seeking penalties up to a fine of IR£ 1 500 or six months imprisonment. Summary procedures must be brought quickly, though, and thus they may not be appropriate for complex cases, which will take more time for investigation and trial. Until recently, the Authority had made little use of this power to initiate its own enforcement action in lower courts. The first conviction in a summary action came in October 2000. For more serious cases, the Authority may refer its investigative results to the DPP, who may seek an indictment and bring a case in the Central Criminal Court. Conviction on indictment could lead to fines of IR£ 3 million or 10% of turnover, whichever is greater, and imprisonment up to 2 years. Criminal liability may attach both to individuals and to firms. As of early 2001, no indictments had been authorised yet. In general, courts have rarely imposed high penalties in white collar crime cases.

Resort to courts and criminal sanctions introduces complexities and difficulties. The scope of application of criminal sanctions remains to be determined authoritatively. The Authority's enforcement guidelines highlight the application of criminal sanctions to the hard-core cartel violations, but they do not rule out seeking criminal penalties against other practices, such as conduct whose intent or effect is clearly anti-competitive or conduct that another case has already challenged successfully. There have been few litigated cases, so many judges remain unfamiliar with these novel laws and doctrines. Competition cases may be heard by judges at all levels, which may dilute expertise and efficiency. There is no special rule of jurisdiction for competition cases. The choice of court depends on the general rules of criminal law, so cases may be heard in local Circuit Courts, which sit intermittently. The resulting problems, of lack of continuity and expertise, are not insoluble. But an opportunity was missed in 1996 to assign jurisdiction for all Competition Act prosecutions to the central criminal court, where the president of the Court could assign an expert judge. Providing for general jurisdiction and very broad substantive coverage are evidence that the practical consequences of adopting criminal sanctions were not given enough consideration at the outset.

Application of the law is a reasonably transparent process, because most of it is done through public judicial processes. The Authority's decisions about granting or withholding licences and its advisory reports about mergers are published with full reasoning.[29] But DETE's merger decisions, about whether to refer a transaction to the Authority and about prohibiting a merger or imposing conditions, have not been as transparent. The Authority's decisions about licences may be appealed to the courts, for a full re-examination on the merits (but based on the Authority's factual record). Decisions of trial courts may be appealed or reviewed through the usual judicial channels, from the Circuit Court to the High Court, where the matter may be heard de novo, and from the High Court to the Supreme Court.

3.3. Other enforcement methods

Private enforcement has been unusually significant in Ireland. For the first 5 years after the Competition Act was passed, private actions were the only form of enforcement. Under Section 6 of the 1991 Act, "any person aggrieved" by any agreement or abuse prohibited under Section 4 or 5 of the Act has a right of action for damages, injunctive relief or declaration. Actions against restrictive agreements may be brought in the High Court, while actions against abuse of a dominant position may be brought in the High Court or the (lower) Circuit Court. In the Circuit Court, the amount of damages that can be recovered is limited, but the costs of suit are also lower. Nearly all private cases have been filed in the High Court. The 1996 Amendment Act creates a wider personal liability for directors, shadow directors, managers and other officers of the defendants. Private plaintiffs can now sue those individuals, as well as their firms.

Experience with private suits has been mixed. High costs and legal uncertainty have discouraged some potential plaintiffs. Courts have struggled with the complex economic issues, and the experience has led members of the bar to believe that competition cases are difficult to win. But the private right of action may still have tactical value, in putting additional pressure on adversaries and in gathering evidence (Ireland, 2000). Plaintiffs may complain to the Authority at the same time they are pursuing private relief. (Conversely, defendants in private suits may apply to the Authority for a licence or certificate, to use in defence against the private claim). Most private actions have been complaints by entrants against allegedly dominant firms, including some against former state monopolies, about refusals to supply or other entry-deterring strategies. Although plaintiffs have rarely won outright – the courts often find there is dominance, but not abuse – the decisions have established some sound and useful precedents about the application of the Competition Act. For example, private parties must show not only private injury, but also injury to competition, in order to recover. And the decisions recognise that market power in purchasing can violate the law just as market power in selling can (Fingleton, 2000).

Private suits have accompanied public actions against anti-competitive "private regulation." When the Authority examined a licence application for an unwritten agreement between the state electricity company, ESB, and the Register of Electrical Contractors, it found that the arrangement was already the subject of a private lawsuit complaining that the agreement steered business to RECI members. After RECI ensured that smaller firms could become members, the Authority accepted the safety-based claims about the agreement's public interest justification (OECD CLP 1997). When the Royal College of Surgeons brought a private suit challenging restrictive arrangements for training pharmacists between the Pharmaceutical Society and Trinity College Dublin, the problem also came to the attention of the Authority (OECD CLP 2000). Another private action against private regulation evidently targeted the government as well as the relevant trade association, seeking damages for lost sales because of a rule preventing the sale of non-prescription reading glasses. The Opticians Act was to be amended in 2000 to remove the restriction, but the disgruntled doctor intended to maintain his suit nonetheless.[30]

The option to file a private suit is a valuable safety-valve. A party complaining about a refusal to supply has a credible alternative if the Authority lacks resources to pursue the matter or concludes that the claim is groundless. The disappointed complainant can bring a relatively low-cost action in the Circuit Court seeking an injunction. To be sure, the cost of such a suit is not zero. But it is appropriate for private parties to bear that cost and risk, for these cases are typically about private interests, more than public interests. The CMRG and the Authority have called for permitting private suits involving restrictive agreements to be filed in Circuit Courts, to reduce the parties' costs and make private remedies more widely available (Ireland, 2000).

The Competition Act originally gave full enforcement powers to the Minister for Industry and Commerce. DETE still has these powers, to seek injunctions in court, bring summary prosecutions, and recommend indictments. But the department has never used them, even during the period from 1991-1996 when it had sole enforcement power. The experience, consistent with that in other OECD countries, shows that enforcement is likely to be more vigorous when it is assigned to a body that is independent of the political decision-making process. The CMRG recommends repeal of all provisions authorising DETE enforcement actions, so that the Authority would be the only public body authorised to apply the Competition Act. Repeal would confirm the actual situation and avoid the risk of inconsistency or conflict.

3.4. International trade issues

The competition policy of the European Union applies in Ireland, but the means for applying it are likely to change. At present, the only way to apply EU competition policy through Irish institutions is by private lawsuit. The Authority does not yet have that power, even though the substance of the Competition Act is directly analogous to EU law. The EU has proposed wide-ranging, fundamental changes in the way its competition policy would be implemented. Much of the CMRG report discusses the implications of those changes. Because the proposals are still being discussed and are unlikely to be effective for several years, the CMRG recommendations on this subject are offered as items for consideration, depending on the direction the EU ultimately takes. But its first recommendation, to empower the Authority to apply EU competition law to the extent national agencies may do so, should be adopted regardless of the direction of other reforms.

The Authority's ability to deal with international matters is hampered by constraints on sharing information. The Authority and its members and staff may not disclose information they obtain in the performance of their official functions, except that they may disclose it as necessary in connection with those official functions and enforcement actions (Competition Act, 1991 (Schedule, paragraph 9)). This prohibition nearly prevents exchanging information with the competition enforcement agencies of other countries (Ireland, 2000).

Table 1.   Merchandise trade in Ireland[1]

	Authorised positions	Members[2]	Economists and lawyers[2]	Non-specialists[2]	Vacancies	Budget (IR£)	Expenditures (IR£)
2000 (2Q)[3]	24	5	7	12	8		
1999	24	5	7	12	5	1 083 000	892 000
1998	25	5	7	13	1	875 000	825 000
1997	[4]	24	4	7	13	3	
1996	17	4	1	12			
1995	16	3	1	12			
1994	12	3					

1. At the Authority; in DETE, another 8-9 persons are involved in merger reviews and competition policy.
2. Authorised positions.
3. At the end of June 2000, 5 new professional positions were authorised.
4. Budget not separately identified within DETE through 1997.
Source: Ireland, 2000; OECD CLP, 1995.

In the application of the Competition Act, no concerns have been reported about national treatment of foreign firms or about the consideration of impacts of international trade on competition. The law appears to support extraterritorial jurisdiction, as the Competition Act reaches practices that have the object or effect of impairing competition in Ireland, without regard to the location of the conduct. That jurisdictional claim appears not to have been tested, though. In general, the application of competition policy seems to accommodate the impacts of foreign trade with no difficulties. On a few occasions, issues have arisen due to trade with or competition from firms in the UK. Support for the Groceries Order comes in part from local firms resisting entry by chain store operations based in the UK. In automobiles and some other products, exchange rates and tax policy differences between Ireland and the UK have created arbitrage opportunities, followed by private efforts to suppress them.

3.5. Resources and priorities

Uncertainty about personnel has hindered the Authority's work. As of mid-2000, the Authority was critically understaffed (Ireland, 2000), with 40% of its authorised positions vacant, including 5 of its 7 professional staff positions. Yet the staff had been at virtually full strength in the third quarter of 1999. The principal reasons for the decline appear to be the expiration of limited-term personnel contracts, which had discouraged retention of professional staff, and increased demand for people with these skills at the new sectoral regulators and private sector firms involved with regulation, as well as disruptions that accompanied the resignation and replacement of the chair in early 2000. Appointments restored the Authority to its full 5 member complement in the third quarter of 2000, and recruitment continued to fill staff positions for economists and legal advisors.

The Authority depends on DETE for staff and budget resources. Disagreements about support between the Authority and the department date back to the early 1990s (Competition Authority, 1996).[31] Hiring and retaining economists and legal advisors has proved difficult. It took until mid-1998, or nearly two years after the Authority's enforcement authority became effective, to get the professional staff on board. In addition, DETE set up the staff positions as three-year contracts, rather than as permanent posts, and set the pay at normal civil service rates, rather than meet the salary levels for the relevant skills that are paid by other regulatory bodies or the private sector. In Ireland's booming job market, the combination of limited pay and lack of tenure protection decimated the professional staff. The Authority has lacked the personnel resources needed to do its job, yet it has not been able to spend all of its budget.

The Authority's dependence on DETE needs to be reduced. The Office of the Director of Telecommunications Regulation, which has an independent source of funding, has greater budgetary and operational autonomy from its related Department, as well as more flexibility in hiring and compensating its professional staff (Competition Authority, 1999). The CMRG points out that providing for separate funding authorisation and the same degree of freedom that comparable independent agencies already enjoy would strengthen the Authority's actual and perceived independence (CMRG, 2000, Recommendation 33). Before taking steps to improve the Authority's resource situation, DETE asked for an outside consultant's report. The consultant's interim report resulted in authorisation to hire 5 additional professional staff, 4 of whom are now in place. The final report recommended further strengthening of the Authority's personnel resources by adding another 15 positions.[32]

The available resources have been concentrated on the top enforcement priority, investigating hard-core horizontal cartels (Ireland, 2000). The other principal objects of investigation are resale price maintenance (in part because it may be a means of facilitating horizontal price-fixing) and certain types of abuse of dominance (Ireland, 2000). Confirming that cartels are the top competition issue in Ireland, more complaints are made about price-fixing than about any other kind of violation. Since 1996, the Authority has received 146 price fixing complaints (in many cases, more than one complaint about the same cartel), compared to 127 complaints about abuse of dominance. As staffing fell in 1999, maintaining the cartel investigations required diverting resources from other issues, so the case backlog grew (OECD CLP, 2000). Only one investigation has wound up with a conviction and fine yet, in late 2000; otherwise, the few orders that have been issued in enforcement matters represent settlements.

Table 2. Trends in competition policy actions

	Horizontal agreements	Vertical agreements	Abuse of dominance	Mergers	Other[1]
1999: matters opened	37	29	39	2	53
sanctions or orders sought	3				
orders or sanctions imposed					
total sanctions imposed					
1998: matters opened	34	24	28	5	69
sanctions or orders sought	3		1	1	
orders or sanctions imposed	3				
total sanctions imposed					
1997: matters opened	57	31	48	3	81
sanctions or orders sought					
orders or sanctions imposed					
total sanctions imposed					
1996: matters opened[2]	13	20	12		49
sanctions or orders sought					
orders or sanctions imposed					
total sanctions imposed					

1. "Other" includes complaints about matters judged not to fall under the Competition Act, including unfair competition.
2. The Authority's enforcement powers became effective in the second half of 1996. Before then, the Minister did not undertake any enforcement action.

Source: Ireland, 2000.

The Authority's policy work is being pushed aside because of resource constraints. Previous industry studies such as the Authority's 1998 papers about competition problems in the taxicab and retail drinks industries were influential factors in public debate. One member and one staff economist, devoting together about one-half of a person-year, try to follow advocacy matters (Ireland, 2000). But maintaining this function has been difficult. A general study of surface passenger transport issues, begun in 1999, has been deferred because of lack of resources (Ireland, 2000). Re-establishing this function is a high priority. The chair has created a separate division, overseen by one of the Members of the Authority, to concentrate on government-imposed restraints and advocacy. Currently, 4 staff are assigned to this division, and the chair hopes that this number will be doubled.

4. LIMITS OF COMPETITION POLICY: EXEMPTIONS AND SPECIAL REGULATORY REGIMES

There are no explicit exemptions from the Competition Act, but many other laws and programmes inhibit competition, usually by restricting entry in order to protect incumbent firms. Where these conditions are authorised by statute, the Competition Act cannot correct them.

State-owned firms are subject to the competition law, and some of them have been sued for abuse of dominance (Ireland, 2000).[33] State monopolies may operate under laws that authorise non-competitive practices or conditions, though. The authorised non-competitive practices and conditions in Ireland have included gas and water service, forestry, airport management, and road and rail passenger transport, as well as the telecoms, electric power, broadcast, and postal sectors where reform programmes are making the transition to competitive markets. This list resembles those often found in other countries.

The Competition Act cannot redress the anti-competitive actions of local authorities. These are often taken through advisory boards that include local officials and appointees. Subjects where problems have appeared include land use, health care, and licensing. Some of these are described below with respect to the sectors involved. Anti-competitive decisions by these bodies may not be subject to challenge as violations of the competition law, if these bodies are not "undertakings" pursuing economic objectives. To correct these problems requires advocacy and legislation.

Ireland's competition policy makes no special provision for small business. The Authority has advocated repealing one vestige of small-business protection, the Groceries Order. The Authority's first decision denied that the law should not be concerned about the conduct of smaller firms. On the contrary, in a small country with a dispersed population, consumers may be more vulnerable to anti-competitive behaviour by small firms such as local retailers, professionals, and service providers.[34] Nonetheless, some observers continue to advocate adopting a *de minimis* rule, perhaps to make Ireland's rules consistent with the EU's in this respect. In its interim draft report, the CMRG proposed two possible *de minimis* exemptions, either that liability depend upon showing "substantial effects", or that the law establish a safe-harbour based on market share or turnover. But such exemptions would make it difficult to maintain a clear rule against horizontal cartels. No special rule would be needed about vertical arrangements involving small firms, for those would usually be covered by category certificates. It would be difficult to devise safe-harbour tests that would not shield some notorious competition problems, such as pubs, from effective enforcement. The *de minimis* proposal was dropped from its final recommendations, but the CMRG did propose that the Authority issue guidelines to give smaller businesses more confidence.

4.1. Sector-specific exclusions, rules and exemptions

The extent to which competition in particular sectors is impaired by licence controls and other regulations is not known with certainty. The competition policy office in DETE is undertaking, as of mid-2000, a review of existing legislation and regulatory programmes to identify state-promoted legal and other restrictions on competition in all areas of the economy (Ireland, 2000). The following section discusses developments in some sectors where the issues are already well recognised.

Box 5. Independent regulators and competition policy

Sectoral reforms moving from monopoly toward competition have highlighted the relationships between general competition policy and special sectoral regulators. Independent regulators for telecoms, electric power, and aviation already exist. Responsibility for postal services has been assigned to the telecoms regulator (soon to become the "Commission for Communications Regulation"), and for gas, to the electric power regulator (to become the "Commission for Energy Regulation"). Regulatory arrangements for surface transport and the financial sector are under consideration.

The Authority's relationships with these sectoral regulators are still developing. Efficient sharing of responsibilities is hampered by constraints on sharing information and the lack of clear means for one agency to defer to another about a particular complaint. Disputes between the Authority and the telecoms regulator, ODTR, highlighted the co-ordination problem. In 1999, the Authority initiated proceedings against the incumbent wireline provider, contending that its refusal to unbundle local loop services was an abuse of dominance in violation of the Competition Act. At about the same time, ODTR initiated a process of public consultation to consider whether, and on what terms, the incumbent should be required to unbundle these services by regulation. Concerns about whether there was an adequate, timely effort to co-ordinate these two processes may have lent urgency to efforts to improve the process. Legislative measures to facilitate further co-operation between the Authority and sectoral regulators is under development by DPE and DETE.

As these sectoral regulators have begun to proliferate, Ireland has engaged in a debate about the implications of institutional independence and the relationship with competition policy. Most of these new regulators deal with sectors that are under the jurisdiction of DPE. Thus, the Minister for Public Enterprise called for comment in September 1999 on regulatory governance and accountability. Her proposals appeared in March 2000 (Ireland, 2000*b*). The problem of devising a structure of accountability between her department and these independent bodies echoes the relationship between DETE and the independent Authority. Some of the DPE proposals about appointment and tenure, to balance independence with responsiveness, follow the current practice that applies at the Authority. DPE's proposals include means for promoting accountability to the public, such as formal decision procedures, consultation requirements, comment opportunities, publication of comments and decisions, and protection of confidentiality. Regulators would be accountable to the Minister through regular strategy statements and work programmes. And the parliament could request regulators to account to parliamentary committees at least annually. This review would deal with implementation of plans and overall performance, but not, in theory, with individual decisions (Ireland, 2000*b*).

DPE's proposals for co-ordinating regulation with competition policy are not yet fully formed, though. DPE recognises that regulators' tasks have evolved as traditional state monopolies have become privately owned competitive industries. Those tasks now call for interventions to facilitate entry and ensure fair market conditions and consumer protections. The DPE proposals apparently conclude that Ireland's competition law could not eliminate barriers to entry unless there is a showing of abuse, and that regulation could eliminate even abusive barriers more efficiently and effectively. DPE notes that sectoral regulators have powers over licensing conditions that necessarily involve them in competition issues. This suggests the potential use of those powers to enforce compliance with competition rules, if the enforcement methods of competition law are considered too time-consuming and legalistic. DPE acknowledges that sector-specific rules should not, in principle, conflict with generally applicable competition rules, but rather than try to resolve remaining tensions between them, the proposals take advantage of the contemporaneous appearance of the CMRG report to call for more consultations between the ministries and for continued consultations between sectoral regulators and the Authority (Ireland, 2000*b*). And DPE proposes a periodic review of regulatory structures that would involve regulators, other departments, industry, employee, customer, and consumer interests, the Director of Consumer Affairs, and the Authority.

The CMRG makes detailed recommendations for managing the relationship between sectoral regulation and general competition policy. To emphasise the generality of competition policy[1], the Competition Act should continue to apply to regulated sectors, without any substantive exclusion or exemption. A single public body, the Authority, should enforce it. To avoid putting firms in impossible positions where regulatory decisions overlap competition issues, conduct undertaken pursuant to a regulator's decision or approval

Independent regulators and competition policy (*cont.*)

should not be subject to the most serious sanctions, of criminal liability or damages, though it might still be enjoined as a violation of the law. These recommendations have the net effect of giving competition policy a general priority while leaving to the courts the task of working out the balance between competition policy and regulatory decisions in particular cases. Sectoral regulators could not confer *ad hoc* exemptions from competition law consequences, but firms in the regulated sector would be assured that complying with the regulatory programme would not subject them to disproportionate and unjustified risk of liability because of conflicts among laws or enforcement programmes.

CMRG recommendations would also encourage co-ordination among enforcers, to prevent serious conflicts from developing. The Authority and the sectoral regulators would be required to notify each other when initiating an action that the other might also be able to take, and then to consult to avoid unnecessary duplication or inconsistency, perhaps by one agency deferring to the other. Sectoral regulators would be required to consult with the Authority before taking action about behaviour that could be considered a competition law violation, and to take account of the Authority's opinion about it. To be sure these consultations actually happen, the Authority and the regulators would be required to meet at least quarterly, face to face. The relevant laws would need to be amended to make it clear that the agencies would have legal discretion to defer to each other and to share necessary information about matters that come up within their jurisdictions. Where the sectoral regulatory programme calls for a process of appeal on the merits, one member of the appeal panel would be a member of the Authority.[2]

---

1. The more general problem, of establishing the right balance among independent decision-making and political accountability, is taken up in background report to Chapter 2.

2. One concern underlying the CMRG's recommendations is to avoid subjecting firms to "double jeopardy" in multiple administrative proceedings. Its solution is to put a burden on complainants. The CMRG calls for requiring an "election of remedies", at least to the extent that a complainant could not take its problem to two different agencies at the same time. The prohibition could tend to undermine the CMRG's other recommendations calling for inter-agency co-operation. A complainant who was in doubt about whether its problem was covered by a regulation or by the competition law might want to submit the same complaint to each and let the two agencies sort it out, consulting with each other about the best course to take. Prohibiting simultaneous complaints might tend to discourage simultaneous actions, but it would not necessarily prevent them. The first agency would have better information, from the complainant. But even if the complainant did not tip it off, the other agency would learn of the possible problem at the time of consultation, and could then undertake an ex officio investigation. The CMRG proposes to permit a disappointed complainant to go to the other agency after the first one rejects its case. Permitting sequential complaints might tend to clarify jurisdictional boundaries. Presumably, when the disappointed complainant goes to the second agency, it is because there has been an authoritative ruling that its problem cannot or should not be resolved under the other's jurisdiction, leaving the way clear for the second agency to act without risk of conflict. On the other hand, if the first agency's action concludes or implies that the complainant's problem is not worthy of any relief at all, that finding could tie the second agency's hands.

4.2. Pubs

The most well-known competition problem in Ireland, although perhaps not the one with the greatest economic impact, affects one of its most characteristic institutions, the pub. Both the emergence of the problem and the efforts to address it illustrate the tradition of reluctance to apply competition policy principles. The political influence of the interests who profit from the historic system prevents the most straightforward reform, which would be to eliminate quantitative entry controls. Instead, the government has repeatedly invoked the Prices Act to regulate the industry. This approach postpones fundamental reform, while the rules are modified in ways that preserve or even increase the scarcity value of the publicans' licences. The latest reform package, the Intoxicating Liquor Act, 2000, enacted in July 2000, relaxes some constraints on opening hours and, for the first time, allows existing licenses to be transferred to different geographic areas. But the numerical limit on the number of licenses remains in place.

The Licensing Acts are legion, dating from 1833. There are at least 11 separate statutes called "Intoxicating Liquor Acts." The first law to place quantitative limits on the trade was the Licensing

(Ireland) Act 1902. Before then, anyone who qualified for a licence had the common-law right to enter the business. Over a century, the number of pub licences has continually declined, from about 13 500 in 1896 to just under 10 000 in 1996.[35] (Before the famine of the 1840s, there had been over 21 000 on the island). A host of different kinds of licences has developed. The basic publican's licence permits the holder to operate a bar, offering "on-licence" sale of beer, wine, and spirits for consumption on (or off) the premises. Two kinds of licences permit a hotel to operate a bar, subject to conditions such as having a minimum number of rooms or a maximum proportion of revenues from liquor sales. Restaurants may serve wine, but until the new law of 2000 they could not serve beer or spirits unless they had a "special restaurant licence". This was introduced in 1988 to address the anomaly that pubs could serve food but restaurants could not serve beer.[36] Nonetheless, conditions on the restaurant licence tended to ensure that restaurant facilities do not compete with the pubs' type of service. A *bona fide* private-member "club" is not subject to the licence requirement, but it can only serve its members (and guests in defined circumstances,) not the general public. The licensing laws limit operating hours. A short-term "special exemption" is needed to remain open after hours.

Pub licences have been technically tied to particular premises. They could be "transferred" only through a process that involved extinguishing one or more licences and issuing another licence for the new premises. Until the law was changed in 2000, the rules differed for rural and urban premises. A "new" rural licence required extinguishing 2 existing rural licences. In this context, "rural" was defined formally, so that several densely populated suburbs of Dublin were classified as "rural". A "city or town" exemption was introduced in 1962, so that in theory an "urban" licence could be granted for an area where population had increased since 1902. But the number of licences was not increased; rather, the "new" urban licence depended on extinguishing an existing one, in the same city, town, or parish. Licences could not be transferred from rural to urban areas or between different towns and cities. A blanket "one mile" rule prevented entry that would compete with older, unimproved rural pubs. Incumbents could object to a "new" licence on the basis of the number of pubs already in the neighbourhood or on the grounds that the new licence would be "unreasonably detrimental" to their existing business.

The stated purpose of the 1902 law was simply to "safeguard the public interest" by preventing a "proliferation" of pubs. One concern was apparently to end corruption in the process of issuing rural licences. Presumably, the temperance movement provided some of the support for limiting the number of pubs. Echoing that presumed original concern about the effects of public drinking, some groups contend there are still too many pubs and that they are open too long. The Dublin pub owners' association, whose members are the principal beneficiaries of the market power that their licences confer, admitted that the system increases costs and discourages entry, but it argued that those effects are positive goods, not problems. If entry were easy, quality standards would fall, unscrupulous operators would not keep their houses orderly to protect their investment, and financial stability would be undermined as the asset value of the licences fell. Hotel operators, who also benefit from the limited licences they can obtain, objected to making any changes in the system, predicting that more open entry would lead to more failures and then to dominance by larger, monopolistic operators. The Dublin publicans claimed that prices are not identical at all pubs, so there is adequate competition. Admitting, though, that Dublin prices increased more recently than prices outside Dublin did, they also claimed that this increase was needed to pay for refurbishing amenities that customers demand, and that customers are relatively indifferent to the prices they are paying.

The effect of the limitation on price is revealed by an econometric study that the Authority commissioned. Even after correcting for differences in demand patterns stemming from Dublin's demographics, the study found that Dubliners paid 6% more than consumers outside Dublin for a pint of stout at a pub, and the differential reached 10-12% for other beers and lagers. Underlining the effect of the publicans' market power, the study found that Dubliners paid less for off-licence package products, because of the presence of efficient high-volume retailers in the urban area. Experience with free entry in the UK shows a feedback effect: more demand leads to more pubs, which in turn leads to more demand. The net effect on price in such a situation is unclear, but the positive effect on output is unambiguous. In Ireland, and especially in Dublin, where increased demand could not be met by increasing the number of pubs, the net effect was to increase prices more than to increase output.

The economic significance of the limitation on entry could be measured in the value of a pub licence. The price of a licence varied by locality. The reported minimum, for a rural licence, was IR£ 45 000; for high demand areas, it could range as high as IR£ 500 000. By one report, a rural licence recently sold for IR£ 150 000 (to a firm that may plan to transfer it to another location, under the new legislation), and a pub licence in Dublin may have sold for as much as IR£ 2 000 000. The 2-for-1 rule for rural pubs, recently repealed, meant that the basic licence cost for a "ne" rural pub would have been at least IR£ 90 000. As populations have shifted much more than pub licences, the urban areas, particularly Dublin, have become seriously under-served. A century ago, Dublin had over 1 100 pubs; now, it has 946. Then, the average Dublin pub served 388 people; now, it serves 1 119. In one "rural" suburb, 3 pubs serve a population of 39 000 – 13 000 people per pub. Outside the Dublin area, the average population per pub is 283. The huge investment in a licence calls for investment in a big facility to recover it. Pubs in suburban Dublin are becoming much larger, in response to this demand, and the cost of a licence those areas has increased accordingly. A rough estimate of the value of all the outstanding licences, rural and urban together, under the previous regulatory constraints was IR£ 550 000 000 (Competition Authority, 1998b).

For decades, the government's response to competition problems in this sector has been to impose price controls, rather than to permit entry. These responses may alleviate some of the effects of market power, but they put off adopting a more fundamental and effective solution, and they also tend to encourage industry co-ordination. In 1997, DETE issued a Price Acts order freezing prices outside Dublin for 6 months. But no order was needed for Dublin – because the publicans' association in Dublin had agreed that its members would fix their prices at the previous level. In response to concerns about overall inflation, another Price Acts order froze pub prices in July 2000.

Reform is complicated greatly by the network of interests and investments that have developed over a century based on the expectation that entry would be controlled. For example, the pubs' bankers object that free entry would reduce the value of their collateral. Rather than upset these expectations, reform proposals have often appeared designed to preserve the value of existing licences. Legislation[37] adopted in 2000 permits more transfers of licences and extends pub opening hours. (Some restaurants that are authorised to serve wine would also be permitted to serve beer). But the total number of licences would not increase. Allowing some rural licences that are virtually unused to be transferred to the Dublin area should increase the supply, and hence reduce the value, of Dublin licences, but it will also increase the price of those rural licences, so the net effect is not clear. Meanwhile another commission will be appointed to study the situation further and produce a final report in two years.[38]

The pub situation tests Ireland's commitment to competition policy. It is a well-known problem, which directly affects a large number of citizens. The Authority has called for ending the licensing regime, and it has resorted to law enforcement against the collusion that the present regime has fostered. A successful prosecution, demonstrating how the present system has abused consumers, could change the balance and lead to demands for structural reform. But the industry's supporters could also threaten to undermine the independence of the bodies such as the Authority and the DPP that are trying to correct the problem.

4.3. Taxicabs

The number of taxicabs in Dublin (and some other areas) was controlled by local authorities pursuant to a 1978 law. Virtually no new licences were issued until the Minister for the Environment and Local Government resumed responsibility temporarily in 1991. Between 1991 and 1995, about 150 new licences were issued, the first since 1978. The number of taxi licences was increased a few times, but the ceiling was not eliminated.[39] Regulations returned the licensing and oversight responsibility to local authorities in 1995. Taxicabs could compete to some extent with hackney services, which must

Box 6. **The pub problem: 75 years of studies**

Six studies have examined competition in Ireland's retail drinks industry. Since the 1960s, these studies have identified the licensing system as a critical constraint on competition.

- A 1925 report, examining whether there were too many pubs, proposed a scheme under which a pub's local competitors would pay to buy out the "excess" licencee. This operated only for one year, 1927, and was then abandoned because too much was being paid for marginal licences. That fact already suggests the industry recognised the value of scarcity: competitors found it worth more to buy out a competitor than would appear plausible from the competitor's economic performance alone.

- A Commission of Inquiry in 1957 recommended making new licences available, under a 2-for-1 rule (to get a new licence, 2 old ones had to be extinguished), except that a hotel could have a public bar in exchange for extinguishing 1 old licence. Some of its recommendation appear in the 1960 Law.

- The Fair Trade Commission was asked to study the industry in the early 1960s, after the trade co-ordinated a price increase in the wake of an increase in the excise tax. The Commission found that collective arrangements about retail prices were widespread. Some local associations did not just recommend increases, but took steps to enforce those recommendations. The result of this study was a 1965 Restrictive Practices Order prohibiting collective action about retail drinks prices, which remained in effect (although evidently unenforceable) until the new Competition Act of 1991.

- When the industry applied for a price increase in 1972, the National Prices Commission determined that the licensing system, strong trade associations, and the "closed shop" constrained competition so cost increases were passed on to consumers. The commission denied the full price increase requested, called for price displays, and recommended re-examining the licensing system because it limited competition without evident justification.

- The Restrictive Practices Commission examined the industry again in 1977, in response to a request from the Minister who was concerned about prices and about violations of the 1965 Order. The Commission found that the Order had been ineffective; concerted action continued. The licensing system facilitated collusion about price, seriously distorted the structure of the trade, and increased operating costs and prices (particularly in urban areas). For the first time, the Commission recommended ending the cap on the number of licences and eliminating the explicitly anti-competitive aspects of the licensing criteria. Only the recommendation to introduce restaurant licences was adopted, though.

- Most recently, a select Committee on Legislation and Security was appointed to review the liquor licensing laws, but it did not examine their effect on entry, deferring instead to the Authority's contemporaneous study of that aspect of the problem.

The Authority undertook a new study in January 1997, one of the first to apply its new powers of self-initiated investigation. The study responded to media reports of simultaneous price increases in licensed premises in Dublin. The study's terms of reference were not the conduct behind these particular increases (since that might prejudice any subsequent enforcement action), but rather structural barriers that could be beyond the reach of law enforcement. The Authority's interim findings were published in 1998. The Authority concluded that a serious attempt to reform the licensing laws had to address the fundamental problem, namely the complete barrier to entry. Thus, the Authority recommended revising the laws to repeal the 1902 Act's prohibition against new licences, to repeal provisions protecting existing establishments from entry, and to retain licensing criteria that are directly relevant to the social dimension of the sale of alcohol, such as suitability of the applicant and premises and compliance with health, safety, and planning requirements.

The 1998 report was "interim," because it did not yet include a discussion of how the licensing limits affected firm behaviour. Behaviour had just become the subject of another proceeding: in June 1998, the Authority initiated law enforcement proceedings under Section 4 (Competition Authority, 1998b).

be arranged privately. The extent of that competition appeared limited, though. Increasing the number of hackney licences did not reduce the market value of taxi licences, suggesting that hackney competition did not erode the taxis' revenues and profits.

Limited supply led to long waiting times and poor service. Demand increased 100% over the last 20 years, but the number of licences increased less than 30%. In times of heavy usage, waiting times of 90 minutes are reported (Fingleton, 1998). The Fair Trade Commission criticised the limitation in 1991 and recommended phasing it out. The chairman of the Authority in 1998 again called for phasing out the limits and introducing a more liberal entry regime (Competition Authority, 1998c). The 1998 report pointed out that the impact of the monopoly could be measured by the increasing value of a taxicab licence in the secondary market. A taxi licence was valued at about IR£ 80 000, and the aggregate value of licences outstanding in 1997 exceeded IR£ 150 000 000. The annual monopoly profit was estimated to be IR£ 30 000 000 (Competition Authority, 1998c). There are other, less obvious effects of limited taxi service. Because of the limitations in the regulatory scheme in effect before November 2000, taxis could contribute little to filling Ireland's need for more flexible public transport.

Change is difficult, though, because incumbents resist losing the value of their licences. Reform will require more than simply increasing the number of licences, for it must also deal with the fact that several different local authorities issue licences.[40] Reform efforts have been piecemeal, and they have been stalled by litigation. In November 1999, the government proposed to add about 3 100 new licences, by letting each incumbent buy another, new licence and making another 500 licences available to applicants under the "points assessment" system (which would tend to favour co-drivers under existing licences). All the new licences, like the old ones, would be freely transferable. When the first regulations to implement this reform appeared in January 2000, the taxi drivers responded by threatening to strike,[41] and hackney drivers challenged several aspects of the regulatory authority in court[42] (Ireland, 2000). After the judge ruled in October 2000 that quantitative limits were illegal, the government decided to remove them entirely. The new regulations, issued 21 November 2000, set up a new licensing system that sets uniform national fees and that does not permit local authorities to impose any numerical limits. Owners of taxi licences could recover their investment as a write-off against their tax liabilities. Within days, about 300 applications for new licenses were submitted (and about 3 000 applications were requested). The taxi licence holders immediately went on strike in protest and sought judicial review in the High Court to overturn the new policy and retain their protection against competitive entry. The High Court has heard the case and reserved judgement; meanwhile, the Court has allowed the issuing of taxi licences under the new regime to continue pending its decision. By early 2000, the number of taxicabs doubled.

4.4. Pharmacies

The number of pharmacies is effectively capped. Regulations governing Community Pharmacy Contractor Agreements call for a determination of need.[43] These contracts, which cover pharmaceutical purchases that are reimbursable, amount to a necessary condition for running a viable pharmacy. A "definite public health need" would exist for a service area that has at least 4 000 people and no incumbent pharmacy within 250 meters (in rural areas, 2 500 people and 5 kilometres). Moreover, and regardless of these quantitative rules, local health boards that approve the contracts must consider their effects on existing pharmacies. Entry of a new contractor must not have an "adverse impact on the viability" of incumbents that would affect the "quality of pharmacy services" they are providing. One local health board refused a licence application for a new pharmacy in village that had no pharmacy at all, in part because it would hurt business at an existing pharmacy in another nearby town. The village where the new entry was refused, Knock, is a pilgrimage destination for the sick.

These regulations are relatively new. Entry to the profession in Ireland had been limited for many years until EC mutual recognition requirements and an expansion of university places in the UK increased the supply in the late 1980s. In response, the Irish Pharmaceutical Union, the trade association of established pharmacies, sought protection. Legislation to restrict the entry of foreign-trained pharmacists was rejected because it would be contrary to EC law. But a derogation from the EC mutual

207

recognition requirement limits the ability of pharmacists qualified elsewhere to supervise or manage a new pharmacy in Ireland. And in 1996 the Minister for Health introduced these regulations, which give incumbents power to prevent entry in the planning process. These regulations contradict the policies adopted shortly afterwards in the government's reform process, calling for eliminating licence requirements that prevent competition. Prospects for change appear poor. The Consumer Association of Ireland has tried, without success, to discuss its objections to these regulations with the Minister for Health, while the Authority and DETE have advocated reform.

4.5. Professional services

Many professional sectors are self-regulated, setting and applying their own standards for entry, provisions for professional training, codes of conduct, and recommended fee scales. Examples are the engineering, legal, medical, dental and auditing professions. For many professions, these standards are recognised, at least tacitly, by legislation (Ireland, 2000). The associations for auditors and for solicitors have statutory recognition, while those for architects, engineers, and surveyors are independent (Ireland, 2000). In the health sector, there are several recognised regulatory bodies, for opticians,[44] nurses,[45] hospitals,[46] dentists,[47] doctors,[58] and pharmacists.[49] In October 2000, the Department of Health and Children published for comment a proposed program of statutory registration for health and social professionals. This program would formalise the process of recognising and ensuring competence to practise, by establishing self-regulatory bodies separate from the professions' trade associations. The process would still be dominated by the professionals, though, because the boards would typically have only one consumer member, and a majority would be practising professionals. Competition issues raised by the rules and practices of self-regulated professions are treated in more detail in the background report to Chapter 6, with particular attention to the legal professions.

Box 7.   Advice about retail regulation

To date, retail competition in Ireland has been strong (with some exceptions due to regulatory constraints), and entry has been open to large operations, mostly from the UK. One result was relatively low inflation attributable to consumer prices in the 1990s (EIU, 2000). But land use planning processes give incumbents substantial power to resist greenfield entry in retail.

Small retailers have demanded still more protection. A Report from the parliamentary Joint Committee on Enterprise and Small Business called for a host of constraints: reducing maximum store size (from 3 000 m² to 2 500 m²), requiring in-country purchasing offices and suppliers, prohibiting large stores from opening overnight and limiting their Sunday opening hours, and "monitoring" and discouraging free parking at large stores and encouraging shoppers to park in town instead. And it called for studying means of setting up co-operative trading organisations to reduce the losses smaller stores were experiencing from the shift to centralised distribution.

The Authority argued against a single national rule; rather, a planning-based approach should leave room for local variation and decision, to respond to local concerns and situations. And it objected that rules based only on a store's size would be anti-competitive. Protecting small and inefficient Irish retailers would do them no favours, for in the long run their survival would depend on becoming efficient. The Authority pointed out that efforts to favour Irish firms over foreign competitors would probably violate EU competition principles. And it doubted that city fathers, trying to clear congestion from city-centre streets, would welcome measures to encourage more traffic.

The final Retail Planning Guidelines were issued in January, 2001, after a study was commissioned by the government to examine the likely impact of the proposed guidelines on competition, consumer prices, consumer choice, and suppliers.

Some professions are calling for a kind of exemption from the competition law, by treating their collective actions under the labour law rather than competition law. The Authority is considering a notified agreement that seeks this treatment. The professions that have expressed interest include free-lance journalists and hospital consultants. When the issue arose in a court proceeding against the veterinarians' association, the labour federation did not support a proposal to expand the labour law's coverage.

4.6. Consumer credit

A form of price control applies to certain finance charges. The Office of Consumer Affairs has power, under 1996 regulations, to approve or disapprove credit institutions' charges (other than interest rates). The statute calls for fee increases to be judged with "regard to the promotion of fair competition" between credit institutions, as well as claims of commercial justification, passing on costs to customers, and effects on customers more generally.[50] These regulations were borrowed from banking legislation, and the regulatory responsibility may be transferred to the proposed single financial regulator when that is established. The criterion of "fair competition" among institutions could be misapplied to effect uniformity, rather than rivalry. Rate regulation demanding "commercial justification" seems inappropriate unless there is a showing of market power. To the extent the problem it addresses is consumers' lack of information about charges, that problem would be better addressed by standardised disclosure requirements.

4.7. Other products

A private sector company has enjoyed *de facto* monopoly rights in cement manufacture. Under the Cement Acts, 1933 to 1962, manufacturing cement requires a licence from DETE, and only one firm has a licence. The government proposes to repeal the Cement Acts, and two firms have undertaken to enter, having been assured that the licence requirement will not be applied. Maintaining the monopoly implied an inconsistent commitment to competition as a principle; the promised repeal will be welcome. Wholesale petroleum suppliers must still source 20% of their requirements from the state-owned oil refinery (a figure that had been 35% a few years ago; the government has announced plans to dispose of the refinery and end this requirement). The state forestry operation is a *de facto* monopoly, because private sector forestry is not yet competitive in the Irish Republic. When the firm tried to gain control of a competitor in Northern Ireland, the Authority recommended that the acquisition be blocked, and the Minister followed that advice (OECD CLP, 1999). The operation has now been privatised, but it remains a monopoly. The government continues to study how it should be structured. An opportunity was missed to establish this sector on a competitive basis at the outset of privatisation.

4.8. Other transport sectors

Trucking was liberalised in the 1980s. Attention is now turning to bus services (on inter-city routes). A study by Forfás recommends reforms that would lead to competition for the bus sector, rather than within it. A bottleneck element of the air transport system, airport services, will become subject to a new regulator, who would authorise airport charges, regulate ground handling, allocate slots, and administer some other programmes. Regulation to control monopoly elements of airport service may be called for, because distances and limited land transport infrastructure prevent competition among Ireland's airports for domestic services. A Forfás study suggests that this new regulator also take on the regulatory functions for seaports.

5. COMPETITION ADVOCACY FOR REGULATORY REFORM

The Authority has tried to move into an advocacy role, but making advocacy effective will require more resources and clearer independence.

Although the Authority's predecessors occasionally prepared and issued reports on competition issues, those were not part of a systematic programme of advocacy. The Fair Trade Commission, in its 1989 report proposing a new competition law, recommended that the new competition body "have a responsibility to examine proposed legislation and regulations from a competition viewpoint and to make public statements where, in its view, the legislation or regulations would be anti-competitive" (FTC, 1989). It also recommended that the new agency have similar powers to report about anti-competitive features of existing legislation. But those recommendations did not become part of the new law. Instead, the 1991 law only authorised the Authority to respond to requests from DETE for studies (Sec. 11) or investigations (Sec. 14).

The Authority obtained the power to initiate studies on its own, without waiting for a request from the Minister, in the 1996 amendments. It has applied this power to high-priority problems. The first project it undertook was a comprehensive study of the retail drinks market, and another "discussion paper" targeted the problems of the taxi industry. A study of competition issues in transport had to be suspended because of resource constraints.

DETE, rather than the Authority, is generally responsible for reviewing legislative proposals to assess their effect on competition policy. There is no statutory basis for the Authority to participate on its own behalf in systematic review and comment about legislative proposals. DETE may ask for the Authority's views about draft laws and regulations, which would be transmitted through DETE. In this way, the Authority has commented on proposals about digital TV, superstores, and retail planning guidelines.

Authority comments have aided the process of reforming traditional utility sectors. In 1997, the Authority submitted views in response to a Ministerial request about proposals to reform the electricity supply industry (Competition Authority, 1997b). The comments emphasised that promoting competition could require separating the industry's operations vertically and limiting the amount of generating capacity under one firm's control. The Authority also raised questions about the relative merits of the "third party access" and "single buyer" models. The Authority supported establishing a separate regulatory regime to deal with access charges and output prices, leaving other competition related issues to be addressed under the general competition law. In 1998, the Authority submitted a similar comment to DPE about transmission and pricing issues in natural gas (Competition Authority, 1998e).

The resources available for analysis and advocacy, at DETE and at the Authority, are limited, One economist at the Authority works with policy staff at other departments and regulators, in addition to work on the Authority's other responsibilities. To do the function well, the Authority believes it would need to assign 2 or 3 professional staff. At DETE, only half of the competition policy staff (of 8 or 9) is available, as the rest are involved in merger review. The informal, ad hoc nature of the process makes it harder to use these few resources effectively. Comments are typically requested late, when there is little time for a thorough response – and perhaps little prospect of affecting the outcome, for positions may have already become inflexible.

The Authority would be a more effective advocate if its role were more public and more clearly independent. The CMRG made detailed recommendations to strengthen the Authority's advocacy capability and to help ensure that the competition impact of proposed laws and rules is considered carefully.[51] These fall somewhat short of establishing a completely free-ranging advocacy power, for the Authority could only comment on a proposal if the sponsoring Minister requested it. But concerning primary legislation at least, the sponsoring Minister would have to provide a public justification if the Authority's views were not requested. The CMRG also calls for other measures, and more resources, to clarify and strengthen the Authority's advocacy function, including express statutory power to review and assess the impact of existing, as well as proposed, legislation and of the regulations issued by regulators responsible for particular sectors, trades, or professions. DETE too supports giving the Authority a stronger, more independent advocacy role, even though the result could be to reduce DETE's own influence and control over the process because other ministries would deal directly with the Authority.

6. CONCLUSIONS AND POLICY OPTIONS

6.1. Current strengths and weaknesses

The importance of competition policy in market reform is recognised and supported at the highest levels in Ireland. Competition policy is a principal substantive criterion of regulatory quality in the SMI reform programme of the Prime Minister's office. The Ministers with the largest stake, at DETE and DPE, support the competition policy principles of reform. As in many other countries, reform has been prodded by EU directives. In Ireland, the visibly positive results of liberalising trade, inviting foreign investment, and introducing more competition should help build even broader support.[52] Effective competition policy will be viewed as important to stimulating innovation and production while keeping price increases in check. It can thus help eliminate bottlenecks to achieving growth without inflation.

To achieve the benefits of reform, though, policy must move away from emphasis on protection of incumbents against innovation and competition. The strength of this tendency to protect incumbents appears in the persistence of barriers to new entry in pubs and taxi services, the continued support for anti-competitive regulations like the Groceries Order, and the appearance of new constraints on competition in pharmacies and retail trade. As in other countries, change comes more slowly in such sheltered sectors, where EU institutions are less likely to reach and where producer support for the status quo is strong.

Consumer interests are not well represented in policy debate and deliberation in Ireland, which remain dominated by producer interests. Consultation with consumer groups tends to come late, asking for pro forma comment on a finished product rather than help in creating it. No consumer group is among the nearly 40 bodies identified as participants in the negotiation of the social partners' "Programme for Prosperity and Fairness." The "social partnership" process has expanded beyond the traditional economic interests, but it still does not incorporate the most inclusive interest, with the most to gain from pro-competitive reform, namely the consuming public at large.

In many respects, Ireland's competition policy institutions have followed international best practices. The Authority was established with broad jurisdiction, decision-making independence, and the capacity for sophisticated fact-finding and analysis. Applying modern economic concepts, it has adopted a programme based on consumer welfare and efficiency. After clearing most of the initial flood of notifications and issued a category licence about vertical restraints, it has turned its new enforcement powers to hard-core cartels. Expert observers from the Irish bar find that the Authority's opinions and analysis are first-quality.

But these strengths of laws and institutions have been compromised by a lack of resources, unclear independence, and inconsistent leadership. The Authority's continuing resource problems suggest that the relationship between the Authority and the department that controls its budget and shares many of its powers needs improvement. A dramatic decline in staff, which coincided with the change in Authority leadership in early 2000, called attention to the urgency of this issue. The demand from the private sector and from other, new regulators for professionals with competition policy expertise surely aggravated the Authority's personnel problems.

Competition policy institutions have been employed only sporadically in the process of reforming economic regulations. Responsibilities are spread among DETE, DPE, its sectoral regulators, and the Authority. In policy matters, DETE plays some role, mostly behind the scenes, while the Authority, with limited resources, appears only infrequently. The Authority's well-publicised enforcement stance, and its reputation for being aggressive, may have weakened its appeal as a potential source of policy advice for other agencies.

Reliance on criminal processes and penalties has introduced technical problems that delay the Authority's major enforcement programme. Because well-publicised cases still have not been resolved   211 by convictions, and indeed no criminal sanctions were imposed at all until October 2000, potential allies in the consumer movement believe that the Authority lacks power or will.

For mergers, the decision process appears to permit politicisation and risks some uncertainty. Some provision for public interest judgements may well be appropriate, but the process should be more transparent, and the trade-offs should be recognised more forthrightly.

Ireland now has a modern competition law and enforcement structure, but several opportunities to make policy more effective were missed. The Prices Acts and Groceries Order survived the three major legislative reforms, in 1987, 1991, and again in 1996. Criminal sanctions were created without giving enough attention to the legal tools that would be needed to make them work well in practice. Privatisation proceeded without ensuring competitive conditions in sectors such as forestry.

6.2. Capacities for and impediments to change

As Ireland's economy has prospered, the direction of its economic policy attention has shifted, toward factors that promote efficiency[53] But despite the seemingly rapid changes in the economy itself, policy change in this new direction has been almost deliberately slow and evolutionary.

The institutional basis for incorporating competition into regulation systematically is still under development. The criterion of competitive effect in the SMI checklist remains an exhortation, until it becomes clear that failure to meet this criterion has real consequences. The CMRG proposes a stronger advocacy role for the Authority, but that is still a proposal. DPE took an *ad hoc* approach to the synthesis of competition and regulation in particular sectors. DPE's proposal for a more comprehensive approach postpones addressing this very issue, leaving it for further consultation. Meanwhile, as DPE proceeds to design structures and rules sector by sector, the bodies that are explicitly responsible for developing and applying competition policy play a consulting role, commenting on the proposal but not responsible for it.

The institutional framework for applying competition policy too is a work in progress. The Minister's action in appointing a new chair and supporting proposed reforms to increase the chair's management authority shows support for continued vigour. This degree of centralisation may over-correct for any problem of diffuse leadership. On the other hand, as the Authority's chief function shifts from deciding about applications to investigating and prosecuting, a single-executive structure may be more effective. Other changes may be coming, to adapt to changes in EU process. To deal with them, the CMRG's report, which represents a tremendous investment of intellectual resources, provides many useful ideas and resources. The CMRG recommendations about merger processes and some other subjects should be implemented without waiting to see what direction the EU ultimately takes. For some other topics, though, the CMRG report seems premature and hypothetical. Rather than radically redesign institutions that have hardly been tested, it will be better to give the Authority, the DPP, and the courts more of a chance to show whether the present system can be made to work.

6.3. Potential benefits and costs of further regulatory reform

A major benefit of continued pro-competitive reform could be to help Ireland control inflation. Greater competition can discipline pricing due to market power, and it can improve efficiency and thus productivity, helping keep inflation down while maintaining growth. The extent of the possible benefit is suggested by experiences with other reforms, and by analysis of some of the current problems.

Experience already shows how reform pays off. Opening up the airline market to competition reduced fares and expanded service, and also increased employment in the long run as tourism grew. Reforms in telecoms too have expanded services. The annual benefits from reform in airlines and telecoms have been estimated to be IR£ 1 billion.

Estimates of potential gains if other problems can be solved are also substantial. One example is pubs. The real prices of packaged beer, where retail sales competition is open to new entry, and on-licence beer at a pub, where entry is closed, have diverged over the last 15 years. Prices for package retail sale have declined, while prices in the pubs have increased, so that the indexes of the prices in the competitive package sector and the non-competitive pub sector have diverged by as much as 25%, for a product on which Ireland spends 5% of its GDP (Fingleton, 1997). Another measure of the burden is the rents revealed in the aggregate value of taxi licences in Dublin – some IR£ 200 million (Fingleton, 2000). Estimates based on the aggregate value of the outstanding licences for pubs and taxis conclude that eliminating the constraints on entry in these sectors could produce a one-time saving of .4% of total personal expenditure, in addition to continuing savings from the elimination of market power.

To be sure, eliminating these overcharges and rents would also impose some costs, as the incumbents would lose the scarcity value of their licences, as well as the prospect of continuing to profit from market power. The long-run net effects of these changes on incumbents are unclear, though. Sometimes, eliminating a monopoly has led first to a decline in employment, but that has been followed by expansion of service that more than made up for the initial losses. The same may be true for employment in taxis and pubs.

6.4. Policy options for consideration

– *Remove licensing constraints on free entry, particularly those with quantitative limits.*

The SMI Working Group set this goal several years ago. The problem is not one of repealing explicit exemptions from the Competition Act, for there are none. The challenge is to identify and eliminate regulatory programmes and licensing schemes that have the effect of preventing entry and permitting non-competitive behaviour. The obvious targets are pubs and taxis. More detailed review by DETE is likely to identify other "quota"-like constraints. This review has antecedents. A 1992 report by an independent policy review group recommended a programme to relax controls, restrictions, licences, and other limitations that restricted entry into trades, professions, and services. The Minister for Enterprise and Employment reported to the parliament in 1994 that his Department had conducted "a wide review of regulations and restrictions which operate to restrict competition," requesting other Departments to identify controls or licensing systems in their areas of responsibility. That 1994 statement claimed progress concerning lawyers, opticians, electric power, telecoms, oil, gas, air and bus transport, broadcasting, taxi and hackney licensing, ports, and casual trade licences (CMRG, 1999). Seven years later, constraints on competition persist in nearly all of these sectors, but the recent action to eliminate limits in taxi service is a most welcome development – if it survives the pending challenge in the High Court. The CMRG commissioned a review of statutory controls that inhibit competition in several sectors, too.[54]

– *Eliminate special-interest rules that inhibit efficient competition, such as the Groceries Order.*

The potentially anti-competitive effects of the Groceries Order are well recognised. The CMRG's proposal, to eliminate rules aimed at sales supposedly below cost but retain some rules against anti-competitive discrimination and assertion of buyer power, seems sensible.

– *Apply competition policy against non-transparent, anti-competitive self-regulation of professions and services.*

This subject is treated at more length in another chapter of this study. These problems have already been the subject of enforcement action. Vigorous enforcement may be necessary, but the risk of backlash must also be managed. That is, the professions may seek legislative protection against further enforcement. To resist that plea, the Authority should be able to demonstrate how its action have yielded concrete consumer benefits.

– *Complete the process of introducing competition, and the application of general competition policy, in traditional monopoly sectors.*

This subject is treated at length in other chapters of this study.

– *Improve advocacy powers, with clearer authorisation for more independent, wide-ranging analysis, clearer responsibilities on other agencies to consult with the Authority, and more resources to do the job.*

213

The statute should be amended, if needed to authorise more clearly a broad-ranging analysis and advocacy role for the Authority. The Authority should act on its own right, and it should participate at the outset, rather than offering futile commentary at the end of the process. The CMRG recommendation presents a useful model for advocacy powers. Ministers sponsoring legislation should be free to request the Authority's views directly, without going through DETE, about the proposal's implications for competition. Ministers should explain their views about the proposals' likely impacts and the reasons why restraints on competition could be justified in the public interest, and they should state whether they have consulted the Authority. The Authority's opinion would become public when the bill is published. Similarly, Ministers should be free to consult the Authority about the effects of proposed regulations, and the Authority's views about them would be made public along with the regulations. Providing for more systematic competition analysis of regulations and decisions below the level of legislation could be particularly important. Input from the Authority should be routine before departments adopt rules that limit entry and competition. More broadly, the CMRG calls for empowering the Authority to publish general discussion papers, to participate in the development of national policies that may affect competition, to co-operate with sectoral regulators, and to appear before parliamentary committees concerning issues that may affect competition. To do these things effectively, the Authority will need another economist or two.

- *Clarify the respective roles of sectoral regulators and the Authority to ensure a co-ordinated, uniform competition policy approach in the regulated sectors.*

Here many of the CMRG recommendations should be followed, to provide for a structured process of co-ordination and a legal basis for the agencies to defer to each other without risk and without diluting or compromising the application of competition policy. The Authority and sectoral regulators should advise each other about matters that may come under the others' jurisdiction, and consult when they find they are both pursuing the same matter.[55] To do this meaningfully, they must have the right to exchange information with each other. Having someone from the Authority sit on appeal panels for sectoral regulator decision is an excellent idea for integrating policy perspectives.

- *Clarify and make operational the criteria about competitive effects in the SMI checklist and standards.*

The competition policy criteria in the SMI checklist may be too general to guide non-expert bureaucrats. Either through additional guidance or training, they could be made more practical and specific. For example, they might operationalise the Working Group's recommendation to eliminate constraints that act like quotas limiting entry. And it must be clear that there will be some consequences if a rule, or a proposed rule, fails these criteria. An inter-agency conference might be useful, to show other agencies how to avoid creating competition problems in their regulation.

- *Make merger processes consistent, and eliminate the risks of overlap, uncertainty, and conflict.*

Maintaining two notification systems, reflecting a lingering jurisdictional skirmish, presents an accident waiting to happen. Before it produces an embarrassment such as contradictory orders from two regulators, the process should be streamlined and responsibility for competition policy reviews for all mergers clearly assigned to the Authority. Application of other public interest factors would then be up to the Minister. This change might require transferring some of the personnel at the Department, who now do the initial merger screenings, to the Authority, anticipating that they would continue performing that function there. In November 2000, the government decided to change the review process so that the Authority would have sole decision-making responsibility, except for mergers involving the media.

- *Authorise a "whistleblower" or leniency programme.*

Effective pursuit of the Authority's top priority will be aided greatly by a publicly announced offer of leniency to cartel members to give evidence against their co-conspirators. Implementing this would require close co-ordination between the Authority and the DPP, which would ultimately make any leniency determinations. Here, Ireland may wish to study the Canadian programme, for responsibilities there are also divided between the competition agency and the prosecutor. Generally applicable criminal procedures might support such a programme. If not, then special legislation or an authoritative policy statement would be needed.

    – *Consider ways to develop judicial expertise in competition matters.*

Competition law may still be novel for many Irish judges. The CMRG has recommended that competition cases be assigned to judges on the basis of their expertise in competition matters, both in the High Court and in Circuit Courts. This may accomplish the same thing as establishing a specialised competition court, but without the need for structural changes in the judicial system. Rather, it could presumably be accomplished by court rule, adopted by the judges themselves.

    – *Make the Authority more independent with respect to budget and staffing decisions.*

Advocacy and especially a formal review role could only work if there is a statutory basis for Authority independence, as well as independence from indirect control through the government budget. The Authority should have the same hiring flexibility that is enjoyed by the regulatory bodies under DPE. Permitting the Authority to exceed civil service salary caps could improve its retention experience. After the crisis of 1999 and early 2000, DETE has taken steps to bring the Authority and its staff up to authorised levels. At a minimum, that process should be completed. Additional investigative staff from the gardaí will aid the enforcement program. And additional economic resources will enable the Authority to revive its analysis and advocacy functions.

6.5. Managing regulatory reform

The leading method for advancing competition policy now appears to be law enforcement. The Authority is trying to demonstrate that the new competition policy tools can identify, punish, and correct problems that directly affect consumer welfare. This strategy explains its early and continued pursuit of high-profile enforcement actions, such as the civil actions against the pub associations. By March 2000, newspapers were reporting that the Authority had referred findings about price fixing among wholesalers for prosecution.[56] (The Authority may have missed an opportunity to demonstrate some quick, early successes by bringing more summary prosecutions on its own initiative, which would not have to be referred to the DPP. The first completed criminal case, in October 2000, was a summary prosecution brought by the Authority). There is some risk that this emphasis on enforcement, targeting criminal violations, has positioned the Authority outside the policy debate. To reduce that risk will require devoting attention again to advocacy.

Presenting novel policy ideas effectively requires careful attention to background expectations and traditions. In Ireland, reaction to economic policy steps such as privatisation has been coloured by impressions about the nearby experiences in the UK. Thus, it may be helpful if reform proposals and decisions can be presented and explained in terms of their contrast with UK efforts that seem to have faltered, or their consistency with UK experiences that turned out well. Another background condition is Ireland's tradition of favouring producer interests, in part because of cultural memories of a society dominated by small, family enterprises. Perhaps reforms should be designed and presented in ways that are consistent both with consumer interests and efficiency and with the interests of at least some important producers. Repeal of the Groceries Order may require introducing particular rules about discrimination and unfair transacting practices, to accommodate producers' concerns. Solving the problems in pubs and taxis will probably require compensating the incumbents in some way, although that will dilute the benefits of the reform.

The moment is right to take action with long-term benefits, for prosperity and full employment will cushion short-term adjustment shocks.[57]

NOTES

1. References to the "Competition Act" are to the Competition Act, 1991. All citations are to this Act, unless otherwise noted.

2. Irish Constitution, Art. 45.

3. Unless otherwise indicated, references to the "Minister" are to the Minister for Enterprise, Trade and Employment.

4. Irish Independent, online edition http://www.independent.ie/, 18 July 2000; Irish Times, online edition, www.ireland.com/newspaper, 18 July 2000

5. An association of "undertakings" may itself be an "undertaking", so that agreements entered by the association are subject to the law (as is the overall agreement establishing the association itself) (Fingleton, 1997).

6. This application was withdrawn before the Authority reached a decision.

7. Contractors; CA/836/92, cited in (Fingleton, 1997, p. 101).

8. Optometry; Authority Decision No. 17, 1993, cited in (Fingleton, 1997, p. 101).

9. In addition, the statute provides detailed rules about defensive arguments that could arise in situations involving the licensing process.

10. The CMRG recommends legislation to grant immunity to persons to make complaints or furnish information about violations of the Competition Act, and sets out numerous technical matters and possible resolutions of them (CMRG, 2000; Recommendation 10). The focus of this recommendation seems to be on protecting the "whistleblower" employee who gives evidence against a firm that is in a cartel, rather than on granting lenient treatment to the firm itself. But the latter idea could also be included in the CMRG's proposal.

11. Decision No. 528 of December 4, 1998.

12. Decision No. 336, 1994.

13. One phrase in the law, which is not paralleled in the EU law, implies a limitation in coverage. That is, Ireland prohibits abuse of a position that is dominant "in trade" for goods or services. This phase could imply that a third party, such as a trade association setting standards or terms for its members, that does not itself participate in the "trade" could not be found to be in a dominant position. Such a situation could probably be treated as a restrictive agreement among the association and its members.

14. Criminal sanctions could apply to abuse of dominance (Competition (Amendment) Act 1996, Sec. 2(7)). The Authority has indicated as a matter of policy that it does not propose to bring criminal proceedings for such cases.

15. The CMRG recommends incorporating these criteria into legislation about mergers, subject to their compatibility with Community law (CMRG, 2000, Recommendation 29).

16. text implies that the Minister could act even if the Authority did not find dominance and abuse.

17. In principle, the Mergers Acts do not apply to banks, but because bank mergers are usually accomplished through corporate forms that the laws do cover, the exception has little practical significance.

18. "HHI" is the Herfindahl-Hirschman index, which is computed as the sum of the squares of the market shares of each of the firms in the relevant market.

19. This scheme echoes the thresholds in the US Merger Guidelines.

20. Notification must be made within one month after the parties reach agreement on the transaction (or an offer is made that the other party could accept).

21. In addition, the Mergers Acts apply to any acquisition or merger involving a newspaper or magazine, regardless of size.

22. Art. 13(1)(a).

23. It may be possible to "amend" the Order by repealing parts of it, without repealing it all.

24. The CMRG recommends making the Director of Competition Enforcement a separate, staff-level position, rather than one of the Authority members. One motivation is to separate the functions of investigation and prosecution from decision-making, out of concern that information learned through the process of reviewing notifications could be misused in enforcement proceedings. The CMRG is evidently concerned that firms will be reluctant to notify their agreements, if the information might later be used in a prosecution or to support a decision about a proposed merger. But the notification process is becoming less important, for firms and for the Authority. Another motivation for the proposal could be to reduce the Director's power and the risk of conflict with the priorities of the chair and the other members

25. The Garda Síochána is the national police force; the literal translation is "guardians of the peace".

26. The CMRG's final report makes many technical recommendations to improve aspects of the investigation and enforcement process, about such topics as search warrant standards, the power of "arrest" to lead to admissions, targets' rights to consult counsel in connection with dawn raids, and rules of evidence.

27. For non-enforcement actions, the CMRG recommends establishing a 4 month deadline for Authority decisions on applications for licences (CMRG, 2000, Recommendation 34).

28. The CMRG report tries to correct this lack of consideration, after the fact. Because filing a criminal case after a civil case could force defendants to "give evidence" against themselves in the civil proceeding, the CMRG recommends that the public enforcer should complete its criminal proceeding first. It recommends assigning competition cases in the high court to specially qualified judges. Because there is no provision for exemplary damages or administrative fines in Irish law, to retain the deterrent effect the CMRG recommends keeping criminal penalty despite the attendant procedural and conceptual complications (CMRG, 2000, Recommendation 6).

29. The CMRG recommends that the statute be amended to require the Authority to furnish detailed written reasons for its decisions (CMRG, 2000, Recommendation 36). As a practical matter, this would just ratify current practice. As a legal matter, though making this a statutory obligation could lead to collateral challenges and litigation about the Authority's decision processes.

30. Irish Independent, web edition, 23 March 2000.

31. The relationship degenerated to the point that the Authority chairman brought a lawsuit over the adequacy of benefits. Irish Independent, 2 August 1996; Irish Times, 2 August 1996.

32. There had been discussions about the possibility of adding 5 investigators from the gardaí to the Authority staff, for example. The status of those discussions is unclear.

33. State firms that are engaged in regulatory functions are effectively exempt with respect to those functions, although not with respect to their commercial or revenue-producing operations The exemption follows from the definition of an "undertaking" that is subject to the law and to legal remedies, as an entity engaged "for gain" in production, supply, or distribution of a good or service (Competition Act, Sec. 3(1)).

34. Competition Authority Decision No. 1, Notification No. CA/8/91, *Nallen/O'Toole* (1992). The statement was *dictum* in the particular decision, which approved a non-competition agreement that accompanied the sale of a small repair shop.

35. The total number of retail outlets of all kinds, including hotels, restaurants, and stores selling packages for off-premises consumption, is about 15 000.

36. To serve intoxicating liquor, a restauranteur must either apply for a restaurant certificate in conjunction with a wine retailer's on-licence or a publican's licence pursuant to Section 12 of the Intoxicating Liquor Act 1927, or a Special Restaurant Licence. The Special Restaurant Licence, introduced in 1988, permits the sale of the full range of alcoholic drinks. The Intoxicating Liquor Act, 2000, allows restaurants with full restaurant certificate and wine on-licence to serve beer with a meal, abolishes the requirement that the waiting area be not greater than 20% of the dining area, and abolishes the requirement for a Bord Failte certificate for restaurants operating on the basis of a Special Restaurant Licence.

37. Act 17 of 2000, 30 June 2000.

38. The commission is expected to report on the off-licence sector within 3 months of its first meeting, set for March 2001.

39. There is no limit on the number of licences for wheel-chair accessible vehicles, for which the required fee has been IR£ 15 000; the licensee must also operate a specially equipped vehicle. The aggregate cost of setting up to operate with this kind of licence is estimated to be about IR£ 42 500 (Competition Authority, 1998c).

40. The 1998 paper by the chair of the Authority argued that incremental reform would not work as long as licences remained transferable and thus valuable. Although rapid, complete liberalisation of entry would be even better, it recommended eliminating licence transferability first, in order to begin the process of dissipating the rents and reducing the licence value to 0 (Competition Authority, 1998c).

41. Irish Independent, web edition, 15 January 2000, 17 January 2000.

42. Irish Independent, web edition, 22 March 2000.

43. Health (Community Pharmacy Contractor Agreement) Regulations, 1996 SI No. 152 of 1996; definition of "definite public health need", Regulation 2(1).

44. Bord na Radharcmhastoiri (The Opticians Board), established under the Opticians Act, 1956.

45. An Bord Altranais (The Nursing Board), established under the Nurses Act, 1950.

46. Comhairle na Ospideal (The Hospitals Council), established under the Health Act, 1970.

47. The Dental Council, established under the Dentists Act, 1985.

48. The Medical Council, established under the Medical Practitioners Act, 1978.

49. Pharmaceutical Society of Ireland, established under the Pharmacy Act, 1875.

50. Sec. 149(8), Consumer Credit Act of 1995.

51. Concerning primary legislation, sponsoring Ministers would be free to request the Authority's views directly. Even if they did not, legislative proposals would have to be accompanied by a competitive impact statement, explaining whether the proposal would impair competition, and if so, why the restriction is justified in the public interest. If the Authority's views were sought and obtained, the Authority's opinion should be made public when the proposed bill is published. For proposed regulations, similarly, sponsoring Ministers would be free to request views directly from the Authority, and those views would be published along with the regulations (CMRG, 2000, Recommendation 17).

52. As the chair of the Authority has observed (Fingleton, 2000):

    [I]n the industries where regulatory reform and liberalisation have occurred (such as telephony, broadcasting and electricity generation), competition from new entrants is developing apace. This new environment has forced enormous change on the former monopolies. Substantial growth of many of the markets, something that accompanies increased efficiency, means that redundancies to deal with historic overstaffing have not increased unemployment. Consumer choice has expanded and the quality of service improved as former monopolies switch from a focus on technical and engineering proficiency to an emphasis on the consumer and the market. New product markets and innovative services have developed where entrants see profitable opportunities. Dramatic falls in telephony prices illustrate how competition and regulatory policies can simultaneously be expansionary and counter-inflationary.

53. "[T]here has been a startling transformation in economic policy in which the emphasis has moved from meeting macroeconomic targets to a detailed focus on microeconomic efficiency. Competition and regulatory policies play an essential part in a portfolio that also includes reforms of taxation and company law" (Fingleton, 2000).

54. See (CMRG, 1999), p. 220, No. 350. This report was evidently not published.

55. Making the agencies meet together quarterly to make sure they really do this seems like an oddly precise requirement, but its inclusion in the CMRG recommendation recognises, unfortunately, the history of suspicious relations among these agencies.

56. Irish Sunday Independent, web edition, 12 March 2000, 30 May 2000.

57. From (Fingleton, 2000):

    Although producer interests trump consumer interests, there are signs that this is changing. The positive experience in deregulating areas like telecommunications and air travel makes clear the enormous benefits from reform, and also removes fears concerning the dire scenarios predicted by the vested interests in such markets. As such, this early success builds momentum or constituencies for further change and makes it easier to argue for more extensive reform. In the first half of 2000, the Government finally started to tackle the problem in the Dublin taxi market, and has announced plans to introduce competition in the bus market in Dublin. A major review of competition law has recommended sweeping changes that would also benefit consumers, several of which were mentioned above and includes the abolition of the Groceries Order. On the other hand, greater competition increases the incentive for vested interests to seek protection by special regulation. As a result, we can expect exciting debates that raise complex economic, legal and political issues to continue in this area.

BIBLIOGRAPHY

Competition & Mergers Review Group (1999),
  Proposals for Discussion in Relation to Competition Law, Dublin.

Competition & Mergers Review Group (2000),
  Final Report, Dublin.

Economist Intelligence Unit (2000),
  Ireland: Country Profile 2000, London.

Fingleton, John and Oliver Hogan (2000), *The Economy of Ireland: Policy & Performance of a European Region*, Chapter 5, "Competition and Regulatory Policy", pp. 123-148, Gill and Macmillan, Dublin.

Fingleton, John, J. Evans and O. Hogan (1998), *The Dublin Taxi Market: Re-regulate or Stay Queuing?* Studies in Public Policy: 3, The Policy Institute, Trinity College, Dublin.

Fingleton, John (1997), "Standards of Competition in the Irish Economy," *Journal of the Statistical and Social Inquiry Society of Ireland*, vol. 27, part 4, p. 87 (paper presented 30 January 1997).

Government of Ireland (2000), Communication with OECD Secretariat.

Government of Ireland (1996), Competition Authority, *Annual Report 1995*, March.

Government of Ireland (1997), Competition Authority, Discussion Paper No. 2, *Second Submission to the Merger Review Group*, April.

Government of Ireland (1997*b*), Competition Authority, Discussion Paper No. 3, Patrick Massey, *Proposals for the Electricity Supply Industry in Ireland: Comments on the Consultation Paper published by the Department of Transport, Energy and Communications*, November.

Government of Ireland (1998), Competition Authority, *Annual Report 1997*, March.

Government of Ireland (1998*b*), Competition Authority, *Interim Study on the Liquor Licensing Laws and other Barriers to Entry and their impact on Competition in the Retail Drinks Market*, September.

Government of Ireland (1998*c*), Competition Authority, Discussion Paper No. 6, *Solving Dublin Taxi Problems: Urban-Sharecroppers v. Rentseekers*, November.

Government of Ireland (1998*d*), Competition Authority, Discussion Paper No. 4, Patrick Massey, *The Treatment of Vertical Restraints Under Competition Law*, May.

Government of Ireland (1998*e*), Competition Authority, Discussion Paper No. 5, Patrick Massey & Tony Shortall, *Competition in the Natural Gas Industry*, November.

Government of Ireland (1999), Competition Authority, Discussion Paper No. 9, *Response to the Competition and Mergers Review Group's Proposals for Discussion in relation to Competition Law*, December.

Government of Ireland (1999*b*), Competition Authority, *Response to the Minister for Public Enterprise's Invitation to Comment on Governance and Accountability Arrangements in the Regulatory Process*, December.

Government of Ireland (2000*b*), Department of Public Enterprise, *Governance and Accountability in the Regulatory Process: Policy Proposals*, March.

Government of Ireland (1989), Fair Trade Commission, *Study of Competition Law* (Pl. 7080).

OECD (1997), *The OECD Report on Regulatory Reform*, Paris.

OECD Committee on Competition Law and Policy (1995), *Annual Report on Competition Policy Developments in Ireland 1994*.

OECD Committee on Competition Law and Policy (1996), *Annual Report on Competition Policy Developments in Ireland 1995*.

OECD Committee on Competition Law and Policy (1997), *Annual Report on Competition Policy Developments in Ireland 1996*.

OECD Committee on Competition Law and Policy (1998), *Annual Report on Competition Policy Developments in Ireland 1997*.

OECD Committee on Competition Law and Policy (1999), *Annual Report on Competition Policy Developments in Ireland 1998*.

OECD Committee on Competition Law and Policy (2000), *Annual Report on Competition Policy Developments in Ireland 1999*.

BACKGROUND REPORT ON ENHANCING MARKET OPENNESS THROUGH REGULATORY REFORM*

* This report was principally prepared by **Denis Audet**, Administrator of the Trade Directorate with the participation of **Didier Campion**. It has benefited from extensive comments provided by colleagues throughout the OECD Secretariat, by the Government of Ireland, and by Member countries as part of the peer review process. This report was peer reviewed in December 2000 in the Working Party of the OECD's Trade Committee.

TABLE OF CONTENTS

List of Figures

Executive Summary

Background Report on Enhancing Market Openness through Regulatory Reform

Ireland's stellar growth performance in recent years reflects an array of policy reforms and in particular Ireland's commitments in the context of ongoing integration within the European Union, through the Single European Market Programme and the Economic and Monetary Union. Large and sustained foreign investment in skilled-labour-intensive and export-oriented sectors was a major driver of its economic success and has transformed the Irish production capacity and broadened its trading interest beyond the EU market. Despite the scope and depth of the EU integration process, Ireland increasingly trades with non-EU Member States, taking advantage of competitive input sourcing on a world basis and further re-enforcing the competitiveness of Irish production capacity.

Efforts were recently made to improve the process of elaborating domestic laws and regulations through the use of more rules-based procedures fostering transparency, public consultation and the use of the Quality Regulation Checklist (QRC). Despite positive changes, there are several deficiencies in the enforcement system. The regulatory approach relies only on qualitative criteria and ignores quantitative criteria, such as cost and benefit analysis. Departments have considerable discretionary power for carrying out the public consultation process in terms of the duration of the consultation and the selection of the interested parties that are consulted. It lacks an independent assessment body that would verify the compliance of the completed QRC with the required criteria and lacks guidelines and training for policy makers to assist them in completing the necessary requirements.

Interested parties have no access to the QRC. Improved availability of this regulatory tool to the public would add transparency to the process and act as a powerful way to formalise public consultation and, simultaneously, enhancing the quality of the QRC. These enforcement lacunae raise considerable doubts about the uniformity of application among Departments and the effectiveness of the QRC as a useful regulatory tool to assist policy makers in making the best policy and regulatory choice.

Efforts are made to reduce the role of government in economic activities by exposing previously sheltered sectors to competition forces. Similarly, systemic changes in regulatory functions are occurring through the transferring of regulatory responsibilities for certain infrastructure utility sectors from Departments to newly established independent sectoral regulators. Although the Irish Government is committed to market-based and liberal approaches, the incumbent state-owned enterprises still hold dominant positions in the energy sector and in the telecommunications sector, the former state-owned enterprise is still a significant market participant. Therefore concerns remain about the potential abuse of their dominant positions.

Ongoing economic successes are leading to capacity constraints and are threatening the sustainability of future economic performance. There is a need for balancing growth objectives with sound competitive conditions for ensuring efficient use of resources, labour in particular. Continuing focus on market openness through import competition will contribute to reduce inflationary pressures in wages and costs of building materials and of services. Import competition can play a crucial role in government procurement activities in facilitating the completion of projects on time and keeping downward cost pressures on goods and services purchased. Facilitating labour mobility within the EU and from abroad through the recognition of professional qualifications will be instrumental in improving the availability of required skills and for easing inflationary pressures, particularly in services-related sectors.

Ireland has gained commensurate benefits in pursuing trade liberalisation, welcoming foreign-owned firms and integrating in the world economy. Nevertheless, the recent economic expansion has overshadowed the need to put in place a more rules-based regulatory regime that fosters economic efficiency, minimises obstacles to growth and promotes sound competitive conditions. Ireland would be able to deal more effectively with eventual external shocks and a less favourable global economic environment if it were to strengthen its regulatory approaches. Ireland would maximise the return of its market openness approach by pursuing additional efforts to apply a set of efficient regulation principles as discussed in this review.

1. MARKET OPENNESS AND REGULATION: THE POLICY ENVIRONMENT IN IRELAND

Ireland achieved spectacular growth performance between 1994 and 1999 with an average annual growth rate in real GDP of 8.5%, far outstripping the OECD average of 2.9%, and bringing the cumulative increase to over 50% during this period.[1] An array of factors have contributed to this economic expansion, in particular Ireland's commitments in the context of ongoing integration within the European Union (EU), through the Single European Market Programme and the Economic and Monetary Union. Favourable demographic changes, due to a relatively late baby boom, compounded by qualitative components through human capital accumulation, have also been instrumental for its economic performance – 66% of the population in the 25 to 34 age group had completed at least upper secondary education in 1996. Foreign investors, partly lured by generous incentives, have recognised the attractiveness of Ireland and made significant investment in skilled-labour-intensive and export-oriented sectors that have transformed Irish production capacity and broadened Ireland's trading interest beyond the EU market.

Ireland acceded to the European Economic Communities (EEC) in 1973, ten years after its initial application to join was withdrawn when the simultaneous application by the United Kingdom was rejected. The setback and the search for alternative trade arrangements led to a series of unilateral across-the-board tariff cuts in 1963 and 1964 and the Anglo-Irish Free Trade Agreement in December 1965, which provided for a gradual phase out of reciprocal tariff protection over a ten-year period. Closer economic integration with its main trading partners, through market openness, was considered a necessary policy to improve its economic prosperity and to curb a long-term trend of emigration – in the 1950s, around 1.5% of the population in net terms was departing every year.[2]

With its EU membership, Ireland has foregone the right to follow an independent trade policy but in return it has gained improved market access to other EU member markets and a voice in the process of elaborating the EU's common external trade policy. Accession meant that it had to assume all prevailing EU rights and obligations, the *"Acquis communautaire"*, some of it immediately upon accession and the rest over a transitional period. These reforms rapidly brought positive results with higher economic growth and lower unemployment.

However, the economic progress was eroded and Ireland became almost bankrupt when it pursued a policy of budget deficits during the high interest rate period of the late 1970s and early 1980s. Economic growth resumed in 1987 following broader social consensus for a macroeconomic stability programme based on government deficit reductions.

As EU member countries agreed to further their integration process, Ireland was required to provide free movement in the areas of goods, services, capital and people – the four freedoms – to other EU member countries in return for similar commitments. The Single European Market Programme (SEM), aimed at eliminating internal obstacles to trade within the EU, has acted as a strong policy anchor and was instrumental in the Irish success in attracting foreign investment in projects designed to serve the EU-wide market and beyond. The SEM Directives have had wide spread effects as they put downward pressure on costs and prices and encouraged rationalisation in several sectors. It was estimated that Ireland has grown at about one percentage point faster per year than it would otherwise have done.[3]

Since 1989, Ireland has considerably benefited from the EU structural and cohesion funds aimed at reducing economic and social disparities among EU country members. The annual transfers to Ireland from the Community Structural Funds was estimated at 2.8% of GDP between 1989 and 1993, the level declined afterwards, but still amounted to 2.25% in 1997 and 1998 (Barry *et al.*, 1997). More than half of these transfers was allocated to human resource development and physical infrastructure projects, which enhanced productive potential without adding budgetary pressure. Although Ireland's success has brought its per capita GDP above the EU average, its eligibility under the EU Community Support Framework will continue for the period 2000-2006, but on a different basis than previously, with eligibility criteria now varying depending on the regional location of projects.

With a population of about 3.7 million, the lowest among OECD countries after Iceland and Luxembourg, trade is increasingly important to the Irish economy, with total merchandise trade amounting to 125.1% of GDP in 1999 and up from 102.4% in 1993 (Table 1). This ratio is about twice higher than corresponding ratios for other OECD countries with small population – New Zealand (44.1%), Norway (54.8%), Portugal (58.2%), Finland (60.2%) and Sweden (65.2%). This high ratio reflects the strong and growing integration of Ireland within the world economy with an increasing share of its total trade carried out with non-EU countries (Table 4). In terms of tariff protection, the average nominal rate of duty was estimated at 25% in 1966 and reduced to 5% in 1976 due to various market openness initiatives (O'Malley).[4] In 2001, once all EU tariff reduction commitments undertaken during the Uruguay Round are fully implemented, the average unweighted tariff rate on industrial products is scheduled to be 3.7% (3.0% taking account of tariff elimination commitments of the WTO Information Technology Agreement).[5] Another indicator of market openness is the ratio of customs receipts to merchandise imports which was estimated at 20% in 1960, 13% in 1970 and 0.9% in 1990 (Ó Gráda).[6]

Table 1.　Merchandise trade in Ireland

Trade (% of GDP)	1993	1995	1999
Exports	58.5%	67.2%	75.4%
Imports	43.9%	49.8%	49.7%
Export + Imports	102.4%	117.0%	125.1%

Source:　Ireland's Central Statistics Office.

Figure 1.　**Ireland real GDP growth rates and current account balances**

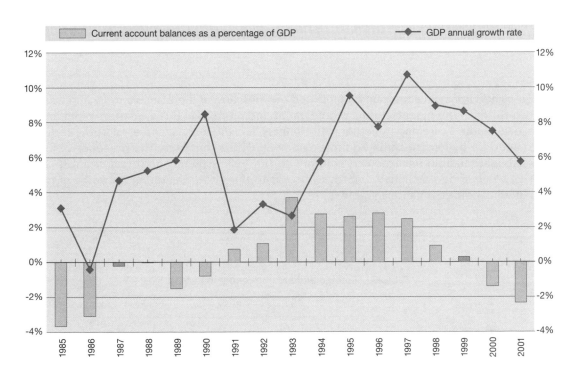

Note:　Data are estimated for 1999 and projected for 2000-2001.

Source:　OECD Economic Outlook (1999), December.

Ireland has long made efforts to enhance its attractiveness as a host country for foreign direct investment (FDI): several restrictions on foreign ownership were removed as early as 1958 and various programmes were set up to encourage FDI. More recently, several factors have been instrumental in Ireland's success in attracting greenfield investments in skilled-labour-intensive and export-oriented sectors, such as information and communications technologies, financial services, healthcare and pharmaceuticals. Among the explanatory factors for its success are: access to the EU-wide market, the availability of high skilled labour at a reasonable cost, a preferential tax system, an industrial agglomeration in electronics and pharmaceuticals, and a linguistic/cultural affinity with US investors. Irish programmes to attract foreign investment have caused some controversy and EU Member States have complained about the competition-distorting impact of the Irish preferential tax system. Prior to 1995, FDI originating from the United States accounted for about half of total FDI and this share has exceeded three-quarters in the period 1995-1998 (Table 2). Reflecting the relative attractiveness of Ireland among OECD countries, Ireland's share of total OECD inward FDI increased by a factor of six during the 1988-1998 period (Table 2).

Table 2.   Foreign Direct Investment, inflows

FDI	1988	1990	1995	1996	1997	1998
Direct investment (Million Irish Pounds)	169	125	235	360	383	415
Origins (% of total)						
Europe	41%	36%	12%	13%	13%	21%
USA	51%	52%	78%	83%	84%	78%
Others	6%	12%	10%	3%	1%	1%
Ireland/Total OECD	0.07%	0.14%	0.27%	0.78%	0.58%	0.48%

Source: OECD, International Direct Investment Statistic Yearbook, 1999.

Foreign-owned firms have profoundly modified the structure of the Irish economy and were responsible for two-thirds of the manufacturing employment and more than three-quarters of its imports and exports in 1996 (Table 3). Ireland, together with Hungary, has the highest shares of both production and trade accounted for by foreign affiliated firms among all OECD countries. The presence of foreign affiliates has brought tangible linkages and spin-offs to the Irish economy, in terms of improved human skills in high value-added activities, improved access to the world marketing networks of these firms and diversified export destinations (Table 4).

Table 3.   Foreign affiliates operating in Ireland

(% of total)	1992	1993	1994	1995	1996
Employees	44.0%	44.4%	46.6%	47.1%	47.0%
Manufacturing prod.	55.0%	58.3%	61.6%	65.2%	66.4%
Exports	76.7%	77.3%	80.0%	82.3%	83.9%
Imports	69.2%	72.8%	74.1%	77.8%	75.4%

Source: OECD (1999), Measuring Globalisation, the role of Multinationals in OECD Countries.

Table 4. Regional composition of Irish trade

(US$ million and percentages of total trade)

Year	1985	1990	1995	1999
Total Exports	10 383	23 713	43 763	69 823
OECD (29)	89.7%	93.1%	89.5%	89.5%
EU (15)	72.0%	78.0%	72.3%	64.3%
UK	33.0%	33.7%	25.4%	21.5%
USA	9.8%	8.2%	8.3%	15.6%
Japan	1.6%	1.8%	3.0%	2.9%
Rest of the World	10.3%	6.9%	10.5%	10.5%
Total Imports	10 050	20 624	32 312	45 645
OECD (29)	93.3%	93.2%	83.6%	82.2%
EU (15)	69.1%	69.4%	56.1%	54.1%
UK	42.7%	42.2%	35.6%	32.2%
USA	17.0%	14.6%	17.7%	16.8%
Japan	3.5%	5.6%	5.3%	5.8%
Singapore	0.3%	0.5%	4.8%	4.9%
Rest of the World	6.4%	6.3%	11.6%	12.9%

Source: OECD Foreign Trade Statistics.

Despite the scope and depth of the EU integration process, the EU's share of Ireland's imports and exports has dropped between 1988 and 1998, with a corresponding increase in exports to the United States and larger imports from Singapore and the rest of the World (Table 5). The Irish trade pattern suggests that the Irish integration process within the EU has not been detrimental to non-EU trading partners. It also highlights that Ireland has gained commensurate benefits in pursuing integration within the world economy on a world-wide basis.

Table 5. Product composition of Irish trade

Composition of Trade (% of Total)	Imports		Exports	
	1988	1998	1988	1998
Agriculture and Food	12.6%	7.4%	26.3%	10.4%
Mineral Products	6.4%	3.1%	1.6%	0.4%
Textiles, Clothing & Footwear	9.8%	5.0%	6.1%	2.1%
Semi-manufactured Goods	21.6%	16.7%	18.3%	34.1%
Manufactured Goods	49.6%	67.8%	47.8%	53.0%

Source: OECD Foreign Trade Statistics.

Changes in the product composition of foreign trade usually provide potentially interesting indications about the relative competitiveness of sectors of the country concerned. In the case of Ireland, the share of manufactured goods in total exports increased from 18.3 to 34.1% between 1988 and 1998, with corresponding reductions in the shares of other categories, i.e. agriculture and food, oil and mineral products, and textiles, clothing and footwear. Among the semi-manufactured goods, exports of organic chemicals and pharmaceutical products accounted for almost a quarter of total exports in 1998.

231

Along with economic growth, Ireland maintained between 1994 and 1999 an average annual rate of employment creation of 5.1%, outstripping the OECD average of 1.16%, and bringing its unemployment rate to 3.7% in October 2000 – down from 15.7% in 1993. Employment grew by 10.2% in 1998 supported by a net migration flow of 22 800 persons in the year to April 1998 and a further 18 500 by April 1999. A large proportion of the immigrants is composed of Irish nationals that have lived abroad and other people of Irish origin. Immigrants are heavily concentrated in the 15 to 44 age group. To ease labour shortages, firms are recruiting on a world-wide basis making use of the EU internal labour mobility provisions and a new work visa that was established to make it easier for people originating from outside the European Economic Area to take up employment in Ireland. As labour shortages are spreading throughout the whole economy, wage and residential cost pressures are creeping up and are gradually eroding some of the perceived Irish comparative advantages. The consumer price index reached 6.2% in the year to July 2000, outstripping the EU average of 2.2%.

In conjunction with a market openness policy that brought foreign-owned firms to a predominant position in the economy, the Irish Government maintains what is referred to as "a pragmatic rather than a theoretical approach" regarding the privatisation of state-sponsored bodies (SSBs). Irish SSBs engaged in primarily commercial operations, such as transport, energy, communications, banking, insurance, hotels and peat moss, employed about 5.4% of total employment in 1995. The main privatisation initiatives that occurred since then were in the telecommunications sector.

Ireland has large budgetary surpluses, so the ongoing debate about the privatisation of SSBs is not driven by fiscal considerations. The privatisation debate is subdued and overshadowed by the ongoing reform in major infrastructure utility sectors, with the setting up of sectoral regulators whose independence is balanced with accountability. Government objectives regarding SSBs are wide ranging and their activities need to be assessed against clear economic benchmarks and subject to appropriate accountability requirements to ensure that a sound resource allocation is achieved.

Various reviews and measures were launched to complement policies aimed at improving regulation and competition in Ireland. These include an action programme of regulatory reform, a review of competition and mergers policy, a public consultation on governance and accountability in the regulatory framework, and the adoption of a public private partnership approach to the funding of certain public capital projects. The Government also released the National Development Plan for 2000-2006, which aims to raise the quality of Ireland's physical, educational and social infrastructure to continental European standards.

Ireland has gained commensurable benefits by pursuing trade liberalisation, welcoming foreign-owned firms and integrating in the world economy. Nevertheless, the recent economic expansion has overshadowed the need to put in place a more rules-based regulatory regime that fosters economic efficiency, minimises obstacles to growth and promotes sound competitive conditions. Ireland would deal more effectively with eventual external shocks and a less favourable global economic environment if it were to strengthen its regulatory approaches. Ireland, being a small open economy, is more vulnerable to external shocks than larger economies.

2. THE POLICY FRAMEWORK FOR MARKET OPENNESS: THE SIX "EFFICIENT REGULATION PRINCIPLES"

An important step in ensuring that regulations do not unnecessarily reduce market openness is to build the "efficient regulation" principles into the domestic regulatory process for social and economic regulations, as well as for administrative practices. "Market openness" here refers to the ability of foreign suppliers to compete in a national market without encountering discriminatory, excessively burdensome or restrictive conditions. These principles, which have been described in the 1997 OECD *Report on Regulatory Reform* and developed further in the Trade Committee, are:

– Transparency and openness of decision making;

– Non-discrimination;

– Avoidance of unnecessary trade restrictiveness;

– Use of internationally harmonised measures;

– Recognition of equivalence of other countries' regulatory measures; and

– Application of competition principles.

They have been identified by trade policy makers as key to market-oriented and trade and investment-friendly regulations. They reflect the basic principles underpinning the multilateral trading system, concerning which countries have undertaken certain obligations in the WTO and other contexts. The intention in the OECD country reviews of regulatory reform is not to judge the extent to which any country may have undertaken and lived up to international commitments relating directly or indirectly to these principles, but rather to assess whether and how domestic instruments, procedures and practices give effect to the principles and successfully contribute to market openness. Similarly, the OECD country reviews are not concerned with an assessment of trade policies and practices in Member countries.

In sum, this report considers whether and how Irish regulatory procedures and content affect the quality of market access and presence in Ireland. An important reverse scenario – whether and how trade and investment affect the fulfilment of legitimate policy objectives reflected in social regulation – is beyond the scope of the present discussion. This latter issue has been extensively debated within and beyond the OECD from a range of policy perspectives. To date, however, OECD deliberations have found no evidence to suggest that trade and investment *per se* impact negatively on the pursuit and attainment of domestic policy goals through regulation or other means.[7]

2.1. Transparency and openness of decision-making

To ensure international market openness, foreign firms and individuals seeking access to a market (or expanding activities in a given market) must have adequate information on new or revised regulations so that they can base their decisions on an accurate assessment of potential costs, risks, and market opportunities. Regulations need to be transparent to foreign traders and investors. Regulatory transparency at both domestic and international levels can be achieved through a variety of means, including systematic publication of proposed rules prior to entry into force, use of electronic means to share information (such as the Internet), well-timed opportunities for public comment, and rigorous mechanisms for ensuring that such comments are given due consideration prior to the adoption of a final regulation.[8] Market participants wishing to voice concerns about the application of existing regulations should have appropriate access to appeal procedures. This sub-section discusses the above transparency and transparency-related considerations in Ireland and how they are met.

2.1.1. *Transparency in the elaboration of Irish regulations*

An important aspect of transparency arises from the administrative procedures put into place for the elaboration and adoption of domestic regulations. It is therefore essential to review some of the key steps involved in order to assess the transparency-friendliness of these procedures. Background report to Chapter 2 provides a detailed discussion of the Irish process for elaborating new regulations and offers detailed recommendations for improving the transparency of the process and the institutional setting.

Recent institutional reforms

Ireland's administrative procedures were reformed in recent years pursuant to the *Strategic Management Initiative* (SMI) launched in 1994, set up to review the government decision-making infrastructure and to recommend proposals for modernising the systems and practices. Many of the SMI objectives have materialised through formal legislation, such as the *Public Service Management Act*, 1997, the *Freedom of Information Act*, 1997 and the *Committee of the Houses of the Oireachtas* (Compellability, Privilege and Immunity of Witnesses) *Act*, 1997.

The work of the *Regulatory Reform Working Group* established in 1996 resulted in recommendations for an action programme that was adopted by the government in July 1999 and referred to as "*Reducing Red Tape – An Action Programme of Regulatory Reform in Ireland*". It sets out new requirements for deepening public consultation with departments' customers and other interested parties. It also modified the elaboration process of new legislation and regulations by requiring the preparation of a *Quality Regulation Checklist*.

As a means to promote transparency of government information relating to individuals, the *Freedom of Information Act* came into force in April 1998. It asserts the right of members of the public to obtain access to official information to the greatest extent possible consistent with the public interest and the right to privacy of individuals. Within its purview, each person has a right to access to government records, to correct personal information, where it is inaccurate, incomplete or misleading, and to obtain reasons for decisions affecting oneself. The Act sets out a series of exemptions to protect sensitive information where its disclosure may damage key interests of the State or of third parties. The Act also provides for appeal procedures, via an independent review by the Information Commissioner.

Systemic changes in regulatory functions are also occurring through the ongoing process of transferring regulatory responsibilities over certain infrastructure utility sectors from government Departments to newly established independent bodies. In June 1997, regulatory functions for the telecommunications sector were transferred to a new independent regulator, the *Director of Telecommunications Regulation*. In July 1999, the *Commission for Electricity Regulation* (CER) was established. In late 1999, a Commissioner-Designate for Aviation Regulation was appointed pending enactment of legislation. In March 2000, the Minister for Public Enterprise published a policy paper "*Governance and Accountability in the Regulatory Process: Policy Proposals*". The proposals are now reflected in the various legislation documents that the Minister has recently brought forward for the regulation of individual sectors. In September 2000, the regulation of postal services was assigned to the telecommunications regulator. Regulatory arrangements for gas and for surface transport are under consideration at present.

Rule-making procedures

The elaboration process of new legislation begins with a memorandum seeking the authority to proceed with specific legislative proposals. The memorandum prepared by the sponsoring Department outlines the principal objectives and intended results of the proposed legislation, referred to as *the Heads of the Bill*. These are transmitted to the Office of the Attorney General (OAG) where consistency with the Constitution and the general principles of law is verified. Other Departments directly concerned with the proposal are also consulted. The final decision to proceed with the legislation is taken by the Government. The sponsoring Department prepares a Cabinet memorandum, containing the final draft legislation, and "as appropriate" the accompanying Quality Regulatory Checklist (QRC) (Box 3), together with six statements of impact assessment covering: relations and co-operation between Ireland and Britain, employment, women, persons in poverty, industry and small business costs, and exchequer costs and staffing implications. The eventual enactment will follow a multiple stage process, including the publication of the draft legislation and subsequently the final legislation in the Irish Official Journal (*Iris Oifigiúil*).

Ireland, unlike most OECD countries, does not have a specific law setting out procedures for the legislative drafting process. Before 1998, procedures were elaborated in a government manual "Government Procedure Instructions". Since 1998, the Prime Minister's Office (*the Department of the Taoiseach*) has published a *Cabinet Handbook* that details the required procedures to present proposals for approval by the government and it is regularly updated to reflect recent modifications to the administrative procedures. The *Cabinet Handbook* is now available on the Internet (www.irlgov.ie/taoiseach/publication/cabinethandbook).

The preparation of regulations, orders, rules and bye-laws, generally referred to as secondary legislation, follows the principles laid down in the *Cabinet Handbook*. Ministers have responsibility to prepare them in accordance to the relevant Act and they usually involve the OAG in the process. Notice of making of regulations is published in the Irish Official Journal and, in many cases, notice is also published in national newspapers. Not all draft regulations are considered by the Parliament but, when they are, resolutions can be submitted to annul them during a period of 21 days after being presented.

Public consultations

Irish Departments are now required to carry out public consultations with interested parties in accordance with the relevant provision of the QRC, which sets out a series of considerations for justifying legislative proposals. Public consultations on regulatory matters were not specifically codified in the law before recent institutional reforms but were nevertheless carried out with social partners on the basis of informal practices. Ireland, being a small economy, the informality of the process was perceived by many as a flexible means for facilitating the emergence of social consensus. Easy accessibility to government information, senior decision-makers and Irish Ministers contributed to this informality, characteristics that are less likely to occur in large size economies. Although informality underpins flexibility and quick responsiveness, it is often mirrored by procedures lacking in transparency with inevitable risks of regulatory capture.

The QRC formalises in some ways the public consultation process by requiring consultation with interested parties and outlining their views in the Cabinet memorandum. However, it is left to each Department to determine whether consultation with outside persons/bodies is necessary, the modalities of the consultation process in terms of the duration and the moment, the selection of the interested parties and the information supplied to them. Interested parties have also no access to the QRC. There are no common criteria for evaluating the quality of either the consultation or the decisions taken by the regulators on the selected consultation mechanism. There are also no specific requirements to ensure that the views of foreign parties are sought and taken into consideration during the process. In one particular case, industry representatives have expressed concerns about the short consultation period assigned for the auctioning of the "virtual independent power producer contracts".

Although Departments rely on an array of advisory bodies, *e.g.* the Tax Administration Liaison Committee and the Small Business and Services Forum (abolished in July 2000), these formal and bodies may not be adequate to deal with a rapidly changing society. A pro-competitive stance should require a re-balancing of power between the views of producers and those of consumers, more broadly the civil society. Economic and social developments also mean that new interest groups can become increasingly effective and thus require further transparency and accountability safeguards to avoid potential risks of regulatory capture.

2.1.2. *Transparency in the elaboration of technical regulations*

Transparency in the area of technical regulations, *i.e.* mandatory product specifications set in regulations, and of standards, *i.e.* specifications established by standardisation bodies for which compliance is not mandatory, has been strengthened by regional and international discipline mechanisms. As divergent national product regulations are considered as major obstacles to access to domestic markets, information in this area is essential to firms as it reduces uncertainties over applicable requirements and more generally facilitates the understanding of market conditions. As part of its notification obligations to the European Commission and the WTO, Ireland provides information to its trading partners on the making process of national technical regulations and standards, and gives them opportunity to comment.

In all EU Member States, when draft technical regulations are not pure transpositions of EU harmonising directives, they must be notified to the European Commission. The obligation gives the European Commission and other EU Member States the opportunity to comment on new or modified national rules for a period of three months, which may be extended for an additional three or twelve months depending on the circumstances. They can, for example, raise questions of interpretation, ask for further details, or challenge the conformity of prospective rules with Community law while they are still at the drafting stage. Failure to notify or to respond to comments can result in the Commission launching an infringement procedure. The National Standards Authority of Ireland (NSAI) is the Irish notifying body under EU directives.

Although first directed at Member States, the procedure benefits the private sector in the EU by opening a window on national regulatory activities. The European Commission publishes regularly the titles of draft national technical regulations in the Official Journal of the European Communities and since 1999 this information is available on the Internet. Any individual or firm interested in a notified draft can obtain further information by contacting the Commission or the relevant contact point in any Member State. This mechanism promotes the awareness of all interested parties, whether European or not, as regard national regulatory activities within the EU.

The notification procedure has enhanced the transparency of the regulatory decision making process all over the European Union, thus reducing the risks of regulatory capture. Since its inception in 1985, the procedure has helped build the principle of transparency into the regulatory practices of European countries as far as the technical rules are concerned. The incentive of countries to notify, and thus the efficiency of the system, has been strongly reinforced by the 1996 "Securitel" decision by the European Court of Justice.[10] The decision established the principle that failure to comply with the notification obligation results in the technical regulations concerned being inapplicable, so that they are unenforceable against individuals.

In the EU, the notification procedure has recently been complemented by a procedure requiring Member States to notify the Commission of national measures derogating from the principle of free movement of goods within the EU.[11] This procedure was established in view of persisting obstacles to the free movement of goods within the Single Market. Member States must notify any measure, other

---

Box 1.   EU notification requirements

Provision of information in the field of technical regulation in the European Union

To avoid erecting new barriers to the free movement of goods, which could arise from the adoption of technical regulations at the national level, EU Member States are required by Directive 98/34 (which has codified Directive 83/189) to notify all draft technical regulations on products, to the extent that these are not a transposition of European harmonised directives. This notification obligation covers all regulations at the national or regional level, which introduce technical specifications, the observance of which is compulsory in the case of marketing or use; but also fiscal and financial measures to encourage compliance with such specifications, and voluntary agreements to which a public authority is a party. Directive 98/48 recently extended the scope of the notification obligation to rules on information-society services. Notified texts are further communicated by the Commission to the other Member States and are in principle not regarded as confidential, unless explicitly designated as such.

Following the notification, the concerned Member State must refrain from adopting the draft regulations for a period of three months during which the Commission and other Member States vet the effects of these regulations on the Single Market. If the Commission or a Member State emit a detailed opinion arguing that the proposed regulation constitutes a barrier to trade, the standstill period is extended for another three months. Furthermore, if the preparation of new legislation in the same area is undertaken at the European Union level, the Commission can extend the standstill for another twelve months. An infringement procedure may be engaged in case of failure to notify or if the Member State concerned ignores a detailed opinion.

Similarly, as far as standards are concerned, Directive 94/34 provides for an exchange of information concerning the initiatives of the National Standardisation Organisations (NSOs) and, upon request, the working programmes, thus enhancing transparency and promoting co-operation among NSOs. The direct beneficiaries of the notification obligation of draft standards are the Member States, their NSOs and the European Standardisation Bodies (CEN, CENELEC and ETSI). Private parties can indirectly become part of the standardisation procedures in countries other than their own, through their country's NSOs, which are ensured the possibility of taking an active or passive role in the standardisation work of other NSOs.

than a judicial decision, which prevents the free movement of products lawfully manufactured or marketed in another Member State for reasons relating in particular to safety, health or protection of the environment. For example, Member States must notify any measure which imposes a general ban, or requires a product to be modified or withdrawn from the market. Whereas the notification procedure for draft technical regulations mentioned above acts on the period preceding the adoption of technical regulations, this procedure deals with measures taken after the adoption of technical regulations. So far, the new procedure has produced limited results. The general level of notifications remains very low (33 in 1997, 69 in 1998 and 26 in 1999) which, according to the European Commission, may indicate that the mechanism is under-used.[12]

To the extent that notified prospective regulations are not based on relevant international standards, the European Commission transmits the information to the WTO Secretariat and other WTO Members in accordance with the WTO Agreement on Technical Barriers to Trade (TBT). Similarly, notification required under other WTO provisions, such as the WTO Agreement on the Application of Sanitary and Phytosanitary Measures (SPS), or regular notifications in the framework of WTO Agreements on Agriculture, Rules of Origin, Import Licensing, etc., is made to the WTO by the European Commission on behalf of Member States. WTO members may comment on the drafts and the notifying country has to react. If not, the case may be raised in the WTO system via the TBT Committee and if this does not lead to an acceptable solution, through the dispute settlement procedure. Following the TBT and SPS Agreements, an enquiry point about standards and technical regulations has been established in Ireland.

2.1.3. *Transparency in the elaboration of standards*

The National Standards Authority of Ireland (NSAI) is responsible for the transposition as Irish Standards of all standards published by European Standardisation Bodies, as well as for their diffusion, promotion and marketing. It is also responsible for managing the public consultation process in Ireland for standards and for preparing indigenous standards consistent with EU requirements under the Single European Market Programme.

NSAI elaborates Irish standards with the open participation of all interested parties, without any nationality-based discrimination. It is the Irish member of the European Committee for Standardisation (CEN), the European Institute of Telecommunications Standards (ETSI) and the International Standardisation Organisation (ISO). Through the Electro-Technical Council of Ireland, with which NSAI collaborates closely, it participates in the International Electrotechnical Commission (IEC) and the European Committee for Electrotechnical Standardisation (CENELEC). It has adopted the WTO TBT Code of Good Practice for the Preparation, Adoption and Application of Standards.

The creation of Irish standards or purely national standards referred to as "indigenous standards" takes place in one of NSAI's 15 principal Consultative Committees (CC) in charge of developing standards in specific fields of activity. The CCs gather manufacturers, consumer associations, government representatives, testing laboratories and certification bodies, and other entities that can be affected by the development of standards. When a draft is under preparation, the firms and other interests, which are considered most affected by the project, are informed and are free to become involved in the work through one of the members of the relevant CC. CCs must consider the participation of other standardisation bodies, which are members of CEN/CENELEC. More broadly the participation of persons, including from outside the European Union, is not restricted. Any business or professional organisations, including any manufacturer or individual, can call for the creation of a standard on the basis of actual technical specifications. NSAI has the obligation to transpose European standards within the time period set by CEN, CENELEC or ETSI, usually six months and to withdraw conflicting national standards.

Once a draft standard is approved by the concerned CC, the public comment stage begins and any individuals and legal entities are invited to submit comments. The time period for public consultation is set on a case by case basis, typically two months. NSAI's publications, *Standards Bulletin and Catalogue,*

237

provides regular information on draft technical regulations notified by all member States of the EU and EFTA and on the ongoing work programmes of CEN, CENELEC, ETSI, ISO and IEC. After examining the comments, the CC prepares a final proposal, which has to be approved by the NSAI governing bodies. Eventually, the finalised standard is notified in the Irish Official Journal and included in NSAI's Standards Catalogue. NSAI publishes a bimonthly *Standards Bulletin and Standards Factsheet*, which are available for subscribers on its Internet website (www.nsai.ie).

The European Commission has also taken further initiatives to promote transparency and facilitate the understanding by market participants of the rules governing the Single European Market and some key issues, such as standards or public procurement. It has created a one-stop Internet shop for business "Dialogue with Business".[13] The site is linked to "Euro Info Centres", which are set up all over the European Union and specialise in standards. They can provide business with information on the application of standards, conformity assessment procedures, CE-marking or quality initiatives in Europe. The European Commission also operates a website in co-operation with the European standardisation bodies, which gives information on European New Approach directives and harmonised standards.[14]

Overall the elaboration process of Irish standards and EU standards are subject to a series of check and balance features that minimise the emergence of obstacles to the free movement of goods within the EU. The world community benefits directly from the application of the transparency and non-discrimination procedures and indirectly through the reduced risk of regulatory capture.

2.1.4. Government procurement

In OECD countries, although government procurement procedures intend to be transparent, the cost of retrieving relevant information can be substantial for small-, medium-sized and foreign enterprises. There are perceptions that specifications with no obvious relationship to the nature of the contract involved can be used to disqualify bids. Appeal procedures may not be clearly established or may seem so burdensome that contractors will not even consider recourse to them in cases of alleged infringement of procedures. In this connection, foreign and domestic participants have legitimate expectations about the appropriate degree of transparency that domestic government procurement procedures should provide.

The Irish legal framework on government procurement procedures transposes the guiding principles provided for in the EU Government Procurement Framework, which is based on six substantive Directives.[15] The substantive Directives apply to procurement procedures of all Member States and their regional and municipal administrations. They provide for the principles of transparency, non-discrimination and equal treatment, which altogether enhance competitive conditions and are mutually beneficial for concerned parties.

In May 2000, the European Commission adopted a package of amendments to simplify and modernise the public procurement Directives. The new legal framework proposes, *inter alia*, to consolidate three existing Directives into one more coherent text, to relax some of the award procedures that are considered too inflexible to achieve the objective of best value for money and to encourage public authorities to make greater use of electronic means. It also provides for the exclusion of former regulated sectors, *i.e.* telecommunications, electricity and water, from the scope of the Directives as these sectors are effectively being liberalised and opened up to real competition. The European Commission recommends that Member States implement the new legal framework by 2002.

Irish public authorities have diligently implemented the relevant EU Directives as illustrated by the near absence of infringement procedures being launched by the European Commission against Ireland for incorrect application of these Directives. The last infringement proceedings occurred in 1996 regarding irregularities dating back to 1994 with respect to the Directive on Public Supply Contracts by the Irish Forestry Board. A voluntary chapter of best practices on debriefing of suppliers was approved in 1999 by the Forum on Public Procurement in Ireland.[16] It provides for common access to information and a common debriefing policy while ensuring the full respect of the confidential nature of information made available to contracting entities by suppliers.

Box 2.   The EU government procurement framework

The transparency principle is applied concretely through various requirements. Contracting authorities must prepare an annual indicative notice of total procurement, by product area and exceeding an annual minimum threshold, which they envisage awarding during the subsequent 12-month period. The annual indicative list and any contract whose estimated value exceeds specific thresholds must be noticed in the Official Journal of the European Communities. Contracts must indicate which of the permissible award procedures is chosen (open, restricted or negotiated procedures) and they must use objective criteria in selecting candidates and tenders, which criteria must be known beforehand. Contracting authorities are also obliged to make known the result of contract procedures through a notice in the Official Journal of the European Communities.

Member States are also obliged to provide appropriate procedures for judicial review of decisions taken by contracting authorities that infringe Community laws or national implementing laws. In particular, they have to provide for the possibility of implementing interim measures, including the suspension of contract award procedures, for setting aside decisions taken unlawfully and for awarding damages to persons harmed by an infringement. The EU Directives require that these procedures shall be effectively and rapidly enforced. The appreciation of these qualitative criteria is likely to be a difficult task in practice due to the diversity of culture and judicial systems among EU Member States.

With respect to the twin principles of non-discrimination and equal treatment, the main requirements involve: the use of minimum periods for the bidding process; the use of recognised technical standards, with European standards taking precedence over national standards; and the prohibition against discrimination as provided under the Treaty of Rome. The latter prohibits any discrimination or restrictions in awarding of contracts on the grounds of nationality and prohibits the use of quantitative restrictions on imports or measures with equivalent effect. It also provides for the freedom of nationals of one Member State to establish themselves in the territory of another Member State and the freedom to provide services from any Member State. The EU Directives on mutual recognition of professional services and the New Approach for technical standards (see Box 5 in Section 2.4) further contribute to minimising potential incidences of discrimination.

In a study commissioned by the Department of Enterprise, Trade and Employment, the proportion of public sector procurement sourced from imports was estimated at 43.4% in 1998.[17] Estimating the import share of total public procurement is an inherently complex task and is based on a certain set of assumptions. For a small open economy like Ireland, a high import share of total public procurement is an expected result, particularly in the current period of capacity constraints. The absence of similar studies for other countries does not permit making reliable country comparisons.

By virtue of the application of the transparency and non-discrimination principles, firms and individuals from EU Member States benefit in terms of opportunities to compete for public contracts from Irish awarding authorities. Non-EU firms and individuals also gain from the overall transparency of EU procurement rules and indirectly through the enhanced competitive conditions conferred by the openness of the Irish investment rules and the non-discrimination principle. The European Commission also undertook specific commitments in the context of the WTO Government Procurement Agreement (GPA), which lists the contracting authorities of each EU Member State, including Ireland, that is subject to the Agreement.

2.1.5. Regions in Ireland

In any country, the possibility exists for conflicting or inconsistent regulations between the central government and decentralised regulatory authorities, which may frustrate the free circulation of goods and services within the country. Ireland is a highly centralised country and its 114 local authorities,

Regulatory Reform in Ireland

including 29 county councils, have a more limited range of powers in comparison to their counterparts in other European countries. Under the general supervision of the Department of Environment and Local Government, local governments provide public services such as social housing, water, waste removal and treatment, roads, fire services and recreational facilities for local communities. In recent years, a certain amount of regulatory responsibility has been decentralised in the areas of environment, urban renewal, housing and general development, while others responsibilities have been transferred to specialised agencies, such as health functions and primary environmental protection. Local governments have limited powers in fields of education, police, health and public transport, except taxis. Their involvement in social programmes is growing. In terms of regulatory powers, local authorities' competencies concentrate on licensing, *i.e.* land use, traffic, parking and control of nuisance and litter.

A number of semi-autonomous public regional bodies operate in the health, tourism promotion and fisheries areas, complementing the role of the local authorities. In the last decade, the government has made important efforts to improve the managerial capacities of local governments' administration. Based on SMI, the programme *Better Local Government* created new advisory bodies that seek to improve co-ordination and to reduce policy and service delivery fragmentation at local level. Within the EU, the Single Economic Market Directives apply to decentralised bodies and large cities of Ireland and contribute to minimise the potential risk of conflicting regulations that would impede the free circulation of goods and services within the country. Assessing the application of the efficient regulation principles by local and regional bodies necessitates resources that are beyond those currently available for this review. The central government should continue to promote the awareness and to encourage respect of the efficient regulation principles by local and regional communities. Background report to Chapter 2 provides more detailed information about the relationships among the various levels of government administration.

2.2. Measures to ensure non-discrimination

Application of non-discrimination principles aims to provide effective equality of competitive opportunities between like products and services irrespective of country of origin. Thus, the extent to which respect for two core principles of the multilateral trading system – Most-Favoured-Nation (MFN) and National Treatment (NT) – is actively promoted when developing and applying regulations is a helpful gauge of a country's overall efforts to promote trade and investment-friendly regulation.

The Irish Constitution does not include a general prohibition against this sort of discrimination. Through membership in the WTO and in the EU, Ireland subscribes to the MFN and national treatment principles. It falls upon the Market Access Division of DETE to act as an oversight agency to ensure that the implementation of non-discrimination and national treatment provisions stemming from the WTO and other international trade and trade-related investment agreements are effectively implemented. Within the WTO dispute settlement process, trading partners have the opportunity to request consultation with Ireland and/or the European Commission, depending on the area of competence, for alleged infringement of any WTO obligations including MFN or national treatment obligations. If the consultation does not lead to a mutually satisfactory outcome, trading partners have the right to request the establishment of panels which will examine the case and prepare a report on the compatibility of the alleged measures with WTO obligations.

2.2.1. WTO *consultations and dispute settlement*

In mid-2000, there were no outstanding consultations or panel deliberations directly targeting Irish policies. The United States has sought WTO consultations with Ireland on two issues since mid-1997, concerning a scheme for special tax rates in respect of trading income from export sale of goods manufactured in Ireland (Special Trading Houses Scheme) and the alleged failure to grant certain copyright and neighbouring rights under Irish intellectual property protection laws – obligations arising under the WTO TRIPs Agreement. The tax issue was solved in 1998 by the agreement to abolish the Special Trading Houses Scheme. Concerning the intellectual property right issues, Ireland undertook a lengthy

240

© OECD 2001

review of its relevant law with a view to modernise its provisions and a legislative package was adopted in July 2000 and intended to comply with its WTO obligations. The new legislation came into force on 1 January 2001.

Given the European Commission competence on trade issues, there were several outstanding dispute settlement procedures in which trading partners are alleging infringement of WTO obligations by the EU. Since the European Commission acts on behalf of its Member States on trade policies, it is not possible to disassociate any Member State, including Ireland, from EU trade policy stances. The majority of the complaints involved the EU agricultural policies and its import regime for agricultural products.

2.2.2. *Corporate tax regime*

Favourable corporate income tax provisions combined with attractive incentive programmes have encouraged foreign investors to locate in Ireland but the European Commission and EU Member States have complained about the competition-distorting impact of the Irish preferential tax system. In July 1998, an agreement was reached between the European Commission and Ireland that removed the discriminatory provisions and addressed the concerns about the state aid aspects of the Irish corporation tax regime. At issue was the contrast between the standards corporate tax rate of 32% on profits of domestic income versus the preferential corporate rate of 10% on profits of trading income. A single corporation tax of 12.5% will be implemented as of January 2003. Transitional arrangements were also concluded to regulate the number of new investment projects that will gain access to the 10% tax rate applied until then. Irish Authority claims that the new 12.5% tax regime will be compatible with the EU Code of Conduct on business taxation which is designed to curb harmful tax measures within EU Member States.

2.2.3. *Preferential trade agreements*

While preferential agreements give more favourable treatment to specified countries and are thus inherent departures from the MFN and NT principles, the extent of a country's participation in preferential agreements is not in itself indicative of a lack of commitment to the principle of non-discrimination. In assessing such commitments, it is relevant to consider the attitudes of participating countries towards non-members in respect of transparency and the potential for discriminatory effects. Third countries need access to information about the content and operation of preferential agreements in order to make informed assessment of any impact on their commercial interests. In addition, substantive approaches to regulatory issues such as standards and conformity assessment can introduce the potential for discriminatory treatment of third countries if, for example, standards recognised by partners in a preferential agreement would be difficult to meet by third countries.

Since its accession to the European Economic Communities in 1973, Ireland has *de jure* participated in all preferential trade agreements entered into by the EU. The most relevant ones are the free trade agreements (FTAs) with the European Economic Area (EEA), several European Agreements with Central and Eastern European Countries (CEECs), Mexico and several Euro-Mediterranean Agreements.[18] The EU has entered into preferential non-reciprocal agreements with several Mediterranean countries, in the context of the Lomé Convention and the EU General System of Preferences (GSP) in favour of developing countries.

To the extent that the various FTAs are comprehensive in scope, the likelihood is that these will generate trade creation processes larger than the trade diversion inherent in any FTA. In the context of the increasing number of FTAs entered into by the EU, Ireland has gradually been exposed to incremental levels of increased competition and, conversely, gained preferential access to new markets.

The attitude of participating countries towards non-members may be assessed against their willingness to extend on a multilateral basis the benefits of their preferential agreements. In this connection, Ireland supports the European Commission's position for keeping the momentum of trade liberalisation with a comprehensive round of multilateral trade negotiations in the WTO. In particular, the

European Commission favours a global approach for WTO negotiations that would seek to improve market access for industrial goods, agricultural products, services and improved multilateral rules in the areas of trade facilitation, government procurement, investment and competition dimensions.

2.2.4. Trade in services

In the context of the WTO General Agreement on Trade in Services (GATS), Ireland has undertaken international commitments in the field of services, including in the sectoral annexes to the GATS and more recently the Financial Services and Basic Telecommunications Agreements concluded in 1997. Under the GATS, specific commitments and the list of exemptions from MFN treatment are made according to four modes of supply for each services sector concerned (cross-border supply, consumption abroad, commercial presence, and presence of natural persons). For the then 12 EU Member States, a single schedule of specific commitments was decided at the EU level and submitted to the WTO on behalf of the EU. The specific commitments are composed of EU-wide commitments and exemptions as qualified by the additional restrictions attached by individual Member States.

To evaluate the extent to which foreign producers have effectively equal competitive opportunities in Ireland in services, it is necessary to examine the range of activities covered in each services sector and the limitations on market access and national treatment pertaining to the different modes of supply, including any specific additional limitations by Ireland. In addition, since the EU has tabled a list of MFN exemptions, this must be examined in order to assess the extent to which the Commission gives preferential treatment to, or discriminates against, one or more trading partners.

While it is not the purpose of this study to examine in detail the extent of EU and Irish commitments and exemptions under the GATS, the following gives some examples. The EU schedule shows that the EU undertook sector-specific commitments in a large number of sectors. However, it did not offer any commitments in the following sectors: postal services; courier services; audio-visual services; other education services; libraries, archives, museum and other cultural services; maritime transport; internal waterways transport; space transport and pipeline transport.

By mode, the EU limitations are mostly at Member State level for cross-border supply (*e.g.*, business and financial services sectors), while consumption abroad is mostly bound with no restrictions. The principal limitations to commercial presence arise from requirements on the legal form of the service provider at both EU and individual Member State level. Some of these are limitations on national treatment, as they apply only to third country providers. Movement of natural persons is subject to general limitations applying to all sectors, with some additional Member State limitations at the sectoral level (*e.g.* education services; professional services; financial services). The list of MFN exemptions tabled by the EU shows a number of sectoral exemptions, which apply in Ireland, including audiovisual services; road transportation services (passenger and freight); the marketing of air transport services; and direct non-life-insurance.

Ireland maintains few additional limitations concerning certain professional services, mainly relating to commercial presence. Market access is limited to partnerships for auditing services. For medical, dental and veterinary services market access is limited to partnerships or natural persons. Regarding cross-border supply, real estate services are unbound. For financial services, the right of establishment in Ireland does not cover the creation of representative offices for insurance companies.

2.3. Measures to avoid unnecessary trade restrictiveness

To attain a particular regulatory objective, policy makers should seek regulations that are not more trade restrictive than necessary to fulfil a legitimate objective, taking account of the risks non-fulfilment would create. Examples of this approach would be to use performance-based, rather than design standards as the basis of a technical regulation, to use tariffs instead of quantitative restrictions requiring the allocation of import permits, or to consider taxes or tradable permits in lieu of regulations to achieve the same legitimate policy goal. At the procedural level, effective adherence to this principle entails consideration of the extent to which specific provisions require or encourage regulators to avoid unnecessary trade restrictiveness and the rationale for any exceptions, how the impact of new regulations on international trade and investment is assessed, the extent to which trade policy bodies as well as foreign traders and investors are consulted in the regulatory process, and means for ensuring access by foreign parties to dispute settlement.

2.3.1. *Regulatory impact assessment*

In Ireland, the principal tools for assessing the potential effects of legislative and subordinated regulatory proposals are the *Quality Regulation Checklist* (QRC) and the six statements of impact assessment (Section 2.1.1.2). The preparation of the QRC provides a structured approach for Irish policy makers to improve the quality of the information on which decisions are based and to integrate efficient regulatory principles into the decision making process of regulatory matters. The Irish QRC integrates many aspects of the OECD *Reference Checklist for Regulatory Decision-Making* for producing efficient, flexible and transparent regulations (OECD 1995).[19] The new requirements are only required since July 1999, which is late compared to similar requirements put in place in most other OECD countries.

The preparation of the QRC statement and the six statements of impact assessment altogether may be assimilated to a Regulatory Impact Analysis (RIA) in the sense of OECD best practices.[20] However, the regulatory approach relies only on qualitative criteria and thus completely ignore quantitative criteria, such as cost and benefit analysis that can be a useful tool for comparing the benefits to specific interest groups versus the costs born by society as a whole. There is an element of discretion with the QRC, which is required "as appropriate" and raises doubts as to whether it is systematically and uniformly applied throughout the administration. The deficiencies in the enforcement strategy are most notable by the absence of an independent assessment body or unit that would verify the compliance of the completed QRC with the required criteria and the absence of guidelines and training for

---

Box 3. Quality regulation checklist

1. Is the proposed legislation and/or regulation absolutely necessary? Is the problem correctly defined and can the objective be achieved by other means (*i.e.* improved information, voluntary schemes, codes of practice, self-regulation, procedural instructions)?

2. Will the legislation affect market entry, result in any restrictions on competition or increase the administrative burden?

3. Is the legislation compatible with developments in the Information Society, particularly as regards electronic Government and electronic commerce?

4. Outline the consideration which has been given to exemptions or simplified procedures for particular economic or social sectors which may be disproportionately burdened by the proposal, including the small business sector.

5. Outline the consideration which has been given to application of the following principles:

    (a) Sunsetting, *i.e.* establishing a date by which the measure will expire unless renewed;

    (b) Review date, *i.e.* a predetermined date on which the efficacy and impact of the proposed new measure will be reviewed;

    (c) The "Replacement" principle, *i.e.* where the body of regulations/legislation in a particular area will not be added to without a corresponding reduction through repeal of an existing measure.

6. Outline the extent to which interested or affected parties have been consulted, including interest groups or representative bodies where such exist. A summary of the views of such parties should be provided.

---

completing the necessary requirements. The poor enforcement infrastructure raises considerable doubts about the effectiveness of the QRC as a useful regulatory tool to assist regulators that they have made the best policy choice.

In principle, the QRC calls upon an assessment of the competition impact of proposed regulations. The competition criteria could be given a wide interpretation by considering the least trade restrictiveness impact of regulations and to encourage regulators to select regulatory instruments that minimise negative impact on competitive conditions. In practice, some recent regulatory decisions regarding the licensing of taxis in the Dublin area and pubs suggest that the competition criterion has not been interpreted in the sense of minimising barriers to entry (see Section 2.6).[21] Although the trade implication in these cases is somehow remote, they nevertheless illustrate that one of the key criteria of the QRC has been ignored in practice. These cases also raise a broader point about the competition criterion that regulators have no incentive to give it a wide interpretation to cover the least trade restrictiveness impact of proposed regulations that have more explicit trade implication.

Ireland should consider bringing together the QRC with the six statements of impact assessment and to complement them with quantitative criteria, such as a cost and benefit analysis. The merged criteria under a revamped QRC would provide a more coherent regulatory tool. Equally important, an independent unit should review compliance of the completed QRC with its guiding criteria. This would act as a major incentive for regulators to take seriously the preparation of the QRC and to better use the criteria as effective tools to guide their regulatory choices. Quantitative criteria should complement the qualitative criteria of the QRC. While it is recognised that the preparation of detailed cost and benefit analysis of proposed legislative and regulatory proposals is a resource-intensive undertaking, the setting up of *a priori* minimum threshold level could be envisaged to avoid making the regulatory process overly burdensome.

Currently there are no formal training programmes or guidelines to assist policy makers in preparing the QRC. Training should be a high priority to ensure more uniform practices and to contribute to put into place a culture of evaluating the impact of legislative and regulatory proposals. Ireland should consider making the QRC more widely available to the public during the consultation process. Improving the availability of this tool to the public would add transparency to the process. As experience will be gained in the preparation of QRC more uniform practices are likely to emerge and to contribute making the QRC an important regulatory tool for mobilising and directing regulatory actions government-wide. The experience with RIA among OECD suggests that an effective RIA programme is both a long-term and far-reaching enterprise, which can be implemented in stages as analytical skills and tools are improved.

The recent economic prosperity has somehow overshadowed the current weaknesses of the Irish regulatory approaches. Current capacity constraints and the emergence of "bottlenecks" in many sectors are undermining the sustainability of the economic expansion and are exposing the fragility of the Irish economic strategy, including its regulatory regime. By strengthening the Irish regulatory approaches based on the above recommendations, Ireland would be better positioned to deal more effectively with eventual external shocks and a less favourable global economic environment. Ireland, being a small open economy, is more exposed to external shocks than larger economies.

2.3.2. *Trade advocacy*

The Trade, Competition and Market Rights Division of the Department of Enterprise, Trade and Employment (DETE) oversees the implementation of transparency provisions relating to Irish obligations contained in the WTO and other trade agreements. This oversight concerns not only obligations regarding transparency but also those concerning non-discrimination and national treatment. The European Commission also plays a similar role at the EU level for subjects falling within its purview. With regard to the elaboration of domestic regulation, DETE has access to all draft regulations and can recommend modifications or deletion of any draft provision that interferes with Ireland's trade and investment obligations.

The DETE also participates actively in the Inter-Departmental Co-ordination for WTO negotiations, which has two main functions. The first is to play a co-ordinating role for determining Irish positions concerning WTO trade negotiations. The second is a co-ordinating role in encouraging government-wide awareness of and respect for international obligations relating to domestic regulatory matters, such as the WTO/GATT Article III (national treatment on internal taxation and regulation) and regulatory commitments arising from other WTO Agreements, such as the Technical Barriers to Trade (TBT) and the Sanitary and Phytosanitary Measures (SPS). Units of the DETE act as the contact points for both the TBT and SPS Agreements.

Throughout 1999 and 2000, public consultations were carried out with representatives from the private sector, non-governmental organisations and civil society with a view to refining Ireland's position regarding a new round of multilateral trade negotiations in the WTO. Ireland supports the launch of a new round with a comprehensive negotiation agenda encompassing tariff reductions, trade-related investment and competition issues, genuine market openness measures for developing countries along with greater recognition for their needs.

2.3.3. Business simplification initiatives

As a business simplification measure pursued under the SMI programme, the process of consolida-tion of Company Law is under way following recommendations made in 1999 by the Working Party on Company Law Compliance and Enforcement. The aim is to consolidate into a single Act all the provisions and related regulations of the Companies Act enacted since 1963, including company regulations made under EU Acts. It is expected that the consolidated company law would contribute to greater transparency and facilitate compliance. The enactment of the Company law Consolidation Bill is expected for early 2002.

The European Commission is also pursuing various initiatives to simplify and improve the Internal Market rules to make cross-border transactions easier and improve competitiveness. In early 2000, the Commission estimated that the regulatory costs and red tape, mostly due to national and regional regulation rather than EC rules, was equivalent to 3-5% of the EU's GDP.[22] One of these initiatives is the *Simpler Legislation for the Internal Market* (SLIM) project, which gathers national regulatory experts and recommends simplification suggestions. Government representatives from DETE will co-ordinate Irish participation in the new group of "better regulation" specialists which will operate under the auspices the EU Internal Market Advisory Committee.

2.3.4. Trade facilitation through customs procedures

In any country, importers can incur significant cost overruns when shipments are held in customs warehouses as a result of inefficiencies in customs procedures. The corruption of Customs officials is also encouraged when regulations provide them with wide discretionary powers. As customs tariffs are generally low within OECD countries, cumbersome customs procedures are increasingly perceived by traders as major trade obstacles and are often assimilated as non-tariff barriers. Lack of transparency or uneven application of customs regulations and procedures between various ports of entry can encourage traders to engage in port shopping to find out which entry ports will provide them more favourable conditions. Inconsistency and lack of transparency undermine the trade policy framework and provide competitive advantages to traders that have benefited from more favourable treatment. Trade flows may then be diverted from entry ports for reasons other than transportation efficiency.

The Irish Customs authorities oversee 41 Customs entry ports distributed throughout the Irish territory. Beginning in 1991, a paper-less system through electronic exchanges was gradually introduced and was fully operational in May 1996.[23] The use of the EU Single Administrative Document (SAD) as a declaration form and electronic exchanges have enabled drastic reductions in the time required for goods to clear customs. Declarations can be customs cleared within a few seconds, instead of six to eight hours per transaction before 1991.

245

The utilisation rate of electronic declaration forms in Ireland grew from 81% to 92% of total import declarations between May 1996 and the end 2000, and from 23% to 80% of total export declarations during the same period. Reflecting its geographical situation, two thirds of total import and export declarations relate to air traffic, percentages that have grown by more than three percentage points between 1997 and 1999. The volume of total customs declarations has more than doubled between 1993 and 1999 reflecting the booming Irish economy.

Box 4. The EU customs procedures

There are over 3 000 Customs entry ports within the European Union distributed within its 15 Member States to respond to air, sea and land border crossing points. EU Customs procedures are carried out in the eleven official languages. Customs officials are not only responsible for the administration of trade policy measures, including customs duties, rules of origin and tariff-quotas, but also for the application of respective national value-added taxes, excise taxes, and a whole range of country-specific national regulations, covering pornography, weapons, health and sanitary protection. In total, EU Customs authorities estimate that they are responsible for the application of over 4 different regulatory measures. The task of managing in a coherent way which ensures an even application of EU customs procedures throughout the 15 different national administrations is therefore colossal, by any standards.

Within the EU, the administration of customs procedures is decentralised among the Member States and the Commission assumes a co-ordinating role. Harmonisation of customs procedures is provided by the application of the Community Customs Code for all Member States and a structure of EU committees is set up for ensuring a proper cohesion. One of these committees is the EU Customs Code Committee, which examines necessary amendments to the Customs Code. The latter contains over 250 Articles and some 900 amendments were approved since 1996. Customs-related legal documents and forms can be retrieved on the Internet (www.europa.eu.int/eur-lex and www.revenue.ie).

Amendments to the Customs Code must be properly notified in the Official Journal of the European Communities before they are enforced. Keeping track of EU amendments is the day-to-day reality for professional customs brokers and their ignorance can imply significant transaction cost overruns and additional administrative burdens on them or their clients.

The implementation of the Single Market in 1993, abolishing all customs checks at the internal borders for the movement of goods, has stretched the limits of the EU paper-based transit procedures and exposed its weaknesses.[1] A temporary Committee of Inquiry was established in December 1995 by the European Parliament to examine the alleged problems with the Community transit system. The four-volume report of the Committee concluded that transit procedures were indispensable for the functioning of the Single Market and recommended a series of recommendations, including the adoption of a comprehensive computerised transit system and the reform of the guarantee system.[2]

The European Commission is pursuing further its efforts to safeguard the uniform application of Community customs law and common trade policy through the ongoing action programme: Customs 2002. This consolidation programme recognises that the abolition of internal borders requires an efficient high-quality control of the external borders to avoid operational divergences in customs matters at national level. It provides for strengthen measures to combat frauds, further developments of common training programmes and more extended computerised procedures at the Union level, including a new computerised transit system.

---

1. The transit procedures aim at facilitating trade within a given customs territory or between separate customs territories. Its essence is to allow the temporary suspension of customs duties, excise and VAT payable on goods originating from and/or destined for a third country while under transport across the territory of a defined customs area.
2. For more details, see Committee of Inquiry into the Community Transit System, Final Report and Recommendations, February 1997, European Parliament, PE 220.895.

2.4. Use of internationally harmonised measures

Compliance with different standards and regulations for like products in different markets often presents firms wishing to engage in international trade with significant and sometimes prohibitive costs. Thus, when appropriate and feasible, reliance on internationally harmonised measures (such as international standards) as the basis of domestic regulations can facilitate trade flows. National efforts to encourage the adoption of regulations based on harmonised measures, procedures for monitoring progress in the development and adoption of international standards, and incentives for regulatory authorities to seek out and apply appropriate international standards are thus important indicators of a country's commitment to efficient regulation.

As an EU Member State, Ireland takes part in the harmonisation process, which was launched in the field of technical regulations and standards to achieve the Single Market. Since 1985, harmonisation has been guided by the "New Approach" adopted by the European Council. Under the New Approach, EU technical regulations no longer seek to define detailed rules, but rather define the "essential requirements" which products placed on the EU market must meet if they are to benefit from free movement within the EU. This more flexible policy approach has replaced the previous guiding policy approach based on the harmonisation of detailed technical specifications for products.

Under the New Approach, manufacturers are free to use any technical specification they deem appropriate to meet the essential requirements defined by EU Directives. Following a mandate issued by the European Commission, the European standardisation bodies have the task of drawing up the technical specifications meeting those essential requirements (such specifications are referred to as "harmonised standards"). Compliance with harmonised standards is voluntary but it grants products a presumption of conformity with the essential requirements. The New Approach benefits European manufacturers, but also non-European manufacturers, as they too are not required to use specific technical rules, but simply have to demonstrate compliance with the essential requirements (for further details on the New Approach, see Box 5).

The notification requirement of national draft standards and technical regulations under EU law aims at ensuring the transparency of national initiatives, but it also plays a role in promoting the European harmonisation process. The notification procedure enables the Commission to propose the approximation of laws in areas where barriers are likely to appear and harmonisation is necessary. The Commission can thus intervene at an early stage and suggest harmonisation before barriers have actually emerged. It can impose a blockage of draft national regulation for twelve months when the regulation deals with a matter covered by a Commission's proposal. The Directive establishing the notification procedure also gives the Commission the possibility to mandate European standardisation bodies with the task of elaborating European standards in a given field. In such cases, standardisation bodies must observe a standstill period during which they cannot carry out any work on the mandated subject.

In Ireland, measures to encourage the use of measures harmonised at the international level are related to the country's membership in the European Union. Integration in the Single Market implies that Ireland adopts European directives, takes part in the harmonisation of technical regulations, and transposes European standards into its own set of standards. By promoting transparency and consultation processes, the EU notification procedures of technical rules provide for safeguards. They put a brake on the elaboration of specific technical rules by national authorities and prevent the emergence of barriers to trade, at least within the Single Market.

Reflecting the harmonisation effort in the EU, Irish indigenous standards account for less than 3% of total standards enforced and published in the NSAI's Catalogue – of about 9 600 standards, there are 286 indigenous standards concentrated in the construction and food sectors. The adoption of an indigenous standard by the NSAI is now a rare occasion, which occurs less than four times a year on average in recent years. These standards are approved only if it can be clearly demonstrated that there is a definite national need for it and that European standards do not exist in that area. New or modified indigenous standards are subject to the notification obligations set up under the EU Directive 98/34.

247

Box 5.   The New and Global Approaches

The need to harmonise technical regulations when diverging rules from Member States impair the operation of the common market was recognised by the Treaty of Rome in Articles 100 to 102 on the approximation of laws. By 1985 it had become clear that relying only on the traditional harmonisation approach would not allow the achievement of the Single Market. As a matter of fact, this approach was encumbered by very detailed specifications which were difficult and time consuming to adopt at the political level, burdensome to control at the implementation level and requiring frequent updates to adapt to technical progress. The adoption of a new policy towards technical harmonisation and standardisation was thus necessary to actually ensure the free movement of goods instituted by the Single Market.

The way to achieve this was opened by the European Court of Justice, with its celebrated ruling on *Cassis de Dijon*,[1] which interpreted Article 30 of the EC Treaty. In effect, the ruling required that goods lawfully marketed in one Member State be accepted in other Member States, unless their national rules required a higher level of protection on one or more of a short list of overriding objectives. This opened the door to a policy based on mutual recognition of required levels of protection and to harmonisation focusing only on those levels, not the technical solution for meeting the level of protection.

In 1985 the Council adopted the "New Approach", according to which harmonisation would no longer result in detailed technical rules, but would be limited to defining the essential health, safety and other[2] requirements which industrial products must meet before they can be marketed. This "New Approach" to harmonisation was supplemented in 1989 by the "Global Approach" which established conformity assessment procedures, criteria relating to the independence and quality of certification bodies, mutual recognition and accreditation.

The New Approach calls for essential requirements to be harmonised and made mandatory by directives. This approach is appropriate only where it is genuinely possible to distinguish between essential requirements and technical specifications; where a wide range of products is sufficiently homogenous or a horizontal risk identifiable to allow common essential requirements; and where the product area or risk concerned is suitable for standardisation. Furthermore, the New Approach has not been applied to sectors where Community legislation was well advanced prior to 1985.

On the basis of the New Approach manufacturers are only bound by essential requirements, which are written with a view to being generic, not requiring updating and not implying a unique technical solution. They are free to use any technical specification they deem appropriate to meet these requirements. Products, which conform, are allowed free circulation in the European market.

For the New Approach, detailed harmonised standards are not indispensable. However, they do offer a privileged route for demonstrating compliance with the essential requirements. The elaboration at European level of technical specifications which meet those requirements is no longer the responsibility of the EU government bodies but has been entrusted to three European standardisation bodies mandated by the Commission on the basis of General Orientations agreed between them and the Commission. The CEN (European Committee for Standardisation), CENELEC (European Committee for Electrotechnical Standards) and ETSI (European Telecommunications Standards Institute) are all signatories to the WTO TBT Code of Good Practice.

When harmonised standards produced by the CEN, CENELEC or ETSI are identified by the Commission, as corresponding to a specific set of essential requirements, the references are published in the Official Journal. They become effective as soon as one Member State has transposed them at the national level and retracted any conflicting national standards. These standards are not mandatory. However conformity with them confers a presumption of conformity with the essential requirements set by the New Approach Directives in all Member States.

The manufacturer can always choose to demonstrate conformity with the essential requirements by other means. This is clearly necessary where harmonised European standards are not (or not yet) available. Each New Approach directive specifies the conformity assessment procedures to be used. These are chosen among the list of equivalent procedures established by the Global Approach (the so-called "modules"), and

The New and Global Approaches (*cont.*)

respond to different needs in specific situations. They range from the supplier's declaration of conformity, through third party type examination, to full product quality assurance.

National public authorities are responsible for identifying and notifying competent bodies, entitled to perform the conformity assessment, but do not themselves intervene in the conformity assessment. When third party intervention is required, suppliers may address any of the notified bodies within the European Union. Products which have successfully undergone the appropriate assessment procedures are then affixed the CE marking, which grants free circulation in all Member States, but also implies that the producer accepts full liability for the product.[3]

The strength of the New Approach and the Global Approach lies in limiting legal requirements to what is essential and leaving to the producer the choice of the technical solution to meet this requirement. At the same time, by introducing EU-wide competition between notified bodies and by building confidence in their competence through accreditation, conformity assessment is distanced from national control. The standards system, rather than being a means of imposing government-decided requirements, is put at the service of industry to offer viable solutions to the need to meet essential requirements, which however are not in principle binding.

The success of the New and Global Approaches in creating a more flexible and efficient harmonised standardisation process in the European Union heavily depends on the reliability of the European standardisation and certification bodies and on the actual efficiency of control by Member States. First, European standardisation and certification bodies need to have a high degree of technical competence, impartiality and independence from vested interests, as well as to be able to elaborate the standards necessary for giving concrete expression to the essential requirements in an expeditious manner. Second, each Member State has the responsibility to ensure that the CE marking is respected and that only products conforming to the essential requirements are sold on its market. If tests carried out by a notified body are cast in doubt, the supervisory authorities of the Member State concerned should follow this up.

---

1. Decision of 20 February 1979, Cassis de Dijon, Case 120/78, ECR p. 649.

2. Energy-efficiency, labelling, environment, noise.

3. See the Council Directive 85/374/EEC of 25 July 1985 on the approximation of the laws, regulations and administrative provisions of the Member States concerning the liability for defective products.

In addition, various initiatives have been developed to promote co-operation in standardisation at the international level. European standardisation bodies have signed co-operation agreements with international standardisation bodies in order to reach the highest possible degree of convergence between European and international standards, and to avoid duplication of standardisation work. In 1991, CEN concluded an agreement with the International Standardisation Organisation (ISO), usually referred to as the "Vienna Agreement". CENELEC and the International Electrotechnical Commission (IEC) have established a similar co-operation agreement (referred to as the "Dresden Agreement"), and ETSI is a party to various international co-operation agreements, notably with ISO, IEC and the International Telecommunication Unit (ITU).

The decline in the production of specific regulations is also reflected in the number of draft technical regulations notified to the European Commission as part of the provision of information in the field of technical standards and regulation (see Box 1 in Section 2.1.2). Since January 1993, Ireland notified 23 technical regulations to the European Commission, compared to a total number of 4 653 for all Member States during the same period. With only three technical regulations notified by Ireland in 1999, the harmonisation process of technical regulations and standards with the EU is almost total.

Overall, the harmonisation process of Irish technical regulations and standards with the EU is comprehensive. However, the latest Single Market Scoreboard released by the European Commission in November 2000 shows that Ireland stands close to the bottom end of the list of EU member states in terms of their score in transposing all Single Economic Market Directives, *i.e.* 12th position. The level of non-transposed Directives during the twelve-month period ending in November 2000 has fallen slightly to 3.6%, compared to 3.9% in May 2000 and 5.4% in November 1999. This reduction has been help by the adoption of the intellectual property legislation in July 2000 and which entered into force on 1 January 2001.

2.5. Recognition of equivalence of other countries' regulatory measures

In cases where the harmonisation of regulatory measures is not considered feasible or necessary, the recognition of other countries' regulatory measures in attaining the same regulatory objective may be the most appropriate avenue for reducing technical barriers related to regulatory divergence. Despite the development of global standards, there are still many specific national rules, which prevent manufacturers selling their products in different countries and from enjoying full economies of scale. Exporters are also increasingly required to demonstrate the compliance of their products with the rules of the country of import through independent testing and certification of the import country, giving rise to additional costs. Reducing trade barriers through recognition of other countries' regulatory measures can be achieved by accepting the equivalence of the standards and technical requirements applicable in other markets, and of conformity assessment results too.

Box 6.   The EU Mutual Recognition Agreements

The EU has concluded MRAs with Australia, Canada, Israel, New Zealand, Switzerland and the United States and all these have entered into force, except the MRA with Switzerland which is underway.[1] The Community has also launched negotiations on "Protocols on European Conformity Assessment" (PECAs) with the Central and Eastern European Countries (CEECs) in view of these countries' eventual accession to the European Union. The main difference between these PECAs and other MRAs is that PECAs are based on the implementation of the *acquis communautaire* in the area of product regulations in these countries.

Each MRA includes a framework covering general principles and sectoral annexes, which contain provisions for facilitation of trade and the mutual recognition of mandatory conformity assessment procedures (for details on sectoral coverage, see Table 6). The framework agreements specify the conditions under which each party accepts the results of conformity assessment procedures issued by the other party's conformity assessment bodies in accordance with the rules and regulations of the importing party. The results of conformity assessment procedures include studies and data, certificates and marks of conformity. The requirements covered by the agreement are specified on a sector-specific basis in the sectoral annexes.

Under these MRAs, there is no recognition between the parties of the equivalence of their respective regulatory requirements. However, if a conformity assessment body in the exporting country certifies that a product covered by a MRA is in conformity to the requirements set by the importing party, this certification has to be accepted as equivalent by the importing party. In the case of Good Manufacturing Practices and Good Laboratory Practices the parties recognise their manufacturing and laboratory practices respectively. Prospective agreements with the CEECs also provide for the alignment of their legislation with the European legislation to allow for their economic integration into the European Union.

---

1.   The MRA with Canada entered into force on 1 November 1998, the MRA with the United States on 1 December 1998 and the MRA with Australia and New Zealand on 1 January 1999.

2.5.1. Mutual recognition within the European Union

Within the European Union the principle of mutual recognition applies among Member States. In its ruling on *Cassis de Dijon*[24] of 1979, the European Court of Justice gave substance to the EU Treaty's principle of free circulation of goods by providing the key elements for mutual recognition. All products lawfully manufactured in one Member State must be accepted by the others even when they have been manufactured in accordance with technical regulations which differ from those laid down by existing national legislation, provided they meet the marketing conditions in the originating Member State. This benefits EU manufacturers and non-EU countries as well since any product, including a product originating from a third country, marketed in one of the EU countries, can circulate freely within the Community (for more details see Box 5 on the New and Global Approaches).

These benefits depend however on the effective implementation of the principle of mutual recognition in each Member State. During the 1996-98 period, the European Commission raised one infringement case against Ireland concerning mutual recognition in the area of products, out of 228 cases for the 15 Member States. Ireland stood in the second place among the Member States, after Luxembourg, for the lowest number of infringements.[25]

2.5.2. Mutual recognition agreements with non-EU countries

As an EU Member, Ireland is involved in the Mutual Recognition Agreements (MRAs) negotiated by the European Commission with non-EU countries. Following the adoption of the Global Approach, when the Council stated the need for the Community *"to promote international trade in regulated products, in particular by concluding recognition agreements,"*[26] the European Commission has engaged negotiation of MRAs in the field of conformity assessment with trading partners. These agreements intend to promote efficient, transparent and compatible regulatory systems, reduce costs and delays associated with obtaining product approvals in third country markets, and avoid duplication of testing procedures and unpredictability incurred in obtaining approvals.

2.5.3. International co-operation in the field of accreditation

The National Accreditation Board of Ireland (NAB) is a member of the two European accreditation organisations: the European Co-operation for Accreditation of Laboratories (EAL) and the European Accreditation of Certification (EAC). These two organisations are now in process of amalgamation into the European Accreditation (EA). The task of the new body is to develop and promote criteria, which ensure equal performance of national accreditation bodies throughout the European Economic Area (EEA). This creates mutual confidence in, and acceptance of, accredited certifications, inspections and test reports. The need for multiple assessments is thereby reduced or eliminated, as a supplier will only need one certificate or report to satisfy several markets. This is laid down in multilateral Mutual Recognition Agreements (MRAs). EA-sponsored MRAs do not only include EEA countries, but also non-European countries, such as Australia, Hong Kong (China), New Zealand and South Africa.

NAB also participates in the International Laboratory Accreditation Co-operation (ILAC) and the International Accreditation Forum (IAF). Many countries throughout the world are represented in these bodies, including USA, Canada, Japan, China, Russia, Australia and New Zealand. These fora aim at promoting confidence in the accreditation systems and at reducing obstacles to trade by supporting the development and implementation of ISO/IEC standards and guides, exchanging information and establishing multilateral agreements on the equivalence of accreditation programmes operated by their members.

2.6. Application of competition principles from an international perspective

The benefits of market access may be reduced by regulatory action condoning anti-competitive conduct or by failure to correct anti-competitive private actions that have the same effect. It is therefore important that regulatory institutions make it possible for both domestic and foreign firms affected by

Regulatory Reform in Ireland

Table 6. Mutual Recognition Agreements concluded or under negotiation by the European Union

	Mutual Recognition Agreements							PECAsc			
	Australia	New Zealand	United States	Canada	Israel	Japan	Swit-zerland	Czech Republic	Hungary	Estonia	Latvia
Construction plant & equipment							✓				N
Chemical GLPa			✓	✓							
Pharmaceutical GMPb	✓	✓	✓	✓		✓	✓			N	N
Pharmaceutical GLPa					✓		✓			N	N
Medical devices	✓	✓	✓	✓		✓	✓		N		
Veterinary medicinal products			✓								
Low voltage electrical equipment	✓	✓	✓	✓			✓	N	N	N	N
Electromagnetic compatibility	✓	✓	✓	✓		✓	✓	N	N	N	N
Telecommunications terminal equipment	✓	✓	✓	✓			✓			N	
Pressure equipment	✓	✓				✓	✓	N			
Equipment & systems used in explosive atmosphere							✓	N			
Fasteners			✓								
Gas appliances & boilers							✓	N			
Machinery	✓	✓				✓	✓	N	N	N	N
Measuring instruments							✓				
Aircraft	✓	✓									
Agricultural & forestry tractors							✓				
Motor vehicles	✓						✓				
Personal protective equipment							✓	N	N		
Recreational craft			✓	✓							
Toys							✓				
Foodstuffs										N	N
Marine safety equipment			N	N							

✓ Concluded
N Under negotiation.
a Good Laboratory Practices.
b Good Manufacturing Practices.
c Protocols on European Conformity Assessments. In July 2000, The European Commission signed agreements with Hungary, the Czech Republic and Latvia in the fields of mandatory approval procedures and mutual recognition of results of conformity assessment procedures. In February 1997 the European Commission signed an agreement with Poland regarding preparatory steps on conformity assessment, precursor for a real PECA.

Source: European Commission.

anti-competitive practices to present their positions effectively. The existence of procedures for hearing and deciding complaints about regulatory or private actions that impair market access and effective competition by foreign firms, the nature of the institutions that hear such complaints, and adherence to deadlines (if they exist) are thus key issues from an international market openness perspective.

In Ireland, complaint about business practices that are perceived to restrict competition may be submitted to the Competition Authority (the Authority). This body was first established in 1991 when a new Competition Act was enacted representing a sea change in policy in that the Competition Act 1991 replaced the former Restrictive Practices Acts and Orders made under those Acts with legislation based by analogy on Articles 85 and 86 (as they then were) of the Treaty establishing the European Community. The new legislation, *inter alia*, prohibited restrictive agreements and abuse of dominance. However, the power to take enforcement action remained the sole responsibility of the (then) Minister of Industry and Commerce. Reflecting increasing concerns about the inability of the Competition Authority to deal effectively with enforcement issues, the Competition (Amendment) Act 1996 brought the enforcement power under its purview. This Act also made all violations of the law potentially criminal offences and set fines and imprisonment as available sanctions. In addition, the government concurrently appointed the "Competition and Mergers Review Group" (CMRG) to examine competition and Merger policy and enforcement processes. The final report of the CMRG was published in May 2000 and contained a series of recommendations concerning enforcement of competition law and the relationships between competition policy and other regulatory institutions. The Irish Government has now decided to draft consolidating Competition Legislation arising from the Report of the CMRG.

The DETE is responsible for policy issues related to the competition law and for consumer protection policy and enforcement. DETE also plays a policy advocacy role in the reviewing of legislative and administrative initiatives, *i.e.* privatisation and deregulation. Consideration of the competition impact of new law and regulation is also a shared responsibility for all departments under the "Strategic Management Initiative". Each department is required "as appropriate" to complete the "quality regulation checklist" for legislative and subordinated regulation and to assess whether its proposals "will affect market entry, result in any restrictions on competition or increase the administrative burden". Despite the pro-competition direction of this regulatory framework, DETE temporarily invoked the Drink Prices Order for a six-month period to regulate drink prices in Irish pubs, instead of eliminating the anti-competitive licensing controls against new entry.

The Irish competition law closely follows the competition policy provisions of the Treaty of Rome (now the Treaty of Amsterdam) and the EU competition law covers practices that affect trade between member States. The European Commission can take actions against practices that limit access of foreign firms to domestic markets. It has done so in several cases involving EU Member States in the past but there are no case involving Ireland. Although EU competition policy applies in Ireland, the Authority is currently hampered in dealing with international matters by constraints on sharing information with competition enforcement agencies of other countries. The European Commission has recently proposed wide-ranging changes in the way its competition policy would be implemented, which could ultimately require modifications in Irish procedures and those of other Member States.

The Authority obtained in 1996 an advocacy power to undertake on its own initiative studies of high priority problems. It initiated a study of the retail drinks market but the study of the bus and rail passenger industry was suspended due to resource constraints. It has also issued a series of discussion papers, one of which concerns the taxi industry. The Authority has no statutory power to initiate on its own a systematic review of, or comment on, legislative proposals. However, DETE may ask for the Authority's views on specific draft laws and regulations, which would be transmitted through DETE.

In this way, the Authority has commented on proposed retail planning guidelines, arguing that efforts to favour Irish firms over foreign competitors would violate EU competition principles. In another case concerning the proposed reform of the electricity supply industry, the Authority's comments emphasised that promoting competition could require separating the industry's operations vertically and limiting the amount of generating capacity under one firm's control. The Authority supported

253

establishing a separate regulatory regime to deal with access charges and output prices, leaving other competition-related issues to be addressed under the general competition law. In 1998, the Authority submitted similar comments to the Department of Public Enterprise (DPE) about transmission and pricing issues in natural gas.[27]

No concerns have been reported that foreign firms would not receive national treatment in the application of the competition procedures when they are seeking redress for perceived anti-competitive problems. One area of particular interest for foreign firms wishing to expand activities in Ireland relates to the Irish merger law. Due to overlapping notification requirements for merger agreements under the Mergers and Take-Overs Act, administered by DETE, and the Competition Act, administered by the Authority, parties are exposed to some legal uncertainty and risk. The CMRG has examined the situation and recommended that a simplified notification process be applied to all mergers over a defined threshold and that mergers no longer be treated as potentially restrictive agreements under the Competition Act. The CMRG also recommended that the provisions of the Competition Act dealing with abuse of dominance should continue to apply to mergers falling below the thresholds for merger notifications, with certain qualifications.

Deregulation initiatives in major infrastructure utility sectors may have created or strengthened the position of incumbents who might be able to impose strategic barriers that raise the cost of entry to foreign and domestic rivals. Furthermore, the advantage so gained in the domestic market may afford an unfair advantage in foreign markets where such firms compete against their foreign rivals. This might be a concern in network industries, such as telecommunications, electricity and airlines. Since 1996, the Authority, its own initiative, went to court for injunctive relief against abuse of dominance in network industries in several cases.

The Authority claimed, in an April 1999 lawsuit, that Telecom Eircom's refusal to grant unbundled access to the local loop constituted an abuse of a dominant position. This suit was intended in part to bridge an apparent jurisdictional lacuna in the rules applied by the independent telecommunications regulator (ODTR) – this lacuna, which existed at the EU level as well, is now being addressed through a regulation on local loop unbundling. The proposed Communications (Regulation) Bill outlined in September 2000 includes provisions for clarifying the relationships between the Authority and the telecommunications regulator (to be renamed the Commission for Communications Regulation).

The Electricity Supply Board (ESB) had proposed a post-liberalisation pricing scheme for its larger customers, which would have given ESB the right to match any lower price offer from another supplier and to lock in customers for 6 months even if ESB did not match the lower price. The Authority's threat of enforcement action led to ESB removing the price matching right and reducing the notice period to 3 months. In 1997, the Authority communicated its concerns to Bord Gais Eireann (gas) about a power plant proposal that could have involved price discrimination among firms that competed at the downstream stage, and that favoured the incumbent supplier's own operations and those of firms in which it had an interest. In 2000, the Authority launched an investigation of the action taken by Aer Lingus in response to the competing service offered by Cityjet between Dublin and London City airports.

Deregulation initiatives in major infrastructure utility sectors have also highlighted the relationships between general competition policy and special sectoral regulators. Ireland has already established several independent regulators and additional regulators are under consideration. The Competition Authority's relationships with these sectoral regulators are still developing. Efficient sharing of responsibilities may be hampered by constraints on sharing information and the lack of clear means for one agency to defer to another about a particular complaint. The Competition Authority considers that these constraints have been addressed in the proposed Communications (Regulation) Bill issued in September 2000 for public consultation.

As these sectoral regulators have begun to proliferate, Ireland has engaged in a debate about the implications of regulatory independence and the relationship with competition policy. Most of these new regulators deal with sectors that are under the jurisdiction of DPE. In March 2000, policy proposals regarding governance and accountability arrangements in the regulated sectors, falling under the responsibility of the Minister of Public Enterprise, were released and are now reflected in specific regulatory measures.

Ireland has obtained commensurate benefits from the participation of foreign firms in its economy. It thus needs to be vigilant to ensure that foreign and domestic firms receive equivalent treatment in procedural and practical terms. It also needs to remain vigilant in applying competition policy to newly deregulated sectors and privatised enterprises to ensure that access and entry are not impeded. Background report to Chapter 3 discusses in greater detail competition and competition enforcement dimensions in Ireland and contains a set of recommendations to further the process of regulatory reform in this area.

3. ASSESSING RESULTS IN SELECTED SECTORS

This section examines the implications for international market openness arising from Irish regulations currently in place for four sectors: telecommunications equipment; telecommunications services; automobiles and components and electricity. For each sector, an attempt has been made to draw out the effects of sector-specific regulations on international trade and investment and the extent to which the six efficient regulation principles are explicitly or implicitly applied. Electricity and telecommunications are reviewed in greater detail in background reports to Chapter 5 and 6 respectively.

Particular attention is paid to product standards and conformity assessment procedures, where relevant. Other issues addressed here include efforts to adopt internationally harmonised product standards, use of voluntary product standards by regulatory authorities, and openness and flexibility of conformity assessment systems. In many respects, multilateral disciplines, notably the WTO TBT Agreement, provide a sound basis for reducing trade tensions by encouraging respect for fundamental principles of efficient regulation such as transparency, non-discrimination, and avoidance of unnecessary trade restrictiveness.

3.1. Telecommunications services

Since 1st December 1998, the Irish market is officially fully opened to competition, in conformity with relevant EU Directives.[28] In mid-2000, there were 70 telecommunications licence holders, of which 45 were operating in the Irish market, most having entered the market after December 1998. Several foreign competitors are now effectively established in the Irish market. Two foreign firms, KPN BV of the Netherlands and Telia AB of Sweden, together hold 35% of total shares of Eircom, the former state-monopoly. British Telecom is active in the mobile and fixed network sectors, through its fixed line subsidiary, OCEAN, and its recent acquisition of Esat Telecom and a shareholding in Esat Digifone. Meteor, the third holder of a mobile licence, is a partnership venture between Western Wireless Corporation of the USA, RF Communications of Ireland and the Walter Group of the USA. The Irish fixed line market is nevertheless still dominated by Eircom with a market share of about 85% (based on revenues) and its affiliated firm Eircell which controls two-thirds of the mobile market.

Ireland had initially negotiated a two year-grace period with respect to EU Directives to complete the liberalisation of national telecommunications markets by 1st January 2000. The delay was sought because of the high debt accumulated by Eircom in delivering universal service and to provide Eircom additional adjustment time to function more effectively within a fully liberalised market. In practice, the grace period was subsequently reduced to 11 months.[29] The completion of the liberalisation of the Irish market brought an end to the historical monopoly for fixed voice telephony by Eircom. Competition was introduced in 1994 for value-added services and in 1997 for mobile telephony when Esat Digifone began operating its GSM license and value-added service providers were allowed to put in place their own networks. The Eircom privatisation process began in 1995 and the government disposed of virtually all its remaining shareholding in July 1999 and furthermore in early 2000 – its remaining shareholding in Eircom is estimated to be below 0.5% in mid-2000.

255

Since full liberalisation, the Irish market has shown dynamic growth in terms of new market participants and investment and development of services. International telephone charges for both business and residential clients are significantly lower than the OECD averages but mobile prices are about 30% above the OECD average (Chapter 6) due to lack of competition exacerbated by delays in the issuance of a third mobile licence (see below). Despite impressive growth, Ireland still lags behind the OECD average in the number of telephone lines as shown in Table 7.

Table 7.   Access lines per 100 inhabitants

Access Lines	1985	1990	1995	1997
Ireland	19.8	28.1	37.0	42.1
OECD average	32.9	39.1	45.6	48.9

Source: OECD *Communications Outlook*, 1999.

The main legislative changes that brought the legal framework for the facilitation of the transition of the sector from a monopoly status to liberalisation, were the transposition of EU Directives into Irish law as well as the Telecommunications (Miscellaneous Provisions) Act of 1996. These regulatory adjustments enabled Ireland to comply with the 1997 WTO Agreement on Basic Telecommunications Services. The EU Directives require the promotion of competition among service operators, the equality of opportunities through the abolition of exclusive or special rights and the promotion of development and use of new services, networks and technologies. The European Commission has therefore played a major role in driving the regulatory reform in Ireland and in other EU Member States as well and it continues to be responsible for guarding against abuse of a dominant position and anti-competitive behaviour at the EU level.

The Department of Public Enterprise has traditionally assumed all regulatory responsibilities over the telecommunications and broadcasting transmission sectors, including the radio frequency spectrum. Pursuant to EU policy where Member States retain ownership of incumbent telecom operators and also carry out regulatory functions, regulatory responsibilities over the sector were transferred to an independent regulatory authority, namely the *Office of the Director of Telecommunications Regulation* (ODTR), which began its functions in July 1997. The scope of the regulatory functions transferred to ODTR is comprehensive and although its decisions and requests for information are binding, enforcement of some decisions has been controversial. The issuance of a third mobile licence to Meteor was appealed regarding the way in which the ODTR's responsibilities were carried out. In the Supreme Court, it was found that the ODTR had acted properly in the matter. However, because the ODTR's decision to grant the licence was suspended while the matter was under appeal, the legal proceedings had the effect of maintaining in the meantime a duopoly situation in the mobile telephony market. As of January 2001, Meteor was still not in operation. Since the introduction of new legal provisions in March 2000, decisions of the ODTR on licensing and interconnection matters, if appealed, can now be implemented by the Director unless the court decides to suspend the decision pending the outcome of the appeal.

Pursuant to the EU Directives on Open Network Provision, ODTR has designated Eircom as having *Significant Market Power* (SMP) in the specified telecommunications markets and imposed obligations, such as offering interconnection on a cost-oriented and non-discriminatory basis for controlling the exercise of their market power. Eircom is a SMP operator in three markets, namely: fixed public telecommunications networks and services, leased line services, and the national interconnection market. Its subsidiary, Eircell, is an SMP operator in the public mobile market and the interconnection market. Esat Telecom's affiliate Esat Digifone was also designated as a SMP operator in the public mobile market. All SMP designations are subject to an annual review by ODTR. Eircom currently has thirteen interconnection agreements with other fixed operators.

In July 2000, the European Commission, following a comprehensive review, published proposals for reforming the telecommunications regulatory framework to accelerate the benefits of competition and enable Europe to reap the benefits of the information society. The plan is that the new regulatory framework will be in place in Member States during 2002. The Irish Government has already outlined legislative proposals to put into effect the new EU regulatory framework in recognition of the expected advantage to be derived from a highly competitive communications sector. Public consultations were launched in September 2000 on the provisions of the proposed legislation.

The proposed Communications Bill also includes provisions to replace the current single Director position with a three-person Commission for Communications Regulation (the Commission). This will help ensure a broad range of expertise and experience at the top level of the regulatory structure and will also make the Commission less vulnerable to any possible future claims of regulatory capture. The powers of the new Commission would be broadened to enable ex-ante regulation to be imposed on specific areas likely to be subject to market distortion and to facilitate dispute resolution. The Bill would also implement several policy proposals pursuant to the March 2000 policy proposals on the *Governance and Accountability in the Regulatory Process*, including the co-ordination of responsibility between the Commission and the Competition Authority.

3.2. Telecommunications equipment

Exports of communications-related equipment from Ireland have tripled in value between 1996 and 1999 (Table 8) and Ireland maintains a sizeable trade surplus in this sector. Imports have doubled during the same period and were instrumental for the vitality and competitiveness of the Irish communications sector.

With respect to the elaboration of technical standards for most radio equipment and telecommunications terminal equipment, the EU Directive (99/5/EC) provides for harmonised European standards and mutual recognition of their conformity. The 99/5/EC Directive replaces the 98/13/EC Directive to account, *inter alia*, for the rapid pace of technical development in this field and that 98/13/EC did not cover a substantial proportion of radio equipment. CEN, CENELEC or ETSI develops these technical standards. As indicated in Section 2.1.3, NSAI must transpose as Irish standards all European standards elaborated by CEN and CENELEC. It is also responsible for managing the public consultation process in Ireland and for adopting ETSI standards. With respect to the elaboration of technical standards for other telecommunications equipment, there are no telecommunications-specific procedures. The generic elaboration procedures for technical regulations and standards, including indigenous standards, apply and are subject to the EU notification requirements (see Section 2.1.2) and EU

Table 8.   Irish trade in communications equipment

Communications equipment (in US$)	HS Numbers	Imports		Exports	
		1996	1999	1996	1999
Telephone equipment					
Telephone sets	85.17.11+19	20 463 637	55 008 473	48 850 781	63 114 933
Switching equipment	85.17.30	09 516 903	16 629 804	39 534 762	24 480 889
Other equipment	85.17.80+90	207 821 369	640 164 664	331 468 463	1782 124 439
Radio, Telephony, Broadcasting					
Tramsmission apparatus	85.25.10.+20	53 373 908	89 801 761	184 038 357	135 194 321
Receivers (radio/tel/broad)	85.27	56 936 948	32 529 664	117 660 998	26 545 242
Television receivers	85.28	66 173 586	67 528 444	05 127 439	77 905 934
Other equipment	85.29	141 291 121	84 538 773	30 461 966	120 124 633
Total		555 577 472	986 201 583	757 142 766	2 229 490 391

Source: OECD, Foreign Trade Statistics, Harmonised System of Classification.

harmonisation as guided by the New Approach (see Section 2.4). At the international level, NSAI is the Irish member of the International Standardisation Organisation (ISO) and of the International Electrotechnical Commission (IEC). A number of mutual recognition agreements are also applicable to telecommunications equipment (see Table 6).

3.3. Automobiles and components

Due to the historic dynamism of global economic activity in the sector and traditionally interventionist policies of some governments aimed at protecting domestic automotive industries, trade tensions related to domestic regulatory issues in general and standards and certification procedures in particular have long figured on bilateral and regional trade agendas. This reflects the fact that automobiles remain among the most highly regulated products in the world, primarily for reasons relating to safety, energy conservation and the environment. Divergent national approaches to the achievement of legitimate domestic objectives in these key policy areas are therefore likely to remain a significant source of trade tension as global demand for automobiles continues to rise.

The Irish motor vehicle industry is virtually non-existent with no domestic production or assembly plants. Harmonised EU safety standards for motor vehicles based on a type approval system and, more recently, the mutual recognition of certification of conformity procedures among EU Member States, have been instrumental for implementing the EU Single Market in automobiles. Buoyant consumer confidence spurred by rapid economic expansion is illustrated by a 40% growth in new motor vehicle registrations in Ireland for the first six-month period in 2000 relative to the same period in 1999 (Table 9).

Table 9.   Motor vehicle registrations in Ireland

New Registrations	1990	1995	1998	1999	2000 (1/2)
Units	109 492	103 303	177 106	212 876	210 380

Source: OICA, Statisticals Yearbook for 1990-98 and the Society of the Irish Motor Industry for 1999-2000.

Within the EU, technical requirements for motor vehicles have been fully harmonised since 1993 – they are not elaborated on the basis of the New Approach (Box 5). Detailed technical requirements are specified in various EU Directives and applicable throughout the EU and EFTA countries. Draft Directives or amendments are submitted by the Commission and published in the Official Journal. During a consultation period, the Commission consults a Working Party on Motor Vehicles composed of representatives of Member States and the EU industry. Following the consultation, the Commission proposes the new Directive or an amendment to the EU Council for approval. The new Directive comes into effect after it is published in the Official Journal.

The certification of these requirements is done through a system of type-approval of motor vehicles. Each vehicle type, whether domestically produced or imported, must be brought to a Regulatory Body testing facility, tested and certified that it meets relevant technical regulations. Each Member State grants the type-approval to any vehicle, which meets the technical requirements of the 54 separate basic Directives for passenger cars. There are also some 100 modifications to the basic Directives. In its Framework Directive (70/156) as amended, the EU has deemed several UN-ECE Regulations to be equivalent to relevant EU technical Directives – in 1999 35 UN-ECE Regulations are recognised as equivalent as well as those listed in Annex II of Directive 97/836.

Since 1996, the conformity of the type-approval certificate for a passenger vehicle delivered in one Member State is valid in all other Member States and the vehicle can be registered or permitted for sale in all EU States. Since 1998, mutual recognition of EU certification of conformity is extended to all vehicles belonging to category M1, including passenger and light commercial vehicles.

Within the EU, motor vehicle distribution must conform to specific legislation as a condition of its exemption from anti-competitive proceedings. The Regulation is known as the block exemption Regulation on the Selective and Exclusive Distribution of Cars, which was renewed in 1995 and extended until September 2002.[30] This Regulation seeks to safeguard consumers' access to vehicle and parts supply in any EU Member State at favourable terms. It provides dealers with enhanced freedom to acquire additional franchises and to resist the imposition of sales targets by manufacturers. Although the franchise agreement can provide for exclusive geographical zones, it is prohibited for dealers to reject sales to a consumer who is a resident of another EU Member State, the so-called prohibition against parallel imports.

The European Commission has sanctioned and imposed hefty fines against Volkswagen in January 1998 (90 million Euro) and the Dutch importer of Opel cars in July 2000 (43 million Euro) for serious infringement of the competition law for having obstructed the proper operation of the Single Market. In July 2000, the fine against Volkswagen, although reduced, was upheld by a decision of the European Court of First Instance.

As a competition enhancement measure, Directorate-General IV (Competition) carries out and publishes a survey of pre-tax retail prices for 73 models applied in each EU Member States. The survey shows the price of individual models in local currencies, in Euro and price indices relative to the country with the lowest price (the lowest price has the reference index of 100%). The last survey carried out 1 May 2000 shows that price differentials among Member States generally vary within an average of 20%. Pre-tax car prices in Ireland are moderate within the EU – 8 models are the referenced cheapest EU prices and two-thirds of the models surveyed are within a 10% price range above to the cheapest EU prices.

Irish consumers are subject to a hefty vehicle registration tax regime under which percentage rates vary depending on the size of the engine (from 22.5 to 30%), plus the regular value-added-tax of 21%. Vehicles in Ireland are right-hand drive, hence Irish consumers have few opportunities outside Ireland and the United Kingdom for testing and ordering their vehicles. Since the UK pre-tax prices are among the highest in the EU, Irish consumers currently have no incentives to buy cars in the UK.

Harmonised EU safety standards for motor vehicles and the mutual recognition of certification of conformity procedures among EU Member States are instrumental in the implementation of the EU Single Market for motor vehicles and contribute to minimise price differential within the EU due to

---

Box 7. Global technical regulations for wheeled vehicles

In recent years, support was voiced for strengthening the legal and administrative capacity of the 1958 Agreement of Working Party 29 of the United Nations – Economic Commission for Europe (UN-ECE) as the principal body for common development of technical standards and regulatory requirements for motor vehicles. A new Agreement was concluded in June 1998 on Global Technical Regulations for Wheeled Vehicles, which shall facilitate the full participation of countries operating either the type-approval or the self-declaration systems of conformity of standards. The UN-ECE Global Agreement is entitled "Agreement concerning the establishment of global technical regulations for wheeled vehicles, equipment and parts, which can be fitted and/or be used on wheeled vehicles". The 1998 Agreement opens up the possibility for establishing "global technical regulations" proposed by its contracting parties and which must be approved by consensus. The new Agreement was ratified by the eight countries or regional organisations, including the EU, the USA, Japan, Canada and the Russian Federation, and entered into force on 25 August 2000.

regulatory factors. While significant price differentials still persist, the European Commission closely monitors these and actually sanctions car manufacturers that infringe on the relevant EU competition law. Ireland only has consumer interests to protect in the automobile sector. It should continue supporting EU initiatives eliminating regulatory obstacles and sanctioning anti-competitive practices in this sector.

3.4. Electricity

Reforming the Irish electricity sector has been on the government's agenda for some time and focuses on the multiple policy objectives of ensuring security, reliability, competitiveness and efficiency in energy supplies while meeting sustainable development and environmental objectives. The reform of the electricity and gas sectors is analysed in detail in the background report to Chapter 5 in this volume. The EU Electricity and Gas Single Market Directives have also been instrumental in reassessing the regulatory framework in a broader context of EU-wide competition conditions and consumer needs. The Irish energy sector remains dominated by the activities of four state-owned enterprises: Electricity Supply Board (ESB) (electricity), Bord Gáis Éireann (BGE) (gas), Bord na Móna (peat) and the Irish National Petroleum Corporation (INPC) (oil) which owns and operates the only refinery on the island. With regard to oil, 65% of the market is accounted for by private sector oil companies, with the INPC accounting for the remaining 35%. The Electricity Regulation Act of 1999 brought the legislative changes to implement the necessary minimum provisions of the EU Electricity Directive before the transposition deadline of February 2000, one year after most other EU Member States. The Commission for Electricity Regulation (the Regulator) was established to exercise regulatory functions for granting and revoking licences, authorising the construction of new generating stations, approving access charges to the transmission and distribution systems and resolving disputes. It is estimated that 31% of total electricity demand was liberalised in February 2000. Although the EU Electricity Directive requires that 33% of respective national electricity market be opened up in 2003, Ireland has announced that the Irish electricity market will be fully opened by 2005.

Ireland has also transposed through various legislative measures and administrative requirements the EU Gas Directive which implementation deadline was set for 10 August 2000. Additional legislative changes are in the offing that would provide for the transfer of gas regulatory functions from the Department of Public Enterprises to the existing Commission for Electricity Regulation by mid-2001 and the transformation of BGE into a public limited company. A consolidated Gas Bill might be considered in late 2001. Since 1995, large gas customer consuming more than 25 million cubic metres per year have been able to choose their supplier which is equivalent to 75% of total Irish gas demand. With the implementation of the EU Gas Directive, choice was extended all gas-fired power generators and free choice for all consumers will be gradually implemented up to 2008, although full market liberalisation by 2005 is under consideration.

Electricity consumption has increased by more than 50% in the 1990s as the economy expanded rapidly. Ireland has few indigenous sources of energy supplies and it relies on imports for about three-quarters of its total energy needs. With the recent determination of commercial viability of the Corrib offshore gas discovery in the West Coast, the reliance on imported energy supply is expected to decline. The development and construction of the connecting pipelines to shore and onshore to the existing network will require considerable investment and is unlikely to be completed before 2003.

With 17% of the country occupied by peatland, peat is used as energy source in five power stations and the electricity produced accounts for about 7% of total electricity production in 1999. A new peat plant came into commercial operation in December 2000 and is operated by the Finnish group, Fortum. ESB also plans to construct two new peat stations, in line with the orderly closure of ESB's existing stations within the next few years. Security of supply and socio-economic factors have been prominent factors in the policy decisions to begin and maintain peat-related operations. The International Energy Agency (IEA) estimates that the cost of generating electricity from peat exceeds by more than 50% the cost of generating electricity from alternative fuel (IEA, 1999).[31] With high oil prices throughout 2000[31], the estimated excess cost would be lower.

Another indigenous source of energy for electricity generation is the gas production from the Kinsale and Ballycotton fields, whose reserves may be exhausted for commercial purposes after 2005. ESB consumes about 50% of total gas demand and it is the largest single consumer of BGE. Since 1993, gas is increasingly imported through a gas interconnector from Scotland with a capacity of 17 million standard cubic metres per day to be achieved by October 2001. Given the strength of electricity and gas demand, total gas demand is soon expected to exceed the interconnector capacity. The Irish electricity transmission system is linked to the Northern Ireland system but net imports account for less than 2% of total electricity supply in 2000. Except for Northern Ireland, there are no possibilities for interconnecting the Irish electricity grid on a commercial basis due to the geographical location of the island. Hence, further developing the interconnection with Northern Ireland offers possibilities for realising added efficiency gains in electricity generation, transportation and distribution on the island.

Table 10.   Electricity production by fuel sources

Fuels	1995	2010
Gas	29%	64%
Peat	11%	5%
Coal	39%	17%
Renewables	5%	8%
Oil	16%	6%

Source: International Energy Agency (1999), Electricity Supply Board, p. 56.

The Irish electricity market is small by EU standards and the prospect for entry of new competitors in the Irish electricity market is linked to the lifting of prevailing market uncertainties about the future sources of gas supply that will be required to meet the expected demand growth. In the meantime, the dominant position of the incumbent state-owned enterprises is likely to remain. Decisions about the timing and magnitude of the potential commercial development of the Corrib gas reserves will influence the consideration of alternative supply sources. With the determination of commercial viability of the Corrib reserves, authorisation and construction of a new supply pipe will be rapidly required.

The Commission for Electricity Regulation, supported by an adequate staff and resources, has a crucial role to play for developing the trading mechanisms needed to encourage and to protect new competitors, particularly small investors, in electricity generation and supply assets. Concerns still remain about the potential abuse of dominant positions by the incumbent state-owned enterprises in the Irish energy sector.

4.   CONCLUSIONS AND POLICY OPTIONS FOR REFORM

4.1. General assessment of current strengths and weaknesses

Ireland's stellar growth performance in recent years reflects an array of policy and sectoral reforms, in particular Ireland's commitments in the context of the ongoing EU integration process with the Single European Market Programme and the Economic and Monetary Union. Efforts were made to improve the education level of the baby boom generation that entered the labour market in the 90s. Large and sustained foreign investment, partly lured by generous incentives, has transformed Ireland's production capacity and broadened its trading interests beyond the EU market. However, economic prosperity has overshadowed the current weaknesses of the Irish regulatory approaches. Current capacity constraints and the emergence of "bottlenecks" in many sectors are undermining the sustainability of the economic expansion and are exposing the fragility of the Irish economic strategy, in particular its regulatory regime. Ireland would deal more effectively with eventual external shocks and a less favourable global economic environment if it were to strengthen its regulatory approaches.

Not all of the six efficient regulation principles examined in this review are expressly codified in Irish administrative and regulatory oversight procedures to the same degree. However, the weight of available evidence suggests that the principles of non-discrimination, use of international standards and recognition of equivalence are given ample expression in practice. Integration in the EU implies that Ireland adopts EU Directives and takes part in the harmonisation of technical regulations.

The content of the Strategic Management Initiatives (SMI) and the ensuing action plan for regulatory reform are broadly in line with regulatory standards in place across the OECD area, albeit there were more recently put into place. The policy fosters transparency and accountability by stressing the need for consultation and rules-based procedures. Although public consultations on regulatory matters have lost a great deal of its informality, it remains that each government Department has discretionary power for carrying out the public consultation process in terms of the duration and the moment of the consultation and the selection of the interested parties. There are no common criteria for evaluating the quality of either the consultation or the decisions taken by the regulators on the selected consultation mechanism. A pro-competitive stance calls for a more formalised public consultation process encompassing the broad range of civil society interests, particularly consumer interests.

The requirement to complete the Quality Regulatory Checklist (QRC) provides a more structured approach for Irish policy makers to improve the quality of the information on which decisions are based and to integrate some of the efficient regulatory principles into the decision making process of regulatory matters. However, the regulatory approach relies only on qualitative criteria and completely ignores quantitative criteria, such as cost and benefit analysis that can be a useful tool for comparing the benefits to specific interest groups versus the costs born by society as a whole.

There is an element of discretion with the QRC, which is required "as appropriate" and raises doubts as to whether it is systematically and uniformly applied throughout the administration. There are several deficiencies in the enforcement system. It lacks an independent assessment body or unit that would verify the compliance of the completed QRC with the required criteria, and lacks guidelines and training for policy makers to assist them in completing the necessary requirements. The poor enforcement infrastructure raises considerable doubts on the effectiveness of the QRC as a useful regulatory tool to assist policy makers that they have made the best policy and regulatory choice.

Although the QRC requires consideration of the competition impact of proposed regulations, some recent regulatory decisions regarding the licensing of taxis in the Dublin (a decision subject to an appeal) and pubs suggest that this competition criteria has not been interpreted in the sense of minimising barriers to entry. These cases highlight the need for strengthened enforcement mechanisms to review the quality of the assessment.

Ireland should consider bringing together the QRC with the six statements of impact assessment and to complement them with quantitative criteria. The merged criteria under a revamped QRC would provide a more coherent regulatory tool. The QRC should be made available to the public during the consultation process. Improving the availability of this tool to the public would add transparency to the process and act as a powerful way to formalise public consultation and, simultaneously, improving the quality of the QRC. As experience will be gained in the preparation of this regulatory tool more uniform practices will emerge and contribute making it an important regulatory tool for mobilising and directing regulatory actions government-wide.

Considerable efforts have been made to reduce the role of government in economic activities in exposing previously sheltered firms to competition forces. An institutional competition infrastructure has been established through the Competition Authority and two independent regulators, for the telecommunications and the electricity sectors respectively. Although the Irish Government is committed to liberalising these two sectors, two large players hold dominant positions in the telecommunications sector and state-owned enterprises still dominate the energy sector. Concerns remain about the potential abuse of their dominant position in these sectors.

4.2. The dynamic view: the pace and direction of change

Ireland has gained commensurable benefits by pursuing trade liberalisation, welcoming foreign-owned firms and integrating in the world economy. Ongoing economic successes are leading to capacity constraints and are threatening the sustainability of its future economic performance. There is a need for balancing growth objectives with sound competitive conditions for ensuring efficient use of resources, labour in particular. Continuing focus on market openness through import competition will contribute to reduce inflationary pressures in wages and costs of building materials and of services. Import competition can play a crucial role in government procurement by facilitating the completion of projects on time and keeping downward cost pressure on goods and services purchased. Facilitating labour mobility within the EU and from abroad through the recognition of professional qualifications will be instrumental in improving the availability of required skills and for easing inflationary pressures, particularly in services-related sectors where demand is expected to remain strong in the foreseeable future.

The recent economic expansion has overshadowed the need to put in place a more rules-based regulatory regime that fosters economic efficiency, minimise obstacles to growth and promote sound competitive conditions. Ireland would deal more effectively with eventual external shocks and a less favourable global economic environment if it were to strengthen its regulatory approaches. Ireland, being a small open economy, is more vulnerable to external shocks than larger economies.

One policy consequence for Ireland and other EU qualified members under the European Monetary Union is that they no longer have the option of devaluating domestic currencies as a policy instrument to improve the international competitiveness of their domestic firms. However, Ireland remains particularly vulnerable, unlike any other EU Member States, to large fluctuations in the external value of the Euro since its largest trading partners are not Euro-members. The United Kingdom and the United States together account for more than a third of total exports and almost half of total imports. In this context, the importance of establishing a sound regulatory framework that minimises domestic obstacles to growth and maximises competitive conditions is more crucial than ever. Ireland would maximise the return of its market openness approach by pursuing additional efforts in applying a set of efficient regulation principles as discussed in this review.

4.3. Policy options for consideration

This section identifies actions that, based on international consensus on good regulatory practices and on concrete experiences in OECD countries, are likely to be beneficial to improving regulation in Ireland. They are based on the recommendations and policy framework in 1997 OECD Report to Ministers on Regulatory Reform.

1. *Enhance transparency through the publication in the Official Journal of the text of draft regulations, with information about the period of public consultation; and through the availability of draft regulations on the Internet.*

   These steps would contribute to improving the transparency of the elaboration process of new regulations by providing information more rapidly to all potentially affected parties, thereby widening the basis for consultation.

2. *Merge together the Quality Regulation Checklist with the six statements of impact assessment and complement the qualitative criteria with quantitative ones, such as a cost and benefit analysis;*

   Adapt the QRC to include explicit references to the "efficient regulation principles";

   Set up a priori minimum threshold level below it the cost and benefit analysis would not required to avoid making the regulatory process overly burdensome;

Establish an independent unit to review compliance of the QRC with its provisions, and establish appropriate guidelines and training programmes to ensure a more uniform application of the QRC;

Make the QRC widely available to consulted parties, possibly through the Internet.

A revamped QRC would provide a more coherent regulatory tool to assist regulators in the exercise of the regulatory choices. Current deficiencies in enforcement of the QRC are undermining its effectiveness as a useful regulatory tool.

3. *Heighten awareness of and encourage respect for the efficient regulation principles by the county councils, regional bodies and large cities in their regulatory activities affecting international trade and investment.*

Through the co-operation institutions between the central government and sub-central bodies, the central government should promote the awareness and encourage respect of efficient regulation principles.

4. *Continue to encourage the use of international standards as a basis for national standardisation activities and to promote international harmonisation in the European and international fora.*

A strong commitment to an efficient and reliable standardisation system not only enhances market opportunities for Irish firms but also greatly contributes to the consolidation world-wide of efficient and transparent markets for industry and consumers.

5. *Continue to support EU initiatives seeking the elimination of regulatory obstacles in the automobile sector and sanctioning automobile distribution practices that are obstructing the proper operation of the Single Market in the automobile sector.*

6. *Encourage a strengthened enforcement of competition policy recognising its increasing importance for market openness; and implement the measures recommended in Chapter 3, including an increase in the professional staff for the Competition Authority to support the Authority's independent advocacy function.*

With the potential privatisation of several state-owned enterprises and sectoral reforms exposing previously sheltered sectors to competition forces, concerns remain about potential anti-competitive practices, including the potential abuse of dominant positions. Therefore, strong enforcement of competition policy is needed to prevent regulatory or private actions that would impair market access and effective competition by foreign firms.

NOTES

1. Due to a significant level of overseas involvement in the Irish economy, the Gross National Product (GNP) is probably a better indicator of economic prosperity in Ireland than the GDP. However, for country comparison purposes, the GDP indicator is more appropriate.

2. The cumulative total of net emigration from Ireland in the 110 years up to 1991 was 2.8 million persons. OECD (1999) Economic Surveys: Ireland, Paris, p. 36.

3. Barry, Frank *et al.* (1997).

4. O'Malley, Eoin (1980), pp. 6-8.

5. In 1997, the EU simple average tariff rate across all products stood at 10%. The average rate for agricultural products (HS 1-24) stood at 20.8% in 1997. See, WTO (1997), pp. 44-45.

6. Ó Gráda, Cormac (1997), pp. 45-55.

7. See, in particular OECD (1998); OECD (1994) and OECD (1995*a*).

8. See related discussion in OECD (1997*a*), Chapter 2: "Regulatory Quality and Public Sector Reform".

9. As provided by Directive 98/34/EC of 22 June 1998. The Directive codified and replaced Directive 83/189/EEC which had established the procedure and had been subsequently amended.

10. "CIA Security International vs. Signalson SA and Securitel SPRL", Decision of the European Court of Justice of 30 April 1996 (Case C-194/94).

11. The procedure was established by a December 1995 Decision of the EU's Council of Ministers and the European Parliament (3052/95) and came into effect on 1 January 1997.

12. European Commission (2000).

13. http://europa.eu.int/business/en/index.html.

14. http://www.newapproach.org.

15. The Public Supplies Directive (93/36/EEC); the Public Works Directive (93/37/EEC); the Public Services Directive (92/50/EEC); the Public Remedies Directive (89/665/EEC); the Utilities Directive (93/38/EEC); and the Remedies Utilities Directive (92/13/EEC).

16. See the Forum on Public Procurement's website http://www.fpp.ie.

17. See *Small Firms and Public Procurement in Ireland*, a Summary for the Study Prepared for the Department of Enterprise, Trade and Employment, Networks Resources Limited, July 1999.

18. In early 1998, the EU had the following free trade agreements: Europe Agreements with Hungary, Poland, Czech Republic, Slovakia, Romania, Bulgaria, Romania, Estonia, Latvia, Lithuania, Slovenia; and Euro-Mediterranean Agreements with Cyprus, Malta, Israel, Tunisia, Morocco and Palestinian Authority.

19. See OECD (1995*b*).

20. See OECD (1997*b*), *Regulatory Impact Analysis – Best Practices in OECD Countries*, Paris.

21. To deal with a constant problem of long waiting times, poor services and monopolistic behaviour reflected by the increasing value of a taxicab licence, the Minister of the Environment and Local Government adopted a secondary legislation in late 1999. It provides for the replacement of current licences for new licences to existing holders and 500 new licences would be made available favouring co-drivers under existing licences. The new regulation was challenged in the Irish High Court. The Court found (delivered on 13 October 2000) that the Minister was not empo-

wered under the Road Traffic Act to make a regulation. The Judge also stated that regulation may indirectly discriminate against EU Member States in a manner which is prohibited under the EU obligation – the great majority of existing licence holders are Irish nationals, thus precluding nationals of other EU Member States from becoming the owners of new taxi licences.

22. See The European Commission, Up Date on the Single Market, Commission moves to simplify single market legislation, 6 march 2000, (www.europa.eu.int/comm/internal_market).

23. The computerised system is based on the United Nations Electronic Data Interchange Protocol and harmonised data-set (UN/EDIFACT) and it enables users to submit their import and/or export declarations to Customs authorities and to receive customs permissions through electronic exchange.

24. Decision of the European Court of Justice of 20 February 1979, Cassis de Dijon, Case 120/78.

25. See European Commission (1999).

26. See European Council (1989), 90/C 10/01.

27. See, Competition Authority (1998).

28. The EU Directives are composed of: Terminal Equipment Directive (88/301/EEC); Services Directive (90/388/EEC); ONP Framework Directive (90/387/EEC) and ONP Leased Lines Directive (92/44/EEC). Other EC Directives include: Satellite Directive (94/46/EC); Cable Directive (95/51/EC); Mobile Directive (96/2/EC); Full Competition Directive (96/19/EC) and Licensing Directive (97/13/EC). Finally ONP Interconnection Directive (97/33/EC): ONP Amending Directive (97/51/EC); Telecom Data Protection Directive (97/66/EC); ONP Voice Telephony Directive (98/10/EC).

29. Extension periods were also accorded to Luxembourg (1 July 1998), Portugal (1 January 2000), Greece (31 December 2000) and Spain (1 January 2003 but full liberalisation effectively occurred on 1 December 1998).

30. The Commission Regulation (EC) No. 1475/95 on the application of Article 85(3) of the Treaty to certain categories of motor vehicle distribution and servicing agreements was adopted in June 1995 and applies until September 2002.

31. International Energy Agency (1999).

BIBLIOGRAPHY

Barry, Frank *et al.* (1997),
  Single Market Review: Aggregate and Regional Impact – the cases of Greece, Spain, Ireland and Portugal, Kogan Page, London.

Competition Authority (1998),
  Patrick Massey & Tony Shortall, *Competition in the Natural Gas Industry*, Discussion Paper No. 5, November.

European Commission (2000),
  Single Market Scoreboard, Brussels, May.

European Commission (1999),
  Principles of Mutual Recognition: Working Towards More Effective Implementation, Single Market News, No. 17, July, Brussels.

European Council (1989),
  Council Resolution of 21 December 1989 on a Global Approach to Conformity Assessment, Brussels.

Greer, Heather (1999),
  Small Firms and Public Procurement in Ireland, a Summary for the Study Prepared for the Department of Enterprise, Trade and Employment, Networks Resources Limited, July.

International Energy Agency (1999),
  Ireland 1999 Review, Energy Policies of IEA Countries, Paris.

OECD (1998),
  Open Markets Matter; The Benefits of Trade and Investment Liberalisation, Paris.

OECD (1997a),
  The OECD Report on Regulatory Reform, Volume II: Thematic Studies, Paris.

OECD (1997b),
  Regulatory Impact Analysis, Best Practices in OECD Countries, Paris.

OECD (1995a),
  Report on Trade and Environment, Paris.

OECD (1995b),
  Recommendation of the Council of the OECD on improving the quality of government regulation, including the OECD reference checklist for regulatory decision-making and background note, OECD/GD(95)95, Paris.

OECD (1994),
  The Environmental Effects of Trade, Paris.

Ó Gráda, Cormac (1997),
  A Rocky Road: The Irish Economy since the 1920s, Manchester University Press, Manchester and New York,

O'Malley, Eoin (1980), *Industrial Policy and Development: A survey of Literature from the Early 1960s to the Present*, National Economic and Social Council, Report No. 56, December.

WTO (1997), *Trade Policy Review*, European Union, Geneva.

BACKGROUND REPORT ON REGULATORY REFORM IN ELECTRICITY, GAS, PHARMACIES, AND LEGAL SERVICES*

---

* This report was principally prepared by **Sally Van Siclen**, Principal Administrator, of the OECD's Division for Competition Law and Policy. It has benefited from extensive comments provided by colleagues throughout the OECD Secretariats, by the Government of Ireland, and by Member countries as part of the peer review process. This report was peer reviewed in October 2000 by the Working Party on Competition and Regulation of the Competition Law and Policy Committee of the OECD.

269

© OECD 2001

TABLE OF CONTENTS

List of Boxes

List of Tables

List of Figures

Note by the Secretariat

Sectoral reforms in Ireland have been an important part of the move toward market-based growth but as yet progress has varied among the sectors. Work by the OECD and by other organisations indicates that a range of key regulatory and competition issues remain in many sectors. In this report, we examine selected issues in electricity, gas and professional services, using legal services and pharmacies as case studies.

ELECTRICITY AND GAS

1. INTRODUCTION

The Irish electricity and gas sectors are dominated by two vertically integrated state-owned entities, the Electricity Supply Board (ESB) and Bord Gáis, respectively. Electricity and gas demand are growing rapidly, reflecting GDP growth. The shift toward gas as the electricity generating fuel of choice mean that incremental electricity generation requires incremental natural gas supply. By 2010, or earlier, 70% of electricity is likely to be generated by gas and in 2000 shortages of gas were projected in winter 2002

Reducing the cost of non-traded, as well as traded, goods and services improves the competitiveness of Ireland. Effective competition in the non-traded sectors reduces costs. In other European Union Member states, the EU directives in electricity and gas have been used as springboards to re-examine thoroughly the structure and regulation of those sectors and, in many cases, to reform and introduce competition that lowers costs. There is in Ireland, while the economy is growing robustly, and before any actual ownership has been transferred from the state, an opportunity for reform that truly promotes the interests of consumers and the competitiveness of the whole economy.

Such reform involves changes in structure, regulation and institutions. Structural change means separation into distinct companies, with distinct commercial objectives and ultimately distinct owners, of electricity generation from supply, and both from the grid business of transmission-distribution, as well as investments in transmission to make significant trade with Northern Ireland and Scotland feasible. It may be advisable to create separate, competing generation companies, or it may be sufficient to develop an all-island market and promote competitive entry into electricity generation. (A fundamental issue in Ireland is the size of electricity demand as compared with the size of existing generating units, the minimum efficient scale of new generating units, and whether the legal framework supports two or more independent owners of capacity at a single generating plant.) In gas, structural change means a similar separation of transmission from supply, or alternatively to retain vertical integration while selling rights to transmission capacity and introducing competition in transmission. Changes in regulation mean proceeding with the transformation of the entities into limited liability companies, and also imposing on their boards commercial objectives and incentives. It means too introducing economic regulation that provides incentives for efficiency and competition, such as a price cap regime. But without private investors pushing for better returns, incentive-compatible regulation like price caps has but an attenuated effect on companies' efficiency. Access to the electricity and gas transmission networks needs to be non-discriminatory, at prices that induce their efficient use, and subject to independent regulation, as is already the case for electricity. Reforming institutions means putting into place an independent regulator with effective regulatory powers exercised within the policy framework with accountability to Government and Parliament, and ensuring that the Competition Authority applies the competition laws and advocates for competition principles in the sectors.

A main obstacle to private investment in the sectors is regulatory uncertainty. Laws and institutions are not yet fully in place in Ireland, and policies not clearly set out. While progress was made in the course of 2000 – the independent regulatory institution was staffed and operating, and had been

273

granted regulatory authority over final electricity tariffs, and access to gas (necessary for new electricity generation) was allocated – as of early 2001 the independent transmission operator was neither incorporated nor staffed and the principles for gas transmission tariffs were under review. Delay favours the incumbent state-owned firms, who due to the implicit state guarantees are relatively unaffected by policy uncertainty. As long as new generating capacity and new gas transmission capacity are put off, the incumbents' dominance if not monopoly are prolonged. Thus, within a framework of market-oriented proposals and widespread consultation, the Government should undertake to reduce the delays and uncertainty in the future legal framework for these sectors.

2. POLICY OBJECTIVES

The Department of Public Enterprise has three main policy objectives. These are: to promote the evolution of competitive energy (and other) sectors to contribute to Irish competitiveness, to manage any change in ownership to "best cater for the development of the sectors and the long term interests of the companies and their employees," and to provide an effective regulatory framework that balances independence and accountability (DPE 1998) More specifically for the energy sector, the objectives are:

- To ensure environmentally sustainable energy production and consumption;

- To develop a competitive energy supply industry;

- To ensure security and reliability of energy supply;

- To maximise energy efficiency; and

- To ensure that energy infrastructure is operated safely (DPE 1998).

The difficulty of reconciling these objectives is acknowledged, and indeed implementation to date reflects tradeoffs. Thus, the objective of competitive energy sectors is to be striven for not by changing the structure of the incumbents, but rather by new entry into the potentially competitive activities of the sectors. But entry is foreseen to be limited: Under a Tripartite Agreement (between the managers and unions of ESB, and government), the incumbent electricity monopoly will seek to retain about 60% share of the electricity market. Security of supply was given priority over competition development in the July 2000 statutory instrument on allocating gas capacity for electricity generation, and, in the event, one-third of the capacity was allocated to the incumbent electricity generator.

However, the DPE has noted that these objectives can be congruent. The DPE has written that, in the long term, the best assured future for the companies for which it exercises ownership and their employees is achieved by planning for inevitable liberalisation and moving ahead of minimum requirements.

3. DESCRIPTION OF THE SECTOR

The Electricity Supply Board (ESB) and Bord Gáis Éireann (Irish Gas Board) dominate all activities in the eponymous sectors. ESB consumes about half of all gas consumed in Ireland. Both the ESB and Bord Gáis are fully state-owned "State-sponsored bodies".[1] (A diverse group of entities has the status of "State-sponsored bodies" in Ireland.) Access to the grids is regulated, by the Commission for Electricity Regulation (CER) for electricity and through Government directives for gas. CER is expected to begin, in 2001, to regulate final electricity tariffs for captive consumers in addition to its current regulation of the of generators and suppliers of electricity. The Government, as owner, controls other aspects of the sectors. Prices of electricity for both industrial and domestic customers are low by European standards, and about median among International Energy Agency members. Two plants, Moneypoint (coal) and Poolbeg (gas) generate more than 20% and about 22%, respectively, of total electricity in the Republic.

Since February 2000, about 30% of electricity demand (nearly 400 large users, using more than 4 million kWh annually) may choose electricity supplier. This is the first step in a phased liberalisation of all electricity consumers by 2005 (ESB 2000). Since 1995, gas consumers with annual usage above 25mcm/year, and since August 2000, all power generators irrespective of size, have been able to choose their gas supplier and transport the gas through Bord Gáis' network. (This amounts to 6 to 8 large users and about 60 small-scale power generators accounting for about 75% of demand.) This degree of consumer liberalisation meets or exceeds that specified in the directives agreed by European Union Member states. The EU electricity directive allowed Ireland an additional year to implement the first phase of liberalisation.

New electricity generators are poised to enter the Irish market, according to market participants. Some already supply power to liberalised Irish consumers, and will have built generating plants in a few years. However, in the short term, gas transmission capacity restricts the number of new gas-fired power plants to two or three.

Ireland's energy sectors are moulded by its location and geology. Perched on the edge of Eurasia, Ireland can, with current connections of 280MW, trade a limited quantity of electricity, and that only with Northern Ireland. While this connection will be upgraded, and a connection between Northern Ireland and Scotland built, their capacity could supply only a small part of total Irish demand. About two-thirds

Figure 1. **International price comparisons**
Industrial electricity prices in selected OECD countries, 1998

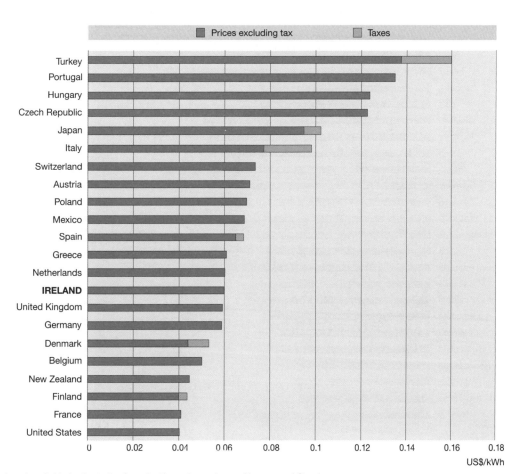

Note: Data not available for Australia, Canada, Korea, Luxembourg, Norway, and Sweden.

Source: IEA/OECD (2000), *Energy Prices and Taxes*, 3rd quarter, Paris.

of natural gas (63% in 1999) arrives via one pipeline from Scotland. Electricity is also generated from imported coal and oil and indigenous peat, which is a soft organic material formed by partial decomposition in water of plants for a few thousand years.

Access to the limited capacity of the gas interconnector from Scotland is key to the expansion of electricity generation in the short term. The existing indigenous gas field is nearly depleted but another, Corrib, was discovered in the 1990s. The press reports that Corrib will be developed. However, if the Corrib field is not developed in time, then a second gas pipeline from Britain will have to be built in the next half-decade. It could be provided without government or other external assistance (IEA, 1999) and a variety of private and public sector proposals have been made – paralleling the current pipeline to Scotland, to Wales, and to Northern Ireland.

There is excess demand for the gas interconnector capacity. By October 1999, *Bord Gáis* had received applications for gas capacity which corresponds to a total of 4 000 MW additional gas-fired generating capacity (DPE, 1999). In July 2000, a statutory instrument was signed (S.I. No. 237 of 2000, Gas (Amendment) Act, 2000, (Section 2) Regulations, 2000, 26 July 2000) that instructed CER to allocate a fixed amount of gas transmission capacity to new power generation. The statutory instrument gave priority to supply shortage considerations over competition considerations. In the event, gas transmission

Figure 2. **International price comparisons**
Household electricity prices in selected OECD countries, 1998

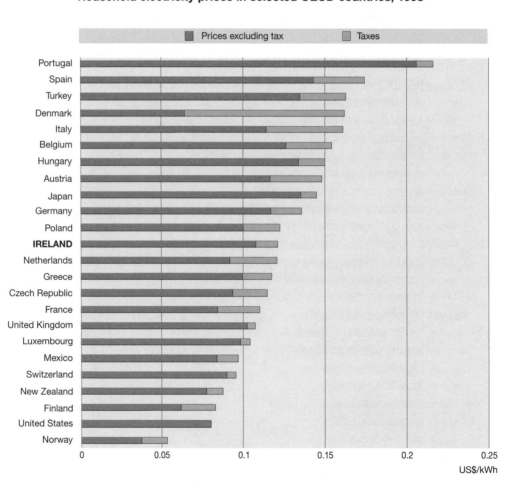

Note: Ex-tax price for the United States. Data are not available for Australia, Canada, Korea and Sweden.

Source: IEA/OECD (2000), *Energy Prices and Taxes*, 3rd quarter, Paris.

Figure 3. **Gas prices in selected OECD countries**

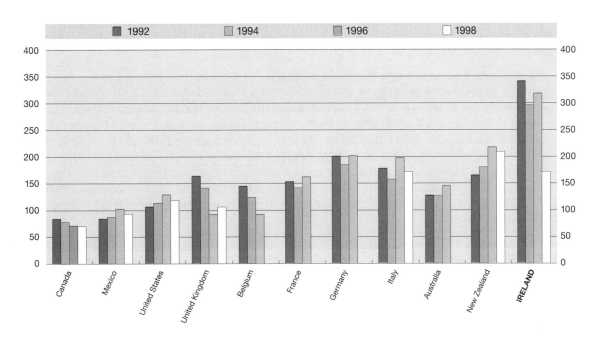

Average price per 10b kcal on a gross calorific basis. All prices in US Dollars
Source: IEA, *Natural Gas Information* (1999), Table 17.

Box 1. Irish electricity and gas sectors at a glance

Electricity

Installed capacity (end 1999): 4 360 MW (of which ESB owns 4 158 MW, excluding Poolbeg steam turbine, 160 MW, commissioned in 2000; remaining 202 MW is small scale generation).

Annual Generation (1999): 20.89 TWh (ESB 20.17 TWh and SSG 0.72 TWh).

Fuel mix (generation in 1999): 32% gas, 26% coal, 28% oil, 7% hydro, 7% peat.

Expected growth is 4.4% per annum, 1998-2006 (It was 6.6% from 1998 to 1999) (CER and ESB, ESB 2000).

Interconnections: 280MW to Northern Ireland, of which 200MW is under long-term contract.

Gas

Imports:	88 099 Terra Joules.
Domestic production:	51 329 GCV.
Total final consumption:	139 428 GCV.
Electricity generation:	69 581.
Distribution losses:	2 597.
Industrial consumption:	18 848.
Commercial consumption:	11 416.
Residential consumption:	17 957.
Non-energy use:	19 029.

---

capacity was allocated to three generators – an ESB-Statoil joint venture, and two new entrants – totalling about 800 MW capacity. In that connection, the Competition Commissioner of the European Union indicated that a substantial change in the structure of the electricity market "can only be achieved by means of new market entries," and that ESB's joint venture with Statoil cannot be considered to be an independent operator (Monti, 2000).[2]

Discussion about how to allocate the limited capacity had centred on the desire to introduce earlier competition in electricity generation.[3] Granting priority to avoidance of supply shortage was seen as further delaying the development of a competitive structure in the generation market by enabling the incumbent to gain access to gas capacity that would otherwise have gone to an independent competitor. (Sunday Business Post, 23 July 2000). The issue had been identified some time ago. The International Energy Agency had noted that investment in new generation would be rationed by the availability of gas supplies and was urging since mid-1999 that the first power stations allocated gas supplies be owned by a company other than ESB. In October 1998, the ESB, in consultation with the DPE, said that in excess of 200 MW additional generating capacity would be required in late 2001/early 2002, and a further 800 MW by 2005.

Electricity transmission. The electricity transmission and distribution system in Ireland needs to be upgraded. *Forfas*, the national economic and technology policy board, recommended in *Enterprise* 2010 that 220Kv supply to all regions be guaranteed (*Enterprise* 2010, January 2000). Some observers note that

---

Box 2.   Description of the electricity sector

The electricity sector has four main stages of production, which vary in terms of their scope for competition and the regulation that can be applied. These stages are:

- Generation – the production of electric power using a variety of fuels and technologies

- Transmission – the high-voltage "transport" of electric power over distances from generators to distribution networks and large industrial customers

- Distribution – the low-voltage "transport" of electric power to smaller customers

- Retailing or supply – a set of services including metering, billing and sale of electric power to final consumers.

A fifth component is system operation. The electricity system must remain in balance, with demand and supply equal at each moment in time. Demand varies unpredictably. Hence to remain in balance, supply must respond immediately to changes in demand. System operation is the control of the generating units and other equipment attached to the transmission grid to ensure this demand-supply balancing, as well as to maintain other quality attributes of electricity.

Transmission and distribution are, for the foreseeable future, natural monopolies at any given geographic location. Further, even where a transmission grid has different owners in different geographic regions, the physical properties of electric power imply not that the sections of the grid could compete but rather that they would each "transport" a share of the power. Consequently, competition in transmission and distribution is infeasible.

By contrast, both generation and retailing are potentially competitive activities and indeed are competitive in many countries for at least some final consumers. It should be noted that generators may be located on either the same or the opposite side of an international border from the users of the electric power.

Behaviour by one user of an electricity system can change the costs of other users. These externalities imply that, at least up to relatively large geographic areas, system operation over a larger area is more effective than over a smaller area. This implies that system operation at any given geographic location is a natural monopoly activity and competition is infeasible.

potential investors do not consider locating in parts of western Ireland due to electricity supply problems (Business & Finance, 23 March 2000, p. 17).

Connections beyond the Republic will be upgraded in the next few years. The ones between the Republic and Northern Ireland are being upgraded from 280MW to 400MW in 2001. CER auctioned off the use of some of the capacity for a year, although there remains some hesitancy, for security reasons, in relying upon the connection. The Moyle Interconnector between Northern Ireland and Scotland will have 500 MW capacity when completed in 2001, although 125 MW has been reserved under long term contract. While these connections will facilitate the reliability of the Irish systems, the nameplate capacities amount to only about one-seventh of installed generating capacity in the Republic, and effective capacities are invariably lower.

Box 3.   The natural gas sector

Like many other industries, the natural gas industry comprises a number of distinct "stages of production", differing in the nature of their regulation and the scope for competition. It is possible to distinguish five broad stages of production, from the point of extraction (the "well-head") to the point of consumption (the "burner-tip").

(a)   Production - which can be further broken down into the exploration, drilling, extraction and processing of gas. For the purposes of this paper, re-gassification facilities for gas in its liquid form (known as LNG) can be included within this stage of production.

(b)   Transmission - the high-pressure transportation of gas to high-volume customers such as distribution companies, large industrial customers and power stations.

(c)   Distribution - the low-pressure distribution of gas to small and medium-volume gas customers.

(d)   Storage - the smoothing of the flow of gas through the transportation network by pumping gas into holding facilities at off-peak times, and withdrawing the gas at peak times.

(e)   Retailing or Marketing - the provision of services of contracting with production, transmission and distribution companies on behalf of gas customers and associated billing and metering services.

In most cases, competition between gas producers is feasible. Competition may not be effective in practice, as one or a few producers may own all the viable independent sources of gas. This is especially of concern when the independent sources of gas are under the jurisdiction of a foreign country.

While gas transmission pipelines exhibit sizeable economies of scale, competition between pipelines may nevertheless be feasible in some countries, according to the magnitude and the geography of demand for gas flows. As a rule, however, it seems likely that for the foreseeable future effective inter-pipeline competition even in fully liberalised markets will be limited to a few geographic locations.

While some gas customers, particularly very large ones, are supplied directly off the high-pressure transmission network, most smaller customers are supplied through local gas distribution companies, known as "LDCs". Like many other network industries, local gas distribution exhibits economies of density - once the costs have been sunk of installing a gas main down a street, the marginal cost of connecting another house or building to the gas main is very small. Because of these economies of density, local gas distribution is, generally speaking, a natural monopoly. Competition would not normally be expected to be feasible in gas distribution.

Demand for gas is highly seasonal. Demand at peak times can be several times higher than at off-peak times. Gas storage facilities smooth the flow of gas through the network, which are filled at off-peak times and drawn down at peak times. Gas is stored in a number of different types of facilities, such as depleted gas reservoirs or disused mines. Although access to certain key facilities (such as depleted gas reservoirs) can be limited, the economies of scale in gas storage are small. As a result, there remains scope for effective competition in gas storage services, with the possible exception of regions with low population density.

Renewable energy generation. Ireland has set an ambitious target for increasing the amount of electricity generated by renewable sources of energy. In its Green Paper on Sustainable Energy, this target was increased by 500MW (about one-eighth of total). Ireland has relied on auctions to build generation using specified technologies (the *Alternative Energy Requirement competitions*). It is expected that these projects and the 2005 target will deliver a total capacity in excess of 600MWe in 2005, the vast majority of which (over 80%) will be wind powered (ESB, 1998). Since February 2000, this mechanism has been augmented by allowing any electricity supplier supplying from renewable energy sources (green electricity) to supply any final consumer. The ERA, 1999 requires the CER to have regard to the need, "to promote the use of renewable, sustainable or alternative forms of energy." CER recently amended the trading regulation to allow green operators to mix with non-green sources, thus facilitating their activities. However, the expansion of wind powered generation is hampered by the lack of verified published data on site-specific and overall grid capacity acceptance limits from wind powered sources. Until resolved, this will hinder growth in the liberalised green market.

Peat, the traditional fuel in Ireland, is supplied by *Bord na Móna*, a State-sponsored body, to ESB under long term agreement.[4] The International Energy Agency estimates that, in 1999, the cost of generating electricity from peat was 50% higher than doing so from alternative fuel (coal). The IEA notes, however, that the producer subsidy for peat was far lower than the producer subsidy equivalent for coal in, say, Germany or Spain (IEA, 1999). Peat emits more CO_2 per unit electricity generated, 1 467g/kWh as compared with 851g/kWh for coal or 492g/kWh for gas (IEA calculation). However, since the exploitation of peat for electricity generation takes place in an area of higher than average unemployment, it was originally considered to form part of the social safety net. Current plans call for the six old peat-fuelled plants to be replaced by two new peat plants, bringing the total to three. The Minister for Public Enterprise may direct the CER to impose on ESB the requirement, as a public service obligation, that up to 15% peat, as a primary fuel source, is used in the fuel mix of electricity generation in any year (ERA, Sect. 39). This requirement is intended to ensure that Ireland is reasonably self-sufficient in electricity generation. Gas from the Irish seabed and from other European Union Members also ensures this self-sufficiency.

Anticipating competition, ESB has already improved its efficiency. A Cost and Competitiveness Review programme yielded net annual cost savings of I£60m. Staff reductions contributed substantially; about 2 000 employees have voluntarily departed since 1996. According to a commitment made under the Cost and Competitiveness Review, 5% of shares will be transferred to ESB staff after ESB is transformed into a limited liability company (ESB, 2000). ESB has set a target of an additional I£100m annual cost savings over the five years from 2000. Meeting this target would mean further staff reductions, greater efficiencies, competitive sourcing of business and purchasing services, and replacement and refurbishment of generating plant (ESB, 2000). These efficiency improvements are being driven by the threat of competition, as they could have been carried out under the existing regulatory regime.

4. REGULATORY INSTITUTIONS AND REGULATION

Three institutions – the Department of Public Enterprise, the Commission for Electricity Regulation (*An Coimisiún um Rialáil Leictreachais* or CER), and the Competition Authority – are involved in regulating the sectors. The Minister for Public Enterprise has overall responsibility for the gas and electricity sectors. She makes policy and, together with the Minister for Finance, exercises the ownership role in ESB on behalf of the state. ESB is a statutory corporation established under the Electricity (Supply) Act 1927 and *Bord Gáis* is a statutory body, established under the Gas Act 1976. (The Department of Marine and Natural Resources is responsible for *inter alia* licensing gas exploration and development.) The formulation of government policy in these sectors could be greatly influenced by the nature of the partnership framework, which includes business and trade union representatives. The Minister, as shareholder, decides on major investments, such as new power plants or gas pipeline extensions. She appoints eight members of the Board of ESB (the four other members are elected by ESB staff) and ESB's independent auditor. She appoints all nine members of the Board of *Bord Gáis*. For both entities, the respective Boards appoint the chief executive and other managers. At present, the Minister gives general directives to Bord Gáis on transmission access pricing and resolves access disputes. In March 2001, the Government proposed the transfer to the Commission for Electricity Regulation of responsibility for regulating gas transmission access, granting consents for gas pipeline construction, and licensing pipeline operation and storage and supply of natural gas (DPE, 2001). However, the policy framework relies on competition from other fuels to limit expressions of monopoly power by Bord Gáis.

The CER regulates network access and entry into electricity generation, and supply to liberalised consumers. Statutory Instrument No. 445 of 2000 provides for CER to regulate final electricity tariffs paid by captive consumers, *i.e.*, those who are not "eligible," after the S.I. came into effect on 20 December 2000.The CER makes the rules for trading in electricity (ERA, Sect. 9) in accordance with the Policy Direction issued by the Minister in July 1999. To secure compliance, CER may apply to the High Court for an order requiring the holder of a license or of an authorisation to comply with its direction (Sect. 26).

The CER has structural independence. Its one to three members are appointed by the Minister for Public Enterprise, after a selection process by an independent body, for three to seven year terms, renewable once. The Minister may remove a member of the CER in event of incapacity or stated misbehaviour, and must state the reason. The CER is independent in the performance of its functions and has financial independence since it may impose a levy on electricity undertakings. The CER must submit to the Minister an annual report on its activities and proposed future work programme. The Minister must provide these reports to each House of the *Oireachtas*. The CER must report to a Joint Committee of the *Oireachtas*, from time to time and as requested, and have regard to its recommendations (Schedule ERA). However, CER's independence from the Minister is mitigated by the fact that its authority to regulate final tariffs to captive consumers and the agreement between the transmission system operator and owner is granted under Statutory Instrument rather than statute, so that the delegation of authority is reversible by the minister. The Government intends to grant the regulatory power to the CER under primary legislation to be prepared later in 2001.

The CER has varying degrees of discretion. Under the gas capacity allocation rules (Gas Amendment Act, 2000), the CER had almost no freedom of decision-making, being limited almost to estimating projects' completion dates. By contrast, the CER is independent in regulating transmission and distribution grid access. It can direct the ESB on the basis for calculating charges for the use of and connection to the grids, on the content of connection and use agreements, and the terms of connection offers. CER may also resolve connection disputes. CER, solely, determines the "appropriate proportion" of costs and the "reasonable rate of return" on capital that enter the calculation of charges for the connection or use of the electricity grids (Sect. 35).

The Competition Authority is the only institution that may enforce the general competition law. There is also the right of private action. While there are no exemptions from that law, where other legislation authorises non-competitive practices and conditions the competition law cannot correct them. (Of course, a damaged person could sue under European Union competition law, provided the transaction in question has a community dimension. In those cases, the EU law takes precedence over the national legislation.) The Authority had two competition matters in the electricity and gas sectors in recent years. Responding to a complaint received May 1997, the Authority expressed its views that, under the Competition Acts, Bord Gáis could not charge different prices to firms buying similar quantities of gas where those firms were in competition with one another, nor could it offer more favourable terms to a firm in which it had an interest where doing so placed a rival firm at a disadvantage. In addition the Authority indicated that Bord Gáis could not set charges to competitors for use of the interconnector and the gas pipeline which were less favourable than those applying to itself. The Authority had ongoing discussions with Bord Gáis regarding the setting of access charges for use of the transmission network.

In August 1998, the Authority received a complaint regarding an "Optisave Contract" that ESB was offering to a number of its larger customers. The Authority objected to a clause which provided that,   281|

after market liberalisation in February 2000, a customer who was offered cheaper electricity by a competing supplier would have been required to give details of the offer to the ESB (while not naming the other supplier) and to allow it an opportunity to lower its prices. The customer would only have been allowed to switch to another supplier if ESB failed to match or offer a lower price, and then only after giving ESB six months notice of termination. Further, customers could not submit alternative offers to ESB before the date of liberalisation. ESB subsequently agreed to delete the clause to which the Authority had objected and to amend the agreements to provide that either party may terminate on giving three months notice.

4.1. Regulation

The regulation of ESB is less formal and complete than that in many other OECD countries. ESB must "break-even." Within that framework condition, the regulation of ESB's tariffs is changing in 2001. Under the earlier system, ESB may apply to the Minister for Public Enterprise for increases in the tariffs charged customers, and the Minister may grant or deny the application. There have been significant delays in consideration of the application: In January 1995, an application for a price increase had been with the Department for seven years (Dail Reports, 21 February 1995, Col. 870 reported in Massey and O'Hare, p. 73). The basis for the decision appeared to include the overall profitability of ESB. (Response to question in Parliament, Minister for Public Enterprise Mary O'Rourke, 29 June 1999, ref. No. 16298/99). However, CER is to acquire the power to set and change tariffs under S.I. 445 of 2000. In addition, the Minister exercising ownership must give ESB prior approval for large capital expenditures, such as to build power plants. Extensions of power lines and new power plants also require planning permission from local government.

Public service obligations. Public service obligations are imposed by order of the Minister for Public Enterprise. These obligations may relate to security of supply, regularity, quality and price of supplies, environmental protection, and use of indigenous energy sources. She may direct CER to require that up to 15% peat as a primary fuel source, is used in the fuel mix for electricity "available to" ESB in any year. Orders under this section shall provide for the recovery, by a levy on final consumers, of the additional costs incurred including a reasonable return on capital (Sect. 39 of ERA). If complete cost recovery were guaranteed, companies fulfilling public service obligations would not be provided incentives to fulfil them efficiently. In addition, where public service obligations receive excessive compensation, market competition is needlessly distorted. In particular, if the amount of the transfer makes it profitable for ESB to exceed the 15% share, or indeed for it to displace competitors' generation, then the transfer increases total cost of the system beyond the limit implicit in the 15% share policy decision.

Transmission pricing. Two issues arise as regards transmission access in Ireland, pricing and access in light of the congested network. Charges for the use of or connection to the grids shall enable the ESB to recover the appropriate proportion of direct and indirect costs incurred, and a reasonable rate of return (Sect. 35). Originally, the ESB had proposed that generators connecting to the transmission grid would be charged on the basis of "deep" connection charging principles. That is, the cost of transmission reinforcement at a distance from the generator would be charged to the generator. Subsequently, the CER issued a Direction to ESB in accordance with Section 34 of the Act to adopt a shallow approach to transmission connection charges. This reduces the connection charge to generators and shifts some costs to "use of system" charges (which are calculated to provide locational signals for generators) paid by all users. The Transmission System Operator, *Eirgrid*, will be responsible for transmission pricing, subject to CER approval. Some concern has been expressed that *Eirgrid* may not be given the commercial objectives or incentives to price transmission to induce lowest total system cost behaviour. The congestion of the Irish transmission network means that there are only a few points where a new generating plant could be physically connected. It is estimated that only two generating plants can be added in the Dublin area, for example. Thus, the granting by ESB of a grid connection to its joint venture with Statoil before other potential entrants could enter a grid connection agreement has been seen by the potential competitors as having serious repercussions on the future development of competition in the Irish electricity market. The EU Competition Commissioner has indicated that the allocation procedure needs clarification (Monti, 200)).

Transitional costs. The Minister for Public Enterprise can, after consultation with the CER and the European Commission, provide for the recovery of stranded costs from final consumers (Sect. 40 ERA). However, Ireland has confirmed to the European Commission that it does not intend to notify a stranded cost recovery regime.

Accounting separation. Integrated electricity undertakings are to keep separate accounts for their generation, transmission, distribution and supply activities. These accounts must be kept in accordance with the Companies Acts, 1963 to 1999, as if they were carried out by separate companies, "and with a view to avoiding discrimination, cross-subsidisation and distortion of competition (Art. 31, S.I. No. 445 of 2000). ESB must also prepare separate accounts, in this manner, for its supply to libe-

---

Box 4.   EU gas directive key features

Third-Party Access Requirement: Member states must allow certain gas customers to buy gas from the supplier of their choice and to have it transported through the existing pipeline network at regulated rates. This right must only be available initially to very large gas customers. For the first five years, only gas customers taking at least 25 million cubic metres (mcm) of gas per year and electricity generators must be eligible; for the next five years the threshold reduces to 15 mcm per annum; in the final 3 years, this threshold reduces to 5 mcm per annum. It is thought that there are 8 gas customers in Ireland who qualify for the first group. Member states may liberalise smaller customers, sooner. Member states can choose between "negotiated access" and "regulated access". Under negotiated access individual customers enter into commercial negotiations to determine the precise terms and conditions. Gas companies are required to publish their "main commercial conditions" for the use of the system. Under regulated access, gas customers have a right of access on the basis of published regulated tariffs.

Independent regulatory institutions: Member states are required to designate competent authorities, independent of the parties, with access to the internal accounts of the natural gas undertakings to settle access disputes expeditiously.

Unbundling: Natural gas undertakings are required to keep separate accounts in their internal accounting at least for their gas transmission, distribution, storage and consolidated non-gas activities "as they would be required to do if the activities were carried out by separate undertakings".

New investment: Member states must allow a general freedom to build and operate natural gas facilities via objective, non-discriminatory and transparent authorisations.

Public service obligations: Member states are allowed to impose on gas utilities, in the general economic interest, public service obligations which may relate to security of supply, regularity, quality and price of supplies and to environmental protection.

Capacity rationing: Natural gas undertakings may refuse access to their system on the basis of lack of capacity, or where the access to the system would prevent them carrying out the public service obligations that are assigned to them.

Derogations: A natural gas undertaking may apply to a Member state for a derogation from the obligation to provide access if it considers that it would encounter serious economic and financial difficulties because of its take-or-pay commitments. The Commission oversees the granting of the derogation. The directive allows a derogation of the market opening requirements for those markets (Finland and Greece) which are dependent on one main external supplier and are not interconnected with the system of another Member State.

Source: OECD (2000a).

ralised consumers and for its supplies to captive consumers. The Eligible Supply Business, a business unit of ESB, is to purchase electricity from its own generators on the same basis as independent suppliers (ESB, 2000).

A generating license condition prohibits generators considered by the CER to be dominant in the electricity generation market from discriminating in favour of affiliates or related undertakings, and prohibits cross-subsidy with other businesses, affiliates or related undertakings of the licensee. For the purpose of this condition, the CER determines what constitutes the market, and whether the licensee is dominant (Electricity Generation License at http://www.cer.ie/new.htm on 12 June 2000).

Gas

Bord Gáis is not subject to economic regulation, except for access to its pipelines. Bord Gáis has split into four business units. The business unit for transmission has a separate management and operates independently of the remainder of the company and, under Bord Gáis' code of practice, is to offer the same services at the same prices to the remainder of Bord Gáis as it offers to third parties and must not share business sensitive information obtained in the course of carrying out its transmission business with other units. Under the corporate governance Bord Gáis has imposed upon itself, each business unit is to operate in a commercial, arm's length and transparent manner, and not cross subsidise. Each business unit keeps separate accounts and presents financial statements as though they were separate incorporated entities. Bord Gáis has had the practice of extensive outsourcing, a practice that allows costs to be more finely allocated and that may have resulted in higher efficiency and lower overall costs (ESRI 1995, p. 18).

There is continuing discussion about how the transmission tariff should be calculated. The interconnector is a significant cost item, so the question of whether all gas sold should contribute towards its costs, or only gas that passes through the interconnector, has been an important point of contention. It is generally agreed in Ireland to not reflect geographic differences in the cost of on-island gas transmission, even though not doing so signals gas users to locate in higher-cost-to-serve places.

The future

Additional reform has been announced. The government has announced that electricity users totalling 40% of demand will be free to choose supplier in 2002, and 100% by 2005. Three auctions for a total of 600MW of "virtual independent power producers" (VIPPs) generation capacity were held in October 2000. ESB and two independent companies won. An auction for 40GWh of "green" energy was also held and won by ESB and an independent company. The VIPP contracts are expected to have a one-year duration, beginning 1 November 2000. In the gas sector, discussion on transmission access pricing continues but no decision has been announced as of January 2001. With respect to gas supply, in March 2001 the Government proposed to accelerate liberalisation by allowing customers with annual consumption below 2 million cubic meters to have regulated access to the gas network (this amounts to about 100 customers) and to aim for liberalisation of all consumers by 2005 (DPE, 2001).

5. EVALUATION OF THE REFORM

Ireland has embarked upon a major reform of its gas and electricity sectors. While much has been accomplished, Ireland is closer to the beginning than the end of establishing an energy sector where private investment, innovation and lower prices are driven by competition.

The discussion of electricity reform has gone on for some time.

– The May 1993 Ministerial announcement of the "unbundling" of ESB into business units said that the objective of the change was "to introduce greater cost transparency and competition into the electricity sector" (Press Release, 21 May 1993, Republic of Ireland, Government Information

Services, on behalf of the Department of Transport, Energy and Communication, cited in Cross, p. 71). At the same time, it was announced that, "The new arrangements will be subject to independent public regulation" (Communication of the Department of Transport, Energy and Communications to the ESB Board of Directors, 21 May 1993, cited in Cross, p. 71).

- A 1995 paper by economists at the ESRI (The Economic and Social Research Institute) argued that "[T]he crucial objective should be to introduce competition into the [electricity and gas] industr[ies] in Ireland *wherever it is realistically possible*. However, it may still be desirable to keep the bulk of the existing physical assets in state ownership while opening up the market to new entrants wherever feasible." They also warned against privatisation of a monopoly and recommended comprehensive regulation by an independent authority (Fitz Gerald and Johnson, 1995).

- The May 1997 consultation document, *Proposals for the Electricity Supply Industry* in Ireland, proposed, among other things, the establishment of ESB as the "single buyer" for captive customers.

- The 1998 *Legislative Proposal for Implementation of Electricity Directive* 96/92/EC would have established an independent regulator (who would have been responsible to control tariffs, as well as network access and entry), put transmission operation (but not assets) into a separate state-owned company, liberalised some consumers and allow ESB to be the sole licensed supplier to captive consumers.

- The 1999 Electricity Act granted the regulator fewer powers than did the Proposal. Specifically, it retained government control over tariffs to captive consumers.

- The 1999 Electricity Act is itself an interim legislation; further legislation is intended.

- The Statutory Instrument No. 445 of 2000 granted to CER regulatory control over tariffs to captive consumers and dispute resolution powers, provided for the establishment of the transmission system operator and specified its objectives, specified that ESB would be the unique transmission system owner and distribution system operator, and provided a framework for the "infrastructure agreement" between the transmission system operator and owner.

The reform proposals were criticised. The Competition Authority pointed out, in 1997, that international experience indicated that breaking up a monopoly firm is likely to be more effective than controlling a dominant firm. It noted too the need for a mechanism for efficiency savings in generation to be passed onto consumers as lower prices. Vertical separation and limits on ESB's market share should be considered, according to the Authority. The Authority said that, "[G]reater emphasis should be placed on promoting competition and some of the structural proposals contained in the paper should be re-examined" (Competition Authority, 1997). The Authority called the 1998 proposal, "a significant improvement compared with what had previously been proposed." It said that, "[C]onsideration should be given to permitting greater competition in the gas and electricity sectors. This would involve vertical separation in gas as in electricity, progressive further liberalisation in gas supply and measures to reduce the ESB's dominant position in generation." It noted too, the need for independent regulation (Competition Authority, 1999). While the Irish Business and Employers Confederation (IBEC) "broadly welcomed" the direction of legislation in a May 1998 consultation paper on electricity, IBEC, noted that lower prices must be and had not been set as an objective In April 2000, IBEC "called for Government to give the development of a competitive electricity market the priority it deserves" (IBEC, 2000).

Some important proposals have been delayed or only partially implemented. For example, the Minister announced on 6 June 1995 that, from 1 January 1998, very large electricity users could buy from generators other than ESB (Massey and O'Hare, p. 84). The change in the law to allow this took effect only in February 2000. The scope of the authority of the independent regulator has been diminished as discussion has proceeded. In 1993 it was announced that the electricity sector would be subject to independent public regulation. In 1998, the Legislative Proposal (paragraph 44(4)(b)) stated that there would be, "periodic review by the [Electricity Regulatory] Authority of, charges or tariffs." In 1999, the Minister for Public Enterprise, responding to a question in Parliament said that "Future price increases, including tariff re-balancing, will be a matter for the new Commission for Electricity Regulation" (29 June 1999, ref. No. 16298/99). But under the Electricity Regulation Act, 1999, the CER (which came into being, rather than the Authority) may only review transmission tariffs; the Government retains the power to regulate captive consumers' tariffs, although the Minister has delegated to CER that power in Statutory Instrument No. 445 of 2000.

As well, there are instances of the reforms being strengthened over time. For example, the single buyer of electricity, as a long-term entity, has been rejected in favour of liberalising all consumers and regulating access to the networks. The announcement of the intention to transfer regulatory authority in the natural gas sector to the CER and to accelerate liberalisation of consumers, points in the direction of strengthening reform.

Delay in finalising and implementing reforms has hindered the development of competition. In spite of earlier warnings, a law that addressed the allocation of gas capacity was passed only after supply shortage concerns had become imminent. This delay benefited the incumbent because competition objectives were subordinated to short-term issues of supply security. Delays and uncertainties about gas regulation benefit state-owned over private, competitive interconnector projects, since their state financing is less sensitive than private financing to uncertainty. Had the uncertainties been resolved earlier, one of the proposed competing privately-funded interconnector might have been built. In the event, in February 2001 it was announced that the incumbent, Bord Gais, will build the second interconnector.

5.1. Structural reform to promote competition

The small scale of the Republic of Ireland's electricity system raises the question of whether a competitive generation market is feasible. Existing plants are large relative to the size of demand, so ESB's plants could, at most, be split among two or three independent companies. Experience in the United Kingdom, Spain and New Zealand indicates that further increasing the number of independent generating companies would induce yet lower prices and higher productivity. Such an increase in numbers of competitors could be effected by having distinct owners of distinct generator sets within a given plant, for example. Similarly, experience in New Zealand showed that imposing a capacity cap and relying on new entrants to provide competition did not develop effective competition. Under a capacity cap, ESB would retain market power even after some years of high demand growth. This is because, during periods of high demand, when small competitors are generating at capacity, ESB will set market prices. Facilitating competition from generation in Northern Ireland, such as through transmission infrastructure investments and compatible regulatory regimes, would introduce two sizeable independent competitors to the market in the Republic of Ireland. "Virtual independent power producers"

Box 5. Effects of competition in electricity

Significant time series on efficiency and prices after the introduction of competition are only available for the United Kingdom. Since 1990, productivity has skyrocketed (as output rose by 8% from 1988 to 1995, employment was reduced by 50%), and prices have plummeted. In real terms, over the 1990-1997 period, household ("domestic") prices decreased by 20%, and prices to other consumers fell 19 to 27% (Littlechild, 1998, cited in IEA, 2000). In 1998, in real terms, the standard domestic tariff in England and Wales was 26% lower, and for industrial customers the price was 23 to 32% lower than in 1990 (Office of Electricity Generation 1998, p. 58) Only shorter time series are available for other reforming countries. For example, 1997 prices in the Australian state of Victoria fell to less than half their 1995 level, reflecting the introduction of competition, privatisation and excess capacity. However, prices in Norway and New Zealand, where the sector remains state owned and there is a high reliance on hydropower – thus subjecting the system to cost variations due to hydrological variations – did not fall with the introduction of competition (IEA, 2000).

(VIPPs), or firms re-selling power generated by ESB, could have some mitigating effect on ESB's market power, but cannot be relied upon to provide competition to ESB. All of these factors indicate that Ireland will have to rely on a basket of structural and regulatory changes in order to introduce effective competition. No single change, alone, will be sufficient.

It has been argued that Ireland's is such a small electricity system that the cost of setting up and running an electricity pool system may outweigh the benefits, and that if some other way of introducing competition can be found, then it would be best to retain a co-ordinated planning model (Fitz Gerald and Johnston, p. 15). The Moneypoint plant accounts for about one-fifth and the Poolbeg plant for almost a quarter of all electricity generated in the Republic. Other authors have observed that, at best, ESB's existing generating capacity could be split into two or three competing companies (Massey and O'Hare, p. 117).

Some other countries and states achieved rapidly a more competitive structure by splitting the incumbent monopolist's generation. The United Kingdom (England and Wales), New Zealand, Australia (three largest states), some states of the United States, and Argentina have split generation. It is planned in Italy and South Korea. But these were jurisdictions where the market was much larger than Ireland's. For example, the capacity of the smallest of the three generating companies expected to be spun off by ENEL in Italy is more than half the entire generating capacity in Ireland. The total capacity of the four smallest of the five generating plants spun off in Victoria, Australia is a bit more than half the Irish total.

Box 6. United Kingdom and Spain

Both the United Kingdom and Spain had electricity sectors with structures more conducive to competition than Ireland will have under present proposals, and in both countries there was evidence that market prices were well above competitive prices. The United Kingdom had three and Spain had two large electricity generators. In the United Kingdom, for some time the main generators were not vertically integrated, but in Spain they were integrated into distribution-supply, and partly owned the transmission grid.

In the United Kingdom, the Office of Electricity Regulation found that the two dominant non-nuclear firms had significantly increased prices and reduced output during the 1997/8 winter. Other competitors expanded output within the limits of their capacity. During that period, the two firms set the system marginal price 70% of the time. The Director-General concluded that the most effective way to increase competition in the short term was to transfer more of the two dominant firms' capacity to competitors (Office of Electricity Regulation, 1998, pp. 8-9).

In the Spanish market, the two largest firms owned 76% of production and, in 1998, provided the marginal capacity 59% and 24% of the time, respectively. Several analyses have been performed for or by the CNSE, the former independent energy advisory body. One, which took into account competition from imports, suggested that either company, acting on its own, could raise prices.[1] Another[2] suggested that such behaviour could lead to an average price 39% above marginal costs. A more recent study of actual Spanish market operation identified market power problems. A study[3] of the Spanish market in 1998 reached similar conclusions. Two reports released by the CNSE in July 1999 identify specific instances in 1998 where the two companies offered very high prices to the spot market for generators located in areas of high consumption and low generation.[4]

---

1. Frankena, Mark (1997), *Market Power in the Spanish Electric Power Industry*, Report prepared for the Comisión del Sistema Eléctrico Nacional, Madrid, March.

2. Ocaña, Carlos, and Romero, Arturo (1998), A *simulation of the Spanish electricity pool*, CNSE, Madrid, June.

3. London Economics (1999), *El sector eléctrico español, Análisis del poder de mercado*, Madrid, February.

4. CNSE (1999), "Análisis de la participación de Endesa en ciertos episodios anómalos en los mercados de energía eléctrica gestionados por el operador del sistema and Análisis de la participación de Iberdrola en ciertos episodios anómalos en los mercados de energía eléctrica gestionados por el operador del sistema," Madrid, 28 July.

Some countries combined capacity caps on the dominant generator with divestiture. Italy, for example, capped ENEL's electricity generation plus imports at 50% and ordered divestiture to attain that cap. This share has been called too large both by the competition authority and the energy regulator. New Zealand initially combined a cap with divestiture, but subsequently ordered further divestiture by the dominant generator because of insufficient competition. If ESB retains, as it aspires to, at least a 60% share of the market then effective competition is unlikely. The comparisons with the markets in the United Kingdom and Spain – which are less concentrated than envisaged in Ireland, and where prices were above competitive levels – are instructive. Under European Union competition law, a company with a market share above 40% would usually be considered dominant and its actions subject to special scrutiny to ensure its dominance is not abused. Even the 40-60-share split would not be attained for a decade, if generation grows at 5% annually, as predicted. If gas supplies constrain capacity expansion, then even this timetable is optimistic. A 40% market share would not allow many independent generators of significant size. Discussions about the allocation of gas pipeline capacity centre around plants of 400 MW, which places them a bit smaller than Poolbeg. While wind-powered generating plants are substantially smaller, their technical characteristics mean they cannot behave strategically in the market.

Three factors largely determine whether the cost of generation would be lower if ESB's generation were split among several companies. Economies of scale imply that the resulting operating units should not be too small; competition implies that the resulting companies should not be too few, and transition costs mean that some splits that would be efficient in the long run may be too costly to implement. Effective competition in generation requires *inter alia* a number of independent sellers along the merit order of generation, that is, from base load (generation that is always operating) through mid-merit to peak load (generation that operates only when demand for electricity is high). Each of these sellers must be of some size for competition to be effective; otherwise, the dominant firm can raise price unilaterally when its small rivals are operating at capacity.

Figure 4. **One and two firm concentration levels for selected countries or regions, 1998[1]**

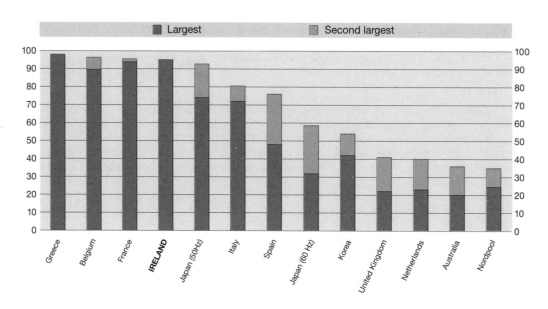

1. Data refers to 1999 for Greece and Ireland.

Source: OECD, IEA, Electrabel annual report (Electrabel + SPE), EdF and Charbonnage de France annual reports, Edison April 1999 presentation to shareholders, Spanish and Korean Ministry of Industry and Energy, Ofgem (NatPower and PowerGen in England and Wales 97/98, NEMMCO, Macquarie and Delta annual reports (SE market only), Nordpool annual report and Vattenfall, Statkraft.

"Virtual" independent power producers

In Ireland, contracts for "virtual independent power producers" have been auctioned. These are financial instruments; neither ownership nor operational control of any generation assets will change hands. The idea is that owners of these VIPP contracts will compete in the supply market to re-sell electricity to liberalised consumers. VIPP contracts for 600MW, plus 40GWh of "green" electricity, or about one-seventh of installed capacity, were offered for auction in October 2000. The auction was won by ESB and two independent companies, Viridian (the Northern Ireland transmission owner), and ePower. (No one could win more than 240MW.) The contracts will be for one year, beginning 1 November 2000, though ESB's dominance is expected to persist for much longer. Further auctions may be held. The capacity and energy charges in the VIPP contracts are the same for all contracts, and energy charges vary by time of day and ESB's fuel costs. These charges were negotiated between the regulator and ESB. VIPPs pay a penalty for taking more energy than contracted, and are prohibited from supplying the same customer by both VIPP and other means.

VIPP contracts have major weaknesses as a tool to promote competition. They have been labelled "not an effective mitigation measure" when offered to the United States' Federal Energy Regulatory Commission,[6] although they were accepted in Alberta, Canada where ESB is the Independent Transmission Administrator. The concern in the United States was that the contracts did not remove the output of the plant from the control of the plant's owner. By retaining operational control, the owner could manipulate downtime to withhold capacity. Further, these contracts do not provide incentives to increase operating efficiency. Over the longer term, the contracts may not last as long as the market power they were intended to mitigate, and it is more difficult to reach agreement on investment decisions – for modernisation, environmental compliance, and so on – for the plant. It may be difficult to oversee these complicated financial instruments. Finally, it is unclear how the incumbent buying VIPP contracts from itself has any effect on competition. However, VIPPs may be able to "package" electricity in ways that better match consumer needs.

By contrast, joint ventures have successfully built and operated generating plants where one parent company is the designated operator. Each owner makes independent decisions about the amount of power to "take." Joint ventures, however, lend themselves to more complex agreements over much longer time spans than do the VIPP contracts envisaged.

Development of an all-island market

The development of an all-island electricity market is necessary to develop competition in generation for consumers in the Republic, as well as in Northern Ireland. In 1999, economists at the ESRI said that an all-island market, "could give rise to substantial savings in the very long run for consumers in both jurisdictions" (ESRI 1999, p. 252). An all-island electricity market is developing. However, before it can proceed, the transmission grid needs substantial reinforcement. Besides enhancing competition, this will also increase security of supply and fuel diversification and reduce the need for, and thus the cost of, operational reserve of generation (http://www.nie.co.uk/ on 12 June 2000). Continuing the co-ordination between the regulators on the island will also aid the increases in efficiency from cross-border trade and investment.

There is already limited cross-border trade between the Republic of Ireland and Northern Ireland and by 2002 Northern Ireland and Scotland will be electrically connected. The Northern Ireland system is smaller than the Republic's, with maximum demand of 1 665 MW and annual sales of 7 291 GWh. Three privately owned generators operate in Northern Ireland, but two plants account for 90% of output in Northern Ireland, and two vertically integrated power companies operate in Scotland. Investment has also crossed the border, with ESB owning 40% of a small power station and planning to develop a combined cycle gas turbine (CCGT). Viridian Group, the owner of the transmission-distribution company in Northern Ireland, has contracts to sell to liberalised consumers and is progressing toward building a gas-fired plant in the Republic.

289

Generators in Northern Ireland would find it economic to supply Irish consumers. A superficial examination of relative prices in the Republic and Northern Ireland might suggest that generators in Northern Ireland would have little interest in selling in the Republic. According to UNIPEDE figures, industrial prices in the Republic are 34% lower than in Northern Ireland and household prices 22% lower (ESB, 2000). The price of electricity sold to households in Northern Ireland is much higher than in Britain (Ofreg, Tackling the High Cost of Generation: Executive Summary). However, these prices are vestiges of vesting contracts in Northern Ireland, so do not reflect marginal costs.[7]

There is greater scope for developing a competitive all-island market than of developing two separate competitive markets. Each of the Republic and Northern Ireland are supplied mainly by two power plants. Four is surely more competitive than two, and by joining the markets entry in one place has a pro-competitive effect across the island. In April 2000, the regulator said of generation and supply in Northern Ireland, "these markets are becoming competitive but competition is still at an early stage and is far from fully developed" (Ofreg 2000a, p. 8). Thus, both the Republic and Northern Ireland would benefit substantially from a single market. The Authorities in the Republic and Northern Ireland are aware of the potential offered by an all-island energy market and the two administrations have jointly commissioned consultants to examine the operation of the markets in each jurisdiction with a view to creating an all-island energy market in a European context. This report is expected in mid-2001.

Vertical integration

Despite accounting separation, both ESB and Bord Gáis continue to be vertically integrated into both competitive activities – generation (for ESB) and supply – and monopolistic activities – transmission and distribution. In the electricity sector, even though ESB and Eirgrid have separate management, they have common owners in the Ministers of Finance and Public Enterprise. The vertical integration means the companies retain incentives to discriminate against non-integrated rivals, and to exercise market power. Three possible concerns are discriminatory operation of transmission, insufficient investment in transmission, and misattribution of costs to the regulated activity. Discrimination discourages entry and increases total system cost, and insufficient investment in transmission – notably electricity from Northern Ireland and gas from Scotland or beyond – reduces competition to supply Irish consumers. Misattribution of costs provides an "unlevel playing field" for non-integrated rival generators or gas suppliers.

Other countries have experienced problems in ensuring non-discriminatory transmission access. Accounting separation is the least effective means of preventing discrimination against non-integrated companies. As noted by the Irish Competition Authority, in the United Kingdom, "both the MMC and Ofgas concluded that accounting separation was insufficient to eliminate the potential for anti-competitive behaviour on the part of British Gas" (Competition Authority, 1998). The CER has noted that regulatory accounts of the separate businesses would provide more appropriate financial and economic information than accounts as prepared under the various Companies Acts (CER, 2000). Divestiture, that is, separation of ownership of generation from transmission, is the only form of separation that eliminates incentives to discriminate. Lesser forms of separation can reduce the ability to discriminate, provided appropriate regulation is in place and the regulator is vigilant.

The shift of operational control of electric transmission to Eirgrid diminishes the scope for discrimination in dispatch and other operations. However, scope for discrimination remains, particularly as the timing and means of maintenance – which ESB is responsible for carrying out – can affect the competitiveness of generators. In addition, it may be very difficult for Eirgrid to induce ESB to make timely grid investments that reduce the profitability of its generating plants. Indeed, ESB has deferred investments in transmission even when there was no competitive advantage to doing so. Statutory Instrument No. 445 grants to Eirgrid responsibility for planning transmission development, ESB an obligation to implement the development plan and CER the power to approve the development plan and regulate both entities. Eirgrid can "step in" and arrange work to be done if ESB delays or defaults in carrying out the development plan. CER should ensure that investments in transmission are timely, particularly those that would facilitate competition from Northern Ireland. In addition, ESB, being responsible for maintenance of the transmission grid, may get access to commercially sensitive information in the normal course of events. Further, ESB would retain incentives to try to allocate as many costs as allowed to regulated activities. In the longer term, if the cost or failure rate of regulation of transmission turn out to be too high then the complete ownership separation of electricity transmission from generation would be necessary.

5.2. Institutions

Independent regulation provides a safeguard to competition especially in sectors where there is an essential facility to which all firms need access. In Ireland, the Minister for Public Enterprise is the primary regulator of gas. The Minister for Public Enterprise has substantial regulatory power as regards electricity, although the Minister has delegated by statutory instrument much of her power to the CER, and the CER has the power to regulate entry into generation, transmission, and electricity trading. More specifically, the Minister has delegated to CER power to regulate final tariffs to captive consumers and the agreement between Eirgrid and ESB. The current intention is that a future law will increase the scope of regulation by the CER.

Ireland is discussing the various regulatory institutions and their characteristics. The focus of the consultation document, *Governance and Accountability in the Regulatory Process*: Policy Proposals (DPE, 2000), is the relationship between accountability and independence. Both of these features, as well as others, are necessary for effective regulation.

A market environment requires regulatory institutions that make decisions that are neutral, transparent and not subject to day-to-day political pressures. In order to make fair and reasonably predictable decisions, the regulator must have analytical expertise and not rely on the expertise of the regulated utilities. Unpredictable regulation discourages private investment, and changing regulation renders sunk investment less efficient. Thus, a greater reliance on independent regulation can reduce regulatory barriers, promote entry and investment, and accelerate the development of competition. The regulator must also be functionally separate from policy-making in order to maintain a neutral regulatory regime. To be seen to be fair, the regulator should have well-defined obligations for transparency, notably with respect to its decision-making processes and information on which the decisions are made. Further, the objectives of the regulator must be clearly stated, more specifically than, for example, "the public interest" and progress towards these objectives should be monitored. Finally, the powers of the regulator should be clearly stated. The combination of transparencies of objectives, powers, processes, decisions and information give the public clear performance criteria to evaluate the extent to which the regulator is fulfilling its role.

Particularly in a country with a state-owned incumbent, there are many potential conflicts of interest. While Government looks after the broad public interest, Government as regulator looks after the interests of consumers and producers of a good or service, and Government as owner ensures the profitability of its firms. When all of these roles are played by a single entity, the inevitable tradeoffs are not subject to public scrutiny and debate. By contrast, an independent regulator can be made publicly accountable to fulfil one or a very few objectives.

Other OECD countries have independent regulators of electricity and gas, including Australia, Finland, Italy, the United Kingdom and the United States. In Germany and New Zealand, the threat of action under the competition law is used, along with information disclosure in New Zealand. While specific arrangements differ in each country the main features of independent regulation are: complete independence from the regulated companies, a legal mandate that provides for separation the regulatory body from political control, a degree of organisational autonomy, and well defined obligations for transparency (*e.g.*, publishing decisions) and accountability (*e.g.*, appealable decisions, public scrutiny of expenditures). Key to independent regulation is independent expertise and sources of information. CER has these attributes; its scope of responsibilities to go along with them should be

291

enshrined in an act. Consultation with the Competition Authority in questions regarding markets, would be one source of independent expertise.

5.3. Regulation

ESB has little persistent external pressure to reduce costs. The mandate that ESB "break even" meant that it was assured of covering its costs with its revenues. For example, during a long period where it was not permitted to raise its tariffs, ESB complied with the break-even mandate by reducing investments, which resulted in lower than desired standards of service in rural areas. But on the other hand, ESB's accounting practice of "double depreciation" allows it to accumulate reserves to finance investment. With rate-of-return regulation, ESB can be expected to under-invest (when the allowed rate islower than the market rate) or over-invest (when the allowed rate is higher than the market rate) in capital.

Some other countries use a price cap methodology to regulate utilities, or those parts that are natural monopolies, because this method, applied to profit-seeking companies, provides them incentives to reduce costs. In Ireland, one proposal would subject Bord Gáis's transmission to price cap regulation. So long as prices remain under their respective caps, and the companies meet other specified criteria such as safety, environmental, universality of service offerings and reliability standards, the companies are free to take actions to increase their profits, often actions that reduce their costs. Where a company is not profit-seeking, these efficiency incentives do not operate. Neither ESB nor Bord Gáis, owned by the state and governed by boards appointed by the state and employees, is profit-seeking (even if they might report substantial profits). Even in these circumstances, price caps can protect consumers from monopoly exploitation.

Where price cap regulation is not used, the regulator needs cost information. Overcoming the information asymmetry between regulator and regulated company is challenging. Two general strategies are to get information from other companies, either overseas or private entrants, and to require accounting that generates information from the regulated firm. For example, the creation of distinct distribution companies may help identify cost-reducing practices in one part of the country that can be applied more widely.

5.3.1. Tariffs

According to ESB, households pay about 10% less than the cost of supply, and industrial customers pay about 10% more than the cost attributed to them. (Without formal regulation, these figures have not been independently assessed.) If effective competition to supply large customers does indeed develop, then ESB will be provided a strong incentive to reduce the cost of supply to them. When all households are offered the choice of supplier, then any system for a "supplier of last resort" will need to ensure that any subsidy required is funded equitably and that the choice of "supplier of last resort" is made competitively. In particular, higher cost-to-supply customers can be expected to use the "supplier of last resort" and the level of subsidy should reflect that propensity. Competitive bidding for minimum subsidy can ensure that the amount of subsidy is not unnecessarily high and that the lowest cost supplier is the provider.

A package of measures to address inflation included a commitment by the Government that it would not approve any new price increases by public bodies during the remainder of 2000. In such an environment, an application by ESB to raise prices would not be considered. While a suitable macroeconomic environment is important, it may be more important to ensure long-term efficiency and investments in regulated sectors.

Transmission tariffs, as well as charges for connections, influence the choice of generators about where to locate and the feasibility of competition by generation located in Northern Ireland. The location of generators affects the overall system cost. Hence, economic efficiency is served by transmission charges that induce entry at low-system cost locations. Some other countries and regions have locational pricing of electricity in order to reflect transmission costs so as to induce efficient use of generation and transmission. This is particularly important in congested systems.

5.3.2. *Regulation of Eirgrid and the energy procurer for efficiency*

It will be difficult to provide E*irgrid*, the transmission system operator (TSO) with incentives for efficiency. Since E*irgrid* should seek innovative ways to reduce system cost, command and control regulation is unsuitable. Performance-related pay of managers might induce the desired behaviour. But a main weakness of E*irgrid* is its relative lack of information as compared with ESB, who will continue to own the transmission and distribution assets and be primarily responsible for their maintenance and expansion. (Although E*irgrid* is "to operate and ensure the maintenance of and, if necessary, develop" the transmission system, generally ESB maintains and constructs the system.) Since this asymmetry is inherently unmeasurable, performance-related pay would have to use more or less imperfect proxies.

The 1998 Legislative Proposal described a Public Electricity Supply Business. From February 2005, the Public Electricity Supplier will have an economic purchase obligation, *i.e.*, it will not be supplied in the first instance by ESB Generation. Such entities are difficult to regulate. While it would seem "fair" to pass onto consumers the costs of the energy procured for them, this would mean the Public Electricity Supply Business would not have incentives to bargain for better prices or to seek alternative lower cost suppliers. Indeed, since its parent company, ESB, owns almost all the generation available, bargaining between units of ESB is probably unlikely. Since captive consumers (generally households) will in general not have time-of-use metering or tariffs, the Public Electricity Supply Business will purchase on behalf of demand that is insensitive to short term price variations. The combination of the Public Electricity Supply Business passing through its cost of energy and buying for price insensitive demand means that it will be profitable for suppliers to charge higher prices.

5.3.3. *Competitive neutrality*

For competition to reward the most efficient firm(s), the "playing field" must be level as regards regulation and other state interventions. In the energy sector, capital constitutes a large part of total cost. As a result, differences in the cost of capital between state-owned and private companies can have a significant effect on total cost. Differences can arise through the implicit or explicit guarantee against bankruptcy enjoyed by state-owned enterprise (enabling a SOE to borrow at lower interest in a more uncertain climate) and though the owner not requiring market-like rates of return on equity.

Other OECD countries, notably Australia, have tried to diminish the differences in cost of capital. In Australia, "government business enterprises" must either borrow at commercial rates or pay the estimated difference due to the state debt guarantee. In addition, GBEs are required to achieve a commercial rate of return at least sufficient to justify the long-tern retention of assets in the business, and to pay commercial dividends to the budget from those returns. The level of estimated dividends (and forecast payout ratio) is agreed annually between directors and shareholder Ministers. In the United States, differences in tax, legal, and regulatory treatment between state-owned and privately owned electric utilities result in significant cost differences, though the extent to which the entire 16-20% difference in costs is accounted for by different treatment is disputed (Regulatory Reform in the United States, p. 293).

Equal treatment as regards land, *e.g.*, the price at which public land is made available, treatment under the land use laws, is also important because the location of a generating plant can greatly influence the cost of integrating the plant into the transmission grid and transmitting the plant's output.

6. CONCLUSIONS

The plans of the current government are encouraging, but reforms of the Irish electricity and gas sectors have only begun. The liberalisation of large consumers is an important first step. It is therefore important that the liberalisation of all consumers proceed as planned and further acceleration might be considered.

293

8

The reforms to date are not sufficient for the development of effective competition. The Competition Commissioner of the European Union wrote in December 2000 that, "The current structure of the Irish electricity market is not favourable to competition" (Monti, 2000). The objectives of the reform have not been clearly set out to promote consumer interests. Further structural change, including the diminution of ESB's dominant position in generation, is an integral part of a reform package. Whether that diminution takes the form of a capacity cap or divestiture, is a decision that needs to rest on the experience of market entry, competition from Northern Ireland generation, and assessments of market prices and performance. Investments in transmission to facilitate supply from Northern Ireland, or even Scotland, can have a positive effect on competition and reliability in both the Republic and Northern Ireland.

Accounting separation has proved, in other countries, to be the least effective way to reduce discrimination against competitors. Where there are significant economies of scope between stages of production, then vertical integration may be superior. But that does not appear to be the case in electricity and gas. Discriminatory access is difficult to police, but if it is detected then that should be a signal to separate the potentially competitive activities – generation and supply – from the networks.

The second integral part of an effective reform package is putting in place appropriate regulatory institutions, in particular an independent regulator. The CER had few resources and little time to prepare for market liberalisation at the outset. Compared to corresponding institutions in other countries, the CER has few resources and limited scope for applying its powers. Independent, well-resourced and well-respected regulatory institutions attract investment since investors can feel they will be treated fairly and consistently. The CER's powers should be expanded, in statute, to cover all aspects of economic regulation of the electricity and gas undertakings. And it should have the resources to do the important tasks assigned it. To the extent that the market is integrated across national borders, such institutions are needed in each jurisdiction, and increasing co-ordination will be needed between these institutions.

No single reform will enable the Irish electricity and gas sectors to become competitive. The economy, and therefore demand for energy, is relatively small on a global scale and the location is not conducive to the importation of much competition. However, by combining structural change in generation, enhanced transmission to allow access by generation in Northern Ireland, and interim gas allocation rules that promote competition, in combination with the institutional and regulatory changes, then the Irish electricity market can become competitive.

Energy might seem an unimportant input into Irish competitiveness – after all, there are world or large regional prices for fossil fuels themselves. But the non-traded aspects of the sectors can result in large cost differences, as noted above. And in Ireland, energy could become a bottleneck that impedes the development of some regions. Hence, the reforms embarked upon should be continued in an integrated way so as to deliver a more efficient, competitive sector.

7. POLICY OPTIONS

1. *Increase competition in the market for electricity by*:

   – Prohibiting, in the short and medium term, further additions to ESB's generating plant. In the longer term, if effective competition develops, then remove this limit on ESB so that all generators can compete across the entire market.

   – Require divestiture of some generation plant by ESB. If market prices to liberalised customers are above competitive levels after the generation fuelled by the existing gas capacity comes on line, and if the amount of entry then expected and import capacity are together insufficient for effective competition, require further divestiture.

- Ensuring by establishment of appropriate access tariffs and terms, that conditions of access to the transmission and distribution grid, including for example ancillary services, are cost-reflective and non-discriminatory.

- Requiring divestiture of transmission from generation if transmission constraints are not relieved or if there is discrimination in access.

- Proceeding with plans to increase the capacity of transmission of electricity between the Republic and Northern Ireland.

- Ensuring that any long-term contracts do not block further liberalisation of consumers.

- Liberalising choice for all electricity and gas consumers by 2005, or sooner if there is evidence of liberalised customers being subsidised by captive customers.

2. *Ensure well-resourced and independent regulation of the electricity and gas sectors by*:

- Maintaining, for electricity, regulatory responsibility for tariffs, specific license conditions and transmission access and, for gas, shifting regulatory responsibility for transmission access, to the Commission for Electricity Regulation.

- Retaining enforcement of the competition law in the sectors, however, with the Competition Authority.

3. *Modify the tariff structure to improve efficiency in the sector by*:

- Making regulated tariffs cost-reflective. Consider eliminating the requirement that tariffs be geographically uniform in light of the non-uniformity of cost of supply.

4. *Reduce barriers to entry for gas importers and sellers.*

- The corporate separation of transmission should be a first step toward ownership separation of transmission from the potentially competitive activities.

5. *Increase efficiency of regional employment support by*:

- Putting into place more efficient support for employment and eliminate the subsidies to peat.

PROFESSIONAL SERVICES: PHARMACIES AND LEGAL PROFESSIONS

A significant part of the Irish economy depends upon, or consists of, professional services. As the economy has boomed, demand for these services has experienced a corresponding expansion. More providers are needed to meet this increased demand, and this has come from several sources: expanding places for professional education at Irish universities and other programmes, Irish citizens going abroad – notably to the United Kingdom – for professional education, return of Irish expatriate professionals, and immigration of already qualified professionals. This report examines the ways in which two professional services are regulated, and seeks ways to reform the regulation so that professional services can be provided more efficiently at an appropriate quality. The report concentrates on the legal professions – barristers and solicitors – and pharmacies.

The discussion of these professions illustrates issues that appear in other professions that are not examined here. The main problems that can affect professions are unnecessarily restrictive conditions for entry and rules about advertising and location, and explicit or implicit collective fee-setting. The high scores on the Leaving Certificate (from high school) now required to enter professional training programmes, and the widespread resort to professional training in the United Kingdom, suggest that demand to enter some professions is highly constrained. The number of training places is often determined by the corresponding professional body, creating a risk of self-interested constraint that would justify a second look, to determine whether the number of places is sufficiently to serve the public interest, would be in order. Self-governing professional bodies may impose further restrictions on practitioners that reduce competition but that may not improve the quality of the service to the public. The problems described in this report are only indicative of a range of practices in professional and other services that may need to be reviewed in order to increase efficiency and eliminate bottlenecks in the Irish economy.

Previous studies have called for reforms in Ireland's professions. During the 1980s and 1990s, the Fair Trade Commission and later Competition Authority undertook several enquiries, in response to a Minister's request to undertake a wide-ranging study. Reports were published on concerted fixing of fees, and advertising restrictions in the accountancy and engineering professions, restrictions on conveyancing and advertising by solicitors, and restrictive practices in the legal profession. In 1993, the Competition Authority issued a Certificate to the Association of Optometrists under the Competition Act, following amendments by the Association to its Code of Ethics to meet the Authority's concerns in relation to the siting of premises, advertising, fees and charges. The Authority also issued reports about practices of architects, surveyors, auctioneers, estate agents and trademark and patent agents. As a result of the Competition Authority's actions, advertising restrictions have been considerably liberalised and fee scales are only allowed only if used as guidelines, and not as minima (OECD, 1997, p. 129). A recent consultant's report on business services in Ireland found that self-regulation was predominant. It recommended independent collection of information, scrutiny by the Competition Authority of codes of conduct of self-regulating bodies with statutory power, separation of the control of education and entry from the profession's self-governing body, and elimination of anything that has the effect of a quantitative restriction on entry. The consultant made a number of other specific recommendations about solicitors, barristers, the court system, auditors, surveyors, and advertising (Bacon, pp. 42-43).

Box 7.   Professional services

The principal reasons to regulate professional services are to correct or prevent market failures that result in inadequate quality or safety. One possible market failure arises when consumers cannot evaluate the quality of the service. In this case, it is difficult for high-quality but high-cost practitioners to sustain themselves in the market and quality can decline unacceptably. Related to this is deceptive over-treatment, when consumers cannot evaluate what services are necessary for the desired outcome, and as a result providers take advantage of their ignorance to supply "too much" service. The two problems may appear in the same market, as consumers can differ in their experience and knowledge. Another possible market failure is for markets to be "missing." For example, potential investors rely upon information provided by auditors hired by the company whose accounts are examined. Even if potential investors desired more information than that desired by management, they cannot hire the auditors to provide the additional service.

The regulatory response to ensure quality or safety against these problems often takes the form of licensing rules that require practitioners to be qualified. Standards for services may establish criteria for maintaining and evaluating quality and for identifying abuses of "over-prescription." Disciplinary rules may expel providers whose quality is inadequate.

But regulatory responses also tend to reduce competition. They may limit entry, control prices, mandate service levels, prevent truthful advertising, and prohibit commercial relationships. In practice, restrictions on competitive practices such as price competition, truthful advertising, use of non-deceptive trade names, and relationships with other kinds of businesses have correlated with higher prices and less innovation, yet without necessarily improving quality. To the extent that quality was actually increased or protected, the costs of ensuring quality have, historically, included higher prices, reduced output, and reduced product differentiation.

8. PHARMACIES

Pharmacies are highly regulated in Ireland, as they are in many other countries. However, the evidence suggests that reform of some of the economic – as distinguished from safety – regulations could bring about lower prices and more efficient provision. The retail margin on medicines in Ireland is higher than in any other EU country (Bacon, pp. 10-11). Community pharmacists can receive salaries high enough to impair the supply of pharmacists to hospital pharmacies and industry [Forum]. Pharmacies are changing hands at high prices, in one famous example in Limerick for IR£ 2.7m in 2000. Competition is limited by preventing new pharmacies from locating near existing pharmacies. Reducing barriers to competition among pharmacists is expected to increase competition, which in turn would induce pharmacists to identify more efficient ways of performing their professional tasks and thus reduce the cost to consumers. A concern is to ensure adequate provision of pharmacy services to people living in rural areas. While 21 new pharmacies have opened in rural or semi-rural areas between 1996 and 2000, reforming economic regulations can improve services at lower cost.

Community pharmacies constitute the bulk of the pharmacy sector, accounting for about 80% of total employment of pharmacists in Ireland (about 1 400 out of just under 1 800 employed pharmacists in 1998). They, rather than hospital pharmacies or industry, are the focus here. In 1993, there were 1.1 pharmacists per pharmacy in Ireland (Bacon, p. 9, citing MacArthur).

8.1. Regulation

Pharmacies and pharmacists in Ireland are subject to two main types of control: (a) control of medicines and (b) control of the practice of pharmacy. The Pharmaceutical Society of Ireland (PSI), the Irish Medicines Board, the local health boards and the Department of Health enforce the law on retail sale and supply of medicines. In practice, the PSI concerns itself with the activities of pharmacists and pharmacies. As regards the practice of pharmacy, there is, as well as primary legislation in the Pharmacy Acts, additional statutory regulation of the Council of the PSI under the Pharmacy Act 1962. There is control of entry by way of the European Communities (Recognition of Qualifications in Pharmacy) Regulations, 1987 and the Health (Community Pharmacy Contractor Agreement) Regulations of 1996.

The legislation sets out the controls on medicines. In effect, "scheduled" prescription medicines for human use can only be supplied under prescription, some of these may only be dispensed in a hospital, and most medicines exempt from prescription-only may only be dispensed in a pharmacy by or under the supervision of a pharmacist (IPU Yearbook, p. 272). Some substances are specifically exempted from the pharmacist-supervised sale requirement, and thus these may be sold in non-pharmacies. They are, notably, aspirin, paracetamol, nicotinic acid, certain vitamins and toothpaste components (IPU Yearbook, p. 273). The supply of medicines by mail order is prohibited (IPU Yearbook, p. 272). Legislation also controls advertising. It prohibits advertising to the general public of controlled drugs and prescription-only medicines, as well as of certain, specified illnesses and the medicines to prevent, diagnose or treat them. Advertising to health professionals should comply with the summary of characteristics incorporated in the product authorisation and present information objectively (IPU Yearbook, p. 275).

The Pharmaceutical Society of Ireland is a public body with statutory responsibility for regulating the qualification of pharmacists in Ireland, as well as for enforcing the law on retail sale and supply of medicines. The PSI has established a Code of Ethics and professional standards guidelines, and may reprimand pharmacists who do not comply. All pharmacists employed in Ireland must be registered with the PSI (Pharmaceutical Society website, Forum).

The General Medical Services (GMS) Scheme provides full medical and surgical services to persons or their dependants who cannot, without undue hardship, provide for these services themselves. Community pharmacists may contract with the Health Boards to supply drugs, medicines, and appliances under the GMS. The provisions of the GMS contract have a pervasive effect on community

297

Table 1.   Summary of market structure in selected OECD countries

	Netherlands	Belgium	Italy	Germany	France
Transmission	A single transmission company (Gasunie) supplies 46% of the gas market directly.	Like the Netherlands, Belgium has a single transmission company (Distrigaz) supplying about half (54%) of the total gas market directly. Distrigaz was privatised in 1994.	In Italy, SNAM, controlled by ENI, is the dominant transmission company (with around 97% of total transmission capacity) and is the only company to have a nation wide natural gas transmission network. EDISON GAS, the second Italian transmission company, has a transmission capacity of around 3%.	Ruhrgas is the dominant transmission company, carrying 70% of the total gas supplies, but there are 17 other transmission companies. Collectively these transmission companies directly supply 32% of the total gas market.	In France there is one dominant transmission company (Gaz de France, "GdF") along with two other smaller subsidiaries (Gaz de Sud-Ouest and Compagnie Française de Méthane). About 30% of the market is supplied directly off the transmission network.
Distribution	35 LDCs, all of which are owned by regional and local authorities.	There are 23 distribution companies, the majority of which (19) have private shareholdings (although even in the cases where private shareholders are in a a majority, the public shareholders keep the the company boards).	A very large number of LDCs (more than 800) are active in the distribution of gas. Around 50% of these are directly managed by municipal local authorities. ITALGAS Spa, the largest company, with a 30% share of distribution nation wide, supplies directly around 92% of the demand of natural gas for electricity production.	There are also a large number (673) of distribution companies. "there is no clear distinction between different types of gas supply companies in the gas chain. Many companies mainly active in distribution are also involved in transmission and vice versa", IEA (1998b), p. 35. Of these is controlled by ENI. SNAM distribution companies, the majority are state-owned. Less than 25% of the companies have some degree of private ownership.	Although GdF is by far the largest company in the gas distribution sector, supplying the bulk of the gas demand of residential/commercial and small industrial customers, there are also 15 state-owned and private distribution companies which supply 2.8% of the market.
Vertical integration	There are almost no ownership links between Gasunie and the LDCs, or between the LDCs and gas producers. The only exception is the minority shares (10%) held by Gasunie in two LDCs (Intergas and Obragas).	There are no ownership links between Distrigaz and the LDCs.	ENI is vertically integrated in production, transmission, and distribution activities. ENI, through SNAM, has a 91% share in the Italian market for natural gas. ENI owns gas import acilities, transmission networks and the largest distribution company ITALGAS. EDISON GAS is also vertically integrated in production, trans-mission and distribution activities through ownership links.	Most of the transmission companies have ownership interests in LDCs. Some of the gas producers have ownership interests both in transmission and distribution companies.	GdF is highly vertically integrated. The other two transmission companies are owner by Elf, Total and GdF.
Horizontal integration	Only 11 of the LDCs are pure gas companies, the majority also distribute electricity and heat.	Of the LDCs only 6 are pure gas companies, the others usually also supply electricity and cable TV signal distn.	The majority of the LDCs. also distribute other services, particularly water and less often electricity.	Only around 20% of the LDCs are pure gas distribution companies. The majority distribute both gas and water or gas, water and . electricity.	GdF is a specialised gas company but the 15 independent LDCs are usually involved in activities other than gas distribution, such as water distribution.

Table 1. Summary of market structure in selected OECD countries (*Cont.*)

	United Kingdom	Australia	New Zealand	USA	Argentina
Transmission	BG Transco (formerly the pipeline operating part of British Gas) provides an integrated transmission and distribution network. There are no other companies providing these services. British Gas was privatised in 1986.	Arrangements differ in the different states. Most transmission pipelines are state-owned, except in Victoria and New South Wales.	One major transmission pipeline network in the North Island owned and operated by NGC (Natural Gas Corporation).	About 45 privately-owned interstate pipeline companies provide transmission services. These are privately owned and regulated entities	Two new pipeline companies where formed in 1992, in the north (TGN) and the south (TGS). These companies are privately owned.
Distribution	BG Transco also operates the distribution network.	Several distribution companies, many of which are private.	Two main distribution companies - NGC and Orion - distributing primarily in the northern half of the North Island. 4 smaller companies. A mixture of private and local government-owned.	Distribution is carried out by local distribution companies which are usually privately owned and regulated.	8 distribution and supply companies were created in 1992. These are privately owned.
Vertical integration	The gas distribution system in Great Britain has historically been the most highly integrated in Europe. In addition to being a considerable gas producer, British Gas was completely integrated from the beach to the burner tip until the early 1990's when competition was introduced. However, in 1997 British Gas separated into a production and marketing company (Centrical) and a transmission/distribution company (BG Transco). BG is also heavily involved in production, with ownership of a significant proportion of the North Sea as fields.	Vertical separation between transmission and distribution in Victoria, whereas transmission is integrated into distribution in New South Wales. There is no integration between production and transmission.	NGC is vertically integrated between transmission and distribution. It also has a significant gas marketing business. All but two of NZ's gas distributors also have a gas retail business.	There is little integration between transmission and gas production and between transmission and distribution.	The Gas Act 1992 prohibits producers and storage companies from owning a controlling interest in a transportation or distribution company.
Horizontal integration	Neither Transcog nor Centrica are involved in other industries although many of the new competitors in the gas marketing sector also provide electricity or water services.		NGC and some other distribution companies are integrated with electricity companies.	Some distribution companies are integrated with electricity companies.	

pharmacists for two reasons. First, at the end of 1999, about 31% of the population is covered by the GMS, and 78% of all prescriptions that are reimbursed are reimbursed under the GMS. Second, and following from the first fact, all but a very small handful of community pharmacists are "contractor pharmacists."

In addition to these three sources of rules, is the Irish Pharmaceutical Union (IPU), representing qualified pharmacists. The IPU's purposes include to promote the economic and professional welfare of members, to negotiate and settle differences and disputes and to regulate the relations between members of the Union and their employers, to represent its members, and to encourage ethical practice of pharmacy. "[M]isconduct includes any act or default likely to bring discredit upon the Union or its members or any part of its members." [63a]

8.2. Entry restrictions

Pharmacists must earn a Bachelor of Science (Pharmacy) degree and complete one-year of practical training under the supervision of a tutor pharmacist, or meet requirements for their foreign education to be recognised. At present, only Trinity College Dublin offers a pharmacy degree in Ireland. The capacity of the course was 50 until the 1997 intake, when it expanded to 70. Nevertheless, the Leaving Certificate score required was one of the highest of any profession. The fact that people with high scores were unable to win a place at the pharmacy school indicates substantial excess demand for places. In August 2000, the Minister for Education and Science announced his decision to increase the annual intake of pharmacy students to 120 and invited the relevant institutions to make proposals to meet the increase.

Despite limited domestic supply of pharmacists, or perhaps in reaction to it, the largest part of recent additions to the PSI Register (about half during 1988-1997 and more than two-thirds in 1998-1999) came from UK universities. Many are Irish citizens. This heavy dependence on training outside Ireland has given rise to complaints that, "It is not appropriate that the State depend on UK universities to continue to provide a very large proportion of the supply needs of the pharmacy profession in Ireland" (Forum).

This substantial labour flow from the UK, or provision of pharmacist education in the UK to Irish students, is made possible by European Union directives. These directives say that persons holding a (specified) comparable certification from a Member State may practice pharmacy in other Member States, subject to some restrictions. In Ireland, the main constraint, in practice, has been that such a person cannot, throughout his career, ever manage or supervise a pharmacy that has been in existence for less than three years. This has been characterised as "an artificial counterbalance to the licensing system perpetuated in some Member States" in a High Court decision (Ailish Young v The Pharmaceutical Society of Ireland, the Minister for Health, Ireland, and the Attorney General, 1992, No. 2098p). This constraint was put into place to ensure that lifting the entry restraints on EU-trained pharmacists would not result in massive opening of new pharmacies in Ireland, openings that were restricted in many other EU Member States. The rules on "contractor pharmacies" perform essentially the same function.

There is also provision for mutual recognition of pharmacy qualifications obtained in Australia and New Zealand. The main requirements are that an applicant have practised as a registered pharmacist for at least one year in the state of registration, and pass an oral examination in the laws governing the practice of pharmacy and the sale of medical preparations and poisons in Ireland (Pharmaceutical Society website). While it is possible to register as a pharmacist in Ireland based on original qualification in pharmacy that was not granted in a European Union Member State or Australia or New Zealand, the process can take two and a half years to complete and requires residency in Ireland to have been already established (Pharmaceutical Society website).

Despite the restrictions on entry, there is not now a mechanism by which pharmacists who have become impaired can be forced to quit practising. The Pharmaceutical Society would like to see "fitness to practise" included in new legislation.

Limits on the location of pharmacies effectively limit the number of pharmacies. Pharmacies that wish – as all but five at present do – to be contractors under the GMS must comply with the location restrictions. New contracts are made with pharmacies on the basis of "definite public health need," which is defined as:

a. The ratio of pharmacies to population at least 1:4 000 in urban areas and towns (over 3 000 population) and at least 1:2 500 in rural areas, and

b. No other pharmacy within 250m in urban areas and towns or within 5km in rural areas, and

c. No adverse effect on the viability of existing community pharmacies in the area, to the extent that it will affect the quality of pharmacy services being provided by them.

On receipt of an application for a new contractor pharmacy, the CEO of the (regional) health board must publish a notice, announcing the receipt of the application and asking for comments, and announcing that additional applications may be made in that catchment area.

Despite the heavy process, since 1996, 27 new contracts have been granted, of which 21 were in rural or semi-rural locations that did not previously have a community pharmacy.

The reasons put forward by the Department of Health for these restrictions were (1) to erect similar controls to those already in place in many EU Member Countries (2) to promote the development of a quality-driven service, and (3) to prevent further clustering of pharmacies in areas already well-served while promoting the provision of services in rural areas.

Before 1996, Ireland did not restrict entry of pharmacies. This resulted in Ireland having one of the highest ratios of pharmacies to population in Europe (Thesing, p. 11). Other countries, including Italy, Spain, Hungary, Norway, France, Australia and, since 1987, the United Kingdom, restrict the number or location of pharmacies. In New Zealand and Spain, only registered pharmacists may own a pharmacy and none may own more than one. Sweden reserves pharmacies to the state. By contrast, the United States, South Korea and Mexico do not have significant entry restrictions on pharmacies. Prescription drugs are delivered by mail in the United States, and future reform may bring mail delivered drugs to the United Kingdom.

8.3. Pricing, mark-ups and dispensing fees

Pharmacies, as implied above, sell both under the GMS and to private patients. Both types of transactions are heavily regulated, at least for medicines dispensed under prescription. In particular, for a sale of a prescription medicine under the GMS, the pharmacist cannot charge a mark-up; he is compensated his cost of the medicine plus a flat dispensing fee. The flat fee can vary if a powder or ointment must be prepared or if the medicine is dispensed at night. For a sale to a private patient, *i.e.*, one not under the GMS, the pharmacist charges a 50% mark-up, under established custom and trade. The wholesale cost of prescription medicine is set by multi-year agreement between the Department of Health and Children and the Irish Pharmaceutical Healthcare Association, representing drug makers.

Other products that pharmacists sell include "over the counter" medicines, *i.e.*, those exempt from prescription-only, as well as cosmetics, toiletries, camera film, and so on.

Many other OECD Members also control retail prices of prescription medicines, and negotiate the wholesale prices with the pharmaceutical companies. Some also restrict prices for "over the counter" medicines.

8.4. Advertising restrictions

Advertising by pharmacies is tightly constrained by the ethical rules of the profession. Listings in the telephone directory and notices in the newspaper cannot advertise more than its existence and hours or change of hours. Special events, such as testing, can be advertised only by a notice in the window of the pharmacy. The cumulative effect of the restrictions means that a pharmacy cannot increase its foot traffic by advertising.

8.5. Conclusions and policy options

The pharmacy sector has a vital role to promote the health of Irish citizens. One reason given for the restrictions is that they will ensure that each pharmacy has sufficient scale to make the investments to strengthen its delivery of more sophisticated health care services such as testing and advising. Another reason given is to improve the delivery of health care services in rural areas. Thus, it is fair to compare the actual effects of the restrictions with these objectives, and to ask whether a different approach might be less costly to society.

The restriction on pharmacists educated in other EU countries, holding certificates that Ireland has agreed certify education comparable to that someone would have received in Ireland, does not promote health care delivery. It simply restricts entry, and thus has anti-competitive effect. In particular, it restricts entry of new pharmacies – those that would have opened if foreign-trained pharmacists were unrestricted – and employment possibilities for a subset of pharmacists. As the proportion of pharmacists with this handicap increase, the restriction may also raise the price of pharmacies operating for more than three years above the price of comparable pharmacies operating for less than three years.

Therefore, the restriction on economic freedom of pharmacists educated in other EU Member countries should be eliminated.

An additional benefit of eliminating this restriction will be to provide a back-up if the number of training places in Ireland does not expand enough. If the expansion were delayed, or if the estimate that 120 will be sufficient turns out to be too low, then the effects will be muted by the flexibility offered by international trade – whether one thinks of the trade as being in pharmacists or pharmacy education.

The logic provided for restricting the location and number of pharmacies is flawed. Incumbents in other sectors in other economies make similar arguments, that if they are protected from competition then they will perform a variety of good works. In fact, competition – keeping up with the competitors – is what induces quality-improving investments. Telephony in many OECD countries provides a good example.

Where there is a genuine public service obligation, such as loss-making provision of a service to rural areas, the solution is not creation of a protected monopoly to cross-subsidise the unprofitable activity. Rather, the solution is to split the task into two parts, of providing the service and of paying for the part that must be subsidised. The provider is chosen by auction for minimum subsidy, where the auction terms specify the services to be provided. The funds are provided either by the statebudget, or by a small fee like a tax on some set of persons. By funding and providing the public service obligation in this way, the subsidy from taxpayers is minimised – the lowest cost provider should win a fair auction.

Pharmacies in Ireland probably do not need such a heavy regulatory structure. Free entry works just like an auction – the most efficient provider enters. Such quality-ensuring characteristics as minimum opening hours, inventory, and continuing education can still be required by regulation. And, since there can be continuous competition among pharmacies, pharmacies will have incentives to provide those quality attributes that are difficult to specify in regulation but which consumers value. If there are rural areas that would not have a pharmacy under such conditions, but that need one according to public policy criteria, those may have to be subsidised directly. For example, the United Kingdom subsidises some pharmacies to be open on Sundays and bank holidays. They already are being subsided indirectly, by consumers and potential pharmacists who endure inconvenience and higher costs. The proposed change would make the subsidy transparent.

Therefore, eliminate the location restrictions on pharmacies. Assess the exit and entry in the sector, and provide transparent subsidies to pharmacies that are desirable on the basis of public policy objectives, but are not forthcoming under free entry.

9. LEGAL SERVICES

The legal profession in Ireland is divided into solicitors and barristers.[8] Solicitors, who deal directly with clients, provide legal advice, prepare the paperwork for legal proceedings, retain barristers, and have overall management of a legal case. Solicitors also advocate in District Court. They also engage in other work not directly related to court, such as property conveyancing, testacy, and commercial contract work. Barristers provide legal advice and advocate in court as well as in tribunals. While the division of which profession advocates in which courts has not been enshrined in law or regulation since 1971, it persists in practice. Other practices which constrain practitioners' commercial freedom include the apparent prohibition of employed barristers appearing in court and the requirement, under their professional rules, for barristers to take work only from solicitors or from members of specified professional bodies.[9] But a client may direct his solicitor to retain a particular barrister. Further, the business form in which barristers and solicitors may practice is restricted: barristers may enter neither partnerships nor companies, whereas solicitors may enter partnerships with other solicitors – but not other types of professionals.

Solicitors and barristers are self-governing through the Law Society and the Bar Council, respectively. Both self-governing bodies are responsible for the certification and discipline of their members. Some aspects of the way in which these tasks are fulfilled can have the incidental effect of restricting entry and some aspects of competition. However, the restrictions differ in their extent and effects in the two professions. Partly, this difference in effect results from the practice of clients not having direct access to barristers, so that the information asymmetry between clients and professionals is limited to the market for solicitors' services.

Both professions restrict entry to the extent that the number of places in their respective professional schools is limited. Under current demand conditions, these entry limits do not seem to be binding on barristers – there is substantial exit – but they seem to limit the number of solicitors below the free-entry level. Before the Competition Act 1991, there was a history of recommended scale fees for solicitors. There is evidence that the since discontinued recommended scale fees for conveyancing still provided a "focal point" from which solicitors discounted their fees some years later. Advertising restrictions can restrict competition. In Ireland, solicitors have substantial freedom to advertise, including fees and areas of specialisation. However, in 2000-2001 legislation to restrict solicitors' advertising of personal injury claims is being considered . By contrast, barristers are prohibited from advertising. The effect of this prohibition is small, though, because barristers make themselves known to solicitors by other means.

Any evaluation of restrictions, regulations and customs must take into account their differing effects on the different types of clients. Clients who are frequent, large buyers of legal services, such as insurance companies and banks, have enough experience to assess the quality of services received. Further, some have sufficient market power to ensure that they receive good value for money. Clients who are involved in the legal system infrequently may be unable to assess quality and have little bargaining power in negotiating fees. This report focuses on the effect of the regulations and practices on small, infrequent clients.

Ireland has already implemented substantial reform in the legal professions. Earlier reforms, which allowed solicitors to advertise and which removed the compulsion of scale fees published by the self-governing bodies, lifted the main hindrances. Further reform of the regulation of the legal professions should focus on removing remaining impediments to competition among solicitors, and providing incentives on solicitors to ensure that even inexperienced clients receive barristers' services at competitive fees. Opening up the service of conveyancing to, for example, banks and financial institutions, would provide additional options to purchases of conveyancing services. Continued freedom of advertising for solicitors will encourage consumers to shop around for cost-efficient legal services, which in turn encourages competition among solicitors. Making solicitors responsible to pay barristers their fee would increase solicitors' incentives to ensure cost-effective barristers services. And enabling clients to instruct barristers directly would increase efficiency. Allowing solicitors and barristers to practice in other business forms could increase efficiency, and other common law systems give legal professional greater scope in this dimension than does Ireland's. Any publication of, *e.g.*, a survey of costs, that could help to form solicitors' or barristers' expectations about a standard price should be suppressed. The control of education and entry of legal professionals should be moved from the self-governing bodies, but close ties as regards quality of entrants and content of education should be maintained.

9.1. Regulatory bodies

Solicitors have a self-governing regulatory body, the Law Society. The Law Society exercises statutory functions under the Solicitors Acts 1954-1994 for the education, admission, enrolment, discipline and regulation of the solicitors' profession.

The Society is authorised by law to consider complaints about inadequate professional services and overcharging. (Solicitors (Amendment) Act 1994, sections 8 and 9) Conflicts about negligence a nd breach of contract are resolved in court. Within the Law Society, the Registrar's Committee is responsible for resolving complaints under the Law Society's self-regulation. Some lay members (persons who are not solicitors) sit on the Registrar's Committee. If satisfied that a bill is excessive, the Society can direct the solicitor to refund immediately some or all of what has been paid, and to waive the right to recover those costs. After the Registrar's Committee of the Law Society has dealt with a complaint, if the person complaining is a member of the public and remains dissatisfied, (s)he may apply to the Independent Adjudicator, who is appointed by the Law Society. The Adjudicator may direct the Society to either re-examine the complaint or to apply to the Disciplinary Tribunal of the High Court. If a complaint has not been resolved or dealt with by the Registrar's Committee, the Society may refer a complaint to the Disciplinary Tribunal. (Complaints may also be made directly by members of the public.) The Disciplinary Tribunal, independent of the Law Society, is appointed by the President of the High Court and includes lay members. The Disciplinary Tribunal decides whether to bring the complaint before the President of the High Court, and if so, recommends the penalty to be imposed on the solicitor. The President of the High Court makes a decision on the basis of the Disciplinary Tribunal's findings or after further evidence in the High Court (Law Society website).

Another way a client can complain about high fees, without going to the Law Society, is to request that the bill be taxed, that is, reviewed by a court official, the Taxing Master. Also, the losing party in a court case against whom the winners' legal fees have been awarded can appeal the amount to the Taxing Master. Statistics on Taxing Masters' decisions show that, from the year 1996-97 to 2000, fees are reduced by 20 to 30%, depending on the year and Taxing Master, in those cases where a complaint was made (Question No. 244.).

The self-governing regulatory body for barristers is the Bar Council. It also represents the interests of practising barristers. The governing body of the Bar Council contains only barristers. The Bar Council promulgates a Code of Conduct and administers the Law Library, of which all practising barristers are members. The Bar Council's Professional Practices Committee considers complaints of misconduct by a barrister made by another barrister; the Professional Conduct Tribunal considers such complaints made by anyone else. The Professional Conduct Tribunal consists of five practising barristers and two non-barristers, one nominated by the Irish Business and Employers' Confederation (IBEC) and one by the Irish Congress of Trade Unions (ICTU). The Tribunal may impose penalties if it finds that a barrister has violated the Code of Conduct or breached proper professional standards (Law Library website).

The Bar Council is a non-statutory body. While both barristers and solicitors are considered officers of the court, judges are traditionally drawn from the ranks of barristers, although District Court judges are frequently solicitors. Control over the education of barristers is not entirely in the hands of barristers, as the Honorable Society of Kings Inns, the educational establishment for barristers is composed of members of both the Judiciary and the Bar.

9.2. Entry

Solicitors and barristers impose exacting entry requirements, including courses, examinations, and work under supervision. Barristers in Ireland are educated at the Honourable Society of King's Inns ("the King's Inns"). To become a barrister in Ireland, one must have a law degree approved by the King's Inns (or pass its Diploma in Legal Studies examination), pass a two-year course at the King's Inns, and work with an established barrister, "devilling," for one year. For solicitors, the entry requirement for solicitors, also, is graduating from university (or being a law clerk with five years experience and meeting other requirements), passing the course at the (unique) Law School and a number of examinations, and serving a two-year apprenticeship with a practising solicitor. Since 1991, any solicitor in good standing in Northern Ireland, England or Wales could apply to the Law Society and be automatically registered. Only about forty persons enter in this way each year. A person who is qualified to practice, in a non-European Union country, a profession that corresponds substantially to the profession of solicitor, may allowed to practice in Ireland. The Law Society may impose obligations of education, training, examinations, and practice in the first three years of Irish practice. (Sect. 52, Solicitors Act 1994) Over the past four years, about 14 to 17% of solicitors admitted were from outside the Republic of Ireland.

Various European Union Directives affect entry. Directive 77/249/EEC, allows lawyers who have obtained their qualification in another Member State of the European Union to provide legal services, with some limited exceptions. Under Directive 89/48/EEC, which deals with the recognition of professional qualifications requiring a period of training of at least three years duration, EU qualified lawyers are, in general, subject to an aptitude test if they wish to become barristers or solicitors in Ireland. Directive 98/5/EC – in the process of being implemented in Ireland – provides a right to EU lawyers to pursue, on a permanent basis under the home State title, in a Member State other than the State in which they obtained their qualification, the professional activities of lawyers in the host State. This right is subject to a registration requirement. A lawyer who has practiced for at least three years in the host State's law, can apply to enter the relevant host State profession without having to pass the aptitude test provided for in Directive 89/48/EEC.

The economic effects of the entry restrictions appear to differ between barristers and solicitors, at least at the present time. For solicitors, the entry barriers seem to be binding. An author in the Law Society Gazette notes, "After the crisis of three years ago when there were so many calls within the profession to limit entry to the Roll of Solicitors, those cries have died down to a whimper. Where once the Law Society maintained a register of solicitors seeking employment, they now maintain a register of employers seeking solicitors (Gilhooly, 1999). This may be a short-term phenomenon, because from October 2000 the capacity of the Law School doubled to 400 places. For comparison, about 7 000 solicitors are on the rolls and about 5 300 to 5 400 practice. In Japan, where entry into the legal profession is highly restricted, only about 500 new lawyers were permitted annually and about 15 000 were already active.

Restrictions on entry into the profession of barrister appear, at present, to have little effect on competition. Each year relatively large fractions of practising barristers enter or leave the profession. Many barristers, especially new ones, cannot support themselves in their chosen profession (Because standards for admission to King's Inns are high, they presumably have enough skills to support themselves in some other profession.) One survey reported that 800 of the 1 300 practising barristers had gross incomes of IR£20 000 or less in 1995 (Bacon). High turnover and low incomes of many practitioners both suggest that entry controls are not restricting competition among barristers.

For more than a decade, reports have recommended that the responsibility for educating and certifying legal professionals be borne by the state rather than the self-governing bodies. "The great danger arising from such control over entry, in the opinion of the Commission, is that that the number admitted might be restricted to a level which was believed to match the perceived requirements of the profession, and not of the public" (FTC, p. 313). "[T]he Government should accept in principle a move away from control of education and entry to a sector by the sector's self-regulating body" (Bacon, p. 42). The argument is that the interests of the public and of the incumbent professionals differ, where the public wants a larger choice of professionals charging lower fees.

Conveyancing is one area of legal practice that is now reserved to solicitors in Ireland. Other common law jurisdictions have opened conveyancing to other professions. All Australian states but

Queensland have done so. One study of New South Wales found that a number of reforms (notably removing most fee advertising restrictions on solicitors and allowing licensed conveyancers to compete with solicitors), resulted in a 17% decrease (1994 to 1996) in the average fees charged by small firms for conveyancing, yielding an estimated annual savings to consumers of US$86 million (Barker, 1996). In the United States, conveyancing is open to non-lawyers, and in the United Kingdom, conveyancing is open to notaries and licenced conveyancers, as well as solicitors. Reform under consideration in New Zealand would open conveyancing to non-solicitors. Thus, the predominant model in other common law jurisdictions is not to reserve conveyancing to solicitors.

Almost anyone who wishes – or must – go to court must employ a solicitor in order to access a barrister. The custom of barristers not taking instruction from anyone but a solicitor (with the exceptions noted earlier), and the practice of solicitors not advocating in courts beyond District Courts, means that any person not in the excepted categories must usually employ a solicitor in order to speak with a court advocate. The exceptions appear to be professionals who would routinely instruct barristers in technical cases, and the exceptions apply only for non-contentious business. It is reasonable to ask whether other professions, or indeed government departments and bodies, would not be in a similar situation and should be accorded similar privileges.

9.3. Fee setting

Clients and professionals are free to negotiate fees. Before the Competition Act 1991, there was a history of recommended scale fees for solicitors. There is evidence that the since discontinued recommended scale fees for conveyancing still provided a "focal point" from which solicitors discounted their fees some years later.

Changes in the law have made it more feasible for clients to "shop around" for legal services. Solicitors must provide to clients, on taking instruction or as soon as is practicable thereafter, the actual charges, or if not feasible an estimate, or if that is not feasible, the basis on which charges are made. (Sect. 68, Solicitors Act 1994) The solicitor must also tell the client the barrister's fees. Reportedly, clients have begun to contact several solicitors to try to obtain a reduction in the fee for conveyancing. This change may be related, too, to the substantial rise in the price of property in Ireland and the fact that the fee for conveyancing is normally expressed as a percentage of the price of the property.

Developments in the market for conveyancing illustrate the practical effect of the recommended scale fees. Before the Competition Act 1991 was introduced, the Law Society set the fee for conveyancing as 1.5% of the price of the property sold for the purchaser and 1% plus IR£100 for the seller. In principle, clients and solicitors could negotiate an alternative agreement, but the scale fee was the maximum that could be charged if no agreement could be reached. After the introduction of the Competition Act 1991, the Law Society could not publish compulsory scale fees, but as late as 1996 the Dublin Solicitors Bar Association published a "Survey of Costs" that included the 1% figure. (The "Survey of Costs" did not contain any recommendation that solicitors actually charge the fees listed.) A study shows that, in 1994, solicitors quoted fees for hypothetical transactions that were discounted from the scale fee. Within each region, discounts were sensitive to location; local markets showed systematic deviations from the recommended fee scale. However, the study could not distinguish between local markets of solicitors being competitive or cartelised. Interviews with solicitors provided support for the view that the discontinued recommended scale fees provide a "focal point" from which solicitors discount in order to set their fees (Shinnick and Stephen, p. 13). (A "focal point" means that there is a particular fee that all solicitors know is associated with a particular task, and know that all other solicitors know it has this association.)

The study of conveyancing raises two points about where competition is likely to be less vigorous. First, the three requirements for successful cartelisation – to reach an agreement, to detect cheating on it, and to punish cheating – would appear to be easier to satisfy in rural areas, where the small number of competitors makes undercutting more detectable. Second, many services performed by solicitors are less standard than conveyancing. Requesting fee estimates for less standardised tasks imposes a time cost, which discourages clients' "shopping around." If fewer clients actually make comparisons, then solicitors may engage in less vigorous competition for non-standard tasks.

Fee setting by barristers takes place in a somewhat different market environment. Solicitors are regularly "in the market" for barristers' professional services, so if solicitors act as clients' agents then they would effectively cumulate their clients' indirect demand for barristers' services and reduce the effect of such a "focal point" in barristers' fees. While a recent study (Bacon) could not rule out some incidence of anti-competitive behaviour among barristers, it concluded that high fees charged by a few barristers could not in the main be attributed to anti-competitive behaviour. The perception that some barristers have "too much" work and others have "too little" supports this view. Also supportive is the absence, or at least weakness, of one of the key requirements for collusion to work, the ability to detect cheating on the cartel.

The Fair Trade Commission's *Report of Study into Restrictive Practices* in the Legal Profession reported that solicitors' representatives said, in 1982, that "in practice the amount of price competition (among solicitors) was limited but maintained that there was instead competition in the quality of service given" (FTC, p. 209). At that time, the Law Society's scale fees were not mandatory minima, and the representatives pointed out that prospective clients could shop around.

It was reported by the FTC in 1990 that the Bar Council had issued a recommended table of fees for certain basic services. The Bar Council had stated that they saw them as useful guides for Taxing Masters – who would not allow fees higher than shown on the scale in the taxation of costs – and that the Circuit Court Rules Committee had, in the past, adopted the table, sometimes with amendment. The Bar Council had stated for the 1990 Report that it understands that, in the main, the tables of published fees are adhered to by the Bar (FTC, p. 210).

The FTC concluded in 1990 that, "Although we accept that there is some shopping around by clients for fee quotations, we now believe that the existence of fee scales in respect of own client charges by lawyers, particularly conveyancing fee scales, is a serious detriment to competition, without compensating advantages, and that such scales are unfair and contrary to the common good" (FTC, p. 219). It went on to recommend that the Law Society be requested to withdraw any recommendations on fees, and that rules regarding fees for conveyancing, and for solicitor's costs and barrister's fees on a party and party basis, be revoked and the power to make such rules be withdrawn (*ibid.*, pp. 220, 223). After the Competition Act 1991, any recommended scale fee would be of great interest to the Competition Authority.

9.4. Advertising

Solicitors may, and do, advertise, but barristers are prohibited from advertising by the Code of Conduct of the Bar Council. A solicitor may advertise her fees for specified legal services and, if qualified under the regulations of the Law Society, may designate herself as having specialised knowledge in an area of law or practice. However, the solicitor cannot assert specialist knowledge superior to other solicitors, and cannot advertise in ways that are likely to bring the solicitors' profession into disrepute. The Law Society may make regulations that prohibit the advertising of fees, but only with the consent of the Minister and where the Minister is satisfied that such regulations are in the public interest (Sect. 69, Solicitors' Act 1994). At present, regulations prohibiting the advertising of fees have not been made. Under the now-replaced Law Society's 1988 regulations, solicitors could not advertise their fees (FTC, p. 254).

There is a concern in Ireland that solicitors' advertising might have induced greater litigiousness, and a recent report recommended consideration of restricting the content of solicitor's advertising aimed at the general public (Bacon, p. 44). However, advertising by solicitors is already required to be not "false or misleading in any respect" (Sect. 69, Solicitors' Act 1994). Because litigation is inherently uncertain, presumably boasts about the likelihood of success in a lawsuit could be prohibited under such a general standard. Further, newspaper coverage about a series of successful plaintiffs, which can induce more people to sue, would not be stifled under these rules. Indeed, advertising by solicitors and newspaper articles both overcome a market failure by providing information about the cost and benefits of professional services, thus expanding services and access to justice to under-served populations. If the underlying issue is too many tort suits damaging Irish competitiveness, then perhaps a more direct reform would result in a more efficient justice system. Hence, any restriction on content of advertising should be circumscribes so as to be least restrictive of advertising that supports the competitive process.

Representatives of the Bar Council argued to the FTC that barristers, in a sense, advertised all the time on their feet in court. Further, solicitors have directories of barristers and their specialities (FTC, p. 248). Nevertheless, the FTC recommended that barristers (and solicitors – the change had not yet occurred at that time) be permitted to advertise fees, since it felt that this would benefit clients and not lead to any diminution in professional standards (FTC, p. 257). A more recent report also recommended that the Bar Council be persuaded to allow comparative advertising by barristers to solicitors and their clients (Bacon, p. 44).

9.5. Business forms

Ireland restricts the form of business in which solicitors and barristers may practice. Solicitors may practice only in partnerships with other solicitors, and barristers may practice neither in partnerships nor companies. New Zealand also prohibits legal professionals from incorporating. By contrast, salaried lawyers in the United Kingdom and in the United States are nevertheless considered to be independent. In both cases, they may work in partnerships with non-lawyers. The professional responsibilities do not seem to have been altered by permitting these other business forms, as the same codes of conduct and disciplinary mechanisms apply regardless.

9.6. Conclusions and policy options

Clients hire legal professionals, making choices among solicitors but, with few exceptions, not among barristers. Solicitors choose among barristers, except when experienced clients make that choice. Hence, from an economic perspective, for inexperienced clients, solicitors compete for clients, and barristers compete for solicitors.

In the market for barristers' professional services, the clients or solicitors tend to be well informed. If an individual solicitor feels insufficiently informed about barristers' characteristics to make a choice in a particular case, then she normally consults others in the same firm or in an informal network. The quality of a barrister's advocacy is relatively apparent to solicitors. Barristers win or lose in public court, where the quality of their advocacy, as well as the solidity of the underlying case, are apparent to observers. In a small legal system such as Ireland's, the repeated exposure of solicitors, especially those who have specialised in an area of the law, to the same set of barristers would allow numerous quality comparisons to have been made. The quality of a barrister's legal analysis would also be signalled in court, but the informal network of solicitors and barristers is also a source of information.

The role of solicitors in the barristers' market – that they make the choice of barrister but do not bear the cost – raises the possibility that barristers' fees could be above the competitive level. If the market for solicitors' services is not competitive, then solicitors would not have incentives to seek the barrister who provides the best value for money because cost would be paid by the client.

But there is little reason to be concerned that barristers' fees are above the competitive level, at least on average. The high rate of exit suggests that barristers' remuneration, at the low end, is not higher than for alternative careers for those with a barrister's training. The correspondingly high rate of entry implies that any excessive remuneration for barristers would be not persist, but would instead be competed away by attracting more barristers into the profession.

By contrast, the market for solicitors' professional services has a different structure from that for barristers. The difference is largely that solicitors' clients – at least those who are infrequent – are relatively uninformed. While clients have begun to "comparison shop" for relatively straightforward tasks, such as conveyancing, this is impractical where the task is non-standardised. Further, at present there is excess demand for solicitors' training. Together, these characteristics mean that the market for solicitors' services raises more concerns than does the market for barristers' services.

Ireland has already implemented substantial reform in the legal professions. Advertising by solicitors is already liberalised. Further, the self-governing body of solicitors has already taken steps to increase the capacity of its Law School. However, further reform is likely to have positive effects.

Entry

Entry and education are in the hands of the professions' self-governing body. While their stated purpose is to guarantee a minimal quality of professional knowledge and skills, the logical connection between the input, education, and output, quality enhancement, is tenuous. The contrast with the absence of mandatory continuing legal education[10] is marked. There is also a difference in the interests of the professional bodies and the public, where the latter would prefer a wider choice of professionals at lower cost.

Therefore, move the control of education and entry of legal professionals from the self-governing bodies, but maintain close ties as regards quality of entrants and content of education and training.

Advertising

Advertising by solicitors encourages consumers to shop around for cost-efficient legal services, which in turn encourages competition among solicitors.

Therefore, maintain the freedom of solicitors to advertise their fees and areas of specialisation.

NOTES

1. In addition to its Irish investments, ESB has significant investments in power generation in UK, Northern Ireland and Spain, and is the Independent Transmission Administrator of Alberta, Canada (ESB 2000).

2. The SI instructs the CER to allocate up to 3.3 mcm/day of capacity to two or more new power generators. (Capacity of the interconnector is planned to be 14mcm/day in October 2000 and 17mcm/day in October 2001) (IEA, 1999). CER evaluated and ranked the applications. Plants that are expected, by the CER, to be commissioned earlier rank higher, and among plants with the same expected commissioning date, larger rank higher. As a general rule, CER is to allocate capacity according to the rank order until the capacity is exhausted. However, if the CER believes that the allocation implied by the rank order "would ultimately result in demand for the supply of electricity in the State not being met," or "would ... result in the promotion of competition in the market for the generation and supply of electricity being adversely affected," then the CER shall alter the rankings.

3. "The main reason why this option [first commissioning date wins] was favoured was that it enables the introduction of competition to the electricity market at the earliest possible time." Also, "In reaching this decision the Minister has had regard in particular to the necessity of establishing new power production capacity at the earliest possible date and the desirability of ensuring the early development of competition in the electricity supply market." [*Policy Statement and response to the submissions received on: The allocation of capacity in the natural gas network for the generation of electricity* 14 December 1999 at http://www.irlgov.ie/tec/energy/Allocat.htm on 2 June 2000). The DPE's strategy statement 1998, published in April 1998 [DPE Annual Report and Financial Statements, 1998, p. 27 at http://www.irlgov.ie/tec/publications/YrReview.pdf on 12 July 2000], says that the DPE would promote competition in electricity generation by encouraging new entrants.

4. To compare size of operation, the turnover of Bord na Móna in the year ended March 1999 was IR£153m, of which some was not from the energy market, whereas the turnover of *Bord Gais* in 1998 was IR£313m (http://www.bge.ie/htm/faces/fac_fs6c.htm on 12 June 2000).

5. Section 21(2) of the Electricity (Supply) Act 1927 requires ESB to fix charges for the sale of electricity and for goods and services rendered by it so that the revenues derived in any year from such sales and services will be sufficient and only sufficient to pay all salaries, working expenses, and other outgoings properly chargeable to income in that year and such sums as the Board may think proper to set aside in that year for reserve fund, extensions, renewals, depreciation, loans and other like purposes (ESB 2000b).

6. Allegheny Energy Inc. and DQE Inc. Docket Nos. EC97-46-000, ER97-4050-000 and ER97-4051-000, Federal United States Energy Regulatory Commission, Order issued 16 September 1998.

7. "The main obstacles to price reduction through competition are the long-term availability contracts for Ballylumford and Kilroot. These contracts – which account for some 90% of Northern Ireland's electricity output – cannot be cancelled before 2010" (Ofreg, Tackling the High Cost of Generation).

8. This study did not address the question of whether the legal profession should continue to be divided into barristers and solicitors.

9. Included are: Ombudsman for Credit Institutions, Ombudsman for Insurance Industry, Association of Chartered Certified Accountants, Association of Chartered Accountants in Ireland, Institute of Certified Public Accountants in Ireland, Chartered Institute of Management Accountants, Institute of Chartered Secretaries and Administrators, Institute of Secretaries and Administrators.

10. "21 Years On: The Changing Face Of CLE" by Sarah O'Reilly in the Law Society Gazette December 1999 on http://www.lawsociety.ie/GazDec1999.htm on 9 June 2000. "The future development of CLE is currently under review by a Law Society task force. The law societies of England & Wales and Scotland have in recent years introduced mandatory CLE. While the suggestion of mandatory CLE in Ireland has previously been discounted, there are some signs of change of attitude among the profession."

BIBLIOGRAPHY

Ailish Young v the Pharmaceutical Society of Ireland (1992), the Minister for Health, Ireland, and the Attorney General, No. 2098p.

Competition Authority (1997),
Proposals for the Electricity Supply Industry in Ireland: Comments on the Consultation Paper published by the Department of Transport, Energy and Communications, Discussion Paper No. 3 (Patrick Massey), November.

Competition Authority (1998),
Competition in the Natural Gas Industry, Discussion Paper No. 5 (Patrick Massey and Tony Shortall), November.

Competition Authority (1999),
Competition and Regulation in Public Utility Industries, Discussion Paper No. 7 (Patrick Massey and Paula O'Hare), July Department of Public Enterprise (DPE) 1998. Strategy Statement at http://www.irlgov.ie/tec/publications/ on 12 July 2000.

Commission for Electricity Regulation (2000),
CER Response to Draft European Communities (Internal Market in Electricity) Regulations 2000 at http://www.irl-gov.ie/tec/energy/cer.htm on 28 January 2001.

Cross, Eugene D. (1996),
Electricity Regulation in the European Union: A Country by Country Guide, Wiley, Chichester.

Crawley, Alison (1998),
Abstract: "Summary of the Testimony of Alison Crawley Before the Multidisciplinary Practice Commission", Center for Professional Responsibility, American Bar Association at http://www.abanet.org/cpr/crawley1198.html on 7 February 2001.

Department of Public Enterprise (DPE) (2001),
Press release "Government approves plans for independent regulation of the gas sector and accelerated liberalisation," 6 March.

Department of Public Enterprise (DPE) (2000),
"Governance and Accountability: Policy Proposals", March 2000, DPE at www.irlgov.ie/tec on 28 March 2001.

Department of Public Enterprise (DPE) (1999),
Discussion Document: "The allocation of capacity in the natural gas network for the generation of electricity", 21 October at http://www.irlgov.ie/tec/energy/Discuss.htm on 2 June 2000.

Department of Public Enterprise (DPE) (1998),
"Statement of Strategy" April, at http://www.irlgov.ie/tec/publications/ on 12 July 2000.

Barker, Joanne (1996),
Conveyancing Fees in a Competitive Market, Justice Research Centre, Law Foundation of New South Wales, Sydney at http://www.lawfoundation.net.au/jrc/reports/conv_web.pdf on 7 February 2001.

Economic and Social Research Institute, The (1999),
National Investment Priorities for the Period 2000-2006, John Fitz Gerald, Ide Kearney, Edgar Morgenroth and Diarmaid Smyth (eds.) Dublin, March.

Electricity Supply Board (ESB) (1998),
Generation Capacity Requirements to 2005 A report produced by ESB in consultation with the Department of Public Enterprise, October, at http://www.irlgov.ie/tec/energy/generation.htm on 2 June 2000.

Electricity Supply Board (ESB) (2000),
Annual Report and Accounts for the year ended 31 December 1999, at http://www.esb.ie/ on 12 June 2000.

311

Electricity Supply Board (ESB) (2000*b*),
    Accounts 1999, Dublin.

Fitz Gerald, John and Johnson, Justin (1995),
    "Restructuring Irish Energy Utilities" in Energy Utilities and Competitiveness, Fitz Gerald and Johnson (ed.).
    Policy Research Series Paper No. 24, Dublin: The Economic and Social Research Institute, April.

Forum on the Need for Pharmacy Graduates (2000),
    Held on 31 May at Jurys Hotel, Ballsbridge, Dublin. Report at
    http://www.pharmaceuticalsociety.ie/forumreport.htm on 5 September 2000.

Gilhooly, Stuart (1999),
    "How to Hold on to Your Bright Young Things," Law Society Gazette, September on
    http://www.lawsociety.ie/Gaz0999(5).htm on 10 June 2000.

Halpin, Tony and James Flynn (2000),
    "Taxing Times," Gazette of the Law Society, January/February at http://www.lawsociety.ie/janfeb2kGaz.htm on 10
    September.

IEA (1999), In-depth Review of Ireland, Paris.

Irish Business and Employers Confederation (IBEC) (2000),
    Press release, "Competition needed in electricity market – 20/04/2000" at http:// www.ibec.ie on 17 October 2000."

Irish Fair Trade Commission (1990),
    Report of Study into Restrictive Practices in the Legal Profession, Dublin.

Irish Pharmaceutical Union (2000),
    IPU Yearbook-Diary 2000, Dublin.

Irish Pharmaceutical Society, The. http://www.pharmaceuticalsociety.ie.

Law Library of Ireland, The. http://indigo.ie/~gregk/.

Law Society of Ireland, The. http://www.lawsociety.ie.

Massey, Patrick and O'Hare, Paula. "Competition and Regulatory Reform in Public Utility Industries: Issues and
    Prospects," Journal of the Statistical and Social Inquiry Society of Ireland, Vol. XXVII, Part III, pp. 71-134.

Mario Monti (2000),
    Letter to Ms Mary O'Rourke T.D. 22 December. http://www.irlgov.ie/tec/energy/mariomonti.htm on 6 February 2001.

Office for the Regulation of Electricity & Gas (Ofreg) (2000a), Transmission and Distribution Price Control Review for Northern
    Ireland Electricity plc: A Consultation Paper, April.

O'Neill, Peter (2000),
    "Future Development of the Natural Gas Industry in Ireland," address at the Energy Ireland 2000 Conference,
    Dublin, 15th June.

OECD (1997),
    OECD Report on Regulatory Reform, Vol. 1: Sectoral Studies, Paris.

Peter Bacon & Associates (2000),
    Final Report: The Requirements for regulatory reform in the business services sector in Ireland, April.

Question No. 244, to the Minister for Justice, Equality and Law Reform, for written answer on 5 April 2000.

Shinnick, Edward and Frank H. Stephen (2000),
    "Professional Cartels and Scale Fees: Chiselling on the celtic fringe?" forthcoming in International Review of Law and
    Economics, Vol. 20, No. 4, December.

Shaw, John (1999),
    "Law Society's New Complaints Procedures," Gazette of the Law Society, May at
    http://www.lawsociety.ie/Gaz0599(3).htm on 10 June 2000.

S.I. No. 237 of 2000, Gas (Amendment) Act, 2000, (Section 2) Regulations, 2000, 26 July 2000 at
    http://www.irlgov.ie/tec/energy/si23700.htm on 9 August 2000.

Thesing, Gabi (2000),
    "Pharmacies – Are They Creaming It?" Business & Finance, pp. 10-13, 24 August.

BACKGROUND REPORT ON REGULATORY REFORM IN THE TELECOMMUNICATIONS INDUSTRY*

* This report was principally prepared by **Takashi Yamada**, of the Directorate on Science, Technology, and Industry, with the participation of **Dimitri Ypsilanti** of the Directorate on Science, Technology, and Industry. It has benefited from comments provided by colleagues throughout the OECD Secretariat, by the Government of Ireland, and by Member countries as part of the peer review process. This report was peer reviewed in December 2000 by the OECD's Working Party on Telecommunication and Information Services Policies with the participation of the Competition Law and Policy Committee.

TABLE OF CONTENTS

List of Boxes

List of Tables

List of Figures

Executive Summary

Background Report on Regulatory Reform in the Telecommunications Industry

The telecommunications sector in OECD countries has seen significant regulatory reform in recent years. Twenty-four OECD countries had, in 2000, unrestricted market access to all forms of telecommunications, including voice telephony, infrastructure investment and investment by foreign enterprises, compared to only a handful just a few years ago. The success of the liberalisation process depends on the presence of a transparent and effective regulatory regime that enables the development of full competition, while effectively protecting other public interests. There is a need to promote entry in markets where formerly regulated monopolists remain dominant and to consider elimination of traditionally separate regulatory frameworks applicable to telecommunications infrastructure and services and to broadcasting infrastructures and services.

Ireland has for over five years been liberalising its telecommunication markets, largely driven by the European Union's policies. Originally, on the basis of a European Commission derogation, Ireland had committed to completing the opening of its market to full competition on 1 January 2000. A turning point was the decision taken by Ireland in May 1998 to end the derogation on 1 December 1998, shortening the remaining period for completing the full liberalisation from nineteen to six months. This acceleration in the liberalisation process brought the Irish regulatory framework on a par with many other OECD countries, and in certain areas ahead of many countries that had opened their markets earlier to competition. Market access in the telecommunications sector of Ireland is among the most liberalised and its regulatory framework has been moving steadily toward implementing best practice regulation.

The Department of Public Enterprise and the Office of the Director of Telecommunications Regulations (ODTR), the independent regulator, have rapidly put in place the essential regulatory measures for fair and effective competition. Nonetheless, the rapid transition to create a competitive environment inevitably left a number of issues unresolved. Price rebalancing needs to continue. Progress on introducing an interconnection framework reflecting best practice methodology needs to be continued, and delays in obtaining capacity from the incumbent reduced. Mechanisms to protect consumer interests must be given greater priority and legislation relating to rights of way for telecommunication operators over public highways should be adopted as soon as possible. In addition, a universal service costing methodology needs to be implemented and, if necessary a universal service fund set up. The enforcement power of the ODTR must be strengthened and it should ensure that it has adequate resources. Ireland's strength is in its recognition that there is a continuing need for further progress and development along with its readiness to implement change and improve institutional and regulatory arrangements.

There are now over forty operators competing in the Irish telecommunications market, and the new entrants' share in the fixed line market has grown to more than 17% (as measured by revenue). Introduction of Wireless Local Loop services and telephony over cable TV networks have already started to develop in the local call market. Competition in the mobile market is weak at present, but a third market entrant entering at the end of 2000 will improve this situation and several airtime resellers are beginning to place competitive pressure on prices.

The stated ambition of the Irish authorities is to reach the top decile of the OECD countries in terms of major indicators. Ireland has the potential to attain this goal, if the government continues to pursue further regulatory reforms.

1. THE TELECOMMUNICATIONS SECTOR IN IRELAND

1.1. The national context for telecommunications policies

The Irish economy has shown remarkable growth since the late 1980's. Growth in output has been on average over nine per cent per year on a GDP basis during the period 1994-98.[1] GDP per capita in terms of purchasing power parity has surpassed the European Union average.[2] The telecommunications sector has increased its weight in GDP from 2.40% in 1985 to about 3% in 1999 as measured by public telecommunication revenue.[3] During the same period, the number of telephone mainlines increased more than twice from 0.7 million to 1.6 million.[4] This corresponds to an increase from 19.8 to 42.2 per 100 inhabitants, but despite this growth Ireland still ranked below the OECD average.

Employment in the Irish telecommunications sector, which was about 16 200 in 1985, had declined to 11 700 in 1997.[5] However, by the end of 1999, the incumbent's employment had increased again reaching a level of 12 606.[6] Telecommunications employment declined as a percentage of total national employment from 1.50% in 1985 to 0.85% in 1997. Public telecommunication revenue per employee in Ireland has increased significantly, as in most other OECD countries, from USD 29.2 in 1985 to USD 192.7 in 1999, but is low relative to the OECD average of USD 269.5.[7]

The incumbent, Telecom Éireann (Eircom since September 1999) was ranked 59th in 1999 among the major public telecommunications operators in the OECD area as measured by revenues.[8]

1.2. General features of the regulatory regime, telecommunications market and market participants

Development and Liberalisation of Telecommunications in Ireland

The main features in the development and liberalisation of the telecommunications sector in Ireland are shown in Box 1.

As in the other OECD countries, Ireland's telecommunications networks were developed by direct involvement of the national government, which created a state-owned monopoly with an "exclusive privilege", based on the argument that the sector was a natural monopoly.

Ireland as a member of the European Union, has gradually opened up its telecommunications market in line with the Union's requirements and has been influenced by other EU members' policy orientations since the 1980s. However, Ireland was not a leading country in terms of taking steps toward market liberalisation and the creation of competitive telecommunication markets in the 1990s. Its request in 1996 for a derogation from the EU's 1 January 1998 full liberalisation was indicative of policies at that time placing emphasis on caution rather than market forces and regulatory reform.

The first major step toward liberalisation of the telecommunications sector was the separation of the government policy function from service operations by establishing Telecom Éireann as a statutory corporation in 1984. The company was wholly owned by the state and was managed by a governing board whose members were appointed by the responsible Minister.

The basic market, regulatory and institutional changes to prepare for liberalisation were enacted in the Telecommunications (Miscellaneous Provisions) Act, 1996, which amended the Postal and Telecommunications Services Act of 1983. The Act's main provisions included establishment of an independent regulator, namely the Director of Telecommunications Regulation, transfer of regulatory functions to the Director from the Minister for Public Enterprise, imposition of levies on telecommunications service providers for meeting the expenses of the ODTR, and tariff regulation.

The Act allowed for a change in the ownership of the incumbent. With a goal to complete the liberalisation process by 1 January 2000, the Irish government in 1996 decided to prepare Telecom Éireann for competition by gradually privatising the company. The first step in this direction was to find a strategic investor. An agreement was concluded with a consortium composed of the Netherlands' KPN and

Sweden's Telia, who acquired a shareholding of 20% in Telecom Éireann (the share increased to 35% – 21% by KPN[9] and 14% by Telia – by 1999).[10]

Another significant step taken in the 1996 Act was the separation of regulatory functions from the policy functions of the Department of Public Enterprise by establishing an independent regulator of telecommunications, the Office of the Director of Telecommunications Regulation (ODTR), with effect from 30 June 1997. The new act also provided for a price cap regime of certain services of Telecom Éireann.

During the course of implementing a number of liberalisation measures between 1997 to 1998 in line with the EU Directives, the Minister for Public Enterprise decided in May 1998 to end the liberalisation derogation with effect from 1 December 1998, leaving it with only about six months instead of one year and seven months to complete the liberalisation process.

Another major step in the liberalisation process of Ireland took place in July 1999, when the government disposed of its majority shareholding in Eircom, reducing the shares to less than 1% by November 2000. The government decided not to retain a golden share, and it has no policy to retain any state shareholding in Eircom.

The ODTR became operational, initially, using to a large extent seconded staff from the Department of Public Enterprise. Both the Department and the ODTR managed very successfully to meet the shor-

---

Box 1.   Important events in the liberalisation of the telecommunications sector in Ireland

1984:   Telecom Éireann was established as a fully government-owned telecommunications operator with an "exclusive privilege".

1992:   Provision of value added services were liberalised.

1994:   Regulatory conditions regarding the supply of leased lines by Telecom Éireann were laid down.

1996:   EC allowed Ireland a two-year derogation until 1 January 2000 to complete the full liberalisation of the telecommunications market.

1996:   Telecommunications (Miscellaneous Provisions) Act, 1996 was passed. It provided the main framework for regulation in the fully liberalised market.

1996:   Telecom Éireann established a strategic alliance with KPN and Telia.

1997:   Competition in mobile phone services started with the entry of Esat Digifone as a second GSM operator (licensed in 1996).

1997:   Alternative infrastructure provision was allowed by removing the monopoly on the provision of satellite-based telecommunications services and the supply of liberalised telecommunications services over cable TV networks and alternative public telecommunications networks.

1997   (June): The Office of the Director of Telecommunications Regulation (ODTR) was created.

1998   (May): The Minister of Public Enterprise decided to end the derogation with effect from 1 December 1998.

1998:   A third mobile (GSM) operator was selected to end the duopoly, but the award of the licence was challenged legally by an unsuccessful applicant which delayed the process for two years until 2000.

1998   (1 December): Voice telephony was fully opened to competition to complete the full liberalisation of the telecommunications market.

1999:   Telecom Éireann was privatised by a public share offering, and its name was changed to Eircom.

tened deadline to complete the opening up of the market fully to competition. Over the last three and a half years they have implemented a number of policy and regulatory measures for liberalisation and transformed EU Directives into national laws and regulations. Considering the short period in which they were required to make changes both of the authorities deserve credit for their efforts and achievements. Nevertheless, linked largely to shortages of experienced staff and the short period given to implement the basic requirements for market liberalisation a number of problems arose. However, from a slow start in the process of market liberalisation, Ireland has made rapid progress helped by the ODTR, which expedited matters and used experience gained by other countries.

At the same time, the Irish regulatory landscape has been characterised by a number of court cases. This has tended to slow down the process of liberalisation and creating effective competition. The Department of Public Enterprise addressed this issue in respect of interconnection and licensing decisions of the ODTR,[11] and also, as noted below, new proposed provisions of the Communications Regulations Act, 2000 will likely act to reduce the resort to the courts, in particular where such legal processes have been used to slow down change. Initial problems arising from poor implementation are also being rectified through provision of appropriate legal power and through increased staffing.

Derogation for the full liberalisation

Ireland was the only one of the five EU countries with a derogation[12] to implement full market liberalisation before the derogation period had been completed. The confidence and willingness of the government to transform their telecommunication market from a monopoly to a competitive market, providing leading edge services, and benchmark themselves with other advanced countries, has characterised policy and regulatory developments since then. But the decision of Ireland to waive the derogation eleven months after the EC's original deadline for other countries, but thirteen months before the specially granted deadline to Ireland, raise a question as to whether the initial derogation was necessary.

The request of the Irish government for the derogation on fully liberalising fixed voice telephony was based mainly on the following reasons:

– Telecom Éireann's high level of debt, due to a significant capital investment required and high cost of delivering telecommunications services in Ireland.

– Necessary structural adjustments of Telecom Éireann to enable it to function effectively in a fully liberalised market while ensuring universal service, increasing telephone density, and re-balancing tariffs.

The European Commission, taking into account the submissions by interested parties in Ireland, examined the issue from the following perspectives:

– To what extent the temporary exclusion of all competition is necessary in order to allow Telecom Éireann to continue performing its task of general interest, *i.e.* universal service for voice telephony.

– The derogation period should be strictly proportional to what is necessary to achieve the necessary structural adjustment for facing full competition, *i.e.* (i) further development of Telecom Éireann's networks, (ii) further adjustment of Telecom Éireann's tariff structure, and (iii) transformation of Telecom Éireann, in particular, further developments of its products, restructuring of its cost base and completion of its organisational change to be market driven and customer focused.

After a thorough examination of the issues covering the factors of universal service, telephone density and penetration rate, re-balancing of tariffs, debt and cost structure, and effect on trade including the possibility of cross-subsidisation for investing in foreign markets, the European Commission reached a conclusion to accept the request of the Irish government as shown in Table 1.

The derogation did require that Ireland should, before 1 April 1998, publish proposed legislative changes to implement full competition, publish proposals for the funding of universal services, and adopt these changes before 1 November 1998.

Table 1. Derogation for completing full liberalisation

	Requirement of EC	Derogation granted	Request of Ireland
Provision of voice telephony and infrastructure	1 January 1998	1 January 2000	1 January 2000
Provision of already liberalised services on own or alternative infrastructure	1 July 1996	1 July 1997	1 July 1999
Direct interconnection of mobile networks	Immediately in 1996	1 January 1999	1 January 2000

Telecommunications market and participants

There are at present around 70 telecommunications licence holders, of which 45 are actually operating, in the Irish telecommunications market, most having entered the market after full liberalisation on 1 December 1998. However, the top two companies – the Eircom group and Esat Telecom group – represent a large part of the Irish telecommunications market at present. Table 2 shows major telecommunications operators and the numbers of residential customers.

Table 2. The major telecommunications operators in Ireland

	Operator	Number of residential customers (as of 31 March 2000)
Fixed line market	Eircom	1 585 000
	Esat Telecom	37 720
	OCEAN	N/A
Mobile phone market	Eircell	1 049 000
	Esat Digifone	550 000
	Meteor	(operation to start shortly)
Cable television market	NTL	356 231 (cable TV)
		0 (telephony)
	Chorus Communications	254 585 (cable TV)
		0 (telephony)

1. Both Esat Telecom and OCEAN are owned by British Telecom, and are in the process of merging.
2. The number of subscribers for Ntl and Chorus Communications are as of 30 June 2000.
3. Eircell is being acquired by Vodafone of the United Kingdom as of December 2000.

Source: Esat Telecom (http://www.esat.com/news/PR20000110-1.asp),
Eircom (Annual Report 2000), Ntl (http://www.ntl.com/ireland/frames/quarterly/1st-00.htm).

Eircom, the former monopoly, has continued to be the strongest player in the Irish telecommunications market since full liberalisation with a share of close to 83% in the fixed line market based on revenue.[13] Eircom's revenue grew by 10% between fiscal year 1998 to 1999. The increase was driven primarily by the mobile sector, which had 40% growth in revenue.[14] Eircom's fixed line retail call traffic, which stood at 10.3 billion minutes at the end of March 2000, has grown by 7.1% over the past year, and its wholesale call traffic, 1.8 billion minutes increased by 129% during the same period.[15] It is expected that new entrants' market share in fixed line services will increase further as the new interconnection regime, based on a long run average incremental costs (LRAIC) methodology, carrier pre-selection, and geographic number portability are introduced and developed.

321

Eircom continues to maintain a strong position in the fixed network market as a result of its nation-wide infrastructure coverage. It provides service in every segment of the telecommunications market, and has the largest share among competitors in each of these segments.

In the domestic fixed network market, Esat Telecom and OCEAN (no longer operating separately from Esat Telecom under the common ownership of British Telecom of the United Kingdom as a result of a merger in early 2000) are the major competitors to Eircom, and are providing services in both business and residential markets, and in all of the local, long distance, and international markets.

There are currently 596 000 homes receiving cable television services in Ireland out of a total estimated television home population of 1.2 million. There are a number of small CATV operators, generally with less than one thousand subscribers, with analogue services.[16] In addition, there are around 120 000 subscribers of Multipoint Microwave Distribution System (MMDS) in rural and non-cabled urban areas. MMDS operators offer both analogue and digital services, and are subject to similar licence provisions with those of cable licences coming under the same regulation. Each cable operator has a monopoly (in-platform exclusivity) granted by the ODTR, which will expire in April 2004. The limited monopoly was granted to upgrade their networks to provide digital services and expand their coverage as required by the licence conditions.

The estimated number of cellular mobile subscribers reached 1.86 million by June 2000, corresponding to a penetration rate of 50%. Of the two mobile operators in the Irish market, Eircell is the larger, but both operators are designated as having a significant market power (SMP) in public mobile telecommunications networks and services. The third licensed operator, Meteor, was not in operation as of October 2000.

There will be four UMTS (IMT-2000) licences awarded. Licences will be awarded in April or May 2001 through a comparative selection process (so called "beauty contest").[17]

New forms of mobile service providers such as airtime resellers, indirect access providers, and mobile virtual network operators (MVNOs) are also expected to develop. The ODTR is expected not to take regulatory action in this area, placing emphasis on commercial negotiations as indicated in their consultation paper.[18]

Operators have been designated as having Significant Market Power (SMP) in four markets by the ODTR,[19] making them subject to additional obligations for controlling the exercise of their market power, under the EU Open Network Provision (ONP) Directive. These are the markets for fixed public telecommunications networks and services, leased line services, public mobile telecommunications networks and services, and the national market for interconnection. Eircom is an operator with SMP in the market for fixed networks and services, in the leased line market, and in the national market of interconnection. Eircell has been designated as having SMP in the mobile market and in the national market of interconnection. Esat Digifone has been designated as having SMP in the mobile market (Table 3). The eventual build-up of market share by the third mobile operator, Meteor, will require a review of SMP in the mobile market.[20]

Table 3. Designation of SMP in the Irish telecommunications market

	Fixed public telecommunications networks and services	Leased line services	Public mobile telecommunications networks and services	National interconnection
Eircom	SMP	SMP		SMP
Eircel			SMP	SMP
Esat Digifone			SMP	

2. REGULATORY STRUCTURES AND THEIR REFORM

2.1. Regulatory institutions and processes

Department of Public Enterprise

The Department of Public Enterprise is the government ministry in Ireland which has the responsibility for overall policy for the telecommunications and broadcasting transmission[21] sectors including the radio frequency spectrum, as well as for policies in transport, energy, and earth resource sectors. As noted previously, the government's regulatory functions were transferred to the ODTR by the enactment of the Telecommunications (Miscellaneous Provisions) Act, 1996 (hereinafter "1996 Act"). Unlike a number of government Ministries in other OECD countries the Department did not attempt to retain regulatory power over the sector.

One of the criticisms made of the liberalisation process in Ireland is that the Irish government, has simply reacted to the European Union's requirements by mechanically transposing them into national legislation and that the objective of the whole regulatory reform process, and thus the benefits of reform, has not been recognised sufficiently. This criticism is unfair in that by shortening the derogation period available the Irish Government did recognise the benefits of competition, but because the process of market liberalisation was started late, there was little alternative to rapidly transposing Directives as well as ensuring that policy frameworks in place met requirements to create a competitive market.

Since 1998 new policy initiatives have taken place in relation to development of the regulatory framework, including publication in March 2000 by the Minister for Public Enterprise of "Governance and Accountability in the Regulatory Process: Policy Proposals", which sets out her proposals for development and clarification of the regulatory framework across the sectors within her remit. In September 2000 the Minister published an "Outline Legislative Proposals in relation to the Regulation of the Communications Sector",[22] which sets out her proposals for legislation in the area of communications regulation, including implementation of the "Governance and Accountability" proposals in the sector. These proposals show a rapid reaction by the Department to perceived weaknesses in the regulatory framework as well as incorporating new EU proposals in legislation. Also, although yet to pass the parliament, the Department initiated and prepared a Telecommunications (Infrastructure) Bill in 1999 to reform the system for telecommunications network operators to access public and private land. As a result of the Department's work and that of the ODTR Ireland's regulatory framework, despite the late start, has caught-up with many of the EU countries that started the liberalisation process much earlier, and in certain policy areas is in advance of these countries.

The National Development Plan 2000-2006 states that Ireland's objectives in communications and electronic commerce policies are (1) the development of the Irish communications sector so that its ranks in the top decile of OECD countries in terms of service range, quality, availability and price, and (2) the establishment of a legal, regulatory and administrative framework which will create a favourable climate for the development of electronic commerce and digital industries.[23]

Office of the Director of Telecommunications Regulation (ODTR)

The ODTR is the independent national regulatory authority for telecommunications regulations including the broadcasting distribution sector. It was established by the 1996 Act and commenced the operation in July 1997. It is headed by one person, namely the Director, appointed after a public competition by the Minister for Public Enterprise with the consent of the Minister for Finance.[24] Regulatory bodies structured on the basis of a single person as the head of the regulatory body are common among the OECD countries, although regulators structured on the basis of a collegiate body are in the majority.[25]

The ODTR's functions and duties are defined by an extensive range of legislation, both primary and secondary. The main ones include the development and implementation of a licensing regime, supervision of the interconnection regime, dispute resolution, supervision of access to networks, management and licensing of use of the frequency spectrum, management and administration of the national numbering resource, setting price caps, and monitoring and enforcing quality of service and performance targets.

The ODTR is wholly funded by income received from the broadcasting, radio and telecommunications industry. The income comprises licence fees in respect of radio licences issued and levies raised on the turnover of telecommunications operators (at a rate of 0.2%) and cable and MMDS television operators (at a rate of 3.5%).[26] The cost of the ODTR's activities for the year ended on 30 June 1999 was approximately IEP 11.1 million and was totally covered by licensing fees and levies (and bank interest)[27]. In the majority of OECD countries regulators use fees and contributions from the industry to support wholly or partly their budgetary needs.

The 1996 Act did not define clearly the objectives of the ODTR. In this context the Director of the ODTR has stated that she is "committed to ensuring [the ODTR] plays an effective role in facilitating the operation and competitive development of the sector, within the parameters of EU and Irish law." and that "Ireland needs cheap, advanced communications to maintain and improve its competitive position in the world economy."[28] Also, the mission of the ODTR as defined under Section 15 of the *Freedom of Information Act*, 1997 states:

- "The purpose of the Office of the Director of Telecommunications Regulation is to regulate with integrity, impartiality and expertise to facilitate rapid development of a competitive leading edge telecommunications sector, that provides the best in price, choice and quality to the end user, attracts business investment and supports ongoing social and economic growth."[29]

The ODTR has focused on the competitive development of the telecommunications sector, which leads to improvement of the competitive position of the Irish economy. However, the ODTR emphasised in its annual report for 1998-99 that "[t]he focus has now firmly shifted to the users of telecommunications services and how they are best served." and that "we have now moved into a liberalised environment offering consumer choice."[30] The new legislative proposals by the Department of Public Enterprise now set out clearly the objectives of the ODTR as follows :[31]

a) "To promote and sustain an open and competitive market in Ireland for electronic communication networks and services with a view to achieving maximum benefits for users in terms of choice, price, quality, value for money and access to a variety of innovative services.

b) To ensure the efficient management and use of the radio frequency spectrum and numbers from the national numbering resource in Ireland in accordance with policy as may be determined by the Minister."

The ODTR is organised around three functional units called Market Development, Market Operations, and Market Framework (in addition to Human Resources, Financial Control, and Legal). It is structured in a forward-looking and flexible manner to respond effectively to the changes and convergence of traditional sectors. Many market participants have criticised the ODTR for not being sufficiently transparent in providing details of its organisation or clearly nominating contact points. There were several reasons for this lack of structural transparency, partly to do with insufficient resources at the ODTR, and partly to do with the use of flexible teams on different projects which meant that a rigid organigramme was not feasible. There is, however, still scope to improve transparency and accessibility. Although the organisational structure and contact points have recently been made available on the ODTR's Web site, it is somewhat terse and provides insufficient information on contact details for different regulatory issues. In contrast, consultations are widely publicised and contact details are provided there for the specific consultation. The greater emphasis of the ODTR, in particular by putting to the forefront the interests of consumers may require a change in the internal organisation by, for example, establishing a unit that deals exclusively with consumer issues.

Starting initially with staff seconded from the Department of Public Enterprise, the ODTR now operates with around seventy staff, whereas it is mandated to have around ninety. Recruitment of staff has been a major issue for the ODTR and there has always been a shortage of personnel relative to the required amount, quality, and speed of work. This has resulted partly from the fact that the staff seconded from the Department have been returning, and also, the ODTR has to compete with the private sector which, resulting from liberalisation, have also increased their demand for skilled telecommunication personnel.

One of the inevitable results has been that the ODTR often has resorted to outside consultants for high quality expertise in specific issues. While it is beneficial to make good use of highly qualified outside expertise, it is necessary as well to develop internal experts and retain an "institutional memory", which the ODTR has been well aware of and has tried to ensure knowledge transfer to the staff.

Relationships between the Minister and the Director of the ODTR

The Minister for Public Enterprise has the mandate to appoint the Director and to remove him or her under certain circumstances.[32] At the same time, the 1996 Act stipulates that "The Director shall be independent in the exercise of his or her functions."[33] It further provides for the involvement of the Minister in certain areas, where the Minister may direct the Director, in relations with public service requirements, international commitments, allocation and use of the spectrum, etc.[34]

The Director must report the performance of his or her functions as well as provide financial accountability to the Minister annually, and the Minister submits the Director's report to the Parliament.[35] This means that it is the Minister who is accountable to the Parliament for the ODTR's performance in general, a common arrangement among a number of OECD countries.

Accountability

Important issues concerning accountability have received much attention in Ireland in recent times and the generic regulatory framework has undergone some development in this regard.[36] The Department of Public Enterprise has been concerned with the issue of accountability of regulators noting the need to overcome a perceived "democratic deficit".[37] The 1996 Act establishing the ODTR did not have a provision regarding their accountability to the Parliament, but such lacuna has been filled in later legislation for other sectoral regulators such as in electricity. Following the publication of its "Statement of Strategy", the Department published, "Governance and Accountability in the Regulatory Process: Policy Proposals"[38] in March 2000 as policy proposals on the governance and accountability aspects of the generic regulatory framework as it applies across all sectors within its remit. The proposals drew on the views expressed in the public consultation and on the experience gained in Ireland and in other countries. In general terms, they develop the regulatory framework so as to resolve perceptions about "democratic deficit" which could have had an impact on the credibility and legitimacy of the new regulatory institutions.[39]

In telecommunications, the Department published in September 2000 a consultation paper of proposed legislation entitled "Outline Legislative Proposals in relation to the Regulation of the Communications Sector", which when enacted will be cited as the Communications Regulation Act, 2000.[40] It reflects the "Governance and Accountability" proposals and those which are of particular relevance in this regard are:

- Replacement of the current single regulator structure of the ODTR with a three-person Commission, bringing postal regulation within the ambit of the regulator.[41]

- Explicitly requiring the "Commission" to report to a relevant parliamentary committee on a regular basis in relation to its plans and overall performance, as is provided for in case of the Commission for Electricity Regulation.[42]

- The proposed legislation is important in tightening up previous legislation (the Telecommunications (Miscellaneous Provisions) Act, 1996) which had not addressed or provided clear guidance for a number of important issues (see below). There is no evidence available from other OECD countries to indicate that a "Commission" structure for a telecommunication regulatory body is more or less effective than a single-person regulator. The latter can be more effective since a single Director is more likely to be able to make more rapid decisions than a

Commission. However, this may depend on how a Commission is structured and frequency of meetings. A Commission may provide for a wider scope of opinions, but again the structure and how responsibilities are allocated within a Commission can play an important role. Criticism that a single person regulator can result in "undue personalisation" may not be of concern if good accountability procedures are put in place. On the contrary, effective regulation may sometimes require that the regulator has an authoritative public profile The proposals in the Communications Regulation Act, 2000, would require that the Commissioners be appointed by the Minister, after a competition by the Civil Service Commission. The proposed terms of office are between three to five years and a Commissioner will be limited to two terms of office. Commissioners can be removed from office only for reasons of incapacity or "stated misbehaviour."[43]

The proposed Act improves accountability of regulation by more clearly defining the objectives of regulation, the powers of the regulatory body, and its answerability. By requiring the regulatory body to provide a general review of its performance to a committee of parliament the proposed Act serves to increase transparency and accountability, and also to enhance the independence of the regulatory body. However, the draft Act states that it should have "regard to any recommendation of such Committee [of parliament] relevant to its functions".[44] In this context it is also important to note that the Minister is responsible for overall policy in the communications sector. This new clause can cause difficulties for the Commission since it is subject to policy directions from the Minister and these policy directions may differ from "recommendations" of a Committee of parliament.

Review of the ODTR's decisions

Aggrieved parties can challenge ODTR's decisions by going to court if they believe there has been an illegality in procedural aspects. Before 16 March 2000, appeals against decisions of the ODTR on licensing and interconnection resulted in suspension of the decision until the outcome of the appeal. Now an appealed decision can be implemented by the Director unless the court decides whether to suspend it pending the outcome of the appeal. As an example, a decision by the ODTR to award the third cellular mobile licence to Meteor Mobile Communications Ltd., in 1998 was brought to court by the unsuccessful applicant, Orange Communications Ltd. This high profile case presented some major institutional issues regarding the review of the ODTR's decisions.[45]

The legal process, which ended when the Supreme Court upheld the original decision of the ODTR in May 2000, delayed the introduction of the third mobile licence, in other words delayed the end of duopoly in the Irish cellular mobile market by around eighteen months, to the detriment of consumer interests. This, and other cases have raised a more general question of challenging decisions of the regulator through recourse to the legal system, which can effectively delay implementation of decisions, and often can impose costs on parties who would gain by the implementation of a decision.

In an attempt to overcome the potential invocation of judicial proceeding in an effort to delay implementation of regulatory decisions, the "Governance and Accountability" document proposed that regulatory decisions would apply when the matter was referred to judicial review unless the court decided otherwise. In telecommunications, the Department of Public Enterprise made amendments to the existing regulations in respect of interconnection and licensing[46] Stepping further, it proposed in the draft Act that this principle applies to the ODTR decision in general. At the same time it is proposed to strengthen the regulator by ensuring that its decisions cannot be questioned other than through judicial review for compliance with legal requirements, and not judicial appeal on the merits, by placing a time limit on applying for a review of a decision, and ensuring that judicial review takes into account "the interests of the public in the efficient regulation of the market".[47] Thus, the new draft rectifies a problem in the original legislation which had not addressed the question of judicial appeal, *i.e.* it provided the courts the opportunity to examine the substantive merits of a decision of the ODTR in all matters.

This initiative of the Department is important in addressing the issue of possible abusive appeals to delay the effective implementation of decisions and by ensuring that courts take into account the objective of ODTR decisions.

Decision making process

Telecommunication regulators in many OECD countries use public consultation as an integral part of their decision making processes. Such consultation helps to improve transparency and to improve decision-making by reflecting a wide range of views. Both the ODTR and the Department of Public Enterprise should be commended for their very effective use of the public consultation process, although there is no such requirement in the relevant legislation.[48]

A difficult challenge is how to better reflect consumer interests effectively in the public consultation procedures. The general public, consumer groups, and small and medium enterprises are provided the same opportunity to comment on a range of issues through public consultation. Moreover, the ODTR invites consumer groups to meet with them and draws their attention to consultations of particular interest to consumers so that the consumer groups are encouraged to respond to the consultations. However, partly because of their lack of expertise in specific areas, and partly because in many cases these groups may not be well organised, these groups generally perceive that their views are not given sufficient weight in the consultation process, although they are often the most widely affected by the decisions.

Co-operation with the Competition Authority

The transition of the telecommunications market from monopoly to competition has been accompanied by increased involvement of competition authorities in this sector throughout the OECD. In Ireland, the Competition Authority (CA), as the agency responsible for enforcing the competition law under the Department of Enterprise, Trade and Employment is mandated to take action against anti-competitive practices in all sectors of the economy. Because of overlapping jurisdiction with the ODTR, there is a possibility that an act specifically allowed or even mandated by the ODTR could inadvertently be in conflict with competition laws, costing and confusing enterprises. Thus, it is important to ensure that decisions are co-ordinated to avoid the possibility of inconsistency and over-burdening relevant parties. In this respect, the Report of the Competition and Mergers Review Group[49] recommends that the Competition Act should be amended "to grant immunity from criminal prosecution and/or liability in damages under the Competition Act in respect of actions taken by undertakings pursuant to and in accordance with a ruling, decision or approval granted by a sectoral regulator." (Recommendation 16(i)), which is likely to reduce uncertainties for undertakings.

Initially, there have been complications in co-ordination. The ODTR had intended to include the terms of Sections 4(1) and 5 of the Competition Act, 1991 (sections prohibiting anti-competitive agreements, decisions, and practices, and abuse of dominant position) as a condition of telecommunication licences. During the ODTR's consultation on the licences, concern was raised about coherence with existing law and clarity for industry players, which led the Director to remove the general fair trading clauses from all licences that would be operational from 1st December 1998, in order to avoid potential conflicts with the CA.

On the other hand the CA has acted while the ODTR has carried out a public consultation on proposed regulatory measures. For example, for local loop unbundling the ODTR, in early 1999 began a consultation process on ULL. Then the EC clarified that the existing EC Directives included only bitstream access within their scope but not full ULL. Consequently the ODTR noted in its Decision Notice on Unbundling published in April 2000 that it did not have sufficient powers under the existing EC Directives to enforce ULL. The Decision Notice set out a work programme for the introduction of bitstream access by April 2001. The CA initiated proceedings against Eircom in October 1998 alleging abuse of its dominant position. At present these proceedings are in the hands of the courts. In December 2000, the EU adopted a Regulation for full unbundling to impose on fixed line operators with SMP the obligation to make available ULL from 1 January 2001. Eircom has published its access reference offer shortly prior to 1 January 2001.

The draft Communications Regulation Act, 2000 explicitly recognises the need to ensure that the ODTR and Competition Authority work together. There are three relevant clauses in the proposed Act at Head 39. The first, which is based on the presumption that both bodies have a good working relationship, states that where a regulatory issue falls within the competence of both bodies one of the regulatory bodies may defer from regulation allowing the other body to take action. The second, and an important clause, requires that the two bodies consult before taking any action in the area of communications regulation if such action is in an area in which the other body also has competence and take into account the opinion of the other body. Effective implementation of this clause may, however, require that the two regulatory bodies agree in advance on their respective fields of competence as regards the communications regulatory area. This could be in the form of a protocol established between the two authorities.[50]

Equally important in the draft Act is a provision allowing the two regulatory bodies to exchange confidential information. This clause is relatively unique in that competition authorities are often constrained to maintain information they obtain in the course of their inquiries confidential. In giving the ODTR powers to collect information and subjecting them to a confidentiality requirement the new Act facilitates such information exchange which will allow for more rapid and efficient decision making.

Lack of sufficient enforcement power of ODTR

The industry has, in general, given favourable ratings to the ODTR in terms of its operations and decision making. However, the ODTR has not been rated highly in the past in terms of its ability to follow-up on decisions, monitor their compliance and enforce decisions. One reason for this has been the lack of staff and the necessity for the regulator concentrate on putting in place the necessary regulatory framework and safeguards, following the Government's decision in 1998 to fully liberalise the market 13 months before the end of the derogation period. A second, more fundamental reason, has been the lack of sufficient enforcement powers.

The new draft Act provides the ODTR with more enforcement power. In particular, penalties have been increased including the possibility of prosecution and conviction on indictment with up to five years imprisonment. Fines up to 10% of turnover or IEP 500 000 (whichever is greater) are being proposed together with a fine not exceeding IEP 5 000 per day for a continuing offence. For lesser offences the regulator will also be given the power of prosecution in certain circumstances so that it can take quick action if it believes an offence is being committed.[51] For summary offences the new law proposed to maintain the existing level of fine (*i.e.* IEP 1 500) and up to three months imprisonment. Although a significant improvement on previous provisions the new proposals do not give the regulator sufficient scope to act speedily to impose fines. This is necessary in view of the costs that non-adherence to a regulatory decision can impose on other market players. The level of fines imposed on summary offences remains quite low and should be more proportionate to the damage that can be inflicted on other market players through non-compliance to regulatory decisions. It needs to be noted as well that there is a constitutional constraint on the imposition of penalties without recourse to the courts, *i.e.* if the fine is above a certain level, the offence must be prosecuted on indictment, which could take a long time.

The ODTR has been able to invoke penalty clauses for failure to meet agreed delivery of leased lines by Eircom to other licensed operators. In September 1999 Eircom, following consultation with the ODTR and industry, agreed to a "service level agreement" (SLA) with other licensed operators which stipulated that Eircom would deliver leased circuits within 26 days of an order, and failing this would be penalised on a capped basis. The SLA, which came into effect in November 1999, also had put forward, improved delivery times declining from 60-40 days to ten days. The penalties were capped at IEP 3 000 per delayed line.[52] The ODTR, arguing that Eircom's performance has been persistently inadequate, decided in September 2000 to uncap the fines and impose higher fines and on a daily basis. Eircom challenged the ODTR's authority to uncap such fines and the matter is before the High Court for hearing in late November 2000.

Handling of consumer complaints

Consumer groups have argued that their complaints regarding telecommunications services have not been handled in a satisfactory manner. Consumer complaints, such as those on billing, have been dealt with primarily by being directed to the telecommunications operators who are the object of the complaint and who have the primary responsibility to deal with them. It should be noted as well that the ODTR requires applicants of telecommunications licences to establish a customer contract indicating how they will deal with complaints. Consumers unsatisfied with the operator's handling have at times requested the intervention of the Office of the Director of Consumer Affairs (ODCA), an independent statutory body responsible for a wide range of consumer protection laws. However, the ODCA does not normally investigate individual complaints, irrespective of the sector. The ODTR, who has regulatory responsibilities in complaints on telecommunications, in many cases has referred problems back to the operators for investigation before ascertaining what action if any can be taken.

This situation has arisen in large part by the lack of a formal mechanism to handle such complaints. Thus, although the ODTR has been mandated to resolve consumer complaints in telecommunications, that do not come within the scope of the Small Claims Court (see below), they have dealt with all complaints to them on an basis.[53] Most of the time, it has meant referring the complaints to the operators in question for investigation in the first instance and asking them for a report on the matter so that the ODTR can ascertain what action is necessary. Other means at consumers' hands at the moment include the use of the small claims procedure within the District Court structure (known colloquially as the Small Claims Court), if the claim does not exceed IEP 1 000.

The ODTR and the Department of Public Enterprise have been aware of these problems, and have been working to establish a formal mechanism to handle consumer complaints. The draft Communications Regulation Act, 2000 provides for a framework to address this issue.[54] The Law would require telecommunication operators to develop and make public an appropriate code of practice for their dealings with users.[55] However, it would be more appropriate if a requirement was made on the industry as a whole to develop a single code of practice for the resolution of user complaints and disputes. The Law would also require the ODTR to establish procedures for examination, investigation, and resolution of consumer and user complaints and disputes, following public consultation, and would give it the authority to make binding determinations. The ODTR has already worked with operators to implement a timeframe for the resolution of complaints. It is important that these time frames are included in any specific procedures to be set out.

It is important for the regulator to supplement these proposed provisions by requiring operators to provide a published report on the number and type of complaints received, and summary data on the time taken for resolution, the number of cases resolved satisfactorily and the number not resolved. In this context, the ODTR plans to do so under a programme called "Measuring Licensed Operator Performance" should be welcomed.

2.2. Regulations and related policy instruments in the telecommunications sector

Regulation of entry and service provision

Full liberalisation of the Irish telecommunications market on 1 December 1998 resulted in a new licensing regime. The ODTR, based on the provisions of the Postal and Telecommunications Services Act 1983, specified two types of licences: a General Telecommunications Licence and a Basic Telecommunications Licence. Their main features are shown in Table 4. There were, as of December 2000, 46 General Licence holders (25 of which were operational), and 31 Basic Licence holders (21 of which were operational).[56]

The Irish licensing regime is open. The standard time to handle the licensing process of four or six weeks is relatively rapid compared to a number of other OECD countries with an individual licensing framework. The regime is in compliance with the EU Licensing Directive.[57] However, in order to further reduce barriers to market entry and attract more investment, as well as to further transparency, simplicity, and efficiency of regulation, Ireland should change its individual licensing regime toward a system of general authorisation. At minimum, the requirement for a detailed and high-level business plan, including details on financial sources and projections, and adequacy of managerial and technical resources,[58] should be reconsidered since a well functioning market would decide whether the entran-

329

t's plan is sufficiently viable. The EU Licensing Directive of 1997 requires that priority be given to general authorisations as opposed to individual licences, and a new EU directive[59] being proposed will require that all electronic communication services and networks are covered under a general authorisation framework. Under this proposal use of licensing would be limited to the assignment of radio frequencies.

The best practice in this regard is found in Denmark. In Denmark, all telecommunications operators, except for those providing public mobile communications, can enter the market freely without the need even to register with the regulatory authority as long as they satisfy the general conditions stipulated in an Executive Order, which follows the essential conditions set down in the EU Licensing Directive.[60]

There are no line-of-business restrictions in the Irish telecommunications market.[61]

Table 4.   Types of licences required to enter Irish telecommunications market

	General telecommunications licence	Basic telecommunications licence
Permitted operation	• Provision of all types of telecommunications networks and services, including voice telephony, to the general public. • Holders can apply for telephone numbers from the national numbering scheme.	• Provision of all types of telecommunications networks and services except voice telephony and services involving numbers
Duration of validity	15 years	Five years
Standard handling of the application	Processed within six weeks after receipt of all information.	Processed within four weeks after receipt of all information.
Main requirements in application	• A high-level business plan for three or more years, including key sources of finance, revenue and expenditure projections. • Adequate managerial and technical resources. • To specify the network or service to provide.	To specify the network or service to provide
Form of licence	Individual licence	General authorisation
Licence fee	Initial: Euro 12 500 Annual: 0.2% of turnover	Initial: Euro 2 500 Annual: 0.2% of turnover
Legal basis	Section 111(2) of Postal and Telecommunications Services Act 1983	Section 111(3) of Postal and Telecommunications Services Act 1983

Source: ODTR.

In order to provide mobile telephony in Ireland, an operator needs to obtain two individual licences as in other OECD countries. They are a service licence under the 1983 Postal & Telecommunications Act and a radio licence for the equipment and spectrum under the 1926 Wireless Telegraphy Act. There are three operators at present in this category: of which, Eircell and Esat Digifone are operational and designated as operators with SMP in public mobile telecommunications networks and services market,[62] and Meteor, the third licensee, is expected to start operation in 2000. Operators of Wireless in the local loop (WLL) need equivalent licences since they need access to radio frequencies. Six of them have been issued to date.

Provision of new mobile service by airtime resellers, indirect access providers, and mobile virtual network operators (MVNOs) is not subject to any special regulations in principle as was made clear by the ODTR's report on the regulatory framework for access in the mobile market.[63]

Entry into cable television market, including MMDS, requires an individual licence granted by the ODTR. Current terms of cable licences, which were issued in 1999, grant cable operators five years of in-platform exclusivity (monopoly in each operating area), out of fifteen years duration of licence, for their provision of programming services. CATV operators are required to pay an annual licence fee of 3.5% of their turnover. Also, specific phased roll-out requirements are imposed.

This policy of limited exclusivity was employed so that the CATV infrastructure in Ireland, particularly for digital services, could develop quickly and licensees could invest actively in building infrastructure requiring enormous capital investment. The licences were granted on first come first served basis subject to meeting certain regulatory requirements. However, even though the granting of an exclusive period might have been necessary to attract investment and to develop the cable infrastructure as quickly as possible, the penetration rate of cable infrastructure including MMDS (multipoint microwave distribution system, or so called "wireless cable") is now relatively high (see Section 3). This suggests that the original aim has been partly achieved. Upgrading cable to provide broadband access and telephony would more likely occur in a competitive market. However, it is now necessary to ensure that cable operators are clearly informed that their exclusive period will end as planned.

Cable operators are also required to obtain authorisation from municipalities from a planning perspective for the installation of equipment such as headends and from a road management perspective in relation to road excavation. When cable operators provide telephony, they are required to obtain separate telecommunications services licences because the cable licences currently do not cover telephony. When the initial period of five years expires in April 2004, licensing for CATV networks should be streamlined and covered by general authorisation.

Terrestrial broadcasting operators first need to obtain licences from the ODTR for the operation of apparatus for wireless telegraphy (under the 1926 Wireless Telegraphy Act). They also need authorisation to provide programming services from the Independent Radio and Television Commission (IRTC) under the 1988 Radio and Television Act. Ireland also has a national public service broadcasting organisation, the RTE (Radio Telefís Éireann), which is a statutory corporation under the Broadcasting Act 1960.

Foreign ownership restrictions do not exist in Ireland. There are certain notification procedures in relation to change of control, ownership or shareholding of a licensee. A number of fully-owned foreign communication companies already operate in the Irish telecommunications market, and foreign investment has played an important role in developing Irish telecommunications. Some examples include KPN and Telia's shareholding in Eircom and British Telecom's acquisition of Esat Telecom in April 2000.

Rights of way

Under a monopoly regime Telecom Éireann (currently Eircom) had the right to compulsorily acquire private land or rights of way, but this right was abolished when it lost its monopoly privilege. As a result, Eircom and other telecommunications operators do not have any rights to compulsorily acquire rights of way over private land. They now need to rely on negotiations with owners of private rights of way.

A major difficulty faced by new entrants is the demands placed by local and municipal authorities on requests for rights of way over public highways. Some municipalities have requested, for example, that extra ducts be provided and made available to other new entrants. The Association of Licensed Telecommunications Operators (ALTO, an association of new market entrants) have made proposals to co-ordinate ducting. Obtaining rights of way to public highways requires, for local roads, permission from local road authorities (there are over thirty of them in Ireland) or the National Roads Authority for national roads. There are a number of legislative provisions, some of which date back to 1863, giving telecommunications operators the right to open public highways for the purpose of laying the infrastructure and provide for the procedure.

The Minister for Public Enterprise prepared a bill, the Telecommunications (Infrastructure) Bill, in 1999 to reform the system for telecommunications network operators to access public and private land. The Bill provided that the network operators could apply for and possibly compulsorily acquire rights of way over private land in the event that negotiations with landowners were unsuccessful. It also addressed the issue of opening of public roads to lay cable, the use of public roads for infrastructure, and provided a legislative basis for sharing of ducts. The Bill proposed to set up a Telecommunications

Infrastructure Board, a quasi-judicial body with the power to adjudicate on access to private rights of way. The Bill also provided for simplification and clarification of the procedures for the operators to access public roads. On enactment, such legislation would have provided a benchmark for many countries with open telecommunication markets in that rights of way, and the lack of an appropriate framework, have become a key stumbling block in the development of competitive networks.

Due to public concerns which were expressed after the Bill was published and proposed to parliament regarding possible compulsory access by telecommunications operators to private land for the purpose of constructing telecommunications infrastructure, the Minister did not proceed with the Bill and withdrew it in December 2000. Instead, the Minister intends to include in the Communications (Regulation) Bill, 2000 those provisions of the withdrawn Bill relating to access by telecommunications operators to public highways and relating to sharing of infrastructure. In other words, the provisions relating to compulsorily acquiring access to private land by telecommunications operators are dropped and such access will continue to be a matter for negotiation between operators and landowners. It is expected that the Communications (Regulation) Bill will be published in mid-2001 and submitted to parliament in autumn 2001. The Bill should help facilitate the rapid construction of alternative facilities, thus helping in developing effective competition and meeting Ireland's broader goals of creating an Information Society. The new Bill does not aim to take away powers from Municipalities, but rather aims to ensure consistency and fairness in access to public ways.

Regulation of interconnection

New entrants still rely highly on Eircom's networks to provide services to end-users. Such a situation is foreseen to continue for some time, especially for the local network. To facilitate competition in telecommunication markets the Irish government has made efforts to provide new entrants access to Eircom's networks at cost based prices so that they have the opportunities to compete with Eircom effectively.

Ireland's interconnection regime is based on the EU Interconnect Directive (Directive 97/33/EC) transposed into the European Communities (Interconnection in Telecommunications) Regulations 1998 (S.I. No. 15 of 1998), which came into effect in January 1998. It provides for certain rights and obligations on licensed operators to enter into interconnection agreements, and the SMP operator such as Eircom is further obliged to offer interconnection on a cost-oriented and non-discriminatory basis as requested. It is also required to publish a Reference Interconnect Offer (RIO) stating all of the terms and conditions. Mobile networks are also covered in this regime because the regulations apply to all licensed operators. Eircom currently has thirteen interconnection agreements with other fixed operators, and a number of new entrants are negotiating interconnection agreements with Eircom and Esat Digifone.

The method used to determine interconnect charges offered by Eircom has been based on historical costs. However, the ODTR has developed an initial bottom up LRIC (Long Run Incremental Cost) model with the assistance of the Industry Advisory Group, and it was used to assess Eircom's RIO rates in establishing the interim rates for 2000 to 2001. The ODTR has finalised the bottom up LRIC model with further inputs from the industry, and Eircom is developing a top down LRIC model due to be out in December 2000. Then the two models will be compared to finalise the current interim rates for 1 December 1999 to 31 March 2001. LRIC will also be used to set up the rates for 2001 to 2002. Table 5 shows the level of interconnection rates in Ireland. Ireland's interconnection rates are below EU benchmarks and one of the lowest among EU members as shown in Figure 1.

A general consensus has emerged among a number of countries on the theoretical superiority of the LRIC accounting methodology as closely approximating costs of the most efficient operators and as bringing the rates to a level of a fully competitive market, while a methodology based on historical cost (FDC or Fully Distributed Cost) tends to overly compensate the incumbent through subsidising inefficient historical costs incurred by it. Thus, many OECD countries have developed or are developing LRIC model for interconnection rates, but few countries have come yet to the point of its implementation as Ireland has except Austria, the United Kingdom, and Portugal. Ireland, at present, belongs to a group of countries with lower rates, but has a potential for further reductions in local and single tandem prices to meet best practice.

Table 5.   Fixed line interconnection charges of Eircom for call termination

Call termination	August 98 Rate per minute (pence)	01/12/1998-1/12/99 Final rates Rate per minute (pence)	1/12/99-31/3/00 Interim rates Rate per minute (pence)
Primary peak	1.02	0.82	0.805
Primary off/peak	0.68	0.41	0.425
Primary weekend		0.33	0.36
Tandem peak	1.54	1.27	1.16
Tandem off/peak	1.03	0.63	0.605
Tandem weekend		0.52	0.52
Tertiary peak	2.31		
Double tandem <50km peak		1.56	1.38
Double tandem >50km peak		1.78	1.58
Tertiary off/peak	1.54		
Double tandem <50km off/peak		0.78	0.72
Double tandem >50km off/peak		0.88	0.82
Double tandem <50km weekend		0.64	0.615
Double tandem >50km weekend		0.73	0.71

Source: ODTR.

Figure 1.   **Comparison of fixed interconnexion charges based on a call duration of three minutes**

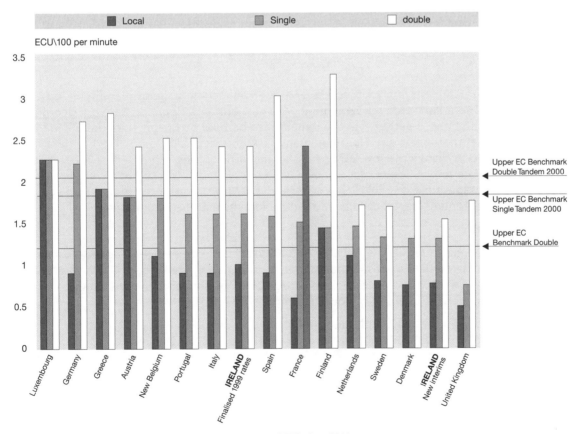

Source: Official Journal of the Europeen Communities March 2000; ODTR, June 2000.

1891 Internet access

Eircom's introduction in January 1999 of a new discounted daytime call charge for accessing certain Internet service providers (ISPs) raised an issue related to interconnection regime. The new service offered end users access to the ISPs with an 1891 access code at a charge less than the cost of a local call.

A number of new entrants objected to what was viewed as unfair discrimination by Eircom in the provision of the 1891 services because:

1. Eircom was providing an interconnection service to its own downstream arm that it was not providing to competing operators.

2. It was providing a service to end users at a retail price that competing operators were not in a position to offer.

3. It was providing a service to ISPs as end users that other operators could not offer.[65]

The ODTR dealt with the issue in a broader context, *i.e.* the interconnect for calls destined for Internet services, and following two public consultations it decided in July 1999 that:

1. Operators with SMP in the fixed market are required to pass 1891 Internet calls over national interconnection links, and allowing a new entrant to pick up a call at a "higher" level would not imply that the call was not a local call.

2. Retail revenue retained on calls destined for the Internet by the originating SMP operators should be cost based.

3. Eircom must offer the services related to calls to the Internet on the principle of non-discrimination.

4. The retail price of calls to the Internet should be under the control of the terminating operator.

The ODTR also decided to establish an industry forum to develop the new interconnect arrangements based on these decisions. The ODTR should also consider how a flat rate (unmetered) Internet call origination can be introduced in order to develop an Internet market more conducive to electronic commerce.

An important requirement in market access and interconnection is the availability of leased lines. Eircom had agreed to a service level agreement with new entrants detailing delivery deadlines and other terms and conditions, together with the penalties to be paid by Eircom to operators in the event of its failure to meet the targets set. However, many new entrants have complained of delays.[66] The ODTR has proposed to change the level of fines as an incentive for the incumbent to meet its commitments. The immediate imposition of these fines has been delayed as a result of a court appeal by the incumbent. At the same time the ODTR has launched a review in order to try and find solutions to improve on the provision of leased circuits and the performance of the incumbent.

Local loop unbundling[67]

The regulator began to tackle the issue of unbundling at an early stage relatively to many other OECD countries. In March 1999 a consultation paper on unbundling was issued, which was followed in April 2000 by a Decision to introduce bitstream access. The Decision also announced that it was planned to develop a framework for full local loop unbundling by April 2001.

The regulator did not initially implement full local loop unbundling arguing that the "current EU framework does not enable the Regulator to mandate this particular form of access at this time (*i.e.* April 2000)".[68] This decision is indicative of the limited powers given to the Regulator under national law. Whereas Austria, Germany and the Netherlands had already implemented full unbundling under national law, the Irish Regulator argued that EU legislation on Special Network Access obligations did not mandate such full unbundling, and neither did Irish law.[69] It is important for the Regulator to have sufficient powers to take innovate decisions which will facilitate the development of competition. The new provisions in the proposed draft Act enhance significantly the powers of the Regulator by laying down clear and specific objectives, by setting down *ex ante* obligations the Regulator can impose on an enterprise designated as having SMP, and by establishing Relevant Markets to allow for regulation of operators with SMP. The Regulator needs powers not only to survey the market, but should also be given sufficient flexibility to initiate change when necessary for the efficient functioning of the market.

Developments at the EU level and the decision to implement full local loop unbundling will be an important step in upgrading the network to provide broadband access and help fulfil Ireland's policy goal to develop a knowledge based economy as well as become a European hub for electronic commerce. It is unfortunate that these wider economic goals were not supplemented much earlier through specific legislation to allow important developments such as full LLU (Local Loop Unbundling) to be implemented thus giving Ireland a head start.

The Regulator should ensure that its policy to give new entrants the opportunity to participate in ADSL[70] trials at an early stage so that they are not disadvantaged relative to the incumbent is being implemented by Eircom. A decision on pricing of unbundled local loops also needs to be made rapidly and in this context price rebalancing will be important. The Regulator has taken a decision that geographic averaging of prices will be retained for unbundled local loops.

Pricing policy

Price regulation in telecommunications services in Ireland is based on the 1996 Act and takes the form of price caps on services provided by an operator with a dominant position and/or where there is no competition in the services. The price cap in Ireland follows the CPI-X formula, where CPI is the consumer price index as calculated by the Central Statistics Office and X is the adjustment specified originally by the Department of Public Enterprise with subsequent modifications by the ODTR. X used to be six, and was changed to eight after the revision of 1999. The actual overall price reduction over a three year period from January 1997 to December 1999 was 22.6% in nominal terms, whereas the required rate was 12.3% reduction. Increased operator efficiency and the development of competitive markets in fixed line telecommunications could account for the further reduction of 10%. There are currently sub-price caps on the prices of individual services within the overall price cap basket of the incumbent's services.

For fixed line telecommunications sector, the ODTR carried out during 1999 a detailed review and consultation process to modify the price cap on Eircom, which had been set three years earlier for a five-year period. As a result, Eircom was found to be dominant in all the relevant telecommunication service markets, including for access. It was determined that price caps continued to be applied to the same services except that international calls were dropped because of the prospect of their becoming competitive within the three years term of the modified cap. It may be opportune to consider whether caps on national calls could also be dropped if the competitive situation warrants this and given that a higher percentage of national calls are carried on mobile networks. The services that the price cap continues to apply in fixed line services are; voice telephony (local and national), the provision of connection, and take-over of telephone exchange lines and ISDN (Integrated Services Digital Network) lines, operator calls, directory enquiry calls, and payphone calls. Under the current regime, the prices under the price cap regulation must be transparent, cost-oriented, and non-discriminatory.

It is important that price regulation encourages full tariff rebalancing in order to promote competition on the basis of efficient price structures. The ODTR has taken into account the need for rebalancing in their examination of price caps. It decided to raise the sub-cap of CPI-0 on line rental charges to CPI+2 to allow progressive re-balancing of Eircom's fixed charges. The ODTR has recognised that the line rental charges of Eircom are below cost. It has however not been clarified if at the end of the current cap period *i.e.* 2002, price rebalancing will have been achieved. Data in Section three show that the incumbent's line rental charges have only been subject to minor changes over a seven year period, although significant changes have taken place in local call charges. It is important for the ODTR to ensure that subscriber line charges are cost-oriented as soon as possible. While it would be preferable

335

that this takes place before full local loop unbundling is introduced, this is unlikely to occur given the low increase allowed by the cap.

There are social and economic considerations that need to be taken into account so that a "one-off" price increase may not be possible. However, an agreed date, which is publicised, to achieve such rebalancing may help to speed up the transition and would forewarn users of scheduled price changes.

There appears to be a consensus among OECD countries that the most effective way to achieve cost-based prices is through effective competition and not through price regulation. However, in tariff re-balancing of residential and local services, the regulator has to handle the particularly sensitive issue of how quickly or slowly to manage the transition since such price changes tend to become highly political. Excessive tariff control can also reduce tariff flexibility and since many new entrants use the incumbents price levels as a benchmark to set prices, such price controls may in fact reduce the impact of competition in pushing down prices. Therefore, constant review of market competition and price developments is important and so are efforts to streamline price control.

In the cellular mobile market, which effectively has been a duopoly up to the end of 2000,[71] there is no price cap regulation on the operators' charges. Instead, price controls on the operators' retail charges are implemented through their licence conditions. Both Eircell and Esat Digifone offered to have retail price control included in their licences when they applied for GSM900 or 1800 spectrum. Specifically, their licence conditions state:

> *The Licensee shall endeavour to reduce, in each of its financial years, the amounts of the charges to its customers so that those amounts are, after allowance is made for changes in the value of money in each such year after the first, lower than those obtaining in the previous such year, and shall endeavour to maintain those charges at or below the appropriate international comparators specified from time to time by the* Director. [72]

Irrespective of this condition, Ireland's cellular mobile prices are well above the OECD average for residential and business customers. It would appear that the licence condition has not played a significant role in reducing prices. Such reductions should occur through competition, as they have in most other OECD countries. And this should begin to occur when the third operator develops its business.

Quality of service

Under the 1996 Act and other legislation the ODTR is responsible for regulating service quality. Licences, both General and Basic, contain conditions relating to service quality, among which are obligations in relation to use of terminal equipment and a requirement to have a Code of Practice for resolution of consumer disputes. Also, the ODTR may issue directions regarding indicators and measurement methods of the quality of telephony services and digital leased lines.

The ODTR developed a minimum set of service level agreements, which became effective in November 1999, to ensure that the new entrants receive the same level of services from the SMP operators' wholesale arm as their own retail arm. Also, in response to the complaints regarding delayed delivery of interconnection links to the new entrants, and delayed dealing with technical faults by Eircom, the ODTR decided to require Eircom to develop service level agreements on interconnection covering, *inter alia*, delivery times, and fault maintenance and restoration, in the context of approving Eircom's Reference Interconnection Offer, which is expected to become effective shortly.

According to the ODTR, they receive complaints covering a broad variety of issues ranging from interconnection, carrier access and selection, numbering, cross-subsidisation, customer service behaviour, Internet, pricing and access. As of May 2000, they had received 48 formal disputes, among which three had been rejected, one withdrawn, 15 issues addressed, three referred back to the operators, two draft determinations, seven final determinations, and 16 ongoing.

On an informal level, the ODTR receives complaints by telephone calls, emails, letters and representations from the public concerning levels of services by the licensees. They receive an average of 60 complaints per week, among which the main complaint for telecommunications services is billing. This might have resulted from customers' increased awareness of charges from itemised billing. Eircom presently charges IEP 3 for itemised billing[73] even though Article 14 of Directive 98/10/EC (ONP to Voice Telephony) states that a basic level of itemised billing should be made available at no charge.

The ODTR has set down key areas for performance measurement by all operators offering public telecommunication services. These include service provision, fault management, complaints and billing. Additional information will be required from Eircom, as the fixed line SMP operator, covering: directory enquiry services, public payphones and quality of service for other licensed operators. Operators will begin publishing these in 2001. Such indicators are important for consumer choice and to ensure continued best practice performance.

2.3. Resource issues

Spectrum allocation

The development of competition, and in particular in mobile communications, has increased the demand for frequency spectrum in many OECD countries, and in Ireland. Increasing demand for spectrum access provides greater pressure for an objective and transparent regulatory allocation of spectrum and for greater efficiency in the use of spectrum.

Responsibility for frequency planning is shared between the Department of Public Enterprise and the ODTR. Under the 1996 Act, the ODTR is required to provide a radio frequency plan and is responsible for the licensing of spectrum, whereas the Department retains the right to issue directions to the ODTR to comply with decisions concerning the allocation and use of spectrum. The ODTR published a detailed Table of Frequency Allocations for Ireland[74] in 1998, and is currently reviewing it with the aim to complete the review in early 2001.

The assignment and licensing of spectrum for the first mobile telecommunications service was to Eircell (then Telecom Éireann), which started analogue (TACS standard) mobile telephony service in 900 MHz band in 1985. Further spectrum was assigned to Eircell (Telecom Éireann) within the 900 MHz band for their provision of digital (GSM standard) mobile service in 1993. There was no competition for spectrum assignment in these cases. The second GSM licence was allocated on the basis of a competitive tender in March 1995 by the Department of Transport, Energy and Communications, where six applications were received. Esat Digifone won the licence in May 1996 (the service was launched in March 1997). Meteor Mobile Communications was selected as the third mobile licensee (GSM900/1800 standard) in June 1998 also through a beauty contest. There were only two applicants (a legal challenge by the unsuccessful applicant delayed the award until May 2000). In addition, the ODTR invited Eircell and Esat Digifone to apply for additional spectrum in the 1800 MHz band for the provision of a dual band GSM 900/1800 service, and subsequently they were awarded the spectrum in late 1999.

Ireland has been one of the OECD countries that began licensing wireless in the local loop technologies at an early stage. The first licences were awarded mid 2000: four broadband and two narrowband WLL licences were awarded.[75] Following this earlier WLL licensing a competition for three further WLL licences is to be held shortly with a view to awarding licences in April 2001.

UMTS (IMT-2000) licensing has been taking place in a number of OECD countries recently, and a number of countries have decided to use auction as a method for spectrum allocation. The financial success of the auctions in some countries (*e.g.* the United Kingdom Treasury earned around USD 35 billion for five licences and Germany around USD 46 billion for six licences using auctions to sell the licences) has also led countries to reconsider methods of licence allocation. In Ireland, the ODTR decided, following a consultation process, to use a comparative selection process (beauty contest) to award four UMTS licences.[76] A comparative selection was chosen over auctions as the ODTR came to a conclusion that the former would best secure the delivery of competitive prices, choice and quality in the Irish telecommunications market. The factors that have counted in reaching a decision in favour of a beauty contest are the following:

- Speedy roll-out and extensive geographic and population coverage would be easier to specify in a comparative tender than in an auction where the costs of market entry are much higher.

- Concerns over high retail prices to consumers because of the very high fees for spectrum access and the higher per capita fixed cost of building the networks, relative to the small size of the Irish market and its population density compared to those of the United Kingdom or other countries.

- A comparative tender provides more incentives for entrants to undertake voluntary commitments for roaming arrangements and third parties' access to the licensees' networks.

- Experience and expertise in Ireland with beauty contests and performance guarantees.

However, even if an auction procedure were chosen, the above performance requirements could easily be included as part of the licence.

The level of UMTS fees are currently being considered by the ODTR,[77] taking into account, *inter alia*, the development in other European countries. The ODTR plans to develop and publish competition details, run the competition, and finally award the licences around April to May 2001. The ODTR should try to maintain or even advance this schedule in order to try and ensure that service provision begins at the beginning of 2002.

Another point to be mentioned regarding the allocation of spectrum is that the new legislative proposals include a provision to enable the Minister to give directions to the proposed regulatory Commission regarding the means by which licences for spectrum use may be assigned.[78] This effectively reduces the existing power of the regulator by returning some of its powers on spectrum allocation to the Minister. This is likely to have an impact on choosing a method to allocate spectrum in the future, in particular on the choice between auctions and beauty contests.

Numbering issues

Management of the Irish numbering resources is the responsibility of the ODTR, which is obliged by statute to put in place procedures to ensure that the allocation of numbers is carried out in an objective, transparent, non-discriminatory, and timely manner.

Call-by-call carrier selection/access services have been available in Ireland since December 1998. All operators have five digit access codes for these purposes. Moreover, full carrier pre-selection was introduced in January 2000, the deadline required by the European Parliament and Council Directive (98/61/EC). Three options are available currently for pre-selection: international calls only, national calls only, and all calls. Customers have a choice of opting for both of the first two options and pre-select different operators. They are also able to override their pre-selection for individual calls by dialling a carrier selection/access code.

Number portability is another important safeguard for efficient competition. Non-geographic number portability, portability of numbers without containing geographic information such as freephone numbers between operators, was introduced on 1 January 2000, in line with the European Parliament and Council Directive (98/61/EC).[79] Geographic number portability is currently being introduced on a phased manner between July and November 2000.

At an initial stage, Eircom was required to provide the capability to export geographic numbers to any other operator who requested them and is willing in return to offer portability by 1 July 2000. In this operator-initiated portability, a new operator can choose not to participate in the regime (*i.e.* to refuse the request for reciprocal portability). The second stage is customer-initiated portability to be introduced on 30 November 2000, where any operator must provide portability when a customer requests it. This requires all operators to equip themselves with networks capable of dealing with importing and exporting numbers. After 30 November, new operators are not allowed to refuse importing and exporting numbers from and to any other operator. There are currently 128 minimum numbering areas in Ireland, within which geographic number portability applies.

For mobile telephony, partial number portability has been available since 1997. It has been partial in a sense that customers changing operator are allowed to retain the subscriber part of their number, but have to change their access codes. As the third mobile operator is entering the market, there is a more pressing need for full portability of mobile phone number, and the ODTR is currently working to introduce it.

2.4. Universal Service Obligations (USO)

Ireland's current universal service regulations, effective from 15 April 1999, are based on relevant Directives of the European Commission, namely the Revised Voice Telephony Directive (98/10/EC) and the Interconnection Directive (97/33/EC), which have been transposed into Irish national regulations.[80] The Directives define universal service as "a minimum set of services of specified quality which is available to all users independent of their geographical location and, in light of specific conditions, at an affordable price", and the Irish transposed regulations are in this line. Based on the transposed regulations, Eircom was designated as having the obligation to provide universal service by the ODTR on 14 May 1999.[81]

Telecommunications services covered within the universal service obligations (USO) in Ireland are in line with the relevant EU Directives and comparable to those of many OECD countries. These services are access to the fixed public telephone network and services, directory services, and public pay telephones. The first of the three is an obligation that the USO operator (Eircom), so far as it considers reasonable, must meet any request by a person for connection to the fixed public telephone network at a fixed location and provide access to fixed public telephone service. As a safeguard, the ODTR is authorised to overrule a refusal by the USO operator to provide such services. USO in directory services are the provision of directory services, *i.e.* compilation of and access to directory information, and of comprehensive public directories in printed or electronic form. USO in public pay telephones are the obligation imposed on USO operator to provide public pay telephones in sufficient numbers, taking into account the population density to satisfy all reasonable needs for them throughout the area.

Regarding a funding mechanism of USO, the USO operator may receive funding for the net cost of meeting the USO, taking into account any obligations on such an operator.[82] The "net cost" is defined in the regulation as "the cost, if any, having regard to the direct and indirect costs and revenues associated with the provision of universal service including in particular, any market benefits accruing to a person arising from its obligation to provide universal service."[83] Eircom requested such funding for the period from December 1998, when the market was fully liberalised, to May 2000, and the ODTR is currently reviewing this request. If the ODTR determines that there is a net cost and if such a cost is determined by the ODTR to be an unfair burden, Eircom is reimbursed by either of the following two mechanisms. The first option is establishing a fund to which all operators contribute and from which the USO operator is reimbursed. The second is that a supplementary charge is added to the charge for interconnection to the public telecommunications network.[84]

Experience from other countries has shown that the first option tends to be preferable since it avoids distortion in interconnection, tends to be more transparent and allows designating another operator, instead of the incumbent, to provide universal service in specific areas. Principles of transparency, non-discrimination, efficiency, and proportionality should apply in the management of the compensation mechanism, and accounting separation should be ensured to prevent the possibility of cross-subsidisation with other competitive services offered by the USO operator. The second option, if implemented, should clearly separate interconnection payments from any access deficit charges. This option could create structural inflexibility in prices and in the way interconnection is charged.

2.5. International aspects

Ireland imposes no restrictions on market entry by foreign operators. In the European Communities' commitment to WTO agreement on basic telecommunications concluded in February 1997, Ireland made exemptions to delay the implementation of full liberalisation in public voice telephony and facilities-based services until 2000, and to delay the liberalisation of internationally connected mobile and personal communications services until 1999. However, as already noted, Ireland implemented the WTO commitment earlier than the scheduled deadline.

2.6. Consumer protection

Consumer interests are best enhanced through effective competition, which will deliver lower prices, improved choice and better quality. However, there is a continuing role for the government to ensure that consumer interests are protected. While the government and the ODTR have worked to ensure that consumers benefit from increased competition, including by inexpensive switching of service providers, and from customer charters, improved performance of operators, etc., some aspects of consumer protection have been left behind in Ireland as seen in the earlier sections, such as the lack of a formal and clearer mechanism to handle consumer complaints. However, the proposed legislation provides for frameworks for resolving this and other issues on consumer protection.[85]

It is also a welcome move that the ODTR is strengthening its focus towards enhancement of consumer interests as a general policy, and the efforts to establish concrete mechanisms within the general framework to be provided by the proposed legislation to address consumer complaints are understood in this context. Also, their efforts to establish quality of service indicators in fixed line services to be published (see Section 3) are a positive step in enhancing consumer choice and information. The ODTR should establish concrete procedures with standard time frame for handling consumer complaints. It is the intention of the new legislation to do so. The procedure should be speedy, simple, and inexpensive for ordinary consumers. It should also ensure under relevant legal provisions to come into place that telecommunications operators implement and make public an appropriate code of practice for consumers.[86] It is preferable that an industry wide code is available to ensure consistency in the market. Operators should be required to provide a published report on their handling of the complaints, and in this regard it is a welcome move that they will be required to do so under the ODTR's Measuring Licensed Operator Performance programme from June 2001.

2.7. Streamlining regulation and application of competition principles

The Irish competition acts, namely the Competition Act, 1991 and Competition (Amendment) Act, 1996, apply to telecommunications sector with no exemptions. As in other OECD countries, these acts prohibit anti-competitive agreements and abuse of dominant power in all industries. As noted earlier, some overlap of jurisdiction between the agencies to administer the competition acts and the telecommunications acts is inevitable and a framework of co-operation is essential and the right of an aggrieved party to pursue a case in either the Competition Authority or the ODTR should be respected.

Regulatory streamlining

While sector-specific regulations are necessary to steer and facilitate the transition of the market from monopoly to full competition, it is also necessary to consider when it is appropriate to streamline regulations and to withdraw sector specific regulations as the market becomes fully competitive. It is important to review regulations on a regular basis and determine whether they should be maintained, modified or streamlined and are proportionate to their stated aim and take into account the degree of competition in the market in question. Determination of when and to what extent the sector-specific regulations could be withdrawn needs thorough examination and evaluation of a number of factors related to the actual situation and functioning of the market.

The ODTR's practice of conducting and publishing a quarterly review of the Irish telecommunications market is commendable from this perspective.[87] The review focuses on monitoring the market to allow the ODTR to discharge its own responsibilities. However, the review should focus as well on the impact of market changes on users and the benefits that they are deriving from competition. It would also facilitate an evaluation of the market and of the impact of regulation if data on the market shares of individual companies and quality of service of market players, particularly for fixed voice communications, were published.

The use of industry self-regulation, rather than imposition of regulations by the government is becoming more common in OECD countries, for example, in management of numbering. Self-regulation is generally viewed as having advantages in providing more flexibility to rapid changes and in ensuring better compliance by the industry. The ODTR should consider how it could provide an incentive to encourage industry self-regulation where it is practical. The success of such regulation will clearly depend on having an open dialogue between the incumbent and new entrants.

Transparency

The existing telecommunication legislative provisions in Ireland are spread over an enormous number of statutes inevitably as a result of consecutive amendments and enactment over a hundred and forty years. Consequently, it is not easy to access and understand the overall legislative framework. The practice in the past of amending existing legislation has also led to difficulties in having access to a comprehensive legislative framework. It would help ensure further consistency and greater transparency of laws and regulations if the Department and the ODTR consolidate these into a single document available to the public.

The ODTR, although not legally required, uses a process of public consultation extensively, and publishes its findings. ODTR's website is well organised helping to ensure greater transparency by providing information on regulations issued, documents and consultations. ODTR needs to provide better information on contact points for specific issues for the industry and other market participants to be able to obtain further information.

2.8. Convergence in communications markets

Convergence between telecommunications and broadcasting sector is advancing rapidly at the technological, service, and market level in OECD countries, posing a number of regulatory challenges for many member countries. In Ireland, regulation of infrastructures including broadcasting, namely television and radio transmitters and equipment associated with terrestrial services and CATV networks fall under ODTR's jurisdiction. The ODTR is not organised internally along the traditional separation of the communication sectors, but along functional divisions (*i.e.* Market Operations, Market Development and Market Framework), within each of which both telecommunications and broadcasting issues are dealt with. This helps in dealing with issues where convergence is an important factor. A number of recent decisions have been relevant to convergence. For example, licences were issued in 1999 that provide for digital cable and MMDS. In addition a consultation is under way on the implications that convergence and, in particular, the use of ADSL technology will have for the legal and regulatory frameworks covering telecommunications and broadcasting. The ODTR also took steps in 1999, much earlier than many other OECD countries, to provide wireless in the local loop licences.

Programming services or content of private broadcasting services are regulated by the Independent Radio and Television Commission (IRTC) under the 1988 Radio and Television Act. The operation of the state broadcaster, RTE, as a statutory corporation, falls under the supervision of RTE Authority (a commission comprising nine members) under the Broadcasting Act 1960.

3. MARKET PERFORMANCE

3.1. Introduction

The rationale for regulatory reform is the increase in the efficiency in the provision of services and the beneficial effects it is expected to deliver to users and consumers. This section assesses the performance of the Irish telecommunications industry in the delivery of those benefits to users and consumers, using indicators related to network penetration, investment, price, and quality.

The main elements of market performance examined below are:

– Network development and modernisation.

– Services based on leading edge technology and infrastructure.

– Lower prices.

– Improved quality of service.

– Increased customer choice.

– Benefit to users.

Since full liberalisation of the Irish telecommunication market in late 1998 the market has shown dynamic growth in terms of new market entry, investment and development of services. Nevertheless, the less than smooth market opening has also slowed potential growth and benefits to users. This is most apparent in the cellular mobile sector where the third licence is only now becoming operational because of litigation lasting well over a year. This has had a negative impact on price performance and mobile penetration rates.

Ireland has had the ambition to become a communications hub linking Europe and North America. It also has placed much emphasis on the creation on the development of electronic commerce. It is thus important, if these objectives are to be met, that the full benefits of competition are realised and passed on to users. The efficient working of the market will allow this to happen, but in the shorter term as the telecommunications market is transformed from a monopoly to a competitive market, effective regulation will play a key role. In this context, as well, having good benchmarking data is important for effective regulation and the ODTR needs to improve on its ability to obtain and publish such benchmarks.

3.2. Market development

The telecommunication service sector, as measured by telecommunication service revenues, in Ireland has increased from IEP 1 094 million in 1995 to IEP 1 407 million by 1997. By 1999 revenues had reached IEP 1 716 million (Table 6). The telecommunication sector increased its share in GDP from 2.4% to 2.9% during the 1985-97 period. In 1999 telecommunications revenue accounted for 2.6% of GDP. With emphasis on network expansion and digitalisation during the 1990s, public telecommunication investment ranged around 3% of national gross fixed capital formation, reaching 4% in 1997.[88] Over the period 1997-99 telecommunication investment averaged 3.4% of GFCF.

The number of telephone mainlines expanded significantly during the 1990s, from 983 thousand lines in 1990 to 1.6 million by 1999. As a result the penetration rate increased from 28.1 access lines per 100 inhabitants in 1990, well below the OECD average, to 42.2 per 100 inhabitants by 1999, although still below the OECD average. In terms of access channels (i.e. including ISDN lines) per 100 inhabitants Ireland was below the OECD average with 46 channels compared to 54. Telecommunication employment, which stood at 16.1 thousand in 1985, has declined steadily to around 11.7 thousand in 1997, increasing to 1999 to attain 12 600.[89]

The incumbent, Eircom, was ranked 59th in 1999 among the major public telecommunication operators in the OECD area as measured by revenues. Mobile services now account for 20% of its revenue. The increase in Internet traffic has been important and by the first quarter of 2000 accounted for 30% of local call traffic. Competition has also benefited the incumbent, for example, they have experienced extremely high growth in the wholesale traffic market, which amounted to 17% of retail fixed line traffic at the beginning of 2000.

Table 6. Eircom: main telecommunication indicators

	1995	1996	1997	1998	1999
Telecommunication services: revenue (IEP million)	1 094	1 230	1 354	1 435	1 551
Total employment	12 025	11 918	11 705	11 911	12 055
Operating revenue per access line (IEP)	833	885	938	1 055	1 059
Operating revenue per employee (IEP)	90 990	103 205	120 229	120 476	128 660

Note: Total employment includes mobile and fixed services.

Source: OECD, Telecommunications Database 1999, ODTR.

Network development and modernisation

Ireland, in the mid-1980s, had a relatively low telecommunication penetration rate. High investment led to a growth in telecommunication access at a compound annual growth rate of 6.9% during 1987-92 and 6.1% during the 1992-97 period.[90] However, this growth was insufficient to close the gap between Irish penetration rates and the OECD average (see Figure 2). In terms of access lines per 100 inhabitants, Ireland ranked 21st in the OECD in 1997 with a penetration rate of 42 lines per 100 population (compared to an OECD average of 49). By 1999 the penetration rate had increased only slightly.

Table 7 indicates that in Ireland, public telecommunications investment (*i.e.* Eircom's investment) as a percentage of revenue weakened in the early 1990s and only began to pick up as the threat of competition began to become a reality. In addition, increases in investment over the last several years reflect investment in mobile activities.

Figure 2. **Access lines 100 inhabitants**

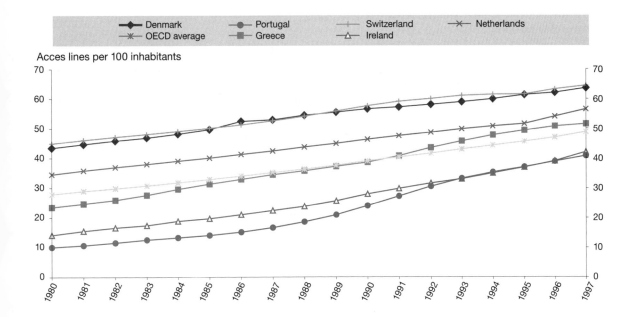

Table 7. Public telecommunication investment as a percentage of revenue

	1986-88	1989-91	1992-94	1995	1996	1997	1998	1999
Ireland	24.0	21.0	17.2	16.4	24.1	27.6	34.3	23.9
OECD average	26	27	25	24	25	24	25	27

Source: OECD (2001), *Communications Outlook 2001*, Paris.

Digitalisation

In contrast to network expansion, Ireland has rapidly digitalised its network and by 1998 had attained 100% digitalisation as shown in Table 8. New technologies have emerged with digitalisation, in particular ISDN. National coverage for ISDN was achieved by 1998.

Penetration of ISDN increased from 4 184 subscribers in 1995 to 27 522 basic rate access lines by the end of 1999 or about 0.5% of main lines. By the end of the 1999 the number of basic rate ISDN connections was 76 000 customers (or 5% of main lines). Commercial ADSL services had not yet been made available in mid-2000 although pilot trials were being held. By the end of 1999 Ireland had 596 000 CATV subscribers, a 38% increase since 1997. The CATV penetration rate as measured by the proportion of households with access to cable was 49%.

Table 8. Eircom's rate of digitalisation

	1993	1995	1997	1998	1999
Ireland	71.0	79.0	92.0	100.0	100.0
Czech Republic	10.0	17.0	54.6	64.1	74.4
Greece	22.0	37.1	47.1	74.5	90.6
Poland	9.5	48.0	58.0	62.0	68.0
Portugal	59.0	70.0	88.3	98.0	100.0
OECD average	58.8	74.8	87.5	92.1	94.2

Source: OECD, *Communications Outlook 1999*, and *Communications Outlook 2001*.

Cellular mobile services

Between 1985 and 1997, when the second GSM mobile licence became operational, the mobile market developed in a monopoly environment. Telecom Éireann launched analogue service in 1985 and it was also provided with a GMS licence launching service in 1993 (as Eircell). In March 1997 a second GSM licence was awarded to Esat Digifone. Cellular mobile penetration has increased from 14.4 per 100 inhabitants in 1997 (OECD average 15.6) to 42.7 by 1999 (OECD average 32.4). Prepaid subscriptions have played an important part in mobile growth, for example, prepaid subscribers account for 60% of Eircom's total cellular mobile subscribers.

Table 9. Cellular mobile subscribers

	1997	1998	1999	2000 (June)
Eircell	405 747	707 000	1 049 000	1 100 000
Esat	105 000	239 000	551 000	744 000
TOTAL	510 747	946 000	1 600 000	1 860 000
Market penetration	14.4	25.5	42.7	49.7

Source: *Company annual reports*, ODTR.

By mid-2000 the number of mobile subscribers had reached 1.9 million or 49.7 subscribers per 100 inhabitants, that is higher than the penetration rate for the fixed network. Eircell has the largest market share with 60% of subscribers. Nevertheless, it has lost about seven percentage points of market share since 1999.[91]

Development of competition

Although there has been full liberalisation for only 18 months some benefits have accrued to Irish consumers and users (see Section 3.4 below). These have been mainly from price decreases, and an expansion in the range of services becoming available. The delay in the third mobile licence becoming operational has reduced the impact of price competition in that market, in particular for subscribers on monthly plans (prepaid call prices declined substantially during the first half of 2000).

Alternate communication infrastructures are developing quite rapidly in Ireland. Cable television infrastructure has been developing relatively rapidly and is providing bundled broadband services, including voice at reasonable prices.

A number of new entrants have entered the Irish telecommunications market since full liberalisation took place in 1 December 1998. Around forty-five operators were providing telecommunications networks and/or services as of September 2000. Eleven of them offer fixed services to residential customers at least in international calls markets, and eight offered integrated local, long distance, and international services.[92]

In the fixed network sector, the share of new entrants, based on operators' revenues, is estimated to be in excess of 15% as of June 2000, whereas the equivalent for March 2000 was in excess of 10%. The market share of new entrants for international telephone services rose to around 9% in terms of minutes of international traffic in 1997 from 0% in 1996.[94] The development of competition for international calls resulted in the ODTR removing these services from price cap regulations.

The licensing of wireless local loop services will also ensure the more rapid development of competition in the local market. The ODTR has issued wireless local loop (WLL) licences for broadband services to four entities, two of which also have been granted WLL licences in narrow band, earlier than many other OECD countries. As noted in the previous section, full local loop unbundling is expected shortly.

Price performance and rebalancing

Price levels in other countries provide an important benchmark to assess relative performance of telecommunication markets. For these purposes the OECD collects the prices of a basket of telecommunications for residential and business customers in each of the twenty-nine OECD countries.[95] Ireland is ranked 12th for the business basket and 13th for the residential basket among OECD countries as measured in terms of purchasing power parities (see Figures 3 and 4).

Important changes have taken place in Eircom's prices. However, fixed charges have hardly been adjusted unlike other countries where price increases have taken place mainly in fixed prices. National call charges have become distance insensitive and international call charges have been adjusted downward. Local call charges remain high and rather than using a call set-up charge a minimum charge is being used. However, per second charging has been introduced. In October 2000 new call charges were introduced but only for off-peak local calls. These new call charges were in response to competition from new entry. For example the cable company, NTL, has offered its customers a bundled package costing IEP 20 per month which includes two telephone lines, cable TV and unlimited and unmetered Internet access. Telephone call charges will be at a minimum rate of 3.5p.

International telecommunication prices

Ireland had relatively high international collection charges, which were above the OECD average in the past, but continuous reductions since 1994 (mainly through indirect competition *e.g.* call-back services) have improved Ireland's relative position quite significantly.[96] The OECD basket of interna-

345

Figure 3. **OECD Composite Basket of business telephone charges,**
November 2000 (in US$/PPP)

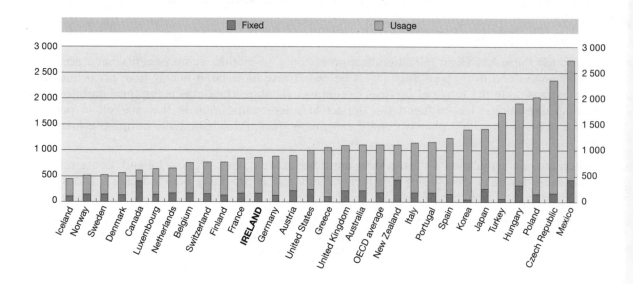

Note: VAT is excluded; calls to mobiles are excluded.
Source: OECD.

Figure 4. **OECD Composite Basket of residential telephone charges,**
November 2000

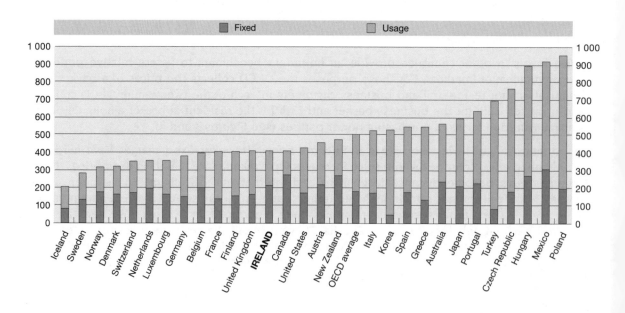

Note: VAT is excluded; calls to mobiles are excluded.

Source: OECD.

tional telephone charges[97] as of August 2000 shows that Ireland has international charges of less than a half of the OECD average both for business and residential calls in USD/PPP (Table 11). Accounting rates with the United States have also declined and are comparable with other heavier traffic routes (Table 12).

Leased lines

The availability of leased lines and their price levels are important for the development of competition since new entrants initially will rely on these circuits to develop service. Leased circuits have also become important for the development of Internet services. Relative to other OECD countries prices Ireland has the eighth lowest tariffs of national leased lines of 64Kbit (Figure 5).

Cellular mobile prices

Ireland has high prices for mobile telephone services offered by the incumbent. The basket of consumer mobile telephone charges shows Ireland as the ninth most expensive OECD country (in PPP), above the OECD average (Figure 6). Equivalent charges of the business basket are also high (the ninth highest at USD/PPP1 146) and above the OECD average of USD/PPP1 072. The relative lack of mobile competition in the Irish mobile market which had a monopoly until 1997 and a duopoly since then is the main reason for the lack of price competition.

Internet developments and performance

The number of Internet subscribers in Ireland is estimated to be around 405 000, of which 243 000 or 60% are Eircom's customers.[98] This corresponds to 11 per 100 population, which is about the OECD average.[99] The number of Internet hosts per 1 000 inhabitants has been growing, and reached 36.4 in January 2000, which is below the OECD average of 59.3. The increase between July 1999 and January

Table 10. Local telephony charges

	1992	1993	1997	1998	1999	2000
Connection charges (IR punts)			145.00		99 (incl. VAT)	99 (incl. VAT)
Monthly rental charges (IR punts)	10.00	10.00	10.00	10.00	10.24 (excl. VAT)	10.92 (excl. VAT)
Charge for 3 minutes (IR pounds)					9.5p minimum charge (per second pricing introduced) [3.31p/min charged	
Peak	11.17 (for 15 minutes)	9.5			above initial charge - 0.83 offpeak]	5.0 (incl.VAT)
Off-peak	11.17 (for 30 minutes)	1.9				1.0) (incl. VAT
National calls (pence per minute)	22 for over 80km				8.26	7.38 (incl. VAT)
					5.50 evening	4.84 (incl. VAT) offpeak
					0.83 weekend	1.0 (incl. VAT) weekend

Note: In 1990 business and residential customers were charged the same for line rental. Local call timing was first used in 1992.
In 1996 local call areas expanded to include calls up to 27km. In 1998 per second charging introduced (but minimum fee applies).
Source: ODTR.

347

Table 11.   OECD basket of international telephone charges, August 2000

	Business Excluding tax		Residential Including tax	
	USD	USD PPP	USD	USD PPP
Australia	0.80	1.03	1.12	1.44
Austria	0.80	0.87	1.21	1.32
Belgium	1.17	1.34	1.56	1.79
Canada	0.21	0.26	0.74	0.92
Czech Republic	1.18	3.11	1.26	3.31
Denmark	0.50	0.44	0.81	0.71
Finland	0.77	0.74	1.08	1.04
France	0.60	0.65	0.75	0.81
Germany	0.79	0.86	1.16	1.26
Greece	0.89	1.26	1.35	1.90
Hungary	1.11	2.77	1.77	4.43
Iceland	0.79	0.63	1.25	1.00
IRELAND	0.55	**0.65**	0.76	**0.89**
Italy	0.93	1.18	1.35	1.71
Japan	2.90	1.78	3.25	1.99
Korea	2.38	3.83	2.77	4.46
Luxembourg	0.52	0.58	0.66	0.74
Mexico	3.25	4.51	3.94	5.47
Netherlands	0.33	0.38	0.48	0.55
New Zealand	0.77	1.09	1.06	1.50
Norway	0.46	0.40	0.71	0.62
Poland	1.49	2.87	2.35	4.51
Portugal	0.97	1.49	1.38	2.12
Spain	1.09	1.49	1.52	2.08
Sweden	0.39	0.35	0.61	0.56
Switzerland	0.30	0.25	0.37	0.31
Turkey	1.67	3.10	2.07	3.84
United Kingdom	0.87	0.80	0.94	0.87
United States	0.55	0.55	0.87	0.87
OECD average	1.00	**1.35**	1.35	**1.38**

Source: OECD and Teligen.

Table 12.   Accounting rates with the United States (US$)

	1996	1997	1998	1999	2000
Ireland	USD 0.35	0.33	0.19	0.19	0.20
France	USD 0.35	0.26	0.21	0.20	0.20
Greece	USD 1.01	0.86	0.55	0.30	0.26
Italy	USD 0.52	0.33	0.22	0.22	0.21
Portugal	USD 0.83	0.60	0.43	0.30	0.29
Spain	USD 0.64	0.48	0.26	0.27	0.27
United Kingdom (BT)	USD 0.36	0.20	0.21	0.21	0.20

Source: International Bureau, Federal Communications Commission, US.

Figure 5. **Comparison of OECD leased line tariff baskets,**
November 2000 (in USD/PPP)

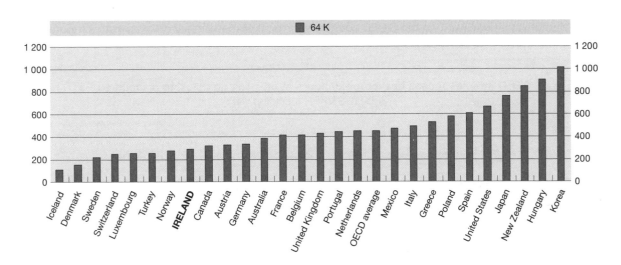

Note: The basket includes 50 minutes per months and excludes international calls. VAT is included.

Source: OECD and Teligen.

Figure 6. **OECD Basket of consumer mobile telephone charges,**
November 2000 (in US$/PPP)

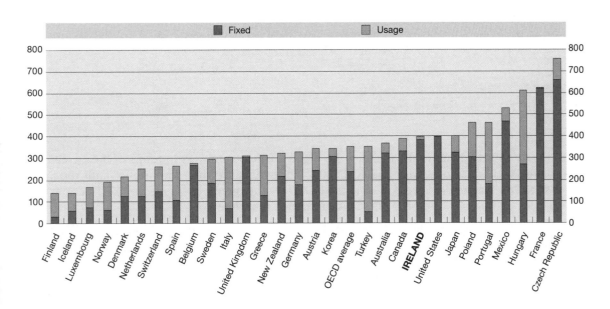

Note: The basket includes 50 minutes per months and excludes international calls. VAT is included.

Source: OECD and Teligen.

2000 of 7.7% is also below the OECD average of 12.2%, or below the equivalent average among OECD members with metered local access charges of 8.6%.[100]

Access price of the Internet as measured by the OECD basket for 20 hours shows that Ireland has the sixth highest charges among the OECD countries for peak times, but for off-peak times Ireland's performance is better (Figure 7).

Figure 7. **OECD Internet access basket for 20 hours at off-peak times using discounted PSTN rates,** 2000 (US$/PPP, including VAT)

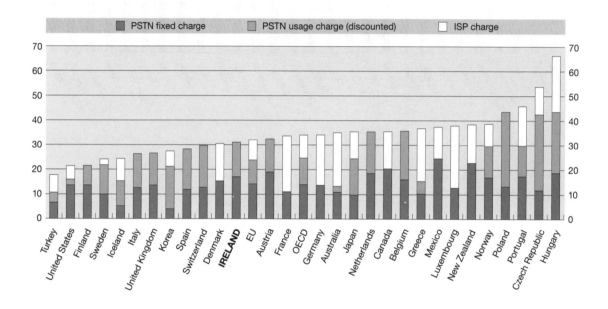

Note: PSTN fixed charges include monthly rental fee. The basket includes 20 one-hour calls. Off peak is taken at 20h00. In some countries, ISP and PSTN usage charges are bundled and included under either the ISP or the PSTN charge.
Source: OECD.

Quality of service

In the early 1990s Ireland ranked among the highest OECD countries in terms of the percentage of faults repaired within 24 hours with a rate of 100%. However, since then the rate for fault repair declined in 1997 to 76%, one of the lowest rates in the OECD.[101] The number of faults per 100 lines per annum was 15 in 1997, or 13th of 17 reporting OECD countries at that time.

The ODTR, following a public consultation, issued a report[102] in January 2000 to develop parameters to measure fixed line operators' performance in a comprehensive way. An industry forum has been working to agree on detailed definitions for performance parameters, and it is expected that the results will be published in mid-2001. Main parameters include service delivery, fault management, complaints, billing, and disconnection. These efforts are likely to help improve the quality of service significantly.

The current focus in these efforts is to measure the performance of fixed line services and do not cover mobile operations. As a future step, the ODTR should also develop, and publish, quality of service parameters for mobile services.

4. CONCLUSIONS AND RECOMMENDATIONS

4.1. General assessment of current strengths and weaknesses

The regulatory regime in Ireland displays a number of strengths (see below). These strengths are based above all on the emphasis the government, and the regulator, have been placing on the importance of market forces and the readiness and flexibility to adopt best practice regulation. Ireland introduced full liberalisation of telecommunications market on 1 December 1998, later by eleven months than many other European Union countries. As one of the five countries that was granted a derogation up to 1 January 2000 by the EC for full liberalisation, the decision taken in May 1998 to fully open the market to competition 13 months earlier than necessary was courageous, even though it was to give rise to a number of shorter term problems. The government's decision was commendable in understanding the importance of competition and in understanding that the technological speed of change in the telecommunication sector can only be mastered and benefited from in a competitive environment.

The early opening of the market to full liberalisation before the regulator had completed the task of putting in place the necessary safeguards forced the regulator to divert very scarce human resources to immediate problem areas where emphasis was needed on building a sound regulatory framework. Inevitably this led to dissatisfaction from all parties in the market, placing even further pressure on the regulator. The last year was essentially a period of adjustment for the regulator in trying to cope with a framework, which was not yet complete. The government has rapidly put forward new measures to ensure that the regulator has sufficient tools available to take and enforce decisions, as well as measure which aim at trying to ensure that benefits from liberalisation accrue to the consumer.

The courage in opening the market early to competition has proved to be a success. There are now more than forty operators providing telecommunications networks and/or services in Ireland despite the relatively small size of the country. Price reductions, including for local call prices are beginning to take place benefiting consumers.

Market access in telecommunications is open in Ireland, as exemplified by the number of new entrants offering range of services in the past two years. Despite the number of new entrants the question of whether an individual licensing system is required remains. It is timely to move to an even more open market entry framework based on a class licensing system. Market entry is not limited through any discriminatory restrictions on foreign participants, and in fact all major operators in Ireland, including the incumbent, are largely owned by foreign companies. In the mobile market, which has been a duopoly, the late licensing of the third operator that occurred in June 2000, resulted from litigation brought against the original licence award made in 1998.

The Department of Public Enterprise and the ODTR have quickly recognised weaknesses both in regulations as well as institutions, and have showed readiness to take rapid action to bring about

---

Box 2. Strengths

Emphasis on market forces shown through shortening of derogation period for full liberalisation by thirteen months.

Emphasis on open market access.

Awareness of a continuing need for further progress and development in the regulatory system.

Responsiveness and flexibility in regulatory reform.

Transparency of regulatory decision making supported by extensive use of public consultation. Regular review and evaluation of the market.

351

necessary changes. For example, the government is already preparing major legislation since the enactment of the Telecommunications (Miscellaneous Provisions) Act, 1996 to make major changes in institutional and regulatory frameworks.

The government and the regulator have used quite effectively public consultation process both in the development of legislation and in regulation. There is general consensus that the ODTR has acted fairly and independently of politics and of industry. Emphasis has also been placed on market evaluation as a basis for making timely and appropriate regulatory decisions. In this context, the practice of the ODTR to conduct quarterly reviews of the market is commendable.

There are, however, a number of weaknesses that need to be addressed:

Although the strengths of the Irish regulatory framework provide the potential for the creation of a competitive and efficient market which will bring benefits to Irish consumers and the economy at large, there are some regulatory issues that need to be addressed. The ODTR needs to be strengthened in terms of its powers to make binding decisions and enforce them. The recent outline of legislative proposals in relation to the regulation of the communications sector in fact addresses this weakness and some of the others noted above. This proposed legislation would, if successfully implemented, go a long way to allow for the development of a more open market without the danger of constant litigation slowing down regulatory reforms.

High quality in policies and regulation is not possible without adequate human resources. The brief history of the ODTR, as noted earlier, is commendable in light of the insufficient resources available. ODTR has had support of staff seconded from the Department of Public Enterprise, who have gradually returned to their Department, and outside expert consultants. ODTR needs to continue its focus on completing its staffing needs.

Lack of staffing is partially responsible for the fact that the ODTR has not been sufficiently pro-active in certain areas, *e.g.* in consumer protection and enforcement of the decisions. Another reason for this, as noted previously, has been the early liberalisation, which resulted in emphasis being placed on implementing the Directives and the Decisions of the European Community as well as some basic regulatory requirements. Improvements in institutional relations with the Competition Authority are necessary. The last year has already led to some improvements and the proposed draft legislation also addresses this issue. Both institutions have recognised past deficiencies and seem prepared to make improvements. In this regard, it should be acknowledged that the Competition and Mergers Review Group, a consultative body for the Minister for Enterprise, Trade and Employment, made co-ordination proposals, where both the ODTR and the CA made inputs, and both agencies incorporated them in actual practice. It is also incorporated in the new proposed Communications Regulation Bill, 2000.

Despite rapid growth in the cellular mobile market, resulting mainly from pre-paid cards, insufficient competition has developed in mobile markets and prices remain high. Entry of the third operator is

---

Box 3.   Weaknesses

Inadequate powers of the ODTR.

Insufficient human resource with ODTR.

Greater focus needed to ensure benefits to consumer of competition.

Further improvements required in institutional co-operation.

More competition needed in cellular mobile sector.

Completion of price rebalancing.

---

expected shortly. This should improve the situation, but the ODTR needs to maintain this market under review to ensure that a competitive market for mobile services develops. This will be assisted by the announced intention to offer four licences for the UMTS services.

Price rebalancing should be completed as rapidly as possible to ensure attainment of cost-orientation and elimination of any cross-subsidies. This will also facilitate the implementation of local loop unbundling.

It is also necessary that the ODTR place greater focus on consumer interests. It is understandable that the ODTR has generally focused on development of the industry and setting up a framework to develop a competitive market. In itself this has brought benefits to consumers, but a more direct focus is needed on consumer interests and the implication of changes of regulation on consumers. In particular, an effective framework is needed to handle consumer complaints and resolve disputes. Benchmarks for quality of service and the publication of relative quality of service indicators can also facilitate consumer choice. To their credit, the ODTR is already aware of some of these deficiencies, and has been working to address them.

4.2. Potential benefits and costs of further regulatory reform

As indicated in previous sections, the Irish industry and consumers have in the past benefited from declining prices and an increasing variety of services. However, as described in Section 4.1, there is still room for improvement in the regulatory framework of Ireland in order to achieve fair and effective competition in a market, which is still in transition, and exploit its potential fully. The consultation paper on draft changes to legislation goes a long way to meet present problems and concerns. The government should, however, take opportunity of this draft to introduce new streamlined licensing system and procedures in line with proposals of the European Commission.

Improvement in the regulatory landscape and enhanced competition would bring further benefits to consumers through price reduction, better quality and more choice. From this perspective, it is suggested that Ireland consider the following recommendations.

4.3. Policy recommendations

The following policy recommendations are based on the "Policy Recommendations For Regulatory Reform" set out in the OECD "Report on Regulatory Reform" (OECD, June 1997).

1. *Ensure that regulations and regulatory processes are transparent, non-discriminatory, and applied effectively.*

    – The licensing regime should be streamlined using general authorisations, rather than individual licensing.

Ireland needs to shift further towards a framework for market entry based on general authorisation rather than individual licensing. This will help to further reduce barriers to entry and to free scarce human resources in the ODTR. The requirement for a high-level business plan with the financial sources and projections, as well as for adequacy of managerial and technical resources, in obtaining a General Licence is questionable.

    – The ODTR should establish concrete procedures with standard time frame for handling consumer complaints. The procedure should be speedy, simple, and inexpensive for ordinary consumers. It should also ensure that telecommunications operators implement and make public an appropriate code of practice for consumer. Operators should be required to provide a published report on their handling of the complaints.

The Department of Public Enterprise and the ODTR have been aware of the problem in dealing with consumer complaints and this issue has been covered in the draft legislation. The ODTR should develop concrete procedures to deal with consumer interests. The telecommunications industry, in particular, should be required to develop adequate and simple procedures to resolve disputes and respond to co plaints.

- Accelerate the introduction of appropriate rights of way legislation to facilitate the construction of new networks on public lands.

The Irish government proposed benchmark legislation in 1999 to reform the system for telecommunications network operators to access public and private land. The Telecommunications (Infrastructure) Bill provided that the network operators could apply for and possibly compulsorily acquire rights of way over private land in the event that negotiations with landowners were unsuccessful. It also addressed the issue of the use of public roads for infrastructure, and provided a legislative basis for sharing of ducts. The Bill proposed to set up a Telecommunications Infrastructure Board, a quasi-judicial body with the power to facilitate access to private land. Now that the Infrastructure Bill is withdrawn because of the issues over compulsory access to private land and the provisions relating to access to public highways and sharing of infrastructure are included in the new Communications (Regulation) Bill, the government needs to take appropriate action to ensure its enactment.

2. *Reform regulations to stimulate competition and eliminate them except where clear evidence demonstrates that they are the best way to serve the broad public interest.*

    - The "in platform exclusivity" granted to cable operators should not be continued after the five-year period has expired in April 2004. The industry should be informed of such a decision at an early stage.

Intended as a means to provided an incentive to develop digital networks, the "in platform exclusivity" period also serves to limit competition. As a tool to stimulate investment, the strength of the policy lies in the time limitation imposed. Clarifying that the exclusive privilege will not be extended is more likely to provide CATV operators with incentives to upgrade their networks for broadband access and telephony.

    - The costs of providing universal service should be determined on an agreed methodology. If net costs are found and deemed as an unfair burden on the incumbent then a universal service fund should be created through contributions of market participants.

Appropriate policies to rebalancing prices should be given the first priority in the context of universal service. A methodology agreed to by the industry should be used to determine the cost of providing universal service. If the ODTR determines that the costs of universal service are high, taking into account any benefits that may accrue to the incumbent from providing universal service, then a funding system should be implemented to allow for appropriate compensation. If this is required, it is more appropriate to set up a universal service fund to which market players contribute than to use access deficit charges, which would also be in line with the European Commission's proposals in the draft new Directive on Universal Service.

3. *Review, and strengthen where necessary, the scope, effectiveness and enforcement of competition policy.*

    - Explicit and concrete provisions governing forbearance and withdrawal from sector specific regulation should be developed. From this perspective, the ODTR's practice of reviewing the telecommunications market should be strengthened and enhanced as a measure to enable the ODTR to evaluate the state of competition in the market to determine when and how sectoral regulations can be withdrawn leaving incumbent power to be disciplined by the market and the general competition law.

Even though there may be scope for the introduction of further regulations in the market, the requirement to streamline regulations and forbear from regulation, when and where appropriate, remains an important task for the ODTR as does the need for continuous consultation with the Competition Authority. The market reviews of the ODTR are an important initial step in this process. These should be strengthened and the ODTR should be required to undertake regular reviews of regulation to ascertain where streamlining can take place.

NOTES

1. OECD (1999*a*), p. 9.

2. I*bid*.

3. OECD (2001), *Communications Outlook* 2001, forthcoming.

4. I*bid*.

5. OECD (1999*b*), p. 208.

6. OECD (2001).

7. I*bid*.

8. Ireland, with the exception of Luxembourg and Iceland, is the smallest OECD country in terms of population.

9. KPN plans to dispose of all of its shares to institutional and private investors as of September 2000.

10. This agreement for a strategic alliance also involved co-operation in a transformation programme of Telecom Éireann to improve its market focus and the cost base. In parallel to the agreement, the Irish government arranged for the acquisition of 14.9% of the shares of the company by a trust on behalf of Telecom Éireann's employees in return for changes in work practices as well as for financial interests.

11. European Communities (Interconnection in Telecommunication) (Amendment) Regulations, 2000 (S.I. No. 69 of 2000), and European Communities (Telecommunications Licences)(Amendment) Regulations, 2000 (S.I. No. 70 of 2000).

12. Other countries which were granted similar derogation were Greece, Luxembourg, Portugal, and Spain. The derogations differ in length and scope from country to country.

13. ODTR (2000*b*), p. 10.

14. Eircom (2000), p. 3.

15. I*bid*, p. 4.

16. Most of such operators are TV deflector operators who deliver services by analogue means using UHF broadcasting bands. Many of them had been providing services illegally for many years, but a short-term licensing system for such operations was established by the ODTR with the consent of the Minister for Public Enterprise, in 1999.

17. ODTR, Media Release of 26th July 2000.

18. See, ODTR (2000*c*), 00/53.

19. See, ODTR "Significant Market Power in the Irish Telecommunications' Sector, Decision Notice: D 15/99 & Report on the Consultation Paper ODTR 99/59", December 1999, Document No. ODTR 99/75.

20. ODTR Decision Notice: D 15/99 & Report on the Consultation Paper ODTR 99/59, "Significant Market Power in the Irish Telecommunications Sector", ODTR 99/75, December 1999. All markets in respect of which the ODTR designate SMP operators are reviewed annually by the ODTR.

21. Non-transmission aspects of broadcasting policy such as cultural and public service issues are responsibilities of the Department of Arts, Heritage, the Gaeltacht and the Islands.

22. Department of Public Enterprise, "Outline Legislative Proposals in relation to the Regulation of the Communications Sector /Consultation Paper" September 2000.

23. Ireland (1999), "National Development Plan 2000-2006", 15 November, p. 68.

24. First Schedule of 1996 Act at item 1.

25. Other OECD countries whose telecommunications regulator is headed by one person are Belgium, the Czech Republic, Denmark, Germany, Hungary, Iceland, Luxembourg, Norway, and the United Kingdom. Other countries with an independent regulator have a collegiate body.

26. The levy on cable operators is a licence fee in relation to the provision of programme services, The telecommunications levy is a levy on telecommunication service providers in relation to the provision of telecommunication services.

27. ODTR (2000a), p. 49.

28. ODTR, "Introduction by the Director" at <www.odtr.ie/new/flash_theoffice.html>.

29. ODTR http://www.odtr.ie/foi_mission_statement.asp.

30. ODTR, op. cit., note 26, p. 5.

31. Department of Public Enterprises, op. cit., note 22.

32. First Schedule of 1996 Act at items 1 and 4.

33. Ibid at item 10.

34. Sections 3(7), (8), (9), 4(8), (9), (10), (11), 6(5) of the 1996 Act.

35. First Schedule of 1996 Act at item 16.

36. In telecommunications, the issue of ODTR's accountability received much attention in 1998 when the Director declined to appear before the relevant parliamentary committee on the grounds that there were no statutory requirements for this. However, the Director has in fact appeared before parliamentary committees on several occasions since then.

37. See, Department of Public Enterprise (1998), "Statement of Strategy", April, at the section "Accountability of regulatory system" available at www.irlgov.ie/tec/publications/dpe13.htm.

38. Available at www.irlgov.ie/tec/publiccations/regulatory.htm.

39. For a fuller discussion of "democratic deficit" in the regulatory process, see Ferris, Tom (2000), "Why Regulate Irish Utilities?", paper delivered to the 23rd Annual Economic Policy Conference of the Dublin Economic Workshop, October.

40. This document is available on the website of the Department of Public Enterprise at www.irlgov.ie/tec/communications/commconsultation.pdf. The discussion and analysis in the "Governance and Accountability" document is of a cross-sectoral, generic nature, but implementation of the policy proposals is being done by means of sector-specific measures.

41. The Department of Public Enterprise, op. cit., note 36 at Item 3(a)(b). Postal regulation has already been transferred to the ODTR under a Statutory instrument of 27 September 2000.

42. Ibid at Item 4(h).

43. Department of Public Enterprise, op. cit. note 22 at Head 10.

44. Ibid. at Head 25.

45. Incumbents, who are usually subject to a decision by the regulator, have an interest to appeal to the courts to delay implementation of a decision. Cost savings from delaying implementation are often significantly higher than court costs.

46. See note 11.

47. Department of Public Enterprise, op. cit., note 22 at Head 44.

48. Both the Department and the ODTR are subject to extensive Freedom of Information legislation, which provides access to decision-related information.

49. Available at http://www.entemp.ie/tcmr/cmrg1.pdf.

50. For example as in the Netherlands. See, OECD (2000), "Telecommunications Regulations: Institutional Structures and Responsibilities", at pp. 22-23.

51. Department of Public Enterprise, op. cit., note 22 at Head 46.

52. Eircom has paid in the last year approximately IEP 5 million in fines for delayed lines.

53. According to the ODTR, 75% of complaints referred to it are resolved within ten days. It has also agreed with various operators upon an acceptable timeframe for the resolution of complaints. Another point to be noted here is that the proposed legislation will remove the provision limiting the mandate of the ODTR to handle complaints which are within the scope of the Small Claims Court under Regulation 28 of the European Communities (Voice Telephony and Universal Service) Regulations, 1999 (S.I. No. 71 of 1999), and will explicitly provide the new Commission with responsibilities in this regard.

54. Department of Public Enterprise, *op. cit.*, note 22 at Head 40.

55. It should be acknowledged that condition 6.9 of the General Telecommunications Licence requires that operators implement and make public an appropriate code of practice for their dealings with users.

56. ODTR, *op. cit.*, note 13.

57. Directive 97/13/EC of the European Parliament and of the Council of 10 April 1997 on a common framework for general authorisation and individual licences in the field of telecommunications services, Official journal L 117, 07/05/1997 pp. 0015-0027.

58. ODTR (1998), "Application for a General Telecommunications Licence", October, Document No. 98/46R at 3.8 and 3.9; ODTR (1998), "Telecommunications Licences: Guidance Notes for Applicants", October, Document No. 98/44R at 3.5 and 4.3.

59. Proposal for a Directive of the European Parliament and the Council on the authorisation of electronic communications networks and services, COM(2000) 386 final.

60. OECD (2000*a*), at 18.

61. The derogation required that the CATV subsidiary of Telecom Éireann, Cablelink, be managed at arm's length. This company was eventually divested by the incumbent.

62. Eircell is also designated as having SMP in national interconnection market.

63. ODTR, *op. cit.* note 18.

64. SPs wishing to operate using the Eircom's 1891 service must obtain an 1891 number from the ODTR and must have a Point of Presence in the local call area of the end user.

65. ODTR (1999), pp. 29-30.

66. The ODTR states that in September 2000, delivery of circuits was 20% less than in August 2000, and 25% less than the target for September set by Eircom under its transformation programme. See ODTR (2000*d*).

67. Local Loop Unbundling (LLU) refers to a mandatory opening-up of the local loop (the last part of physical telecommunication circuit leading to the subscriber's premises) to enable new entrants to access customers directly over the incumbent's networks. The ODTR found that one of the three forms of the LLU, bitstream access, was within their mandate to implement, but the other two, direct access to raw copper and line sharing were not supported by the EU legal framework. See, ODTR Decision D6/00 (Document No. ODTR 00/30) for further details.

68. ODTR, Press Release of 19 April 2000.

69. As a result of the Regulator's position the issue of unbundling was examined by the Competition Authority who took legal actions against E*ircom* to mandate unbundling. Although a court ruling has not yet been made, events at the EU level where final action has been taken to require unbundling have made such a ruling academic.

70. ADSL (Asymmetric Digital Subscriber Line) is one of the digital coding technologies that utilise an existing telephone line of copper for high-speed data communications. ADSL has been commercialised the most extensively among various DSL technologies and the word "Asymmetric" comes from the fact that downstream data flow (downloading) of up to 8Mbps is faster than that of upstream (uploading) of up to 1Mbps.

71. The third licensee started operations in November of 2000.

72. Section 1, Part 7 of Schedule of Mobile Telecommunications Licence to Esat Digifone, January 2000, Document No. ODTR 00/03.

73. Some Eircom discount schemes currently include free itemised billing. An examination of whether regulatory action is required in this area is being carried out by the ODTR in conjunction with their work on access costing and universal service.

74. Document ODTR 98/03.

75. Eircom, Esat, Formus Communications and Prince Holdings obtained broadband licences, and Eircom, Esat, Formus and Prince Holdings also obtained narrowband licences.

76. See, for details, ODTR Press Release 26th July 2000.

77. Fees for telecommunications licences are subject to the consent of the Minister for Finance.

78. Department of Public Enterprise, *op. cit.* note 22 at Head 30 (Paragraph 2).

79. The incumbent had to process orders manually until a fully automated system was introduced in April 2000.

80. European Communities (Voice Telephony and Universal Service) Regulations, 1999 (S.I. No. 71 of 1999), and European Communities (Interconnection in Telecommunications) Regulations, 1998 (S.I. No. 15 of 1998).

81. Eircom also had universal service obligations prior to this designation under Section 14 of the Postal and Telecommunications Services Act, 1983.

82. Regulation 5(1) of the European Communities (Voice Telephony and Universal Service) Regulations, 1999 (S.I. No. 71 of 1999).

83. *Ibid* at paragraph (17).

84. It should be noted however that the European Commission, as part of its proposed regulatory package published in July 2000, proposes to remove the second option (a supplementary charge to interconnection) in its proposed new Directive on Universal Service. That new Directive when adopted after discussions (and possibly amendments) in the Council of Ministers and in the European Parliament will replace the Directive on which current Irish regulation, *i.e.* European Communities (Voice Telephony and Universal Service) Regulations, 1999 (S.I. No 71 of 1999), is based.

85. Department of Public Enterprise, *op. cit.* note 22 at Head 40.

86. At present operators with General Telecommunication Licence holders are required to implement their own appropriate code of practice for the resolution of customer disputes under its condition 6.9.

87. However, it is not evident that a quarterly review is necessary. With resource constraints that has affected ODTR's ability to act in certain areas, a less frequent review would be sufficient.

88. OECD, "Communications Outlook 1999", Paris, Table 4.11 at 81.

89. Eircom only.

90. OECD (1999*b*), Table 4.1 at 97.

91. ODTR "The Irish Telecommunications Market/ Quarterly Review" for September 2000.

92. *Ibid* at Table 3.2.

93. ODTR "The Irish Telecommunications Market/ Quarterly Review" for September 2000 and for May 2000.

94. OECD (1999*b*), Table 2.2.

95. The basket includes a number of calls distributed at different times of the day, different days of the week, and over different distances. The statistics are prepared in US$ using both purchasing power parity (PPP) and current exchange rates. In general, it is considered that the PPP figures provide a more reliable comparison.

96. See, OECD (1999*b*), Table 7.9.

97. OECD countries are divided into three regions (Europe, North America, Asia-Pacific) and international call destinations are assumed to be distributed equally to each area.

98. OECD (2001).

99. *Ibid.*

100. OECD (2000*b*), p. 60.

101. OECD (1999*b*), Table 8.5, p. 199.

102. ODTR (2000), "Measuring Licensed Operator Performance: Report on Consultation", 27 January, Document No. ODTR 00/04.BIBLIOGRAPH

BIBLIOGRAPHY

Department of Public Enterprise (1998),
   Statement of Strategy.

Department of Public Enterprise (2000),
   Outline Legislative Proposals in relation to the Regulation of the Communications Sector, Consultation Paper.

Eircom (2000),
   Annual Reports and Accounts 2000.

Government of Ireland (1999),
   National Development Plan 2000-2006.

ODTR (2000*a*),
   Annual Report & Accounts 1998-1999.

ODTR (2000*b*),
   The Irish Telecommunications Market, Quarterly Review, Document No. ODTR 00/91, December.

ODTR (2000*c*),
   "The Regulatory Framework for Access in the Mobile Market – Report on the Consultation", No. 53, July.

ODTR (2000*d*),
   Consultation Paper on Service Levels Provided to Other Licensed Operators by Licensees with Significant Market Power,
   ODTR 00/78.

ODTR (1999),
   "Interconnect for calls destined for Internet services and number translation codes/Consultation paper", April,
   ODTR 99/25.

OECD (1999*a*),
   Economic Surveys – Ireland, Paris.

OECD (1999*b*),
   Communications Outlook 1999, Paris.

OECD (2000*a*),
   OECD *Reviews of Regulatory Reform*, *Regulatory Reform in Denmark*, "Regulatory Reform in the Telecommunications
   Industry", Paris.

OECD (2000*b*)
   Local Access Pricing and E-Commerce, Paris.

OECD (2001),
   Communications Outlook 2001, Paris.

OECD PUBLICATIONS, 2, rue André-Pascal, 75775 PARIS CEDEX 16
PRINTED IN FRANCE
(42 2001 07 1 P) ISBN 92-64-18704-9 – No. 51891 2001